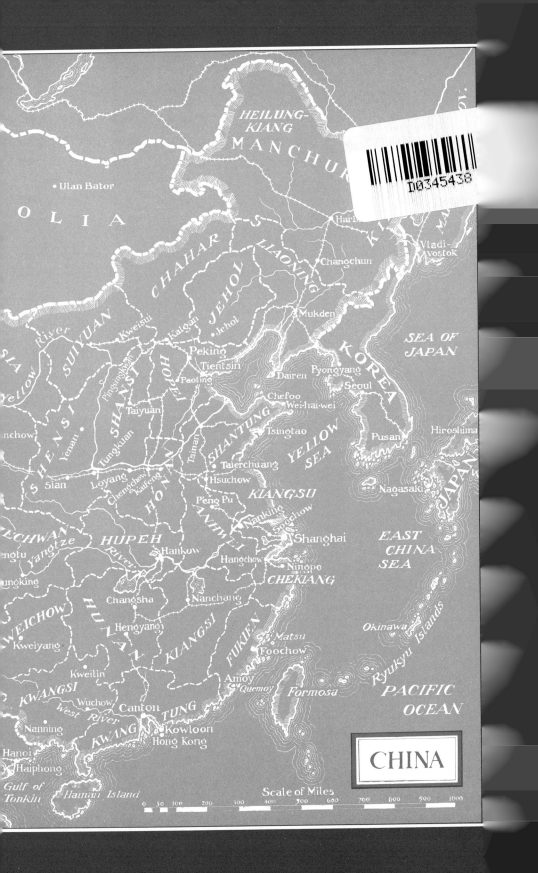

CHINA

Also by BARBARA W. TUCHMAN

General Joseph W. Stilwell after the victorious attack on Myitkyina airstrip, Burma, 1944.

STILWELL AND THE
AMERICAN
EXPERIENCE
IN CHINA, 1911-45

STILWELL AND THE

BARBARA W. TUCHMAN

With a new introduction by John K. Fairbank
and a new afterword by the author
Illustrations selected specially for this edition
Joan Paterson Kerr, Picture Editor

AMERICAN
EXPERIENCE
IN CHINA, 1911-45

THE AMERICAN PAST

Book-of-the-Month Club, Inc., New York

FRONTISPIECE

North corner, Peking wall, photograph by Felice A. Beato, October 1860.

Contents

II

Illustrations

The Book-of-the-Month Club is indebted to the members of the Stilwell family—Nancy Stilwell Easterbrook, Winifred Stilwell Cox, Alison Stilwell Cameron and Dr. Benjamin W. Stilwell—for their generosity in making available many previously unpublished pictures of General Stilwell's life and military career; to the Hoover Institution Archives, whose Stilwell Collection also contains a large number of rare photographs from the late Mrs. Joseph Stilwell; and to the Yale University Archives, which houses the collection of the author, Barbara W. Tuchman. We also wish to thank the many individuals and picture sources listed below.

PAGE i

Stilwell at Myitkyina, Burma. *U.S. Army Photograph*

PAGES ii–iii

Peking wall. *Collection of Paul F. Walter*

PROLOGUE

1. Stilwell on a road in China. *Stilwell family*

PART I

CHAPTER ONE

2. Great Wall of China. *Wide World Photos*
3. Stilwell aged four. *Stilwell family*

CHAPTER FIVE

CHAPTER SIX

CHAPTER SEVEN

CHAPTER EIGHT

PART II

CHAPTER NINE

Maps

Maps drawn by
Brigadier General Frank Dorn, U.S.A. (Ret.)

Introduction

by John K. Fairbank

Barbara Tuchman's *Stilwell i*s a classic for a number of very different reasons, each one quite adequate to make it endure. First of all, it is high drama. It gives us a close-up biography of a quirky but genuine hero, one of America's greatest field commanders. When the U.S. Army staged war games in Louisiana in 1940 to find talented commanders, Joe Stilwell was so lightning quick, imaginative and unorthodox, already a master of the blitzkrieg, that he was rated the best of the Army's nine corps commanders and selected to command the invasion of North Africa. He might have become the Bradley or the Patton of the European theater. But instead, because of his China experience, he had to be sent to handle the crisis there.

But the American war effort in China was largely wasted—even allowing for the fact that warfare is itself the most highly organized form of human wastefulness. The adventure against odds of General Stilwell, who achieved miracles by sheer devotion to his task, is highlighted by the crumbling environment of Free China under Generalissimo Chiang Kai-shek, to whom Stilwell was nominally "chief of staff." What a contrast!—the hard-bitten American idealist, determined to train Chinese troops and "beat the Japs," and the crafty military politician, equally determined to stay in power by not mounting any further Chinese war effort. The Stilwell-Chiang stalemate encapsulated the frustration of America's war aims in China.

Stilwell, however, is more than a fast-paced narrative of colorful events shadowed by tragedy. Back of the war story looms the long-term American effort to help China be more like us—a quixotic endeavor with nine lives that now flourishes again. The reader will find this volume ends very appropriately (as of 1971): "In the end China went her own way as if the Americans had never come." But nearly fifteen years later another cycle of contact, tourism, exchanges, investment and diplomacy is well under way. High time for the American public to look back, Chinese-style, "at the tracks of the cart that went this way before." Especially when we find that in helping our allies the Nationalists we set ourselves against the Communist Chinese revolution, and worst of all, for us, the revolution succeeded.

In short, after setting out, as we said, to help China, we let our "national interest" in the power politics of the cold war line us up against the Chinese people. Was it really in our national interest to do so? Especially when it was the prelude to our wars in Korea and Vietnam? Barbara Tuchman's *Stilwell* leaves us with a residue of questions very pertinent today.

But the real attraction of this book is that it is a first-rate historical narrative by a self-assured master of the art. Early on, Barbara Wertheim Tuchman moved naturally into the American aristocracy of the intellect. Her grandfathers had been liberal leaders among New York's men of affairs. One was Henry Morgenthau, Sr., whose son, her uncle, became Roosevelt's Secretary of the Treasury. While still a student at Radcliffe she accompanied her grandfather to the World Economic Conference at London. High policy and public personalities were part of her inheritance.

At Radcliffe she concentrated in the combined and rather special field of history and literature. Graduation in 1933 ushered her into a world soon obliged to mobilize against fascism and militarism. Gifted with a self-propelled, lucid and unafraid mind, she became a researcher in the Institute of Pacific Relations, during 1934 in New York, in 1935 in Tokyo. The IPR was a pioneer "think tank" and conference organization originally put together in the 1920s by ex-YMCA secretaries at Honolulu. It consisted of a dozen national institutes in all the major Pacific rim countries including the European colonial powers. Alone in the Pacific area, it inaugurated the kind of contemporary research and periodic international discussion that is now pursued by centers and associations every day of the week. From militaristic Tokyo, Barbara Wertheim visited pre-Communist China in 1935.

Back in New York she joined the staff of *The Nation,* of which her father had once been publisher, and then went to Madrid to report the grim civil war in Spain during 1937–38. Returning to New York as American correspondent for the *New Statesman* of London, she married Dr. Lester Tuchman in 1940 and soon had three daughters. From 1943 to 1945 she worked on the Far East news desk of the Office of War Information in New York.

Such an early career might have prepared a well-to-do and busy mother to grace the New York establishment at meetings of the Council on Foreign Relations and little more. Barbara Tuchman, however, was just beginning to hit her stride. In 1956, continuing an earlier interest, she published *Bible and Sword: Britain and Palestine from the Bronze Age to Balfour*, an historical account down to 1918. Thereafter she avoided topics that engaged her personal feelings and found her own style as a writer of histories that reached the public.

A critic who called these books "popular history" would be saying as much about himself as about the books. They are, to be sure, "non-academic" in the sense that they are not mainly devoted to discussion of historical "problems," so many of which have been derived from the infiltration of history by the social sciences. This invasion of history in the universities by seekers after the uniformities of science puts a premium on generalizations, patterns of events and comparative schema. It may well have contributed to the recent decline of student interest in history. At any rate, Barbara Tuchman has been a vocal, incisive and widely persuasive advocate of history as a readable story. To her, questions of social mobility, legitimization, investment ratios and the work ethic are of secondary interest to how people felt and acted, what they did and said. She reaffirms the uniqueness of all happenings, persons and places.

Of course the struggle in history between the claims of the particular and of the general has gone on for ages. We cannot hope to crack this hoary philosophical chestnut here in a few words, however well chosen. We don't have to, for Barbara Tuchman's history stands on its own feet and needs no theoretical support. It simply fascinates readers by bringing them as close to past reality as they are ever likely to get.

Her secret lies first of all in prodigious hard work. Her research exhumes the record down to the smallest scrap of paper. *Stilwell* was four years in gestation, the same as her earlier best-seller and Pulitzer Prize–winner about the first month of World War I, *The Guns of August*. By 1967, when she began on *Stilwell*, a number of careful studies had traced out the diplomatic-bureaucratic intricacies of America's China policy in World War II. Two very competent military historians had produced three solid volumes on Stilwell's operations in his China-Burma-India (CBI) theater. The framework of events had been set up. Most valuable of all,

General Stilwell's extensive diaries and personal records were made available by his family.

By centering on Stilwell, Mrs. Tuchman could find her way through the mine-sown sea of *ex parte* testimony, recrimination and self-serving memoirs that had accumulated over two decades since the United States' alleged "loss of China." Moreover, a focus on Stilwell enabled her to explore the really central conflict of interest between the United States and its ally the Nationalist Government of China. It avoided the distraction of the dire struggle between the Nationalists under Chiang Kai-shek and the Chinese Communists under Mao Tse-tung, which broke loose and embittered American domestic politics after Stilwell's sudden death of cancer in 1946.

Another palpable secret, allied to hard work, is Barbara Tuchman's mastery and use of the record to provide what she calls "corroborative detail." Supposing she has already perceived how certain events interrelate, it is still necessary to convey this to the reader in evidence from the scene—words quoted, a fact, a happening that makes the point self-evident. This detail brings events closer. Since she is telling a story, not building a case, Barbara Tuchman scorns the paraphernalia of computer printouts and also the quoting of other historians. "I could never see any sense whatever in referring to one's neighbor in the next university as a source. To me that is no source at all; I want to know where a given fact came from originally, not who used it last."* Fortunately, this provocative independence of spirit (she is not a professor) is combined with a keen eye for the very same political, economic and social institutions or "factors" that preoccupy so many academics. For example, her analysis of Chiang Kai-shek's precarious and enervating balance of power within China is one of the clearest elements in the book. Her picture of Stilwell's early career—his talent for languages and foreign travel, his athletic activism, his exploration of China in the 1920s and '30s—is both biography and social history, the man and his times. With her skill in getting at and using the record, Mrs. Tuchman has put the story together.

How do Stilwell and the American experience in China look from the perspective of the 1980s?

In the long view, the era 1911–45 saw the new Chinese Republic's stumbling efforts to create a new polity. Eventually, in 1928, the Kuomintang (Nationalist) party dictatorship emerged to take the place of the monarchy. But from 1931 China's political life was still made a shambles by the Japanese invasion.

---

* "History by the Ounce," *Harper's Magazine*, July 1965, p. 74.

During all this era of political disunity and weakness, foreigners—and especially Americans—had unusual opportunities to take part in Chinese life. To many Chinese patriots the Americans' treaty-based privileges seemed like a continuation of the late-nineteenth-century imperialism of the Europeans and the Japanese. The idea that General Stilwell should command all the Chinese armies against Japan, which President Roosevelt actually proposed in 1944, was certainly a climactic point in the long imperialist story. Since 1949 the Chinese Communist revolution has changed all that. And yet . . .

If in the 1980s China's polity seems self-contained and independent, her economy still seems to need foreign trade, technology and investment. The population has more than doubled since 1949, eating up the gains of the revolution. China's poverty is still visible, especially to patriots who see material affluence abroad. Chairman Mao's anti-foreign egalitarianism, like his social revolution against ruling class privilege and bureaucratism, had to give way to Deng Xiaoping's industrial-technological revolution. The People's Republic now has to increase production with foreign help. Once again Americans, including well-heeled American tourists, are special people in poor China. Once again we may become closely involved in business and friendship with ruling-class Chinese. Once again our Chinese friends may become targets of an anti-foreign populist movement.

We of the 1980s have seen in China's revolution something that Stilwell did not live to see—a dynamic alternation between the social and the industrial revolutions, between the aspirations of the countryside and of the city people. There is a seemingly built-in pendulum that leads China on a zigzag course like that of a blind man who must first try to mobilize egalitarian social change among the peasantry and then veer off to train a new ruling class in the modernizing technologies. The record of the last third of a century does not augur a humdrum stability.

What new understanding have other historians produced in the years since Barbara Tuchman wrote? Much has appeared about Mao and the Chinese Communists, who won the future, but little about the American war effort of the 1940s. Perhaps the most illuminating study is Michael Schaller's *The U.S. Crusade in China, 1938–1945*,* which uses hitherto secret government archives liberated under the Freedom of Information Act. Schaller's study only deepens the disillusion with American aims and actions in wartime China that emerges so clearly from Tuchman's *Stilwell*.

To cite one example: he documents the work of Navy Group China under Commander Milton Miles, who kept ahead of the U.S. Army by

* Columbia University Press, 1979.

getting a secret agreement signed by President Roosevelt in April 1943 to let the U.S. Navy import arms to China in their own planes and help Chiang's secret police chief, Tai Li, train his men and attack their Chinese Communist enemies. Miles seemed to have the Boy Scout virtues, and certainly the appearance. From Naval Academy days he was known to his friends as "Mary" for his dimpled likeness to the stage star Mary Miles Minter. In Free China between 2,500 and 3,000 Americans served under Miles. Some assisted Tai Li's anti-communist program of assassination, poisoning, imprisonment and suppression. Top-level U.S. Navy support of Miles, time after time, thwarted Stilwell's efforts to get his operation under control. Miles felt a "magnetic attraction" for Tai Li, who, he explained, "being the liberal, democratic individual he was . . . only established concentration camps that were fully legal . . . and he loved his mother and supported education for women."* Miles, according to his critics, participated in mass trials conducted by Tai Li, after which political prisoners were buried alive. Having inaugurated the cold war in China way ahead of time, this romantic and dreadful naval officer developed megalomania and was shipped home in September 1945. Chinese Communist protests about his activities had been thoroughly justified.

The Miles episode shows how Stilwell's war effort in China was stuck between Nationalist apathy and Sino-American counter-revolution. A great trainer of soldiers, Joe Stilwell wanted to teach China's conscripted farm boys how to defend their country. He personified what we like to think of as the American virtues of democracy and dedicated activism. His story shows what one gifted individual of superhuman grit could, and could not, achieve.

It is undoubtedly fortunate that Stilwell never became commander of China's armies against Japan, as President Roosevelt proposed just before Stilwell's recall in 1944. It would have put him between the Nationalists and the Chinese Communists, neither of whom wanted at that time to fight the Japanese. Chinese patriotism was on the rise and the Nationalist-Communist civil war had already started. Stilwell's appointment to command, which Chiang Kai-shek refused, might have fatally involved the United States in a postwar super-Vietnam in China. Even as it was, thirty years were to pass before the United States would recognize the Chinese revolution.

John K. Fairbank
Professor of History, Emeritus, Harvard University

* Schaller, p. 241, quoting Miles in August 1945.

Foreword

by Barbara W. Tuchman

The theme of this book is the relation of America to China, in a larger sense to Asia. The vehicle of the theme is the career of General Stilwell. Why Stilwell? Because he combined a career focused on China with background and character that were quintessentially American; because his connection with China spanned the period that shaped the present from the dramatic opening moment of 1911, year of the Revolution, to 1944, decisive year in the decline of the Nationalist Government; because his service in the intervening years was a prism of the times—as language officer from 1920 to 1923 in the time of the warlords, as officer of the 15th Infantry in Tientsin from 1926 to 1929 at the time of the rise to power of Chiang Kai-shek, as Military Attaché from 1935 to 1939 at the time of Japanese invasion, lastly as theater commander in World War II; because in the final and critical years of this period he was the most important figure in the Sino-American relationship. Impatient, acid, impolitic, "Vinegar Joe" was not the ideal man for the role. But in knowledge of the language and country, friendship for the people, belief and persistence in his task, combined with official position and power, he personified the strongest endeavor and, as it was to prove, the tragic limits, of his country's experience in Asia.

I am conscious of the hazards of venturing into the realm of America's China policy, a subject that, following the defeat of Chiang Kai-shek by the Communists and the waste of an immense American effort, aroused one of the angriest and most damaging campaigns of vilification in recent public life. Nevertheless, since China is the ultimate reason for our involvement in Southeast Asia, the subject is worth the venture even though the ground is hot. It is only fair to add that this book, which ends in 1946, is concerned with origins that reach back beyond yesterday. "You will hear a lot of talk," General Stilwell wrote for the graduating class of West Point in 1945, "about how this or that generation messed things up and got us into war. What nonsense. All living generations are responsible for what we do and all dead ones as well."

I should like to add a word of explanation about General Stilwell's diaries, which were naturally a major source for his biographer. I became thereby a trespasser since the diaries were intended for no eyes but his own. "This little book," he explicitly warned on the flyleaf of the pocket diary for 1906, "contains None of Your Damned Business!" Believing in the right of privacy, I do not share the view that posterity has some sort of "right" to know the private life of a public figure if he wishes otherwise but in Stilwell's case the needs of history had already prevailed over privacy. After the war it became important and necessary to let Stilwell's voice speak for itself about the events of his controversial command. With the consent of his family his wartime diaries and letters for the period 1942-44 only were edited by the former correspondent in China, Theodore White, and published under the title *The Stilwell Papers* in 1948. The originals together with other wartime documents were also made available to Charles Romanus and Riley Sunderland, authors of the official Army history of the China–Burma–India theater, and were subsequently donated for public use to the Hoover Library in Stanford, California. This decision having been taken, it was logical to give a biographer access to the rest of the Stilwell archive covering his career prior to Pearl Harbor. Mrs. Stilwell made available to me the diaries, letters, documents, scrapbooks, family albums and other material in her possession, hitherto unpublished. These are described further in the Bibliography.

The Stilwell Papers was a sensation and a best seller and has been a source of invaluable fact and enlivening quotation for historians ever since. Yet in this case a man's own diaries, paradoxically, do not represent the real, or at any rate, the entire, man. Taken alone they give a one-sided view because Stilwell consciously used his diary to vent his "bile," as he put it, of which he had a large natural endowment augmented by a peculiarly frustrating situation. Not content with diary entries, he rewrote and expanded his notes afterwards in larger notebooks or on loose sheets of paper, all of which he kept. Sometimes the process itself was recorded: "Wrote and wrote. Terrible." Or, "I am just scribbling to keep from biting the radiator." All this turmoil, which in other men would have been ephemeral, has become historical record. The acid, which in life was balanced by other qualities, has survived in undue proportion.

Finally, I am aware that this book by the nature of its subject does injustice to China and the Chinese people. Because it concentrates, especially in the second half, on a low point in China's history and on the military function which has never been of high repute in China, the negative aspects predominate. The likableness, the artistic vision and philosophic mind, the strength of character, intelligence, good humor and capacity for work which have put the Chinese in the forefront of the world's civilized peoples, have not come through in proper proportion. The author can only acknowledge this with regret.

Documentation will be found at the back of the book, with the relevant phrase and page number as the indicator.

ACKNOWLEDGMENTS

This book has had many contributors for whose help and advice and criticism I would like to express my gratitude and thanks. These go first to Mrs. Joseph W. Stilwell for permission to use and quote from all of her husband's papers and family letters in her possession and for her friendly hospitality while I was engaged in their study; to Mrs. Bettye (the former Mrs. Benjamin) Stilwell for her devoted work in transcribing the diaries and arranging the papers in order; to Mrs. Nancy Stilwell Easterbrook, the General's eldest daughter, and her husband, General Ernest Easterbrook, for their insights and information throughout the course of my work; to Mrs. Stuart Wilder, the General's sister, for her recollections.

I owe a special debt to Professor John King Fairbank of the East Asia Research Center, Harvard University, for the gift of his knowledge and time in reading and commenting on the manuscript; to Brigadier General Frank Dorn, Stilwell's senior aide and colleague in other capacities over many years, for the same, as well as for a constant and generous supply of information; to Colonel David D. Barrett, who served in China from 1927 to 1945, for most of the time in association with Stilwell, for his lively guidance and earnest endeavor to persuade me to "keep down the charisma"; to Dr. Forrest Pogue, biographer of General Marshall, for his ungrudging response whenever queried; to Lieutenant General Raymond A. Wheeler, former chief of the Service of Supply in the China–Burma–India theater, for his warm interest and help in arranging interviews and introductions.

My thanks and appreciation are due also to many who participated in the events of this history and who personally answered my questions, supplied explanations, recalled experiences and provided other varieties of help, viz.: to Colonel Trevor Dupuy and General Samuel B. Griffith, who separately and coincidentally supplied the initial push to a project that was then only lurking in the back of my mind; to Shang Chen, former Chief of Foreign Liaison of the Ministry of War, Yü Ta-wei, former Director of Ordnance, Chang Kia-ngau, former Minister of Communications, Horace Eng, formerly with CBI Headquarters; to the four former officers of the Chinese 38th Division, veterans of the Burma campaign, who were good enough to give me in Taiwan their first-hand views and information, and whom with great reluctance I must leave anonymous to protect them from possible embarrassment; to the former foreign service officers in China, and on the China desk, Edmund Clubb, John Service, John Paton Davies, John Emmerson, Philip Sprouse and John Carter Vincent, for their intimate knowledge of circumstances and persons, and to Mrs. Clubb, Mrs. Service and Mrs. Vincent, who supplemented it; to President Roosevelt's associates, Ambassador Averell Harriman, Judge Samuel Rosenman, Benjamin V. Cohen and the President's daughter, Mrs. James Halsted; to Earl Mountbatten of Burma, who spared a morning out of a very crowded schedule and filled it with sparkling reminiscence; to John Keswick and Peter Fleming for further views from the British side and hospitality in addition; to the journalists who served in China or CBI, Edgar Snow, Theodore White, Tillman Durdin, Brooks Atkinson, Eric Sevareid; and to the following fellow-officers, friends and other associates of General Stilwell: General of the Army Omar Bradley, Generals Jacob Devers, Matthew B. Ridgway, Maxwell Taylor, Albert C. Wedemeyer, Major Generals Frank Roberts, Thomas Timberman, H. L. Boatner, Brigadier Generals Thomas Arms, Thomas Betts, W. E. Crist, E. J. McNally, Frederick Munson, Ambassador Henry A. Byroade, Colonel George Demetriadi, Colonel Thomas Arms, Jr., Mrs. John Magruder, Mrs. Simon Bolivar Buckner, Mrs. James McHugh, Mr. and Mrs. Paul Jones, Dean Rusk, Joseph Alsop, Dillon Ripley, Richard M. T. Young, Roger Hilsman, and members of the family, Colonel and Mrs. Ellis Cox, Dr. Benjamin Stilwell and the late Mr. Charles Duell.

I am particularly grateful to Ambassador Chester Bowles for making it possible for me to go to Assam and to Mr. and Mrs. J. L. Watt for their hospitality and Mr. J. Phookan for his escort while there. For assistance in Taiwan I am indebted to Colonel Harry Collier and Mr. Fox Butterfield, and in Hong Kong to Mr. Alan Whiting of the American Consulate and Colonel William Whitson.

For assistance in research my primary thanks go to Mr. John E. Taylor of the Military Records Division, National Archives, and to Dr. Kenneth Glazier of the Hoover Library at Stanford. I am especially indebted to my predecessor on the Stilwell trail, Mr. Charles Romanus, co-author of the inexhaustible Army volumes on CBI, for his welcome and his elucidations; also to his colleagues in the Office of the Chief of Military History, Dr. Stetson Conn, Mr. Charles MacDonald and Mrs. Hannah Zeidlik; to Colonel Thomas Griess, professor of Military Art and Engineering at West Point; to Mr. Joseph O'Donnell of the Archives and History Section, USMA Library; to Mr. Leon Williams of the Film Division, National Archives; to Mr. Seymour Pomrenze and his staff of the Adjutant General's Office, Department of Defense; to Colonel Fant, Colonel Webb, Miss Urban and Miss Sprigg of the Book and Magazine Division (in its various incarnations) of the Department of Defense; to Miss Elizabeth Drewry, former director of the Roosevelt Library at Hyde Park, and her successor, Dr. James O'Neill, and their staff; to Miss Julie How and Mrs. Elizabeth B. Mason of the East Asia Oral History Project of Columbia University; to Dr. Herman Kahn, director of Manuscripts and Archives of the Yale University Library, and his assistant, Miss Judith Schiff, for searches in the Stimson Papers; to William Franklin, chief of the Historical Division, Department of State; to the staff of the Reference Division, New York Public Library; to Miss Dorothy Borg and Professors Theodore Ropp of Duke University, Doak Barnett of Columbia, James MacGregor Burns of Williams College and Lyman Van Slyke of Stanford.

For indispensable readership of the work in progress, without which a writer—or this one—would dry up, and for valuable criticism, I am most sincerely grateful to my daughters and son-in-law, Lucy and David Eisenberg, Jessica and Alma Tuchman, and my husband, Dr. Lester Tuchman.

Prologue:

THE CRISIS

IN July 1944, at the height of the Second World War, the United States Government officially requested Generalissimo Chiang Kai-shek to place an American, specifically Lieutenant General Joseph W. Stilwell, in command of all China's armed forces. The proposal was unprecedented: no American had ever before directly commanded the national forces of an ally. It was the more extreme because General Stilwell, already a figure of accomplishment, controversy and feuds in the China–Burma–India theater, was known to be *persona non grata* to the Generalissimo who had previously asked for his recall.

China's case, however, was considered "desperate," demanding "desperate remedies." To keep China in the war, salvage something of her combat potential and prevent the consolidation of Japan's hold on the mainland were objects essential to both American strategy and postwar policy. "The future of all Asia is at stake," President Roosevelt said in his message to Chiang Kai-shek, "along with the tremendous effort which America has expended in that region." He was fully aware, he added, "of your feelings regarding General Stilwell" but "I know of no other man who has the ability, the force and the determination to offset the disaster that now threatens China."

A sweeping offensive by the Japanese into hitherto unoccupied China had precipitated the crisis. Launched in April with rapid successes, and advancing implacably against feeble and yielding Chinese defense, it threat-

I

Major Stilwell, on his first assignment to China, 1920–23, walking up a Chinese road (1). The photograph is from one of the many albums Stilwell kept during his lifetime.

ened to choke off Free China and overrun the area where American air bases were located. At this stage of the war Japan was on the defensive against the westward American advance across the Pacific and her supply lines by sea were dangerously weakening under American air attack from the bases in south China. The purpose of the Japanese offensive was to wipe out the American airfields, assure a linked-up overland route from Manchuria to Southeast Asia and isolate Free China from contact with a possible American landing on the China coast.

Were these gains to be won, as the enemy's rapid successes and lack of coordinated Chinese defense indicated they might well be, the war would be prolonged for no one knew how long. Japan could knit together her communications, eliminate a future base of American action and so strengthen her hold on the mainland that her Government might retreat there even if the home islands were lost.

Beyond that a darker prospect loomed. If China collapsed, the whole goal of American policy in the Far East could well be lost. That goal required, after victory, a Chinese nation strong and stable enough to take Japan's place and keep the peace in the Far East. Far from strong after resistance to invasion that had lasted for seven years, longer than that of any other nation, China was battered and blockaded, its economy ruined by enemy occupation, its Government tired, corrupt and deteriorating. National war effort was paralyzed by fear of the internal challenge of the Communists whose annihilation Chiang Kai-shek had vainly pursued for ten years before a truce in 1937. If his Government should now fall, China would disintegrate in civil strife. Even if the Nationalist Government survived in an area reduced and fragmented by the new Japanese inroads, defeatism and decay from within would be accelerated. In the end, would the ravaged China that emerged from the war be capable of enforcing Japan's surrender and maintaining her own integrity? If not, who then would be the foundation of stability in Asia?

These were the disturbing questions that shadowed American policy and that by negative outcome could nullify the tremendous effort of the war. The hope of a strong China as one of the four cornerstones of the postwar peace had formed Roosevelt's policy from the beginning and dictated the effort to sustain China through the war. Military strategy ran parallel. It intended that China's manpower, not America's, should fight on the mainland; it needed China's territory as a base of present air, and future ground, operations; above all, it depended on China's continued resistance to hold down a million Japanese troops on the mainland. Otherwise they might be released against the Americans' perilous progress from island to island across the Pacific. The collapse, surrender or collaboration of the Chungking Government, representing the last free nation of the Far

East, might induce the other nations of Asia to come to terms with Japan, realizing Roosevelt's greatest fear. These were the reasons that dictated the long-bedeviled campaign to supply, invigorate and mobilize China and reopen the back door through Burma which had been General Stilwell's task since Pearl Harbor.

The Government in remote Chungking beyond the gorges of the Yangtze had no plan of defense to stem the Japanese advance. The Generalissimo whose genius was political rather than military had relied for defense on the air power of the American Fourteenth Air Force and the assurance of its confident commander, General Claire Chennault, that if adequately supplied by his countrymen he could contain, even defeat, the Japanese. This program perfectly suited the Generalissimo because it provided him with a surrogate to fight Japan while allowing him to hoard China's limited military capacity for use against internal enemies. His best divisions were not in action against the Japanese but holding a frontier against the Communist area in the north. Dissidence in other quarters, too, chronically haunted him. Old antagonists among the southern regional commanders, growing restless under the many failings of Chungking, were promoting another of the separatist movements that had long been China's bane.

Under these pressures Chiang wished neither to risk loyal troops in costly battle against the Japanese nor allow troops of doubtful loyalty to be trained, armed and equipped by the Americans lest some day they be turned against himself. He desperately wanted all the American help in arms, money and supplies that he could get, not for use against the common enemy whom he expected his allies would defeat in any event, but for the purpose which he, as its chief executive, considered most important for his country—survival of the Nationalist regime. This was the web in which he was caught and which fixed the terms of the long-existing struggle between himself and Stilwell.

Stilwell offered no surrogate. He had long maintained that an air force was no better than the ground troops that defended its airfields. The Japanese advance now gave his thesis alarming cogency. His object and assigned mission was to enable the Chinese ground forces to fight efficiently; to so train, arm and equip the Chinese soldier, and assure his pay, food and medical care, as to create an effective military arm. "If I can prove the Chinese soldier is as good as any Allied soldier," he told a correspondent, "I'll die happy." He had proved it could be done by the performance of two Chinese armies under his command in Burma, but his training programs with American instructors and equipment for 60 divisions in China were a ceaseless battle against frustrations and delays, not all of them natural.

To Chiang every unit trained by the Americans was one that loosened his control. He could not reject the program since he was utterly dependent on American aid but he could stall and thwart and divert supplies. For more than two years two unyielding men, equally determined, mutually hostile, supposedly allies, wrestled over the fate of China. Three times Chiang asked or induced others to ask for Stilwell's recall. Stilwell in his turn despised, as he tactlessly did not conceal, the Generalissimo.

Known with reason as Vinegar Joe, Stilwell was a man of high performance and utter integrity, too quickly disgusted with anything less in others. His particular animus was reserved for persons in high places. He could no more ingratiate himself with someone he did not respect than the dumb could speak. He would have liked to do the job proposed for him if he could have done it without the office. He was already Commanding General of U.S. forces in the CBI theater, Deputy Supreme Allied Commander in Southeast Asia, Commanding General of the Chinese Army in India and its field commander in Burma, nominal Chief of Staff to Chiang Kai-shek for the China theater, chief of the Chinese Training and Combat Command and Administrator of Lend-Lease to China—each of these with its appropriate staffs, pomp and paper work. Since he hated palaver and loathed pretensions, it was understandable that he preferred war in the jungles of Burma among leeches, mildew and outright enemies.

At the front, like General U. S. Grant, he shed insignia of rank and made himself comfortable out of uniform. In nonregulation sweater, GI boots and his old stiff-brimmed campaign hat from the First World War, he could be found within a few hundred yards of the firing line, standing beside a Chinese battalion commander, chewing gum, smoking from a cigaret holder and talking Chinese. He was sixty-one, a slight figure, lean and bony, five-foot-nine, with short-cropped gray-black hair, a hard, lined, decisive face and a deceptive appearance of physical fragility. He was in fact as fragile as steel wire. He had served in China at different periods through the days of the warlords, the rise of the Kuomintang and the Sino-Japanese War. As an officer his persistent concern for the welfare of the men, whether Americans or Chinese, was not journalists' copy but lifelong, unfailing and on occasion explosive. To the American public he was the hero of the celebrated walk out of Burma in a time of defeat, to the GIs he was Uncle Joe, to the British, whom he insisted on disliking except for those he liked, he was "difficult," to *CBI Roundup,* the theater journal, he was remarkable for singleness of purpose and a sense of humor which "only fails him in case of the monsoon and stuffed shirts." His motto was *Illegitimati non carborundum,* personally translated as "Don't let the bastards grind you down."

To make his proposed appointment more palatable to Chiang Kai-shek, Stilwell was promoted to four-star general, equal to the rank then held only by Generals Marshall, Eisenhower, MacArthur and Arnold.

A foreigner in command of China's armed forces was not a proposition that could be made palatable to Chiang Kai-shek in any form. Nevertheless Roosevelt's tone, harsh and almost insulting from one head of state and ally to another, suggested an ultimatum. The United States held the upper hand but all China's history weighed in the scale against compliance. Chiang accepted "in principle," proposed modifications, shifted ground, insisted on control of Lend-Lease, twisted and temporized. The Chinese from necessity had made manipulation of the strong by the weak into a fine art and Chiang played every stratagem and every maneuver. In response to his request for a special envoy to "adjust relations between me and General Stilwell," Washington sent a former Secretary of War, General Patrick Hurley. Chiang enveloped him in seductions and evasions; Washington's impatience and pressure increased. After two months the issue was still unresolved. On September 12 Hurley returned from an interview discouraged, reporting the Generalissimo to have been "very difficult" and the matter no nearer to settlement. Chiang's parting remark, half Oriental pretense of humility, half genuine bitterness, was "General Stilwell has more power in China than I have."

The facts were otherwise but that the statement could be made was a strange destiny for an American who five years earlier had left China, as he then supposed, at the end of his career and for the last time.

I

1

Foundations of an Officer

LIEUTENANT STILWELL, aged twenty-eight, met China for the first time in November 1911 at the moment when the most ancient of independent nations stumbled into the twentieth century. Six weeks before he came, revolution had erupted half by accident, and spreading from city to city in swaying battle against the Imperial forces, was about to overcome the decrepit Manchu regime. Haphazard in outbreak it was to be imperfect in triumph for it failed to fill the void left by what it swept away. The monarchy which had held together a quarter of the earth's population found no firm successor. Fragmenting under rival claimants and already penetrated by a maze of foreign inroads into her sovereignty, China with lost cohesion and damaged confidence moved into the oncoming storms of the world's most violent age.

The visitor, on leave from military duty in the Philippines, was as pure Yankee in heritage as it was possible to be. He was the eighth generation in direct descent from Nicholas Stilwell, who had come to America from England in 1638 and acquired property in Staten Island, Long Island and Manhattan. His mother's forebears named Fowler had also arrived in the 1630s and over succeeding generations had gathered in the major strains of colonial America: English, French Huguenot and Dutch. Nicholas Stilwell had produced some 1,600 descendants by the time Joe Stilwell was born, of whom two, Colonel Richard Stilwell and General Garrett Stilwell, fought in the American Revolution.

9

Chinese troops using the ages-old Great Wall as a roadway during the early stages of the Sino-Japanese War in 1937 (2).

A military career was not so much chosen by Joe as thrust on him by paternal whim. His father, Dr. Benjamin W. Stilwell, was a clever and handsome gentleman of authoritative character, comfortable circumstances and a variety of talents not carried too far. He was the son of John Stilwell, a dry-goods merchant of "business sagacity and exemplary habits" who had retired with a considerable fortune derived from investment in real estate and settled in Yonkers where he built an attractive house overlooking the Hudson and became a director of the Bank of Yonkers and a pillar of the Methodist Church. The family home remained in Yonkers thereafter.

Benjamin Stilwell took a law degree at Columbia when he was twenty-one but did not establish himself in practice. Following his marriage in 1880 to Mary A. Peene, and the birth of a daughter, he moved to a plantation near Palatka, Florida, with the intention of developing a lumber business in southern pine. Here on March 19, 1883, his first son was born and named Joseph Warren for the friend and physician who attended at his birth. The name had been inherited from the original Dr. Joseph Warren of Boston who, refusing the post of Surgeon General for a more hazardous active command, was killed in the Battle of Bunker Hill.

Abandoning the venture in lumber, Benjamin Stilwell returned with his family to Yonkers where he now took up the study of medicine and obtained a degree, but this profession too failed to attract him into practice. In 1892 the family, enlarged by a second son, John, and a second daughter, Mary, moved to a farm near Great Barrington in the Berkshires where Dr. Stilwell decided to take up the role of country gentleman. After four years he came to the conclusion that he was failing in the duty he owed society to make use of his endowments and so returned once again to Yonkers where he now accepted a position with a public utility, the Westchester Lighting Company, ultimately becoming vice-president.

Having at last satisfied the prodding of the puritan conscience which will not allow a man to live guiltlessly without a job, Dr. Stilwell enjoyed life thereafter as one of Yonkers' distinguished citizens, holding office as president of the school board and various directorships of Westchester banks and companies. With his imposing but genial presence and considerable charm, Dr. Benjamin Stilwell was accepted at face value by his family and community as a superior person. "Father was *impressive*" was the verdict of a daughter. He had the manner and means to carry off the posture of prominence as well as the evident abilities which he never used to their fullest or tested in a more exigent world than Yonkers. He took his family to Paris in the centennial year of 1889, conducting them through England, France, Belgium, Holland, Germany, Austria and Italy and sending home a series of entertaining and well-written travel letters to the

Two uncharacteristic portraits of young Joseph Stilwell, as a starched four-year-old (3) and as a proper West Point cadet in full dress (4). He spent the major part of his childhood in this wisteria-laden house in Yonkers, New York (5).

3

4

5

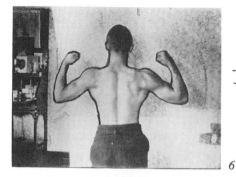

6

Hercules in disgust —

W. Point

Y.H.S.
TRACK TEAM

7

'98

'98

CHAMPIONS OF '98

8

Yonkers Statesman. He painted and played the piano, maintained a strict hand and high moral tone over the upbringing of his children, presided and asked the blessing three times a day at the family dining table, entertained the family with a flow of stories, wit, advice and instruction, and enjoyed the devoted admiration of his sons and daughters, who believed, or were educated in the habit of believing, that Father was wonderful—and always right.

Joe Stilwell, called Warren by his family, was an active, driving, sharp-witted boy who climbed rooftops, drowned rabbits in the horse trough and exceedingly disliked Sunday services which he was required to attend three times in the day, including church, Sunday school and a sermon at vespers. Writing to his own daughter when he was over sixty, he recalled the "criminal instincts I picked up by being forced to go to Church and Sunday School, and seeing how little real good religion does anybody, I advise passing them all up and using common sense instead."

Like his father, Warren had facility with words, but his heart and energy went into athletics. He played tennis, rowed a shell on the Hudson and played quarterback on the Yonkers High football team of which, in the words of a classmate, he was "the motive power, inspiration and field general." When under his generalship the varsity of 1899 defeated all the prep school teams of New York City and Westchester, the public high school of Yonkers was so pleased that it paid its players. On the track team Warren's specialty was the quarter-mile and his interest carried over to organizing track meets of the Westchester Inter-Scholastic League which he helped to form and serving as reporter of athletic events for the *Yonkers Statesman.* Organizing athletics was to remain a lifelong activity along with a passion for keeping himself in physical trim at the athlete's level.

At the end of his senior year in 1899 the final report of the principal, Dr. Thomas O. Baker, described a model boy—as it proved, a little prematurely. The subject maintained "a high standard in all his studies," possessed "energy and executive ability . . . useful in advancing the interests of the school," had "no bad habits" and was "entirely worthy of confidence."

Dr. Stilwell had chosen Yale for his sons but he now decided that at sixteen Warren was too young to go to college and, on the theory that the right place for every child was at home, he ordained that his able, bright, extra-energized, highly effective son should take a postgraduate year at Yonkers in the same school system in which he had been, with a brief interval, since he was five. Ironically, it was this over-protective gesture which diverted Joe Stilwell to a military career. Predictably bored, he soon departed from his estimable record. Forming a club of friends called the "Big Four," he constructed a hideaway in the school loft with

Stilwell often wrote captions on the backs of photographs and in this case also outlined his lean torso in ink (6). In the picture of his high school track team (7) he stands second from right, front row; in that of the football team of 1898, he sits second from left, front row (8).

boards laid across the rafters where the group played cards and on one occasion suspended the principal's desk by ropes from the ceiling. In another venture they spread Limburger cheese on the pupils' desks, and in climactic naughtiness, at the senior dance of 1900, perpetrated what came to be known as the Great Ice Cream Raid. Led by Warren, the four marauders assaulted the refreshment table and after doing battle with the defenders, in the course of which Dr. Baker was inadvertently "slugged," made off with the tubs of ice cream and trays of cakes. A special meeting of the Board of Education to deal with the scandal was summoned the next day, at which the guilty boys were variously suspended, expelled or not allowed to graduate, leaving Warren, who had already graduated, a special case.

Though at first unable to believe that a Stilwell could be guilty of misbehavior, Dr. Stilwell upon investigation confirmed the unhappy truth. He decided discipline was needed: Warren must go into the Army. He seems not to have taken a severe or punishing attitude for he told Warren (according to a version adopted if not authenticated by the family) that "there is a nice place up the Hudson where you can play tennis." Although his father's decision cost Warren the chance to play football at Yale, he made, as far as is known, no objection. Indeed, with the United States having recently tossed off a "splendid little war" in Cuba and still engaged in fighting Insurrectos in the Philippines, and with American infantry at that moment shooting their way along with other foreign troops to the rescue of the Legations besieged in Peking by the Boxer Rebellion, the prospect of being a soldier may have appealed to a boy suffering from both paternal smothering and a surfeit of high school.

In any event he seems to have plunged with characteristic intensity into the endeavor of gaining admission to West Point; a neighbor remembers his having stayed in bed for a week on the interesting theory that he could in this way stretch himself a quarter-inch to meet the height requirement for a cadet.

As it was already late to apply for an appointment to the Military Academy, Dr. Stilwell pulled wires. Through a neighbor across the street who was a friend of President McKinley, Warren was given an appointment as an alternate-at-large. On the application form Dr. Stilwell lightly penciled in the blanks before allowing his son to copy them over in ink. At the ordeal of the qualifying examinations Warren thought he had failed in mathematics, but when the names of those failing to qualify were mercilessly read aloud, he found himself, to his surprise, left in line with the successful remainder.

The student body in which he was now included did not represent a military caste such as was built into European society. Out of close to 4,000 officers who had graduated from West Point by the year 1900 only 139 or 3.5 percent were the sons or grandsons of previous graduates. Traditionally suspicious of "militarism," Congress had retained the power of appointment to the Academy, and from fear of allowing a military caste to develop, tended to lean away from the sons of officers in favor of civilians' sons. Its nominations brought together a group mainly of conservative, native-born, middle- and upper-middle-class background. Ages ranged in the first year from seventeen to twenty-two, with Stilwell among the youngest. The newest recruits on that July day in 1900 raced to the telegraph office to notify their families and then, as Stilwell wrote in his diary, "went back to hell."

For plebe year at West Point in 1900 the description was not inappropriate. Hazing had reached an extreme at this time which, after the withdrawal and subsequent death of two cadets from causes attributed to hazing, brought on a Congressional investigation in February 1901. Among those required to testify, much against his will, was Douglas MacArthur, in the class a year ahead of Stilwell, who had lain on his cot in convulsions after a session of "exercising." Plebes were made to squat over bayonets, to run naked while buckets of cold water were thrown at them, to be hanged from their thumbs or to stand on their heads in the bath, to hold a rifle on extended arms for long periods, to be "sweated" (wrapped in blankets and raincoats in July), to swallow Tabasco sauce or eat vast quantities of a food such as a plateful of molasses or two hundred prunes, to engage in forced fights or eat meals under the table and to suffer various other humiliations.

The practice was not entirely wanton. Its excuse was that, like the rigid routines of the official regime, it was said to teach self-control, resistance to panic and, above all, acceptance of authority. The core of the military profession is discipline and the essence of discipline is obedience. Since this does not come naturally to men of independent and rational mind, they must train themselves in the habit of obedience on which lives and the fortunes of battle may some day depend. Reasonable orders are easy enough to obey; it is capricious, bureaucratic or plain idiotic demands that form the habit of discipline. Of these, bracing at West Point—a frozen stance with shoulders squeezed back, chin and stomach sucked in—was the symbol and the essence.

"Brace, brace, brace," Stilwell wrote in his diary, "drill, drill, drill. Oh, Lord. . . . Sink, setting up drill, drink, rest, squad drill, dinner, clean guns, squad drill, retreat, company drill around the area before supper. . . . Taps, oblivion, reveille at 4:30, brace all the time, at meals between every mouthful, had to brace on toes for an hour-and-a-half once." Upper-class-men made bracing a constant torture. Sometimes plebes had to work "holding tissue paper between shoulder blades (a cinch when wet)." During tent camp in summer he was subjected to a "soiree" of hazing which he could describe only incoherently as "smoking and poking skags at your chin. And hell sauce. Oh, joy. Rat funerals and bugs. Watch 'em with crossed bayonets for hours." Joe (as he was now and hereafter known except to his family) was homesick, miserable and constipated, a condition with which he was often concerned throughout life. "Overslept once till guns went off—scared to death. . . . Made beds, swept up tents, looped up walls, dragged water, put in collars and cuffs . . . cussed out all the time."

He found escape in adventure stories borrowed from the library, among them *Kidnapped, The Luck of Roaring Camp, King Solomon's Mines, Under Two Flags, Les Misérables* and a sport on this list, De Quincy's *Confessions of an Opium Eater*. He kept the last out for the longest time, two weeks compared to two to five days for the others.

Eventually plebe year was over, and like coming into the sunlight out of some dark tunnel, he emerged an upper-classman. The curriculum of the Military Academy at this time was designed to produce an officer *ab ovo* and concentrated on the technical knowledge needed by a soldier with little attention to the possibly wider needs of a citizen. A student emerged marvelously proficient in drawing maps and terrain features but less well versed in the history of man and his institutions. The humanities were confined to one course in history and one in English language, literature and composition combined. Otherwise the cadet took French and Spanish, math, chemistry, law and "natural philosophy" (which meant a smattering of the physical sciences), plus his military subjects. In addition to drill regulations, these were ordnance and gunnery, surveying, fortifications, tactics and two years of drawing which included topography and plotting of surveys, shades and shadows, linear perspective, theory of color and laying of tints, field reconnaissance contouring, history of cartography, engineering and ordnance drawing, freehand landscape and enough more to equip a Leonardo.

The capstone of the cadet's military studies, taught by the Department of Military Engineering, was "The Art of War." Originally called "The Science of War" in the days when the only element considered teachable was fortifications, the course had been transformed and developed by one of the Academy's great teachers, Dennis Hart Mahan, into a study of the principles of tactics and strategy drawn from lessons of past battles and great captains. During Mahan's tenure from 1832 to 1871 Napoleon's campaigns were the model and the offensive spirit was the theme. Emphasis was on speed, mobility, surprise and other components of attack. By Stilwell's time as a cadet the Civil War had superseded Napoleon. Even the dubious experience of 1898, which provided more lessons to shun than to emulate, had reached the classroom.

Joe revealed a proficiency in languages, standing number one in French in his second year, and managed well enough in his other studies, but he lacked the high seriousness and self-belief that had led such predecessors as Robert E. Lee, John J. Pershing and Douglas MacArthur to graduate number one in military aptitude. Twice Joe received demerits for "laughing at drill," which is not the stuff that makes First Captain. Other demerits incurred were for "throwing food in mess hall at supper," "shouting and creating disturbance in bathroom upon departure of baseball squad," "prearranging organized fistic combat between two cadets" and "cat in quarters at P.M. inspection."

Besides these pursuits his athletic activities continued prodigious. He formed the habit of running several miles before breakfast, served as captain of the cross-country team, won the mile in 1903, scored the winning points in the track meet of 1904 and rowed in two boat races the day after. He is credited with introducing basketball at the Academy and he coached and played on, as well as managed, its first team in 1903-04. Despite the handicap of slight stature, he earned his letter in varsity football in his final year. With what energy was left over from athletics he served as his company's "hop" manager, or representative for social activities, for two years in a row.

Having achieved the rank of Lieutenant of Cadets, he graduated decently if not brilliantly as 32nd in a class of 124. This was considerably short of the top ten, who, as the first to exercise choice of their branch of service, invariably took all the available places in the Engineers which offered the most interesting work in peacetime. The Cavalry was not for Joe either; although he rode, he hated horses. He called them "oat blowers" and said the shape of their heads showed they had dinosaur brains. He chose the Infantry, and on June 15, 1904, aged twenty-one, received his commission as second lieutenant. Described in the yearbook as "one of the few who puts down his ancestry as Yankee," he was at this time a straight, taut figure of five-foot-nine weighing 145 pounds, with neat head and features, cropped hair, a straightforward look and serious dark eyes. "Sheepskin at last" was the only comment in his diary on graduation day. Then as later, memorable events caused him to lapse into the laconic.

While Stilwell was at West Point preparing to enter it, the Army was undergoing the greatest shaking up in its history. From an unexacting career in 1900 it had been purged, reorganized and reformed into a profession by 1904, at least in theory. If the change was still mostly on paper, the foundations of professionalism had been laid. The transforming cause was not so much the recent war as the Secretary of War, Elihu Root.

The chaos of mobilization for Cuba in 1898 revealed the hopeless inadequacy of the Army's executive system. It had no General Staff but operated under ten virtually autonomous Bureaus—Quartermaster's Paymaster's, Commissary, Ordnance and so forth. No unit of the armed forces could be activated by a single order since its arms and supplies and auxiliaries and transport each required the orders of a different Bureau. The officers administering the Bureaus held permanent staff jobs, which tended to nourish inertia.

Appointed Secretary in 1899 to reform the system, Root went to work on the basis of a truism and a principle: that "the object of having an Army is to provide for war" and that the Regular Army could only be a nucleus, "never the whole machine with which any war will be fought." His primary reform, based on blueprints drawn 20 years earlier by General Emory Upton, one of West Point's most remarkable graduates, and by an Englishman, Spenser Wilkinson, was the establishment of a General Staff. The Staff, in the title of Wilkinson's book, was to serve as "The Brains of the Army." It was to exercise the executive function in place of the Bureaus and it was assigned a task new to the American Army—war planning.

Root created the Army War College to educate for the strategic function and he improved the postgraduate courses for line officers in the Artillery, Cavalry and Infantry schools and at the Command and General Staff College at Fort Leavenworth. He introduced examination as a criterion for promotion and established the principle of rotating service between line and staff duty. The whole system was to be regularly tested by field maneuvers. Root succeeded in pushing his reforms through Congress in the sessions of 1901-03. Although the grip of the Bureaus could not be loosened all at once, he laid the framework for a centrally organized Army.

In size the Army had increased from a prewar strength of 28,000 men and 2,000 officers to a total of 100,000 at the peak of action in the Philippines. Against cries of "militarism," Congress authorized a minimum of 60,000 thereafter. By 1904, the year that Stilwell entered it, the Army had shrunk back to about 50,000 men and 3,000 officers. On paper it was organized into 31 regiments of Infantry and 15 of Cavalry, which together with the Artillery Corps and the Corps of Engineers were distributed over some 45 posts in the United States and overseas. The framework of a regiment was three battalions which at full strength numbered 800 men each, divided into four companies. In the peacetime reality of 1904 the average garrison was merely the nucleus of a regiment amounting to about 700 men, or less than a battalion.

Except in the Philippines where sporadic fighting still continued, garrison life in the United States was not challenging. The last armed clash with Indians had taken place in 1890, but local districts and their representatives in Congress resisted attempts to abolish the "hitching post" forts or to consolidate their areas. The little garrisons droned on with whatever routines of drill and rifle practice, polishing and cleaning and rote-learning of the Manual could be devised to keep men and officers busy. Emphasis was on exactness, and marksmanship was a fetish at which the American soldier attained greater skill than the European. The working day was over at noon. Enlisted men lived in quarters known as Soapsuds Row from the days when their wives worked as laundresses for the officers. Pay ranged in 1904 from a private's $13 a month to a minimum of $45 for a first sergeant, with an extra $2 for qualifying as a marksman, and $5 for expert rifleman. The quality of enlisted personnel was rough and they did not command the affection of the public.

America did not on the whole admire its Army. Having deliberately eschewed spiked helmets and cuirasses, bearskin hats and scarlet facings, it did not feel the love and respect these accouterments evoked in Europe. After the short-lived imperial enthusiasm of 1900, Congress resumed being as stingy as possible with appropriations. Troop trains on the railroads rated after freight cars in priority and had to wait on sidings to let passenger and freight trains go by. The public attitude was such that Congress felt required in 1911 to provide a $500 fine for any public place of entertainment that discriminated against men in uniform.

Against the long horizon of peace as viewed from 1904, the officers' corps to which Stilwell now belonged could look forward to an assured and reasonably comfortable but small-time life with little scope for strong ambitions. Pay was not princely, ranging from $1,400 a year for a new second lieutenant to $4,000 for a colonel. Life was dominated by rank, and promotion in 1904 was stagnant. Descending step by step from the commanding officer—and the commanding officer's wife, referred to as COW—rank determined everything in both official and social life, including living quarters. Within any grade it was refined down to seniority by date of appointment so that an officer promoted as of June might find himself ousted from a desirable house by a new arrival who had reached the same grade in May. At afternoon receptions the highest ranking officer's wife poured coffee rather than tea because, since coffee was the more popular drink in America and more people tended to congregate at that end of the table, it was considered to outrank tea.

With place of work and residence combined, with schools located on post, with frequent changes of post preventing ties with the local community and throwing officers on each other's company, with lives crossing and recrossing, and the social notes in service journals keeping everyone apprised of marriages, card parties and who entertained whom at what post, the military career evolved into a closed, and as regards the tensions and political antagonisms of civilian life, an almost innocent society. Regardless of jealousies and intrigues engendered by rank, a strong *esprit de corps* existed whose sign was the salute, proclaimed by the Manual as "the signal of recognition and greeting between members of the military brotherhood." The code instilled by the Academy prescribed that officers were gentlemen joined by common principles of honor and behavior and by personal loyalty toward brother officers. Loyalty owed to the CO, whether regimental colonel or Commander-in-Chief, was considered to be personal no less than official.

In its special relationship to the Commander-in-Chief as "the right arm of the Executive," the Army acknowledged itself subordinate to the civil power. It was very conscious of its position as servant of the state. Beginning at West Point with the motto "Duty, Honor, Country," the operative concept of the officer corps was duty. To be able to respond to a call to duty at any time by whatever Administration, and perform that duty effectively, the military was supposed to cultivate a nonpartisan frame of mind in which it could carry out orders without questioning. In theory it considered itself set apart under an obligation to renounce the ordinary political passions much as a religious order renounces the flesh. "There shall be no discussion of politics" was a bylaw of the West Point Association of Graduates. Army personnel, according to the *Military Services Journal,* were "scarcely conscious" of their right to vote and rarely exercised it.

Given his natural bent for action, Stilwell chose the Philippines, the only place where U.S. forces were then actively engaged, for his first service as a fledgling officer. As a West Point graduate, especially one in the first third of his class, he could express his preference of post. Assigned to the 12th Infantry, he sailed in October 1904 aboard the troop transport *Sheridan,* one of three former transatlantic cattleboats purchased by the Army in 1898. With a stopover in Hawaii, the transports took from 30 to 40 days to make the passage to Manila. Joe managed to pass the time exercising on deck, reading, sleeping, eating, boning up on his Spanish, "bellyaching" with friends, talking with officers' wives and writing letters — "8 good fat ones and 16 postals" in one day. His ease and flow with pen and paper, which he was to retain through life, was already established. He recorded another characteristic: not joining "the booze fighters who get tanked up every night," among them Captain H., "soaking like a piece of milk toast." Though never a teetotaler nor one to make an issue of liquor, Stilwell's drinking remained minimal.

The embarrassment of the United States at finding itself involved in foreign conquest just like any wicked land-hungry power of the Old World was great, the more so since the conquest was being actively resisted. For the sake of the American conscience the Government had hurried to install civil rule in the Philippines and to declare the rebellion over before in fact it was. Although broken as an organized national movement after the capture of Aguinaldo in 1901, many of the island tribes refused his plea to surrender. With lethal bolo knives replacing their dwindling supply of firearms, they were still conducting a guerilla resistance and erupting every now and then in fierce raids on the occupied areas. On Cebu alone, Stilwell noted in his diary, 803 Moros had been killed in "scraps" during the three months before he arrived.

He was soon on active service and while on a march to the coast was "scared to death of getting a bolo rush." In February 1905 his unit, D Company of the 1st Battalion, was sent on an expedition up the Gandora River in Samar against the rebel Pulajanes. He marched "up and down over mountains toward San Jose, swamps, vines, mud, hills, slips, falls. . . . Camp in the woods at dark. Men slept as they stood. Rained all night. Men wet, mud, etc. OH HELL!" Again the next day through rain they climbed a very hard trail, men were dropping out, and they found San Jose deserted. Filipino scouts were sent ahead, they flushed out a band of Pulajanes and a skirmish followed. Later they encountered 50 bolo men who ran off. After two weeks in the bush, Joe recorded, "Took big drink of booze—phew!" During respite in camp by the river, he at once began to organize athletics. "Fixed up a *baroda* with seats, oarlocks, oars—funny as hell, the first 8-oared shell in Samar."

When the march resumed, Joe learned in a few hours of active duty a lesson in command no war college could have taught him. On the second day out the company was without water and the Captain, anxious to reach a source, moved ahead fast, telling Joe to drop behind and keep the rear of the column closed up. In the hard hot going Joe, leading a Pulajan prisoner tied by a rope, came upon the First Sergeant lying by the trail, collapsed from heat exhaustion. During the few seconds he stopped to try to arouse him, the column moved ahead and his shouts to halt it, muffled by the thick brush, went unheard. With the unconscious Sergeant loaded alternately on the prisoner's shoulders and on his own, he struggled forward, losing the faint trail, backtracking to pick it up, badly off for water, and armed with only a .38-caliber Colt, expecting all the time the Pulajanes to "jump out of the brush to cut us up." No message came back from the column. Increasingly exhausted and hoping desperately to get some-where before dark, he finally heard a clatter ahead and stumbled into camp to find the company eating supper and the Captain unconcerned. "You're here, are you?" was all he said. No one had been sent back to look for the missing Sergeant and Lieutenant; only Joe's physical stamina had brought them through. Had he fallen from fatigue in hostile territory, his life might have ended there in Samar within two days of his twenty-second birthday. This experience of a commanding officer's responsibility—or lack of it—made a profound and lasting impression which continued to haunt him. "I don't know to this day," he wrote 30 years later, "if we hadn't gotten in, whether Captain Falls ever intended to do anything about it."

On post at Camp Jossman on the tiny island of Guimaras off Panay, life was less strenuous. An evening at the General's was quickly caught in a few words: "Talcum powder belles, uniforms, waiter, English Lancer." Everything in the native surroundings interested him, from fern leaves used by the children as kites to the native method of stealing grain by letting it drain from a hole in a sack through the slatted floor to a bag held under-neath. Tactical exercises, drill and regulations, rifle practice and pistol shooting, tennis, sailing and encounters with "cavalry stiffs" filled his time. Joe organized hikes and games, arranged decorations for the company dance and translated for the War Department a French pamphlet on the siege of Port Arthur in the current Russo-Japanese War and a Spanish treatise on "The Military Geography of Chile." As first member of the Club executive committee, he "decided to stir things up a little." One form this took was an episode in his running battle with the Cavalry in which he undertook to prove the superiority of the Infantry. Lining up his men in a trench, he provided them with a number of bed sheets. When the Cavalry charged, they stood up and waved the sheets, frightening the horses into a mad shambles, to Joe's infinite delight. In spite or because of such exploits, his Efficiency Report from the Captain of D Company rated him "Excellent" in all categories and "Exceptionally bright, hardworking and efficient."

In February 1906, after 14 months in the Philippines, he received notice that he was being detailed to West Point as Instructor in the Department of Modern Languages. "First man in 1904 back," he noted as a cause for pride. Revealing a supersensitivity, he added a list of seven names from whom he had received congratulations and nine from whom he had not.

He immediately seized on the appointment in languages to apply for two months' leave with permission to return via Europe in order, as he wrote, to improve his French by traveling from Saigon to France on a French liner with opportunity for "everyday intercourse and conversation

with Frenchmen." Fallen among the Bureaus, the request was still unanswered, despite his urgent cables, by the time he was due to sail on the
April transport. At Nagasaki in Japan, where the transports stopped to
coal, he tried again and at last received a reply which proved that inefficiency still defied Root's reforms: it was in a code that no one in Japan
was equipped to read. Joe perforce sailed eastward with the transport, and
only at the next military post in Hawaii, which had the right key for the
code, found that the message read, "Leave granted, return by Europe." By
then it was too late, and with feelings apparently too strong for comment,
he returned home via San Francisco.

In the military profession, where the opportunity to learn through actual
practice is undependable, teaching and training in one form or another was
a major occupation of the officer in peacetime. During his first three years
as an instructor Stilwell taught English, French and Spanish. In the fourth
year he was given additional duty as Instructor of Tactics and transferred
from languages to teaching history. Already impatient with slow minds or
lack of effort or anyone "not on the level," he was quick to help anyone
who was really trying. He served in the Department of Tactics throughout
the period as coach of basketball, baseball and track and in the fourth
year as assistant football coach. "It was due to Lieutenant Stilwell's untiring work," reported the Army Athletic Association for the 1908-09 season,
"that the [basketball] team was so successful." Whether team sports were
assigned to the Department of Tactics for reasons of convenience or of philosophy is moot, but they represented tactics, especially football whose pattern often appears later in the plans and discussions of Stilwell and other
commanders. As a coach, according to General Jacob Devers of the class of
1909, Stilwell was "sarcastic but in a way that made you want to perform.
I would have done anything for him."
    The Academy, however, could not fill his horizon, the less so for being
next door to home. Restless and inquiring, he requested leave for each of
the summers of 1907, 1908 and 1909 to go "beyond the seas," with
Spanish as the excuse. With better luck than he had had when he applied
for leave to improve his French, he succeeded in making three voyages to
areas of Latin America. The first was at Government expense in the form
of a "Confidential Mission" to make a topographical survey of Guatemala.
Ordered to travel under an assumed name, carrying nothing that would
reveal his identity or show him to be a Government agent, he was to fill
in skeleton maps with an accurate rendering of the topography, and supply
information on bridges, fords, ferries, railroads, roads, wagon carts, draft
animals, harbors, landings, fortifications, telephone and telegraph lines,

rivers, lakes, canals, cities, towns and villages, garrisons, occupation and density of population, food, fuel, forage, political conditions, diseases and climate. Six weeks were allowed for the mission.

Stilwell's wanderings by foot and mule in Guatemala were full of discoveries. He found the country flea-bitten and unappetizing, fell ill with dysentery and fever and after a few weeks longed to go home. Yet he was constantly observing, filling his notebooks with facts and comments, finding himself stirred by the same aspects of oppression that were to become familiar in China. They evoked a sympathy with the common man and anger with his rulers that he would not have felt at home. The Guatemalteco, he noted, would not work more than he had to because everything he made was stolen by Government officials who were often "thieves and even worse." Stilwell formed a very "unfavorable opinion" of the officials, landowners and professional classes. Keeping the peasant illiterate and uneducated, he wrote, "suits very well the purpose of the Government which takes him from his farm at any time and puts him in the Army for an indefinite period, not caring whether or not his family starves. Yet . . . he says nothing, enduring it all in silence." These were sentiments that were to repeat themselves in China. As a close friend said, "Stilwell was liberal and sympathetic by instinct. But he was conservative in thought and politics."

The next year, 1908, he spent his summer leave traveling through Mexico with a friend and classmate, Lieutenant Francis Honeycutt, nicknamed "Hungry." They made a militant pair for Honeycutt was reputed to be the best swordsman in the Regular Army while Stilwell, who had qualified as expert marksman and member of the Army rifle team, was reported by a contemporary newspaper to be "one of the 20 premier rifle shots in the United States." Starting in Washington, they visited the War College and the Congressional Library, "which is a peach," Joe noted, giving it his highest praise. Things he really liked were "peachy."

In Mexico they traveled on foot and horseback for two weeks while Joe made copious notes on Mexican culture, history, customs, agriculture, religion and Aztec hieroglyphics. After their return home via Cuba he and Hungry carried the Mexican theme to a costume party at Lake Placid at which they appeared "dressed as 2 femmes with bare legs and bellies. Made quite a hit as Montezuma's daughters." The party was the highlight of a fortnight of fun in the Adirondacks in August which finished off their leave. They charged without pause through picnics and tennis, hikes and dances, sports with friends and jaunts with girls. Containing for once no caustic comments, the diary recorded a rare acknowledgment of a good time among "fine people, cordial and friendly."

Just before leaving for Mexico, Stilwell at twenty-five had met the girl

Second Lieutenant Stilwell's first post was in the Philippines in 1904 (10). In 1908, during summer leave, he traveled through Mexico with classmate Francis Honeycutt, sending back a picture postcard to Honeycutt's mother (9) and pasting in his album a picture of himself fording a river (11).

9

10

11

Stilwell married Winifred A. Smith of Syracuse (13) in Octob[er]
1910 (12) and was shortly thereafter reassigned to his regiment [in]
the Philippines where she accompanied him (15). In 1913 Stilw[ell]
was back at West Point, this time as a happily married man a[nd]
father (14).

he was going to marry. She was Winifred A. Smith of Syracuse, a classmate at boarding school of his younger sister Mary. So far, except for a girl whose picture he had carried to the Philippines (with the approval of his parents who believed it would "help to keep him straight"), Joe had had no serious romances. Not the shadowy girl of the photograph, but his sister, then only thirteen, had been his date at the West Point Hop in the year he graduated. Now returning the compliment, Mary invited him to her school's June dance and asked him to bring Hungry along for her friend Win, a very pretty young lady of nineteen with vivacious eyes and curly hair.

Lieutenant Honeycutt wore elegant blues with the red stripe of the Field Artillery, but it was Mary's brother in starched summer whites to whom Win was more attracted. She thought she had "never met anyone so handsome or with such wonderful deep brown eyes." They felt happy together and he asked if he could write. A year later he invited her to the Officers' Hop at West Point but her mother, suspicious of Army men, refused permission. He came, however, to her graduation dance at finishing school and later, chaperoned by her mother, she visited the Point and met his family. A letter from him addressed "Sweet Peach" embarrassed her but in the spring of 1910, after she attended the Hop of that year, they became engaged and were married in October. In a letter to her before the wedding he wrote, "I will love you more as my wife than I ever have as my fiancée— lots more. . . . I am going to do my very best to take care of you and make you happy. But I am *very* far from perfect. I'll want your help many times —when I get impatient, grouchy, gloomy. . . . If at times I am unbearable please remember, dear, that I'll come out of it and that my one wish will always be your happiness. For I love you with all that is in me."

Even in love Stilwell had not been content to stay home but, moved by his annual yearning to go "beyond the seas," had spent his summer leave of 1909 in Central America, and in 1910 had again applied for a topographical mission for the months between his engagement and marriage. Citing his qualifications in Spanish and previous experience in a letter to the War Department, he stated combatively if somewhat obscurely that he was indifferent to the nature of the work "so long as it takes me to those countries in the interests of the United States and against *them*." Despite these fighting sentiments the request was disapproved by both the State Department, which wished to avoid complications owing to "the late friction" with Nicaragua, and the Chief of Staff, who objected rather cryptically to sending young officers on these missions "on account of the effect it has had upon some of those who have been there in the past."

Shortly before his marriage Stilwell had been caught up in the new rules enforcing rotation between detached service and regimental duty. These required that in peacetime line officers under the rank of major must serve two years out of every six with their regiments. Designed to limit tours of detached service in Washington to four years, the rules were codified by act of Congress in 1912 and thereafter were known as the Manchu Act in tribute to the common uprooting of Army bureaucrats from Washington and Manchus from Peking. Stilwell's first term with the 12th Infantry being found short of the requirements, he was reassigned to his regiment and sailed with his wife for the Philippines on the transport *Sherman* in January 1911.

His second tour in the Islands proved to be routine post duty at Fort William McKinley, a trolley ride from Manila. Marked only by his promotion to first lieutenant in March, it was a daily round of drill which the company could do with its eyes closed, of garrison school which succeeded in killing time until 1 P.M., and of efforts to vent unused energy in organizing boat races in native *bancas* for his men and teaching them to build bamboo bridges over the river. With his eye on the current revolution in Mexico, he agitated for transfer to "activities" on the border but without success. By September, having three months' accumulated leave saved up, he determined to spend it seeing more of the Orient with his wife before she was to go home to await the birth of their first child.

They sailed for Japan on September 14, arriving at Nagasaki from where they toured the shores of the Inland Sea as far as Hiroshima. Stilwell raced up every mountain in sight. After climbing to the top of Miyajima in an hour and a half, he recorded "the guide's admiration for my legs knew no bounds." In the next six weeks, pulled by his endless curiosity and energy, he and Win saw Japan intensively. He began at once to learn the language, causing titters at a railroad station when he asked to buy milk. Checking in the dictionary later, he found he had asked for "mother's milk." His recorded comments were exhaustive but at this stage of his acquaintance with Japan they were confined to descriptions without judgments or opinions.

Although the newspapers were full of the startling events of the Revolution in China, Stilwell was evidently too absorbed to notice, for his diary makes no mention of them. He saw his wife off for the United States in mid-November and continued on to see China by himself.

Visitor to Revolution:

CHINA, 1911

S TILWELL entered at Shanghai, epitome and greatest of the Treaty Ports. His first sight was of the fleet of foreign warships—two Japanese, two French, one British, one German and one American—riding the coffee-colored waters of the harbor not as visitors but as occupants. Developed by foreign enterprise, the great metropolis and business capital of China was governed in major part as a concession under foreign control. It lay at the mouth of the Yangtze, central artery of the country and busiest river in Asia; half of China's industry was contained within its limits and half of China's trade passed over its wharves. Stilwell saw his first rickshaw at Woosung and sampans and sailing junks in the river. Coming into Shanghai proper, his first impression was "a shock," as it was to most foreigners on arrival who, unconsciously expecting something Oriental and exotic, saw instead the solid hotels and banks, the broad streets and parks of a Western-style city. From the hotel window Stilwell thought it looked like Philadelphia. In the streets of the International Settlement he was struck by the tall turbaned Sikhs imported from British India who served as police.

The Revolution added a touch of excitement for Stilwell without seriously inconveniencing him, for like most momentous upheavals it was less noticeable to the eyewitness than it would be to history. On a tour of the Old Chinese City he saw rebel recruiting stations under the flag of the Revolution whose twelve-pointed black sun on a red ground had replaced the Imperial yellow dragon. He talked with some of the soldiers, noting that they carried Chinese-made Mausers and seemed "fine-appearing lads." He saw beggars thick as flies lying in rags in the gutters, vile, filthy canals clogged with refuse, a coolie taking a mountain of trunks from wharf to hotel for 30 cents, a street vendor selling oranges by the section, mourners dressed in white in a temple, "dames of fortune lined up in the doorway under a light, gaily dressed and bejewelled but solidly listless faces." Visiting an old teahouse dating from the Ming dynasty, he noted that the bridge leading to it was built in zigzag form to thwart evil spirits who, unable to maneuver angles according to Chinese belief, would fall into the water at the turns. Elsewhere observing the number of gods and shrines in all the houses, he remarked that the main point of religion in China "seems to be an effort to scare away evil spirits who are continually trying to do them harm."

By chance or perspicacity he had hit upon a central fact of Chinese life—fear of the host of demons, ghosts and devils who bring evil upon men. Foreigners, as indicated by the term "foreign devil," sometimes modified by "long-nosed" or "hairy," were associated in Chinese minds with evil spirits. The instinct of China had been to keep her precincts immune from foreign infection. The Manchu Empire before 1898 had no Ministry of Foreign Affairs to conduct relations with other countries because no such relations had been wanted or considered necessary. Aliens desiring to trade, preach or otherwise establish contact had been dealt with by the Hall for Governance of Barbarians.

Throughout her history China had believed herself the center of civilization, surrounded by barbarians. She was the Middle Kingdom, the center of the universe, whose Emperor was the Son of Heaven, ruling by the Mandate of Heaven. Convinced of their superior values, the Chinese considered that China's greatness was owed to principles of social order formulated by her sages and administered benevolently by a learned elite over a harmonious whole. All outsiders whose misfortune was to live beyond her borders were "barbarians" and necessarily inferiors who were expected, and indeed required, to make their approach, if they insisted on coming, bearing tribute and performing the *kowtow* in token of humble submission.

From Marco Polo to the eighteenth century, visiting Westerners, amazed and admiring, were inclined to take China at her own valuation. Her recorded history began in the third millennium B.C., her bronzes were as old as the pyramids, her classical age was contemporary with that of Greece, her Confucian canon of ethics predated the New Testament if not the Old. She was the inventor of paper, porcelain, silk, gunpowder, the clock and movable type, the builder of the Great Wall, one of the wonders of the world, the creator of fabrics and ceramics of exquisite beauty and of an art of painting that was sophisticated and expressive when Europe's was still primitive and flat.

Vast and grand and faraway, a land of dragon-roofed temples, bridges of marble, terraced rice fields and many-tiered pagodas, dominated by a fabulous monarch and splendid court, supported by a limitless mass of hard-working laborers, unravaged by the religious wars of the West, ancient and supreme outside the Christian sway, boasting a love of order, respect for learning and contempt for war, she was reported by European travelers as a kind of utopia which seemed indeed, as her philosophers claimed, to have found the secret of rational government. In that case the paradox of mass penury was puzzling. Some observers were troubled too by the recurring phenomenon of corruption and dynastic decay and by evidence of a culture that was endlessly turning like a wheel without gears in the grooves of the past. But such doubts did not greatly disturb the Western habit of idealizing China to suit Western theories of a particular time.

When at the end of the eighteenth century Western ships and merchants surged against China's shores, eager for tea and silk and cotton, they found no reciprocal enthusiasm. Enclosed in the isolation of superiority, Imperial China wanted no influx of strangers from primitive islands called Britain or France or Holland who came to live off the riches of the Middle Kingdom bearing only worthless articles for exchange. They had ugly noses and coarse manners and wore ridiculous clothes with constricting sleeves and trousers, tight collars and coats that had tails down the back but failed to close in front. These were not the garments of reasonable men.

A past-oriented society, safe only in seclusion, sensed a threat from the importunate West. The Imperial Government raised every barrier possible by refusals, evasions, postponements and prohibitions to foreign entry or settlement or the opening of formal relations. Splendidly remote in the "Great Within" of the Forbidden City of Peking, the court refused to concern itself with the knocking on its doors. It would admit foreign embassies who came to plead for trade treaties only if they performed the ritual of three genuflections and nine prostrations in approaching the Son of Heaven. British envoys, after surmounting innumerable obstacles to reach Peking, balked at the *kowtow* and turned back empty-handed.

Since Western merchants paid in silver for Chinese goods they were not banned altogether. Under a set of regulations designed to bar their intrusion but not their money, they were confined to the southernmost port of Canton, as far as possible from the capital at Peking, and were required to do business from "factories"—a combination of dwelling, office and

warehouse—outside the city walls. To discourage their permanent settlement they were not allowed to bring in their women. To keep them from
learning the language it was made illegal for Chinese to serve them as
teachers.

Even so the trade grew—to be paid for, fatefully, in opium. The demand
in Europe and America for tea and *chinoiserie* made the traders' prospects
rich but a one-sided exchange of money for goods could not expand
profitably. The foreigners had little to bring that the Chinese wanted
until they introduced opium grown in India and Persia. As the Chinese
demand spread, the drug became the main cargo of shippers licensed
by the British East India Company as well as of American clipper trade
which followed in its wake. Fortunes were made, commerce multiplied
and British rule in India came to depend on the income.

The Chinese too grew rich on the trade although they declared it illegal.
Dealers and middlemen took their commissions and officials at every level
took a consideration for administering permissively the grand fraud. They
surrounded the smuggling with an elaborate pretense of pursuit, chasing
the clipper ships at a safe distance and firing loud cannonades, duly
reported to the distant Emperor as victories. In the context of the East
where form rather than substance is the reality, these engagements satisfied
the Chinese requirement of face. Lush in opportunities, the opium trade
extended the deepening corruption of the Manchu regime. The Westerners,
pricked now and then by a sense of shame, found it could be subdued by
counting the gains. For both sides the vast masquerade was not a good
school of mutual respect.

Out of this situation came the Opium Wars of 1839-42 and 1856-60,
the matrix of intercourse thereafter between China and the West. Because
of the loss of customs revenue, the growing ill effects of opium-smoking
among the people, and the fear that the cordon against foreigners was
breaking down, the Imperial Government decided that the opium trade
must be brought to an end. The British, eager to sell their cotton and
other manufactured goods, were pressing for the opening of other ports
and for the right of trade to be confirmed by treaty. Basically the issue
was not simply opium but the fact that the Chinese wanted to restrict,
and the West to expand, their intercourse. The West prevailed.

Against British armed frigates China's antiquated coastal cannon,
left to rust by Manchu ineptitude, were useless. The First Opium War
ended in the Treaty of Nanking which in effect opened China to the West
and broke ground for all foreign inroads thereafter. Besides ceding Hong
Kong in perpetuity, it opened five coast towns from Canton to Shanghai,
later known as Treaty Ports, where the British could maintain homes (with
wives), establish consulates and courts to try their own law violators under

their own laws, and carry on trade under a fixed tariff of 5 percent. The Second Opium War, in which Imperial forces armed with spears were defeated by an Anglo-French expeditionary force outside Peking, confirmed and extended the principle of extraterritoriality. Foreigners gained access to ten more Treaty Ports and the right to navigation of the Yangtze and to travel anywhere in China. They were yielded the awesome right of diplomatic representation and residence in Peking and the right of missionaries to own property outside the Treaty Ports. In final submission opium was legalized. America and Russia shared in negotiation of the treaties if not in the active belligerence. Throughout the process of the opening of China, the United States followed through portals cut by the British, avoiding the aggression and inheriting the advantages.

China's Imperial Government had ruled by prestige which defeat by the barbarians gravely undermined. In the years following the First Opium War disasters multiplied, taxes were increased upon the peasantry, corruption in the governing mandarinate became systematic, respect for authority declined, power decentralized, banditry flourished, sovereignty rotted at the center. In 1850 all these decays and discontents coalesced in a great popular uprising known as the Taiping Rebellion which was to last 15 years and cost 20 million lives before it was over. Drawing strength from the oppressed, the Taipings succeeded in establishing a rival capital at Nanking. The recurring moment seemed at hand when the Mandate of Heaven had been withdrawn from a dynasty proven unworthy. But the foreigners, in order to ensure the privileges they had exacted by treaty, shored up the Government. With their aid Nanking was retaken to the accompanying massacre of 100,000 Taipings. China's failed French Revolution was suppressed.

Preserved by foreign help, China's Bourbons thereafter began to lean upon their encroachers. One form that dependence took was in the vital area of revenue. During the chaos of the revolution the British and the Americans had taken over the collection of customs dues on behalf of the Government, and as a result of greater efficiency and less graft, Peking enjoyed a larger income from this source than ever before. The system was extended by agreement to all Treaty Ports and put on a permanent footing with a foreign staff under a British Inspector General.

Many Chinese were coming to believe that their country, while remaining true to its own concepts, must arm itself with Western techniques if it was to cope with the Western threat. It must reform or perish. Western methods appeared as something that could be picked out of context and borrowed for limited use. Leaders of this "self-strengthening" movement managed to introduce Western training programs for the Army and Navy, arsenals for Western weapons and, against the bitter resistance of the conservatives, a college in Peking for the study of Western subjects to supplement the ritual learning of the classics which was the substance of Chinese education. As the first essential for a country largely dependent on wheelbarrows for land transport, they advocated railroads as well as telegraph lines, factories, machines, a postal system and above all a modern school system. But reactionary objection was strong, and lacking a mover of vigorous conviction like the current Emperor Meiji in Japan, the program of modernization had no engine and developed no power of its own. The Imperial circle, personified in the narrow mind and majestic presence of the Empress Dowager Tzu Hsi, was able to deflect the efforts of the reformers.

Her Government rested on a medieval-minded princely clique and on a mandarinate grown slack and inefficient. Energy for change was in the foreigner. Railroads were the channel of penetration for foreign capital and influence. The Government sold concessions for the railroads to the foreign powers, who scrambled for them. Foreign advisers were increasingly employed; missionaries proliferated, asserting by their presence China's need for salvation; foreign cotton and other products were imported, causing the decline of cottage industry. China's resentment increased in proportion to her dependence and expressed itself in "incidents," each ending helplessly in another "unequal" treaty, another round of sovereignty sliced off, another toe of extrality* inserted, another Treaty Port door wedged open by a foreign foot. Foreigners developed China's resources but sapped her will and capacity to use them.

Western imperialism reached its rampant age in the 1880s. The Manchu Empire, fighting bitterly but ineffectively, lost two tributaries to the West in 1885—Tonkin and Annam to France, and north Burma to Britain—plus ten more Treaty Ports to Britain in the same year. A third tributary was lost within the decade to another species of barbarian, near neighbors whom the Chinese customarily referred to as the "dwarf slaves" or "dwarf bandits." In 1895 Japan suddenly stood up in new strength and, easily victorious in war with China, forced her to release Korea (under the euphemism of "independence"), as well as Formosa, the Pescadores, a large indemnity and—severest loss of all—the strategic Liaotung peninsula on the mainland. This was the door to Manchuria and the control point of the seaward approach to north China.

Startled at this rival apparition, the European powers, urged on by Russia who wanted no one else in Manchuria, hurriedly combined to make Japan disgorge Liaotung, and then separately rushed in to exact from a China still quivering in defeat various leaseholds, concessions and special

---

* This shortened form of extraterritoriality was generally in use at the time and has been adopted here.

privileges for themselves. Russia moved in where Japan had been pushed out and took leasehold of the tip of Liaotung where she built herself a naval base at Port Arthur and a commercial port and railway terminus at Dairen. Across from Port Arthur Britain took Wei-hai-wei on the Shantung peninsula, giving herself a naval base in the north. Germany acquired a naval base and railway terminus at Tsingtao on the underside of the Shantung peninsula facing the Yellow Sea, plus mining concessions. In the south Britain took Kowloon on the mainland opposite Hong Kong and France acquired her naval base at Kwangchow Bay on the coast adjoining Indochina and also the concession to build a railway leading from Indochina into Yunnan in south China.

Next they all quarreled over shares in the foreign loans through which China was to pay the Japanese indemnity. Loans were the favored form of penetration after railroads. Competition sharpened greed and the powers settled down to staking out "spheres of interest" where each secured a recognized prior right to develop resources and a foothold for future annexation should China ever be partitioned. As the predatory spirit sharpened, talk of the partition of China was increasingly heard, causing an agony of concern to the United States, caught between hunger and principle.

America in the flush of post-Civil War boom had joined in the exploitation of China without compromising her scruples against taking territory. In 1898 this combination of profit and principle was elevated to a doctrine of foreign policy by John Hay. Called the Open Door (though not by him), it managed to sound generous, high-minded and somehow protective of China while meaning, if anything at all, that the door for penetration should be opened equally to everybody.

American infiltration of China by this time was a two-pronged affair of business and the gospel. Agents of Standard Oil purveying kerosene for every household lamp in China may have found more receptive customers, but the missionaries were to leave a greater mark on relations between the two countries.

China's vastness excited the missionary impulse; it appeared as the land of the future whose masses, when converted, offered promise of Christian and even English-speaking dominion of the world. Disregarding the social and ethical structure which the Chinese found suitable, the missionaries wanted them to change to one in which the individual was sacred and the democratic principle dominant, whether or not these concepts were relevant to China's way of life. Inevitably the missionary, witnessing China's agonies in the nineteenth century, took these as evidence that China could not rule herself and that her problems could only be solved by foreign help. Zealous and ubiquitous, American missionaries took "America Assists the East" as their mandate and made it the refrain of their reports to the congregations at home. As they were personally dependent on the home constituencies for financial support, they had to be convincing in arguing the cause to be worthwhile. Congregations all over the United States listened to the returned missionary with his lantern slides tell of the deserving qualities of the Chinese people and of the great reservoir of future Christians. Along with the public impression that America had saved China's integrity by the doctrine of the Open Door, missionary propaganda helped to create the image of China as protégé, an image which carries an accompanying sense of obligation toward the object of one's own beneficence.

For a brief hopeful hour in 1898 China grasped for modernity. Following the defeat by Japan, the shock of the despised neighbor's transformation into a modern military power had revived the Chinese reform party which, with the support of the young Emperor Kuang Hsu, proposed a large program of modernization including development of transport and industry, establishment of schools and newspapers, civil service reform and, most drastic of all, abolition of the old examination system based on calligraphy and the Confucian essays. The Emperor issued the necessary decrees, the old shell cracked and for a hundred days a new China struggled to be born. But the old clique controlled the strongest armed force. In a sweeping coup the Empress Dowager arrested the reform leaders, executed six of them, imprisoned her nephew in an island palace on a lake of the Forbidden City and reseated herself on his throne. A painted, brocaded despot amid her eunuchs, she presided over the final sinking years of the Manchu dynasty, lapped by approaching ruin.

Out of accumulated frustration and humiliation the great crisis of the Boxer Rebellion burst in 1899-1900. Xenophobia was the cry if not the entire cause. The instigators were a train of secret societies called "Harmonious Fists" (translated "Boxers" by foreign newsmen) led by fanatics who blamed all China's ills on the foreigner and aroused the populace with incitements to massacre and promises of magic immunity to bullets. They were the Chinese equivalent of America's Know-Nothings in the 1850s. Not a true rebellion, the movement was a wild and murderous extravaganza that flamed in the north and claimed to fight not against the Manchus but in the name of Empire and Dynasty. It rested in fact on support by the Government which saw in the Boxers both an opportunity to divert popular discontent upon a scapegoat and a last mad hope of sweeping out the foreigner altogether. In separate outbreaks through north China the Boxers murdered over 200 missionaries and their families plus 20,000 or more "secondary devils—that is, Chinese converts—before converging upon Peking in a siege of the foreign Legations. Trembling

The Boxer Rebellion of 1899–1900 focused accumulated Chinese frustration on foreigners. Companies of Boxers like these (16) attacked the section of Peking in which Western diplomats and merchants lived, leaving parts of it in ruins (17).

The Empress Dowager Tzu Hsi (18), her royal eunuchs (20) and her trusted councillors (19).

19

21

22

On the death of Tzu Hsi in 1908, power passed to her three-year-old great-nephew Pu-yi (21). In 1911 the dynasty offered the presidency to its strongest partisan, Yuan Shih-kai (22).

with the gathered hate of 60 years, the court, though divided in counsel, declared war on the Western powers at last.

A foreign force made up of six national contingents fought its way through from the sea to rescue the besieged Legations. Afterwards in revenge for the Boxers' attack, the rescuers burned and looted and killed in wanton punitive forays. "Every town, every village, every peasant's hut in the path of the troops was first looted and then burned," wrote an eyewitness, the veteran journalist, Thomas Millard. The path of the foreign contingents, he concluded, "will leave a taint in the moral atmosphere of the world for generations to come." Inside Peking, according to the American Minister, foreign soldiers and civilians from general to private, from minister to attaché, from bishop to missionary, have "stolen, sacked, pillaged and generally disgraced themselves." Terms imposed by the victors were harsh. Twelve powers signed the Protocol which pronounced China guilty of crimes "against civilization" and against the laws of nations. The Legation Quarter in the heart of Peking was yielded up to extrality under control of foreign garrisons. Importation of foreign arms was prohibited for two years and China's forts from Peking to the coast were razed, with foreign troops given the right to keep the way to Peking open. A huge indemnity was levied with China's customs revenue as security. Four Imperial officials were executed, others dismissed or permanently exiled.

Foreign enterprise, however galling, dragged China into the twentieth century, developing her economy, awakening political consciousness and breaking down her seclusion. As the need to adapt to modernity became obvious, the desire to get rid of the Manchu incubus spread. The first secret society dedicated to the overthrow of the Manchus, the *Hsing Chung Hui* or "Revive China Society," was organized in 1894 by a twenty-eight-year-old Western-educated Christian, Dr. Sun Yat-sen. A native of Canton, the area longest open to Western influences, he had received Western schooling in Honolulu and Western medical training in Hong Kong. His followers were part of the movement toward modernity that was surfacing in many forms—in daring students who cut off their queues, a symbol of submission to the Manchus, and in a literary renaissance that was breaking the rigid mold of the classics. Even the mandarinate, not all of whom were diehards, began to move and in 1904 established the first national public schools. In September 1905, by Imperial edict, the classical examination system in force since the first century B.C., the Great Wall of the country's culture, was abolished. The Manchu court, willing to adopt a new facade in order to preserve the power of the throne, promised a constitution in five years and elected assemblies after a suitable period to allow for education of the people. Western subjects were introduced into the school curriculum

After the Boxer Rebellion the Legation Quarter in Peking was yielded to extrality under the control of foreign garrisons, including those of the Germans, whose cavalry is depicted here arriving in Peking in 1901 (23).

and missionary schools expanded as sources of the new learning. Progressive Chinese, like the Japanese, were attracted to Western methods because they saw in them the means of meeting the Western challenge.

Japan's startling success in the Russo-Japanese War of 1904-05 gave impetus to the "self-strengtheners." The Japanese example appeared as something to emulate. Students seeking a higher education in tune with modern times went to Tokyo. A powerful impulse to nationalism was given by the United States Exclusion Act of 1904. Brought on by heated agitation against cheap "coolie labor" imported to lay the transcontinental railroads, the act ordained specific and permanent exclusion of Chinese workers, but not other classes. Resentment in China burst into a boycott of American goods in 1905 which spread to 25 cities from Peking to Canton and merged with revolutionary sentiment against the Manchus. Now the enemies were combined; usurper and foreigner together would be swept away in a general overturn of all that bound China down. The boycott did not, however, extend to Western ideas; modern-minded Chinese continued to regard Westernization as the necessary vehicle of change.

The returned students from the United States and Europe, with their degrees in engineering or agriculture or political science, their Western clothes and eyeglasses and earnest look, formed a new class as distinct in spirit from the silk-gowned mandarin with the button of rank on his skullcap and long mustache hanging to his chest as they were in appearance.

America at this time, newly directed toward Asia by the recent acquisition of Hawaii and the Philippines, was dazzled by the vision of the opportunities for her enterprise and outlets for her commerce in the Far East. China seemed the area of America's future and took on vast importance. John Hay was credited with having said that whoever understands China holds the key to the world's politics for the next five centuries. "Our future history," declared President Theodore Roosevelt in 1905, "will be more determined by our position on the Pacific facing China than by our position on the Atlantic facing Europe." In 1908 he remitted America's share of the Boxer indemnity, the unpaid portion to be allocated for the education of Chinese students in the United States. As a visible gesture this was an act of advertising genius which for long afterwards was to be cited by Americans and Chinese as the sign of a special relationship between their countries.

American dollar diplomacy, less altruistic, shared with other powers in the frenzied activity to force loans on China for construction of railroads at highly profitable interest rates. Wherever a Chinese looked, some part of his country's body or sovereignty or essential services was in the hands of foreigners. Their steam vessels navigated her inland waterways under treaty rights. Their banks financed her industry and trade and controlled both the proceeds of her Maritime Customs and the interest payments on her foreign debts. They also provided a trusted place for the deposits of her wealthy citizens. Foreign courts administered extraterritorial law and foreign post offices distributed extraterritorial mail. In the foreign settlements of Shanghai a Chinese resident paid taxes but could not vote or enter certain of the public parks although he could be arrested by a foreign policeman.

In the Treaty Ports, many located in the interior on rivers, the foreign Customs Officer in uniform was a familiar presence and an extraterritorial area was set aside for foreign business and residence. In the Chinese section all was bustle, crowds, smells and the incessant din of voices calling, quarreling and laughing. Steamboats jostled junks and sampans at the wharves where boatmen yelled and passengers picked their way between bales of cargo. Streets were filled with outdoor vendors, rickshaws, wheelbarrows, sedan chairs of the rich surrounded by bodyguards shouting for passage, coolies with twin loads bobbing from bamboo shoulder poles, thin dogs prowling underfoot for scraps and men squatting over open drains.

All this stopped at the canal crossed by a bridge. On the other side everything was suddenly quiet and clean, with neat streets lined by shade trees, a guard in a white uniform dozing in a chair and a little white gunboat with shiny brasswork anchored off the Bund. Outside the settlement a recreation ground usually called Victoria Park provided tennis courts, cricket field and clubs. In any club controlled by the British, as were most of them, no Chinese were admitted. Every afternoon the Concession's elite rode out to the park in sedan chairs whose Chinese bearers wore the various uniforms of the consulates and mercantile companies—red facings on white for the British Consul, white on blue for Jardine Matheson's, the great British trading company. In case of riots, bandits or other threats, a small landing party of blue jackets from the gunboats made a show of drill on the Bund. For foreigners in the "outports"—these isolated enclaves in the vast uncertain mass of China—life would have been precarious without the migratory visits of the little gunboats with their birds' names—*Snipe, Teal, Sandpiper, Woodcock.*

Revolution now seemed to many the only way to restore China's independence and equality among nations. Although the foreign Concession was the enemy, Sun Yat-sen himself was too Westernized to be antiforeign, and indeed firmly believed that his country's dependence was too ingrained to do without foreign loans and skills to help her modernize. He regarded the Revolution as primarily anti-Manchu because China would remain weak as long as she remained under the usurping dynasty responsible for her decline, "and her weakness will endanger world peace by exciting the greed of other nations." By giving China a strong modern regime, the Revolution, he believed, would be furthering the peace of the world and would welcome the foreign aid which the powers, in recognition of its role, would certainly offer. "He did not have a Chinese mind," according to his wife, "he had a world mind."

Through the first decade of the twentieth century the illegal Revolutionary societies, operating first from Japan and afterwards from offshore and overseas communities, grew and gathered adherents on the mainland, especially in the two southern provinces of Kwangtung and Kwangsi. With Canton, its capital, commanding the trade through Hong Kong, Kwangtung was the richest province in China and its people were sympathetic to the Revolution because they wanted a country that could maintain prosperity. Six uprisings, directed by Sun Yat-sen from Hanoi, took place in the south in 1907-09 with no fixed objective except the hope that one or another would catch on. Through 1910, while Dr. Sun was in Europe and America collecting funds, the tempo quickened. Coups were attempted in Canton, Hankow and even Peking where Dr. Sun's lieutenant, Wang Ching-wei, went to blow up the Prince Regent and was discovered and sentenced to life imprisonment in chains. Owing to arms shipments that did not arrive, leaders who missed arranged times, and other mishaps and blunders, all the uprisings failed but they dramatized the cause, attracted recruits and spread the spirit of insurrection.

In October 1911 the Revolutionists planned another coup in the focal triple-city of Hankow-Hanyang-Wuchang (otherwise known as Wuhan) astride the Yangtze. An arsenal was located in Hanyang and Revolutionary conversions had been made among the Imperial regiments at Wuchang.

An accidental explosion went off, prematurely disclosing the preparations. At once the decision was taken to attack the Viceroy's headquarters and seize the garrison. On the tenth day of the tenth month, ever afterwards celebrated as the Double Ten, the venture miraculously succeeded. The regiment mutinied and the Viceroy and garrison commander fled in panic to Shanghai, leaving the Revolutionists masters in the heart of China—without a chief. Assembling to elect a leader, a Revolutionary council chose the Colonel of the regiment, Li Yuan-hung, and despatched a delegation to inform him of his fate. Hearing the approach of his visitors, the Colonel, expecting the worst, hid under his bed where he was discovered by a tell-tale foot, and on being pulled out was ceremoniously petitioned to lead the Revolution or be shot. He took the sensible choice and as Generalissimo of Revolutionary Armies proclaimed the overthrow of the Manchu dynasty.

Within two days the whole of the triple-city was in rebel hands. The comrades in Canton rose in response, effectively at last, and succeeded in assassinating the garrison commander and setting up a Revolutionary Government. These events set off a train of insurrections elsewhere in China; provincial capitals burned, governors were murdered, regiments mutinied. Within a month nine provinces had declared their independence of the Imperial Government, though not necessarily their common adherence to one Revolutionary regime. Separatism had begun.

The dynasty, alarmed at last, called upon its strong man, Yuan Shih-kai, a short, thickset man with alert eyes and a mustache, who looked like Clemenceau and like him was exceptionally able and ambitious. Yuan recaptured Hankow at the end of October with accompanying massacre of all who had cut off their queues or otherwise come out in support of the rebellion. The Revolutionists meantime had moved their base to Shanghai, ironically finding asylum under the extrality of the foreign Concessions. A deal was arranged whereby Shanghai with its money, industry, arsenals and dockyards accepted the Republic on November 3. Yuan Shih-kai, appreciating the trend, offered to negotiate on the basis of a constitutional monarchy for whose throne, as the future was to show, he had himself in mind. The Revolutionists, fatally lacking a prepared and solid base or a single strong-minded leader, bargained. While insisting on a republic, they offered Yuan the presidency if in return he would bring north China under the new regime. Peking offered him the post of premier, putting him in the position, possibly unique in history, of being sought for leadership by both a revolution and a counter-revolution at the same time. Yuan accepted the premiership from the Manchus and resumed the struggle. The Revolutionists now mounted an offensive from Shanghai up the Yangtze against Nanking.

Behind the main events the old structure was coming apart in chaos, provincial oligarchs were seizing what power they could, rebel forces burned and slaughtered in the cities they took and the Imperialists did likewise in the cities they held. Refugees in destitute hordes were roaming the land. The countryside suffered more than ever, for now wandering bands of soldiers as well as bandits plundered stored grain and livestock. Bandits flourished as unpaid soldiers sold them cartridges or joined forces with them. Villages fought with hoes, pitchforks and sticks, barred their gates, built up their walls and let in travelers by lowered ropes. The collapse of government seemed imminent but the Revolution carried small assurance of anything stable to take its place. Its aims, though worthy, wrote an American correspondent, "are brought to nought by lack of cohesion, lack of funds and lack of a leader. . . . This great nation, long dormant, is erupting in passions, terror and fanaticism."

At this stage, on November 23, Stilwell reached Shanghai for what was to be a total of 17 days in the country. He barely saw the surface of the turmoil and arrived at no profound judgments, but he observed and noted with tireless curiosity. The view he obtained exhibits a truth often missed by historians—that under the shadow of awful events ordinary life goes on, as it must, much as always. After visiting Shanghai he continued by ship to Hong Kong and was impressed by that daring city "apparently hung on the hillside" over its magnificent harbor. Here as elsewhere east of Suez the British flag was planted with a flair for imperial showmanship upon the highest ground. Thirty-six ocean-going steamers were in port as Stilwell came in. Sampans swarmed around his ship, each one a household including chickens. "Wife steers and kids push on the oars. Everyone does something." After Thanksgiving dinner in a family boardinghouse kept by Americans, he took the Peak tram to the summit where the famous view over the harbor was "superb, the best panorama I can remember."

He remarked on the queer appearance of Chinese who had just cut off their queues and admired the English drill sergeants who "for commands, appearance and results beat our average officer 500%." The English officer, on the other hand, he decided, in the first statement of what was to become a historic prejudice, "is a mess. At least here in Hong Kong. Untidy, grouchy, sloppy, fooling around with canes, a bad example for the men." The cane was the irritant. All his life the sight of an officer of whatever nationality slapping his boot with a swagger stick caused Stilwell the most intense disgust. In Hong Kong, he concluded, all the enlisted men were more soldierly than any of the officers he saw.

While he was there the newspapers were full of reports of chaotic conditions in Canton, fighting in the streets, armed bands of hoodlums looting the shops, bystanders killed, the Revolutionary regime wholly inefficient, the city practically in the hands of brigands and pirates swarming in the West River. They were said to have cut off Wuchow and murdered the chief officer of a British riverboat. Deciding that "all the trouble was worked up by the bloody British who are trying to make things as bad as possible to justify intervention on their part," Stilwell promptly went off to Canton and up-river to Wuchow to see for himself.

All the color and vitality, the physical welter of smells, sounds and bodies, the antiquity and infinite ingenuities, the charms and horrors of Chinese life engulfed him in Canton. He saw a cat and dog market where cats were cooked, split and hung up for sale and dog stew dished out of a pot; a waterclock dating from 1325 in which water, trickling through a series of pans and activating an upright arm on a float, told the time, "accurately too"; a temple roof decorated with exuberant carved dragons painted in brilliant colors and two big and fierce red lions peeking over the gate. He wandered through a maze of narrow stone-paved streets and alleys filled with Chinese running into each other, "hurling imprecations and warnings and crying their wares" with shouts, chants, tinkling bells or the clacking of sticks on blocks of wood. Sellers and buyers of everything conducted business in the streets, weighing and bargaining, women picking over chicken bones in a basket, a tailor sewing, a man stuffing straw into pots, another weighing fish, another selling human hair ("Chink cuts off his hair, puts it on newspaper and has a store."). He took note of opium smokers, ducks raised on junks, singsong girls, burial mounds, joss sticks burning in doorways, idlers gossiping while they deloused the seams of their clothing and ate the findings, eggs hatching in rice straw, pawn shops, pet larks in cages, the squeal of pigs and cackle of hens, the smell of urine and of the public closets which were "just a row of stalls with a log to squat on, in places kids defecating in the streets." China was a contrast between a man making ornaments of kingfisher feathers cut and pasted in tiny pieces of pale blue and mauve to imitate enamel, and "puddles, mud, filth, refuse, rags, glimpses into mysterious interiors."

He talked to the "rebs, a motley gang," some of whom "looked like good hombres but most of them were pirates for fair." They attempted a uniform—pale blue blouse and trousers with red trimmings, khaki strap, puttees and brigand wrappings. "Many had new ammo belts and plenty of cartridges, some were standing around pistol in hand, finger on trigger. . . . I showed them I was a reb by my red tie and blue shirt and that quite tickled them. All bowed and said goodbye." The Canton Bomb Corps, he noted, consisted of 300 men of good standing, all sworn to do or die, whose weapons were small homemade bombs containing a tube of mercury fulminate and Vaseline. He went to Shameen Island, the foreign Concession, and visited the Club where the foreigners "just fight booze." Bullion and valuables worth between two and six million, he was told, were stored by wealthy Chinese on Shameen. He collected Chinese legends and superstitions and a variety of stories exhibiting missionaries in an unfavorable light. He traveled for a day in the company of an American booster of missionary efforts who harangued him about all that Protestant Christians were doing for the people and told him, "When we step in here we bridge over in a second twelve hundred years of history."

After seeing Canton Stilwell boarded a steamboat for the 200-mile trip up the West River to Wuchow, convoyed by the *Sandpiper,* a British gunboat of 85 tons. Tales of pirates proved to be no fantasy. At one stop they met "Rebs" in a fleet of two gunboats, three launches and five or six junks just returning from a scrap with river bandits. They saw corpses floating by in the water and learned the details of a big scrap two weeks earlier in which Wuchow's forces attacked a band of pirates, took 66 prisoners whom they beheaded the next day, afterwards cutting out their hearts which they roasted and ate. It was a common thing, Stilwell learned, to eat the hearts or livers of executed pirates, or in one case, he was told, the whole man; "they ate him so he could not be reincarnated as a pirate." With understandably heightened imagination he awoke in a fright when the anchor dropped at Samshui. "Thought sure we were being attacked. Hopped out of a sound sleep and grabbed for my gun."

By the time he returned to Canton he had spent a week on the river, watching life and death along its banks and on the water, absorbing all he saw or was told, making notes on habits, methods and the prices of everything, being informed that a duck will cackle at a foreigner's approach and concluding that the average Chinese flies into a fury of passion which passes off in words. He had not seen a fight in spite of innumerable collisions.

When still in Hong Kong he had noted in his diary, "400 heads a day in Nanking." This was the harvest of the fall of the ancient southern capital to the rebels on November 27. The event proved a catalyst. Hoping to hold rule for the dynasty, the Regent resigned in favor of the late Emperor's widow but the Revolutionary south declared it would accept nothing less than total abdication. An exodus of Manchus took the road for Manchuria whence long ago they had come. Mongolia declared independence. Despite some apoplectic sentiment in the Treaty Ports for intervention against the rebels, the powers kept hands off. There was a general sense that the Revolution, as Western-oriented, would be less antiforeign than the old regime which, with Boxer days a recent memory, the powers felt no great desire to preserve. There was a sense too that China was drifting into political chaos in which intervention could be disastrous. The future weighed heavily and moved one sober voice* to say, "It has never been doubtful to men who have given the subject careful study that the relations of Asia to the rest of the world constitute the most difficult problem of the twentieth century."

Others, stirred to enthusiasm by the Revolution's promise of liberal, Western, parliamentary ideas, were more optimistic. "We thought high and noble thoughts," wrote one American trader, "about China and the new era that was dawning." This was the attitude, on the whole, of the American public which wanted to believe what the missionaries were always promising, that China of the 400,000,000 was about to transform itself into that desirable and familiar thing, a democracy. That the 400,000,000 were a people 70 to 80 percent illiterate, who on the average had no milk and virtually no other animal products in their diet, who had no sanitation, no running water, no privacy, no electricity, no vote, whose industry was still 90 percent handiwork and whose transportation was still largely conducted by human muscle, was not considered, if considered at all, incom-

* John Foord, Secretary of the American-Asiatic Association.

President Sun Yat-sen, in civilian clothes at center, addressing members of the new government (24).

patible with democracy. When a rebel leader in Hankow, out of Oriental politeness which believes in telling people what presumably they want to hear, said to reporters that "the object of our revolt is to make the Government of China like that of America," nothing could have seemed more natural to American readers.

Stilwell left China to return to Manila on December 9. The Revolution wobbled forward. Negotiations took the place of a military solution and resulted in Yuan Shih-kai formally recommending to his principals the necessity of accepting the Republic. Meanwhile Sun Yat-sen had finally arrived in China on December 25 and was duly elected President of the provisional Republic established at Nanking. For the Manchus support had run out and the end had come. On February 12, 1912, the Empress Regent abdicated on behalf of the dynasty.

China was now a Republic. As such she was welcomed by Joint Resolution of the United States Congress: "Whereas the Chinese Nation has successfully asserted that sovereignty resides in the people" and whereas the American people are "inherently and by tradition sympathetic to all efforts to adopt representative government," therefore the United States "congratulates the people of China on their assumption of the powers, duties and responsibilities of self-government" in the hope that under a republican form of government ". . . the happiness of the Chinese people will be secure and the progress of the country insured."

It was not to be that simple. Yuan Shih-kai remained in control of north China, which he withheld from accession to the Republican regime. He maneuvered and waited. Lacking united support or firm authority or a reliable military arm, Sun Yat-sen could not prevail. More negotiations ensued with unavoidable result. On March 12, 1912, Dr. Sun retired as President in favor of Yuan Shih-kai, who reestablished the Government at Peking. In this unstable mongrel resolution China's modern age began.

3

The Great War:

ST. MIHIEL AND SHANTUNG

T o the American Army officer the years 1912 to 1917, when Stilwell was twenty-nine to thirty-four, were not challenging and offered little opportunity to exercise the energies maturing in a man of that age. Although the military profession in Europe met its ultimate challenge halfway through this period, the American Army remained a millpond barely ruffled by the transatlantic breeze of war.

Stilwell had returned to the United States from the Philippines in January 1912. He remained for another year with his regiment, still as a lieutenant, in a dead calm of duty at the Presidio of Monterey in California. His first son, Joe Jr., was born in Syracuse in March and Stilwell did not see him until six weeks later when mother and child came out to California for the summer. During this summer the Stilwells saw for the first time the little village of Carmel, then still undeveloped and unprettified, on the coast just below Monterey. Taking picnics on the beach and wind-swept walks on rocks pounded by the Pacific, they decided that here was the place where they wanted to live someday and make their home after retirement.

Restless as ever, Stilwell agitated for appointment as Military Attaché to Santo Domingo, without success. He was requested, however, by the Military Academy to return as Instructor in the Department of English and History and took up his duties once more at West Point in August 1913. Although duty at the Academy was better than the tedium of an Infantry post, it did not absorb his energies. He was "a very capable officer," reported his superior, but "he did not impress me as being enthusiastic over his work in the Department of History." He coached basketball and football and saw the addition to his family of a daughter, Nancy, born in June of the following year. But his role as a father had not yet assumed the paramount importance that it would come to have for him when the children grew older and more were added. Before a year had gone by at the Academy, Joe, as his wife remembers, "was wild to get away from West Point."

His chance came in the summer of 1914 when, having been transferred to the Department of Modern Languages to teach Spanish, he contrived an assignment to Madrid for further language study. On June 29, while in Spain, he closed an account of a day's excursion to the countryside with a parenthetical note, "(Assassination in Bosnia)." For the next few weeks, like most of the world, he gave no further thought to the incident at Sarajevo until July 30 when he read the news of Austria's bombardment of Serbia. "Very serious war news. Seems a dream that Europe is about to jump into the abismo."

Returning to the old routine of teaching at the Academy was not exhilarating and nothing happened to change the routine during the next two years. Stilwell's efforts to get overseas as an observer with the French Army were in vain. In reply to his application the War Department stated in December 1915 that it had already sent five officers abroad to observe the European war (which now engaged the armies of ten nations from the Channel coast to Mesopotamia) and "it is not planned to send any more."

But the movement for preparedness was gaining and in April 1916 brought about passage of the Army Act authorizing a doubling of Regular Army strength to a maximum of 288,000 over a period of five years. Stilwell's first war service was as an instructor in the summer of 1916 at Plattsburg, New York, where the first training camp to prepare Reserve officers from civilian life was established. In September after twelve years as a lieutenant he was at last promoted to captain.

In April 1917 the United States, with an Army of 133,000 men, entered the war in which the belligerents had more than six million men engaged on the Western Front alone. The European national forces were organized into armies each containing three to five corps, each corps usually consisting of two divisions. The American Army had no organized military unit higher than a regiment. Although the divisional structure existed on paper, no American soldiers since the Civil War had taken the field as a division, with all the coordination of infantry and artillery, of staff and field, of intelligence and operations, that that requires. All this had to be learned and put into practice. A national army fleshed out to ten times the size of its existing regimental skeleton had to be created, which meant recruited, officered, trained, equipped, shipped overseas, assembled, supplied, coordinated in its arms and branches, and further trained before it could fight. For this task the General Staff had made no arrangements or any general plan of mobilization.

The issue having been forced, a Selective Service Draft law was enacted in May 1917 authorizing conscription of a million men. After investigation in Europe it was realized that plans for the future should be based on three times that number. The specter of the number of officers required for this newly hatched giant of an army—about one for every twenty men or 50,000 for an army of a million—appalled the Regulars. In the first year of war, training camps in a series of three-month courses turned out 57,000 officers, ten times as many as West Point had graduated in all its history.

Training was the tremendous task that dwarfed everything else. To create through training an army that could take the field effectively was to be the central purpose a quarter-century later of Stilwell's work in China, as it was now that of the United States. The first essential in war is an army that will not run away, which can only be assured by training. Without training, a soldier is not worth what it takes to put him in position, an officer is useless, an army is a rabble. General Hunter Liggett, head of the War College, soon to command the 1st Division and ultimately the American First Army, unsparingly estimated that one well-trained, well-equipped foreigner could whip ten good but untrained Americans. An untrained American Army of 5,400, he pointed out, ran away from 1,500 British Regulars in the War of 1812 and did not stop until they were 15 miles on the other side of Washington. In the three days it took to reassemble them the British burned the capital. To create an American force capable of playing an independent American role in the war rather than serving as a depot of fillers for Allied ranks (which was what the Allies wanted) required training as American units under American officers. Professional officers at once became precious assets and they were soon so widely scattered in training duties detached from their own units that half of them were never to go overseas at all.

Though first requested as an instructor for the training camps, Stilwell escaped that fate when other orders detailing him as brigade adjutant to the 80th Division at Camp Lee in Virginia took precedence. Promoted to the temporary rank of major, he arrived at Camp Lee on August 25, 1917, missing by a hair another proposal that might have changed his career. His persistence over the years in visiting Spanish-speaking countries now bore fruit in the offer of an appointment as Military Attaché in Spain. This was "no swivel chair job," wrote his correspondent in the War Department; on the contrary, "Spain is full of spies and German agents," and a good man was needed "for the purpose of running an Espionage system." Stilwell was asked to reply by telegram "right away," but on the day the letter was despatched he had already reached Camp Lee.

Four months later in December 1917 he received orders to go to France to report to the Commanding General AEF for Intelligence duty. He was to be a staff officer. That a man of his physical energy and aggressiveness should find himself assigned to staff instead of line was the ironic yet reasonable result of the course his career had already taken. Though not a graduate of the command and staff courses at Leavenworth and the War College, whose graduates were now filling all the higher posts in the AEF, his command of French was badly needed.

From the day America entered the war the Allies brought unremitting pressure upon everyone from President Wilson down to feed American soldiers in battalion or smaller units into the thinned and battle-worn Allied divisions. Their lack of training would be made up, it was insisted, by serving with seasoned troops, no time being lost in the process.

General John J. Pershing, the iron-willed cavalryman who commanded the American Expeditionary Force, was adamant in refusal. Politically he was carrying out the mandate of his Government, for it was clear that to allow integration of American soldiers into Allied ranks would be to commit America's fortunes to the Allies' and preclude the United States from determining her own policy and from playing a major role at the peace table. Militarily he had his own reasons. He believed the deadlock of trench warfare could only be broken and victory won by restoring a war of movement, that is, by abandoning the offensive of limited objectives followed by consolidation of position, which had become the pattern of the Western Front, in favor of open warfare whose aim was to penetrate rather than consolidate. He intended to accomplish this by an American injection of the offensive spirit and an American philosophy of warfare prescribing maximum initiative in the field by troops and subordinate officers who would be trained to exploit every opportunity. Pershing wanted brief orders, concentrating on the objective, rather than the Allied practice of detailed, phase-by-phase plans and rigidly controlled movements. Since British and French training had become adapted to the methods and weapons of trench warfare, he could only prove his program by American training and only implement it by an independent American Army operating in an American sector. The spirit and method of this program was what Stilwell, a Pershing without an AEF, tried to transplant to Chinese troops one war later.

Arriving in France with his Headquarters staff in July 1917, Pershing looked for a sector where a decisive military result could still be gained. He fixed on the triangle below Verdun and Metz where the German-held

St. Mihiel salient had protruded since 1914. The salient controlled both the rich Briey iron basin and one of two vital railroads supplying the German armies in France. Here, Pershing considered, was the enemy's solar plexus. Metz was the crux of the German defense system and a penetration on either side of it would open the way to Germany. An offensive here, Pershing believed, could only be carried through by the impetus of a fresh army. Heavily fortified by the Germans who realized its vulnerability, the St. Mihiel salient had defied the Allies who had never mustered the force to attack it.

Meanwhile he had to create an army. After the hurrahs for the 1st Division, hurriedly put together and rushed to France in July, no more followed for three months. Shortage of ships and muddle in the War Department as well as lack of trained men caused the delay. Three more American divisions arrived in October but all these, according to Pershing's schedule, still needed three and a half more months to complete their training. By April 1918, a year after the declaration of war, only seven divisions had reached France.

Gloom pervaded the Allied camp at the time Stilwell arrived in France on January 21, 1918; pessimism was general, defeatism appearing. The withdrawal of Russia from the war, promising release of German divisions to the Western Front, was an immense disaster. The Allies' offensives of 1917, bull-headed plunges into mass casualties with no strategic advantage gained, had so reduced reserves that commanders feared they would not be able to throw back a major German offensive if it came. With America's troops withheld from them and unready for battle on their own, the Allies' belief that they could sustain a war of attrition until American strength tipped the balance was shaken. To win by taking the offensive, a 20 percent superiority was considered necessary, which could not be attained without the addition of the Americans and they could not be ready before next summer. Since the logic of this was not lost on the Germans, they were not expected to be quiescent until summer came.

Another belligerent was prepared to take advantage of the hour. This was Japan, one of the Allied powers, who from the first had seen the embroilment of the white nations as her opportunity for expansion in China and the Pacific. In the words of Count Okuma, Premier in 1914, Japan was determined to become one of the world's "governing nations." China, appearing senile and beyond salvation, was marked for the role of first colony. The chief obstacle in the way was not China herself but the other powers. When they turned upon each other in 1914, Japan joined the Allies and as her contribution to the war effort seized Germany's leased territory with its railroad and other concessions on the strategic Shantung peninsula. She also took from Germany the Marshall, Mariana and Caroline Islands in the Pacific, placing herself across America's road to the Philippines.

Japan's next move, the Twenty-one Demands, was designed to put her in administrative and economic control of China. Presented to Yuan Shih-kai in 1915, the demands required China to confirm Japan's assumption of German rights in Shantung, extend her lease on former Russian rights at Port Arthur and Dairen to 99 years, concede various trade, land-owning, rail and industrial concessions in Manchuria, Inner Mongolia and the Yangtze valley, agree not to contract concessions or loans with any other power without Japan's consent, and finally, in a fifth group which amounted to relinquishment of sovereignty, accept Japanese military, political and financial "advisers" and joint Japanese control of arsenals, police and schools.

Yuan Shih-kai, who was preparing to restore the monarchy with himself as Emperor, required support for his ambitions which were not popular. This was Japan's opportunity and the Twenty-one Demands were her price. Yuan protested and resisted feebly but he could expect no aid from the Allies who were not prepared to thwart Japan for fear of causing her to change sides in the war to a more natural alliance with Germany. The United States, equally unwilling to interfere, created for the occasion the doctrine of nonrecognition to the effect that she would not recognize any arrangement imposed upon China in violation of the Open Door. This affected events no more than most statements of principle. Yuan maneuvered, managed to fend off the crucial fifth group of the Twenty-one Demands and succumbed to the rest. The anger and outrage felt by the Chinese when the agreement became known fostered a sense of nationhood. From that date on, China was to be on the whole anti-Japanese although groups who believed in accommodation continued to exist.

Three months after the Twenty-one Demands Yuan declared himself Emperor. While his instinct for a central authority may have been right, the form it took was unacceptable. The Revolution to that extent had been genuine. Public opinion exploded, provinces seceded. Yuan was forced to cancel the decree in 1916 and died two months later of "disease and chagrin," to be succeeded as President by Li Yuan-hung, the Colonel who had been pulled to prominence from under the bed.

He could control nothing and the rout began. China fell prey to the rival ambitions and private armies of the *tuchuns,* translated rather too grandly into English as "warlords." Some were able governors and predators combined, others ignorant ex-bandits and adventurers tossed to the top in the general broil. Appointed military governor of a province by the nominal government in Peking, either in recognition of existing control or in consideration for support, the *tuchun* furnished and paid—or failed to pay—his own military forces. Chinese soldiers no longer served the state but feudal overlords who in constantly changing alliances traded and fought for power, gnawing like rats at what was left of the Republic. The "Government" of China recognized by the powers remained in Peking in the hands of a group of northern warlords known as the Anfu clique (from the provinces of Anhwei and Fukien) who owed their hold on office to Japanese support and loans. They adopted the terminology of republican government with a president, premier, ministers and a puppet parliament.

The Peking Government was declared illegal by the Kuomintang regime reestablished by Sun Yat-sen in Canton. He had returned in 1917, summoned the remnant of the original Kuomintang parliament to Canton and declared it to be the only constitutional government of China. Though his party had been born of Western ideas, and offered the only promise, if not the capability, of a new political order for China, it attracted no foreign support. From political inertia and natural preference, the foreign powers continued to deal with whatever *tuchun* group held the titles to office in Peking because this required no unsettling break in the succession. It is not in the nature of established governments to opt for change, even in their own interest. Sun Yat-sen maintained virtually a separate state dependent for military support on uneasy alliance with southern warlords. For the next decade, one of the most ruinous in China's history, fragmentation proceeded, puppets and warlords held sway and the mandate of heaven held itself hidden.

As for Shantung, Japan knew that what counted to make her hold secure was confirmation by the powers. In March 1917, playing on, not to say encouraging, the fear that she might change sides in the war, she extracted secret agreements from Britain, France and Italy to support her claim to the German succession in Shantung and the Pacific islands at the peace table. When the United States entered the war Japan wanted to add American confirmation as well and succeeded in obtaining, in November 1917, the Lansing-Ishii Agreement, one of the most peculiar departures in all American diplomacy. Reversing the principle of the Open Door (while paying respects to it in name), the agreement acknowledged that as a result of "territorial propinquity" Japan "had special interest in China, particularly in the part to which her possessions are contiguous." As the document was public, except for a secret protocol containing acknowledgment of Chinese sovereignty to satisfy official American conscience, it represented or, what is equally important in making history, seemed to represent American acquiescence in Japan's assumption of a special position in China. Viscount Ishii returned from America in triumph and China's dismay was proportionate. The Chinese Government had of course already acquiesced in the same thing when it signed the Twenty-one Demands, but for America to do so appeared like betrayal. The explanation lay in the dark time of November 1917 when America no more than the Allies could afford Japan as an enemy.

While all this was going on, China too, which is to say both the Peking and Canton regimes, entered the war in August 1917 on the side of the Allies. Among the convoluted reasons for this decision, involving various Chinese, Japanese and Allied aims and schemes, the dominant concern was the peace table. Again equating form with substance, the Chinese supposed that the form of becoming one of the Allied and Associated Powers, regardless of military reality, would endow them with the substance of equality at the peace table. There they could claim, as China's reward and right, an end to the unequal treaties at last, and possibly even reclaim Shantung. Since the Allies wanted labor battalions from China and especially the chance to eliminate all German concessions and commercial competition, they did nothing to discourage China's hopes.

As chief Intelligence officer for the IVth Corps, Stilwell played his major part in the war by preparing the American offensive at St. Mihiel. Staff work for combat was performed chiefly by G-2 and G-3, the Intelligence and Operations sections of the General Staff. Each of the larger units, from division through corps and army to Headquarters, had its own Chief of Staff with Assistant Chiefs of Staff in charge of sections. The Intelligence section was responsible for the collection of all possible information leading to a picture of the enemy's disposition, intentions and weaknesses. It must organize a steady flow of information from the units at the front back through each next higher headquarters to GHQ as well as sideways to neighboring units. At the regimental and battalion level combat intelligence was obtained by scouts who accompanied all patrols and raids, and by the Observation Posts (OPs) which kept track of enemy movements. At the division level listening posts, captured documents and prisoner interrogation supplied further information. At the corps level material was assembled from balloon and airplane reconnaissance and serial photography, which was new and required new techniques and study to interpret the results. All the bits and pieces had to be assembled, evaluated, transformed into graphic representation on maps and distributed to the proper persons. Prior to the war the American Army had had two officers and two clerks of the War College division of the General Staff engaged in Intelligence.

To assemble a force capable of acting as an independent army Pershing's training program had to be continued in France. Besides the staff for GHQ, staffs had to be organized for future corps, each to be composed of four divisions plus one in reserve and one in depot. A corps, when filled out, would contain about 6,000 officers and 170,000 men, larger than the entire peacetime Army before the war. The direct need was for staff officers at division and corps levels, and since they did not exist, they had to be made. A General Staff school as well as schools for other arms and branches was established at Langres near American GHQ at Chaumont, southeast of Paris.

Contemplating these beginnings of war without an existing General Staff, the Allies felt added reason to urge the integration of American combat troops within their system. To organize a General Staff in the European sense with plans drawn for mobilization and campaigns "takes thirty years," a French general told Pershing. "It never took America thirty years to do anything," Pershing snapped.

Stilwell was assigned first to brief duty with the British 58th Division to acquaint himself with actual conditions at the front before taking the Intelligence course at Langres. He reached the headquarters of this division at Noyon, furthest penetration of the Hindenburg Line, on February 10, 1918. Around him was desolation: villages in ruins, some marked only by the foundations of walls and debris; the ground everywhere intersected by old trenches and pitted with shell craters. The staff of the 58th, his first active Allies, he found both obnoxious and agreeable. "These English are beyond me—most of them so very pleasant and some of them so damn snotty . . . too god-damned indifferent and high and mighty to bother about an American officer." He contrasted them unfavorably with the French, whom he found willing, polite and helpful: "Me for them." He spent five days with the British becoming acquainted with every operation of a front-line sector—trenches, dugouts, OPs, night patrols, camouflaging of roads, study of maps and aerial photo reconnaissance. Observing, learning, talking and taking notes, he sufficiently forgot his annoyance with his hosts to wire for permission to stay an extra day and to note gladly, "They said OK!"

A brief stay at Langres coincided with that of Colonel Henry L. Stimson, former Secretary of War under President Taft, now at fifty an Artillery officer, who as Secretary of War a second time was to be a significant figure in Stilwell's future. With the need acute at Chaumont, Stilwell was pulled out after a week to assist in the organization of the G-2 section at GHQ. After three weeks he was again reassigned for schooling of a direct kind to the French XVIIth Army Corps at Verdun. Here half a million men, attackers and defenders, had died over the past two and a half years. Here the French slogan, "They shall not pass" had been born and the "sacred road" for supply and reinforcements kept open. The threatened

In 1914 First Lieutenant Stilwell was at West Point as an instructor of English and history (25), when the war abroad was creating a movement at home for preparedness. He transferred as instructor to a training camp in 1916 (28) and joined the Third Battalion, 5th Training Regiment (second from left), in 1917

25

26

27

(27). At some point before going overseas he returned to Yonkers to be photographed with his father and his brother John (26).

28

30

German breakthrough was barred, yet as if uncontent with the greatest slaughter the world had ever known, the guns still fired.

In a skirmish on March 20, the day Stilwell arrived, the French suffered 20 casualties and there were 42 dead Boches in front of one small sector. The Colonel made him feel welcome, arranged for him to join a bridge game after dinner and, unlike the British, did not avoid personal conversation. "Are you married?" he asked. "Have you children? Are they yours?"

While he was at Verdun the front further to the west erupted under a gigantic assault. This was the opening of the great German offensive of 1918, Ludendorff's fierce effort to end the war in a last grasp at victory before American forces could be brought to bear. His armies were now reinforced by an extra 42 divisions released from the Russian front, whereas the Americans at this stage had added no more than eight divisions to the Allied armies, of which four were still in training camps. Ludendorff's aim, for which every reserve of strength had been assembled, was to split apart the British and French, and by a series of offenses at different points rather than a single head-on collision, use up the Allies' depleted reserves and break through their defenses at last.

Lasting with intermissions from March through July, Ludendorff's effort almost succeeded. The Germans smashed through Allied lines for the largest territorial gains since the beginning of trench warfare, took prisoners and inflicted casualties by the hundreds of thousands, recaptured Noyon 60 miles from Paris, brought Paris under bombardment by long-range cannon, flung the British back against the Channel and in May came again to the Marne where they had been foiled of victory four years before. The crisis forced the Allies into the last resort which they for so long, through so much vain slaughter, had evaded: unified command, to which Foch was named on March 27 in the midst of battle. Even Pershing gave way and allowed American units to serve temporarily under Allied command. Thrown into these battles to help stem the German advance, American divisions fought at Château-Thierry, Belleau Wood and Cantigny.

At Verdun, where he remained for six weeks, Stilwell had no share in the first stage of this drama. He was assigned to the office of Major Armand Belhomme, the G-2 section chief of the XVIIth Corps, but spent the major part of his time out on rounds of forts and command posts which were still under daily bombardment. From a dugout beneath the death-filled pile of Fort Douaumont he saw a "lunar landscape. . . . The whole terrain is churned up, a mixture of wire, tools, shoes, shells, bones, uniforms, cartridge boxes, grenades, helmets, wheels, stakes, iron fragments . . . plentifully sprinkled with lime up front to keep down the boche cadavers." Inside the underground tunnels of Douaumont the place was damp, muddy, stink-

Major Stilwell (front row, center) with the French XVIIth Army Corps at Verdun (29) and in the field inspecting a fortification (30). On the back of one photo (31) he wrote: "Gyp the Blood in foreground. Best pilot in the French air service, Adjutant d'Alegrac in background."

ing and impossible to keep clean. At Fort Vaux fog enabled him to wander in front of the lines where he saw "heads lying around still in helmets, hunks of bodies, thigh bones, jaws, hands, pieces of old rags hanging to them" and in a dugout a leg sticking out on which a soldier had hung his musette.

One patrol took him within 60 yards of the German lines and he returned at 2 A.M. after being on foot since 9 A.M. "Fell in mud holes, boche fuses going up all the time, munitions gang at work, all the night life of the front." After being trapped by shelling all day in a dugout just big enough for two with, as he judged, 150 to 200 77s coming over, luckily aimed too low and to the left, Stilwell's comment was, "Very interesting day." This was not false bravado for he never hesitated to write in his diary "scared to death" when that was how he felt. "Scared" generally meant fear of attack or capture or anticipation of something to come, whereas being under fire seemed not to bother him. During the many reconnaissance trips they made together when action was heavy, Major Belhomme wrote long afterwards, "we learned to appreciate his culture, his cartesianism and his equanimity."

His French hosts made him acquainted with all departments of staff work in the corps, with infantry work in the line and with the functioning of the intelligence service at every echelon. He was the first American to serve with the XVIIth Corps and his command of French opened the way to cordial relations. "They treated me like a long-lost brother," he wrote to his wife, "showed me everything and took me everywhere." His experience was like that of the correspondent Heywood Broun, who wrote at the time, "The Frenchman is the ideal soldier. Not only can he fight, but he can tell you about it." A flight was arranged for Stilwell in an observation plane, and though he got dizzy in the course of a spiral, he decided the aviator's was a soft life, "clean clothes, no wind, short hours, agony over quickly, back for lunch."

Food, as always, interested Stilwell and the recording of meals in his diary was a lifelong habit. At the XVIIth officers' mess they appear to have been worth recording. One evening he dined at the mess of Colonel Cantau, a bald, fat officer of sixty who wore enlisted man's cap, rows of decorations, hazed the servants, ate well and "doesn't give a damn." It being a meatless Friday, the meal consisted of two kinds of omelet, fish and rice, vegetable salad, white and red wine, champagne, two cordials and cheese. The orderly was made to salute and announce, *"Madame est servie."* When Stilwell asked why Madame, the Colonel asked in turn, "Are you married?" "Yes." "Where is your wife?" "In the United States." "No, she is in your heart; therefore she is here. That is why I have him announce, *'Madame est servie.'* " It was no wonder that Stilwell found the French sympathetic.

His own wife was much on his mind and he recorded the receipt of every letter.

On his departure to return to Chaumont he was sent off with a flourish at a farewell party tendered by the corps staff with three *chefs de bureau* heading a full mess, and flowers on all the tables. A wonderful centerpiece of nougat crowned with the French cock and the American eagle decorated his table; champagne flowed all evening and flattering speeches made him blush. All insisted on having his signature on their menus and he was presented with an inkwell made of a Boche shell and a picture of himself among the staff with everyone's names signed on the back. One officer was moved to write a poem which he left on Stilwell's desk. Glowing from a sense of being liked and appreciated, Stilwell replied in slangy and fluent French, thanking them for all he had learned and promising that among all the *emmerdement* awaiting him at Chaumont he would look back to his good friends of the XVIIth "with all the pleasure in the world."

He returned to American GHQ on April 29 in the rather sour expectation of red tape, poor food and stuffed shirts. He hated the time spent as "a damned waffle-tailed clerk in a bloody office . . . grinding out rot about things I know nothing about and surrounded with desks and typewriters and stuff." The coming and going of line officers, many junior to him at West Point and already lieutenant colonels or colonels while he was still a major, was galling and served as a constant reminder of the faster promotion that went with command of troops at the front. His efforts to obtain line duty were frustrated by the greater need for capable staff officers. Certain officers from civilian life sporting superior rank were another irritant, including one described as a "shifty-eyed smiler from the Peanut Club." The Peanut Club was Stilwell's designation for "millionaires, politicians and social darlings who have been given commissions of Major and up, and soft jobs." During the intense fighting for the bridgeheads of the Marne Stilwell's desk-tied frustrations grew. "Things look *bad*. . . . Talk of giving up Rheims . . . French and British howling for our troops. . . . At office, deadly as usual."

At last a transfer came which put him at the heart of the American offensive planned for the reduction of the salient at St. Mihiel. For the next eight weeks Stilwell's task was to prepare the intelligence operations for the coming action and to organize the divisional G-2s as well as the schools to train their staffs. The work kept him constantly on the move from one divisional headquarters to another and back and forth to Chaumont, Langres and IVth Corps headquarters at Neufchâteau.

Information on enemy lines and defenses inside the salient had to be collected, estimates of enemy strength calculated from various indications, daily and weekly summaries of enemy artillery fire distributed, topographical surveys issued, maps on various scales and grids made and delivered. Fifteen tons of maps were ultimately prepared for St. Mihiel.

Meanwhile in the desperate resistance to the Ludendorff offensive the tide had turned; initiative passed to the Allies who moved into counterattacks all along the line, restoring old positions. The enormous German effort since March, which had broken the deadlock, swallowed up miles of territory and inflicted almost a million casualties, had used up its strength and in so doing plowed the ground of its own defeat. While Ludendorff acknowledged as much to the Kaiser on August 8, Foch was planning the series of attacks by which he expected to end the war in 1919. The first was to be the American assault on the St. Mihiel salient scheduled for September 7.

To conduct the assault Pershing, on August 10, formed the First Army, the grand objective of all his planning, of which Stilwell's IVth Corps was one component. Totaling 500,000 men (including one French corps), it was the largest force so far assembled under the American flag and its action was to be the first major battle planned by an American staff. A major part of the planning was the work of the First Army's Assistant Chief of Staff for G-3, Lieutenant Colonel George C. Marshall, who was to play a definitive role in Stilwell's later career. The salient to be taken was a triangle with sides 25 miles long and a 35-mile base. It had been fortified since 1914 by successive bands of barbed wire, concrete pillboxes and dugouts, tunnels in the hills, narrow-gauge railways and carefully selected field-gun and machine-gun emplacements for crossfire. In the effort to achieve tactical surprise the Americans attempted the secret concentration at night of 14 divisions along with their supplies, but security was ragged and the movement was soon being talked of in the streets of Paris. "Worked away on the big dope," Stilwell recorded. "Great secrecy here and barber at Neufchâteau knew all about it. . . . Any boche plane who cannot see our bustle and preparation must be blind. Trucks rushing back and forth, columns of men, railroad trains, autos, motorcycles, etc." He was on the move day and night, visiting OPs for a view of the terrain and going up in a balloon for a wider view.

Visiting the divisions made him "homesick for soldiering," the more so as he did not find the company congenial at corps headquarters with its "son-of-a-bitch cavalry club running things." In contrast to the congenial atmosphere of a French mess and the fun and carousing with friends at Langres, he was as bored and irritated at the IVth Corps mess. *"Terrible* session at chow with old B. Was bored to death, meal was endless." His disparagements would become particularly heated after he had brought visitors to dinner, as if he were ashamed of the lack of interesting conversation. Then the diary growled with references to the "gloomy" or "punk" or "G-D bromide, uncongenial, s.o.b. mess." Stilwell could never suffer bores at all and was made instantly impatient by fools, snobs, stuffed shirts or anyone he conceived to be such.

On September 11, the day before the battle, his promotion to lieutenant colonel came through. Rain had been falling steadily, heightening the tension on the eve of the American test. Stilwell sat up all night finishing last odds and ends. The IVth Corps had never fought as a corps before but it contained two of the AEF's oldest and most battle-wise divisions, the 1st and the 42nd ("Rainbow") Division, of which Douglas MacArthur was Chief of Staff. Poised on its right was the Ist Corps, commanded by General Hunter Liggett.

In darkness artillery opened the battle. "Out at 1 A.M., as the first big one boomed over by St. Mihiel. From then on till 5 the sky was one continuous flash of light. . . . Our men moved up to the jumpoff trenches through the muck and rain. At 5 they went over and from then on it was one continuous round of phone calls and messages. Steady, rapid progress everywhere. . . . Everything went beautifully. *Les exécutants* put it over. . . . 1st and 42nd came through beautifully. 89th sadly lacking through some skullduggery or other." He went down to the 89th's command post to see what was the matter and found "a hell of a condition—no reports." In contrast, at 1st Division command post there was "a quiet capable appearing bunch. . . . The wounded lying outside, howitzers going full blast, tanks, infantry moving up in good style through the shrapnel, boches pulling out, guns going. . . . French sergeant very enthusiastic, *'Magnifique! Magnifique!'* " He escorted some enemy officers from a large haul of prisoners back to the prisoners' cage for interrogation, then went out again to investigate the caliber of shells reported to be bombarding Toul. "Our planes owned the air today, all the Woevre towns on fire. First day's objectives all passed and pushing on to second day's. . . . Got sore and blew up topog. section and was ashamed of it afterward. . . . Ist and IVth Corps had entire success. Great day." The IVth had in fact met sterner resistance than the Ist but reached all of its objectives by noon of the first day.

In the wake of the advance Stilwell made his way through burned-out tanks and trucks, overturned gun carriages, refugees, dead horses and all the strewn litter of war to examine enemy emplacements, and stayed up two nights in a row to write his summaries. While officers gathered for critiques of the action, the general enthusiasm was high. The wiping out of the oldest, strongest and last German-held salient gave a great lift to Allied morale even though the enemy at St. Mihiel was not, as General Liggett wrote, "at his best nor his second best." Composed largely of second-class replacements, the German troops were inferior in number to the Americans and low in morale. Although American performance fell short of expectations in plan and execution, the battle had a decisive effect: in demonstrating to the Germans that an American Army was a reality in the field, it made plain the inevitability of defeat. Hope of a stalemate against the worn-out British and French, permitting at least a satisfactory peace, faded in the face of a new army. From this point on, with desperation lending them fury, the German effort was to fight for withdrawal to a position from which they could negotiate and avoid surrender.

Apart from his work as G-2, Stilwell carved his initials on the battle in a moment of inspiration known as the Schmeercase affair. In the early stages of the battle, when reports were meager, his fellow G-2 at Ist Corps, Colonel Sherman Miles, kept calling him every hour for news of any special developments until Stilwell, exasperated, suddenly obliged: "Yes, the great Otto Schmierkäse, the German bichloride gas expert, has been captured." Great excitement at the other end of the wire: "Spell his name; spell bichloride." Hardly expecting such success for a fiction with the German name for a soft cheese, Stilwell was caught up by his own invention. He added details of such verisimilitude that Colonel Miles announced he was sending over his gas officer to interview the prisoner and hung up before the hoax could be confessed. When the gas officer arrived, it was explained to him that Dr. Schmierkäse had just five minutes before been sent back under guard to G-2, First Army, for interviewing. Thereafter the elusive prisoner had to be kept one move ahead of would-be interviewers. Word of Stilwell's hoax spread through corps and division headquarters, causing some hilarity at the expense of Colonel Miles who not unnaturally resented it. Picked up by Reuters, the Schmeercase (as it was now spelled) report appeared in the papers of Paris, London and New York, establishing as history that "One of the leading German gas experts has been captured by the Americans according to word from the St. Mihiel front. He was arranging a gas projector when nabbed." To his wife Stilwell wrote, "Otto is my own creation and I am getting more proud of him every day. . . . Everybody in AEF knows Otto now."

A general Allied offensive all along the front beginning with the American attack in the Meuse-Argonne sector was lauched at the end of September. The vigor of the American assault, despite fresh tactical errors which caused the relief of seven generals, frustrated Ludendorff's last hope of an orderly withdrawal to a firm position on Germany's frontier. On October 5 came the "TREMENDOUS NEWS," as Stilwell recorded it, that the Germans had appealed to President Wilson for an armistice. Wilson turned it down on the ground that armistice could only be granted by the

Allied Commander-in-Chief. For another month, behind the crescendo of guns in the continuing battle, the Germans maneuvered desperately for position until no room for maneuver was left. Emissaries were sent to ask an armistice of Foch. On a winter morning in the fifth November of the war the Western Front at last fell still.

The IVth Corps was assigned to occupation duty in the Coblenz area with headquarters at Cochem on the Mosel. A man of many distastes, Stilwell made no exception of the enemy. On the march into Germany he described the Burgermeister of Nonweiler as a "typical savage, bowel-less, brutal, grouchy, sullen, boche son-of-a-bitch. He got up and bowed when we left."

While the statesmen assembled in Paris, Stilwell fumed in Cochem. "Sitting, just sitting," he wrote to his wife in January, "and hoping our addle-pated boob of a president will soon weary of the applause, homage, and other mush that he is receiving so that peace negotiations can begin and the American Army can go home." A stream of distinguished personages came to visit including the Prince of Wales whom Stilwell, of all people, was detailed to attend. Fortunately he found him "quiet, unassuming, well brought up, well-mannered and likeable." George Marshall too came by and, evidently not amused, "sounded off about Schmeercase and named the author."

On the recommendation of General Briant Wells, who had joined the IVth Corps as its new Chief of Staff in October, Stilwell was promoted to the temporary rank of full colonel and received the Distinguished Service Medal, a newly created order to reward noncombat service. Wells developed a great liking and admiration for Stilwell whom he reported to be "unusually intelligent" and "one of the most capable G-2 officers developed in the war." "Nothing but praise of your section," he wrote, "has come from any of the Divisions that have served with the Corps."

On May 7, 1919, the draft of one of history's more fallible documents, the Treaty of Versailles, was completed. Upon the anticipated signing of the Peace Treaty, the IVth Corps was deactivated, bringing Stilwell's occupation duty to an end. Like many others during those disillusioning months of 1919 he had not been edified by the spectacle of the Peace Conference and his taste of inter-Allied cooperation was sour. "They are *all* trying to belittle our army and our achievements. . . . Bickering and trading back and forth. . . . Incident of French and Belgians dickering about Luxembourg three *days* after the Armistice. . . . Nothing *generous* or *spontaneous* in relations between Allies . . . watching each other, always trying to put something over." He prepared to go home in a frame of mind he would find already growing in America, "thoroughly convinced that what we want to do is stay home and mind our own business and get ready to pound *anybody* that gets in our way. League of Nations!"

Among the disappointments suffered at the Peace Conference none was greater than China's. The trouble with the terms of the Peace Treaty was not inherent iniquity but the gap by which they fell short of the expectations aroused by President Wilson. Wilson's promises of a just peace, self-determination and all the rest of the Fourteen Points, which had so lifted the spirits of the world and fired the nationalism of ardent young Chinese as of other hopeful peoples, withered at the touch of hard realities. One reality was Japan's secret agreements with the Allies about Shantung. In addition, though Japan had contributed nothing to combat, she was a military and naval power to be reckoned with. China's only reality was her wants. Her bill for cancellation of the unequal treaties was simply ignored, which made her concentrate with all the more fervor on Shantung. She had a weak case in law, having had herself reaffirmed the transfer of German rights to Japan in return for Japanese loans. But she had a strong case in public opinion based on natural sovereignty and the spirit of the Fourteen Points. Her strongly nationalist delegates, all graduates of American universities, made the most of this at Paris.

Angered by the refusal of the Conference to make a declaration of racial equality, the Japanese too turned all their pressure upon Shantung. It became a major issue of the Conference and the source of exquisite embarrassment to President Wilson. His own principles, the advice of his delegation, the passionate pleading of the American Minister to China, Paul Reinsch, and the force of American public opinion aroused on the Shantung issue by missionary societies, all urged China's cause. But Japan's case, in which the Allies had been snared and tied, could not be denied without disrupting the Conference. Torn by all its other quarrels, the Conference was on the edge of disintegrating anyway. Wilson had staked his political life, and indeed his soul, on obtaining the Covenant of the League of Nations—the cure, as he saw it, for all international ills—as part of the Peace Treaty. When Japan threatened to bolt unless given what she wanted, thus providing the excuse for other defections, Wilson saw the prospect of the whole structure that was to save the world and make him immortal collapsing. Against the advice of Secretary Lansing and the other American delegates, who believed the proposed Japanese bolt to be a bluff, he yielded. At its last meeting on April 30, 1919, the Council of Five confirmed Japan as successor to all German concessions in Shantung. As a conciliatory gesture Japan offered the verbal promise to "restore eventual sovereignty" to China. In turn, Wilson took comfort in the theory that once the League existed, it could correct any unfortunate sacrifices incurred in the process of creating it.

Uproar greeted the event in China. Public fervor had already been excited by reports of the dispute in Paris. Students of the National University of Peking, center of the progressives and intellectuals of Young China, were organizing a demonstration for "National Humiliation Day" on May 7 to commemorate the signing of the Twenty-one Demands. When news came of the Shantung award and of its acceptance by pro-Japanese members of the Anfu government, the students assembled in a mass meeting of 3,000 on May 4. Shouting "Down with the traitors!" "Return Shantung!" "Boycott Japanese goods!" they paraded through the streets and attacked the homes of the puppet ministers. The protest spread overnight to Shanghai, Nanking, Hankow and Canton, with shops closing everywhere as students swept through the streets calling for the boycott. The students, who commanded the traditional Chinese respect for scholars, exercised a forceful influence and the boycott they started was taken up by the merchant class and newly formed labor unions. The May Fourth movement developed into a conscious effort to destroy Japan's market in China that was to last for a year. In providing the rallying point for reinvigorating the nationalism of the new China it had a wider effect than anything since the Revolution. Unable to repress it, the Government was finally forced to dismiss the most compromised ministers and approve the refusal of the Chinese delegates at Paris to sign the Peace Treaty.

In America the fate of a remote peninsula in the Yellow Sea became the focus, however artificial, of a tremendous struggle in domestic politics. Since President Wilson had made the League of Nations inseparable from the Peace Treaty, his opponents in the Senate were obliged to defeat the Treaty and for this purpose fastened on Shantung as its "outstanding iniquity." The oratory swelled noisily. "A conspiracy to rob," "an infamy," "shameless," "damnable," "inexcusable" resounded in the Senate and the press. Especially the Western Senators exploited the issue in response to anti-Japanese sentiment in their states where the Oriental Exclusion League was agitating for bills against alien land ownership. Shantung became a double-barreled gun against Japan and Wilson.

Japan's rise as a naval power, her real and supposed activities in Mexico and possible threat to the Panama Canal, her seizure of the Pacific islands, her too eager intervention in Siberia, all combined to give a picture of general aggressiveness which was exciting American antagonism. A powerful Japan whose aim was world hegemony was seen as a direct threat to American interests in the Pacific and Far East, a subject to which the Senate gave great importance and the Hearst press gave its most horrendous attentions. It proclaimed China to have been "outrageously robbed" by a "wily, tricky, fight-thirsty Japan" and suggested "implications of actual war" in American relations with Japan. Senator Hiram Johnson of California, home of the Oriental Exclusion League, orated weekly on the "blot on American honor." But no one equaled the pitch of moral indignation reached by Senator Borah who denounced the Shantung clause as "so immoral and unrighteous that . . . we dread even to think about it. We loathe to be forced to attempt to defend it." He loosed his horror for Wilson and the League in a tirade of exaggeration: ". . . dishonor and degrade . . . war will inevitably follow . . . revolting injustice . . . outside the pale of respectability . . . shocks the conscience . . . naked, hideous and revolting . . . a monster . . . no parallel."

When the press and public men could expend such passion on Shantung and even talk of war, the public could hardly be blamed for assuming the issue to be a major American interest. A few voices, who could not match the boom of Borah and the other "Irreconcilables," suggested that China's case did not altogether justify all the emotion. "Why," asked the editor of *Current Opinion,* "should America shed blood to protect China, as Senator Borah suggests, when she is unwilling to protect herself, unless our own interests are involved to a sufficient extent to justify it?" The echo of that fundamental question would go on resounding through several decades.

The mark left by Shantung on both America and China was historic. Besides aiding American rejection of the League, the issue gave Americans a sense of guilt about China and it gave the Chinese a new injection of nationalism which revived the failing and dispirited Kuomintang, preserving it for eventual power.

In the midst of this tumultuous struggle Stilwell returned home in July 1919. By September, in the general reduction of temporary ranks, he was once again a captain as he had been before the war began.

From maneuvers in California in 1912, Stilwell sent his parents a postcard with the message "This is Josie indicating the range . . ." (32).

4

Assignment to Peking:

YEARS OF THE WARLORDS, 1920-23

T EN days after his return from France Stilwell's career took the decisive turn that connected him thereafter with China. He could see as soon as he came home that a swollen army, combined with the war-disgusted mood of the United States, did not offer a promising outlook for advancement in a military career. Not possessed of a temperament to wait patiently for fate's offerings, he went down to Washington on July 25 to take a hand in his next assignment. He called on a former classmate, Chauncey Fenton, now an officer in the personnel division of the War Department, and asked bluntly, "How about sending me as far away from home as possible?"

"That's a funny thing," Fenton replied. "We were just talking this morning about sending men to Japan and China." He told Stilwell about the program of the Military Intelligence Division (MID) for sending officers to these countries for language training. With both proficiency in languages and previous service in Intelligence, Stilwell was a natural candidate. He asked for Japan. "All the Japan jobs are filled," Fenton said. "How about China?"

"All right, make it China," Stilwell agreed, and so it was arranged. As of August 6, 1919, he was appointed the first language officer for China to represent the Army.

With the Intelligence Division much enlarged by the war, the General

Staff had decided to put the gathering of information by military attachés, hitherto haphazard, on a systematic basis. MID planned to develop a well-chosen, well-trained corps of attachés having, it hopefully prescribed, "detailed knowledge of the language, military establishments, political conditions and customs of foreign nations" and "a true appreciation of . . . their probable reactions in peace and war." As things worked out, the coveted appointment as military attaché which, at least in the larger posts, required a private income, continued to be handed around among a small group who made up the "attachés' clique." But apart from the attaché himself, graduates of the language program were needed to serve the enlarged scope of the Intelligence Division, in particular its Far East section.

Qualifications for the post were general "military efficiency"—meaning the sum of an officer's rating on his Efficiency Report—language proficiency, availability and willingness. The age limit was thirty-five and appointees were to be drawn only from the combat arms: Infantry, Cavalry and Artillery. At thirty-six Stilwell was overage, but since he fitted the qualifications as if carved for them in every other respect, his nomination went through with remarkable and unbureaucratic despatch.

At this moment China was making front-page news. Headlines flared the "Rape of Shantung," the "Crime of Shantung," the "Shame of Shantung" and various other heated pejoratives. Even after Shantung helped to accomplish defeat of the League and the ruin of Wilson, the issue was carried over into the Presidential campaign of 1920 and the wrong done to China was used by the Republicans as a favorite stick with which to beat the Administration. From his front porch Harding presented China as America's ward, now betrayed. As a result of the return of the Boxer indemnity, he said, China had placed her faith "in the example, in the democracy, in the justice of the United States" only to find that several millions of her people were delivered over to a rival nation at Paris. But in the Senate, Harding went on, some steadfast Americans had said "No" and had "kept the plighted faith in the lesson we taught China some twenty years ago."

As the Chinese saw it and as the leaders of the May Fourth movement tirelessly preached, the lesson America had taught in 1919 if not in 1900 was the perfidy of the Allies and the folly of relying on foreign friends. To Americans, however, Harding's version was the governing concept of their relation to China at the time Stilwell entered the Chinese phase of his career.

With his wife and children Stilwell left in August 1919 for California where he was to spend the first year of his Chinese language studies at the University of California at Berkeley. It took him less than a month to conclude that the course there was inadequate and progress frustrated because there was no one to talk Chinese to after school. He reported to MID that he and his fellow-officer in the program, Captain Lloyd P. Horsfall, would do better to transfer to school in China at once where they could hear and practice the spoken language. Though his recommendation was confirmed by other language officers no action was taken.

Of all languages Chinese, because of its tone system, needs to be learned where it can be heard and spoken in daily use. The meaning of a word depends on which of four tones in Mandarin and which of eight tones in Cantonese is used to express it. The difficulty of the written language derives not so much from the several thousand individual characters that must be learned by sight as from the complications involved in using and understanding them in combination. A well-educated man may know 6,000 characters, a scholar 8,000 or 9,000, while for ordinary daily use 3,000 are adequate. These can be recognized with knowledge of about 1,000 basic forms.

Chinese characters are composed of any number of brush strokes, from one, as in 一, meaning "one, unity, all, uniform," to more than 20, as in 灣 (22 strokes), meaning "bay, bend of a stream." Although they seem to the Western eye a mysterious forest with no clue to the maze, they contain a definite principle of order. They are classified in dictionaries under 214 radicals, such as 男, "man"; 女, "woman"; 口, "mouth"; 山, "mountain"; 工, "work" or "workman" (originally a carpenter's square); 宀, "roof"; 車, "cart" (a two-wheeled vehicle viewed from above). The radicals were originally pictographs which gradually became stylized. The rest of the language is represented by the addition of what are called "phonetics" to the radicals; for example, the character 論 (*lun*), meaning "to discuss, discourse" is made up of the radical 言, meaning "words," plus the phonetic 侖, pronounced *lun* and meaning "to arrange, set in order," which indicates both sound and meaning: "to set words in order," i.e. "to discuss." Not all phonetics, however, are so helpful or logical. Some indicate neither sound nor meaning.

There are approximately 880 phonetics which together with the radicals (some of which double as phonetics) make up the 1,000 basic forms a student must know to be able to read and write all Chinese characters. The task requires persistence, hours of practice and constant review, which obviously limits not only the number of foreigners willing and able to accomplish it but the number of Chinese who could achieve literacy before *pai-hua,* a written form of the vernacular, was introduced.

Mandarin or official Chinese was the normal language of the provinces north of the Yangtze (and of some in the south) and the administrative language for the country as a whole. All officials were supposed to be able to speak it. While Mandarin and Cantonese and various other dialects

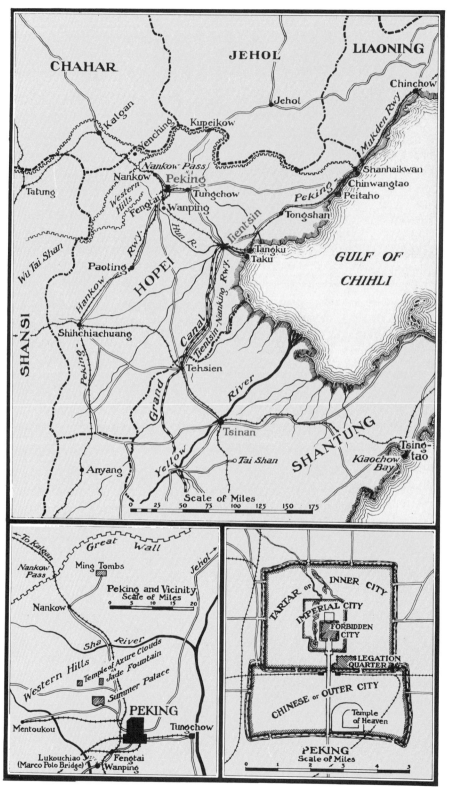

North China and Peking

were mutually unintelligible, all of literate China was united by the written language.

While in California Stilwell spent his summer leave of 1920 at Carmel where he purchased a tract of five lots on the Point overlooking the ocean for a future home. Promoted to major in July, he sailed with his family and the Horsfalls for China on August 5, 1920.

On September 18 the Army transport rounded the Shantung promontory just at dusk when the jagged coastline and the brown batwing sails of Chinese junks were outlined against a rose-colored sunset. Two days later the ship came into Chinwangtao, a Treaty Port at the northern frontier of China proper near where the Great Wall comes down to the sea and the mournful chant of fishermen hauling in their nets rises twice a day. A 250-mile railroad trip southward via Tientsin brought the travelers to their destination, the famed city in the plain, Peking.

Stilwell spent the next ten days looking for a house and exploring one of the great capitals of the world. Here the old mandarin class mingled with venal adventurers, the new China throbbed with plans and hopes of reform, foreigners lived a charmed, hedonistic existence and the silent Altar of Heaven lay in eternal marble perfection open to the sky. Within moats was the Forbidden City with enameled tiled roofs of Imperial yellow and three artificial lakes dotted with islands. On the islands were pagodas and painted pavilions and the palace where the last Emperor had been imprisoned by his aunt. Gnarled willows and cypresses grew along the shores, and miniature hills with rocks and caves simulated the mountain scenery beloved by Chinese painters. An ancient carp caught in one of the lakes, it was said, wore a gold plate engraved with the name of Yung-Lo, a Ming emperor of the sixteenth century.

Upper-class residences were hidden behind walled streets. Each had its courtyard garden with lotus pool and teahouse, peonies in flowerpots, honeycombed rocks carved by hundreds of years of trickling water, and a moon window in a wall. Springless covered Peking carts bumped over the cobblestones, camels from the northwest moved with the haughty dignity of the desert, Buddhist priests in saffron robes stood among the red columns of the Lama Temple, dust storms blowing off the plains periodically tortured the capital and its residents. Outside the walls the plain stretched away to the Summer Palace and the Western Hills where the Monastery of the Azure Cloud and other temples were sheltered by ancient pines. From the Hill of the Jade Fountain springs flowed down to fill the lakes and moats of the Forbidden City.

Within the Legation Quarter were the foreign residences and hotels, the polo grounds, the stately American Legation at the top of the street, dignified banks and business offices, but none of the roaring commerce of

Shanghai. Peking was not like the Treaty Ports; foreigners here even held intercourse with educated Chinese. Peking was the center of intellectual as well as official life. It was the site of the National Peking University, the Peking Union Medical College founded by the Rockefellers, Tsing-Hua College founded by American Boxer indemnity money, Yenching and many other missionary-founded colleges. It was the fount of the renaissance movement dedicated to making China over through the written vernacular *pai-hua,* considered by its promoters the single most important instrument for modernizing the country. *Pai-hua* would make possible the spread of literacy and give popular access to modern newspapers, a recent Western import regarded by the conservatives with the utmost repugnance.

Besides diplomatic corps and journalists, educators and missionaries, the capital attracted art collectors and sinologues, travelers who came through and never left, and retired foreigners who settled here from choice because life was gracious and placid and money went far. With abundant servants, a summer home in the western hills, the Golf Club and Race Club for the Legation set, picnics in summer and pheasant hunting in fall, Peking for the foreigner represented, in the phrase of a nostalgic resident, "the years that were fat."

The Stilwells and Horsfalls together took a Chinese-style house outside the Legation Quarter at No. 3 Pei Tsung Pu Hutung near the east wall. Like all Chinese houses it was built on one floor in a series of connected quadrilaterals, each around a courtyard, and had paper in the windows instead of glass. A house with four bedrooms, dining room, living room, library, office and servants' quarters cost at this time $15 in American money a month, with cost of servants in proportion. The usual officer's family employed five or six servants at a cost of about $35 in American money plus squeeze, the commission on every transaction that is the heart of Chinese life. At the time of the birth of their fourth child, a daughter named Alison, in February 1921, the Stilwells employed a number-one boy who was butler, manager and general factotum, a second houseboy, two cooks, a wash amah, a baby amah and a coolie.

Language officers studied at the North China Union Language School, founded in 1910 to teach missionaries and later expanded to include the many foreign advisers in the Chinese service as well as businessmen and any others who wanted to learn. Employing 100 teachers for 300 students, the school taught the direct method by ear for fast results. The first-year course, with five hours of classes a day, began with six months of listening and speaking and drill in the sound and meaning of words. This was followed by six months of reading, translating and conversing with tutors. At the end of the year the student was supposed to know 700 characters and converse without pain. He also attended seminars and lectures on

Chinese history, religion, economics and current affairs. The language officer, after his first year, added study of technical and military terms. Travel, both for his further acquaintance with the country and for fact-finding missions in the service of the military attaché, was part of his duty. He was required to take examinations each year and at the end of his three- or four-year tour he was supposed to know 3,000 characters and speak fluently.

Dr. William B. Pettus, founder and director of the school, complained that Stilwell and Horsfall had picked up a bad accent in California which could lead to confusion, for even the most fluent foreigner could encounter difficulties. Dr. Edward Hume, an old-timer who spoke perfect Chinese, told Stilwell that once in the countryside he had asked two farmers the way to Changsha. They looked blank, and after repeating his question several times he gave up. As he walked on, he overheard one farmer say to the other, "It sounds just as if the foreigner were asking, 'Is this the road to Changsha?' "

Stilwell acquired, like all foreigners, a Chinese name derived from the sound of his own, in his case Shih Ti-wei, written 史 迪 威. The surname meant "history" and the first name "to direct" or "lead in the right direction"(to) "majesty" or "prestige"—a provocative collection. Between classes he enjoyed wandering through the fairs and markets and streets of shops. His first purchase was some carved ivories and he began to collect inlaid fan handles and to accumulate Chinese furnishings for his future house in Carmel.

He met the charm and cruelty of China side by side. Kite-flying was a favorite sport with kites fashioned in the form of dragons, castles or butterflies with gauzy tinted wings. Hung with whistles or bells or wooden chimes, they filled the air with color and motion and, as an observer described it, "a soft unearthly music . . . as of oriental cherubim." Executions were equally popular, watched by eager crowds as the victim with hands bound was kicked to his knees and his head severed by a stroke of the heavy sword to admiring shouts of *Hao!* When the blood spurted women and children rushed forward to dip strings of copper coins in it which were then hung around the children's necks to frighten away evil spirits. Nearby under a roofed plaza might be found a storyteller in gown and skullcap holding in rapt attention an audience of perhaps a hundred coolies and workers who squatted in total silence as they listened to a tale of ancient heroism and legendary deeds. The narrator softly clapped bamboo sticks in rhythm to his recital or changed into song for philosophical passages or beat a drum for the martial parts.

The seduction of China was at work. Stilwell had been in Peking less than a month when he answered a War Department questionnaire on preference of service by marking "Military Attaché, China," as his only desired post; all others, including "West Point," he marked "No."

Two months before Stilwell arrived, three warlords, each a remarkable personality, had combined in alliance for just long enough to oust the Anfu government and had then turned upon each other to vie for the dominant power that went with control of the capital. The winner who now held Peking was Marshal Wu Pei-fu, a gentlemanly mandarin and graduate of the classical examinations; the loser was Marshal Chang Tso-lin, ex-bandit and lord of Manchuria; the holder of the balance of power was the "Christian General" of peasant birth, Feng Yu-hsiang.

Wu Pei-fu sincerely regarded himself as a public servant with concern for public order and the hope, larger than personal ambition alone, of restoring national government to China. A slender fine-boned man with amber eyes in a narrow head and the aquiline nose that indicated well-born lineage, he spoke in the cultivated vocabulary of the mandarin and was regarded by the diplomatic corps as the favored candidate for the strong man China so badly needed. For the benefit of an American journalist he exhibited a picture of George Washington on the wall of his *yamen** and told his visitor that it was his desire to do for his country what Washington had done in uniting the thirteen colonies. He maintained discipline among his troops and even regularly paid them their whole pay which earned him the dislike of other chieftains but gave him an army that would not readily desert and won him the allegiance of the countryside which was spared the curse of marauding soldiers. In an effort to reconstruct representative government Marshal Wu recalled the parliament of 1913 and restored the ever-available Li Yuan-hung. But though a lion in war, Wu was infirm in politics; his arrangements proved unstable and the "Mukden Tiger," Chang Tso-lin, was waiting in the wings.

Small and delicate in physique, the renowned Manchurian Marshal had started life as a common soldier in the Sino-Japanese War of 1895, progressed to bandit, accepted an offer of amnesty, and in return for bringing in his troops received command of a garrison outside Mukden. From this base he acquired wealth by supplying first the Russians and then the Japanese in the Russo-Japanese War. He now wore on his black satin skullcap a famous pearl said to be the largest in the world. His halls in Manchuria were filled with carved black teak furniture, silken rugs, bronzes, jars of jade, scroll paintings and precious porcelains. He shared his domain in delicate balance with the Japanese, who maintained in Mukden the headquarters of their growing industrial development of Manchuria.

---

* Residence headquarters.

Dr. Sun Yat-sen with his bodyguards in 1924 (33). Standing directly behind him is his thirty-seven-year-old disciple Chiang Kai-shek. In that same year Dr. Sun and his second wife, Ch'ing-ling Soong, traveled by boat from Canton to Peking (34).

33

34

35

Prominent Chinese warlords during Stilwell's first assignment to Peking 1920–23 included Marshal Chang Tso-lin, seen here with his son (35) and his artillery arriving at a railway station (36). Marshal Wu Pei-fu (39), with his troops on parade (37); "Christian General" Feng Yu-hsiang (38) with his troops at trade school (41); and Yen Hsi-shan (40), the "Model Governor" of Shansi province where Stilwell was assigned to build roads.

38

36

37

39

40

41

Around these two Marshals in the struggle for control of north China other factions and *tuchuns* combined and recombined. The most considerable was Feng Yu-hsiang, less because of his prodigious stature than because, like Wu, he took care to build up a loyal and effective army. As a young soldier in the armies of Yuan Shih-kai he had become converted not only to Christianity but also to the gospel of the Revolution according to Sun Yat-sen, and he believed that moral indoctrination in addition to food, clothes and pay was necessary to make good soldiers. During the shifts and confusions of the Republican years he had joined forces with Wu Pei-fu and in 1920 was appointed Military Governor of the northwest province of Shensi. He married the Chinese secretary of the YMCA in Peking, baptized his soldiers with a hose and taught them to sing evangelical hymns and marching songs to the words "We must not drink or smoke" and "We must not gamble or visit whores." He disapproved of Wu's drinking and as a hint once presented him at a banquet with a rare porcelain vase from which Wu poured a glass to drink a toast to the donor, only to spit it out at the first mouthful on discovering it to be water. While Feng did not altogether approve of Wu, he believed him to be working for the same ultimate object as himself—a unified China free of foreign control—and this being the case was more inclined to side with him against Chang Tso-lin than vice versa.

In the years 1920-23, when Stilwell was in Peking, Feng fought in alliance with Wu first against a combine of various *tuchuns* and then in 1922 against Chang Tso-lin when the Tiger renewed his bid to gain north China. Often the military engagements were fought within ten miles of the capital, sometimes causing the city gates to be closed for a week at a time. At night residents could watch the tracers of artillery fire from the roof of the Peking Hotel. At the boom of cannon the hotel trembled as if from a minor earthquake. Once when Stilwell was absent bullets came flying through the streets, some passing through his house. Mrs. Stilwell placed all the children under tables and ventured out to the neighboring home of a missionary from which she could telephone to the Legation to report being under fire. The danger was taken casually: she was advised to return home and let it pass.

The subject of study of a military attaché and his staff is the soldiery of the host country. Stilwell began his acquaintance with the Chinese soldier, whom he was one day to command, under the conditions of the *tuchuns'* strife. He saw Wu Pei-fu's men march off to war in a long gray file accompanied by mule-drawn two-wheeled carts carrying ammunition, bedding and supplies. These were superior arrangements; the average warlord's troops had only squeaking man-powered wheelbarrows for supply trains. Many in Wu's army, as in others, were barely more than fourteen

These pictures from one of Stilwell's albums show Chinese peasants during the famine of 1920, reported to be the worst in forty years (42–45).

years old but they were well equipped with knapsacks, trench picks, shovels, lanterns, teapots, oiled paper umbrellas, alarm clocks and hot-water bottles. They were followed by coolies bearing coffins on poles as reassurance to the soldiers that, if killed, their bodies would not be left unburied on the plains. On the gray cotton uniforms, padded in winter, common to all Chinese troops, Wu's men wore red armbands to distinguish their allegiance. As a rule these armbands were not sewed on but fastened with a safety pin for easy removal when armies changed sides.

Military performance of the average army was not sharp. When soldiers reached the field of battle they would stand for a few moments, look around, unsling their rifles, fire a haphazard shot or two without aiming through the sights and then sit down. Cannon were fired recklessly, often missing their targets by a quarter-mile or more. If it rained the paper umbrellas blossomed down the line like a sudden sprout of mushrooms and fighting ceased. Wu's army was better than most and in 1922 in combination with Feng's drove Chang Tso-lin back to Manchuria.

In his effort to form a national government Wu Pei-fu had invited the adherence of Sun Yat-sen, but Sun, who held the title of President of China, conferred by the rump Kuomintang parliament, refused. He wanted to unite China under the Three Principles of the Kuomintang program: Nationalism, Democracy and the People's Livelihood. But all his schemes and alliances failed and his various partners turned against him. He repeatedly proposed to the American Minister his grand plan for the Western democracies to invest in a new government for China but it found no takers. The plan hardly fitted with Sun's unabated nationalism but in the heartbreaking decade since the Revolution he had come to believe that China could not be lifted by her own bootstraps. In the hope of gaining the north he even entered, at one point, into a far-fetched alliance with Chang Tso-lin which, not surprisingly, had no practical results.

Failed by the West and by his own countrymen, he turned for help where it was offered, to revolutionary Russia, and made alliance with the Comintern in January 1923. In 1919 Soviet Russia had announced the waiving of all Czarist treaties and concessions, causing a tremendous impression in China as the first Western power to give up anything voluntarily. When it came to the practice, the Soviets had second thoughts and proved unwilling to give up the Chinese Eastern Railway in Manchuria or their rights in Mongolia. Nevertheless, to Chinese disillusioned with the progress of their own Revolution, the attraction of Moscow was strong and conversions to Communism began. On its side the Soviet Union was looking for friends and for another base for the ultimate advance of world revolution. While acknowledging that under present conditions China was not ripe for Communism, the U.S.S.R. agreed to aid the Kuomintang to achieve national unity and independence. Under the terms of the alliance with Sun Yat-sen, the Chinese Communists, who had formed their own party in 1921, were admitted into the Kuomintang as collaborators in the goal of regenerating the country and for the time being agreed that the Kuomintang should assume the leadership of the national revolution.

Sun Yat-sen no more than any of the warlords was able to establish himself as a national ruler. He had a political philosophy but no power; the warlords had power without a program. He founded and formulated the Revolution but fell short in command and organization. He was, a contemporary suggested, part St. Paul, part William Jennings Bryan, but even had he been part George Washington, part Lenin, he would have been hard put to prevail over his old and intractable country. In the absence of a monarch, sectional interests prevailed; functioning statehood eluded the nation's grasp.

Stilwell had been in Peking only six months when he found an opportunity to break away from Legation life and become acquainted with China on a working level. Following the severe famine of the previous year, 1920, the International Famine Relief Committee asked to borrow him from the Army to serve as Chief Engineer of the road-building program in Shansi. He was to be in the field for four months from April to July 1921, working daily with Chinese officials, village magistrates, contractors, construction bosses and laborers, sleeping and eating the Chinese way, supervising the work on foot or horseback, bossing, cajoling, bargaining, playing the game of "face," learning Chinese habits and characteristics and interrelations. He had no training or experience in engineering beyond what he had learned as an undergraduate at West Point, but he had self-confidence, and like Ulysses he was never content to stay long in one place. Hearing of the road-building project and eager for a chance to move out and use his newly acquired Chinese under real conditions, he asked for the job. Leading as it did to a mission of greater consequence the year afterwards, the road-building in Shansi played a significant part in deepening the Chinese channel of Stilwell's career.

The Shansi road was designed partly to give work to famine refugees but chiefly as a step in long-range famine control through improved transportation so that in the future surplus grain could be imported into the stricken areas from the northwest provinces which never suffered famine. Away from the railroads and rivers, China was virtually without roads for wheeled transportation. The Chinese Government did not make a habit of relief projects. Emergency distribution of food stores, if undertaken at all, was never done in time to prevent mass starvation. Accustomed to the Western impulse to "do something," China let the foreign activists do what

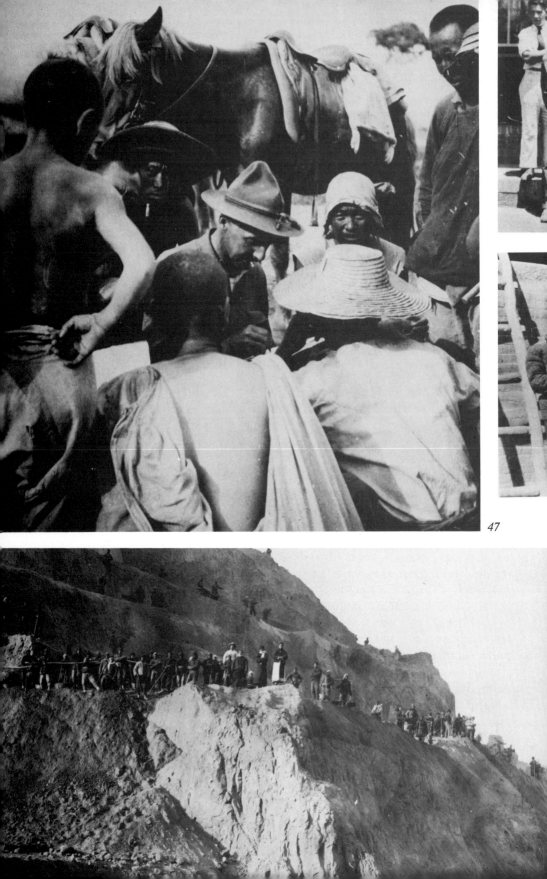

47

48

49

50

51

h the exception of one (46), all these pictures (47–53) come from Stilwell's album of 1921–22
umenting his work as chief engineer of the road-building program in Shansi province in 1921. He
be seen at work on the Yellow River Road (47) and with a group of children (50). His engineers
and foremen (49) posed for group pictures. In 1922 he was asked to build a proper road from
ng Kuan to Sian in Shensi province. His crew can be seen at work on the border of Shensi and
nan (46).

52

53

they could but the Oriental attitude did not insist on man conquering his circumstances. Centuries of calamities inured the Chinese to their recurrence; masses would die but more masses would be born. In the famine of 1920, reported to be the worst in forty years, "incredibly filthy and ragged bands of staggering skeletons with staring eyes, no longer human beings," headed in long lines for the towns and crowded the small railroad stations. The countryside was sere with no sign of spring grain; only the grave mounds stood out against the brown earth while the wind whirled clouds of yellow dust over deserted homes.

The International Famine Relief Committee meeting in Peking heard reports of bungled food shipments, of incompetence and graft among officials and of profiteering in grain. The Committees took the "hopeful view," however, that official China had at last awakened and "will leave the work for foreign committees and the American Red Cross, trusting no more to county and provincial officials." This was the pattern of Western activism and Chinese acceptance. Appealing to the American public for the Chinese Famine Relief Fund, President Wilson in a classic statement of the American point of view said, "To an unusual degree the Chinese people look to us for counsel and for effective leadership." The Chinese themselves never confused material aid which was what they looked to America for with either counsel or leadership. Spurred by the missionaries, the campaign in the United States brought such an outpouring of funds that a surplus resulted and this made possible the road-building program.

Stilwell himself believed that the missionaries deliberately exaggerated reports of the famine, justifying themselves on the ground that by bringing in money and food in a time of distress they were furthering the cause of Christianity. Having to work "against the passive resistance of officials," he wrote, they had a chance "to do something for the people that the government could not or would not do."

Out in the field where the provincial interest was paramount, he found the local officials of Shansi more ready to help than hinder the work of the road-building. This was owing to the influence of the *Tuchun* of the province, Yen Hsi-shan, a progressive and practical materialist who enjoyed the title of "Model Governor." He had the wit to see that he could draw more strength and wealth from the province by improving its conditions than by squeezing it dry. When he explained the benefits of the proposed road to landowners whose property stood in the way, they made no resistance and allowed the road-builders to cut through old grave mounds and even, in the case of recent deaths, willingly moved the graves.

The projected road link was to be 82 miles long, starting at Fenchow and finishing at Jung-tu on the Yellow River. Stilwell's instructions were to make it 22 feet wide with a gravel surface, keep the grade under 6 percent and finish the job by August 1. He had twelve foreign assistants including a Standard Oil civil engineer, a Swedish mining engineer, two Norwegian missionaries and an Anglo-Indian reserve officer. The country was rocky and mountainous with rich agricultural valleys where crop failures were unknown. Everywhere the Chinese farmer could be seen "with his patient cow and B.C. plow," as Stilwell wrote, turning over furrows on hillsides so steep that "the daily struggle even to reach his fields would appall a white man."

The trace ran along a river valley, over a pass, down into another valley and "after that to be determined." Riding or walking miles every day, sleeping in a different place every night—often outdoors to avoid bedbugs and lice—Stilwell directed the work of 6,000 men, showing the Chinese surveyors what to do, helping the section engineers, locating the work gangs, deciding on grades, crossings, cuts and fills, and trying to master the local dialect. Fortunately many spoke Mandarin.

Homes in the area were mostly caverns in the hills lined with stone arches and closed by stone walls in front. Stonemasons were plentiful. Stilwell dealt with small contractors for rock-breaking, lime, marking stakes, mules, water buckets and road labor, avoiding the sleek, silk-gowned businessmen from the towns who offered to take on the whole contract. He preferred to deal with Li Mou-lin, in patched breeches and dirty shirt, than with the fat gentry "so refined and elegant that they cannot walk up six steps without puffing."

Most of the pick-and-shovel men were small farmers earning extra money. They were organized into work groups of about 30 men with an overseer and one or two cooks. The *tuan chang* or overseer carried a cane, wore a straw hat and clean clothes and usually snoozed in the shade with sentries posted to whistle at Stilwell's approach. When the work was poor the battle of face began. Stilwell would reproach the overseer, who in turn would roar at the work gang, who in their turn "rather enjoy the play: they know it is all for effect and if favored with a wink from the foreigner from behind the overseer's back will break into broad grins." When "the Chief Engineer meets man after man who can see through a joke, even when it is on himself and laugh as heartily as the bystanders, his heart warms to the whole race."

In Yungningchow Stilwell was welcomed by the local colonel and magistrate and served an honorific banquet of 57 known and unknown dishes alternating with thimble-glasses of raw alcohol. He was invited to review the cadets of a local military school who paraded to the blare of bugles "blown up and down the scale regardless of consequences." In the morning he was conducted ceremoniously to the city gate while the colonel in spic-and-span uniform and the burly magistrate in brocade gown "bow low as the foreign devil departs in old clothes on a scrawny horse wanting his morning coffee but surfeited with honor."

In Shansi Stilwell could see, unfiltered through the pleasant life of Peking, the raw wants of China: all that it lacked, all that it needed and how one local strong man was attacking the problem. Yen Hsi-shan had carved his way to power by an exemplary and successful opportunism. Appointed Military Governor of Shansi by Yuan Shih-kai in 1912, he chose the right moment to make arrangements with the Anfu clique, and as a result in 1917 took on the added post of Civil Governor. As a rule the civil and military governors of a province acted as a check upon each other but, as Stilwell later wrote in a profile of Yen Hsi-shan for the *Infantry Journal,* "When one man occupied both offices, he had control of all the machinery of government and could do exactly as he pleased." For the next ten years Yen Hsi-shan kept himself and his province out of the struggle for national power and devoted his efforts to producing a healthy revenue from his own domain.

He constructed roads and bridges, laid miles of irrigation ditches, encouraged reforestation and cotton and silk culture, borrowed methods tested in California for arid land reclamation, imported merino sheep and grains and grasses from various countries, promoted literacy and public health, established primary schools and trade schools, campaigned against queues, foot-binding and opium, and published a manual of citizenship which all of Shansi's ten million population were supposed to read or learn. Material welfare was a concept of the new China. Traditional Chinese reform concerned itself with conduct and morals. Not neglecting this aspect, Yen organized a "Heart-Cleansing Institute" with himself as president. His program for the people's welfare did not go so far as to include reduction of land rents and taxes.

Amid the general anxiety to discover a possible leader for China, Yen attracted much attention. "Has China Found a Moses?" queried an American journal. "Will he lead his people out of the wilderness?" Many foreign visitors came to see and were entertained by the "Model Tuchun," a big man of obvious culture with hard eyes in a puffy face. Flanked by his Oxford-educated Chinese secretary, he presided at a dinner table set in foreign style with damask, silver, garnet-colored crystal wine glasses and napkins intricately folded in the shape of roses, birds and pagodas. After dinner, guests were escorted through moonlit gardens by servingmen carrying lanterns of painted gauze suspended from tall poles. Governor Yen told them he hoped to make Shansi a leavening agent for his country but added realistically, "China is a very large loaf."

Out in the dust and heat of the road, traveling with chopsticks, sweater, canned food and a change of socks in his musette bag, Stilwell enjoyed none of these amenities. However, in the spring-fed valley of Yu Tao Ho, a summer resort favored by missionary families, he found a pleasant place to bring his family for the summer where a temple or an old mill could be rented for the season for about $40 in American money.

He returned to Peking in June to bring the family back with him. After reaching central Shansi by train, the trek continued in a stripped-down old Ford with wife, children, amah and baby in a basket installed on wooden planks for seats, bracing themselves while Stilwell at the wheel maneuvered over ruts and holes. Servants and household luggage followed in carts. Farmers came running over fields ripe with grain, trampling the wheat in their excitement to see the "firewagon." At stops along the way, as Mrs. Stilwell wrote, "we were surrounded by gaping awestruck faces; whenever I nursed the baby, which was often to keep her from screaming, the populace surrounded us to see if the foreigner did it the same way." When the truck got stuck, the country people pushed it up steep grades or hauled it out of ditches, laughing at its misadventures. "Whenever they helped, Joe would pass out coppers and they never failed to try to give them back." Smiling faces, dirt and disease were the rule; one cheerful old lady had a goiter under her chin the size of a bag of oranges.

The Stilwells settled in a mill with large, airy, whitewashed rooms, rough beams and morning glories climbing the wall. Outside were trees and song-birds, a spring of clear drinking water, grass spotted with buttercups, and flocks of sheep and goats. At the end of July Stilwell turned over what remained of the road job to one of his assistants and retired to the mill for the rest of the summer. In the time between picnics and tennis with other foreign families, he pursued his habit of writing short stories and sketches of foreign life as he had seen it. He sold an article on the road-building to the magazine *Asia* for $100. But a second one on "Glimpses of Chinese Life" was rejected, which may have discouraged him from further attempts at publication. Nevertheless, he continued to write, and in these sketches of Chinese life the circumstances of his own travel come through vividly: at a railroad station arriving and departing passengers meet in two streams, "screaming and struggling," yelling for coolies, throwing boxes, baskets and bundles out the window while others throw theirs onto the train and force their way aboard. Somehow the chaos settles, the passengers "stow themselves and their baggage away and begin politely to ask one another their names, home provinces and businesses."

At an inn "the courtyard is full of mules, packs and pack-saddles, chickens and pigs. . . . The patrons at various plank tables in a single big room crouch over their bowls of noodles, drawing the food into their mouths with the aid of chopsticks and suction. . . . The cook dishes out noodle stew from a tremendous iron pot a yard wide, serves it in a bowl

which has just been used by a previous customer and which he cleans by
wiping with a dark object like a piece of garage waste. He wipes a pair of
chopsticks on his trousers, puts them in the bowl, hands it to a serving boy
who presents it with a flourish to the customer." The foreigner prefers
to clean his own bowl with boiling water "which he pretends to empty on
the cook's head. With this wonderful joke he is accepted by all present
as a great fellow with a keen sense of humor and thereafter can do as he
likes, even to scraping the chopsticks with a penknife before using them.
. . . Avoiding the *k'ang* with its inevitable bedbugs, he sets up his cot in
the courtyard and watched by an interested crowd, dozes off lulled by the
squeal of pigs, haw-haw of mules, yelling of coolies and occasional tinkle
of camel bells as the night traffic passes by."

He wrote about the Chinese people, not sociologically or analytically but
directly out of his own encounters, with such simplicity and pure ear for
dialogue that they come alive as humanly and visibly as Chekhov's peasants.* There is the mayor of Ch'i K'ou who wants the new road to come
through his town instead of the neighboring town, because if it went there,
Ch'i K'ou's fame as a Yellow River port would be overshadowed. There is
the old grandmother who runs the inn at Kao Chan and draws the foreigner
into a room filled with flies and curious onlookers with confidence that he
will know what to do for a sick child. There are the people of the countryside: the quiet polite farmers of Shansi who graciously reply to his request
for directions and invite him to stop and drink hot water before he travels
on. There are the road children with baskets who scramble out after the
pack trains have passed "and hunt down with unerring eyes anything that
the animals may have dropped. Each road-apple is picked by hand and
gently dusted off before being put in its place in the basket. When the road
is thoroughly looked over, the treasure trove is carried to the old women,
who carefully spread it out to dry."

Social life in Peking was as agreeable as Stilwell's temperament would
allow. The Military Attaché and Assistant Attaché were friends from West
Point until the latter was succeeded by Major John Magruder whose career
in Chinese affairs was often to cross Stilwell's. New language officers and
their wives and others in the American community, including the daughters
of the American Minister, Jacob Gould Schurman, and their friends and
suitors, provided a circle for exchanging dinners and visits. But Win did
not play bridge nor her husband polo and they were regarded by the
regular Legation set as somehow "different." Stilwell enjoyed dancing with
his wife at either of the two hotels and he even contrived to get drunk one

---

* Three of his dialogues are reprinted in the Appendix.

night on crème de menthe at the Hotel Wagons-Lits. An evening of Mah-Jongg proved "not so deadly as anticipated" and a dinner for twenty-five at the Schurmans' was actually "a very pleasant affair." As always, he was quickly bored by dull or pretentious people. "He's a pompous ass and she's a complacent numbskull," he wrote of one couple.

He preferred the company of his family. His occupation and pleasure as a father had increased as his children grew older. He taught the two eldest, Joe and Nance, at home, worried about their illnesses, took them for walks on the city walls and on trips to the Ming tombs, composed an illustrated bestiary in rhyme and directed the children in homemade plays.

In November Stilwell took a group of journalists and members of the Relief Committee in the first party of motor cars over the road. Eleven years later his friend John Goette, correspondent of the International News Service who had been in the group, sent him a clipping from the *North China Daily News* on the habitual Chinese failure to keep roads in repair. It reported that Stilwell's road from Fenchow to the Yellow River, having never received the slightest attention, "has practically ceased to exist."

In 1922 the road's Chief Engineer was an object of interest to the warlord of the neighboring province, Feng Yu-hsiang, the Christian General of Shensi. This province, the earliest center of Chinese civilization, was a region of hills and caves and terraced agriculture where in the next decade the Long March was to bring the Communists to settle around Yenan. With cotton, wool, wheat and mountains rich in minerals, Shensi should have been prosperous but was not, owing to opium-smoking and banditry, but fundamentally to lack of good communications. There were no railroads in the province and only one "so-called road" about 90 miles long from T'ung Kuan at the bend of the Yellow River to Sian, the provincial capital. This was hardly more than a track shoveled out without any surveying. Negotiations ensued between Feng and the Famine Relief Committee which undertook to build a proper road from T'ung Kuan to Sian with Stilwell again as Chief Engineer.

He traveled as far as he could by train which came to an end in Honan about 100 miles from the border of Shensi. From here he continued in a convoy of 50 mule carts plus assorted camels, pack animals, wheelbarrows, pedestrians and an escort of twenty soldiers to conduct them through bandit country. "Off we go in a cloud of dust, a chorus of yells and much cracking of whips. . . . We look like the flight of the Kalmucks or a squad of 49ers on the way to California." Moving at a slow pace over a horrible road, the convoy constantly tangled with wheelbarrow traffic coming in the opposite direction. The barrows carried loads of cotton with babies tied on the side, mothers sitting opposite, fathers pushing, and one or two little boys out in front pulling. Congestion was thickened by beggars lying along the road and farmers' boys with four-pronged forks and baskets picking up the droppings of draft animals and humans. Progress was a "constant succession of struggles between straining, sweating chinks and their unwieldy machines and unwilling beasts." When amid shrieks and vituperation two wheelbarrows conflicted, the remaining traffic "just stops and waits for them to get through. How anyone gets anywhere is a wonder until you see them do it. It is simply because everyone is willing to wait a little or give way a little to help the other fellow along."

It took four days of such travel to reach the border of Shensi and four more days to reach the capital. To escape the awful jolting of the cart Stilwell walked eight, ten or twelve miles a day, trudging through ruts and mudholes and swallowing dust. Nights were spent in a "dirty fleabitten town" or a "filthy inn" or in one case in an opium den where hard-worked coolies "kept trooping in for ten, fifteen, or twenty coppers' worth, put their money and their little pots down and got their poison." Ten coppers, Stilwell noted, was 30 percent of their daily wages, representing a "terrible drain on their resources to say nothing of their health." The poor of China took to the drug because it dulled the pain of hunger. From surcease it grew to addiction and where it obtained a wide hold, drained energy and spread apathy. "Why doesn't Feng stop it?" Stilwell wrote angrily. "Seize the opium and burn it and lead the sellers out and shoot them." He supplied his own answer: Feng would have a revolution on his hands if he tried, and besides he obtained a large revenue from the opium tax, of which he sent a percentage to Wu Pei-fu and used the rest to pay his men.

Crossing into Shensi, Stilwell at once saw signs of the Christian General's rule. Soldiers sang hymns as they marched through the streets. "Hark the Herald Angels Sing" was sung around the theme of "save your ammunition" and the Doxology as an appeal to save the country from decadence. Admonitions painted in blue characters on whitewashed walls exhorted citizens: "Do not smoke cigarets, do not drink wine," "Be honest in business," "Honor thy father and mother," "Plow land, weave cloth, read books." Stores displayed signboards quoting all kinds of proverbs of good advice. "But is it such a simple thing," Stilwell wondered, "to change the habits and mode of life of this to say the least rather stubborn people?"

Feng's efforts were not confined to exhortation. His soldiers were required to learn two new characters before each meal in the literacy campaign that was to fit them to become citizens of a modern state. Officers and even their wives and daughters joined the classes to learn to read and write. Courses for civil administrators, magistrates, police and public health officers were part of Feng's program as well as public works in irrigation and land improvement of the kind Yen Hsi-shan was conducting in Shansi. Stilwell saw little sign of these in his dusty progress toward

Sian. But the *pings* (soldiers), he noted, were "all snappy and their guns are clean."

Exasperations were many: rotten roads and lame mules, lazy carters "still snoozing and unwilling to go," innyards that were open repositories of defecation, pestilential beggars, dust storms for two or three days at a time, then days of rain turning to snow. There were also violets along the road and Ming monuments and a fine view from the top of a pass of the Yellow River with the sun shining on low flats green with young crops on the far side. Ahead to the west were mountains glinting with snow in the clear air.

Entering bandit country the convoy passed a man's head hanging on a tree and that night the *tu fei* (bandits), disguised in uniforms, killed a lieutenant and a soldier. Farther along, outside a town, they passed a dead bandit recently shot and left for all to see. Death was as common as the windblown dust of China, its reminder everywhere in the grave mounds that would wear away over the centuries to be plowed back into the fields, its visible presence in the corpse of a girl baby, victim of infanticide at birth, laid out unburied between the grave mounds for dogs to eat.

At a hot springs, one day's journey from the capital, Stilwell learned that the *Tuchun* had sent orders for him to use his special tub. It was his first bath since leaving Peking.

On April 3 he entered Sian, ancient capital of the Han and T'ang dynasties. Its walls were the highest and thickest in China but they now enclosed large waste spaces, including the old Manchu quarters where there were only fields of a vegetable oil plant resembling mustard. The main business streets were paved with huge old stone blocks but the few new brick schools and government offices were an architect's nightmare, "with facades that look like a mixture of Spanish mission, country garage and Hose Company No. 2." Coal, sold by the pound at a street-corner market, was the city's fuel supply brought in by wheelbarrow from T'ung Kuan 90 miles away. Hides were drying on outdoor frames and the main streets were crowded and busy, filled with *pings* carrying umbrellas. Stilwell found it hard to glimpse an idea of the former greatness of the city, but even in decline the people of Sian devised pleasures. They tied bamboo whistles of varying pitch to the tail feathers of pigeons so that when circling in hundreds overhead the birds made the sound of a flying pipe organ.

Stilwell was taken to meet the *Tuchun* at his headquarters in the old Imperial City which he had reconstructed into neat clean barracks and drill grounds using soldier labor and bricks from the ruins. Feng Yu-hsiang, a big man of forty-one who abjured the usual warlord's grandeur, lived in a "neat little brick shack and is a slow spoken bird . . . a solid sort of guy with no airs who makes friends." Discussion of the road project was begun but Feng did not seem very interested. The reason, as Stilwell discovered in further conversations, was that "he cares not if I build the road or not; he wants dope on military affairs." Feng invited Stilwell to return next day to inspect his arsenals and meanwhile showed him through barracks and workshops.

In the barracks the soldiers' rooms were each adorned with a map of China showing in vivid red the territories lost in the last 50 years— Indo-China, Korea, Formosa, Port Arthur. Maps of Shensi, of China and of the world were painted on the ends of buildings. The men, much neater and cleaner than the average Chinese soldier, were practicing giant swings on the horizontal bar and their proficiency was something of a shock. "Show me any other organization in the world where man after man can get up on the bar and do a giant swing." It was another shock to see men at rest studying the bible. In classrooms they were being taught to read and write and in the workshops they learned a craft, as weavers, carpenters, cabinetmakers, shoemakers, tailors and blacksmiths. In the shoemakers' shop an officer was in charge, working with the men. "This is also a shock. To see a captain pasting uppers doesn't fit in with ordinary notions of military procedure." Stilwell found that promising privates or noncoms were appointed lieutenants without examination. After rising to captain they attended a six-month course of instruction, the only theoretical training they received.

General Feng's Chief of Staff came next day to ask "a lot of questions about planes, tanks, rifle grenades, etc.," followed by the *Tuchun* himself, who talked to Stilwell for an hour about weapons. "They haven't the slightest idea of the uses of the new inventions and talk of guarding a bridge with a tank." Stilwell "doped out a Stokes mortar" for Feng and "tried my best to explain what airplanes, tanks and rifle grenades were designed for and could do, and how useless it was for him to waste money on them. With his infantry and machine guns, there is nothing in the province that he could not clean up in short order." This was not what Feng wanted to hear but Stilwell persevered "in the hope of keeping this really admirable man from wasting his resources on what, to him, would be the frills of war."

He took dinner with Feng that evening, which to his surprise turned out to be excellent. Because of his much-publicized Christianity and characteristics of the peasant hero, Feng was a favorite of the foreign press which liked to portray him wearing a simple cotton gown and eating the same fare as his men. But Stilwell found the dinner was "none of this 'all same soldier' stuff but soup with meatballs, fresh vegetables, chicken, frizzled mutton, lotus seeds, scrambled eggs and *mantou* [steamed wheat bread]."

After four days in Sian, conferring with contractors and Chinese and foreign engineers and assistants, Stilwell collected forty noncoms assigned to him from Feng's army as construction bosses and moved out to the construction site 20 miles north of the city. He had the foremen build a model of the road which was to lead eastward from the Wei, a branch of the Yellow River, and was actually satisfied with the result. The men seemed unusually intelligent and he had hopes that after a little training they would do well. The ford at the river was a chaos of six to eight flatboats jammed with mules, carts and people, pushed by boatmen from the stern, with mules falling overboard, boatmen yelling and laughing and falling into holes as they walked across. Stilwell was carried ashore on a coolie's shoulders.

Work began on the road with 800 laborers armed with "T'ang dynasty picks," wooden shovels, too few baskets and no tamps. Under the circumstances it proved hard to get the road work under way; the workmen proved poor and the foreman disappointing. After a week they were "no good yet. Won't make the men work. . . . Still cutting wrong after being told twenty times. . . . Work all bitched up." But gradually "chaos begins to give way to order" and Stilwell could feel that the work was really progressing. Just at this juncture the renewed war of the northern warlords intervened.

Rumor spread that Chang Tso-lin was "starting things" and Feng's division was sent for to help out Wu Pei-fu. Files of Feng's troops were marching east, Stilwell's carts were commandeered, his foremen were disappearing and it was plain the project would have to be abandoned. Feng's Chief of Staff came to invite him to accompany the army. On April 21 he started east again, brushing aside frantic but incomprehensible pleas for delay by his courier. After two miles an exhausted messenger on a bicycle caught up to Stilwell, bearing on his back a rug as a gift from the *Tuchun*. The bicyclist presented it and collapsed on the ground. Pushing on, Stilwell passed a group of Feng's staff, "all down in the mouth and bemoaning China's fate." He shared their melancholy. If Feng had been left undisturbed for a period of years, he could have established control, wiped out the bandits and attacked the opium traffic with some prospect of success, Stilwell thought. But now "the only man who has shown any likeliness of standing for law and order and decent government" was pulled back into the endless wars of faction and Shensi was left to revert to the old ways.

At T'ung Kuan, an old frontier fortress at the elbow of the Yellow River with big gates and stone-paved ramps leading up to them, Stilwell had a farewell dinner with Feng in an old temple. The *Tuchun* summoned a regiment for review by his guest, whom he introduced to the soldiers as Shih Ying-chang (Major Stilwell) of the *Ou Chou* (European) clan. To a provincial Chinese a foreigner was a foreigner; particular nationality was rarely differentiated.

The return trek following the valley of the Fen, a northeast tributary of the Yellow River, to Taiyuan, capital of Shansi, took 18 days. Past barren land and good land of crops, trees and grapevines the group plodded on through the same dust and rains, smells and dirt, as on the way out but with hot weather now added to the discomforts. At one inn Stilwell was bitten by a scorpion and "lay awake in a sweat all night feeling them all over me." Along the way he was struck by the number of old arched stone bridges, usually with half the arch gone: "Repair? God no, why repair?" His conclusion, that present-day Chinese were a "sad throw-off from the people who built these bridges," was not the whole explanation. Public services were missing because lower officials received no salaries but lived off what they could tax or squeeze from the people with the result that the repair of roads and bridges or the construction of sanitation systems was left undone.

Yet Chinese stamina and good humor were admirable. When one particular carter persistently drove into every gully, the others "cheerfully helped him out of each one as he got in." In order to haul out the carts, "they hitched three mules tandem with a man between the traces" and pulled away, "screaming, yao-ho-ing, laughing and slipping in the mud." For a makeshift bridge they "take the wheels off a cart, turn it upside down and lay it across the gap. Bridge is now built." Though in an exasperated moment he listed "carts, mules, carters, in that order of intelligence," he grew fond of his "pair of jokers, Old Kuo and Old Kuang, both under forty and proud of their profession." He bought them each a pair of shoes and another time treated six carters to breakfast.

After days of alternate jolting and trudging, of dirt and heat and overnight discomforts, and on one occasion following a cloudburst, of walking the last two hours through a foot of water in the dark and finding the gate of the town closed on arrival, Stilwell at last reached Taiyuan where he boarded the train for Peking. He had not built a road this time but he had lived and worked with the Chinese soldier and common man and made a friend of an outstanding leader. On the return trip to Peking Stilwell saw Chang Tso-lin's troop trains heading south from Manchuria toward the confrontation with the forces of Feng and Wu Pei-fu that ended in his defeat. Two years later Feng was to turn against Wu and emerge as the leader of the north, going on to become a crucial figure in the decisive years of the late twenties when Stilwell was again in China. They were to meet again at that time and whenever Stilwell was in China. Long afterwards, a few days after her husband's death, Mrs. Stilwell was upstairs at her home in Carmel when a visitor was announced with some confusion as "the

Christian." Mystified, she went down to find in the hall the huge figure and cannonball head of Feng Yu-hsiang, who said, "I have come to mourn with you for Shih Ti-wei, my friend."*

The Far East, during the winter of 1921-22 between Stilwell's two road-building trips, was the focus of greater international attention than at any time since the Siege of the Legations by the Boxers. The Washington Conference of that winter, halfway in time between the Boxer Rebellion and Pearl Harbor, established the conditions of much that was to follow. Initiated by the United States in consultation with Britain, the Conference was primarily an Anglo-American effort to stabilize a safe balance of naval power in the Pacific without the expenditure of a naval race. Since the American public was distinctly not prepared to pay for a massive naval building program to outmatch the Japanese, the only way to secure and fix a favorable naval ratio and safeguard the Philippines was by agreed limitation. At the same time the Conference was intended to reach a general settlement of interests in the area on the basis of an international treaty. Superseding the Anglo-Japanese Alliance which was up for renewal, this would have the added value of affording Britain a graceful exit from an unwanted attachment—a goal as anxiously sought by the United States and Canada as by Britain.

The American interest was also to encourage a settlement of Sino-Japanese conflicts, hopefully one strengthening China's position. A further motive in the minds of the chief promoters—Secretary of State Charles Evans Hughes and former Secretary Elihu Root—was, by taking the lead in international effort, to exhibit America's responsibility in world affairs and expiate for rejection of the League.

Shantung lay on the American conscience. The Republicans had made heavy use of it in the campaign to elect President Harding—to the point that a Democratic official claimed it was "the best vote-getter the Republicans had." This may have left the Republicans under a sense of obligation to do something about the injustice they had so loudly condemned, but conscience does not often convene international conferences. Secretary Hughes wanted China on the agenda because Japanese expansion threatened to dominate the area, ultimately cutting out American and other foreign interests, and he hoped to limit this expansion by international support of China's "independence" and reaffirmation of the Open Door.

Concern with China's "independence" and "integrity" was chiefly an American policy in which Britain joined, without warm conviction, for the

* Feng was on his first trip to the United States. He went on to visit the U.S.S.R. and was killed en route in a fire on a Soviet ship in the Black Sea.

sake of other gains she expected from the Conference. British interests in China, far larger than the American, were governed by the Treaty Port view of China as permanently incapable of self-rule. Many Americans shared this view but American public opinion on the whole responded to the belief of missionaries and educators in the regenerative power of Western teaching and Western methods. These, exercised through their pupils, the Western-educated Chinese like Dr. Sun and his disciples, would establish a stable government if given a chance, and validate the missionary endeavor.

The real proof of her independence that China wanted—and loudly demanded at the Conference—was cancellation of the unequal treaties. Although American public opinion tended to support the aim, Secretary Hughes and his fellow policy-makers, who would be answerable in the end, were not prepared to go that far. All the more reason, therefore, that China should at least regain Shantung. Hughes insisted on it. "I am an old man," he was quoted as saying (he was sixty), "and I want to see the Shantung Question settled before I die."

Japan had not yet fulfilled her promise to restore the leased area to Chinese sovereignty despite chronic American prodding but she was not fixed in a course of single-minded aggrandizement nor, in 1921, in single-minded hostility to the West. There were two Japans, one militant, the other liberal. Like the thin man inside the fat man crying to get out, Japan's thin little liberal alter ego emerged in the 1920s for a brief beleaguered heyday before it was regorged. The victory of the democracies in the war had impressed Japan and endowed her parliamentary parties and moderate leaders with new prestige. They had no great appetite for a naval race or for aggressive militarism and they advocated a settlement of goodwill with China. They were anxious about the alliance with Britain and they wanted to obtain American recognition of Japan's mandate of the Pacific islands. Japan came to the Washington Conference for these reasons.

The Conference lasted not quite three months, from November 1921 to February 1922, half as long as the Peace Conference at Paris. Nine powers attended including France, Italy, Belgium, Holland and Portugal for various reasons of national pride, naval power or interests in the Far East. Russia, whose interests were both contiguous and persistent but whose Government was not recognized, was not invited despite her angry protest. China's delegates came bent as ever on treaty revision, tariff autonomy and Shantung. It took Secretary Hughes' utmost persuasion to induce them to enter negotiations on the rather shady rights, loans and leases involved in Shantung directly with the Japanese rather than publicly at the Conference table. They finally agreed on condition that Hughes and Arthur Balfour, the chief British delegate, would be present as observers. At the first scheduled meeting they failed to appear and on investigation were found besieged in the bathroom of the Chinese Legation by a group of angry Chinese students opposed to direct negotiations with Japan. Thereafter it took 36 meetings before a settlement was reached by which Japan again agreed, for the first time by treaty instead of verbal promise, to restore the leased territory while retaining certain economic reservations.

Results of the Conference as a whole were embodied in a Four-Power Treaty establishing a naval ratio of 5-5-3 in the Pacific for the United States, Great Britain and Japan; a Five-Power Treaty on nonfortification of possessions in the Pacific; a Nine-Power Treaty on China, plus various separate agreements on Shantung, on withdrawal of Japanese troops from Siberia, on the troublesome island of Yap and a final removal of that old burr under the American conscience, the Lansing-Ishii Agreement. The naval limitation, beginning with Hughes' spectacular opening proposal to scrap planned battleship construction by the three chief naval powers amounting to 66 capital ships and other vessels, was the most dramatic. But the nonfortification agreement by which Japan undertook not to fortify the mandated islands, the United States not to fortify the Philippines, Guam and the Aleutians, and Britain not to strengthen Hong Kong, was more fateful.

The Nine-Power Treaty was the crown. Its four principles in magnificent language laid down all that was necessary for the achievement of that elusive goal of universal—or almost universal—desire: a strong, independent, united China. It pledged the contracting parties: (1) "To respect the sovereignty, independence and territorial and administrative integrity of China. (2) To provide the fullest and most unembarrassed opportunity to China to develop and maintain for herself an effective and stable government." (3) To maintain the principle of "equal opportunity for the commerce and industry of all nations. . . ." (4) To refrain from taking advantage of conditions in China "to seek special rights or privileges" which would abridge the rights of citizens of friendly states.

What this amounted to was a pledge by the signatories to respect the integrity of China without a pledge to defend it if violated. By giving the force of treaty to the American doctrine of the Open Door, it reaffirmed in the American mind a feeling of moral guardianship for China. It expunged the guilt for Shantung without costing any commitment to action. It was at once so high-principled, so innocuous and apparently so pro-Chinese that the Senate, whose way with treaties was not usually so amiable, voted to ratify it 66 to 0. In the absence of a reliable government of China, the signatories did not offer to give up the unequal treaties but they made gestures toward modification. They promised to convene a commission to "examine" extrality and another to "review" the customs problem and grant an increase in customs revenue if not the tariff autonomy that China asked for. Both these bodies eventually met in 1925 and 1926 and reached decisions but by that time new eruptions of domestic chaos and Chinese-foreign conflict prevented their taking effect. A promise by Britain at the Conference to restore Wei-hai-wei was ultimately fulfilled in 1930.

The Washington Treaties taken together seemed a grand self-denying ordinance, a miracle of respect for international order. Everyone who wanted to believe in peace and collective effort could believe that the treaties had indeed achieved disarmament, international equity and the safeguarding of China. Their structure was a general forswearing of aggressive intentions which, lacking sanctions or guarantees, would last only as long as community of interest lasted. While Japan's reigning moderates at the time had as much reason to be satisfied with the results as the other signatories, her nationalists of the Army and Navy regarded the Washington Treaties with malevolence. They resented Japan's inferior position in the restrictions, as they regarded them, on their freedom of action in China. Their hostility was given added cause within a year. In November 1922 the United States Supreme Court confirmed an earlier Act of Congress limiting acquired citizenship to "free white persons," thus in effect ruling that Japanese could not become American citizens by naturalization. In 1924 after clamorous agitation by the western states, Congress enacted the Japanese Exclusion Bill. As a gesture hardly conducive to goodwill, it did not augur well for the Washington Treaties.

As an agent of the Military Attaché, Stilwell was sent to report on one provision of the Washington Treaties: Japan's evacuation of Siberia scheduled for September 1922. In that month he went north on a journey that took him to Manchuria, Siberia, Korea and Japan.

The focus of present ambitions and future conflict, Manchuria was China's wide frontier region north of the Great Wall. Larger than France and Germany combined, it was rich in fertile grasslands, coal and iron, grain and water power. It was the heartland of rival colonialisms, Russian and Japanese. Russian territory curved around it like a horseshoe, reaching on the east to the Maritime Province on the Sea of Japan. The Russian-controlled Chinese Eastern Railway crossed Manchuria from west to east and the Japanese-controlled South Manchurian Railway (SMR) from south to north. Japan's interests in Manchuria were in the hands of the Kwantung Army, a virtually independent force like the Anglo-Indian Army. Mukden, the capital of Manchuria, headquarters of the Kwantung Army and the railway, was Stilwell's first destination.

He disliked it at once. "No Chinese mail goes out from this buggerly place, only Jap mail. I went till I found a Chino letterbox, by god." As the center of the coal and steel empire of the SMR, the city was "buzzing . . .

with big business chances. Everybody has a scheme to get rich but there is always some drawback." He went on to Harbin, center of 100,000 White Russians, and from there east by train to Vladivostok. Japanese evacuation, as he noticed in towns along the way, seemed to be in no hurry. In fact the troops appeared to be "evacuating from east to west. No one knows what they are doing. . . . Two planes buzzing around. No ships in to take them off." The area was still in the aftermath of war and revolution. Exploring, talking and walking around, Stilwell found "Japs digging away on hill to west of town just over Amur bay. The arrogant little bastards were . . . all over town this a.m. in American cars, posting M.P.'s and sticking out their guts. . . . They need a kick in the slats in the worst way. . . . They have systematically bothered and annoyed Americans about passports . . . and seem to go out of their way to make people despise and hate them."

The impression was reinforced after a week's visit to Japan and a week in Japanese-governed Korea on the way back. He found an aggressive chauvinism in Japan that was lacking in China. As the only people of the East to be completely sovereign in their own land and effective in modern terms as well, the Japanese were feeling the pricking in their blood of the master-race sensation. Besides requiring a subject people to validate it, this expressed itself in seizing every available bureaucratic contact to annoy and domineer foreigners who had for so long walked the East as superiors. "Made to wait for meal on boat," Stilwell recorded, "Japs already eating." "Serving Japs first and out of turn, e.g., at ticket window, etc. Close scrutiny of papers. Insistence on lengthy questioning. Open sneers met everywhere." He recognized these as "petty annoyances" and they did not interfere with his pleasure in visiting remembered places in Japan. In the fragrance and quiet of the pine woods on the hills about Miyajima with its view over the straits, he felt, "I could lie on the back of my neck here for months." He liked the country but not the people who reminded him of the Germans. They were, he decided at the end of his visit, "pale imitations of the Germans without the latter's brains and ability. Patriotic, well-organized, brave, artistic, swellheaded and stupid."

In 1923 before his tour as language officer was due to end, Stilwell reported on two more journeys to widely separated regions of China. In April, traveling by riverboat and on foot without interpreter or companion, he went on a month's tour of three provinces on the south bank of the Yangtze: Chekiang on the coast and Kiangsi and Hunan inland. Here there was no scope for road-building for the population owned no wheeled vehicles except wheelbarrows. Goods were water-borne or carried on shoulder poles along trails that followed the dikes between liquid paddy fields or climbed straight up mountainsides. Filtered through mist, the mountains suddenly and surprisingly were seen to be Chinese paintings come true. The countryside was more appealing than the north, with chestnuts in blossom, sails of junks moving along the canals, decorative clumps of bamboo, pagodas with tinkling windbells and the springtime fragrance of beanflowers. Water buffalo, guided in circles by boys stretched lazily on their backs, turned waterwheels to fill an endless chain of buckets for irrigating the fields.

Stilwell reported a heavy traffic in opium protected by the local *tuchun's* troops, in contrast to Japan where the drug had never taken hold. In Hunan the official opium inspector, charged with suppressing the trade, was paid 40 coppers a day by each of the 100 opium shops for protection. Stilwell's boatman was an addict and Stilwell had to buy him some smokes "to keep him from crying. 50 coppers a day, two or three smokes or he is miserable."

He met and mingled with every kind of Chinese from tycoons in the boat cabin adjoining his, "with all the fixings including slaves . . . and four-storied dinner pails," to the "cheerful boat crew, wet or dry, hot or cold, hungry or fed, always on the jump and always jollying each other." The boat was filled with "syphilitics and Chinese violin players." Leaving the river, he hiked through the countryside for several days, covering twenty or thirty miles a day. The populace suffered from oppression by local troops, "mostly rape and robbery." Roads were mere wheelbarrow tracks in appalling condition. Only a Chinese could have the patience and energy to push a heavily loaded wheelbarrow over them. The people appeared friendly to foreigners and, Stilwell reported, "universally consider the U.S. the best friend of China. They nowhere evince the slightest interest in the politics of their own country and ask only to be left alone to make a living as best they can."

Coming down to Hangchow, which Marco Polo had declared unsurpassed in magnificence, Stilwell was disappointed. He thought the West Lake, famous for the beauty of its temples and pagodas, was pretty enough but overrated, with "a lot of Chinese-foreign monstrosities of houses . . . like a second rate American seaside summer resort." He finished his trip at the city celebrated by Arnold Toynbee a few years later as

> You Smyrna weeping London's tears
> You London racked by Smyrna's fears,
> Busy, detestable Shanghai,
> Our anchor's up, Thank God. Good-bye.

Stilwell's opinion matched Toynbee's, if for different reasons. "This town would ruin anybody in no time. The babes that twitch around the hotels need attention so badly that it is hard not to give it to them."

Outer Mongolia, where he went a month later in June 1923, was as

---

The U.S. Army transport Grant *was the ship on which the Stilwell family generally traveled to and from China (54).*

remote in kind as in distance from the fleshpots of Shanghai. Urga, the capital, was 650 miles and three days' journey by car from the rail terminus at Kalgan on the Great Wall. Stilwell slept in Mongols' *yurts* on the way, or when these were unbearable, in the open. Sovereignty of the area as between China, Russia and "independent" Mongolia was moot. No one seemed to know who was head of state; the government was a farce. He reported that the Mongols were determined not to let the Chinese regain control and he believed the country would remain permanently detached. In Urga the hand of Russia was everywhere visible. Five hundred Red troops, both infantry and cavalry, equipped with some machine guns dominated the situation. Their ammunition was meager. Owing to lack of railroads and deficiency of other transportation, campaigning in the area would present great difficulty. He watched the lamas, who numbered 15,000 in Urga, at their prayers and thought them "dirty, depraved and degenerate." Syphilis was rampant, the women barren and, he rather sweepingly reported, "the almost entire absence of children make it possible that in fifty years more the Mongols will be extinct."

Four years had now passed since Stilwell received the China assignment in 1919 and his tour as a language officer had come to an end. On the roadbeds of Shansi and Shensi, in the villages and squalid inns of his one-man travels, he had come to know men and places far outside the foreigner's usual circle of Treaty Port, Legation Quarter and missionary compound. He had functioned with Chinese under Chinese conditions.

On July 9, 1923, he sailed with his family for home, four months after his fortieth birthday. "Here it is," he wrote on that day, "middle-aged man now."

THE "CAN DO" REGIMENT AND THE RISE OF CHIANG KAI-SHEK, 1926-29

O^N his return to the United States, Stilwell at forty went back to school. There was not much else to do in the American Army in 1923, four years after the Great War was won. Whereas defeat in war galvanizes military development, nothing contributes to military desuetude like total victory. Withdrawn again behind its oceans, with no visible menace on the horizon, with Japan seemingly taken care of by the Washington Treaties, the United States basked in the Coolidge sun. The stockmarket climbed, flappers and bootleggers flourished and the Army moldered. A reduction of forces in 1922 had slowed promotions to an imperceptible crawl; American forces were not in action anywhere; the only hope of advancement lay in postgraduate training.

While still in China Stilwell had requested assignment to the Infantry course at Fort Benning in Georgia, which admitted 250 Infantry officers divided into the company course and the advanced course. Stilwell applied for and was assigned to the latter whose leading graduates usually went on to the Command and General Staff School at Fort Leavenworth in Kansas. Unless an officer had passed through Leavenworth he was unlikely to be a candidate for high command. Stilwell took the Infantry course at Benning in 1923-24 and stayed on an extra year as Assistant Executive Officer to the Commandant, General Wells, his friend and admirer from the World War.

He reached Leavenworth for the school year of 1925-26. What Leavenworth taught was "solution of the problem" based on statement of mission, analysis of the enemy, choices of action, solution, decision and plan. In lectures, map problems and terrain exercises the course covered mobilization, movement of units, march, relief, supply, reconnaissance and security, delaying action, withdrawal, change of direction, pursuit and all those maneuvers which man has indefatigably devised to make a science out of fighting. The course was exacting and the pressure to excel so great as to cause a series of suicides in the 1920s that later led to the closing of the school.

Officers stayed up to study until 2 A.M., wives grew bored and irritable, but Stilwell, though he called it a "hell of a year," did not join the frenzy. Older than the average as he had been younger than the average at West Point, he was more than twenty years out of the Academy and did not consider it worth bucking for the highest grade. He knew he would pass and that was enough; the rest was "rot." He studied what was necessary and almost insulted his colleagues by going to bed at ten. Among the hard workers in his class, Dwight Eisenhower, West Point Class of 1915, graduated number one. Stilwell emerged with the Commandant's notation on his report, "Common sense and a sense of humor."

Seized by his periodic urge to remove himself from the United States, he had applied for the Ecole de Guerre, the French staff college. The assignment had already been approved when he learned of a chance to return to China. Willie Whipple, a West Point classmate now at the War Department, sent word of an opening as battalion commander in the 15th Infantry, the American regiment stationed by Boxer Protocol in Tientsin. Would he like to have it? Stilwell threw France over and grabbed for it. Eagerness came to the surface for the first time since he had come home and throughout his term at Leavenworth he pelted Whipple with anxious queries. His friend assured him there would be no hitch. "You are considered the most qualified field officer for this duty, being such an excellent Chinese," he wrote in February, but Stilwell continued to fuss. "Don't worry," Whipple soothed in March, "Nobody else is going to get it. . . . Have no fear regarding the birds who have Senators in back of them. . . . You have me in back of you. It is all settled." When orders had not come through by April, Stilwell resorted to telegrams. "Keep your shirt on," replied Whipple, the orders would come, as they did before the term was over. After a summer's leave spent at Carmel, the Stilwells once more, on August 20, 1926, boarded the Army transport for China. "We all felt," wrote Mrs. Stilwell, "we were going home."

Tientsin spoiled that illusion. Shorn of its walls after the Boxer Rebellion, it represented the foreign foothold in north China where foreign troops were stationed. The Concession area had been razed and rebuilt in heavily ugly late-Victorian Western style. Life there had not the charm of Peking and China was not the China the Stilwells had left three years before. Momentous change was boiling in the south, about to bring forth a leader, a climax of strife and a national government at last.

It began with the order to "Fire!" given by a British Inspector of Police against Chinese students and workers demonstrating in the course of a textile strike in Shanghai on May 30, 1925. Twelve Chinese were killed and 17 wounded. The Shanghai Incident, as it came to be called, was only one incident in a train of history but, like those other shots from British rifles called the Boston Massacre, it was fuel for an upheaval that led to sovereignty.

The Kuomintang, by this time infused with new strength by its alliance with the Comintern, was already on the way up. The most significant help Sun Yat-sen had received from the Russsians came in the form of two foreign advisers, Michael Borodin for civilian affairs and a man known as Galen for military affairs, who later as Marshal Vassili Bluecher was to command the Soviet Far Eastern Army. Borodin was a calm and deliberate man with a long view of history whose influence over his clients grew until he came to be called the Emperor of Canton. The Russian advisers, together with Russian arms and other material support, marked the turning point in Kuomintang fortunes. Revolution, Dr. Sun was told, was not to be accomplished by relying on opportunistic alliances without a common goal. Its first requirement is an indoctrinated armed force of its own. Accordingly a Military Academy with thirty Russian instructors under the direction of Galen was founded at Whampoa in 1923. For reciprocal indoctrination and military training Dr. Sun sent a mission to Moscow headed by a thirty-seven-year-old disciple of outstanding qualities, Chiang Kai-shek.

In 1924 Dr. Sun had proclaimed his program of the Three Principles—Nationalism, Democracy and the People's Livelihood—with inspiring effect throughout China. But lured as ever by the prospect of power through arrangement, he accepted an invitation from Chang Tso-lin and Feng Yu-hsiang in Peking to join a conference of "reorganization" for national union. While in Peking he died of cancer on March 12, 1925, leaving behind his Principles, a movement and a successor already steeped in the realities of Chinese power politics.

Chiang Kai-shek was not one of the Western-educated group nor did he become Soviet-oriented, but rather the contrary, during his sojourn in Moscow. Born in 1887 of petty bourgeois origins in Chekiang, whose rather plebeian accent he never overcame, he had received a military education at the Paoting Academy and the Tokyo Military Academy. When in Japan he joined Sun's party and later participated in the Revolution.

In the decade afterwards he appeared and disappeared, sometimes sharing in Sun's attempted coups, sometimes moving in the Shanghai *mafia* world of the Green Society, the archetype *tong* which controlled various rackets as well as the Chinese version of ward politics. He made connections with a leading Chekiang businessman, Chen Chi-mei, who became Dr. Sun's principal financial patron, and he served for a while on the staff of the Fukien warlord who was alternately Sun's ally and enemy.

Appointed head of the Whampoa Academy upon his return from Moscow in 1924, Chiang enjoyed the prestige of the Teacher to whom the highest loyalty of a Chinese is given. By virtue of control of the Revolutionary Army which went with the Whampoa post, he emerged the dominant figure in the Kuomintang. Advised by Galen, he led the first class of Whampoa to the first test of the new Army, winning a victory over provincial forces in the south. In these years the alliances of the Whampoa clique were formed which gave Chiang Kai-shek his band of adherents. He attracted loyalty and respect not through political inspiration as Sun Yat-sen did, but by the magnetism of an impressive personality. He was slim, laconic and expressionless except for alert dark eyes which seemed to pierce through as if from an inner head behind a mask. His great talent was not military but political, exercised through a mastery of balance among factions and plots so that he came to be called the "Billiken" after the weighted doll that cannot be knocked over.

As soon as Sun's death removed restraint, a schism between right and left wings within the Kuomintang came to the surface, with Chiang as leader of the right. He and his associates wanted national sovereignty while the Communist-Left coalition concentrated on social revolution. Cabals and intrigues, arrests and assassinations marked the internal struggle for control of the Party.

Revolutionary effort among China's proletariat, laboring twelve hours a day seven days a week in textile mills and dockyards, provided the tinder for the Shanghai Incident in 1925. Hatred of the foreigner, drummed on by agitators, spread north and south, surpassing anything since the Boxer outburst. More shots were fired and men killed at a riot in Hankow on June 11. At Canton a great parade of workers, students and soldiers led by Whampoa cadets along the Bund drew fire again—with some provocation—from British and French marines lined up opposite. This time 50 were killed and 100 wounded.

A paralyzing boycott of the British in Hong Kong followed that was to last 15 months, cost the British millions of pounds and, with servants deserting and goods and services withheld, emphasize to every foreigner in China his final vulnerability. Missionaries in the interior as in Boxer days suffered harassment and attacks forcing some to close down or flee. Living as they did in Western-style houses in their own walled compounds, the missionaries appeared to the Chinese as much the exponents of the unequal treaties as the consuls or the agents of Standard Oil and Jardine Matheson. Missionary presence was more of an insult, despite the medicine and schooling they offered, because its basis was the assumption that Chinese ways of worship were inferior and should be discarded for those of the West.

The Kuomintang found its opportunity in the antiforeign furor and in July 1925 proclaimed itself the Nationalist Government of China. Rivalry for the succession to Sun Yat-sen was not yet resolved and leadership was shared in fragile partnership between Chiang Kai-shek as military chief and the good-looking, persuasive, French-educated Wang Ching-wei as political chairman. Wang was the man who as a young revolutionist had suffered imprisonment in chains for his attempt to assassinate the Prince Regent in 1910. Chiang soon ousted his partner and in March 1926 attempted a purge of the Communists which ended in a draw. The movement was still revolutionary. Communist members were active in the Hong Kong boycott and in organizing peasants and labor unions. Political advisers of the commissar type headed by Chou En-lai were attached to the faculty of Whampoa and their slogans appeared on the walls: "Down with Imperialism! Laborers of China Arise! The World Revolution Will Save You! Down with Foreign Cultural Aggression! Destroy the Unequal Treaties!" The walls of the Whampoa auditorium were adorned by three large paintings of foreign oppression: the burning of the opium in 1842, the shooting and bayoneting of Boxers by Allied soldiers as they entered Peking in 1900 with the gates of the city burning in the background, and the Shanghai Incident of 1925 with foreign machine guns (replacing the original rifles) mowing down students, women and children. Though propaganda, they epitomized the profound underlying antiwhite temper of China so seldom appreciated or acknowledged by the West.

By the spring of 1926 the adherence of the two progressive leaders of Kwangtung and Kwangsi, Li Tsung-jen and Pai Ch'ung-hsi, gave the Kuomintang the base and the strength it needed for the march north to national power. For the next twenty years Li and Pai were to be linked to Chiang in the peculiarly Chinese seesaw of enmity and alliance. The time for the Northern Expedition, which Sun Yat-sen had so often tried and failed to launch, had come. It began in July 1926 with the three great cities of the Yangtze valley, Hankow, Nanking and Shanghai, as the objective of the first stage. The Kuomintang Nationalist forces numbered under 100,000 with Chiang Kai-shek none too solidly in control as Commander-in-Chief. Their opponents, composed of various forces of the *tuchuns*, numbered over a million. These were joined by the crisis in an

In 1925 Chiang Kai-shek became military chief and Wang Ching-wei political chairman (57) of the new government. With Chiang on the Northern Expedition were Russian advisers Borodin (far left) and Galen (in uniform with Chiang) (55). Feng and Chiang at memorial service for Dr. Sun (56).

55

56

57

Stilwell's regiment, the 15th Infantry, marching through Tientsin (58) and being entertained in the American compound by the city's civilians, 1927 (59). The missionary establishment was at a peak during this period, with 8,000 Protestants and half as many Catholics, such as this priest teaching catechism to eager young Chinese students (60).

incompatible union of old antagonists, all of whom had fought each other at one time or another. The union embraced Chang Tso-lin, Wu Pei-fu, Chang Tsung-chang—the notorious warlord of Shantung, said to have "the physique of an elephant, the brain of a pig and the temperament of a tiger" and to be "dangerous even to look at"—and Sun Chuan-fang, warlord of five provinces in the Shanghai area. Off in the northwest Stilwell's two former clients, the Model Governor Yen Hsi-shan and the Christian General Feng Yu-hsiang, watched and waited; Yen as a highly uncertain ally of the other *tuchuns* and Feng as an intended ally of the Nationalists.

The Kuomintang soldiers, following the revolutionary doctrine of not molesting or preying upon the people, swept forward during the first months in a series of triumphs. Many units of the northern armies came over to them or fell back without fighting. They took Hankow by September, the month in which Stilwell arrived, and scattered Wu Pei-fu's forces in October. Chiang Kai-shek's First Army suffered a setback in Kiangsi but otherwise the advance, like a flooding river, spread outward and northward toward Nanking and Shanghai. Its way was opened by the hopes and hospitality of a people weary of oppression. The Kuomintang's promise of "better days" to come, not its military prowess, accounted for its easy success. As it entered Hangchow, 100 miles from Shanghai, thousands of spectators lined the streets with smiling faces to watch the well-equipped troops parade through the city. Never before had soldiers been welcomed by the populace. Chiang Monlin, a future Chancellor of Peking University, stood among the crowd "with my heart thumping against my ribs in ecstasy . . . as the good name of a modern army in China was once more established." His feelings confirmed Chiang Kai-shek's assertion, "I expect to win the war 30 per cent by fighting and 70 per cent by propaganda."

By January 1, 1927, the Nationalist Government had moved up to Hankow where the left wing gained control. While Chiang concentrated on his drive toward Nanking, former southern capital, and Shanghai, the locus of money power, Hankow seethed in the ardent atmosphere of international revolt. Borodin was the gray eminence and real leader, Mme. Sun Yat-sen, nee Soong Ch'ing-ling, the presiding spirit, and Eugene Chen, reputedly the best brain in the Kuomintang, the new Foreign Minister. Small, clever, venomous, West-Indian born of part-Negro parentage and Western-educated, in gold-rimmed spectacles and white spats, Chen, who could not write Chinese and scarcely speak it, was famous for his grandiloquent English and consuming hatred of the foreigner, which soon made itself felt.

Among Americans and other foreigners in China the rise of the Nationalists precipitated a violent quarrel between the Treaty Port community which took a colonial view of China and the missionaries who for the sake

of their own survival championed China's rights. The missionary establishment was at a peak at this time of 8,000 Protestant missionaries in 1,149
stations with half again as many Catholics. If they were to exorcise the
hostility of the Chinese, the missionaries had to divorce themselves from
the foreign treaty system even though this was what protected their position in China. Supported by the liberal foreign journals, they argued for
China's right of self-determination and presented her cause as one concerned with "the same questions for which we fought when we separated
ourselves from Great Britain." They persuaded themselves that the Kuomintang, with its source in the Christian Sun Yat-sen, was the sincerely
progressive force that would at last end civil strife and bring good government to China. They castigated businessmen and diplomats for taking the
cynical view and pleaded China's rights in letters to their boards and
churches, in magazine and newspaper articles, lecture tours and public
conferences.

Their view of China was naturally echoed in America by the large
constituency from which they drew support. When the Federal Council of
Churches of Christ speaking for 20 million members petitioned the United
States Government to relinquish the unequal treaties, it represented a
China lobby of significant size. A major assembly of groups with interest
in China met at Johns Hopkins in 1925. As spokesman, John Leighton
Stuart, president of Yenching University and a future Ambassador to
China, called on the United States to take the lead by "an act of aggressive
good" toward ending the treaty system. Only through American action, he
argued, could the powers' relations with China be reformed.

Campaigns such as these infuriated the Treaty Ports whose existence
depended on the unequal treaties. They saw in them a sinister exercise of
the missionaries' "powerful influence." The Treaty Port press, aroused to
a frenzy, accused the church groups of "unwarrantable impertinence,"
"meddlesome interference" and "unspeakable drool" about China's rights
and aspirations.

The "man in the club," who personified the business community, upheld
without question the right of the West to arrange conditions favorable to
the well-being and commerce of Westerners wherever they might be.
Chinese effort to curtail Western privileges was regarded as "encroachment
on foreign rights" and mission-fostered Western education blamed for
breaking down the old Confucian morality and raising up ideals inappropriate to China.

"Elected assemblies and democratic institutions," wrote J. O. P. Bland,
the tribune of the Treaty Ports, "are wholly inapplicable because unintelligible, to the race mind of Asia." That was true enough but it led
men like Bland, who believed that democracy was the proper form of

government, to the conclusion that since Chinese found it unsuitable, therefore Chinese were "manifestly incapable of self-government."

That view did not appeal to the American public. Americans saw in the Chinese a people rightly struggling to be free and assumed that because they were struggling for sovereignty they were also struggling for democracy. This was a delusion of the West. Many struggles were going on in China—for power, for nationhood, even in some cases for the welfare of the people—but election and representation, the sacred rights on which Westerners are nursed, were not their goal.

The American Government, like its people, leaned toward China's rights, at least in the abstract. But it was saved from doing anything positive by a policy which required evidence of a stable and responsible government in China before extrality could be relinquished. In 1926 when the two commissions promised by the Washington Conference were meeting in Peking and Shanghai to review tariff autonomy and extrality, China hardly had a government. The Kuomintang was still a pretender and the *tuchuns'* puppet government in Peking, after the last change of partners in the annual square dance of the northern warlords, had virtually disintegrated. A regency cabinet set up by Chang Tso-lin and Wu Pei-fu was not recognized by the treaty powers; consequently they could claim the moment was not ripe for abandoning treaty rights.

The year 1926 was to be the last chance for the "act of aggressive good," the act of voluntary relinquishment. The treaty powers were not obtuse and some gestures were made. Chinese members were added to the Shanghai Municipal Council. The Tariff Conference agreed that tariff autonomy should be restored by a target date of 1929. The Extrality Commission, however, reached the expected conclusion that China must make progress toward rational judicial and governmental procedures before extrality could be yielded. Its report was issued in September 1926 just as the Nationalists swept into Hankow. After that the choice would no longer be voluntary; China began taking back her sovereign powers without asking.

In October when Eugene Chen announced the intention to levy taxes on foreigners, the Legations in horrified concert agreed that unless forcibly opposed this meant the beginning of the end of treaty rights in China. They were right but their governments could not agree on joint action. Neither Britain nor the United States was disposed to resort to arms against a people on the march to sovereignty. If in the past they had not been prepared to yield their privileges, neither were they now prepared to use force to preserve them.

Taking the lead away from the Americans, the British formulated this conclusion in a statement of policy known as the Christmas Memorandum which called on the powers to recognize the "essential justice" of the claim for treaty revision and meet the "legitimate aspirations of the Chinese people." In America the House of Representatives followed with a resolution urging the United States to end the unequal treaties and renegotiate treaties with the Chinese on an "equal and reciprocal basis." Americans equated China's revolution with their own. The Nationalists represented, according to the *Baltimore Sun,* "a spirit as fine as anything that animated the revolutionary troops of George Washington." The press as a whole (inevitably excepting the Chicago *Tribune*) refused to respond to the Red scare. "Chiang's army is as red as Washington's at Valley Forge," stated the New York *World,* which, considering the presence of the Communists, was an understatement. Led by predisposition in China's favor, American public opinion for the first time in history was moved to minimize rather than inflate the Red menace.

The 15th Infantry in Tientsin felt the vibration of these events without greatly concerning itself, being precluded by American policy from playing any role that might involve it in Chinese affairs. Planted in the midst of the Concession area, it was quartered in three-story brick barracks buildings facing a parade ground. Its officers attended to regimental affairs, tea and dinner dances and polo at the race club; its enlisted men enjoyed a venereal disease rate three times that of the American Army as a whole; its weekly journal, *The Sentinel,* published news under the heading "Domestic" which referred to the United States. The paper could have appeared without change at any regimental post in America.

Tientsin, located 60 miles up-river from the sea, was the main port and business center of north China. As in Shanghai, the Concession area was policed by Sikhs provided by the British, and had its advantages for the Chinese. During the warlord era two presidents, a premier and 26 provincial governors at one time or another took refuge there. The Concession's main street was named in its different sections Kaiser Wilhelmstrasse (renamed Woodrow Wilson Street), Victoria Road, Rue de la France and Via Italia. The United States had not taken a territorial concession until after the World War when it took over a section of the former German Concession, about a city block in area, now called the American Compound. Besides the barracks, the Compound housed the post hospital, service club and recreation hall where the heartbeat of America throbbed through a change of three or four American movies a week. Stilwell, who had contrived to remain unacquainted with Tientsin during his previous tour, had specified a Chinese-style house and was disgusted to find nothing but Western-style available. He had to settle for a "horrible 3-story house," ponderously furnished, at 242 Race Course Road in the British Concession.

One battalion of the 15th Infantry had served against the Boxers in 1900 but the regiment had not taken up its station in China until after the Revolution of 1911. Its regular complement was three battalions, of which one remained in the Philippines. The two in China totaled about 50 officers and 800 men, somewhat less than the British and French contingents in Tientsin and approximately the same as the Japanese at that time. The 15th's motto was "Can Do," taken from the pidgin phrase used by Chinese to express, as the regimental manual put it, "ability to carry out the mission." At the end of the training year a Can Do Week was held with track, field and marksmanship events, horse and transportation shows and much awarding of trophies and medals. The duty day, dominated by the sergeant and taken up with rifle and machine-gun drill, was short, generally over by noon, with little field exercise because the area for maneuver was limited. The regiment maintained a subpost at Tongshan, 85 miles to the southeast, to guard the railroad shops of the Peking-Mukden Railway, a summer training camp near Shankaikwan on the seacoast, and a Mounted Patrol of ex-cavalrymen on Manchurian ponies. The entire regiment was served by coolies, each company having its number-one boy dressed in long blue gown and black skullcap. The coolies pitched officers' tents during field exercises, waited on their mess and performed all the menial tasks, even sometimes cleaning the enlisted men's rifles. Soldiers' reenlistment was high, too high for the Army's liking, since it testified to "cohabiting with low caste native women," according to General Castner, the overall commander and a choleric man. "Women, intoxicants and narcotics can be obtained in their vilest forms for a few cents," he indignantly reported. In an effort to keep down the venereal rate free rickshaws were sent to bring home the men from bars at closing time.

The regimental commander was Colonel Isaac Newell, formerly Military Attaché in Peking, tall, gray-haired and dignified, a polished model of the attaché type, admired by the regiment, with a wealthy and stately wife who suited 15th Infantry traditions. Some of these were not of a nature to be endearing to Stilwell. According to a prescribed custom, officers when in uniform and not under arms "will carry a riding crop or swagger stick of standard 15th Infantry design." All officers and first sergeants wore sabers when on duty. Courtesy calls at "frequent intervals" were encouraged, to develop "regimental esprit and unity." Boxer service graves were visited on Memorial Day. During his tour each officer received one month's detached service for travel in north China.

A program to teach officers and men the rudiments of spoken Chinese had been introduced in 1924. Lessons, held one hour a day four times a week, were compulsory for officers but voluntary for the men, and all who passed the examinations were entitled to wear a sleeve patch with the character 中 (Chung) in red on a green ground. As the first character of 中國 (Chung Kuo, meaning "Middle Country," namely China), the Chung by itself adorning the American uniform and signifying "middle" caused occasional puzzlement to Chinese observers. The effect of the language program on the enlisted men was evidently not spectacular for Stilwell after a time found it necessary to persuade one of the younger officers, Lieutenant Timberman, who had achieved some fluency, to teach the noncoms enough Chinese to ask their way.

The overall command, established for reasons of rank and prestige, was held by a brigadier general designated commander of United States Army Forces in China (USAFC). This post was held by General Castner, an overwrought and unstable man in his sixties who wore unkempt clothes in contrast to the 15th's reputation for classy dressing and was not from West Point. The regiment came under his direct control in December 1926 when headquarters of the 15th Infantry and USAFC were merged. Proud of his physique and prowess in walking, Castner had a passion for physical exercise which may have been one reason why Stilwell understood him and was one of the few officers with whom Castner never quarreled. Coming from a command in the wilder reaches of Alaska, he was going to teach these tea-drinking s.o.b.'s some real soldiering and "reduce the fat men of the regiment to a workable condition." To prepare for the worst, in the face of the Red antiforeign crusade which he, and indeed many others, saw overwhelming Peking as in the days of the Boxers, he resolved to train the regiment to relieve the Legations in three days of forced march. As he explained to the War Department, it might be a "vital necessity" in the future and he personally trained for the event by walking daily around the Tientsin Race Course.

Service in the 15th Infantry offered certain noticeable contrasts to service in America. On field exercises the campsite was policed, according to U.S. Army traditions, down to the last horse dropping, potato peel, wisp of straw, tin can and piece of string, and the latrines duly filled in, until on one occasion a delegation of elders from a nearby village waited on the commanding officer to ask politely if the campsite could be left unpoliced as they could make use of the debris. After that, latrines were left unfilled and refuse ungathered. Within minutes after the troops' departure the place was as clean as a kitchen floor.

There was small opportunity to apply the principles of soldiering taught at Leavenworth. Because the regiment's original mission was to protect the Legation staff in Peking, it was considered an organ of the Legation and in 1922 had come under the control of the State Department. It served under the rather paradoxical injunction to avoid conflict, imposed by American policy which was concerned not merely to keep out of trouble but also to avoid inhibiting Chinese national development. As a result the regiment was militarily incapable of carrying out its mission in a crisis. If challenged, it could only bluff, a maneuver which it had performed with éclat during the recent war of the northern *tuchuns*. In 1924 destitute and disorganized units of Wu Pei-fu's army were streaming toward Tientsin, raising the prospect of sack and plunder. Asked by the city for protection, the 15th Infantry scouted the enemy, which proved to be a wounded and bandaged battalion mostly between the ages of fourteen and eighteen, with one donkey cart of pots and blankets as supply train and one officer on a pony. Setting up five outposts where rice, cabbage and tea were dispensed to the forlorn soldiers in exchange for their arms, the 15th managed to divert and partially disarm them. In gratitude the citizenry presented the regiment with a white marble memorial gate which thereafter stood in the Compound in proud testimony of Can Do's deeds.

The limits permitted to the 15th Infantry were distilled in an order given to an officer in the winter of 1925-26 when Chang Tso-lin's troops were reported marching toward the restricted zone outside the city. Captain Matthew B. Ridgway, a future four-star general, was told to take as many men as he needed and go out and "divert" a force of 12,000 of Chang's troops. He was to use "bluff, expostulation or entreaty," but under no circumstances to fire. In view of these limits he took only two men on Manchurian ponies, shadowed the marching Chinese column all day and returned home, mission accomplished.

Given the inherent contradictions of its position, the regiment's withdrawal had been recommended by Castner's predecessor, General William D. Connor, when he went home early in 1926 to become Commandant of the Army War College. One of the select brains of the Engineers and a former number one at West Point, Connor had looked around him while in China and noted a "spirit of nationalism" developing. In recent brushes with warlords' forces, he pointed out, "we escaped conflict by as narrow a margin as I considered possible." He urged withdrawal of all foreign garrisons simultaneously, and if that were not practicable, then of the American alone, "for I believe that all things considered our continued presence there is harmful to the interests of the United States." The War Department agreed with him on "the wisdom of eventually withdrawing from Tientsin" and periodically discussed the matter with the State Department and the Legation. But the point of decision was never reached and the regiment was to remain for twelve more years until new events made its helplessness unmistakable.

When Stilwell came to Tientsin as battalion commander in 1926 he found the person and formed the connection that was to be decisive for his future. This was his acquaintance from World War days who was now serving as Executive Officer of the 15th Infantry, Lieutenant Colonel George C. Marshall. Their tours in China overlapped for only eight months, but it was long enough for what had been mere acquaintance to grow into a bond of mutual respect. Of any other two men the relation might have been called friendship, but these two closed personalities left few references to each other at this stage, and Marshall was not a man easily claimed as a friend. A graduate of Virginia Military Institute, courtly and distant, closing all conversations with his cool "Thank you very much," he hardly ever used a man's first name and rarely got the last name straight. As befitted Pershing's particular protégé, he was, in the opinion of one soldier of the 15th Infantry, "the most military looking man in the entire army."

The Stilwells took tea at the Marshalls' two days after their arrival and went again to a "special court dinner" in the same week. Stilwell felt sufficiently easy to borrow his host's coat. At a dinner party given by the Marshalls on another occasion one invited couple was late and after a brief wait the host announced they would go in to dinner. Just after soup was served the doorbell rang. Stopping the number-one boy as he was going to answer it, Marshall went to the door himself and the guests heard him say, "I'm sorry, but dinner is nearly over," and then the door was firmly closed. As a childless man, Marshall became fond of and friendly with the Stilwell children but with most adults he remained aloof, leaving an impression of someone "higher up."

Seen through Marshall's eyes (Stilwell's diary at this time was limited, for unexplained reasons, to laconic references to handball) the Nationalists' Northern Expedition appeared likely to "leap into control of North China any month," as he wrote to Pershing, and the Legations "have the wind up pretty badly." Even as he wrote mobs spurred on by radical agitators overran and looted the British Concessions at Hankow and at Kiukang farther down the river. Britain evacuated her nationals rather than make an issue of Hankow and decided to concentrate reinforcements at Shanghai. In their first yielding of territory since the Opium Wars, the British negotiated with Eugene Chen the relinquishment of the Hankow and Kiukang Concessions while diehards thundered red-faced in their clubs and the Empire quivered. Elsewhere missionaries, for all their efforts to be differentiated, were again being assaulted like any other foreigners and driven to evacuate many outlying stations.

As Chiang Kai-shek's troops advanced on the key city of Shanghai their battle was fought for them and the way opened by Communist-organized strikes and demonstrations involving 100,000 workers which the defending forces of the warlord Sun Chuan-fang, despite savage efforts and a hundred beheadings, were unable to suppress. The Concessions saw the specter of revolution. Frenzied consultations took place among the treaty powers. Britain announced the sending of three brigades. The United States, shrinking from the prospect of armed intervention in China, cautiously moved 250 Marines from Guam as far as Manila and only after three weeks' hesitation moved them on to Shanghai. As Chiang's troops reached the outskirts and a state of emergency was declared, 1,500 more Americans and 1,500 Japanese were landed to supplement 9,000 British and the Shanghai Volunteer Force. Foreign residents prepared for siege and employed the labor of hundreds of Chinese to dig trenches and put up barbedwire barricades and concrete blockhouses.

At the height of the crisis 5,000 American Marines arrived led by the Congressional Medal hero General Smedley Butler, veteran of every Marine engagement from the Spanish-American to the World War, including the Siege of the Legations. He promptly exasperated fellow commanders by his unheroic declarations to the press. His mission, he announced, was solely to protect American lives, not treaty rights. This was the principle steadfastly maintained throughout the Chinese turmoil of 1925-28 by Coolidge's Secretary of State, Frank Kellogg, a self-taught lawyer and former Senator from Minnesota. American forces in China, he insisted, were not sent to fight for the International Settlement or any other treaty provision but only to safeguard American nationals directly threatened. General Butler refused to give Shanghai hope of anything more. Asked by the press how many troops would be needed for an armed invasion of China sufficient to suppress the Nationalist movement, he replied with a sound sense of realities, "Half a million and it would probably require a million more before the end of the first year."

On March 24, a day before the Marines landed, Nationalist forces entered Nanking and let loose a day of fearful terrorism against foreigners that was to go down as a date of reckoning in the relations of China and the West. In a campaign deliberately but anonymously instigated, troops rampaged through the city, yelling and shooting, attacking foreigners, looting and burning foreign homes, killing six foreigners including the vicepresident of Nanking University, John E. Williams. Others took refuge on Socony Hill, the Standard Oil property, from which they were able to escape over the walls to gunboats in the river only when the British and American commanders, after an agony of hesitation, opened fire to keep off the attackers. A missionary's wife, Pearl Buck, cowering with her family in the tiny one-room hut of a poor Chinese woman she had befriended, listened to the ferocity outside and thought, "The whirlwinds were gathering . . . and I was reaping what I had not sown. . . . We were in hiding for our lives because we were White."

After Nanking the missionaries could no longer dissemble. They were reaping what they, no less than all foreigners, had sown—the failure to treat Chinese as equals. As news of the "massacre" of Nanking leapt by telegraph across China and other outbreaks followed, they fled to the rivers and gunboats and protection of the Treaty Ports. Eventually 2,500 took refuge in Shanghai and other Concessions and 5,000 left the country. Schools, colleges, hospitals and YMCAs closed down or were taken over by the Nationalists. Later in the early 1930s the missionaries began coming back but were never to reach the numbers of the period before Nanking.

Meanwhile the Treaty Ports were in full outcry over the Nanking outrage and clamoring for a "strong" policy. The Legations urged punishment of the guilty, indemnities, ultimatums and sanctions and, in case of noncompliance, plans for punitive action. The difficulty was that no one was sure, then or since, where to place responsibility: on the local commander, known to be feuding with Chiang Kai-shek, or on the Nationalist command or on the Communists and radicals of Hankow who presumably provoked the attacks in order to embroil Chiang Kai-shek with the foreigners. The last was the explanation put forward by the Japanese who feared the revival of Russian penetration of China via the radicals and believed Chiang Kai-shek represented a group with whom they could accommodate. "Steps already taken by the Japanese with Chiang," reported the American Minister, John V. A. MacMurray, "seem to give confirmation of a relationship between them."

A steady advocate of the hard line, MacMurray insisted that the situation, if not "resolutely met, will mean the downfall of western influences and interests in the Orient." Kellogg refused to be stampeded, the more so as startling events in Shanghai now revealed Chiang Kai-shek as a leader to be encouraged, not embarrassed. He appeared not only as the harbinger of "order" in China at last, but also of order in alliance with the right people.

Until their entry into Shanghai, the Nationalist advance was generally regarded by the Treaty Ports as "the Red Wave on the Yangtze." The profound split between right and left in the Kuomintang was not yet known to foreigners. The Hankow government, with Borodin and Bolshevik influence dominant, appeared to be in control. But Chiang Kai-shek and his supporters, if they were to achieve power in their own right, had to have the revenue and loans they could only obtain in alliance with capitalism. Labor troubles, peasant uprisings and antiforeign riots alarmed property-owners in their own ranks and property-owners whose support they needed. Communists working with the Kuomintang, including Mao Tse-tung, were busy organizing rent strikes and anti-landlord demonstrations among 2,000,000 peasants of Hunan, and Mao was promising that soon all over China "several hundred million peasants will rise like a

tornado . . . and rush forward along the road to revolution." Chiang needed
the support of landlord families. Communist organizers were equally active
among the proletariat and labor unions of Shanghai. Chiang was determined that the great metropolis of commerce, banking and foreign trade
must not fall like Hankow under left-wing control. Shanghai was where
the break had to be made.

Nationalist forces numbering about 3,000 had entered the city on
March 22, less by their own military prowess than by virtue of the strike
action inside the city and the demoralized flight of Sun Chuan-fang's forces.
Arriving by gunboat, Chiang Kai-shek made contact with merchants and
bankers through his former connections and secured a loan on the security
of his assurances. As Commander-in-Chief he had already absorbed into
his army and given commands to apostate officers of the northern forces,
many of them fellow-alumni of Paoting Military Academy, whose presence
strengthened his hand against the left. Through agents he learned of the
plans of the revolutionaries who were collecting arms by night for the
coup by which they hoped to capture control. At this point, on April 6,
a raid by Chang Tso-lin's police on the Soviet Embassy far away in Peking
disclosed documentary evidence of the extent of Soviet penetration under
Borodin's guidance of Chinese affairs. Besides the documents, nineteen
Chinese Communists including the leader of the party, Li Ta-chao, were
arrested on the premises and subsequently executed by strangling on
charges of treason.

Chiang Kai-shek made a wider sweep. On the night of April 12-13,
assisted by agents of the Green Society and police of the French Concession, he carried out a bloody purge of the left, disarming and hunting
down all who could be found and killing more than 300. The revolution
was turned from Red to right. Chiang's coup was both turning point and
point of no return. He was now on the way to unity but he had fixed the
terms of an underlying disunity that would become his nemesis. Hankow
expelled him as a traitor but he had the advantage in armed force and
established his own government at Nanking.

Chiang was now seen by foreign watchers as no Red after all but, as
Secretary Kellogg discovered with pleasant surprise, "apparently a leader
of the Moderates." American policy consequently leaned over backwards
not to embarrass him with responsibility for the Nanking outrages. Resisting MacMurray's insistence on punitive measures, Kellogg put forward
the sensible principle that "leadership inheres in moderation as well as
forceful action." President Coolidge was equally calm. In times of revolution it was not always possible to protect the lives and property of
foreigners, he said in a speech to newspapermen at a dinner of the United
Press, and he had "no doubt" that when a real government emerged in

63

64

In 1927 foreign residents of Shanghai prepare for siege by the revolutionists and put up barbed-wire barricades (61). Chinese loot British stores in Hankow (62) as the Cantonese Revolutionary Army enters that town (63). Nationalist forces under Chiang Kaishek carry out a bloody purge of the left. Stilwell's album contains many pictures of their executions (64, 65).

65

In 1927 Communists working with the Kuomintang, including Mao Tse-tung (third from left, 6
were organizing the peasants of Hunan. Chiang Kai-shek (67) and Michael Borodin (68), befc
their split, addressed crowds during the Hankow riots. Brigadier General Smedley Butler (69) arriv
in Shanghai with 5,000 American Marines to protect American lives. Stilwell became friends w
Lieutenant Colonel George C. Marshall, executive officer of the 15th Infantry, pictured standing w
Colonel Isaac Newell (left), the regimental commander (70).

66

69

70

China it would "make adequate settlement for any wrongs we have suffered."

So much sweet reasonableness was possible because public opinion was not calling for anything else. "We were convinced that the country at large would be wholly opposed to applying any sanctions whatever," Under Secretary Joseph Grew told the French Ambassador. No demagogue came forward to make political cause of the defense of Western treaty rights in China. On the contrary. "Four hundred million people," trumpeted Senator Borah, "imbued with the spirit of independence and national integrity are in the end invincible. There is no power that can master them or hold them in subjection."

Stilwell and other foreigners living in China could not be so objective. The Nationalists, having crossed the Yangtze, were now continuing their northward march and foreign residents of north China visualized a repetition of the Nanking "massacre" taking place in Tsinan, Tientsin and Peking. By temperament an anticipator of trouble, Stilwell wrote of speculating on the loyalty of his servants, of plans for flight at a moment's notice to the Concessions at Tientsin, of "a sick feeling of apprehension . . . for risking wife and children in such a country at such a time."

Confidence in the northern armies was minimal. Wu was not cooperating with Chang Tso-lin who had been named northern Generalissimo, and the associated warlords were regularly falling out with or withholding support from each other. The 15th Infantry and other foreign garrisons held anxious conferences on how to ensure protection of their nationals in Peking and recommended a doubling of the strength of each. In order to hold the railroad open, a total force of 25,000 would be better still, General Castner informed the War Department. He suggested that the next Army transport, due in May, should bring in troops from Manila and take home American women and children from north China. The Japanese moved a brigade down from Dairen to Tsingtao in Shantung and General Butler, deciding that the situation in the north was now more critical than at Shanghai, brought a full brigade of 4,000 Marines to Tientsin.

Equipped with 20 airplanes and a number of light tanks, which none of the other foreign contingents could boast, the Marines were the wonder of Tientsin much to the annoyance of the 15th Infantry. As they briskly and efficiently went about unloading field artillery, mortars, howitzers, machine guns, sandbags for barricades, trucks, tanks, planes and piles of supplies, the infantrymen stood watching with studied carelessness and inner rage. Butler warned that he would tolerate no clashes with the Chinese people and that "if a Marine so much as laid a hand on a rickshaw coolie he would be court-martialed." Nevertheless he spared no effort in his preparations to relieve Peking at a moment's notice. His trucks with machine guns, ammunition and ten days' rations were kept fueled and ready to move. Highway bridges were reinforced to carry the tanks. An airfield was built near the mouth of the Pei Ho and Butler flew back and forth between Tientsin and Taku to keep watch. When winter came he kept fires going day and night to ensure that motor fuel would be usable. With these arrangements, a battalion could start in trucks for Peking within 14 minutes of receiving the alarm and planes within five minutes. The plan arranged with the Legations in case of an antiforeign outbreak was to seize the park of the Temple of Heaven as an assembly point for the foreign residents from where they could be evacuated by truck and plane to the coast.

In May anxiety heightened as the advancing Nationalists approached Hsuchow, the crucial junction of the main north-south and east-west railways just below the border of Shantung. Dating back to legendary times, the battle for Hsuchow was customarily considered the climax of every change of dynasty. According to an old Chinese saying, "who holds Hsuchow holds *T'ien-hsia*," meaning "under heaven," that is, China. It was now held by the forces of the ogre of Shantung, Chang Tsung-chang, the man who was "dangerous even to look at" but who in the war had not made a firm stand yet. If Hsuchow fell, Shantung would be invaded, and if Shantung were overrun, the southerners would be at the gates of Tientsin. Should foreign women and children be evacuated now? What plans should be made? How far would the southern effort go? If, as Stilwell wrote later, "the push had run its course, it would be unseemly to call our nationals in and run for the sea. But if not, and the invasion reaches us even in the northern treaty ports, then what? Who would be responsible for a repetition of Nanking?"

The American Legation needed to obtain at first hand a reliable estimate of the real strength of the southern forces, not to mention the northern. Reports from newspapermen, consular agents and missionaries were so unreliable that it was impossible to judge the situation. Though the mission would be dangerous, given the rising mood of antiforeign fanaticism, an American military man must go in person. The choice fell not on the Military Attaché, Major John Magruder, or any of his staff, but on Major Stilwell of the 15th Infantry. Besides a knowledge of China and Chinese, a record of previous adventurous journeys and a recognized toughness of spirit, Stilwell possessed a further essential qualification—willingness to go, though he would be leaving behind four children and a wife shortly expecting a fifth.

On arriving in Hsuchow he was to present his credentials in person to the famed and terrible Chang Tsung-chang. A former wharf coolie in his youth, nearly seven feet tall, Chang bore the nickname "Three Things Not Known,"—how much money he had, how many soldiers and how many concubines. Of the latter he was said to maintain a stable of 42, including Chinese, Japanese, Korean, 21 White Russians and one bedraggled American, whom he hauled along to his wars in two private railroad cars. He was also known as *Lao pa-shih liu* or "Old Eighty-six" because the height of a pile of that number of silver dollars reputedly represented the length of the most valued portion of his anatomy in action. He supported a luxurious *yamen* thronged with officers, and dined lavishly with brandy and champagne from a Belgian cut-glass dinner service of 40 covers which he boasted cost $50,000. A magnificent carved and lacquered teakwood coffin accompanied him on board a flatcar of his private train. It was his boast that he would return from battle inside it if he failed to conquer, but he returned from Shanghai sitting on the coffin, smoking and slightly tipsy. Under his reign Shantung was plagued by famine in 1927, brought on not by flood or drought but by the *Tuchun's* rapacity.

Stilwell caught the evening train for Hsuchow on May 26. With him went Chao, his Chinese servant without whom, as he wrote afterwards, he might not have returned. "Why should Chao poke his nose into danger and risk his life in loyalty to a *lao mao tze* [Old Hairy One, a common designation for a foreigner] when all his own countrymen were screaming 'Kill them'?" Stilwell could supply no answer but he acknowledged his respect for "a game and loyal man" who when the situation became nasty could easily and safely have run out, but did not.

As the train rattled across the border into Shantung, Stilwell saw telltale signs of trouble. Carts with safe-conduct flags waited for hire at the railroad stations, an indication that local security was nonexistent. The carts were in fact a racket run by bandits who took squeeze from the cart-owners. Villagers with worried faces were mending their mud walls. There was "an ominous quiet when there should have been a hubbub about small things." As the train progressed, soldiers of the northern army began to be seen, "unconcerned, apathetic . . . in a jungle of units . . . no evidence of any organization of positions." Rolling stock in railroad yards was in "terrible condition . . . one or two wrecks in every round house."

After dark of the next day they reached Hsuchow and found it crowded with soldiers of all arms and ranks. Drunken *pings* and scowling White Russians of the warlord's cavalry reeled in the streets. The travelers met surly replies and no room at the inns. Chao suggested the local YMCA and they slept at the home of its secretary, Mr. T'ang. Hsuchow, as they discovered the next morning, was a "wreck," washed over time and again by the wave of war. The homeless, evicted by famine or soldiers, were camping where they could, food supplies were giving out, dead bodies were lying in the streets where they had fallen. "We stepped over them with the other passers-by and went our way." Stilwell saw 15 blind women leading each other around; otherwise no other women but a few old crones were visible in the streets, all being hidden away behind closed doors in fear of the soldiers. The refugees, possessing nothing but the rags they stood in and a few clay pots for cooking, "did not beg; they simply sat and looked out with hopeless eyes at an incomprehensible world." They were fed a meager ration of pressed cake, the residue after oil is pressed from beans, which in Manchuria, Stilwell noted, was broken up for fertilizer or fed to pigs. Once hard-working and industrious farmers, the refugees had seen "their carts and animals seized for armies, their sons drafted, their grain eaten up by locust hordes of soldiers, their homes pulled to pieces for firewood, their women mistreated, their children perhaps scattered— this is the saddest side of Chinese wars." Face to face with the old and limitless misery of China, Stilwell wrote with truth and understanding in contrast to the rather banal ideas he expressed on social problems in America.

After trying in vain to see Chang Tsung-chang, he prowled around the city. "Russky cavalry," the feared and prized adjunct of a northern war-lord's army, galloped through the streets. They wore dark green, almost black, uniforms with yellow leather boots reaching to their thighs, and carried an armory of weapons: pennant-tipped lances in their stirrup sockets, long-barreled Mauser pistols in wooden holsters and the *da-dao* or Chinese beheading sword, like an oversize machete, strapped over the shoulder in a canvas scabbard. Merciless and fierce, men without a country, they were "the toughest eggs I ever laid eyes on." Besides the cavalry troop of about 100, a Russian Infantry Brigade under General Netchaeff of about 3,000 men with four armored trains served with the *Tuchun's* forces.

At the railroad yards Stilwell found 200 cars, 20 locomotives and three armored cars with Russian crews. While trying to identify troop units and estimate numbers he calculated that out of every 100 soldiers, 30 had rifles. In drill units half had guns and half had none. In one "scarecrow" company of 200 to 250 men, 20 percent were under four-foot-six, many under fourteen, all dirty, some barefoot, with a total of fifty rifles among them. "The wildest stretch of the imagination could not envision the rabble in action except running away." An informant told him that the northerners would not fight; they were all afraid of the Red Spears. These were bands of resistance fighters drawn from the country people who, made desperate by marauding soldiers, had organized the Red Spear Society to prey upon whatever small groups of soldiers they could handle. They killed without mercy, inflicting wounds that left their victims alive for three or four hours before they died.

Each day food grew more scarce. Chao scrounged and brought in some canned goods. Preparations for a general movement were increasingly evident. Stilwell kept watch at the two railroad stations and yards, counting guns and calibers, recording troop trains and trying to "dope out" from the chaos what Chang Tsung-chang was planning. From the *pings* he learned that some units had not been paid for five months, some not for a year. Their ration was *mantou,* rice and water. He picked up the news that Feng Yu-hsiang had taken Chengchow which dominated the western end of the transverse railway. This was both true and important.

After a year's absence in Moscow, Feng was once more in command of the Kuominchun (National People's Army), the well-armed and disciplined force of over 200,000 which he had built up in Shensi and which figured in Comintern strategy as the northern arm of the revolutionary forces in China. To make junction with this force was the essential goal of the Kuomintang, but whether Feng would opt for the Communist-left coalition at Hankow or for Chiang Kai-shek was as yet uncertain. Trying to keep up with Feng's permutations which were bewildering even for China, Stilwell reached the verdict, "He double crosses everybody—is strictly for himself." But he also acknowledged that Feng was a "real fighter" who "never allows his troops to abuse the people" and that if China could find ten more commanders like him her troubles would be over. While Hankow and Chiang Kai-shek were both negotiating for his alliance, Feng as a result of various defaults by the northerners, captured Chengchow, causing the northern army in the area to retreat behind the Yellow River, which in turn uncovered Hsuchow. This development decided Chang Tsung-chang to retreat.

Stilwell hurried to the telegraph office to send word to the Legation but he was too late. The office was closed and the operators had fled. Next day, his fourth in Hsuchow, there was no doubt any longer; the northerners were pulling out. He counted six trains leaving in half an hour. When they were gone, the southerners would flood in and a foreigner might likely as not be lynched. His object now was to get out with Chao as soon as possible. The *Tuchun's* train was in the yards, but they were not allowed on, and when they attempted to push their way on board one of the crowded troop trains, they were thrown off. They tried offers of money in vain, the soldiers being themselves too anxious to leave to yield their places. As the *Tuchun's* train pulled out, Stilwell could feel panic rising in the crowd of soldiers around him. "How soon would their officers get them out of this? ... control would now be difficult ... everyone is ugly." The troops crammed on the remaining cars with "latecomers scurrying frantically to get aboard and perch anywhere—on the end-ladders or between the cars. Many will be shaken off...." As he watched, one man fell under the moving wheels and was left to die, "no doctor, no help of any kind, just a crowd of curious coolies jammed around him."

Now it was too late to leave with the northerners. What should he do? Walk? Could he reach Feng Yu-hsiang, some 50 miles off to the west? But the Red Spears were in between and "they will not discriminate in our favor." To the east, more Red Spears, "and the Russians, I am afraid of the Russians." The only alternative was to sit still and wait for the southerners "and that scares me as badly as the Russians do." Mr. T'ang, the YMCA secretary, confessing himself a southern sympathizer, advised staying as safer than going.

For two days after the trains left, "the town waited, holding its breath for the next wave to break over it. . . . One scourge gone, only to make room for another?" The northern rearguard came through, shooting, looting and yelling and doubling the turmoil at night. After them came "the pitiful remnants of a retiring Chinese army: the sick and wounded, dragging themselves along with only the prospect of death from the Red Spears ahead of them." Shops shut, mules sold for $300 and food was not for sale at all. At night "hell let loose; an engine screeching the alarm, *pings* yelling and firing field-guns, rifles, pistols. Only a few bullets whizzed our way." A plane came over and dropped a few bombs. The Russians who had stayed behind in their armor-plated train were the worst. They ran the train, equipped with machine-guns and a naval gun mounted on the rear car, up and down the line, "terrorizing the people by shooting and then stealing everything moveable." When the country people pulled up the track to block the train, the Russians "just about massacred the village" nearest the break. Keeping his daily watch at the railway yards, Stilwell saw another boy soldier run over by a train and laid on a mat to die. Rage and pity welled up in him at the callousness of China and vented itself savagely: "After a month or so you want to stick knitting needles in their balls."

On the morning of June 2 Mr. T'ang came in to report that the Kuomintang Army had arrived. They were behaving well, no beating, no looting, but Chao insisted that Stilwell stay out of sight. Everyone in the neighborhood knew there was a foreigner in Mr. T'ang's house and Stilwell wondered when his presence would be reported to the soldiers. He imagined the squad that would come bursting in, yelling for the foreigner, and he tried to put his mind on something else. After four days of hiding with nothing to do but draw pictures, he felt desperate. "Must do something; hike south seems to be the only feasible plan." After another day when he resorted to jumping over wooden horses for half an hour "to keep from going nutty," he decided he "must get out of here somehow." Mr. T'ang was growing cool and might be regretting having given shelter to a foreigner. On the sixth day of hiding, Chao at last agreed to take a chance. They walked out and made acquaintance with the southern *pings,* "a cheer-

71a

b

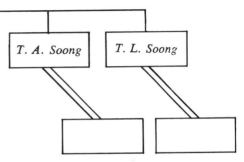

| T. A. Soong | T. L. Soong |

Of the six children of Charlie Soong (71a), the wealthy, American-educated former missionary, and Mme. Soong (71b), whose family had been Christian for centuries, four were to play major roles in the history of modern China. Ai-ling (71c), the eldest, married the influential banker H. H. Kung (71f); Ch'ing-ling (71d) married Dr. Sun Yat-sen (71g) and became a political opponent of the rest of the family; T. V. (71e) became China's Foreign Minister under the rule of his brother-in-law, Chiang Kai-shek, who is seen here on the occasion of his marriage to the youngest Soong daughter, Mayling (71h). T. L. and T. A. Soong made no mark in Chinese history.

h

ful gang, mostly boys hardly 16, little runts with narrow shoulders,
no weight. . . . All the *pings* have been filled full of pro-American propaganda. They think America will actively help them." The city was hung
with Kuomintang flags and welcome signs, shops had reopened, women
reappeared in the streets, carpenters were busy repairing damage, but the
dead and dying still lay in the alleys, and starvation, filth and disease filled
the makeshift shacks of the refugees. "The sights in this town are terrible."

The Kuomintang troops proving less murderous than he had expected,
Stilwell made up his mind to leave via the south for Shanghai. The northerners had taken with them all the rolling stock they could collect but
word came that a southbound train would be going through next day.
Through a crush of frantic people waiting to get on, a wild scramble and
a pall of garlic fumes, he and Chao fought their way on board. After three
hours of suspense in the station waiting for the train to move and a journey
of agonizing halts and delays, they came to a stop at 3 A.M. at P'eng Pu,
still a long way from the Yangtze and possible foreign warships. Passengers
were cleared out, it was obvious the train would go no farther and they
were left standing on the platform in the dark.

For the next 36 hours the sickening emotion of fear was to be Stilwell's
companion. Hungry and thirsty and stranded in a strange place, he and
Chao did not know whether another southbound train would be coming
through and did not dare ask questions for fear of drawing attention. They
could not risk going to look for food or drink for fear of missing a train.
They feared to wait until daylight brought new crowds and made Stilwell
more visible but they had no other choice. At 6 A.M. some freight cars
were pushed onto the southbound track. Among new crowds they struggled on board, while trying to remain inconspicuous, and found places on
the floor of an old coal car. Feeling the other passengers' eyes on him,
Stilwell expected at any moment the sudden shout *"Lao mao tze!"* or the
advent of a guard or official who would haul him off for examination.
Baking in the heat, the car became "filthy with eggshells, snot, seeds, tea,
water, spit, rinds and all the other trash that chinks can throw." Mixed
with "spitting, coughing, belching, nosepicking, sucking and grunting," this
was bad enough, but worse were the whispers and looks cast in his direction. Hunger and thirst increased but they dared not get off at any of the
stops for fear of not getting back on.

Fear materialized in the person of an inspector, "a truculent coolie,
dressed in a little brief authority," who, on frisking Stilwell, triumphantly
discovered and took away his pistol, flourishing it before the passengers
as if to unmask a criminal, a spy, an assassin come to kill Chiang Kai-shek.
Murmurs rose. "What shall be done with him? Take him off and shoot
him." Disarmed, alone except for Chao, Stilwell felt hostility closing in.

At the next stop the inspector got off to report and the hostility became active. Umbrellas poked into him, tea was spilled on his leg, someone spat on his back. Suddenly the realization flooded over him: "They were trying to make me react. They wanted me to resist," as an excuse for attack. It could end in murder. "Chao's warning look proved it; he slowly turned his head back and forth to signal 'No.' He was deathly afraid, not for himself but for me." The prodding and sly tricks and insults continued. With rage in his heart Stilwell contained himself. At a halt the crowd argued whether to "take us off now and shoot us or turn us over at P'u Kow," the last stop. Catching at the straw, Chao demanded, "Yes, arrest us; turn us over to the authorities at P'u Kow. We demand it. The foreigner has great influence and there will be a great deal of trouble for anyone who harms him." He was cursed for being a running dog for a foreigner but before the crowd could take action the train moved. Chao had found his cue. He demanded to be taken before Chiang Kai-shek himself. "We will make complaints; we will report everything." The insults and the prodding stopped but the threat of arrest at P'u Kow abided.

Stilwell decided to give the crowd no time to test its intentions. As the train pulled into P'u Kow, on the Yangtze opposite Nanking, he and Chao jumped off before it came to a stop, and pushing past astonished people, ran for the river feeling pursuit at their heels but not daring to look behind them. They scrambled aboard a ferry and on the other side walked slowly past suspicious glances in search of lodging. Money persuaded a fearful innkeeper to give them a room where, exhausted and dehydrated, they drank teapot after teapot. Stilwell was embarrassed to find his hand trembling when he held out his cup for more. Tension did not let down, for word of the foreign devil's presence brought a crowd gathering in the street and Stilwell once more imagined capture or lynching. Worry, bedbugs and fleas allowed him little sleep. In the morning came another trial of the streets, but without interference they reached the station and boarded the train for Shanghai. The journey was hot and tense. On arriving, their eyes met a huge poster on the wall showing a fat and repulsive foreigner prone on the ground with Chinese soldiers sticking bayonets into him, blood spurting out and a caption exhorting all patriots to kill the foreign swine.

Through the exit, past the sentries and across the square Stilwell could see the barbed-wire fence of the International Settlement and safety, 100 feet away, a matter of 30 seconds. "We crossed the square with 50 pound weights on our feet, passed through the wire . . . and stood at last on our own side." A sampan rowed them out to the cruiser *Pittsburgh* where at the top of the gangway a Marine was standing guard, and "I, an Army officer, felt like throwing my arms around him and giving him a hug!"

It says much for Stilwell's military objectivity that the report he submitted on his return gave the southerners a favorable judgment. Their morale, discipline and confidence were high, he stated, they gave cheerful obedience, did not loot and were welcomed by the populace as shown by the reappearance of the women. Their company officers were students of eighteen to twenty-two, determined and convinced in contrast to the "trash" in the *Tuchun's* army who at the company and battalion level were largely uneducated coolies. Although deficient in armament compared to the northerners, the southern army was capable of beating the *Tuchun's* "rabble" in any clash but he predicted they would not be able to operate beyond Hsuchow for lack of rolling stock. They had brought none across the Yangtze, moving supplies by cart and pack animal, but as soon as they could use the railroad they would roll north with no likelihood of firm resistance. Chang Tsung-chang's army had no fight in it, except for the Russians. "In my opinion a determined southern attack will mean Chang's collapse."

At the Legation MacMurray welcomed the first authentic information on the situation. He listened to Stilwell's narrative and read his report with "great admiration" for his "intrepid personal qualities." General Castner gave his formal commendation for "the highest type of efficiency, military intelligence, splendid determination and courageous conduct"—and for something more. This man of troubled mind understood the true rarity of Stilwell's exploit: that "courage in battle when accompanied by comrades is often seen but a much higher courage is required by any individual who attempts what Major Stilwell accomplished—the close contact alone and unaided, with hundreds of ignorant, hostile anti-foreign Chinese troops of two contending armies." Stilwell was probably the only man with the necessary combination of military knowledge, Chinese knowledge and that "higher courage" who could have carried out the mission to Hsuchow and returned.

Stilwell's second son and fifth child, Benjamin, on whom he doted thereafter, was born in July, a month after he returned. In September he took off on a three weeks' vacation to Korea and Japan. In Korea, he climbed mountains, passed pool after pool of clear water, "took a plunge . . . sat on a rock naked eating lunch." In Japan he enjoyed himself nosing around Kyoto, eating, talking, noticing, shopping and collecting. On his return he found, as he had predicted, that the Northern Expedition had come to a halt at Hsuchow. Suffering from more problems than lack of rolling stock, it went no farther in 1927 and almost foundered in factional strife before the end of the year. The adherence of Feng Yu-hsiang gave the upper hand to Chiang Kai-shek in June. The Hankow Government, already ravaged by doctrinal quarrels, was split by ill-conceived orders from the Comintern causing the left wing of the Kuomintang to break way from the Communists. When Hankow's military arm, the renowned "Ironsides" Fourth Army of General Chang Fa-kwei, resumed independence and went back home to Kwangtung, the regime in ruined and terror-stricken Hankow disintegrated and the united front of the revolution came to an end. Not yet ready to give up, the Communists established a short-lived regime at Nanchang, capital of Kiangsi, attempted a coup that failed, retreated further south and made a last mad effort in the three bloody days of the Canton Commune. Hunted and decimated by Chiang Kai-shek's forces, the remnant retreated into the countryside of Kiangsi and Hunan to gain what foothold they could for survival.

Chiang Kai-shek had already begun to lose the first bloom of public welcome. He was trapped by his alliance with the capitalists into a campaign of Communist suppression that took on all the aspects of a white terror. Searches, seizures, censorship, arbitrary arrests and executions frightened and disillusioned many who had believed in the Kuomintang promise of something better. Taxation was as heavy, armed force as pervasive as ever. The Nationalist movement, overtaken by the compromises and corruptions of the climb to power, began to seem no different from anything else since the days of Yuan Shih-kai.

Facing a renewed challenge for control by Wang Ching-wei and the left wing, and suffering a military setback in August, Chiang resolved the problem by resigning and waiting in Japan to be called back as indispensable. Disunity and chaos rushed in to fill the vacuum. Wang Ching-wei and Mme. Sun's brother, T. V. Soong, set up yet another separatist regime in Canton. But necessity drove and the call to Chiang came in November. While all parties thrashed out the deals and terms for unification during December, the leading figure perfected his position by marrying Miss Mayling Soong,* sister of T. V. and Mme. Sun, and a very remarkable person.

The Soongs were a Shanghai Christian family of wealth, Western education and hallowed affiliations with Dr. Sun Yat-sen. The mother's side had been Christian for 300 years dating back to the earliest conversions by Jesuits. The father, C.J. or Charlie Soong, a friend and supporter of Sun Yat-sen, had been brought up and educated in the United States. He returned to China to work for a missionary but enlarged the family's fortunes instead, built a handsome foreign-style home with formal gardens and a tennis court in the French Concession and fathered six children, all of whom were educated in mission schools and American colleges. The eldest daughter, Ei-ling, had married H. H. Kung, a banker and Oberlin

---

* Western-educated Chinese preferred the anglicized version of their names.

alumnus, who came of a substantial Shansi family which claimed direct descent from Confucius. The second, Ch'ing-ling, became the second wife and widow of Dr. Sun. The youngest, Mayling, combined graduation from Wellesley College with the instinct for power of the Empress Dowager. All three were intelligent, beautiful and, like many Chinese women in contrast to Japanese, strong-willed.

Chiang Kai-shek was sufficiently interested in these assets to have reportedly proposed marriage through a middleman to Mme. Sun after she became a widow. On rejection he transferred his attention to Mayling. To win her, he disposed of an earlier wife as well as the Japanese mother of his son, and at Mme. Soong's insistence was converted to Christianity, acquiring as no small by-product the permanent favor of the missionary establishment. A private Christian ceremony in the Soong home on December 1, 1927, was followed by a very public civil wedding in Western dress in the ballroom of the Majestic Hotel with 1,300 guests including Admiral Bristol of the American Asiatic Fleet and foreign consuls, a large portrait of Dr. Sun flanked by Kuomintang flags, scores of detectives and bodyguards, and a bell-shaped canopy of roses to shelter the ceremony performed by the Minister of Education in the Nanking Government. Attended by four bridesmaids in beaded peach charmeuse and two pages (the son and daughter of Mme. Kung) in black velvet and white satin vests, the bride was given away by her brother, T. V. Soong, while a tenor sang "O Promise Me" and motion-picture cameras recorded the scene. Chiang's position was now impregnable. In January 1928 he was redesignated Generalissimo of the Nationalist Army, chairman of the Central Executive Committee and as such chief of the reorganized and reunited Nationalist Government at Nanking. The march to the north, assisted by revenues found by T. V. Soong through his financial connections, was resumed in April.

In the north, with Wu Pei-fu having retired from the coalition, Chang Tso-lin was the reigning Generalissimo of the *tuchuns'* forces gathered under the name Ankuochun, or Pacification Army. Having declared himself dictator in December, Chang Tso-lin became infected with the disease of Yuan Shih-kai and nourished the ambition to be Emperor. He held court seated on a throne-like chair flanked by two lifelike stuffed tigers. He appointed a Board of Rites and Ceremonies to prepare court procedures, commissioned artists to design a new set of Imperial porcelains and followed the traditional Imperial custom when moving through the city of causing streets to be closed, shop windows shuttered and pavements strewn with "golden sand." For a brief glimmering moment hope revived in the breasts of surviving Manchu aristocrats and old conservatives but Chang's fate, though momentous for China, was not to be the throne.

In January 1928, as the result of feuds at 15th Infantry Headquarters, Stilwell was transferred at the request of General Castner from troop duty to General Staff duty as acting Chief of Staff to the Commanding General. The appointment became official in the following July. Castner's quarrels with Colonel Newell and other officers including his Chief of Staff had grown sharper and for a while the General suffered, according to Stilwell's diary, from a "nervous breakdown" with hallucinations. In the odd role of pacifier Stilwell was the only officer whom the disturbed and difficult commander trusted. His eccentric tyrannies continued to increase antagonism which came to a head over his insistence on training the men at a faster marching pace than the regulation two and one-half miles an hour. Twice a year, grimly setting the pace himself, he led out the entire regiment, with officers dismounted, on forced marches which, while never achieving his goal of 100 miles in three days, succeeded in reaching a rate of 35 miles in ten hours—at considerable cost. Exhausted men staggered to the finish, some dragging or carrying their comrades, determined not to give Castner the satisfaction of seeing a single soldier failing to complete the course. Many in the regiment thought the purpose of Castner's marches was to try to make the suave Colonel Newell fall out, but he never did. Stilwell naturally went along without trouble.

When Colonel Newell and others attempted to bring about the General's removal on charges of mental incompetence, Castner turned to Stilwell for testimony in his behalf. Turmoil matching China's continued to brew at USAFC Headquarters during the rest of Stilwell's tour. Marshall was gone, having left in May 1927 to become Assistant Commandant and academic head of the Infantry School at Fort Benning where he embarked on an ambitious program to reform the course and teaching staff. He wanted Stilwell as head of the Tactical Section, the post next in importance after his own, and was holding the position open for him until he could return to take it.

In May 1928 Stilwell was promoted to lieutenant colonel, receiving *The Sentinel's* congratulations as "one of the most popular officers of the command." Considered the Infantry's expert on Chinese affairs, he was already functioning in the role of teacher. Besides serving as President of the Language School he gave a monthly briefing in the Recreation Hall on the situation in China, impressing one listener as a "brilliant and incisive" speaker with an awesome knowledge of the Chinese tangle. More important was his influence on *The Sentinel,* which in the midst of a country heaving in national agony at last undertook to recognize its surroundings in the form of a weekly front-page article by Stilwell on "Who's Who in the Chinese Situation." The series reflects events as seen in their own time by an American in China who had to deal with them. If it sometimes distorts history from being too close, it is innocent of the equal distortions of hindsight.

Stilwell's series opened in January 1928 with an article on Chang Tso-lin for whom the outlook, he concluded, was not bright. Writing from week to week through the fateful six months from January to June 1928 when the situation was in flux, Stilwell leaned to the Legations' cynical view of the Nationalists and rejected the "sentimental" view of the home-based American who, he believed, knew nothing of China and misunderstood the Revolution.

Adding his own concern for "Old Hundred Names" (the Chinese common man), he wrote of people taxed unmercifully, of life and property insecure, of railroads ruined, trade suffering, banditry universal, famine common and "not a single province . . . where the rights of man are respected." The traditional man of destiny, always supposed to be produced by national emergency, "has not yet appeared." Two months later in an article devoted to Chiang Kai-shek in April 1928, Stilwell described him as head of a faction rather than chief of a party but nevertheless a man who could prove to be the one to put China's house in order. He accorded Chiang admiration for his "determination and energy" and offered the judgment that if he wins "it will be largely on account of resources he can find within himself." His northward advance, however, was "more in the nature of a parade than a campaign," making its progress against unpaid northern troops who "oozed out of town" ahead of it.

From his observations Stilwell distilled a basic principle of Chinese warfare when he wrote that Chang Tsung-chang, the *Tuchun* of Shantung, was living up to his reputation as the greatest Chinese master of "the strategic retreat." Strategic retreat was to be a major source of Stilwell's own future frustration. As opposed to the offensive spirit in which he had been indoctrinated at the West Point formed by Mahan and in the AEF under Pershing, it represented a cultural clash that was fundamental.

Suddenly in May 1928 a sharp intervention took place whose significance for the future Stilwell immediately recognized. The Nationalists had now resumed their advance northward. As they moved up the railroad from Hsuchow toward Tsinan, capital of Shantung, the Japanese accused them of attacks on Japanese nationals and despatched 2,000 troops out of 5,000 previously landed at Tsingtao to the "rescue." In the course of several clashes, with deaths on both sides, the Japanese murdered the Nationalist Commissioner for Foreign Affairs of Shantung along with his wife and fourteen officers in an effort to provoke retaliation and an "incident" sufficient for open hostilities. The clash was followed by an ultimatum to the Nationalists to withdraw from Tsinan.

The prospect of a unified China whose nationalism might extend to Manchuria had begun to worry Japan. Baron Tanaka, progenitor if not author of the famous plan of conquest called the "Tanaka Memorial" of 1927, was then Premier and Foreign Minister. The plan that bore his name expounded the military concept of Japan's destiny which was to be mastery of Asia achieved through successive penetration of Manchuria, Mongolia, north China, all China, and Southeast Asia. Chiang Kai-shek had no desire to make a test of it. Six Japanese warships, eight troopships and eleven freighters crammed with munitions and supplies were at that moment anchored off Tsingtao. Whatever Chiang's pretensions to great captainship, he did not delude himself that his troops were any match for the modern army of Japan. He held to his aim of Peking and unification and prudently saved his army by turning away from Shantung, crossing the Yellow River and moving on Peking from the west. But the incident was not so easily swallowed by the Chinese people. The "unbearable sting" of the Japanese insult to national pride revived all the anti-Japanese feeling of the earlier Shantung affair and was fanned by posters and slogans into another year-long boycott.

In *The Sentinel* for May 11 Stilwell put his finger on Tsinan as a situation "probably as critical as any that has arisen for many years." He had little sympathy for the anti-Japanese agitation which he saw as making ultimate settlement more difficult, for even if all Chinese factions should stand together, "they are no match for an organized power like Japan." The Chinese, he wrote, "can contemplate with equanimity the most terrible injustice and cruelty inflicted by Chinese on Chinese" but as soon as there is trouble with a foreigner "a patriotic orator is found on every street corner ranting and roaring about foreign oppression and the rights of the native." He pointed out that the Japanese, if provoked, could without serious hindrance occupy key points from Tientsin to Shanghai with control of railroads and the Yangtze—a program which ten years later they exactly carried out. "Events of far reaching consequences," Stilwell believed, would ensue from Tsinan.

Within a month came the first. In the collapse of northern resistance Chang Tso-lin saw his imperial vision vanish and realized that he must protect his own domain, if indeed he had not already waited in Peking too long. He retreated to Manchuria in his private train of 20 cars fully loaded with personal property and followed by most of the rolling stock of the Peking-Mukden Railway. For three days locomotives, coaches, cabooses, deluxe wagonlits and freight cars packed with men rolled through the Tientsin station where, in the vacuum of power left by his departure, the 15th Infantry and other garrisons stood guard. On June 4 as the lead train approached Mukden it was blown up by a bomb and Chang Tso-lin

Early scenes of the Chinese war in 1927 in the south, where Stilwell was sent to obtain a reliable estimate of the real strength of the southern forces, including those of refugees fleeing by rail from Chengchow (72) and of families preparing to leave the ruins of their homes in Wuchang (73). Northern forces moved south to P'u Kow on the Yangtze to prevent any surprise attack from the Red Army of the south (74). On October 10, 1928, Chinese students celebrated the seventeenth anniversary of the overthrow of imperial rule (75).

74

75

was killed. That the Japanese had eliminated him no one doubted, either because they feared he would come to terms with Chiang Kai-shek or because he may have refused to cooperate with them on terms they demanded. In either case they overreached themselves—for the time being—for Chang's son, the Young Marshal Chang Hsueh-liang, contrived the assassination some months later of the two leading pro-Japanese ministers and raised the Nationalist flag over Manchuria.

In Peking at last, the Northern Expedition had reached its goal. After arrangements with local *tuchuns* the Nationalists took over the former capital officially on July 3, marching down Legation Street to the "thunderous silence," as an observer wrote, of expressionless onlookers. In contrast to the big northerners, Chiang's troops "seemed small and campaign-worn." Simultaneously they took over Tientsin in a blaze of sunshine that sent the mercury up to 111 in the shade. Talking, shouting and the intervention of strange and complicated political committees and governmental bureaus occupied the next days, as reported by the American Consul, "and we are becoming settled to the new disorder of things." Chiang Kai-shek paid a ceremonial visit to the grave of Sun Yat-sen in the Western Hills to report the consummation of his dream of China united—at least nominally—under the rule of the Kuomintang.

Cancellation of the unequal treaties remained a primary object and the powers were amenable to some concessions on the theory that this would give prestige to the new government and assist stability. As the first to negotiate a step toward revision, the United States signed a treaty on July 25 restoring tariff autonomy to China as far as America was concerned. On October 10, the 18th anniversary of the Revolution, the Nationalist Government assumed the rights and titles of national government based on a one-party system and on the period of "tutelage" which according to Dr. Sun's plan was to follow military unification. Sovereignty resided in the Party, executive power in the Central Executive Committee of 36 members and real power in the Steering Committee whose chairman was the Commander-in-Chief of the armed forces, Chiang Kai-shek. If this was not exactly the democracy that China's Western friends had in mind, they pretended that it was, and China under the influence of the Western legacy adopted the nomenclature. The concept itself remained where it had always been, outside the Chinese frame of reference.

Peking was renamed Peiping, meaning "northern peace" instead of "northern capital," for it was not to be the seat of the new regime. The Government remained at the southern capital of Nanking, partly because it did not feel safe away from the territory of its own troops and could not afford to maintain rice-eating southern troops in the north, and partly because the status of the Legation Quarter of Peking was a "face-destroying" factor.

To protect his victory Chiang Kai-shek moved swiftly in an effort to control a crucial danger—the private armies whose numbers despoiled the country and whose existence deprived any central government of secure authority. He summoned Feng Yu-hsiang, Yen Hsi-shan and Pai Ch'ung-hsi, each of whom controlled an army of about 230,000, to a Disbandment Conference in Peking in July. A national army not to exceed 60 divisions of 15,000 men each, or a total of 900,000, was agreed on, as against an existing total of 2,225,000 men under arms. Six disbandment areas were drawn up, but in the test none of the generals proved willing to carry out the reductions. A second Disbandment Conference held at Nanking in January 1929 also failed to accomplish results. The chieftains returned each to his own base to operate as independent and uncertain allies, or sometimes opponents, but not as subjects. In the coming years alliance, schism and rebellion went on as before. In the south the Kwangsi-Kwangtung armies of Li Tsung-jen, Pai Ch'ung-hsi and Chang Fa-kwei, and in the north those of Feng and Yen, were to move in and out of armed dissidence, in shifting combinations with and against each other, with and against Chiang Kai-shek, but never, ever, in common cause. Canton in 1931 for the nth incredible time supported a separatist regime under the persistent Wang Ching-wei. Chiang Kai-shek's Government was never to be free of these challenges by rival members of the pack, never to be wholly secure in authority. The necessity of bargaining and maneuvering to keep the challengers off balance and maintain his own was the condition of his rule.

As 1928 came to a close, Stilwell, recognizing disbandment as the "real problem," pointed out in *The Sentinel* that the announced agreements were only on paper and that the private armies were in fact recruiting, not disbanding. Summarizing the new regime, as he saw it, he wrote that it was now the fashion to expect the best of the Nationalist Government, to believe that China was now unified, the Government competent and responsible and the period of reconstruction fairly begun. "Cold facts," however, should be examined. The outer provinces were still carrying on private wars without allegiance to Nanking. Conflict between radicals and conservatives within the Kuomintang was unresolved. Until the military was subordinated to the civil authority disbandment would not be achieved. Eighty percent of tax revenue which should have gone to industrialization was absorbed in support of armed forces. Though the Kuomintang now enjoyed favorable propaganda abroad, Stilwell remained skeptical of the likelihood of real progress.

In the Tsinan Incident and the problems of disbandment—or nondis-
bandment—Stilwell had fixed upon two factors whose development would
be critical for China and ultimately affect his own history along with hers.
This took no gift of second sight but interest, awareness and readiness to
observe at first hand the realities of China during the two and a half climactic years of her modern history.

Stilwell returned to the United States in April 1929, taking with him as a
small dividend the handball championship of the Orient.

76

77

*General Joseph C. Castner, the
overall commander of the U.S.
forces in Tientsin, with Secretary
of War George H. Dern and regimental commander Colonel Isaac
Newell. In the rear at right is Stilwell with a man not identified (76).
Chang Tsung-chang (77), the famous and terrible Shantung warlord, and Chao (78), Stilwell's
Chinese servant who accompanied
him to Hsuchow.*

78

6

"Vinegar Joe," 1929-35

WHEN Stilwell came to the Infantry School at Fort Benning as head of the Tactical Section in July 1929, the "Benning Revolution" under Marshall's impetus was in progress. The object of the revolution was to teach by practical experience instead of by the field manual and the classroom battle. Tactics, as the heart of the military art, the area where a man must think on his feet, was the key faculty.

Benning was the basic tactical school of the Army. Under the old system the officer was trained to solve a book situation on the basis of information about the enemy far more complete than would have been available to him on a real battlefield. At exercises of the 15th Infantry in China Marshall had watched an officer who was supposed to envelop the flank of an enemy become paralyzed because he could not draft a written order for 70 men on the basis of the inadequate data on the terrain given to him. When he learned that this officer had stood first at Benning he formed "an intense desire to get my hands on Benning." Once in charge, he threw out the book in favor of realistic exercises that would train for initiative and judgment rather than for the correct solution.

Marshall needed men of similar mind on his staff who would be willing to experiment, to accept new solutions, to welcome the unorthodox if it showed that the student was thinking for himself in the field. Knowing Stilwell to fit this prescription, he held open for him the principal staff post as head of the First or Tactical Section. Stilwell shared Marshall's belief, inherited from Pershing, in short simple orders focused on the objective to be reached without detailing every step on the way. On the real battlefield where the enemy does not wait, quick decision at the company and battalion level was needed. The purpose of Marshall's revolution was to unparalyze this ability and prepare a body of combat officers for the actual duty of leading troops.

From experience in the World War Stilwell knew that the methods and principles of command had to be suitable for the rapid training of officers from civilian life who could again be called upon in another war. It was necessary to develop, as he put it, "something easy to teach a big emergency force." Simplicity was his key. Wars are not won by "fancy tactics. . . . Only simple and direct measures have any chance at all." He condensed military power at the tactical battlefield level to "Move, shoot and communicate."

The Marshall years at Benning, open to new ideas, argument and active thinking about military development, were stimulating for their own sake. In the presence of a future wartime Chief of Staff they were incomparable as a nursery of high command. Marshall in his own words had a "wicked memory." Though mediocrity made little impression on him except as a "momentary irritation," he never forgot an impressive performance or an unfortunate dullard. Among the officers who served on his staff or in the Advanced Course at this time were the future Generals Omar Bradley (as head of the Weapons Section), Matthew B. Ridgway, Courtney Hodges, J. Lawton Collins, Walter Bedell Smith and many others who were to become army and corps commanders.

Stilwell left classroom lecturing largely to subordinates but himself supervised every tactical exercise. His habit was to propose a "screwball idea," ask for reactions and test them out. Student officers found that his tactical problems presented challenging situations requiring original solutions. He taught by applying principles in action and "throwing out anything that does not make common sense." In actual maneuvers he showed what the classroom could not—that field telephones break down, runners get lost, orders are misunderstood, maps are often wrong and complicated movements "always go wrong."

Benning prepared officers for the company and battalion, not the headquarters, level. The view from a battalion command post, as Stilwell wrote, is not the same as the view from a division or corps. What is a line on the map to the higher command is a sector to the combat officer, with particular terrain features that determine his action. A unit never gets lost on a map as it can on the ground, especially at Benning where most of the terrain resembled a jungle. Stilwell constantly emphasized evaluation of terrain as the basis for decisions. The pine forests around Benning, making it impossible to observe artillery support, obstructed the use of field artillery and required the infantry to depend on mortars for "quick action up front in thick country"—exactly the situation he was to meet in Burma.

Mechanized warfare and the immense tactical changes it would bring dominated military thinking. Stilwell studied the theory of combined mobility, penetration and surprise that was to become the blitzkrieg in action and he contributed occasional articles to the *Infantry Journal* but his thinking remained essentially pragmatic rather than speculative. "Don't assume anything—Look!" summed up his creed as it did his critique as umpire of maneuvers in 1932.

After the first year Marshall described him as "a genius for instruction." In reply to the routine question on an Efficiency Report as to the highest command the officer could be recommended to hold, he wrote "qualified for any command in peace or war." Sensitive to Stilwell's inability or reluctance to talk about himself, he commented that "modesty and unassuming methods have prevented this officer from being widely known as one of the exceptionally brilliant and cultured men of the army." He judged him "farsighted. Highly intelligent . . . a leader . . ." and even rashly added "tactful," which during the rest of Stilwell's four-year tenure at Benning proved to be not the most enduring of his qualities.

When Stilwell met ineptness or stupidity he could be acid and it was one such occasion at Benning that earned him the famous nickname. After a particularly caustic critique of performance in field exercises, a student officer returned to barracks and drew a caricature of Stilwell with a none-too-benevolent expression rising out of a vinegar bottle with three Xs on the label. Pinned on the bulletin board, it was widely appreciated, not the least by its subject who asked if he could keep the original and had photographs made of it which he sent to all his friends.

The vinegar element in his character was best understood and explained by his steady friend, General Wells, who wrote to him many years later apropos of a "sour" newspaper picture, "Whenever you wear that expression it is because something or somebody has created a situation that is inherently cock-eyed—at times, even, it stinks." Among Stilwell's other characteristic expressions, Wells went on, were "one of utter hopelessness and one of disgust. . . . It was when decisions or actions taken were so obviously screwy but which nevertheless had to be endured, that developed on your countenance some of the pain that was in your soul. . . . It isn't Vinegar, Joe—it's just something else that looks like it." Wells' conclusion was perhaps too charitable for undeniably there was acid, though balanced by humor and human kindness, in Stilwell's makeup, as he himself recognized. He liked to tell a story of himself when once in a bitter black mood he was walking alone in a Chinese town and was accosted by a Chinese merchant who bowed and said, "Good-day, Missionary."

"Why do you address me as 'Missionary'?" Stilwell asked with a terrible scowl.

"Because you look like one," the Chinese replied.

"And why do I look like a Missionary?"

"Because of your calm benign expression, Sir," was the reply.

"So don't suppose the Chinese lack a sense of humor," Stilwell would add when he told the story.

In an essay written for his family about himself and his wishes for them, he admitted having been at times "unreasonable, impatient, sour-balled, sullen, mad, hard, profane, vulgar. . . ." It was a formidable list for a man to acknowledge and all of it true. Though he was a gentleman when he chose, in society that he enjoyed as with the French at Verdun, and perfectly at home with good manners, he allowed himself to give an impression of boorishness with certain people. It was his way of expressing dislike, and perhaps unconsciously, uneasiness. His use of profanity, too, was a kind of verbal thumbing his nose at pretentiousness. His language when the occasion was suitable could be coarse and in his diary the four-letter words were chronic. Scatological rather than sexual, they give an impression of a rather large fund of hostility.

Stilwell seemed to enjoy the sensation of dislike, and in his diary would work himself up to it, starting out with a reasonably biting remark and then, as if led on by the taste, going on to more and crueler slurs. The inspiration was generally people he regarded as putting on airs such as "nauseating" Americans who pretended to an English accent.

The rich and the snobbish he especially excoriated, often with what seems superfluous vigor. From some hidden source in his nature or past experience he had acquired a chip on his shoulder about the rich. Having been brought up himself in comfortable circumstances, he had as a result of a certain rigidity on his father's part no private income of his own as a mature man. On his father's death in 1933 his circumstances did not change appreciably because, except for a few stocks to his son, Dr. Stilwell left the bulk of his estate to his widow who was to live until 1942. Living on an Army officer's pay with five children, Stilwell doubtless felt at a disadvantage during the prosperous 1920s, but during the depression when an officer was at least assured a secure job and a fixed income, the military felt better off than many others.

The Stilwells did not have expensive tastes. He did not join other officers in hunting or polo, neither did his wife ride nor did they play bridge nor, when in China, join in the club life of the foreign colony. When they entertained at home they served, to the horror of harder-drinking friends, sparkling burgundy. The horse, perhaps because it was the traditional appendage of the rich and snobbish, continued to excite Stilwell's extreme antipathy. Bored on one occasion by a fellow officer's interminable talk of horses, he exploded in a letter to his wife, "If there is anything that gets my goat it is one of these idiotic horse-lovers. . . . If there is a woodener, less intelligent animal on earth than a god-damned hammer-headed horse, show him to me. All prance and fart and no sense." Having vented his feelings, he immediately apologized for a "vulgar" letter.

Lesser vulgarities he used easily and seemingly without pejorative content: limeys for the English, frogs for the French ("met a frog and his wife on shipboard"), huns and squareheads for Germans, wops for Italians, chinks or chinos for Chinese, googs for Filipinos, niggers or coons for Negroes. Terms not commonly used by a man of Stilwell's class and education, they convey, like his swearing, the impression of a person not on the whole charmed by his fellowman. He was in fact "pretty close to a misanthrope," in the words of a fellow-officer. But the source of the misanthropy was hidden and after long acquaintance the colleague confessed that in the end there was always something elusive about Stilwell; he had never figured him out.

The pleasures Stilwell enjoyed were homemade or self-propelled. He was an indefatigable organizer of amateur theatricals and pageants, played tennis for casual sport and kept in physical trim by regular cross-country running or handball, two of the most energy-consuming of all forms of exercise. In khaki pants and T-shirt he could be seen two or three times a week trotting smoothly and easily through the pine woods at Benning. In a five-mile race he came in a mile behind at the finish but reported to his children that he felt few could do it at all at the age of forty-eight.

His family was his citadel where he felt secure against what appeared to be a hostile world, where he loved and felt loved and could shed his defenses. It was a place of jokes and laughter, companionship, mutual entertainment and unbuttoned ease. He never felt really comfortable when away from his family and yet within its bosom for too long, which might be anything more than a few months, he invariably became restless and anxious to get away. In marriage he and his wife Win were joined into a genuine couple. Married to a dominant personality, she took on many of his attitudes and tended to reflect and reinforce rather than soften his hostilities.

His notebooks filled up with evidence of his constant and primary concern for his five children: their heights and weights with annual and sometimes monthly gains, their allowances and accounts, schools and travels, their first words and bright sayings with age and circumstance noted for each remark. "You're old, we're new" was one of Joe Jr.'s at age five. When away from home he always remembered their birthdays in his diary. Even during the chaos of Hsuchow June 1 did not pass without the note, "Nance's birthday." When schools were not satisfactory or when once in China his youngest son and daughter, scolded by their teachers, came home in tears, he swore no one should treat his children like that, took them out of school for a year and taught them at home. Handwriting exercises written out in a large and beautiful script for his eldest daughter Nance to copy reveal something of the "genius" Marshall saw in him as a teacher; how he could charm a pupil with humor and irreverence:

> Begin with short words like Cat.
> Pretty soon you can write hippopotamus
> Hip up on top of the whole lot of us. . . .
> Sit close to the table and sit erect.
> Throw your food up in the air;
> And bite it as it comes down.
> All your friends will be pleased.
> They will think they are at the circus. . . .
> Stab a potato with a knife, and then—
> Swallow it whole. Save the knife.

He could sit for hours with the youngest, Ben, drawing fantastic animals and by a system of cutouts transform a shark into an airplane or a three-headed dragon into a series of marvelous mutations. The family nickname of Ol' Pappy was acquired at Benning when the children were performing an imitation of the local Georgia "crackers" and "reckoned as how ol' pappy would go out and catch hisself a rattlesnake and skin it alive." Delighted with the image, they took to calling their father by the new designation and it stuck.

Stilwell was always writing things down. In addition to diary, letters, essays and sketches, he wrote what he called "Random Notes" or "Odds and Ends" on sheets or scraps of paper dealing with thoughts, dreams, stray ideas, jokes, anecdotes, remarks, quotations or anything that was passing through his constantly ticking mind. A characteristic scrap, verbatim and in entirety, reads,

Henri Fabre's insect study
History of the eel
History of the bowler hat
What to do with Waterloo
Tall men and tall houses least furnished in upper stories—Bacon
Wells's "outline of the arts"
"Fix Bayonets"

Another scrap records his mental struggle with a fundamental problem of democracy, still unsolved. Headed "$=$ and $\neq$ Suffrage," it reads,

```
For  — Everyman one vote. But some more than—
         Ignorant should be < powerful than educated
         Intelligent should be able to offset numerical advantage of masses
Vs   — Difficult to find standard of awarding extra votes
         Property? (Often an accident. Foreign to dem. spirit).
            (Rep. in upper houses)
         Education. (Not nec. true. Uned. more insight at times).
```

Another note headed "Recall, Initiative and Referendum" suggests that he was examining, besides insects, eels and the arts, the constitutional process. He copied passages from Shakespeare including inevitably and predictably Hotspur's outburst, "For he made me mad . . . to talk so like a waiting-gentlewoman, of guns and drums and wounds. . . ."

Intelligent without being profound, Stilwell was a quick thinker usually ahead of the other person in any conversation which he would continually punctuate with a staccato and impatient "Yeh yeh. . . . Yeh, yeh." Apart from intermittent bouts of questioning, the general tenor of his social and political ideas was conventional. Though he had reacted against his father's religious piety, he retained the family Republicanism and joined naturally in the exhilarating exercise of Roosevelt-hating. Despite its nonpartisan traditions, the Army when it "mumbles in its beard," as a fellow-officer put it, shared the ordinary political passions and Stilwell was no exception; indeed, being Stilwell, his sentiments were harsh.

Among other written records were his dreams, reported clearly and fluently, often with perfect candor and confidence in letters to the person who figured in them. To Win before their marriage he wrote of a dream of intimacy which though delicate and tender was still startling to write to a fiancée in 1910 when reticence was the usual rule. To his father he reported a dream in which after a scuffle with his brother he was being chased by his father with intention, as he thought, "to beat me to a pulp. . . . When you caught up . . . instead of beating me you pulled out a coin and handed it to me. I stood looking at it stupidly and finally asked what it was. You said 'A coin of this realm' in a sad way. Well, I was so broken up about that 'coin of this realm' that I woke up and couldn't get to sleep for some time." The dreams frequently were of struggle and physical effort, of "Climbing a big mountain to get to some country. Only way in. Mountain side kept crumbling and getting steeper and steeper." Or of watching with his mother a boy struggling on top of Croton Dam with a stone cannon and being propelled nearer and nearer the edge until he fell over. " 'Don't look' I said. Went down slowly climbing to stone. Struck and never moved. Red stain under him. 'Killed him instantly,' I said." Others were of climbing down from an airship on ladders or of underwater struggle or of a melee of beasts in China in which "the whole struggling lot came crashing down a rocky slope in a grinding mess of broken legs and necks and crushed carcasses. Phew. I woke up scared stiff."

At Benning, even among familiars and equals where there was no group like the diplomats or the British to make him feel uncomfortable or to resent, he could still become difficult and hostile. Marshall acknowledged afterwards that he was three times asked by the Commandant, General Campbell King, to relieve Stilwell. One cause of the animosity he aroused in some officers was the extreme strictness of his standards which would not allow him to give a "Superior" on an Efficiency Report unless he considered it thoroughly deserved. The result was that few officers under his supervision could go on to the War College, whereas in the more routine Weapons Section "Superiors" were freely given, easing the advancement of the recipients' careers. This puritanism of Stilwell's about promotions and awards continued to leave patches of resentment behind him in his future service as commanding officer and theater commander. It was not surprising that Marshall's rating for Stilwell's tact went down a point in the second year at Benning. A faint note of long-suffering was detectable behind his further comments: "High principles. Too hard-working. Nervous temperament. . . ." Yet Marshall held on to his thorny colleague whom he also recorded as "Ahead of his period in tactics and technique."

Stilwell drew on his Chinese experience for examples to illustrate his teaching and also to awaken awareness in the officers of a country with which, as he underlined, *we may all have something to do someday.* In a lecture to the School in 1929 under the title "Psychology of the Oriental" he fixed on a fundamental difficulty between West and East, so obvious that it is usually ignored, when he said that the reason Westerners apply the cliché "inscrutable" to the Chinese is that they find them "different from us." Why are they different? Because having been "cut off" as Stilwell put it, from our civilization for so many centuries, they have developed under different conditions a civilization of their own. "How then can a Chinese be expected to react like a Westerner? . . . Answer, he can't." This was a principle more important than it sounds. He also made the point that owing to a society so old and fixed in its patterns, the Chinese have "a conservative complex . . . whose inertia is simply enormous." Discussing the Oriental concept of "face," he said enough to show that his future mishandling of Chiang Kai-shek was not from ignorance: "Dignity, then, is their most prized possession and he who strips them of it makes bitter enemies. . . . In dealing with Chinese don't take their face from them unless you want to humiliate them and unless you do not care if you make enemies."

In talking of China to colleagues he stressed the country's tremendous needs, especially in every form of communication from roads to radios. His interest, as a friend said, "was in what China could develop *into*." He believed that the current effort in civil reform would permit "the thorn of extrality to be removed from her side" and he persuaded himself intermittently that the new Government might really succeed in modernizing China and mobilizing her potential. "With the right direction," he would say, "four hundred million people with their working and manufacturing ability will dominate and we'd better be with 'em."

While at Benning his notes show that he read—though disappointingly without comment—the historic document that marked the beginning of China's new travail. This was the Report of the Lytton Commission of the League of Nations on the Manchurian crisis, the event whose train of consequences was to engulf the world.

On September 18, 1931, the Japanese Kwantung Army, using the arranged pretext of a bomb explosion on the tracks of the South Manchurian Railway, seized Mukden in "self-defense," and spread out swiftly to the military occupation of Manchuria. The move was a larger successor to the murder of Chang Tso-lin in 1928, and this time accomplished its purpose. It was precipitated by Chiang Kai-shek's efforts in 1929, in collaboration with the patriotic Young Marshal, Chang Hseuh-liang, to reimpose Chinese sovereignty over Manchuria. Directed first at Russian control of the Chinese Eastern Railway, China's challenge had provoked instant retaliation by Soviet troops ending in the defeat and humiliation of the Chinese—and alarm to the Japanese. The revival of both Chinese and Russian pretensions determined the Japanese military, who were the expansionist force in the nation, to consolidate Japan's "special position" in Manchuria. Operating on the principle of direct access to the Emperor which allowed them to act independently of civilian control, the military acting through the Kwantung Army engineered the Mukden Incident, raising issues of tremendous import at home, in China and, in view of the Washington Treaties and the Covenant of the League of Nations, in the West.

When the attack came Chiang Kai-shek's military energies were absorbed in the third of his extermination campaigns against the Communists. Moreover, the country was suffering from a disastrous flood of the Yangtze which left thousands of square miles inundated, two million dead and countless destitute. No attempt to organize military resistance in Manchuria was made. On the contrary, Chiang Kai-shek ordered Chang Hsueh-liang who had 400,000 men under arms both south and north of the Great Wall "resolutely" to follow a policy of "non-resistance." Though his troops were numerically superior, he knew they were no match for the Japanese in training or armament and he preferred a strategic retreat to a military show-down with Japan. His guiding principle was to let nothing deter him from his main purpose of eliminating internal rivals.

Chiang had made up his mind that "pacification" must come before everything; before social and political reform or resistance to the invader. If there was one thing that could qualify Chiang for greatness, it was the fixity with which he gripped and held a conviction, once formed. Against the Japanese he could use China's eternal advantage, her infinite room to retreat, while concentrating on his aim of uniting the country under Kuo-mintang rule. When this was accomplished China could cope with the Japanese; meantime Manchuria, presumably, would satisfy them.

History is the unfolding of miscalculations, and Chiang had made several. Successful aggression is rarely self-terminated nor is the desire of a people to repel the invader so easily denied. Chiang, however, had little choice and his task inside the Wall was great enough. His first year of rule had been plagued by revolts of the leaders who had helped him to power and then resisted disbandment. At various times during 1929-30 the Kwangsi Generals Li Tsung-jen, Pai Ch'ung-hsi and Chang Fa-kwei and, in the north, Feng Yu-hsiang, had challenged the Government in armed conflict and had to be defeated or bought off. The outer provinces, Yunnan, Szechwan and Sinkiang, because they were outside the Govern-ment's control, remained sources of possible opposition. Canton continued to be intermittent host to a kind of subgovernment maintained by the leaders of the still viable left wing, Wang Ching-wei, Eugene Chen and Sun Fo, the son of Dr. Sun Yat-sen. Peiping reverted for a while to a seces-sionist regime under Wang, Feng and Yen Hsi-shan but, with the help of Chang Hsueh-liang, the Central Government reestablished control. These various struggles preoccupied the Kuomintang to the exclusion of social change, and as soon as they seemed settled or quiescent Chiang set himself to quell another set of domestic enemies, the Communists, who were dug into the countryside of Kiangsi. Three successive "Bandit Suppression" campaigns, as these operations were called, absorbed the Government's military effort and brought it unpleasant defeats from the Communists' guerilla tactics in the year before the Japanese struck.

Three times in eighty years, in a country in desperate need of reform, the revolutionary surge had been frustrated. Chiang was concerned with piecing together political power, not with rooting it in a new social foundation. Land rent reduction could not be pursued by a Government that had reverted to the old alliance between officials and landowners. In

Chekiang, where a program of rent reductions was genuinely attempted, its moving spirit and sponsor was assassinated and the program abandoned. Under the formula of "tutelage" the Government remained a one-party autocracy and became increasingly authoritarian and repressive, sowing the wind of rebellion. Deprived of the possibility of reform within the framework of government and hounded as outlaws, the Communist movement according to the American Vice-Consul in Hankow, Edmund Clubb, "has been forced . . . into a bitter rebellion which is sweeping the oppressed—liberal students and all—with a savage hatred of the existing regime in China." All the while the regime clung to the Three Principles of Sun Yat-sen as a kind of incantation to substitute for practice. To fill the vacuum left since the collapse of the throne, Sun was made a cult. His portrait was omnipresent and his will containing the Three Principles was recited at weekly memorial services, at all public meetings, political assemblies and patriotic holidays and by schoolchildren every Monday morning. His body was removed from Peiping to a $6-million mausoleum built into the side of the Purple Mountain at Nanking.

Modernization if not social revolution was pushed in the form of roads and airlines, electrification, new railroads, improvement of agriculture, codification of law, new schools with modern curricula and that basic requirement for all modern organization—a logical method of arranging the language to make a filing system possible. The absence of an alphabet in China was probably as disabling as the absence of roads. Varying from province to province some programs made progress, others did not. There was so much that China needed and the age allowed so little time.

After the seizure of Mukden the Japanese Army, regardless of divided councils at home, pushed ahead to attack Chinchow, Chang Hsueh-liang's provincial capital just north of the Great Wall. They captured the city in January 1932, driving the Young Marshal out of Manchuria. The "independence" of the new state of "Manchukuo" was proclaimed in February and Henry Pu-yi, last relic of the Manchu dynasty, was installed as Regent in March. The Japanese Government, under the necessity of accommodating to the stranglehold of the Army and Navy ministers, was dragged forward by *faits accomplis* and by the blackmail of violent nationalism. Because it was anxious not to give the League of Nations or the signatories of the Nine-Power Treaty a reason to declare that a state of war existed between Japan and China, Tokyo attempted to legalize each forward move on the mainland as "self-defense" and "self-determination" by the people of Manchuria. Behind the facade an intense struggle was shaking Tokyo. The Government resigned in December 1931. In naming a moderate, Ki Inukai, as the new Premier, the Emperor tried to brake the headlong course. Inukai was informed that the Emperor hoped he could curb the Army's "meddling in domestic and foreign politics"—a dangerous assignment that was to prove the Premier's death warrant. Unknown to the West, Inukai in his first month of office sent a secret envoy to Chiang Kai-shek to negotiate a settlement in Manchuria but control of Japanese policy was no longer really in civilian hands.

The effort of the Western powers to deal with the situation over the 17 months from the Mukden Incident to the adoption of the Lytton Report was crucial for the twentieth century. It brewed the acid of appeasement that gutted the League, encouraged further aggression and opened the decade of descent to war. Statesmen are not seers and their actions are taken in contemporary context with no view over the hill. The working out of a crisis takes place in stages without history's advantage of seeing the event whole and its aftermath too. It is doubtful if any stage of the Manchurian crisis could have happened otherwise, for in the course of the process there were no likely alternatives that could have been seized, no might-have-beens just barely missed. Some periods breed greatness, others feebleness. The Manchurian crisis was one of the causative events of history born, not of tragic "ifs," but of the inherent limitations of men and states.

China rested her defense on the guarantees the world had devised for just such a situation: the Nine-Power Treaty, the League Covenant and the newly added Kellogg-Briand Pact signed at Paris in 1928 by which 15 nations including Japan undertook to renounce war as an instrument of national policy, and to agree that the settlement of all disputes "shall never be sought except by pacific means"—except of course in case of "self-defense" and "vital national interest." China formally appealed to the League five days after the initial attack. Aggression had not yet tested the collective will; this was to be the first major case. Although there was eager sentiment at Geneva for doing something "wonderful" for world peace, no one was anxious to do anything specific. The year 1931 cowered under economic blizzard. Britain, the major Western power in the Far East, was in the midst of political and financial crisis and about to go off the gold standard, the bourses of Europe were trembling on the edge of panic, the Weimar Republic was dying and the United States was sunk in the slough of depression. Japan's act was indeed embarrassing in view of all the machinery set up to restrain aggression but as the French Premier André Tardieu said, it was "a long way off."

It seemed immediate and compelling to the American Secretary of State, Henry L. Stimson, an outstanding advocate of disarmament and of the collective effort to outlaw war. As Governor General of the Philippines in

1927-29 and chairman of the American delegation to the London Naval Conference in 1930, Stimson had been closely engaged in the problems of the Pacific. He had seen the London Naval Treaty, outcome of his work, arouse savage resentment in Japan because it prolonged the halt in naval building and the hated 5-5-3 ratio of the Washington Treaty for five more years. The wrath of Japan's superpatriots culminated in the assassination of Premier Hamaguchi who had strongly supported the Treaty and had advised the Emperor to ratify it.

Through Stimson the attack on Manchuria reactivated the United States in world affairs, ultimately with disillusioning result that was to play its role in renewed isolation. Stimson had two objectives in the crisis: to prevent further Japanese expansion on the mainland of Asia as had been the American effort since 1917, and to uphold the system of collective security. But when the League, in the hope of sharing or possibly devolving responsibility on the United States, was prepared to invite ad hoc American adherence to the Council, he shied off, not wishing to find this baby "dumped," "deposited," or "left," as he variously complained in his diary, in or on his country's lap or doorstep. He wanted Japan to be curbed by the "vigorous judgment" of world opinion, not by the United States alone.

What Japan's move implied—whether temporary occupation or something more—and whether it represented concerted policy by the Japanese Government or another wild move by the militarists acting through the Kwantung Army, was by no means clear to the West. Through the remaining months of 1931 Stimson acted in the hope that "mobilization of public opinion against Japan" backed by threat of economic sanctions could strengthen the parliamentary parties and lead to the conclusive curbing of the military. Throughout the first four decades of the twentieth century it was always this beckoning figure of the liberal thin man inside the Japanese body politic and the hope of his reemergence that lured American policy. In 1931 who could say whether international condemnation of the Manchurian adventure, backed by threat of sanctions, would strengthen the hand of the moderates or unite Japan behind the superpatriots?

Lacking any stiffening by the British, the "vigorous judgment" of the powers that Stimson hoped for would not congeal. British foreign policy was then directed by the parent of appeasement, Sir John Simon. He was Britain's foremost lawyer, a man simultaneously cold and unctuous, with a cautious mind, a head too small for his body and a perpetual smirk, who as Foreign Secretary did more to make his country unpopular than anything since the Boer War. Records have since been interpreted to suggest that he too wished to curb Japan, but he gave Geneva the contrary impression and caused Stimson to conclude that Britain would be content to see Japan absorbed in Manchuria rather than competing with British dominance in the Yangtze valley or reaching out toward Australasia or India.

Stimson himself did not speak for a country ready to back words with a big stick. President Hoover was very worried by the idea of economic sanctions which, unless backed by the ultimate sanction of force, he characterized with some justice as "sticking pins in tigers." Stimson argued that the risk must be weighed against the "terrible disadvantages" which Japan's action, if unrestrained, would do to the cause of peace. It must also be weighed against the danger "that Japan was setting on foot a possible war with China which might spread to the entire world." As Japan moved deeper into Manchuria he grew increasingly concerned at the threat both to world peace and to American interests in the Far East. He believed it would cause "incalculable harm" to American prestige in China if, after long association, America were now to "cynically abandon her to her fate."

Failing the joint voice of the Nine Powers or of the League or of the Kellogg-Briand Pact, he determined on some form of unilateral action but the best he could do was to dig out of the files Secretary Bryan's statement at the time of the Twenty-one Demands in 1915 which, reenunciated on January 7, 1932, came to be known as the Stimson Doctrine of Non-Recognition. It notified Japan and China that the United States "cannot admit the legality nor does it intend to recognize" any arrangement between those countries which impaired the Open Door policy or "the sovereignty, the independence, or the territorial or administrative integrity of the Republic of China" and which might be brought about by means contrary to the Kellogg-Briand Pact to which China, Japan and the United States were parties. The statement was resounding, unequivocal and, as an instrument of restraint, without practical effect. This being apparent, the League two months later accepted a resolution offered by Sir John Simon to concur in the doctrine.

In China a national anti-Japanese boycott was proving so effective that it brought on a Japanese attempt to end it by punitive action at Shanghai, center of the boycott movement. Providing themselves with the usual "incident" as pretext—this time a murdered Japanese monk—they attacked Chapei, the Chinese district of Shanghai, with planes and troops landed from warships. The air raid on Chapei of January 29, 1932, was the first terror bombing of a civilian population of an era that was to become familiar with it. The rain of bombs, the thousands killed, the ruins and wounded and refugees, under the eyes of the foreigners of Shanghai, appalled and alienated Western sentiment. Reminded of the German invasion of Belgium in 1914, Stimson determined not to be another Wilson "who did nothing

Fort Benning, Georgia, 1932: Lieutenant Colonel Stilwell, Colonel George Marshall and Major Omar Bradley (79). Caricature of "Vinegar Joe" drawn by a student officer (80). An illustrated rhyming bestiary made by Stilwell for his children (81), all seen in this family group (82).

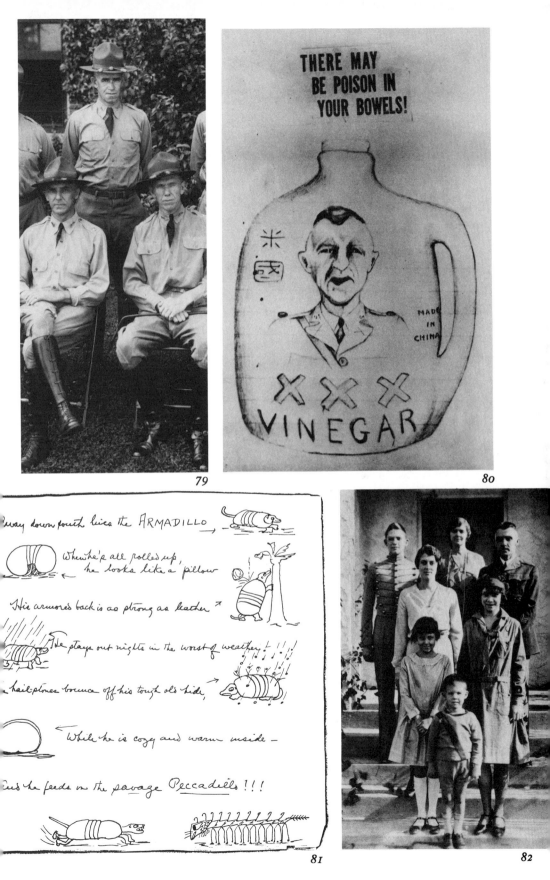

THERE MAY
BE POISON IN
YOUR BOWELS!

MADE
IN
CHINA

XXX
VINEGAR

79

80

'way down south lives the ARMADILLO →

When he's all rolled up,
he looks like a 'pillow ←

His armored back is as strong as leather ↗

He stays out nights in the worst of weather !!!!

hailstones bounce off his tough ol' hide, →

While he is cozy and warm inside —

And he feeds on the savage Peccadillo !!!

81

82

84

Japanese officers in bulletproof vests led their troops on a punitive attack on Chapei, the Chinese district of Shanghai, in 1932 (83) as refugees swarmed into the International Settlement for protection (84) and Chinese troops took cover behind a hastily constructed trench (85).

to show the shame that we felt in regard to Belgium." Chapei, plus a Japanese declaration that the clauses of the Nine-Power Treaty regarding the integrity of China were obsolete, convinced him that Japan had gone past the point of restraint by half-measures. Yet since punitive measures were beyond his power or the world's willingness, he had to choose between the inadequate or nothing, and chose the former.

Making a further attempt to obtain British collaboration, this time to invoke the Nine-Power Treaty, he found Sir John "soft and pudgy" and "very cold-footed." Again Stimson resorted to unilateral warning. He issued a public statement in February declaring the "abiding faith" of the American people in the future of China and reaffirming the principle of the Nine-Power Treaty—that China must be given the opportunity to develop into a "modern and enlightened state." He intimated to Japan that the Washington Treaties were interdependent and that nullification of the clauses relative to China could be considered as canceling the naval and nonfortification clauses. But it was an empty threat for his country was not prepared for the iron alternative of an arms race. Later, when Stimson was occupied at the Disarmament Conference, President Hoover informed Japan that the United States would not resort to economic sanctions.

The crisis was beginning to expose the soft core of the American commitment: that in underwriting the integrity of China, America had espoused a policy not sufficiently in her vital interest to fight for. The Open Door had been the triumph of a phrase. Not only had its syllables a superb and simple euphony but it also conveyed an impression of something brave and free, of wide-open opportunity that appealed to two basic American concepts, the frontier and free enterprise. As Hay said of another of his classic formulations, it had "an uncalled for success." In the long run it enmeshed the United States in that most entangling of alliances—not with a country but with a doctrine. It imposed a sense of obligation to intervene in an issue—the integrity of China—in which American security was not at stake.

With China's appeal still pending, the League faced the uncomfortable necessity of living up to the Covenant. The problem of how to restrain, or failing restraint, how far to condemn Japan without driving her out of the community of nations disturbed and bewildered the powers. The various pretexts and legalizations Japan raised always left a case to be argued. To investigate the facts the Lytton Commission was sent to Manchuria. Meanwhile fighting had spread. A Manchurian leader, General Ma Chan-shan, emerged to cause the Japanese trouble. At Shanghai a brave and unexpectedly effective resistance by the Chinese 19th Route Army, virtually defying Chiang Kai-shek, drew the Japanese into a fight they had not counted upon. Having all they could handle in Manchuria, they were glad of an excuse to withdraw from Chapei on the basis of peace terms arranged by the local foreign powers.

The Mukden Incident had by now gathered self-propelling consequences. Between February and May Japanese ultranationalists successively murdered the Finance Minister, the head of the Mitsui industrial empire and Premier Inukai whose assassins were army officers in uniform. Giving way to a series of national governments, his death marked the end of the political party system. In Japanese opinion Stimson was the evil agent of events, responsible for the world's misunderstanding of Japan and for ill feeling in the United States. Japanese publicists began speaking of an "Asiatic Monroe Doctrine" and suggesting that any attempt by the United States to interfere with Japan's "destiny" in Asia would be cause for war. Anticipating an unfavorable report by the Lytton Commission, Japan challenged it in advance by according *de jure* recognition to Manchukuo in September.

The Lytton Report was submitted in October. Though phrased as decently as possible in the pale hope of saving enough face for Japan to make it possible for her to accept it, the report unavoidably found that Japan had acted in violation of the treaties and that the two pillars of her case, "self-defense" and "self-determination," were unsupported by the facts. It recognized that a return to the *status quo ante* was not feasible and it recommended an autonomous administration under restored Chinese sovereignty with special provision for Japan's economic interests. Through long debate on adoption of the report, the League endeavored somehow to escape the pincers of the dilemma closing in on it: whether to condemn aggression, which was likely to force Japan into a break with the West and a back-to-Asia policy; or to paste over the episode by some legitimatizing formula that would keep the League's structure, if not its purpose, intact.

With the Lytton Report lying on the table no escape was possible. It was adopted in February 1933 and on the following day, after a speech of passionate self-righteousness and warning by the Japanese delegate, Japan withdrew from the League. To underscore her defiance and the futility of international words without teeth, Japanese troops took over Jehol, another province north of the Wall, and then crossed over into Hopei, where they established a demilitarized zone 30 to 40 miles wide between Peiping and Tientsin into which Chinese troops could not enter without Japanese consent. Here this phase of Japan's destiny came to a halt for the time being, legalized by the Tangku Truce negotiated with, or imposed upon, the Chinese Government. It was accepted by Chiang Kai-shek, who, in the same month that the Japanese invaded Hopei, launched 250,000 of his best troops in a fourth Bandit Suppression campaign against the Communists in the south. He had made the same choice as his predecessor, Prince Kung,

Regent at the time of the Taiping Rebellion, who said the rebels were a disease of China's vitals, the barbarians an affliction only of the limbs.

The Manchurian crisis left China's integrity henceforward dependent on the size of the bites Japan could digest. It brought about the supremacy of the military in Japan, but this was an internal process which would have taken the same course even if Japan's fellow-nations had not condemned her action. It left the elaborate structure of the Washington Treaties a hollow shell and exposed the weakness of the collective will. The League, the Nine-Power Treaty and the Kellogg-Briand Pact, separately or together, had not been enough. Between desire for collective security and its implementation the gulf was now painfully apparent. Men began to doubt whether any action short of force could deter a nation from aggression it had determined on. After the Manchurian crisis the nations found themselves, as Stimson confessed, "baffled and pessimistic."

In May 1933, the same month as the Tangku Truce, Stilwell's tour at Benning came to an end accompanied by just such an episode of infuriating bureaucracy as General Wells meant when he wrote of those actions that develop the "pain in your soul." Joe Jr.'s graduation from West Point was to take place within two weeks but owing to the need of officers to staff President Roosevelt's emergency creation of the Civilian Conservation Corps, routine leave between posts was canceled. Every officer was required to report directly to his next station and could not go off duty for any reason. All Stilwell's requests for delay, including, as a last resort, one to General Douglas MacArthur, then Chief of Staff, were turned down. Prevented from attending his eldest son's graduation from his own alma mater, the father was left with what ire can be imagined. He naturally laid the blame on that man in the White House. Mrs. Stilwell and her second daughter, "Doot," represented the family at West Point while Stilwell set off for his new post in California in the car with the two youngest children and Nance and the dog. He arrived after a week of driving to find his predecessor still in place, no orders awaiting him and nothing for him to do. A telegram from Win on the day of Joe's graduation, sharpening the fact of his absence, made him write, "Well, this puts a final touch on my disgust with the machine."

After a period just short of four years at Benning, from which Marshall had departed in 1932, Stilwell had grown restless, to the point of describing his own departure as "Escape from Bondage." He had not wanted to put in for the upper-level staff course at the Army War College, even though it was the acme in status, and when his colleague and fellow-Infantry officer Omar Bradley applied for it, Joe said to him, "Brad, why do you want to go to the War College to learn to do what you don't want to do anyway?" He had been unsuccessful in obtaining foreign service for his next detail, but the War Department had satisfied his second preference for "any duty on the West Coast" by assigning him to San Diego to train the Organized Reserves of the IXth Corps Area. Although the duty was disappointing, it had the advantage of bringing the Stilwells closer to their property at Carmel where they intended to build a home.

During the two years while he was at San Diego Stilwell did his best in another teaching job to transfer the principle of realistic field exercises to the Reserves. In a time of isolationism, enthusiasm for military training was not high. Men from office and salesroom on two-week duty did not offer Stilwell the most professional material but he knew they were the country's resource in war and as one of them said, "He took us seriously. He was probably the best man we ever had." By bringing together the various components of the Army in the area to train together and by giving common-sense instruction in the real tasks of command, he aroused the men's interest. "We have never received better instruction than we are now receiving," one group stated in a resolution of appreciation.

Privately Stilwell was bored and discouraged. He felt that if the War Department thought no more of him than to put him in this kind of job, he could not, at fifty-one and not yet a full colonel, look forward to a military career of much promise. "There will never be a single work of history with me in it," he wrote in a personal summing up. Many times "disgust with the machine" had brought him to the verge of retirement and he now began to discuss the possibility seriously with his family. The house at Carmel, built in 1934 at a cost of $27,000 with money from the stocks left to him by his father and to Win by her mother, was ready and Stilwell hoped to live on savings, retirement pay and what work he could find to employ his talents as a teacher. In the gloom of the depression, however, the outlook was dim and held him back from taking the plunge into retirement precipitously. Colonel Marshall was similarly fretting at this time in a post with the Illinois National Guard. Angry at the stagnation in the promotion system, Marshall wrote to a friend in 1934 that he was "tired of seeing mediocrity placed in high position with brilliance and talent damned by lack of rank to obscurity."

At a low point for Stilwell, the opening came. Previously he had never thought of himself as eligible for the post of military attaché because it had always required a private income. But in 1934, in order to extend its choice of qualified officers, the War Department added an expense allowance to the post. At once friends in the Department queried whether he wanted the appointment to Peiping (where the Legations remained) and, given his qualifications, easily obtained it for him. Although a military attaché's duties are assigned by MID, he serves as a member of the diplomatic mission. Receiving his appointment from Secretary of State Cordell Hull in January 1935, Stilwell found himself, of all things, a diplomat, but that misfortune was bearable for the sake of return to China. "How intensely interesting the international situation is in the Orient at this time," a fellow-officer wrote in a letter of congratulations. "No one can tell how soon we may be mixed up in that situation."

The signs were certainly provocative. In 1934, in a historic statement announcing her intention to control China, Japan slammed shut the open door. Voiced by a spokesman of the Japanese Foreign Office, Eiji Amau, the statement proclaimed it to be Japan's purpose to act as "guardian of peace and order in East Asia." As such, Japan claimed the right to oppose loans or any other form of support by other nations to China and denied China's right to "avail herself of the influence of any other country to resist Japan." The Amau Doctrine startled the world; nevertheless American reaction was held to a low key. With the energies of the Roosevelt Administration strained in the tremendous effort of domestic reform, the Government was not looking for a foreign quarrel. Secretary Hull's policy was to abate the ill feeling left by Stimson. His reply, while necessarily putting America on record as rejecting the Amau Doctrine, was issued, as he said, in a "respectful and friendly spirit."

In practice the Japanese continued their penetration of Inner Mongolia and north China through political arrangements with puppet governors and economic flooding by organized smuggling of opium and Japanese goods. While the north eroded, Chiang continued passive to the Japanese while reorganizing and retraining his army with the help of German advisers for use against the Communists. In 1934 with a mobilization of 700,000 he launched the fifth Bandit Suppression campaign against Communist forces which numbered about 160,000. This time, with artillery, planes and German coaching, he was at last able to overcome the enemy's guerilla tactics. A cordon of blockhouses gradually tightened was designed to force the Communists into positional warfare or else annihilation by siege and starvation. The policy practiced by the Nationalist forces was to exterminate the local peasantry who had amalgamated with the Communists and turn the region into a wasteland incapable of supporting the guerilla troops. Houses were burned, cattle and people driven away, fields left untilled, while piles of bodies rotted in the villages. Through execution or starvation the Nationalists wiped out countless fellow-Chinese. In October 1934 the Communist remnant of some 90,000 to 100,000 broke out to the west and, scattering to escape Chiang's planes, set forth on the Long March through China's outback. After 5,000 miles and a year's duration, the trek brought them to a new revolutionary base in northern Shensi. They had been uprooted but not exterminated and the problem remained.

In December 1934 Japan gave notice of intention to terminate her adherence to the Washington Naval Treaty when it should come up for renewal two years hence. Under the constant pressure of the militarists' demand for naval parity and an end to the yoke of 5-5-3, the last treaty tie with the West was now severed.

On board ship for China in June 1935 Stilwell drew up his estimate of the situation under the title "Future Developments in China." Revealing how closely he had been studying events, it was an analysis of sound strategic and political judgment. He recognized that Japan's goal was to be "the major power in the Far East" with control of eastern Siberia, Manchuria, Korea, China, Formosa, the Philippines and Netherlands East Indies. Because of the development of air power, Japan would endeavor to make her home islands invulnerable against Russia by "pushing her front out to the Gobi desert and make Russia operate from the other side." This required gradual encroachment on and control of Inner Mongolia and north China, which was already evident in the "demilitarizing," that is the substituting of Japanese for Chinese force, of the Peiping-Tientsin area. The program would be extended in the northern provinces until Japan arrived at complete control north of the Yangtze with all the commerce of north China in her hands, leaving Shanghai to the "so-called Nationalists."

"Is there any possibility that this encroachment will be stopped? No, not by the Chinese," Stilwell wrote. Now was the vital time to resist, otherwise it would be too late, but Chiang Kai-shek showed no signs of being willing to risk an open break with Japan. "He knows that he would be defeated which would mean that revolt would break out behind him. Therefore he will sit tight, hold on to what he can and count on foreign influence to help him retain Shanghai where so much foreign business centers."

All of Japan's acts in China, Stilwell believed, were premised on the necessity of creating a "solid western frontier" against Russia. North China, he assumed, would be lost to the Chinese. The foreign powers would do nothing more than "fuss and fume," the United States "would do nothing more than write notes," and "a fait accompli will again be accepted." Japan would not be seriously opposed by China or by the world at large.

Stilwell's final comment showed him possessed of that unusual talent— the capacity to understand a historical process while it was happening. "Paradoxically," he wrote, "each successful encroachment will be accepted more and more as inevitable and the foreign powers will be less and less inclined to call a halt." This was a classic definition of the appeasement era before history gave it a name.

7

MILITARY ATTACHÉ:
China's Last Chance,
1935-37

W HEN Stilwell, promoted to full colonel, came back to Peiping on July 7, 1935, the future of China, the expansion of Japan, the implications for the United States, were spread before him to study as military observer. The capabilities and intentions of the host country are the military attaché's subject. He serves as an intelligence officer whose function it is to keep his War Department informed of factors and developments of military significance. His sources are official and unofficial: inspection of troops, attendance at field exercises, contact with the right people and cultivation of foreign colleagues, study of the press, reports of private agents, and general circulation with open eyes and ears. Ordinarily, the aspect of his task most seriously pursued by the military attaché is the social, on the theory that parties are work. But society was not Stilwell's forte; he avoided the Peking Club and was not felt to be "one of us" by its frequenters. But he was agreeable to a Chinese aristocrat like Mme. Dan, a Manchu princess, former lady-in-waiting to the Empress Dowager, and one of the most distinguished and educated women of the old nobility, who was often entertained by the Stilwells. He cultivated other Chinese acquaintances as diverse as Chiang Monlin, Chancellor of Peking University, and Jade Joe, a dealer in art objects. As Attaché he lived in a 100-year-old house built for a Viceroy of Canton with many courts and lacquered pillars. He commissioned a Chinese painting for one wall of the drawing room, enlarged his collection of ivory fan handles, purchased

Mongolian saddle blankets, a magnificent robe of the Empress Dowager and other treasures.

The charm of life in China that for many Westerners counterbalanced the filth, the cruelty, the indifference to misery and disregard for human life was the quality of her people. It was also true that foreigners, including missionaries, enjoyed China because they lived better, with more status, servants and comfort than at home. But for people like Stilwell the added attraction was to be in contact with a highly civilized society. The Chinese had innate dignity and self-respect, humor, stamina, quickness of mind and lovely women with exquisite figures. Stilwell's Assistant Military Attaché, Captain David D. Barrett, the most accomplished linguist among the American military, considered the Chinese "the smartest, in many ways the most civilized, in general the most charming (especially when they want to be) and certainly on the average the best looking people in the world."

If they seemed deficient in what Westerners call loyalty, indulged in official corruption as a matter of course, did not stress honesty among their virtues, were sometimes arrogant and sometimes supersensitive, they made up for it as heirs of an old and sophisticated culture that compelled admiration. Sun Tzu, a fifth century B.C. writer on military theory and practice who anticipated much of Clausewitz and more of Napoleon, could be read by Stilwell and his professional colleagues with profit.

Under Japanese pressure the integrity of north China was crumbling like the sand cliffs of a battered coastline. Since halting their military advance in the Tangku Truce two years before, the Japanese Army had been conducting a campaign of steady intimidation with the object of detaching north China as an "autonomous" state like Manchukuo. On the day before Stilwell arrived, another portion of Chinese sovereignty fell away, in an episode recorded by history as the Ho-Umezu Agreement. On the grounds that China had violated the Tangku Truce by "lack of sincerity" in suppressing anti-Japanese activities, the Kwantung Army presented a set of demands requiring all anti-Japanese officials to be removed, puppet officials substituted and the remaining Nationalist troops in Hopei withdrawn. General Ho Ying-chin, the Generalissimo's deputy in Peiping, signed the conditions. Bitterness accumulated against Chiang Kai-shek. The fiercely independent ruler of Shantung, General Han Fu-chu, who hated Japan and Chiang Kai-shek equally, refused to allow Nationalist troops withdrawing from Hopei to cross his borders. In Hopei the unhappy local Governor, General Sung Che-yuan, loyal to his country but required to collaborate with its invaders, was left to maintain the fiction of Chinese sovereignty under daily humiliations at the hands of the Japanese.

Lieutenant Colonel Stilwell, as military attaché in Peiping in 1935 (86), lived with his family in a hundred-year-old house with many courts, as seen in the painting by his daughter Alison (87) and in the photograph of the gateman sweeping the snow (89). In 1936 the Stilwells, six visiting relatives and fifteen servants posed for this group portrait (88).

86

87

88

89

Kuan Hsien-sheng had been one of Stilwell's teachers at the language school he attended in 1920 (90 When the family returned to China in 1926, Stilwell brought Kuan to Tientsin as a private tutor an majordomo of the household servants. He resumed this post in 1935 when the Stilwells came back t Peiping. Here he reads to Ben.

For the past two years Japan had been exerting every form of political and economic pressure to force Nanking into a "rapprochement," meaning in effect submission to Japanese penetration and control. China's withdrawal from the League was demanded, her efforts to obtain loans or other help from the West frustrated. She was to be cut off from outside assistance. Convinced of China's military and industrial inferiority vis-à-vis Japan, Chiang Kai-shek believed he had no choice but to follow a policy of compliance and conciliation while hoping for time to bring a change of fortune. But time was running the other way. With Fascism on the rise in Europe and isolationism in the United States, neither Britain nor America was in a mood to court trouble with Japan by overt help to China. In March 1935 Hitler, having previously withdrawn Germany from the League, repudiated the Versailles Treaty and declared Germany's intention to rearm. In May Italy attacked Ethiopia. In America, following public shock at the Nye Committee's disclosures on the relation of the sale of arms to involvement in war, Congress was drafting neutrality legislation against aid to belligerents.

With the Japanese military pervading north China, strutting the streets, knocking Chinese out of their way with blows of their rifle butts, dictating to puppet governors and officials, summoning press conferences and issuing fire-eating statements about Japan's "divine mission" to lead the peoples of Asia, the daily reality of China's subjugation was more apparent in Peiping than in Nanking. Although branch offices of the foreign missions had been opened in Nanking under consuls and chargés, the diplomatic corps was not eager to uproot itself and move down to the muddy city on the Yangtze where it rained all year, new premises would be hard to find and the permanence of the Government was dubious. Owning property in the Legation Quarter of Peiping, comfortable in their clubs and summer homes in the Western Hills, the foreign missions preferred to stay in the Imperial City where life was still pleasant even as its end visibly approached.

Nanking had not been used as a capital for hundreds of years and was inhabited by "those nasty Yangtze Valley people," as Stilwell called them, who compared unfavorably with the agreeable northerners. Among residents of Peiping it was an article of faith that the farther south, the worse the inhabitants. The Kuomintang, however, pressed hard for transfer of the Legations as evidence of foreign recognition of its stability, and this much courtesy after eight years could not be indefinitely withheld. With reluctant feet the official transfer was to be accomplished in 1936. American Legation quarters in Peiping became a Consulate-General with some of the diplomatic staff remaining, including, happily for Stilwell, the Military Attaché. Given the trend of events, it was considered advisable to keep a military watch on north China.

In 1935 the only encouragement Britain and America could offer Nanking was to raise their Legations to Embassies so as not to be outranked by the Japanese who had already made the change. In September, shortly after Stilwell arrived, the American Minister Nelson T. Johnson, accompanied by his staff, presented his credentials as Ambassador in a formal ceremony in the capital. A group photograph which recorded the occasion shows Stilwell in dazzling whites and decorations looking the outward perfection of a suave attaché.

In the following month he thoroughly enjoyed the part on a visit to Siam to which he was accredited along with China. His predecessors had not troubled to visit the exotic little kingdom which owed its independence, unique in Southeast Asia, to the fact that British and French imperialisms advancing from opposite directions had met there and, after lopping off border provinces suitable to each, had allowed the kingdom to stand as a convenient buffer. Stilwell traveled on the U.S.S. *Augusta*, flagship of the Asiatic Squadron, which was making an official visit. To his surprise he enjoyed his contact with the Navy. "Everybody treats me as if I were visiting royalty instead of a damn Army passenger," he wrote to Win. Bangkok, being something of a diplomatic backwater, outdid itself to entertain the party from the *Augusta*. Between banquets and parties and royal receptions, Stilwell managed to inspect Infantry, Cavalry and Air Defense regiments and file an exhaustive report on the training, composition and defenses of the Siamese Army.

By the time he returned to Peiping in November, a new move by the Japanese brought the situation in north China once more to a crisis. Determined to accomplish the separation of the five northern provinces (Hopei, Chahar, Suiyuan, Shansi and Shantung), the Japanese had massed troops north of the demilitarized zone in ostentatious menace and were bringing extreme pressure on General Sung Che-yuan to declare the region's independence of Nanking. A large man of Shantung peasant stock, with the calm impressive face of a Buddha usually adorned by a fat cigar, Sung had been approved by the Japanese as chairman of the Hopei-Chahar Political Council because they thought they could manage him. He was in fact his own man who, when Japanese bribes and lures or threats became importunate, would retire to his native village to perform the customary duty of sweeping the tombs of his ancestors. Nominally he commanded the 29th Army of four divisions or more than 60,000 men, but under Japanese terms he could keep only 10,000 stationed in northern Hopei. Under the renewed pressure in November, he bent and twisted, never quite yielding, hoping for a decision from Nanking to resist. With reason to believe that the Japanese Government was again divided on how far to support the Army's action, Chiang Kai-shek stalled.

Anxiety about the Generalissimo's intentions was rising. Some argued that he would not risk direct confrontation with the Japanese, others that at some point he would turn and retreat no more, if only because driven by popular insistence. "This is a time for fighting," T. V. Soong said to the *Times* correspondent, Hallett Abend. "If we do not resist now our chance may be lost for good and all. Even a defeat, after all, is something. It is better to fight and to lose than to give up everything without a struggle." This was a romantic Western notion which had no appeal for Chiang Kai-shek. Although Chiang and Soong shared, according to Ambassador Johnson, the "only backbone" left in the Government, they worked at cross-purposes. American policy depended on which purpose won.

The view of China received by Washington from its observers in the Embassy and the many consular outposts was pessimistic. Since 1934 their reports had expressed increasing discouragement in the Kuomintang as the force for unifying and reforming China. One ardent Chinese shared the disillusionment. The Kuomintang, said Hu Shih to an American friend, "is dead but not buried and all unburied things cause trouble for the living." The Kuomintang had never succeeded in filling the centralizing function of the throne. Nor was it only the monarchy that had disappeared, but also its instrument of government, the Imperial Civil Service, leaving no adequate replacement. Meanwhile Kuomintang leadership had deteriorated and the regime had hardened in the authoritarian and military stage with no progress toward the promised second and third stages of people's welfare and democracy. China was still a country where half the people died before reaching the age of thirty, where 75 percent of deaths were due to preventable diseases mostly filth-borne, where a peasant could be subjected to 44 different taxes—often collected years, even decades, in advance—on everything from his land to his bedding and kettle and for everything from eleven varieties of military aid to nine varieties of public expense. When this did not suffice, a "temporary expenses tax" or an "extraordinary tax" was thrown in. As always, "Old Hundred Names" paid for the Government, whether of Emperor, warlords or Kuomintang. Chiang Kai-shek spent 80 percent of this revenue on military establishment.

Efforts of university faculties and cooperatives and reformers to improve and modernize, to abolish illegal taxes and help the peasantry to buy back lost land were valiant but frustrated by the impassive rigor of the old ways. Administration continued corrupt and inefficient. Since 1927 the province of Hupeh had suffered five changes of governor and Anhwei six, with bureau chiefs, district magistrates and all local functionaries replaced at each change because of the patronage involved and because the Central Government used these posts as rewards for favors or for loyalty. Gossip of corruption in high places was a frequent theme of foreign service reports to Washington. While her husband was Minister of Finance, Mme. H. H. Kung was "credited with receiving a moderate but invariable commission on all purchases of military planes." She and her sister, Mme. Chiang Kai-shek, were whispered to have manipulated Government bonds and raked in huge profits from speculation in silver in the course of currency measures put through by Dr. Kung. Ambassador Johnson considered that Dr. Kung and his brother-in-law T. V. Soong could not give "unbiased consideration" to China's problems because of their various personal financial interests.

Ambassador Johnson (who as chief of mission was officially Stilwell's superior), though he had lost his original faith in the Kuomintang, still believed in Chiang Kai-shek as the only ruler who could hold China together. A stout middle-class man of forty-eight with a large, plump face, thinning hair and a rather Germanic if good-natured appearance, he had begun his career in China as a language student in 1907, and had served as Consul in cities from Hankow to Chungking. From the consular service he had risen to become chief of the Far East division of the State Department in 1925-29 and as such had opposed the urging of Minister Mac-Murray for intervention against the Nationalists in 1927. Succeeded at the Far East desk by Stanley Hornbeck who was to be autocrat of the Far East desk for the next 15 years, Johnson returned to China as Minister in 1929, the first Chinese-speaking envoy to occupy the post in many years. He possessed a wide if not profound knowledge of China, was not pretentious and did not give white-tie dinners nor frequent the social fleshpots of Peiping. Johnson had adopted as his motto the Taoist saying *Wu Wei Erh Wu Pu Wei,* meaning "Through not doing, all things are done." In fine calligraphy adorning the wall of whatever office he occupied, it suited his temperament.

As a result of the "panic and fear" instilled by the Kwantung Army in Chinese leaders, Johnson reported, "every bit of leadership that was openly hostile to Japan has been eliminated from north China," and according to all reports "the Government at Nanking has been reduced to a jelly." Japan's smuggling campaign, aimed at destroying China's economy and cutting off her revenue from customs, was intensifying. Bales and ship-loads of cotton goods, rayon, sugar, kerosene, cigarets and other manu-factures were smuggled in by armed truck from Manchuria and the seaports. Local officials were bought or bullied into connivance. An enor-mous business in heroin and morphine was conducted through the Japanese

Concession in Tientsin. The attack upon the Chinese Customs, Johnson wrote in 1936, "has been as cold-blooded an act by one country against another as any I have read of and I have no doubt that it will succeed." From Embassy Counselor Willys Peck in Nanking, who had been in China since 1907, came equally gloomy reports. In the midst of a routine report on the difficulties of reconstruction in China, he suddenly erupted, " 'Too late, too late, the Captain cried!' " Washington was hearing little to encourage a policy of active support for China.

When in November 1935 the Japanese issued their ultimatum for the separation of north China, Johnson predicted they could succeed, unless China by gathering resistance "forces them to use force," thus presenting the world, especially the League and the United States, with a very "embarrassing" situation.

The Roosevelt Administration was doing its best to avoid being thus embarrassed. The President in his first term was absorbed in domestic struggle with no mind to challenge his country's strong distaste for entanglement in other people's troubles. What concern for foreign affairs could be spared was concentrated on the Good Neighbor policy with Latin America. Stimson's effort had produced only a negative result; without helping China it had antagonized Japan, and his successors felt no disposition to repeat the exercise. The new Administration's policy concentrated less on curbing Japan than on keeping out of conflict with her. The British, too, favored discretion. Facing enough trouble in Europe, they did not want another area of conflict in the Far East.

Yet there were hostages: the Philippines, Hong Kong, commercial interests—and the moral issue, both as regards traditional support for China and collective security against aggression. The Western powers were not ready to be pushed out of the Far East nor to make up their minds to abandon China. Up to this time it had been a principle that China's independence was essential to the Open Door. But various efforts made by the powers to shore up her independence by loans and credits and other forms of collective aid provoked such Japanese roars that they were abandoned. Persistent efforts of the American Secretary of the Treasury, Henry Morgenthau, to arrange financial help also came to nothing. Motivated by a certain degree of American guilt because of the Senate's unfortunate silver purchase policy which had disrupted China's silver-standard currency, Morgenthau's crusade foundered in the soggy ground of China's unmanageable finances.

To keep China independent, much less strong, was becoming difficult and, in view of the Japanese hostility it provoked, dangerous. Under the influence of the growing pessimism about China's capacity to control her own destiny, some policy-makers were beginning to wonder whether the effort was worth it, whether China's integrity was really necessary to foreign commerce on the mainland, whether one might not, after all, do business with Japan. Why activate Japan's enmity by helping China if China could not or would not help herself? Now that evidence for the negative was desirable, it was discovered that the original rationale for the Open Door—the supposed enormous opportunity for American commerce —had proved a mirage. Neither the Far East as a whole, nor China in particular, had fulfilled the exuberant predictions of the imperialists of 1900. Of America's total foreign investments in 1935, the Far East represented 6 percent and China 1 percent. Of America's total foreign trade in the years 1931-35, China's share was under 4 percent of the total. With her famed 400,000,000 customers, China took a share of American trade and investments ranging from a third to a half of the share that Japan took with a population of 70,000,000.

Britain with a large and real stake in the Far East was beginning to question whether Chinese weakness did not pose a greater threat to her interests than Japanese expansion. Failing a China strong enough to maintain sovereignty, the vacuum would have to be filled by some authority for the sake of peace in the Far East. Considering the dangers of the present situation, suggested Sir Alexander Cadogan, the British Ambassador, to Ambassador Johnson, "perhaps the only solution lay in allowing Japan a free hand in Asia." But it was difficult, he admitted, "to prepare to retreat before this advance."

In Washington the dominant factor determining policy was fear of provoking Japan to war which, in the fanatical state of Japanese nationalism, as Ambassador Joseph Grew repeatedly warned, was entirely possible. Inaction became the guiding principle. When Japanese penetration of north China continued without overt military act, the United States kept quiet in the hope, constantly nourished by the Japanese moderates, that the Japanese militarists if not antagonized would gradually recede. Throughout the 1930s, wrote Secretary Hull, "Japanese diplomats always took care to represent to us that there were two elements in Japan: one liberal, peaceful and civilian; the other military and expansionist. . . . If we did not irritate the military by denying them the right to expand in the Far East, the peaceful element could eventually gain control of the Government and ensure peace. It was therefore up to us to prevent the worst from happening in Japan."

Alarmed at American quiescence, China made anxious inquiries, even suggesting that she might be forced into alliance with Japan. Her hint evoked no reaction. Secretary Hull was determined to nudge relations with Japan onto a less dangerous footing. In a statement to the press on Far

Eastern policy in December 1935, he tiptoed around the issues in a manner so exceedingly nonprovocative as almost to assure Japan of noninterference.

The act that twisted the course of events came from the people of China, or a vocal segment of them in Peiping. The arrogant Japanese presence in north China had brought into being the one thing that could frustrate the Japanese plan—an active nationalism. Nanking's effort to censor and repress its overt expression only increased the seething beneath the lid. When the Japanese ultimatum demanding the declaration of an "autonomous" north China by December 10 was made public by desperate Chinese officials, the demand for resistance broke into the open, given voice by a massive student protest on December 7 in Peiping. Watching crowds applauded, then joined the march, defying the police; even rickshaw coolies shouted the forbidden patriotic slogans. The demonstrations spread to other cities; a second and third were held in Peiping and Tientsin with tens of thousands of participants. Petitions poured in on Nanking. Students commandeered trains on the Shanghai-Nanking run and exhorted people along the way to compel the Government to stand firm against Japan. A National Salvation League was organized and over the next months 30 groups and associations for patriotic defense and a "people's front" or "united front" against Japan were formed.

Communist agents and propaganda helped the growth of the movement. A "united front" against Fascism was by now official policy of the Comintern, proclaimed at its 7th Congress in July-August 1935. For Russia the revival of a militant Germany on her western front combined with a militant Japan at her back on the mainland of Asia had become the dominant fact of life. A Russo-Japanese conflict was widely expected.

Throughout all the adventuring of the Kwantung Army on the northern mainland, from the Manchurian crisis on, observers were never sure whether Japan intended to pursue a course leading to a clash with Russia or continue the effort to swallow China. Since the Kwantung Army and militarists of Tokyo were themselves of two minds, either was always a possibility. It was in Russia's interest to deflect the Japanese southward where they would be absorbed in the quicksand of endless struggle with the Chinese. Arousing anti-Japanese sentiment and stimulating China's will to resist thus became a Communist interest. The Chinese Communists advocated resistance not simply as tools of the Comintern but in their own interest because if Chiang Kai-shek were forced to take up arms against Japan, he would be required to leave off his relentless campaign against themselves. Besides, they recognized, as an axiom of history if not of Marx, that national war has a wider appeal than class war and that the patriotic cause gave them a channel to the people of the north.

As Johnson had predicted, the development of national resistance was the factor that would force the Japanese to use force, again "embarrassing" the world. After the December demonstrations the clamor could not be ignored and a Japanese-prompted declaration of "independence" by north China could hardly appear to be self-determination. It was called off and the Japanese had to content themselves momentarily with establishing a Hopei-Chahar Political Council as their base of control. Hereafter all anti-Japanese activity was denounced as Communist; Japan became the champion of anti-Communism in Asia and endeavored to press Chiang Kai-shek into an anti-Communist alliance. This had its attractions for many Chinese no less than coming to terms with Hitler had its charms for the right wing in England and France. But Chiang Kai-shek could not come to terms with Japan, as he well knew, without risking national leadership. To do so would give the Communists and his many other rivals a rallying cry against him. Already the Li-Pai group in the south was using the demand for action against Japan as cover for another attempt to oust him.

Chiang kept his balance by continuing privately to talk of armed resistance without actually undertaking action except against the Communists. Not to be diverted from pursuing their annihilation, he arrested and imprisoned the leaders of anti-Japanese sentiment and suppressed the National Salvation League. As against the invaders his policy was to postpone the problem as long as possible. Though afraid of the Japanese, he and his countrymen never ceased to think of them as a temporary curse whom the Chinese by virtue of superior wisdom, not to mention numbers, would outlast. Chiang had no thought of giving in to them but on the contrary was already promoting development in Szechwan with the intention, if too strongly pressed, to entrench his Government in its remote city, Chungking.

In the hope that America could be prodded into assistance sooner rather than later, Chiang sent word to Ambassador Johnson that his policy was to "continue" armed resistance to Japan. It was important for the United States to know how realistic was this intention and what was the likelihood of being "embarrassed" by active Chinese resistance. In so far as military preparedness would supply a clue, it was the military attaché's function to find the answer.

As in the past, Stilwell undertook to see for himself on a series of journeys that ranged from south China to Manchuria. The first one in April 1936 to Canton and the Kwangsi-Kwangtung region where the rebellion of Generals Li and Pai was simmering was not definitive. He traveled not by the direct rail route but through the interior by bus, car, riverboat, ferry and foot. After a 30-mile hike from one remote country town to the next on the way to Kweilin, an acquaintance wrote, "You are probably the only one in the American Embassy who ever travelled over that part of the country." In a third-class train with 125 people in one car he not surprisingly concluded that "the people of South China are terrible and there are too many of them." From Canton, where he inspected the officers' training school, he went on by riverboat to Wuchow and from there by local bus to Nanning where he visited Li Tsung-jen, co-leader of the separatist faction. On the way north, in Hankow, he made the acquaintance of the American Consul Robert Jarvis who "seems to have brains, thus standing out in Hankow."

From Hankow he took the train back to Peiping. The taste of coffee at breakfast in the dining car, like Proust's *madeleine,* took him back in memory to his first arrival in Peking in 1920—"the cool crisp days of fall with a breeze in the trees and the sun still strong, good breathing air, the newness of everything. The kids were little and we had a lot yet in front of us. Not so good now. . . . What made up that feeling? The newness of things? . . . No worries; promise of strange and interesting things to come. The kids were little. Plenty of TIME in front. . . ." When he wrote this passage with its poignant phrase, "Not so good now" and its curious premonition of too little time, Stilwell was fifty-three with but ten years to live.

It was on his second trip in June that he found the evidence to answer the question whether the Government was preparing for serious military resistance. The answer was no. Setting out to estimate Chiang Kai-shek's plan from the disposition of his forces north of the Yangtze, Stilwell traveled over the east-west Lunghai line from Hsuchow, which he found "booming" in contrast to 1927. He went west to Kaifeng and Loyang through northern Honan—"flat, dirty, dusty, sandy"—and after returning to Hsuchow traveled north by freighter on the Grand Canal. After locating and identifying army units he was able to report, "No evidence of planned defense against further Japanese encroachment. No troop increase or even thought of it. No drilling or maneuvering." Either the Chinese had made military preparations and "concealed them more skilfully than any other military power has yet learned to do or they have made none at all." A copy of his report, in addition to its regular routing to MID, was sent by Johnson to the Secretary of State.

From the deployment of troops Stilwell formed a low opinion (expressed in his private notes) of Chiang Kai-shek's generalship. "He can have no intention of doing a thing or else he is utterly ignorant of what it means to get ready for a fight with a first class power. . . . If he intends to fight along the Lunghai line he's either a goddamned fool for not getting ready or else he's a g-d fool to think he can jump in and hold off after the show starts." Judging from the inactivity, "it looks as if the Japs had told him they wouldn't go any further just now." But for the future, if

Chiang hoped to hold the Lunghai line, he should be improving his line of communications: "Do something to the railroads. Build feeders to the south. A motor road net back of the railroad. Nothing is being done."

Instead, he noted disgustedly, "Chiang goes around getting up new clubs for this and that. 'Don't spit on the floor. Don't squeeze.' " Like most Westerners, Stilwell was exasperated by the slogans of the New Life movement launched by Chiang Kai-shek in 1934 to take people's minds off Japan. Directed toward the improvement of behavior, manners, social service, cleanliness, honesty and the elimination of opium smoking and graft, it represented the Confucian pursuit of "right conduct," and as such it had meaning for some Chinese. To the Western mind not native to the phenomenon, admonitions against spitting and noisy eating and exhortations to "Be prompt," "Correct your posture," "Kill rats and flies" seemed frivolous at a time when something more was needed to meet the national peril.

According to Stilwell's estimates of China's military forces, listed by province and broken down into corps and divisions with names of commanders, places of headquarters, and varying numerical strengths of the units, the Central Government had under arms in August 1936 a total of 1,300,000 troops plus another 360,000 under provincial control, exclusive of irregulars. Under the guidance of General von Falkenhausen who had replaced General Hans von Seeckt as his military adviser, Chiang was working hard to train and equip an effective army. Thirty German instructors now staffed Whampoa Academy in place of the one-time Russians, and the purchase of German arms was arranged through their connections. Yet without a real change in the political system, there was no way of welding the Chinese forces into a national army. Chiang Kai-shek's authority, like that of Europe's medieval kings, rested on the more or less voluntary fealty of provincial barons. As to reform at the base, in the conditions of life from which the common soldier came and would be asked to fight for, little was attempted. Chiang was not an activist possessed of compelling energy to overturn the old. He changed nothing. He was a holder with no goal but to hold.

"Unfortunately for China," as Stilwell had written in a G-2 report the year before, "there is no other influential leader in sight . . . who can take his place and carry on with anything like the prestige he has gained." The lack of alternative leadership was a weakness, he noted, "common to all dictatorships."

Stilwell continued his researches on two trips to Nanking in July and September where he inspected the Infantry and Artillery Schools and made the acquaintance of various Chinese officials including General Ho Ying-chin who was to be his bane in later years. He began collecting information on the Communist Fourth Army and on Chang Hsueh-liang's Tungpei Army of Manchurian divisions now based at Sian. According to informants, the Young Marshal had cut out opium but "does nothing with his troops. Just flies around in his private plane."*

Nanking held no charms. "What would I do if ordered to Nanking?" Stilwell asked himself and wrote down as a preferable alternative, "Go home and retire." Even Peiping's charm was fading under the deep Japanese inroads suffered since the establishment of the East Hopei Political Council. On the north field of the Legation Quarter Japanese infantry and cavalry engaged in daily exercises to the accompaniment of shrill bugling. Japanese officials in cars bearing the flag of the Rising Sun sped through the streets. Japanese officers rode about on horses invariably too large for them which they could not mount without assistance; in case of need orderlies trotted along behind on foot. Japanese businessmen and other civilians filled the hotels, opened their own cafes and brothels, played on the golf courses. Groups of Japanese schoolchildren on conducted tours of Manchukuo and north China visited the Temple of Heaven and Summer Palace. Stilwell, needless to say, resented them as did every other devotee of China, but with his extra supply of animus, a little more so. During his trip through Honan he had encountered some Japanese being hazed by the local police and recorded, "I enjoyed that and egged them on."

In this state of mind a tour through Manchukuo required a certain self-restraint. He interviewed the Vice-Minister for Foreign Affairs of the "autonomous" state who turned out, by no great surprise, to be Mr. Ohashi, a Japanese. "We are all that stands between Russia and her goal of the sovietization of Asia," this official announced. In reply to Stilwell's questions Mr. Ohashi said that "of course the Russians intend to expand further" in the Far East and that the situation was "extremely critical for Japan." If Manchukuo and Japan were defeated, China would fall an easy victim; therefore Japan faced a "terrible crisis" which must be decided within the next five years one way or another. The date was then September 1936. Stilwell's report to MID on the interview was widely circulated within the Government.

In October Chiang Kai-shek was assembling his forces for a sixth and

---

* Known as the Flying Palace, this was a twin-engine monoplane, silver outside, lined with red plush inside, equipped with two full-length sofas, an ornate writing desk, upholstered chairs, radio and icebox. Though he employed an American pilot, Royal Leonard, Chang often piloted the plane himself, with his long robe tucked up around his knees and his purple Moslem bell-boy cap awry on his head. On inspection flights over his domain, he communicated with his troops by dropping messages to which they replied by spreading out cloth panels on the ground, or failing these, by throwing themselves on the ground in the proper arrangements.

final extermination campaign against the Communists during which he hoped Japan could be kept quiet by the good offices of Britain and the United States. The United States was asked by the Chinese to urge a policy of moderation on Japan, but was not anxious to interfere. When the Chinese Ambassador called to inquire what would be the American attitude in the event of a clash, Secretary Hull could only reply that "our country is of course intensely interested in peace" and that "we earnestly hope no clash will occur."

Stilwell too was prodded. A Chinese colonel came to him with a proposal from his superiors for an "understanding" between the United States and China to stop Japan, to be followed by the establishment of a mixed Sino-American General Staff in Washington to devise military plans. "America can stop Japan if she takes action," Stilwell was told, but if she failed to act Japan would gain control of China's resources to America's detriment. Stilwell commented in his report, "It looks like another manifestation of the Chinese desire to get somebody else to do something they are afraid to do themselves," and he added shrewdly, "possibly an intimation that they have no intention of offering resistance unassisted."

He too had been struck by the Taoist motto on the virtues of inaction which he had copied down from an example in the Great Audience Hall of the Forbidden City. Only the first two characters for *Wu Wei,* or "Do nothing," were given there, leaving the Chinese viewer to add mentally, "and all things will be done." Deciding that "Do nothing" exemplified the Chinese character, Stilwell concluded, "They are constitutionally averse to influencing events." Though there were increasing exceptions to this proposition, his finding represented a fact of life in the Orient that made for infinite impatience among Westerners, as Kipling noted when he wrote the epitaph, "A fool lies here who tried to hustle the East." By contrast, Europeans and their American descendants had been driven by the impulse to change the unsatisfactory, to act, to move away from oppression, to find the frontier, to cross the sea. They were optimists who believed in the efficacy of action. The people of China, on the other hand, had stayed in one place, enclosed by a series of walls, around house and village or city. Tied to the soil, living under the authority of the family, growing their food among the graves of their ancestors, they were perpetuators of a system in which harmony was more important than struggle.

The international horizon was darkening in 1936, with Fascism emboldened and the democracies infirm. In February extremist Japanese officers attempted a *coup d'état* by multiple murder of elder statesmen which, though it failed, had a subduing effect on opponents of militarism. In March Hitler occupied the Rhineland unopposed. In May Mussolini annexed Ethiopia; the League's empty sanctions against Italy were called off and the British fleet, not to be provocative, withdrew from the eastern Mediterranean. Chiang was not the only one who failed to resist. At Geneva a small lonely cloaked figure, the exiled Haile Selassie, in a last appeal to the powers to come to his support, warned, ". . . and if they do not come, the West will perish." In July rebellion of the right, supported by the dictators, brought civil war to Spain. Here resistance, abetted by the Communists, began. The passion of the world's anti-Fascists focused on Spain, the "united front" became an active force, and though the democracies behind a screen of "nonintervention" tried not to look, sides were being drawn for the coming struggle. This was clear enough to Japan which in November joined Germany in the Anti-Comintern Pact.

In China the Communists appeared to be bearing the torch of resistance. They made a notable impression by launching an offensive in Shansi in 1936, ostensibly against the Japanese, but actually to reconnoiter base areas, recruit peasants and collect grain and money. Their military engagements took place chiefly against the local forces of Yen Hsi-shan, but their propaganda for patriotic resistance to Japan, combined with some shooting of landlords and tax collectors, aroused wide enthusiasm in the region.

Stilwell went to Taiyuan and Fenchow in northern Shansi early in March to investigate this adventure and concluded that despite its slogans of "Down with Yen Hsi-shan" and "Down with Japan," the Communists had been motivated by food shortage in Shensi and had "no definite goal beyond the search for new areas where they can subsist." In his G-2 report he pointed out that the penetration had been made easy by the poor performance of Yen Hsi-shan's troops. One brigade took no part in trying to prevent the crossing into Shansi "because it was not in their sector." Another was ambushed by the Reds "as a result of a telephone communication from the Fenchow garrison commander who thought he was talking to his own troops." "If China's armed forces are to be judged on the basis of performance, it is idle even to speak of resisting Japan."

The Communists nevertheless augmented their propaganda campaign for resistance. In August they issued an open letter to the Kuomintang expressing their willingness to join forces in an All-Chinese Democratic Republic for resistance to the invader. Since a genuine coalition of implacable enemies was not a real possibility, their ulterior object was to push Chiang Kai-shek into open conflict with Japan.

"What carries the Communists?" Stilwell asked himself in an undated note. "Some moral support there. What is it?" The question is followed by a tantalizing suggestion, "How about a letter to Ho Lung asking him?" Ho Lung was commander of the Communist Second Red Army who had operated in the Hupeh-Honan border region from 1928 until November

1935 when he set out with his troops on the Long March a year after the
main group. When or where Stilwell made his acquaintance or how he
proposed to get a letter to him is not mentioned in his papers.

"They have good intelligence work," his notes continued, "good organization, good tactics. They do not want the cities. Content to rough it in the
country. Poorly armed and equipped, yet scare the Government to death."
These were the factors, in visible contrast to the decline of the Kuomintang, which impressed foreign observers. Stilwell had been learning what
he could about the Communists for some time and evidently sharing his
information with fellow attachés. A note from the British Embassy in
February 1936 thanked him for "a most interesting brochure on the
Chinese Communist situation."

Familiar with the plight of the Chinese peasant and unfamiliar with
Marxism, Stilwell regarded the Communists as a local phenomenon and
a natural outcome of oppression. "Carrying their burdens of famine and
drought, heavy rent and interest, squeeze by middlemen, absentee land-
lordism," he wrote of the farmers, "naturally they agitated for a readjustment of land ownership and this made them communists—at least that is
the label put on them. Their leaders adopted the methods and slogans of
communism but what they were really after was land ownership under
reasonable conditions. It is not in the nature of Chinese to be communists."

This analysis was a normal one of the time. Foreigners who would have
considered Communists at home a vicious menace looked on them locally
as an indigenous product of the ancient wrongs of China and as reformers
who were trying to do something about it; "not Communists at all," as
Consul Jarvis said to Stilwell. *The Shanghai Evening Post and Mercury,*
organ of the American business community, which at home would have
taken the view of the Chamber of Commerce, declared that the Chinese
Communists had some "very intelligent notions . . . not primarily communist at all but open to anyone." In short, they were practicing obvious
measures of reform. Their military organization and treatment of enlisted
men in contrast to the usual Chinese habit impressed Colonel George A.
Lynch, commander of the 15th Infantry during Stilwell's tenure as Attaché
and a fellow West Pointer. Observing them in Kiangsi in 1932 when he was
traveling in China on leave from the Philippines, he found they did not
press-gang soldiers, did pay them and did not let them prey on the
civilian population. "This procedure presents a very strong contrast to that
of the territory under the control of the Nanking Government," he reported
to MID. As a result, desertions from the Kuomintang forces to the Communists were numerous.

Two years later Arthur Ringwalt, American Vice-Consul in Yunnanfu,
describing what he saw of the Long March as its units passed through the

southwest, wrote of the strong morale and "almost fanatical unity of purpose" exhibited by the Communists. Though poorly equipped, underfed and worn out by years of fighting, they were led by men seasoned in hardship and as a group showed "a dedication and disinterestedness not seen in a large body of forces in China since the Taipings."

The foreign public knew almost nothing of the Communists. It was thus a sensation—and an unpleasant one in Nanking—when in November 1936 the *China Weekly Review* published a sympathetic series of interviews with Communist leaders and an eyewitness report of their substate at Yenan in Shensi by the first foreign journalist to have visited them, Edgar Snow. Reprinted widely both in China and abroad, published in book form as *Red Star Over China,* Snow's account gave the world its first news of the heroic Long March and the first pictures of Communist personalities, way of life, beliefs and intentions. He made the most of their espousal of the anti-Japanese cause, which in the climate of the 1930s, when people felt fiercely about the fight against Fascism, exercised a strong appeal and overshadowed their Marxism.

As Mao Tse-tung explained it in his interview with Snow, the defeat of Japan took precedence over social revolution because it was necessary first to defeat foreign imperialism and win independence; only then could the struggle for socialism succeed. For that reason he was willing to join forces with the Kuomintang against the imperialist enemy. Mao was very convincing. "For a people being deprived of its freedom, the revolutionary task is not immediate Socialism but the struggle for independence. We cannot even discuss Communism if we are robbed of a country in which to practice it." He stated frankly that the defeat of Japanese imperialism in China would hasten the victory of world socialism by destroying one of imperialism's most powerful bases. "If China wins its independence the world revolution will progress very rapidly."

Other American journalists followed Snow to Yenan and found their simple-living hosts attractive. Sharing the work of the soil, earnest in talk, brave in experience, they appeared in refreshing contrast to the faded promise of the Kuomintang. Since they seemed to put revolution second the foreign journalists gave it scant attention; "Communism" appeared, as it had to Stilwell, just a label.

In December 1936 Chiang Kai-shek went up to Sian to unloose the sixth anti-Communist offensive, and stepped into the most bizarre experience ever to befall a modern chief of state. He was kidnapped by Chang Hsueh-liang, intended commander of the offensive, in an endeavor to persuade him to abandon the civil war and agree to the united front against Japan. The Young Marshal's troops, exiles from their Manchurian homeland, were not anxious to fight the Communists. With tanks, bombers and

No authentic photographs exist of the Long March undertaken through China's outback by some 90,000 Chinese Communists in 1934 to escape the Nationalist forces. These pictures of Chiachin Mountain (91) and the caves in Yenan (93) show part of the terrain they were forced to cross and their final destination. The Chinese Communist Army had tried to draft everyone, even thirteen-year-old boys (92). Its leaders, Mao Tsetung and Chu Teh, are photographed in Yenan after the incredible 5,000-mile trek (94).

92

93

94

95

In December 1936 Chiang Kai-shek was kidnapped by Chang Hsueh-liang. Before Stilwell and other foreign military attachés could intervene, the "Young Marshal," on Chiang's right, released Chiang and flew him to Loyang, to everyone's relief (95).

ten divisions mobilized, Chiang had come to insist that they take the field. The drastic kidnapping followed, appalling China and astounding the world.

Chiang's death was momentarily expected, not the least by himself, and indeed advocated by some of the Young Marshal's associates. What saved him was that he was necessary. All at once men in Sian, in Yenan, in frightened Nanking, above all in Moscow, saw the same prospect—chaos in China if Chiang were eliminated, with extended civil war and no gainer but Japan. Before his kidnapping Chiang was neither popular with the public nor enthusiastically admired by his supporters but he was the repository of the habit of obedience to the head of the family, and the sense of security under that authority which in the political life of China is transferred to the head of state. There was no one of enough stature to succeed him and no party that could have held office for more than three months. If the civil war was to be stopped and the country's united energies turned against Japan, only Chiang could do it. Ironically the Communists, who joined in the negotiations that followed the kidnapping, became the instrument of his survival, less through their own volition than because Moscow insisted on it. Acting in their national interest the Russians preferred Chiang Kai-shek to chaos in China with its resulting advantage to Japan.

While Chiang's fate was still uncertain, the foreign military attachés were ordered to Loyang, nearest Nationalist base to Sian, which was in the hands of the rebels. Though less crucially concerned than Russia, the Western powers too feared chaos in China and hoped the attachés by their presence might exert some pressure for Chiang's release. The trip proved superfluous. Stilwell reached Loyang on Christmas Day just as the Generalissimo, followed to the world's astonishment by his erstwhile captor, flew in by plane. News of the release brought wide popular demonstrations of joy and relief. Chiang Kai-shek's prestige was enhanced and Chang Hsueh-liang was placed under house arrest which was to last, in greater or lesser degree of surveillance, from that day to the present.*

Although every effort was made for the sake of face to avoid giving the impression that Chiang had entered into any bargain for his release, in fact he had agreed to call off the sixth extermination campaign and arrange some form of nominal coalition against Japan with the Communists, who in turn agreed to desist from war on landlords and submit their armed forces to Nationalist command. Intricate negotiations on conditions were conducted during the following months with neither side having reason to

---

* He lives in Taiwan and is seen from time to time on Sundays in the same church attended by the Generalissimo.

trust the other and with neither having abandoned the goal of the other's ultimate destruction. The Kuomintang understood well enough that the Communists wanted active battle against Japan as a stage on the way to their own victory and were consequently determined not to be drawn so deeply into resistance as to play their opponent's game. Chiang Kai-shek's aim was still to avoid and postpone outright conflict with Japan until the foreign powers should become involved and bring him enough help to defeat Japanese and Communists both, leaving him at last a clear and independent victor.

The West was impressed by the evidence of national unity and joint effort after Sian. Communist divisions were formed into the 8th Route Army under the authority of Nanking and maintained offices and even published a newspaper in the capital. To Washington it appeared from the reports of Ambassador Johnson and others that real change, real effort to democratize the regime, real cohesion, might at last be under way.

The Japanese too saw a signal in the outcome of Sian. They recognized that the Chinese were developing that sense of national unity which as their Minister of War, General Sugiyama, put it in May 1937, could "obstruct Japan's peaceful advance at its very foundation." The Kwantung Army and militarists in Tokyo began to press for direct action.

Stilwell was not overimpressed by the facade of reconciliation after Sian. "The present talk of democracy in China is glib and meaningless," he wrote in an estimate of the Sino-Japanese situation early in 1937. He expected the Government would "follow a policy of delay, insisting that they are preparing to fight but with no intention of doing so. They hope to have their problems solved by someone else." China's deficiencies were so great that outside help appeared to be the only solution. Vis-à-vis Japan, he wrote, China's only assets were "numbers, hate and a big country. She has neither leaders, morale, cohesion, munitions nor coordinated training." Furthermore, in a war Japan could blockade her ports.

But Stilwell knew too Chinese native capacity which made him believe in the Chinese potential. In studies of the Taiping invasions of the north in 1853-55 and of the campaign of the Imperial General Tso Tsung-t'ang to suppress Moslem rebellion in Chinese Turkestan in the 1870s, he found a "lesson for those who believe that the Chinese have degenerated beyond hope." To anyone who doubted Chinese military ability, Tso's campaign, "one of the most remarkable in history," offered proof to the contrary. Combining "caution with daring" and "initiative with perseverance," Tso had shown "a complete grasp of the situation," executed well-planned actions with "prompt and vigorous pursuit," and found solutions that might have baffled more celebrated leaders. Giving credit to the soldiers as well as their commander (not a habit of military historians), Stilwell

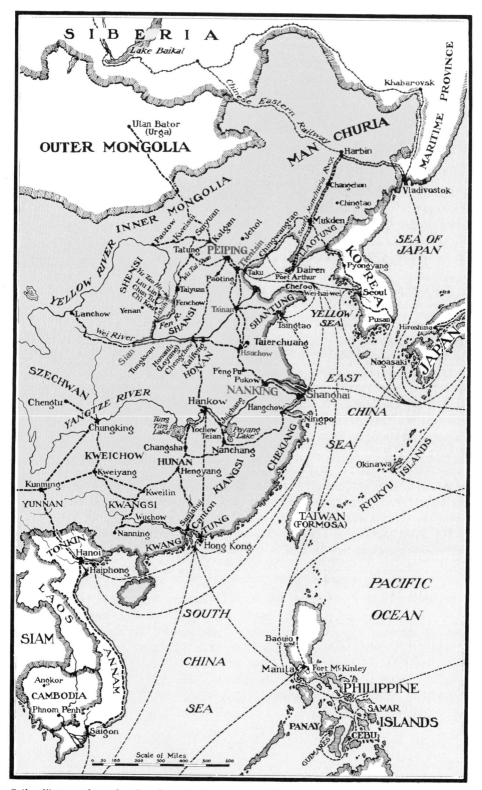

Stilwell's travels on land and sea in the 1920s and 30s

found it difficult to overrate the Chinese troops and their leader "for this brilliant piece of work." These studies clearly helped to shape the convictions he brought to his future role in China.

He felt the outlook for China was black and in June was glad to get away on a trip to Suiyuan and Mongolia with his friend Colonel Sabatier, the French Military Attaché. He expected to go to Wu Tai Shan and walk from there to the railroad, a distance of about 150 miles, he wrote to Win.

His reputation as an expert was growing. Colonel Lynch, on returning to Washington from the 15th Infantry, reported that Stilwell "knows China and the Far East better, in my opinion, than any other officer in the service." His explorations through the country "have given him a background that no one else possesses."

In June 1937 Stilwell, with his companion Gus Soderborn, was entertained in a Mongol yurt near Pailing Nuai (96).

8

MILITARY ATTACHÉ:
Sino-Japanese War, 1937-39

O N a lantern-lit Chinese barge poled by boatmen over the dark Pei
Hai Lake in the Imperial City, a party from the American Embassy
enjoyed a serene excursion under a full moon on the evening of
July 7, 1937. In the group were Colonel and Mrs. Stilwell and their
daughter Nance, Ambassador and Mrs. Johnson, Colonel John Marston,
commander of the Marine Embassy Guard, and his wife, and Stilwell's
friend John Goette. The Ambassador had brought his guitar and played
his favorite song, "Down That Weary Road," as the boatmen paced
rhythmically up and down the side of the deck. Light from the boat's
lanterns glimmered in the water, and lit by the moon the softly gleaming
white marble tower of the Dagoba rose out of the darkness like the vision
of a Buddhist Grail. The party felt themselves surrounded by the spirit
of ancient Peking until reality glided by in another boat carrying a group
of Japanese officers.

Colonel Marston mentioned that as senior officer of the foreign detachments he had been notified by the Japanese that their troops would be
leaving the city that evening for night maneuvers at the railroad bridge
at Lukouchiao, twelve miles to the west on the Peking-Hankow line. The
Japanese had been holding maneuvers in the area for two weeks, causing
worried speculation in the local press. The railway was the only remaining
access to Peiping not under Japanese control and Lukouchiao was a key
junction where a shuttle connected with the railway to Tientsin. Alongside

the railroad bridge, a stone bridge 800 years old with parapets adorned by marble lions spanned the river on 30 graceful arches. One of China's most beautiful monuments, admired by the first Westerner who crossed it in the thirteenth century, it was known in his honor as the Marco Polo Bridge.

At 8 o'clock on the morning after the boat ride Stilwell's office learned there had been a skirmish at the bridge. The Japanese, claiming to have been fired on by troops of Sung Che-yuan's 29th Army garrisoned at nearby Wanping,* were now besieging Wanping with mortar and artillery fire to enforce surrender of the officers they charged were guilty. On Stilwell's orders the Assistant Attaché, Major Barrett, drove out with Goette to investigate. The scene was quiet with only an occasional rifle shot disturbing the calm of a beautiful summer morning, but they found cause for disquiet in the body of a dead Japanese soldier guarded by a platoon. Realizing that this would be made the pretext for extreme Japanese demands, they knew they stood in the presence of an Incident. It proved to be the start of the war.

The Chinese garrison commander had refused the Japanese terms and for the moment was holding a parley. By the time Barrett returned to the office, Stilwell was already receiving reports of Kwantung Army units moving in strength through the Great Wall. Despite the show of negotiations at Wanping, he and Barrett agreed that the Japanese were opening their definitive move to take over north China. The atmosphere in Peiping was tense; no one knew if there was real purpose behind the skirmish or what Chiang Kai-shek would do. Stilwell drove out to Wanping on the third day to try to make contact with the Chinese garrison but as he crossed the last 500 yards both sides opened heavy fire. The driver turned the car around without stopping and "we got out on two wheels."

Reports reaching his office indicated 10,000 Japanese troops were crossing the Wall into Hopei; troop trains were passing through Shanhaikuan at half-hour intervals. To report on the situation as it developed he organized an intelligence network of the five senior language officers who served under his command as assistant attachés and whom he stationed in various cities. Four of the group had already served with the 15th Infantry and two, Captain Frank Roberts and Captain Frank Dorn, were in later years to serve under Stilwell again in the Far East. His son Joe Jr., then in Tientsin with the 15th Infantry, was also enlisted as an informant, as were journalists, consuls, Standard Oil men and whoever was in a position to extract evidence from the fog of rumor. The larger outlines of what was happening could only be estimated by putting together

* See map on page 64.

the hard details: the number of Japanese planes in the air over Tientsin, the frequency of rail and truck movements of Japanese men and matériel, the location of Chinese units and—most elusive—any evidence of Chinese troop concentration or other clues to the Government's intentions.

Stilwell adopted the unorthodox practice for a military attaché of keeping a file of his radios to G-2 on the table in his office for journalists to consult. His object, he told Barrett, was to make available as much accurate information as possible "so that the world would get a true picture of Japanese aggression as it developed south of the Wall." Identifying with China he felt deeply the crisis that gripped her.

The silence from Nanking was not promising. Chiang Kai-shek was not even in the capital as far as anyone knew. The Japanese had issued an ultimatum that was to expire on July 18. Chiang Kai-shek spoke at last, from Kuling, a mountain summer resort where foreigners and upper-class Chinese, carried up by sedan chair, escaped the sickening summer heat of the Yangtze valley. Without voicing a call to action or precluding a settlement, Chiang declared that no further positions in north China could be surrendered and that a settlement with Japan must not invade sovereign rights or territorial integrity. It was a statement that China's limit of endurance had been reached and that she was accepting the necessity of armed resistance. When Chiang's words were broadcast in Peiping, bugles sounded and gongs clanged as excited people filled the streets.

A few days of enthusiasm were all they were to have for the Government had made no plan or preparations for the event of national resistance and the Japanese took over control of Peiping within the week. Stilwell's temper mounted at their charges of Chinese provocation, claims of "self-defense," acts of brutality and at his own country's lack of response. When Secretary Hull held a press conference without taking a position Stilwell commented, "Mr. Hull again says we are against fighting. That ought to stop it quickly."

Alone, without his family who had gone to the coast to see the two older daughters off to America and remained at the seashore at Chinwangtao until mid-August, his mood was low. "The atmosphere is sad and gloomy," he wrote to Win, "and there is a pall over everything. Jesus, to think that the blow has actually fallen already is enough to make you sick physically. . . . This may be the end of this chapter or only a lull before a bad storm—no way of telling yet. In any case, North China is gone."

Sporadic fighting continued outside Peiping although General Sung Che-yuan's intentions were uncertain and there were rumors that he had "gone over." On July 29 Japanese planes bombed Tientsin concentrating on Nankai University. For four hours their squadrons, taking off in relays from an airfield three miles outside the city, "systematically and unhurriedly" rained incendiary bombs on the university buildings which, as Japanese Headquarters informed the press, had to be wiped out because they harbored "anti-Japanese elements," namely the students. They were the most potent agitators of nationalist sentiment. The bombing was designed to destroy the students' base of operations so that they could not mobilize demonstrations or print propaganda leaflets. Throughout their campaign in China, as formerly in Korea, the Japanese intentionally attacked places of education as the source of national consciousness.

On the road to the Temple of Heaven, the Japanese ambushed a Chinese unit, leaving 500 to 600 bodies on the ground, mostly unarmed and many blown to pieces, minus heads, arms and legs. Going out with Barrett to investigate Stilwell saw 30 truckloads of soldiers killed to the last man with parts of bodies plastered against the sides of the trucks and drivers dead at the wheels. Villagers said the Japanese had offered to let the troops surrender if they gave up their arms, and when they emerged from the village, mowed them down with machine guns and grenades. Dead horses were bloated in the hot July sun and dead men lay in the ditches, "one with his eyes wide open and flies walking on them."

At Tungchow, site of the Hopei-Chahar puppet government, the local constabulary, believing rumors of Chinese "victories" around Peiping, mutinied, massacred Japanese and puppet officials and attempted to hold the garrison. The attempt was smashed when Japanese reinforcements wiped them out and laid the city in ruins.

Within four days all Chinese troops were withdrawn from the Peiping-Tientsin area leaving the Japanese in control. The lack of a concerted policy or plan of defense and the vain sacrifice of the men at Lukouchiao and Tungchow enraged Stilwell. The Chinese had missed so many good opportunities that "you can't help getting thoroughly disgusted with them." They could not have defeated the Japanese, he wrote, but they could have inflicted heavy losses if action had been coordinated and the order to attack ever given.

Though late, the Central Government was pulling together the forces for defense. Imprisoned leaders of the National Salvation League were released and the ban on resistance songs and slogans lifted. Now they were sung openly in the streets and broadcast officially on the radio. From the south Pai Ch'ung-hsi flew to Nanking to pledge the services of the Kwangsi-Kwangtung group after eight years of opposition. To consolidate the alliance he was appointed Chiang Kai-shek's Chief of Staff. Provincial warlords of Yunnan and Szechwan rallied to the Government. By the end of August all military forces including the Communists—reorganized as the 8th Route Army—were incorporated in and supposedly responsible to the central command.

106

The start of the Sino-Japanese War, 1937: Chinese commander of Wanping locking city gate after skirmish at Marco Polo Bridge (97); Stilwell later at same gate (99). Chiang deliberately precipitated battle in Shanghai to induce foreign intervention, which did not come despite signs of American presence such as the flag floating near Chinese defense line in Chapei (98). A huge flag was used to identify a boat taking American refugees out of Shanghai (101), but despite flags painted on its decks the Japanese bombed and sank the U.S.S. Panay (102–105). Japanese marines took many prisoners (100), and crowds of Chinese fled to the International Settlement (106).

103　　　　　　　　　　　　*104*　　　　　　　　　　　　*105*

A first small but heartening victory which aroused Stilwell's interest was won at Pinghsingkwan in the mountains of north Shansi by a division of the 8th Route Army commanded by Lin Piao. Using mobile guerilla tactics from village bases with the support of a friendly population, the division attacked the Japanese at a pass in the Great Wall and wiped out a brigade, capturing its headquarters and provisions. Though only a temporary check, it suggested that the Communists had developed methods worth investigating, and several months later Stilwell spent half a day analyzing the battle of Pinghsingkwan with Agnes Smedley, a free-lance correspondent who had spent months with the Communists in the north.

On September 24 the Japanese took Paoting, Sung Che-yuan's headquarters on the Peking-Hankow Railway. The fever of savagery bred by their own campaigns burst out in a week's rampage of murder, rape and pillage by 30,000 soldiers. A self-defeating ferocity accompanied them like a hyena of conquest, growing more ravenous by what it fed on. The Japanese knew that a hostile China must ultimately defeat their aim to become leader of Asia. Throughout their years on the mainland nothing so maddened them as the constant reappearance of "anti-Japanese" sentiment. Annually they insisted on the necessity of forcing China to be "sincerely" cooperative. Intending to attach China, they found themselves forced to conquer, arousing increasing hatred with each advance and employing increasing brutality in response. At Paoting in addition to physical terrorism they burned all the schoolbooks in week-long bonfires as well as the library and laboratory equipment of the Hopei Medical College. A decade's records of crop statistics at the Agriculture Institute, the basis of its program for improved farming methods, were also deliberately destroyed.

In mid-August the still undeclared war entered the Yangtze valley, but not by Japanese design. When the campaign opened at Marco Polo Bridge, the Japanese had intended to finish off the separation of north China in a campaign of perhaps 90 days. They believed the Nanking Government would helplessly acquiesce as before, or, through extension of Japan's control over cities, industries and communications, could be forced to give up and cooperate as a puppet regime. Chiang Kai-shek deliberately precipitated battle in Shanghai, supposedly to harden nationwide resistance by drawing the Japanese down to the heart of China, more likely in pursuit of the strategy he never gave up—to engage foreign intervention. From first to last Chiang Kai-shek had one purpose: to destroy the Communists and wait for foreign help to defeat the Japanese. He believed battle at Shanghai, the international city with its large foreign investments, would lead to mediation and possibly even intervention by Britain and the United States and other powers.

He sent his best German-trained divisions from Nanking down to Chapei on the borders of Shanghai where, he may have considered, any fighting would be likely to produce an incident involving foreigners or foreign property. The Japanese had a marine garrison in the International Settlement and had filled the river with their warships whose menacing naval guns were intended not to fire but to overawe, while in the meantime the Kwantung Army fastened its hold upon the north. But the challenge of the Chinese advance on Shanghai provoked the bursting sense of mastery of the Japanese. They landed troops and extended their lines with intention to disperse the Chinese, and suddenly found themselves thrown back under ardent attack. From then on a battle of suspense and tragedy was fought out under the eyes of the foreign bystanders. In the first week the vigor of the Chinese assault drove the Japanese almost to the river's edge. With the advantage of naval guns and command of the air, the Japanese were able to reinforce and counterattack and eventually to land forces to outflank the Chinese position. Under incessant bombing by the enemy's Formosa-based planes and the shelling by warships in the Whangpoo, the Chinese held their lines for three desperate months in the most visible and publicized and important battle the world had seen since the smashing of the Hindenburg Line in 1918.

The flames and gunsmoke that enveloped Shanghai drew world attention if not help. Commanded by Chang Fa-kwei, leader of the famed Ironsides Army of 1927, the Chinese demonstrated a will to fight both to their countrymen and to the world. At a terrible cost in casualties, greater than any since Verdun and the Somme, they were kept in position against the urgent advice of Pai Ch'ung-hsi and others long after that position was hopeless. Chiang Kai-shek had no other military plan at Shanghai than that of the death stand, but he was playing for world opinion. For prolonging the defense he was to be bitterly condemned and never forgiven by many Chinese. Tenacity was his governing characteristic and he may have believed that the agony of the defenders must finally move the foreign powers.

Toward the end, under attack by Japanese divebombers and field guns fired at a range of 60 yards, the Chinese lines were collapsing from exhaustion, starvation and losses. The last few days of the defense added nothing and wrecked the army. By the time the order for withdrawal was given, Japanese reinforcements had landed down the coast to outflank the line of retreat. Under enemy fire "the tragedy of the retreat," in the words of a Chinese commander, "was beyond description." Sixty percent of the force was lost including 10 percent of the entire trained officer corps.

The defense of Shanghai made the world China-conscious. One of the most memorable war pictures ever published humanized the war for Amer-

"One of the most memorable war pictures ever published humanized the war for Amer

ans" (107). A crying baby sits in ruins of bombed North Station, Shanghai, 1937.

icans in the figure of a crying baby sitting on tracks in the middle of a blasted emptied street in the wake of an explosion. Journalists flocking to the drama and richly nourished twice daily at Chinese Government press conferences reported tales of heroism, blood and suffering. China was seen as fighting democracy's battle and personified by the steadfast Generalissimo and his marvelously attractive, American-educated, unafraid wife. In their image Americans saw China strong in will and united in purpose. Once firmly fixed, this impression was unaffected by the military blunder of the withdrawal from Shanghai, or by the fiasco of the Air Force, which, after trying vainly for weeks to hit the Japanese warships in the Whangpoo, by mistake loosed bombs that caused 2,000 casualties including 900 dead among their own people and hit the U.S. liner *President Hoover*.

Beyond Shanghai, 200 miles up the river, was Nanking. Drawn in more deeply than they had planned, and sensing the growing danger of becoming overextended, the Japanese determined to end the adventure at the capital. Their statements on the necessity of "subduing completely China's will to fight" took on a frenzied tone. The Nanking Government, having "embarked on an anti-Japanese campaign of the most vicious kind," Premier Hirota told the Diet, must be "compelled to mend its ways" and to "act in unison for enduring peace in East Asia through sincere cooperation between Japan and China." Air raids on Nanking, Canton and 20 cities of east China followed, "in order to conclude hostilities as soon as possible," according to the Japanese announcement. Chiang Kai-shek, still unswerving, chose to defend Nanking in a decision that was militarily indefensible since equal time could have been bought, tremendous sacrifice spared and a firmer stand made behind Nanking than in it. Again his purpose was to engage world attention and possibly foreign involvement because of the presence in Nanking of the Embassies.

In Peiping where streamers from Japanese balloons floated overhead announcing the capture of Chinese cities along with the legend, "The Japanese Army Preserves the Peace of East Asia," Stilwell faced the professional necessity of getting on with north China's new masters. To have to ask their permission to visit the front was almost too much for his temperament. "Arrangements generally seemed to go wrong when he was with them," sighed his friend Goette. To improve the situation Stilwell asked for a Japanese-speaking assistant and was lent one of the language officers from Tokyo, Captain Maxwell Taylor, a Leavenworth graduate then thirty-six who 20 years later was to be United States Chief of Staff. Warned that he would find his new chief an unusual officer, able but irritable and hard to get along with, Taylor was surprised to find Colonel Stilwell waiting to meet him on his arrival at the railroad station.

Appreciating the courtesy and confounding predictions, he discovered a man he liked. He saw Stilwell as a man of emotion and action rather than reflection, a doer who when he saw something wrong wanted to correct it right away. He thought Stilwell used bad judgment when in a bad temper, but had the soldier's virtues of bravery and determination.

Taylor could act as a buffer and make arrangements if not control results. Conducted by a Japanese colonel on a tour of Kalgan after its capture, Stilwell confessed to having been thrown out of General Suzuki's office for asking embarrassing questions. He steeled himself to the necessity of professional relations, but after a call on General Takashita, Win recorded, Joe was "quite ready to retire today and go to Carmel." Peiping under the control of the "arrogant little bastards" was hard to bear. They buzzed the American Embassy in planes at 150 feet "to show us what they think of us." They forced students to march in parades "celebrating" the fall of Paoting so that the Japanese could take pictures of the enthusiastic support of the population. "They are more insufferable than ever and I have to deal with them and smile." Duty required that he persist even to the point, persuaded by Taylor, of giving a lunch for five Japanese officers. Two accepted the invitation but failed to appear, one neither replied nor came and of the remaining two Stilwell's only comment was, "The hell with them!"

Humiliation, imposed by Washington's anxiety to avoid trouble, was shared by others. Colonel Alexander McAndrews of the 15th Infantry, citing his instructions from the War Department—"Nothing should be done to involve us in a quarrel"—told Stilwell apologetically that he felt required to call off G-2 observation of Japanese troop movements because of a Japanese vice-consul's veiled threat.

Since the Chinese preferred their war to be observed through the medium of official communiqués, Stilwell could not get to the front with them or with the Japanese and his repeated "blasts" to Washington to exert pressure brought no results. He had to make do with a Japanese-conducted tour of Paoting where his hosts, according to their own statement, had killed 25,800 Chinese in the course of taking the city. Stilwell could find no damage to the walls or other evidence to indicate that the Chinese had put up a strong, or any, defense. Annoyed at being kept from the active front 50 miles away, he considered himself "practically in arrest the whole time and told them I realized it." Not surprisingly he was informed three days later, when another tour was arranged for the foreign attachés, that he was not to be included, "so I guess I am washed up for this war. I am spotted as a friend of the Chinese and a moral leper." He felt let down, too, and unreasonably nagged by MID, "the pack of fools in Washington" with whom his relations were to grow steadily worse in the coming months.

Taken altogether, he wrote to his two oldest daughters then in America, "I have released enough bile since July 8 to float a battleship."

At the end of August he noted, in sad epitome of China's fate, "a nice crop of radishes" on the grave of thirty Chinese soldiers killed in a last skirmish four weeks before. Every day groups of foreign families departed while amahs stood weeping, husbands wiped tears from their eyes and the band helpfully played "Auld Lang Syne." The State Department, nervous lest some accident to its nationals involve America in the conflict, was encouraging departures. So many left, including Ambassador Johnson's wife and children, that Win found herself the ranking American lady in Peiping. On September 7 a Presidential order required all American civilians to leave and at the same time State and Navy ordered out their families but the War Department "hasn't put its finger on us." Stilwell's family, later rejoined by the two daughters from America, remained in China until the end of his tour.

Although China's leaders exasperated him, Stilwell understood that "their moral standards are totally different from ours, therefore their moral strength is not sapped by what to us would be gross national cowardice. . . . Where we would fight to the last man over an invasion of our territory, they are concerned with the continuance of the race, and to keep Chinese coming into the world they will accept temporarily any form of government they have to. Under it the main stream flows on." Even so, Stilwell would become exasperated and allow himself tirades about China's "oily politicians . . . treacherous quitters, selfish, conscienceless, unprincipled crooks." Asked by G-2 after the fall of Paoting when the Chinese would stand and fight, he radioed in reply, "Not until they lose their inherent distaste for offensive combat."

He considered Chinese military weakness to be the result of reliance on winning by outlasting. And the Chinese tradition which puts the local interest ahead of the interest of the whole could be seen operating in one of the gravest of military faults—mentioned in reports from the Shanghai front—the failure of flank units to come to the aid of another unit under attack. The low quality of the professional officer corps on the whole was equally serious. "The educated Chinese is astounded to be told that the Chinese officer is no good," Stilwell wrote. They readily understood his explanations of the value of initiative, selection of point of attack, concentration of means, and then their question became, "Can we produce officers in five years? So I tell them two generations might do it."

Yet he had confidence in Chinese soldiers as fighting material and believed that if properly led they could become the equal of any army in the world. Hardy and uncomplaining, accustomed to long hours, scanty food, hard work, sickness and wounds and no pleasures, yet able to "make a joke of the merest trifle and remain cheerful under the most discouraging circumstances," the Chinese soldier with officers in whom he had confidence "will go anywhere." Regarding Japanese culture as artificial and imitative, Stilwell had more confidence in China, especially in the north Chinese. He discussed his theories with Captain Taylor while out on field excursions to identify Japanese troop units. Walking through villages he would pick a piece of fruit, wipe it with a handkerchief and eat it, to the horror of his companion who felt obliged to do likewise. Once, resting beneath the statue of a Buddha after a long day without finding any clues, they looked up to find that three Japanese soldiers had scratched their names *and* units on the statue's behind.

They watched endlessly for troop trains. Sitting on a hilltop one day they saw in the distance a slowly moving elongated object with legs like a centipede's. It proved to be a train of freight cars being pushed on each side by a company of Chinese soldiers. Contemplating its snail-paced progress in silence for a while, Stilwell said, "That's the spirit that will conquer Japan in the end." But he was inclined to be caustic when the Generalissimo gave an interview calling on the signatories of the Nine-Power Treaty to come to the aid of China. "CKS screams, 'We are fighting the battle of the world. Intervene for Christ's sake!' " was Stilwell's version.

For those who saw Western democracy threatened by the rise of Fascism, intervention to halt the aggressors was the central problem of the time. The Isaiah of this view was ex-Secretary Stimson who spoke out against "amoral drift" and tried to persuade the President of the need for more outspoken guidance of public opinion.

President Roosevelt, though starting out as a supporter of Stimson's Far Eastern policy, had since then acquiesced in, without actively initiating, the American withdrawal from involvement in China. His chief concern with the Far East, after naval limitations came to an end in 1936, was concentrated on building up the Navy. In March of 1936 at the London Naval Conference, convened to discuss renewal of the Washington Treaty, the United States and Great Britain refused to accord parity to Japan, upon which Japan bolted the Conference, and the Treaty, already moribund, expired for good. Given Japan's fanatic mood, Ambassador Grew urged, and Roosevelt and Hull accepted, the necessity of building a navy "so strong that no other country will think seriously of attacking us." But accomplishment was far off and appropriations for a major building program were not voted until 1938. In the meantime the primary object of American policy in the months after Marco Polo Bridge was to keep out of conflict with Japan.

Beneath the official surface the sounds of history were stirring the President and activating in him the ideas that were to shape American policy over the next eight years. Roosevelt was more concerned with the threat of Japan than with the integrity of China per se, although he loved to dwell on the Delano family's connections with the China trade and tell stories of their dealings with Chinese merchants and dignitaries. His mother's father, Warren Delano, had been a partner in the leading American trading firm, Russell & Company, founded in 1824, soon as affluent and influential as the East India Company with branches in all the Treaty Ports where its partners acted as American consuls. They sailed the fastest clippers, sometimes beat the British to London with the first tea of the season, built the first telegraph line in China, set up the first steamship line to run regularly up the Yangtze and dealt in opium as well as in tea and silks. Sara Delano, Roosevelt's mother, lived for several periods during her girlhood at the family home, Rose Hill, in Hong Kong. Her two oldest sisters were born there and married partners of Russell & Company, and one of them, Mrs. W. H. Forbes, continued to make her home at Rose Hill for 35 years.

At Hyde Park Roosevelt was brought up among Chinese furnishings, among them a large blue and white porcelain garden pot in the library which according to family tradition had been used at Rose Hill for bathing the children. A bronze Chinese bell used as a dinner gong had been acquired by Roosevelt's grandfather from two coolies who were carrying it away from the sack at Soochow in 1863. Roosevelt's stamp collection was founded on Chinese and Hong Kong issues given to him by his mother when he was ten. Defending his support of the Stimson Doctrine in 1933, Roosevelt told Raymond Moley that because his ancestors had traded with the Chinese he had always had the deepest sympathy with the Chinese people and did not see how anyone could expect him not to support China against Japan. This was ingenuous; Roosevelt was a Stimson supporter because he was of like mind, not because of his ancestors. After his election in 1932 he conferred with Stimson on Far Eastern policy and on taking office announced his intention to adhere to the policy of nonrecognition.

Privately he told Stimson that he had been profoundly impressed by the seizure of Manchuria because of his recollection of a Japanese fellow-student at Harvard in 1902 who had told him of Japan's schedule, drawn up in 1889, for a 100-year program of expansion in twelve steps. Beginning with a war in China and absorption of Korea, it was to proceed to war with Russia, annexation of Manchuria, then of Jehol, then a protectorate over north China from the Wall to the Yangtze, ultimately acquisition of Australia, New Zealand and the islands of the Pacific including Hawaii, and culmination in a protectorate over all the yellow races. In the stages already carried out the President saw ominous implications.

In the years after Manchuria Roosevelt became "even more incensed" by Japan's conduct, according to Sumner Welles, his closest adviser on foreign policy, and by 1937 was "far more preoccupied" with the threat of Japan than with the threat of Germany. He kept trying to think of ways to halt Japan's advance. After the attack at Marco Polo Bridge he asked the Navy for some large-scale maps of the Pacific which he placed on a stand in his office, and discussed with Welles the possibility of placing an embargo on Japanese trade to be enforced by units of the American and British fleets. Deprived of access to raw materials, Japan would be forced to pull back and would not, he believed, be provoked to war because she was so heavily committed in China. But in the isolationist state of public opinion, the President realized, a measure involving risk of war would not be permitted by Congress.

With his penchant for private informants Roosevelt was receiving news of China from one of the most romantic American observers ever to report from that country—Marine Captain Evans F. Carlson, the Assistant Naval Attaché. Later famous as leader of Carlson's Raiders, a battalion he formed using methods and the motto *Gung-ho* (work together) learned from the Chinese Communists, Carlson was a sincere man of intense convictions and courageous enterprise. He was an American Candide who was able to believe that "mutual confidence obtained between the Generalissimo and the leaders of China's Communist Party" because "both had the welfare of China at heart." Interpreting everything he met in terms of the ideals he was brought up with, he saw both Chiang and the Communists "aiming for representative government." He could not present a lily without gilding it. Mme. Chiang radiated not only the "consciousness of being an instrument of destiny" but also "the mature graciousness of an inward peace."

The son of a Congregationalist minister, Carlson had begun his military career as an enlisted man, and served with the Marines in China under General Smedley Butler in 1927-29, and again at Shanghai and Peiping in 1933-35 when he undertook the study of the language. Roosevelt met and formed a warm attachment to him beginning in 1935 when Carlson commanded the Marine guard at the President's retreat at Warm Springs. He was included on friendly and intimate terms in the Warm Springs circle and on leaving for China in June 1937 was urged by the President to write to the White House. He arrived in mid-August at Shanghai where American interests during the battle were directed by a triumvirate of Admiral Harry E. Yarnell, commander of the Asiatic Fleet, Consul-General Clarence Gauss and Colonel F. B. Price of the Marines who met every morning in Gauss' office. Reporting these dramatic and tragic days in weekly letters, Carlson wrote vividly of the Chinese soldiers whom he observed directly at the front. Never had he known a time "when all prominent Chinese were working together in a common cause," even the "so-called Communists."

The President was so interested that during a month-long hiatus in the correspondence in October he made inquiries of Carlson's whereabouts. "My Chief loves your letters," Missy LeHand wrote, and "asks me to tell you please keep it up."

At the end of November 1937 Carlson took off for Yenan in Shensi to find out how real were the legends of the Communists' guerilla warfare against the Japanese. As evidence he sent the President captured Japanese documents, a diary and a fur-lined uniform. Later when he came inevitably to write a book his point of view appeared in the title he gave to his chapter on Yenan, "China's Fountainhead of Liberalism." His views, expressed more floridly in the book than to the President, typified one kind of American approach to China. He had undertaken the journey, he told the Governor of Shensi, "From the heart . . . in the name of liberty." In his own country people regarded liberty and equality as "inalienable rights" and he had observed "this same love of liberty and equality" in China, "the same spirit which had animated our own ancestors at Lexington, Trenton and Valley Forge." This was China filtered through the rhetoric of the American dream, not necessarily the most appropriate framework for policy in Asia.

Although he had invoked the Neutrality Act prohibiting trade with belligerents in regard to the civil war in Spain, Roosevelt chose not to apply it in the case of Japan and China because it would have worked to the advantage of the aggressor and disadvantage of the victim. Shipment of arms under the American flag to China or Japan was banned, but not the sale. In exercising the discretion allowed him by the Act, Roosevelt had begun to move ahead of prevailing isolationist sentiment. Of 2,000 letters received by the White House and State Department in one week of September 1937, mostly instigated by peace societies, 95 percent demanded that the United States remain at peace, 80 percent were in favor of peace at all costs, 70 percent urged immediate application of the Neutrality Act and only 15 percent were opposed on the ground that it would benefit Japan to the detriment of China.

Worried by the trend the President determined on a speech emphasizing international cooperation. At Chicago on October 5 Roosevelt suggested a collective "quarantine" of the forces breeding "international anarchy" whom he likened to the carriers of a disease. The result was a historic boomerang. Declaring that the President was "pointing" the people down the road to war, six major pacifist organizations launched a joint campaign for 25 million signatures to "Keep America Out of War." The A. F. of L. disapproved the speech, Representative Fish proposed the President's impeachment and a poll of Congress showed two to one against joining the League of Nations in collective action in the Far East. "It's a terrible thing," the President said to a friend, "to look over your shoulder when you are trying to lead—and find no one there."

The United States in consequence drew back from leadership of the Nine-Power Conference which convened in Brussels on October 6 in an effort to resolve the Sino-Japanese conflict. Since Japan rejected in advance any third-party mediation and since economic sanctions depended on common action and mutual guarantees by the Nine Powers in which the United States, among others, was unwilling to join, the Conference disbanded without result. To people who felt a desperate sense of the need to resist aggression, the time seemed under a pall. Stimson in a public letter urged a trade embargo of Japan. Despite the Neutrality Act, he wrote, the United States was not bound to "a passive and shameful acquiescence in the wrong that is now being done." The crucial question of the era was presenting itself again: when does resistance to wrong become a national interest?

In China the Government, followed by the diplomatic corps, withdrew from Nanking to Hankow 400 miles up the river where Stilwell came in the first week of December 1937. With the rail routes from Peiping blocked by the battle front, the journey now took eight days, first by sea around the Shantung peninsula, then via the Lunghai line to Chengchow, then southbound to Hankow. Already "quite fed up with everything and everybody," as Win wrote to her daughters, Stilwell boarded the train at Hsuchow in a swarm of refugees: "13 occupants in 8 seats, didn't dare get up to go to the toilet. Cold . . . no food, no water." After two days and two nights he drank the cold tea from a sleeping passenger's teapot, for the first moisture in 44 hours.

For the next eight months Hankow (or, in its triple character, Wuhan) was the capital of unoccupied China. The Generalissimo had his headquarters across the river in Wuchang on the south bank. In Hankow itself the foreign missions crowded into the Western-style buildings of the Concessions facing the river where the U.S.S. *Luzon,* flagship of the Yangtze patrol, lay at anchor. The city was a chaos of thousands of people rushing around "like ants on a hot rock," in Stilwell's phrase: officials, hangers-on, journalists, profiteers, refugees, welfare committees and all the hectic influx of war. Devotion and energy mixed with laxity and indifference. As always, the uncaring treatment of the common soldier excited Stilwell's wrath. "The wounded left in the north station and everywhere. Not wanted, and they realize it and expect it and pay the price of living by dying. . . . Why didn't CKS organize a medical service or at least a stretcher bearer service?"

A week after Stilwell reached Hankow, on December 13, 1937, Nanking fell in circumstances dreadful even for China. During the time bought in the trenches at Shanghai no preparations for the defense or evacuation of Nanking had been made with the result that losses in men and matériel when the capital fell were enormous. The arsenal was taken intact as was the Red Cross Hospital with all its precious supplies and the wounded in their beds, as well as the rolling stock in the railroad station and vehicles and stores of all kinds. With no defense lines established to cover the withdrawal of soldiers or civilians, the human loss was as great.

Determined to make an example of the capital that would bring the war to an end, the Japanese achieved a climax to the carnage already wrought in the delta below. Fifty thousand soldiers hacked, burned, bayoneted, raped and murdered until they had killed, by hand, according to the evidence witnessed and collected by missionaries and other foreigners of the International Relief Committee, a total of 42,000 civilians in Nanking. Groups of men and women were lined up and machine-gunned or used alive for bayonet practice or tied up, doused with kerosene and set afire while officers looked on. Reports by missionary doctors and others dazed with horror and helplessness filled church publications in America. Much of the photographic evidence that later reached newspapers abroad came from snapshots taken by the Japanese themselves which they gave for developing to ordinary camera shops in Shanghai, whence copies made their way to the correspondents.

In the Yangtze delta whole towns were devastated with acres of houses left in smoldering ruins or in rubble from bombing. In deserted streets the only living creatures were dogs unnaturally fattened by feasting on corpses or a few starving humans wandering like ghosts among the debris. The population that survived disappeared from the area in a mass migration. Rice crops rotted in the fields. Along the roads past blackened ruins and burned-out farms, Japanese troops moved, driving stolen donkeys and water buffaloes, artillery wagons tied with pigs and chickens, and carts loaded with loot pulled by peasants lashed between the shafts.

Not a few Chinese including members of the Government believed peace with Japan preferable to ruin but the majority would not have permitted a surrender or settlement. "CKS can't quit," wrote Stilwell. "Called on the country, it responded. Now he must go on." Japan too had to go on although dangerously extended and with no definite goal in sight. After Nanking, on December 17, Chiang Kai-shek publicly reaffirmed his decision to continue resistance to the utmost by a strategy essentially Chinese. "The time must come," he explained, "when Japan's military strength will be exhausted thus giving China the ultimate victory."

In reply Japan severed relations (up to now maintained), and frustrated and angry, caught in the fatal entanglement of war without limits, drove on, forced to send more and more divisions until their strength on the mainland numbered more than a million. As time went on repeated peace overtures were made to Chiang Kai-shek, first through the German Ambassador in China, later through an American, Dr. John Leighton Stuart, president of Yenching University, but on terms that would have left Japan in control of the country. Whether because he would not or could not, Chiang did not give in. As Ambassador Johnson reported, "The present Chinese Government is in no position to make peace and it is not in a position to make determined war."

On December 12 the event most dreaded by the American Government —an incident involving American bloodshed—occurred. Coinciding with the fall of Nanking, the Japanese in an excess of arrogance bombed and sank the U.S.S. *Panay* a few miles above the capital, causing two deaths and 48 casualties. After the first attack in which the *Panay*'s captain was wounded and the guns put out of action, low-flying planes came back on a second run to bomb the already sinking ship and to damage two Socony tankers and smaller craft alongside, all of which like the *Panay* had American flags painted on their decks and awnings. *Ladybird* and *Bee* of the British Yangtze patrol were also damaged. Japanese shore guns fired on the ships after the planes flew off and Japanese motorboats pursued the escaping crew with machine-gun fire. Because of Washington's anxiety to keep Americans out of trouble, the ships of the Yangtze patrol were being used as bomb shelters for the Embassy staff during the air raids on Nanking, and the Japanese Army and Navy had been supplied with maps showing their exact location and movements. So deliberate was the attack, it could not seem like anything but a direct challenge.

Stilwell's recorded reaction, characteristic of him in fateful moments, was reduced to a minimum: "Panay bombed and sunk yesterday. Great to-do." Almost anything might follow, including war. For the moment Stilwell was beset with anxiety about one of his Assistant Attachés, Captain Roberts, who was on board the *Panay* at the time and, as it later developed, took charge after the disabling of the skipper and led the escape of the crew ashore. By afternoon he learned Roberts was safe and became furious at the Ambassador who had known since morning and had failed to inform him.

Next day tension eased slightly when, as Stilwell put it, "Japs apologize. 'Very sorry for you.' Couldn't see the insignia. The bastards." He did not mention the *Panay* again but it cannot be doubted that the necessary swallowing of this incident by his country added to his black mood at this period.

The *Panay* touched off nothing for when there is no will to war, war does not happen, and neither Japan nor America was ready for confrontation at this time. Alarmed at the wild exploit, the Government in Tokyo apologized promptly and within ten days accepted in full American demands for indemnities. Many Japanese in Tokyo went to the American Embassy to express regrets. Roosevelt considered seizing Japanese assets as a form of preventive sanction against further provocation but he was forestalled by the full apology. Otherwise official American reaction was restrained. In the armed services, which were conscious that American naval forces were inadequate to force the Japanese to behave, the feeling prevailed that anything that might touch off a showdown should be postponed. Public reaction in so far as it was represented by Congress was not to roar but to shrink. The House immediately took up the Ludlow Resolution requiring a national referendum before a declaration of war could become effective. Previously its sponsor had been unable to collect the necessary number of signatures to bring the measure before a Committee of the Whole. Two days after the sinking of the *Panay* he had more than enough and the resolution was later defeated only after heavy pressure by the Administration and only by 21 votes.

A notable result of the *Panay* affair, in order to remove a further possibility of friction with the Japanese, was the withdrawal from China two months later of the 15th Infantry. Long under discussion in Washington and urged by the Army because of the tight restrictions on the regiment, it was a case, according to one American newspaper, "of doing the right thing at the wrong time." To the tears of local women the Can Do troops marched out, played through the streets of Tientsin by the bands of the other foreign regiments and even serenaded by Japanese bugles.

Stilwell's vinegar was at a high level during the winter in Hankow, "the bunghole of creation." He was depressed by the climate, "raw, grey, drizzly, chill," by China's situation, by the endless frustrations in the way of carrying out his professional task and by the blank incomprehension at the Washington end. The Chinese War Ministry had refused permission to visit the front and Stilwell could get no reliable information on the military situation in Hankow nor could his assistants in the field, probably because, as Captain Roberts suggested, the Chinese had none. Stilwell believed they were "entirely at sea about future Japanese operations" and were not anxious to have foreign observers at the front see and report on the poverty of command and poor performance. Since Stilwell had officially asked for permission to visit the front from the Foreign Minister, he could not "slide out" to the front unofficially, as Captain Dorn had discovered to be the best method. Dorn managed to skip back and forth from the Japanese to the Chinese side six or seven times in the course of his duty and bring back the first accurate reports of Chinese troop movements. His chief glowered in Hankow. "So I sit here and chew my nails," and comparing the surroundings to his house in Peiping, "work myself into a black rage."

Especially he was galled by the badgering of MID, which in the hands of a petty despot and pedantic bureaucrat, Colonel E. R. W. McCabe, pestered him with demands for daily operational reports, questioned every expense, issued orders to his staff without consulting him, made demands without relation to the battle situation or even to the normal geography of China and informed Stilwell that it was "embarrassing to receive so little information" from him. "Bastards in Washington don't like me," Stilwell concluded with some truth for there was certainly a quality of vendetta in McCabe's treatment, although he was hounding other attachés too. He kept a little black book called his "SOB book" in which to record his dislikes.*

In Consul Jarvis' apartment, where Stilwell had found living quarters, he felt at ease—"he and I talk the same language"—and at the office where they shared a room, "we say 'Christ' together frequently." But with others of the "embassy bunch" he felt there was "always a strain in the air. . . . I have the feeling that I don't really belong." He had forgiven the Ambassador who was always kind, pleasant, ready to talk and to call Stilwell in when visiting personages came. With the Government now preparing to withdraw to Chungking and Johnson under instructions to go when they did, he left Stilwell free to decide for himself and thus rated along with Jarvis in the category of "good egg." Nelse, as he had now become, confided that he had met the same difficulties in dealing with the Chinese as Stilwell had. Offering to explain these to the War Department, Johnson wrote a "masterpiece," causing Stilwell to regret he had composed and mailed to his wife an uncomplimentary poem about the "Ambastardor." Unable to resist a punning nickname, he had "thought that one up on the train and my trouble is now *not* saying it—it comes out too easily." This was indeed his case. When Win replied that she had not received the poem Stilwell was appalled at the possibility that it might have fallen into the wrong hands—and promptly rewrote and mailed her another copy, tempting fate again.

Friends and cordial hours were part of his life too. Some of the Chinese, especially the mayor, were "delightful" and he enjoyed a reunion with Feng Yu-hsiang, his road-building client of 15 years earlier who was in town to join the "dicker" over reorganizing the Government to let in the Reds. "The old boy looks well and hopeful. Says they can go on for six months."

---

* McCabe's predecessors as head of MID, Brigadier General H. E. Knight in 1935 and Colonel F. H. Lincoln in 1936, had found Stilwell "especially well suited" for his assignment and "keenly intelligent" with "a love of and flair for this work."

Nor were Stilwell's prejudices inflexible. "The pleasantest people in town are the British Navy people," he reported astonishingly. Invited to lunch by their Admiral Crabbe, he enjoyed it and pronounced his hosts "good eggs. . . . The French are okay too." Even the "limey consul" was a good egg. He found his most congenial company among certain of the journalists, usually the more venturesome free-lances sympathetic to revolutionary China who, like Carlson, roamed the country "from the heart." Agnes Smedley and Jack Belden were of this company. Belden especially, a great romantic and idealist aged twenty-eight, moody, driven, alternately gay and despondent, "a sad, ragged, torn, incredible character," as a friend described him, became a close companion and valued informant. Failing to obtain a job after graduating from college at the bottom of the depression, he had shipped as a seaman and jumped ship at Shanghai in 1933. Since then he had explored China and learned Chinese, living by a variety of fringe jobs in journalism until hired by the United Press after the Japanese invasion. He would periodically disappear on excursions through the intricate corridors of Chinese affairs, bringing Stilwell reports of Chinese movements and intentions and an abundance of material on the reputations of commanders and the inner relationships that governed them.

Agnes Smedley whom Stilwell often met to talk about the Communists found him "tough, gruff, battle-scarred . . . direct and honest," and was struck by his compassion for the wounded. Working then for the China Aid Council, she was packing supplies on a truck one day when he came by and demanded, "What are you doing?"

"Loading this truck with medicine. What are you doing?"

"I'm standing here watching you," he said scowling. "I'm also telling you that the warehouse of the International Red Cross is jammed with a new shipment of medicine including the new sulfa drugs." He told her to go there and demand some for the troops.

In January 1938 his pressure finally broke through obstructions and he was able to go on the first of many journeys which over the next year and a half were to take him to embattled areas in many parts of China. On a bitterly cold trip through Kiangsi and Hunan, he found the active front had melted away but there was no peace talk anywhere in the area. The provincial governors talked in terms of three years' resistance and had begun training programs in guerilla tactics. The Chinese were sold on guerilla warfare, Stilwell noted, but munitions and equipment would be a serious problem. When asked by a Chinese officer what his own strategy would be, his reply, "Make use of numbers and attack," was not welcomed.

Through a friendship formed with General Shang Chen, commander of the 20th Army Corps in Honan, Stilwell was able to leave again, this time for Kaifeng and Hsuchow, western and eastern ends of the Lunghai line.

He was so glad to be leaving the miasma of Hankow that a last-minute message from the War Department suggesting that he go to Lanchow "on the way back" from Kaifeng caused more of a shrug than an explosion. He merely commented, "I wonder if they know where it is." Lanchow, port of entry for Russian supplies coming across central Asia, was close to the border of Inner Mongolia, 600 miles northwest of Kaifeng.

In Honan his confidence in the Chinese revived. They were gaining experience, organizing and improving the flow of replacements, and he began to believe that if they could reach the point of taking the initiative and attacking, which might be within the year, "the turning point will be reached." The trip was so cold that he did not take his clothes off for a week nor his shoes for fear he would not be able to get them back on. Frozen feet caused a few days' agony but afterwards "I was all set for 30 or 40 miles." Accompanied to Hsuchow by Shang Chen, whom Stilwell considered one of China's dependable commanders, he was finally able to see China's army at the front, upon which his pessimism returned. He decided "the offensive is not in them." If they would attack at night they could "nullify the Jap superior gun power by reaching the position at day-light" but they will not. "CKS is no soldier. Shang Chen is good. And Pai— that's all."

A talk with a Kuomintang officer, General Liu, recorded with Stilwell's remarkable gift for catching character in dialogue, distilled for him the attitude of the governing class. Yes, losses had been heavy, General Liu admitted, about 600,000, but that was "really a good thing. . . . The Chinese soldiers are all bandits, robbers, thieves and rascals. So we send them to the front and they get killed off and in that way we are eliminating our bad elements." Asked how much pay a soldier received, he replied $8 a month and "if he got any more he wouldn't fight." As to the duration of the war General Liu thought at least one year or two. By that time the Japanese would be broken financially, their soldiers would be homesick and the foreign powers would have entered the war. Actually the more ground Japan occupied the better because they would be that much more easily absorbed. "In the long run the Japanese will disappear, absorbed by the Chinese as were the Mongols and the Manchus." Asked what China would do for salt and motor fuel if blockaded, he replied that the more territory Japan occupied the smaller would be the part left to China, "so we won't have to move around so much then" and would need less gasoline.

Asked why greater use was not made of the educated class as officers, General Liu replied that "University students and graduates are all cowards. They would run. I know because I am a University man." Besides, "The Chinese learned long ago to make the lower classes do the fighting. At first the nobles fought but they soon got over that and made the people do it for them." The English used Indians to fight for them, he pointed out, the French used Moroccans and Annamites and now the Japanese were using Mongols and Manchurians.

Knowing and talking to the China of General Liu, Stilwell was not prone to see the country as fighting democracy's battle, the favorite theme of ideologists like Carlson. Of Carlson himself whom he came to know in Hankow his opinion was kindly. He was "a good scout, not overeducated ... but a solid citizen and a soldier" and, though he wore all the wrong clothes at dinner, "a gentleman anyway." Privately he called him "Captain Courageous" and was not impressed by Carlson's glowing reports of the 8th Route Army's military training methods which Stilwell told him he had seen in practice under Feng Yu-hsiang 15 years before.

Though it was the fashion to say "aren't the 8th Route wonderful," Stilwell was skeptical but professionally interested. Through Agnes Smedley he became acquainted with Chou En-lai, second to Mao in the Communist hierarchy and its representative in Hankow, and with Yeh Chien-ying, the Communist Chief of Staff. He thought the Communists' political demands for "liberation of military policy" and "mobilization of the masses" were "very vague—the usual slogans," but personally, after visiting and dining with Chou En-lai and his entourage, he found them "uniformly frank, courteous, friendly and direct. In contrast to the fur-collared, spurred KMT new-style Napoleon—all pose and bumptiousness." Handsome, cultivated and urbane, Chou En-lai was a favorite of foreigners. Yeh Chien-ying made the select category of "good egg, like most reds." Talking to these intense and energetic men, pursuers of China's old unsatisfied need of revolution and as yet uncorrupted by power, Stilwell realized the "wide chasm" between them and a man like General Liu. He felt sure that if China emerged from the war with Japan, "there will be trouble again internally."

Few could doubt it for a sense of decline in the Government and ruling society pervaded Hankow that winter. Stilwell expressed it when after the fall of Nanking he wrote of "the rotten shell of administration primarily responsible for the current debacle." In the same vein Carlson was writing to the President at this time that he was "disgusted with the attitude of the intellectual class, even the middle class. The town is filled with men and women who take no apparent interest in the war. They have no feeling of responsibility for the future of their country." When Carlson at a Chinese dinner party in Hankow offered a toast to "Old Hundred Names" as bearing the brunt of the war, it fell very flat according to Ambassador Johnson who was present. Johnson too felt that the general attitude was "Let us fight to the last drop of coolie blood" while "in the midst of it all the Soong family carries on its intrigues which sometimes disgust me completely."

The fervor of the Kuomintang's youth had passed to the Communists

leaving Chungking with history's most melancholy tale: that every successful revolution puts on in time the robes of the tyrant it has deposed.
Madame Chiang Kai-shek in a rare moment left a brief acknowledgment.
When a number of journalists returned from Yenan with enthusiastic reports, she invited them to tea, though disbelieving, to hear what they had
to say in person. After listening to their glowing tales of the Communists'
integrity, idealism and sacrifice for a cause, she said it was impossible for
her to believe them. Walking to the window she stared out across the river
in silence for several minutes and then turned back to the room and spoke
the saddest sentence of her life: "If what you tell me about them is true,
then I can only say they have never known *real* power."

Just as Stilwell was about to leave for the Anhwei front to observe the
13th Army under General Tang En-po, he was balked by the War Department which ordered him to go to Lanchow instead to report on Russian aid
reaching China. Furious at the cancellation of a tour which had taken a
great deal of arranging and represented the first time in eight months of
the war that a foreign officer had been able to get accredited to a unit in
the field, Stilwell offered every kind of excuse almost to the point of insub-
ordination to avoid going to Lanchow. He was ordered to comply. The
War Department was acting, as it happened, at the desire of the President
who had asked for a report on the nature and amount of arms reaching
China through all avenues: Hong Kong, Indochina and Burma as well as
overland from Russia. Stilwell was not told this and indeed the whole
Lanchow affair, which brought his resentment to a peak, could have been
mitigated, like the rest of his troubles with MID, by a simple personal
communication. He went off "sick unto death of the interfering bastards
in Washington," and in a mood, as he wrote to Win, to retire, at once or
next year, "whatever the family decides." He passed his fifty-fifth birthday
en route to Lanchow feeling that, in view of his relations with the War
Department, his career henceforward held little promise.

Stilwell was the first foreigner to visit the Russian air base at Lanchow
and bring back evidence to show how far Russia was concerned to help
China. Making his way by train as far as Sian where he visited 8th Route
Army headquarters, and from there to Lanchow by bus and truck, he
hunted down clues, bribed employees of the Russian guest house for figures on arrivals, questioned sentries, police, bus drivers, innkeepers, servants, the Governor of Kansu and his secretaries, missionaries at Sian, a
Tibetan interpreter, an automobile dealer, Chinese officers, student aviators
and local Mongols. These last, "sturdy, dirty, hard-bitten, weather-beaten,
with faces like Sitting Bull," he entertained to tea at an inn; afterwards when
encountered on the street they were "all smiles and howdy." Though his

movements were watched and his conversations listened in on, he was able to inspect the flying field and ascertain that 300 Russian planes had been delivered, of which 30 were still at the base for training Chinese pilots. Russian aviation personnel, though physically impressive, with huge appetites, consuming four meals a day, were "a sour and surly lot . . . I never saw one of them smile." He collected figures on the Russian truck convoys which brought in munitions and fuel, worked out estimates of the monthly deliveries on the basis of distance traveled and turn-around time, and was able to specify types of munitions "though unable to get box markings or broken boxes." The total was little in comparison with what could be brought in by ship at Hong Kong and he concluded the route had been established primarily for aviation fuel and as an emergency inlet in case Canton fell.

By the time he returned to Hankow on April 15 China's mood had undergone a dazzling change caused by her first real victory, at Taierchuang in Shantung on April 6-7. The whole country went "mad with joy." The Japanese were not invincible after all; a new hope in resistance swept away pessimism. It was the first cause for rejoicing since the war began.

Taierchuang was a town on the path of the enemy's advance to Hsuchow whose fall would have put the Japanese on the Lunghai line, opening their way to the interior. Under the command of the Kwangsi General Li Tsung-jen, its defense was turned to counterattack, according to a plan of the German advisers, with an army of reinforcements brought up to cut off the enemy in the rear. General Tang En-po's army, which Stilwell would have been accompanying had he not been ordered to Lanchow, played this role. Thrilled by the phenomenon of reinforcements, the defenders rushed forward to join the attack with "battle cries that shook the skies." They were able to slaughter the Japanese infantry who had been cut off from their supply of ammunition and fuel for their tanks and proved unable to withstand a determined attack without mechanized support. At the end of the 17-day battle the Japanese had suffered 16,000 casualties and the loss of 40 tanks, 70 armored cars and 100 motor vehicles besides guns and other arms in their first notable defeat since their creation of a modern army. The Chinese sustained equal casualties.

Like all China's partisans Stilwell wanted deeply to find cause for optimism and was moved to write after Taierchuang when friends now said they thought China would win, "So do I." At the same time he knew that militarily the Chinese had lost their advantage by failing to pursue. General Falkenhausen, the chief German military adviser, was "tearing his hair" at frustration of his plan. "I tell the Generalissimo to advance, to attack, to exploit his success. But nothing is done. Soon the Japanese will have 8 or 10 divisions before Hsuchow. Then it will be too late." Analyzing the battle with Stilwell and the German advisers, Pai Ch'ung-hsi was not interested in the lesson of attack. He reverted to the theory of winning by outlasting. "We can afford to lose four men if the Japanese lose one," he said, adding that Chinese losses would be of "no significance" until they passed 50 million. The Chinese, Stilwell commented, "cannot get the idea of the offensive into their heads."

Visiting the scene at Taierchuang, he talked with the commander Li Tsung-jen. In one of the few recorded views of Stilwell through Chinese eyes, Li described him as "outspoken" in manner with sympathy for China's cause but with "great pessimism over the future of China's resistance." This pessimism Li ascribed to the "materialist civilization" in which the American Colonel had been educated. He urged Stilwell to recommend to his Government a large loan to China for the purpose of war supplies, arguing that help for China was the best insurance the United States could take out for herself.

Ironically the effect of Taierchuang confirmed Chiang Kai-shek in his overall policy of the defensive because the victory seemed to suggest that the Japanese had exhausted their impetus. Within weeks they returned to the attack, broke through the line and advanced upon Hsuchow which fell at the end of May. With another Japanese army coming down from the north to cross the Yellow River above Kaifeng, the whole region between the rivers, including Hankow itself, was in danger. In a desperate expedient Chiang Kai-shek called not on China's armies but on China's Sorrow— the Yellow River. He ordered General Shang Chen to blow up the dikes at Chengchow behind the Japanese vanguard. Repeatedly he telephoned in anxiety to learn if his orders had been carried out while Shang Chen delayed until his army could be moved out of the way. Then the dynamite was exploded. Jack Belden who was present reported how, for moments of agony to the watchers, the silt-filled waters flowed steadily on their old course, swirling and bubbling against the broken dikes, then suddenly with a "terrible roar" ripped through the breach and spread over the low ground on a rampage eastward to the sea. Eleven cities and 4,000 villages were flooded, the crops and farms of three provinces ruined, two million people rendered homeless, and in that vast and sodden wasteland another fund of animosity stored up against the Government. The Japanese were bogged down and perhaps three months' time bought in the process.

China's battle was making an impression on America. Out of sympathy with her resistance or investment in her affairs, correspondents, missionaries and other observers concentrated on the admirable aspects and left unmentioned the flaws and failures. An idealized image came through. Generalissimo and Mme. Chiang Kai-shek as "Man and Wife of the Year" for 1937 gazed at Americans in sad nobility from the cover of *Time,* sober and steady, brave and true. *Time*'s publisher, Henry Luce, had been born in China of missionary parents, so this worshipful view of the Chiangs was no accident. The missionaries, and behind them the Foreign Missions Conference of North America, the Federal Council of Churches of Christ in America, the YMCA and China Famine Relief rallied to the cause of their wards with warmth, energy and all their considerable influence. As a result of a century of missionary effort Americans felt a responsibility for China which they did not feel for other countries. Whether or not the missionaries had made an impact on China, commented a European observer, "they certainly made an impact on the United States." They rallied to the Chiangs in self-interested loyalty because the Chiangs' Christianity at the helm of China provided such gratifying proof of the validity of the missionary effort. They overpraised Chiang Kai-shek and once committed to his perfection regarded any suggestion of blemish as inadmissable. "China has now the most enlightened, patriotic and able rulers in her history," proclaimed the *Missionary Review of the World.*

The same journal presented the Communists too in acceptable terms as a group trying to bring about "social reform compatible with the aspirations of all progressive people." This picture of "determined oneness of purpose" was necessary not only to the church groups heavily engaged in raising money for China relief but also to the envoys and propagandists of the Nationalist Government who were exerting pressure for American loans and intervention. To acknowledge the deep schism in Chinese society was not convenient. Therefore the Communists were not to be considered irreconcilables but respectable social reformers within the fold. Correspondents were asked by the Kuomintang not to refer to the Communists as Communists. "There are no Communists left in China," Chiang Kai-shek told a German newspaperman in 1939. Everyone assisted in this illusion, including the Communists themselves because it fitted the party line of the united front. Although they did not deny their Marxist ideology, they talked in terms of the "new Democracy" as a stage on the way to their eventual goal.

The rise of international Fascism shaped America's view of China and the fervent syllogism at its core: democracy was threatened by the aggressor nations; China was under attack by an aggressor nation; therefore China was a democracy and her battle was the battle of world democracy. To all men of goodwill convinced of the indivisibility of the world struggle, this appeared self-evident, and help for China therefore obviously in America's self-interest. Strategically this was valid, if not ideologically. But strategy is more attractive when dressed in ideology and people on "our side" are considered to be democrats regardless of their political experience. Americans

Stilwell on a troop train en route to Kaifeng in 1938 (108) and with Captain Maxwell Taylor and the Japanese military attaché (109). Stilwell became acquainted with Chou En-lai, Mao's representative in Hankow (110), and was given this portrait of Li Tsung-jen, hero of China's victory over Japanese (111).

108

109

110

111

112

113

11

115

find it difficult to remember that Thomas Jefferson did not operate in Asia.

Democracy became the theme of China's partisans. The United Council for Civilian Relief in China, incorporating various committees under an imposing roster of prominent directors, unearthed the 25th anniversary of American recognition of the Chinese Republic in 1913 to celebrate as "Democracy Day" with a banquet and speeches broadcast over a national hookup. The same theme was hammered by all the committees that sprang up to aid China and to oppose the continuing sale of war materials to Japan. It was shared by the church groups (who united under the chairmanship of Harper Sibley, former president of the United States Chamber of Commerce), by lay groups like the American Committee for Non-Participation in Japanese Aggression and by left-wing groups of the united front like the American Friends of the Chinese People. It had ardent spokesmen as diverse as Dr. Walter Judd, a medical missionary from Shansi who returned to the United States to become Chiang Kai-shek's most devout supporter, and Captain Carlson who returned home too to make his views public.

Silenced by Navy censors when he gave interviews to reporters praising the fighting qualities of the 8th Route Army, he seized the pretext to resign his commission in 1938 and go home to persuade the public that China could win if America would stop selling war materials to Japan. The outcome of the Sino-Japanese struggle, he maintained, would determine "whether Eastern Asia will be ruled by a military autocracy, or whether the budding democracy of China will come into full bloom." This was ideology rampant and unreal. Democracy was not budding either in the Kuomintang with its one-party Government and censorship and blue shirts and secret police, or in Yenan grounded in the dogma and dedicated to the goals of revolutionary socialism.

Although China's friends made extraordinary efforts, American isolationism remained stronger than sympathy. Polls showed only 2 percent of the public pro-Japanese against 74 percent pro-Chinese but these sentiments did not include a desire for involvement. At government level a sense of urgency was growing. The President, anxious to keep China on her feet, was abetted on the one hand by Secretary Morgenthau who, with a desperate sense of the need to resist Fascist aggression, believed support for China crucial, and restrained on the other hand by Secretary Hull who maintained an unbudging resistance to any "unneutral" gesture, including economic aid, which might involve the United States in the Sino-Japanese conflict. His caution was such that he refused to accept T. V. Soong as economic emissary because he was too prominently anti-Japanese.

When the Treasury's agent in China, J. Lossing Buck, came to see the Military Attaché on August 30, 1938, to be briefed on the military situa-

Japanese tank unit advancing toward Nanking just before its capture, December 1937 (112). Japanese armies entering the walled city of Hsuchow (113) and a town in Anhwei province (114), 1938. Hsuchow fell at the end of May and gloating Japanese generals toasted its fall (115).

tion, Stilwell put forward the argument of Li Tsung-jen that America should aid herself by enabling China to buy arms. As reported by Buck to Secretary Morgenthau, "Colonel Stilwell . . . feels that the policy of our government should be more positive in the present situation and that help to China in the way of financial loans and military equipment is much better defense for us than only the building of our own defense equipment. A very small proportion of the cost of such defense, if given to China, would be much more effective."

Morgenthau agreed. With strong conviction in the larger cause but limited knowledge of China, he thought there was "a bare chance we may still keep a democratic form of government in the Pacific," and strenuously urged the loan to China upon the President. In December 1938 a loan of $25 million was arranged through the Export-Import Bank.

Despite their successes the Japanese could not end the war and in August 1938 took the decision to drive toward a new objective—Hankow. Stilwell returned there in August from Peiping where he had decided on his own authority to spend the summer with his family. This decision had more than ever incensed MID with whom he was already engaged in continuous quarrel over the assignments of his five assistants. Informed by Colonel McCabe that his return to Peiping in June represented "a serious error of judgment . . . when major military developments are in progress," he was ordered in a tone more suitable for a cadet than a full colonel to go on no further travels without permission and to submit for approval "reasons, route, destination and estimated cost in each case." He was told that the Department undertook to direct his and his assistants' movements because the "coverage, quality and quantity of information received was not (repeat not) satisfactory." Seven thousand miles from the scene McCabe asserted MID's right to "assign you or any other officer in China to any mission it deems fit." In further communications Stilwell was informed that his reports compared unfavorably with Carlson's to the Navy, that the information conveyed did not justify the sums of G-2 confidential funds spent, and that he should explain the "exact nature and value" of the information obtained by these expenditures. McCabe was evidently trying to goad Stilwell into resigning from his post so that he could be replaced by some more intimate associate of the "attachés' clique"; if so, he almost succeeded. Stilwell at one point made up his mind to ask for relief and drafted in fierce angry pen strokes a demand for an inspector "to determine the manner in which I have performed my duty under the conditions that have existed since June 1937." China, however, held him back.

When Tilly Hoffman, secretary of the Military Attaché's office in Peiping, went home on leave she heard a long series of complaints from MID involving actions and decisions of Stilwell's which he had not bothered to explain. Although the staff considered Stilwell one of the best observers and reporters they had in MID, in fact as regards military operations the "perfect observer," they complained of his independence of action. When Tilly asked why someone had not taken pen in hand to write to the Colonel directly, the answer was that there were "strict orders against any officer communicating with anyone except through official channels." That situation continued to the end of Stilwell's tour.

Hankow was now cut off from Peiping by land and could only be reached from the north by ship via Shanghai to Hong Kong and from there by plane. When Stilwell arrived on August 26 the Government had withdrawn and a sense of siege was descending. Remembering the great revolutionary days of Hankow in 1925-26, the Communists wanted to conduct a "people's defense" of the city after the example of Madrid which was still holding out after two years of siege. They urged the Government to organize an army of 150,000 workers, students and townspeople, to be led by an elite corps of youths with "the highest revolutionary consciousness." This project had small appeal for Chiang Kai-shek who had no desire to see workers' cadres established under Communist control and did not believe in any case that the Wuhan cities could be held against Japanese assault. Since two supposedly impregnable Chinese positions on the way up the Yangtze had been, in one case, abandoned without battle, and in the other, taken by ruse from the rear, he had some reason for his belief. But essentially the reason for the military ineffectiveness of China's defense was the deep cultural preference, fully shared by the Commander-in-Chief himself, in favor of outlasting over fighting.

Stilwell started out for the front in a group with the British and French Attachés and the news photographer Robert Capa who had covered Spain for a year and was "quite a guy." Staying on after the Englishman "got mad and bowed out" and the Frenchman fell ill of dysentery and returned, Stilwell can be seen in the pages of his diary: "Moved by night, hard going and guard went astray. Pack transport, coolies, exhausted men curled up to die. . . . Jap plane at 200 feet machine gunning the road. After a few wounded, I suppose. Wild Eagles! . . . Welcome from Chung. Go forward, sure. The nearer the front the warmer the welcome. Had a talk and chow. They got me bedding. . . . Bread and cheese for breakfast, by Capa. Mouldy but o.k. Sat around till 9 then off to the front. Hot as the hinges of hell and hard going. Climbed a high hill and got view along Yangtze to Juichang. Just a sea of rocky hills and scrub brush. Could be held indefinitely. . . . A lot of assorted artillery coming out north of the lake. Why? Kwan and Chang say it can't be used but back of their present positions it could."

Back in Hankow there were "barricades and wire everywhere." Colonel

Rousselle, the French Attaché, was dead of dysentery. It was the seventh anniversary of Mukden and in Europe the powers trembled through the Munich crisis. "My god what a world. If another war starts in Europe where will we all end up? . . . Carmel suddenly seems far off." Japanese bombers blasted the city daily, unopposed. The Chinese Air Force on which Chiang Kai-shek had pinned his hopes never became effective and had few planes or pilots left to defend Hankow. Shortage of fuel was made shorter by the pervading Chinese philosophy of hoarding equipment for a future crisis. "The Chinese can't bear to *use* their stuff," Stilwell wrote after seeing a battery of 75s which had been through the battles of Shanghai and Hsuchow without being fired. "If they put it in, they might lose it and then where would they be after the war, without any matériel?"

Air force personnel was a greater difficulty. Lacking the Americans' affinity for the combustion engine, Chinese mechanics treated their machines with little care or respect; lacking expert maintenance, their planes became rapidly useless. Pilots and navigators, drawn from the educated class, represented a group which on the whole was not martial in spirit and had no desire to die in unequal combat with the well-trained, well-equipped Japanese. Those who did become pilots were valiant but reckless and flashy, and ill prepared by the Italian officers whom Chiang Kai-shek accepted from Mussolini early in the 1930s to train his air force. When Italy withdrew her officers out of deference to growing friendship for Japan, the Italians took with them all the aerial maps they had prepared for their clients, leaving the Chinese, who had left the work to others, helpless.

To take charge of building his air force Chiang Kai-shek in 1937 engaged a remarkable American fighter pilot, Captain Claire Chennault, who had retired from the American Air Corps because of deafness and disagreement. By 1938 Chennault, promoted to colonel in the Chinese Air Force, had begun a major program of airfield construction and organized an effective warning net by radio but he had less success with pilots and was soon to recruit a volunteer force of American mercenaries to defend China's skies. For the present as the Japanese raided Hankow unopposed, the sirens wailed and the streets drummed with the sound of thousands of running feet seeking the safety of the foreign Concession area.

While columns of ragged and bloody wounded straggled in, evacuation of civilians began. In the last weeks 40,000 moved out in boats and junks or overland in trucks and handcarts to Changsha, capital of Hunan. Trainloads of half-starved, tattered war orphans gathered up from the battle zones by a women's committee organized by Mme. Chiang were fed and washed and marched in clean blue overalls to riverboats for evacuation. The dismantling of factories and equipment for the long haul to the interior, organized by the industrial cooperatives, was under way. The wounded looking for some designated hospital already dismantled sat or lay on the pavement, worn out, unable to go farther.

Among the "last-ditchers" of Hankow was Mme. Chiang Kai-shek whom Stilwell visited in September and found "very charming, highly intelligent and sincere." Though he recognized that she "pushed out a lot of propaganda about the way the government is looking out for the common people," nevertheless "she is alright and doing a good job." Mme. Chiang never made an effort to charm without succeeding and the American Military Attaché was worth her effort. He sent her flowers after the interview.

Out again to the southern front in October he observed from a battalion commander's command post a five-day fight for Teian in the path of the Japanese drive southward from the Yangtze against Nanchang, capital of Kiangsi. "Walked to Wang Lia-chi's hq, 15 li. Bridges are all burning, road broken every 200 yards or so. Met Wang. Warm welcome. He has been catching hell—50% losses. . . . No hmg [heavy machine guns]. Small cns [caissons?]. No guns. About 200 rounds apiece. 4 lmgs [light machine guns]. Bridge out. No car. No phone, etc. Slept in the straw." Colonel Wang at first held a hill position but was forced back into the town. The fight continued within the walls. In the last hours Colonel Wang himself led a night attack through the narrow streets. As described by Stilwell afterwards, "The detachment runs into a Japanese machine-gun nest. . . . The Chinese throw themselves prone on the right side of the street. The Japanese open fire but fail to come out into the open where they can rake the street and the shots carom off the opposite wall and hit no one. Quick action is needed here and the Chinese are equal to it. A squad slips around a building and coming in from the rear puts the machine-gun crew out of action with hand grenades. . . . Everything by now is in an uproar and Colonel Wang in the darkness loses touch with them. . . ." For the rest of the night and next day the fight continued with only a few yards separating the two sides until, as the Japanese advanced in force against the weakened garrison, the position became hopeless. A messenger from the division commander, the only one to get through of six who were sent, arrived at 6 P.M. with orders to withdraw. Under cover of darkness Colonel Wang with 65 men rejoined the rest of the battalion and left the field with less than 400 men of his original 1,500. They had been continuously in action for over five days with little sleep, food or water. Of his 1,100 casualties, 600 were dead.

In actions like these Stilwell was forming the judgments that he was to take with him to the Chinese theater four years later. He thought Colonel Wang was brave but his judgment was poor; he should have stayed out of the town which being in ruins furnished no cover and was absolutely dominated from the hills. In a G-2 report analyzing the war from what he had seen at first hand, he described the needless failures inherent in Chinese defensive tactics. In open country against Japanese planes, tanks and artillery, the Chinese, being deficient in these weapons, made only halfhearted defense and readily abandoned positions. In hilly country, however, where concealment was good, they held their ground better, and with only rifle, grenade and machine gun slowed down the Japanese advance. The enemy continued to push against the flanks, often thrusting out a salient that invited counterattack, but instead of seizing their chance, the Chinese "always react to protect their rear." They hoarded their reserves, failing to exert full strength when it could succeed with the result that numbers were more equal than they should have been and Japanese initiative and superior equipment turned the scale. "The Chinese replacement system is cockeyed," he added in private notes, and "this failure to use China's greatest asset—manpower—is the most ghastly failure of all."

The report concluded on his favorite theme: "The Chinese soldier is excellent material, wasted and betrayed by stupid leadership." There was a corollary: "Suppose the Chinese soldier were well-fed, well-armed and equipped, well-cared for and well-*led.* . . .?"

The Sino-Japanese War came to a climax in the five days of October 21-25 when the Japanese took not only Hankow but also Canton, China's last access by sea to the outside world. The key city of the south fell like a ripe pear in autumn. Relying on British presence across the bay in Hong Kong, the Chinese had prepared no defense because they could not believe the Japanese would move in under the imperial shadow of the Peak or that Britain would let the event happen without retaliation. More alert, the Japanese took their cue from Munich. On October 12, two weeks after that day of "defeat without war," as Churchill called it, Japanese troops landed at Bias Bay on the Kwangtung coast 30 miles from Hong Kong. Negligence, corruption and some treachery opened their path and Canton was captured without serious opposition.

The British did not react because they could obtain no assurance of American support if action against Japan should involve them in war. The Chinese felt, according to Ambassador Johnson, "completely let down." In a message to President Roosevelt following the landing at Bias Bay, Chiang Kai-shek urged him to give the British the necessary encouragement for "cooperative intervention" in the Far East. He was not shy about stating his thesis. The problem of Asia, he instructed the President, could only be solved by collective action for which "leadership must come from the United States." That was the American dilemma. The United States was prepared neither to seize the leadership nor to acquiesce in Japanese control of China which must result from failure to seize it.

Japan expected the capture of Hankow and Canton to seal victory at last. With a million men now on the mainland, and desperate to find some end to the war, she made one more effort to force China into a settlement. A New Order for East Asia based on an anti-Communist bloc of Japan, China and Manchukuo was announced and the Chinese Government invited to join on condition of repudiating its anti-Japanese past and "reforming its personnel." Now that Japan had control of China's ports, railroads and major cities and of north China, the Shantung peninsula, the Yangtze valley and the southern coast, the Japanese believed the Kuomintang would have to capitulate. To negotiate the settlement they had won over no less an emissary than Wang Ching-wei, Vice-President of the Kuomintang, who along with others had come to believe the Nationalist cause was lost. Partly motivated by old resentment of Chiang Kai-shek and ambition to succeed him even as a collaborationist, Wang was ready to accept the necessity of Japan as a new ruling dynasty.

For Chiang no acceptable future was possible if he submitted. He remained, as always, impervious to the buffeting of events. Nothing ever changed him. He was welded to the belief that China would outlast Japan and that history must bring him foreign allies. Loosely organized and agrarian, China could sustain herself, even though isolated, in the far west— at what reduced level or cost in suffering did not matter. A slender egress by road into Burma, hacked out of the mountains by hand labor, had just been opened. Chiang would hold out in Chungking beyond the enemy's reach until Japan ultimately clashed with Russia or the Western powers. He rejected all terms.

On the failure of Wang's mission in December 1938 the situation congealed. Japan reaffirmed inclusion of occupied China in the New Order and her resolve to "exterminate" the Kuomintang Government which "no longer exists except as a mere local regime." Chiang Kai-shek publicly reaffirmed on December 26 the resolve to maintain China's independence. Except for local punitive campaigns, military advance came to a stop; Japan had no appetite to go further. The war was left unfinished, the million men remained. In 1940 a puppet government under Wang Ching-wei was installed at Nanking but as long as independent China continued to exist and resist, the occupation troops could not be withdrawn.

The New Order confronted the United States with violation of both the integrity of China and equal opportunity in China, the two basic principles of her China policy for 40 years. Once again the horrid case arose of circumstances which the country could not in conscience accept and was unwilling to use force to resist. Washington chose the middle course of protest. The New Order was declared to violate the Open Door and the Nine-Power Treaty. Japan expressed surprise that the United States had "failed to awaken to the new actualities in the Far East resulting from Japan's successful military campaigns in China." In response to renewed agitation in America for economic sanctions, the Japanese were reported by an experienced correspondent to "have begun to feel that the United States may prove the principal antagonist when the time comes for Japan to make a settlement with China."

Stilwell did not stay to see the Japanese enter Hankow. He left to join Shang Chen's headquarters at Changsha in Hunan, pivot of the new defense line. During the next two months when the situation was in flux he remained on the southern front, moving from place to place along with military units, hospital staffs, stranded officials, foreign colleagues and newsmen and all the displaced flotsam which follow a defeat.

Another movement, a huge slow-motion upheaval, was relocating the working capacity of Free China to the west. A steady trudging toiling stream of people carried goods and equipment and themselves out of the area of the invader into the independent zone. Boats, trains, carts, pack animals and coolies, under repeated bombing, shared in the inland trek from Canton, Nanking, Hsuchow and other cities. Factory machinery, government records, university libraries, the contents of hospitals, arsenals and offices, were transported in boxes slung on shoulder poles or packed in sampans and pulled upstream by straining teams moving foot by foot over the rocks and roadless banks. In the age-old method of moving vessels up the rapids, the great-muscled coolies, hundreds to a load, bent double against the ropes, slowly hauled the burdens to the free land beyond the Yangtze gorges. A whole textile mill was packed into 380 junks of which a third sank in the rapids, were raised, repacked and started on their way again. Some factories were more than a year en route before renewing operation. Faculty and students of the universities, organized into marching sections with foraging squads, police units and pack animals, walked to new locations in the west and southwest. Stilwell watched some of the procession through Hankow and Changsha. "A single coolie would trot by with a length of pipe over his shoulder. A cart would creak along with a load of parts. A boiler would be pulled along on rollers. Some of the machines were pulled by manpower over wooden rollers for 500 miles. When they had gone far enough they dug caves in the rock cliffs along the Yangtze and duplicated the arsenal that six months before had been operating in Canton." The migration, no less extraordinary than the Communists' Long March, was proof of what he had seen in the centipede pushing the freight train—the indomitable labor of China.

Gradually, while keeping track of Chinese divisions, reviewing events with the commanders, struggling for transportation and trying to find

Young Chinese schoolboys scrutinize anti-Japanese posters on Hankow buildings in 1938. Ancient Chinese techniques of design are combined in the posters with a more modern approach to propaganda (116).

119

In 1937 Chiang Kai-shek engaged a former American fighter pilot, Captain Claire Chennault (118), to take charge of building his air force. Chennault began a major program of constructing airfields, such as the one at Chengchow (117), junction of the air routes to Peiping, Nanking, Shanghai and inland to Mongolian Ninghsia.

out through the confusion and fog of rumor what was happening, Stilwell made his way southward through Hengyang to Kweilin in Kwangsi. Finding he would have to wait until February for the next vacancy by plane for Chungking, he managed to obtain a place in a car for the journey over the only motor road through Kweichow and over the mountains. Stopping for the night en route in a one-street town he invited himself to dinner at the local inn "with Hsu, Ti, Chu and T'ang . . . all good eggs," and enjoyed as a roommate an interesting rat he called the Engineer because of its dexterity in solving problems.

On December 28 in Chungking, China's wartime capital for the next seven years, Stilwell was to have a personal meeting with Chiang Kai-shek. By now he had been authorized to return to Peiping preparatory to the end of his tour in May and so his stay in Chungking was short, lasting only from December 19 to 31. It was enough to decide that the remote provincial 500-year-old city with its steep streets and steps climbing up from the river, its open sewers and dank fogbound climate in winter was a "sloppy dump." The meeting with the Generalissimo and Mme. Chiang lasted for only fifteen apparently agreeable minutes. "Very cordial," Stilwell recorded. "Both looked extremely well. They were quite frank. Gave me a photo and their blessing." The signed photograph subsequently occupied a prominent place in Stilwell's living room in Peiping, perhaps more in defiance of the Japanese than from admiration of the Generalissimo.

Summarizing his judgment of China's leader in a G-2 report less than a month after their meeting, Stilwell wrote, "Chiang Kai-shek is directly responsible for much of the confusion that normally exists in his command." The reason, Stilwell believed, was his suspicion of rivals. Fearing to delegate authority or to trust his subordinates, Chiang wished to hold as many strings as possible in his own hands. His "first consideration is to maintain his own control over the best troops and material so that his position cannot be threatened."

In private notes Stilwell added, "He wanted to keep all his subordinates in the dark because he didn't trust them . . . If they all knew nothing they couldn't very well get together and dicker." Describing the factors that were one day to become his own frustration, he wrote that the Generalissimo "never assigned good artillery to divisions because he didn't want to let any get away from him—divisions had only MGs and TMs [machine guns and trench mortars]. The same old mistrust kept him from making his army efficient. He was always thinking of what he could save for later on when perhaps his own position would be threatened." Further, he never had a proper information service. "He had a ring around him, half-informed, and they gave him a distorted view of everything. He never went to see for himself . . . real supervision was always lacking."

Marine Captain Evans F. Carlson (119), the assistant naval attaché, who had a private pipeline to President Roosevelt. The Stilwells often entertained Chinese friends at their home in Peiping. Captain Frederick Munson of Stilwell's staff and Stilwell chat with Mme. Dan (120).

Whatever his opinion of the Commander-in-Chief, Stilwell was thinking in terms of the Chinese as future allies. He believed that the United States and Japan must inevitably come to war. For a long time he had been assembling material and forming judgments of the divisions and commanders which could be most useful in a joint effort. While he had small respect for Chinese military leadership in general, he had a good opinion of individuals' capacities and told his assistant, Captain Dorn, to keep his eyes peeled for capable, forceful commanders. With massive American help in organization, training, equipment and supplies, planning, direction and command, if possible, Stilwell believed the Chinese could fight effectively against the Japanese. The shape of the future was already in his mind. Of a particular general whom he regarded highly, Ku Chu-tung, he wrote that if ever the United States were to fight alongside China against Japan, this man would make a good Commander-in-Chief of Chinese forces "to carry out operations under the direction of American officers and staff." He named his favorite Shang Chen as one who would "work in well as an adviser on the American staff."

On the last day of 1938 he left Chungking by air for Kunming in Yunnan, now the main air base of Free China and the starting point of the Burma Road. At the Hotel du Lac he spent the evening in dinner and long talk with Chennault with no foreshadowing of the conflict between them that was to come.

The last months in Peiping were bitter under the Japanese occupation. Only with the greatest difficulty could his new Japanese-speaking assistant, Captain Frederick Munson, convince him to pay an official call on General Okamura as necessary to the functioning of the Military Attaché's office. Stilwell grudgingly agreed but announced he would not go in uniform, and when argued out of that position, balked at wearing a sword, and when persuaded of this formality, had no reserve left but to refuse positively to go in breeches and boots, the inseparable accessories of the Japanese officer. Grimly in military slacks he marched off to tea with China's conquerors and managed to get into an argument on the innocuous subject of the temple deer at Nara.

Drawing up a balance sheet of Japanese qualities to relieve his feelings in private, Stilwell allowed them six good qualities—industrious, brave, perservering, organized, disciplined, patriotic—as against 26 bad—ranging through arrogant, cynical, truculent, ruthless, brutal, stupid, treacherous, lying, unscrupulous, unmoral, unbalanced and hysterical. Almost any foreigner having to accommodate to the Japanese in China during these years would have shared Stilwell's sentiments, if not his facility in expressing them. To maintain correct relations under the provocative insolence and swagger, and worst of all the stream of bland inside-out distortions of fact, was mortifying to the soul. Even Sir Robert Craigie, British Ambassador in Tokyo, while on a visit to Shanghai described himself as so "utterly weary of the policy of appeasing Japan" and so "nauseated by being polite to the little blighters," that he felt constantly humiliated and "emotionally and even maybe mentally upset." He suffered a recurring dream in which, wearing a general's gold-braided uniform, he commanded a landing party near Tokyo and was suffused by a tremendous joy at the order to go "all out in retaliation against the dirty little bastards."

What really tortured Craigie and Stilwell and many others was the passivity of their own countries in the face of Japanese aggression. Frustration was acute as despotism advanced and the democracies threw it chunks of appeasement to buy themselves the illusion of safety. In addition, Stilwell faced his own depressing professional prospects. The first star of a brigadier general which made all the difference in a military career appeared to have receded beyond his reach. In another year he would have passed five years without a promotion which, combined with more than 30 years in the Army, indicated retirement. His old friend Honeycutt and nine others of his class including two junior to him were already generals. Though he had friends and advocates working for him, writing letters to the War Department, and though their pressure had succeeded in having his name put on the eligible list, McCabe's disparaging Efficiency Reports were a nearly insuperable block. Assigned by his new orders to an unpromising job he believed "they're trying to put me out to pasture" and saw his career ending in undistinguished desuetude among the retired colonels.

The time came for departure on May 1, 1939. Discouragement was in the air. Far away in Chungking the winter fogs had lifted, enabling Japanese terror bombing of the undefended city to begin. America was still selling scrap to Japan. No sign of help for China was in prospect. In nearly two years since the incident at Marco Polo Bridge, the improved and concerted military resistance that Stilwell had hoped for had not evolved.

On their last day in China, on board the riverboat from Tientsin to Taku, the Stilwells joined a friend, Mrs. Edmund Clubb, wife of an Embassy official, who too was going home. As they opened a lunch basket to picnic on deck they saw floating by the drowned body of a man clutching a drowned child still attached by a rope to the piece of wood used by houseboat families as a life preserver. It had been inadequate. As a symbol of everything sad and wrong in China the sight of the dead bodies in the river at that particular moment was unbearable. Wordless, the group picked up their lunch and went below.

In America three days earlier Stilwell's fate was entirely changed by an unexpected development: over the heads of 34 senior officers George

121

*Japanese terror bombing of the wartime capital of Chungking
began in the spring of 1939 (121). Refugees watch their homes
burn to the ground (122).*

122

Marshall was appointed Acting Chief of Staff, to succeed to the full position on September 1. With conflict approaching, Marshall's urgent concern was to replace the Army's dead wood with men of action and initiative. One of the first two names he sent up for promotion to brigadier general was Stilwell's.

On August 3, on board ship just coming into Honolulu after a three-month tour through Siam, Indochina, Malaya and Java, Stilwell learned of his promotion by radio message. "It can't be true," he said to Win. "Don't say a word about it. I'm going up on deck to have a walk and try to digest it." But on the Army transport the news had already spread and people crushed around to congratulate him. Everyone joined in the excitement except for one family who outranking the Stilwells had preempted the best cabin. Now entitled to it, Stilwell had no intention of pressing the claim but told Win during the stay-over at Honolulu, "Let's let them be a little uncomfortable and think we might."

Suddenly in the outpouring of congratulatory letters everything he might have accomplished and every good quality he might claim seemed to be recognized. "Ever since I bit on your damned Smirkäse joke 20 odd years ago I have been convinced you deserved it," wrote Sherman Miles. Common to many of the letters was pleased surprise that an officer of pronounced "independence of thought" and "energy of execution," as a major of the Infantry expressed it, had made it against the odds. The news, the letters said, restored confidence in the Administration; at last Headquarters had made a good promotion in spite of everything: "We knew Marshall would do right by the Army and he has." There was real delight in the messages. "It makes you feel like throwing the old sombrero right through the roof," wrote one friend. "Hot dog—you should have had it long before," wrote Willie Whipple. "I have always said so. So has all 1904." "The average excellence of the general officer list has gone up considerably since yesterday," pronounced a colonel of Artillery.

Evans Carlson wrote, "One of the convictions I carried away from China with me was that the army needed a man such as you as a general officer . . . I hardly need say that I would be proud to serve under you in combat." Other China veterans were happy that the "damned China gang" had received fitting recognition at last. After the long displeasure of MID, it was ironic to learn from an officer of its naval equivalent, ONI, that Stilwell's reports had kept that department "oriented on the war in China." "No one in years received a generalship who deserved it more," this admirer wrote. He knew Stilwell would justify it in the field "if war should come in the near future as it looks like it may."

A month later the war began in Europe.

9

The Rush to Prepare
1939-41

T HE United States Army that Stilwell returned to in September 1939 ranked, with Reserves, 19th among the world's armed forces, after Portugal but ahead of Bulgaria. In percent of population under arms it ranked 45th. The active Army numbered 174,000 men, less than two-thirds the peacetime strength authorized by Act of Congress in 1920. It had only three organized divisions, none of them more than 50 percent complete, whose complements were scattered among a number of posts with no opportunity for divisional training owing to the shortage of motor transport. In addition, there were six partly organized divisions, two Cavalry divisions but not one Armored division. There were no corps troops, army troops or GHQ troop units. Training as a field force was inadequate; equipment, modern in 1919, was obsolete. Owing to shortage of funds, maneuvers were held only once every four years for a two-week period with only five days of "very limited action." The continual paring of appropriations by Congress had reduced the Army, reported its new chief, General Marshall, "to the status of that of a third rate power" with less than 25 percent readiness to fight.

The theory that allowed this condition was that the Army was a last and unlikely resort needed only for defense of the United States which in any case was well protected by its oceans. Military policy did not contemplate another expeditionary force outside the hemisphere. After the last overseas war the national consensus was "Never again." The immediate object

A U.S. Army convoy climbs the famous "21 curves" highway at the far end of the Burma Road en route to supply-starved Chungking (123).

before Marshall was to bring the Army up to strength and make it ready
in training and equipment for modern combat. "To make good soldiers out
of good materials," had decreed General Sylvanus Thayer, father of West
Point, "they must be drilled by competent men; to make a good army
out of the best men will take three years." The task was formidable enough
in itself without the primary difficulty of persuading Congress to supply the
funds.

Brigadier General Stilwell was assigned to command the 3rd Brigade of
the 2nd Division at Fort Sam Houston in Texas. During a month's leave
before taking up the post he lectured on the Sino-Japanese War at West
Point, an occasion memorable for his reply to a Cavalry officer's question
on the role of the horse in the fighting in China. After a thoughtful pause
Stilwell replied, "Good eating, if you're hungry." He went on to Washington
to report on China and to allow himself the agreeable opportunity to "have
it out with McCabe" whom he now outranked. It was a sublime moment;
heads popped out of every door as the new general strode down the corridor, and during his talk with McCabe, unhappily not recorded, Stilwell
took care to leave the door open for the benefit of listeners.

As a general he was now entitled to an aide which presented something
of a problem because an aide, like a swagger stick, was a concept in
conspicuous waste that made Stilwell's hackles rise. Aides were "door-
openers and coat-hangers," but he solved his personal problem by selecting
a congenial spirit, Captain Frank Dorn, who had already served under him
in China for four years. A West Point graduate of 1923, known as Pinky
for his complexion, not his politics, Dorn at thirty-eight was a handsome
humorous bachelor of cultivated mind and versatile talents, gifted as an
artist, with sufficient natural irreverence and intellectual curiosity to make
him a stimulating companion. Stilwell approached the subject with some
embarrassment. "I know what you think of aides," he said to Dorn, "and
I know what you think of generals. I've got a proposition for you. I'll be
a new kind of general and you can be a new kind of aide. Don't answer
now. Think it over and send me a telegram." The proposition was accepted.

Although his promotion to general had eliminated personal bitterness,
Stilwell still felt angry and impatient with American policy. From where he
stood Washington appeared to lack understanding of how developments
in the Far East were affecting America and to be paying too much attention to Europe. Like every other serious foreign service officer he felt his
reports had not penetrated the realm of policy-making, perhaps not even
been read.* He believed the main concern of his country was going to be

_____

* Willys Peck, Counselor of the Nanking Embassy in 1936, wrote of "the bottom of
the void into which (we sometimes feel) we drop our reports to Washington." The

Asia and that the United States in its relative quiescence before the Japanese advance was ignoring a situation that would be more important than Europe in the long run. Convinced that war with Japan was coming, he thought the focus on Europe kept Washington from recognizing the danger. Anyone fresh from the physical presence of the Japanese in China, from the arrests and gun-prodding and purposeful humiliation of foreigners, despaired of conveying the actuality of Japanese menace to officials behind desks in Washington.

Marshall, to whom Stilwell poured out his argument, assured him that his reports had been read, that the situation was understood, if far from met, and that "your job, Joe, is to go on down to Fort Sam and help us out."

Stilwell reached Texas on September 24. As brigade commander he served as second in command of the division to General Walter Krueger. The Army, in search of speed and mobility, was using the 2nd Division to experiment with a streamlined triangular formation of three Infantry regiments amounting to 11,000 men instead of the 22,000 of the old square division. Galvanized by the German blitz in Poland, the 2nd Division and companion units of the Third Army entered into a winter of strenuous training, living in the field, marching and sleeping on the ground, often in rain and freezing weather. In field exercises in January Krueger put Stilwell in command of the attacking "enemy" force, a role which because of the *élan* he brought to it was to become his regular part in maneuvers. American training was geared to repel the invader, and with Stilwell leading the invasion, according to a colleague, "there was never a dull moment." His ideas and surprises and unexpected tactics, witnessed by Marshall on a visit in January, upset routine patterns and broke rules. In Dorn's words, "He wanted to win, not just play."

At the planning level in Washington, although overseas action was not contemplated, the War Department had drawn up a Protective Mobilization Plan for a force of 500,000 in an emergency with an eventual army of 1,200,000. But no action to mobilize the nation's industries for the vast effort to arm and supply such a force had been taken. Roosevelt shied off from the necessity for fear of arousing the public and reviving charges of economic "dictatorship." He was equally reluctant to ask for all the appropriations that Marshall wanted for fear of exciting opposition in Congress just when he was trying to persuade it to revise the Neutrality Act. The prior urgency as he saw it, as the crisis temperature mounted in

---

Consul in Yunnan, A. R. Ringwalt, voiced the same complaint: "Especially in an outpost like this one gets the feeling that one is merely writing for one's own amusement, and that reports when received are merely filed away without any notice having been taken of their content."

Europe, was to obtain repeal of the arms embargo so that when the time came America could aid the Allies to win quickly before she could be drawn into the conflict. It was obvious to the Administration if not to the isolationists that American security depended ultimately on the British fleet. Britain's survival as a sovereign nation was an American vital interest in a sense that China's was not.

The country clung to neutrality, the last nostalgia of the American dream to have done with the Old World's quarrels, as long as it could. Then came September 1939. The smashing of Poland by the frightening armor of 56 German divisions and 1,400 planes shook Congress sufficiently to repeal the arms embargo in November after a month's debate, although the isolationists managed to retain the cash-and-carry provision.

American sentiment was more prepared to be partisan in the Far East than in Europe. Partly this was due to guilty conscience about China and partly to the curious fact that it was permissible to be at once isolationist and anti-Japanese. The old-style thunderers like Senators Borah and Hiram Johnson managed to be both vociferous against war and bellicose against Japan without stumbling over any internal difficulty. Roosevelt had no difficulty at all in July 1939 in getting Congress to agree to give the required six months' notice to Japan of intention to terminate the existing Trade Treaty, opening the way to possible economic sanctions. This gesture, in response to a campaign of extreme harassment that Japan was conducting against American and especially British presence in China, was intended to show that the United States was not going to withdraw and to give Japan some cause for caution.

Senator Vandenberg, a leading isolationist, had already offered a resolution to abrogate the Trade Treaty. Two other Senators had submitted resolutions favoring some form of arms embargo against Japan (the Neutrality Act not having been invoked for the Far East). Ambassador Grew on returning from Tokyo to Washington for consultation was struck by the sentiment and thought "Pressure for an embargo against Japan is going to be great . . . and Congress may demand it." By January 1940 five bills or resolutions for embargoing trade with Japan in one form or another awaited action by the new Congress. They were a measure of the change in public opinion in the two years since Congress scuttled under the Ludlow Resolution at the time of the *Panay* incident. The terror bombings of Chinese cities and especially the sense that America was contributing to them by selling scrap to Japan had had their effect. The medical missionary, Dr. Walter Judd, made the connection vivid when he told of his work as a doctor in Shansi removing "these things" from the bodies of Chinese wounded. His listeners could imagine their own scrapped automobiles converted into Japanese bombs. Although church groups on the whole opposed an embargo against Japan as likely to lead to war, many missionaries campaigned for it, "resolutely backed up by naval force if necessary." Seventy percent of the public favored it according to polls. It was the "American people," Ambassador Grew said in an unusual public speech in Tokyo—another of the cautionary efforts—who objected to Japan's efforts to establish a "closed economy" in Asia and to the "bombings, the indignities, the manifold interference with American rights."

In the matter of the Far East Roosevelt lagged behind public opinion for compelling strategic reasons. Strongly advised by the War and State Departments, he hung back from the embargo for fear of provoking Japan—which was dependent on the United States for oil—into southward expansion to obtain alternate sources in the Netherlands Indies. Southeast Asia, with the oil of the Indies, the rubber of Malaya and the rice of Indochina, held the resources the Japanese needed; in the power vacuum caused by the war in Europe lay their opportunity. Japan's militarists, riding the tide of empire, were urging the adventure. It was the one thing that would be *casus belli* for everyone, excluding Russia. It would threaten all the Western positions from Hong Kong to Singapore including the Philippines, possibly even India. It would mean a two-ocean war for which the British fleet was not adequate and the United States not ready. To avoid it if possible, but in any case to postpone it, was essential.

Use of the American Army overseas was still not contemplated. "It is simply unthinkable," stated Colonel Frank Knox, no isolationist but publisher of the internationally minded *Chicago Daily News,* in a speech on April 3, 1940, "that we will ever again send overseas a great expeditionary force of armed men." Though warning that the Allies had only a 50 percent chance of winning and urging an increase in American air and naval strength, he dismissed "all grandiose plans for a whole nation making war with millions of soldiers in the field . . . as unnecessary for our defense." Six days later the German invasion of Norway and Denmark brought the static period of "phony war" to an end.

At this time the American Army had reached a strength of 241,000 of which only five divisions were organized, though not fully equipped, for the field. The arms and equipment and above all the airplanes for the envisaged emergency force of 500,000, much less for 1,200,000, did not exist. To produce them for the larger number, the War Department informed the President, would require from 18 months to two years. By now the Germans had swept into the Low Countries heading for France. Roosevelt asked for new defense appropriations of a billion dollars and stunned the country with a call for production of the astounding figure, multiplied beyond anything ever before suggested, of 50,000 planes a year.

On May 10—the day the Germans invaded Holland and Belgium—the first genuine corps maneuvers in United States history, engaging 70,000 troops of the Third Army, began in Louisiana. Commanding the "Red" invaders, Stilwell made a reputation that placed him in the front rank of American combat infantry commanders and was to earn him his second star within a year of the first. Because of the impending decision on whether to adopt the triangular division, and the opportunity to observe a demonstration of the Third Army's blitzkrieg tactics, all the Army's important figures were watching. The plan presumed that the Red nation was invading the United States with an army of 30,000 and pushing eastward from Texas across the border marked by the Sabine River into Louisiana. The Reds were to drive upon Alexandria, capital of the "Blue" nation, whose army of 40,000 (the defenders being given the benefit of the larger force) was based 700 miles away at Fort Benning. Represented by the IXth Corps, which included the 2nd Division, the Reds achieved surprise by jumping off ahead of schedule, a breaking of the rules that was almost certainly Stilwell-inspired. It reflected his theory that the way to achieve a successful offensive was to "spoil things as planned."

The Red air force attacking with vigor seized command of the air enabling its ground force to roll back the Blues, capture several key places and forge ahead. Stilwell's specialty was night movements to accomplish envelopment by a wide-end run, bringing him up to hit the enemy on flank and rear. His troops attacked Natchitoches "after one of the most amazing encirclements ever undertaken in the history of the Army," according to an enthusiastic press report. From the takeoff point at the Sabine River his scout cars two abreast dashed across the bridge at 3 A.M., followed by demolition parties despatched to every bridge and crossroads to destroy the possibility of the Blues gaining a flank position. By daylight his advance units had traveled 70 miles in a long dash that "was like a series of crises in a melodrama. . . . Stilwell's invasion was Blitzkrieg at its apogee." At nightfall its movements were lost in the "fog of war" and the question everywhere was "Where is the 2nd Division?"

As the battle expanded his surprises continued. At morning he would appear in the wrong place, that is, where he was not expected, and at one point, infuriating General Krueger, he captured the Headquarters of the First Cavalry then commanded by Jonathan Wainright who was soon to suffer a harder defeat at Bataan. The action was ruled fair by the umpires. Observers were impressed because Stilwell was penetrating and generally winning while most officers appeared to be still mentally fighting the last war.

In sinister accompaniment to the American war games the Panzer divisions were smashing through Holland and Belgium, pointing up in their advance many of the faults revealed in Louisiana. In addition to poor reconnaissance, lack of liaison between units and "painful" lack of artillery support, the chief umpire noted an "extreme disinclination of troops to de-truck" and of the trucks themselves to leave the roads and move across country. Roadbound trucks were sitting ducks and infantry in trucks were "completely helpless." Stilwell too was far from satisfied. In Europe, he noted, "a revolutionary form of attack has been developed. Reconnaissance aviation, scout cars, dive bombers, heavy tanks, motorized infantry, bombing aviation, parachuters, all tied, strike and fan out. Attempt to paralyze enemy rear areas. Do we pay any attention? No."

The difficulty was that many of the officers, like the public at large, still felt no sense of the urgency that Stilwell had acquired after two years of war in China. As the German sickle sliced into northern France trapping the Allies against the Channel, one American divisional commander offered to bet, as casually as if it concerned next day's weather, that if France fell Great Britain would not last six weeks longer.

By mid-June the fall of France was an awful reality. The Germans were actually in Paris. In six weeks they had accomplished what four years of gigantic struggle in 1914-18 had never attained. The comparison was a sudden appalling measure of the democracies' weakness. The British saved their Army at the evacuation of Dunkirk but with loss of all their heavy weapons. Short of rifles and ammunition, almost naked in aircraft, they were left with the Channel and Winston Churchill who spoke the famous words, "We shall fight on the beaches . . . in the streets . . . we shall never surrender . . ."

The fall of France staggered America; suddenly anything seemed possible and the invulnerability of the United States no longer safe to assume. If Britain were defeated, the President admitted privately, the United States would be living "at the point of a Nazi gun." Military opinion was not sanguine. General George Strong, Chief of the War Plans Division, who had been one of Stilwell's anathemas at MID during the reign of McCabe, predicted on June 17 "the early defeat of the Allies." The public having comfortably assumed during the "phony war" that the Allies must win, now assumed the contrary and was moved to panic over the poverty of American defenses. Both President Roosevelt and former President Hoover made national radio speeches to calm what Roosevelt called the "calamity-howlers" and direct the fear toward useful ends. "There is no occasion for panic," said Hoover; "there is need for speed."

The following months boiled with defense programs. The War Department drew plans for an Army of a million by October 1941 and two million a year later which would depend on enactment—in an election year—of that repugnant un-Americanism, compulsory military service in peacetime. The President in a startling move named to his Cabinet as Secretary of War and of the Navy, respectively, two Republicans, former Secretary Stimson, now seventy-three, and Colonel Knox, both outspoken advocates of the Draft. Meanwhile Congress in a rush had voted increased men for the Army and tonnage for the Navy and an extra billion and a half dollars to pay for them. But this was piecemeal. In July the President laid before Congress a "total defense" program of production requirements for an Army of 1,200,000, a matching Air Force and a two-ocean Navy strong enough to meet any combination of powers at a cost of just under $5 billion. Congress was in a mood to vote anything for national defense except the compulsory draft of men to implement it. The country was not ready to face the implication that history was again presenting a bill for foreign war. Through the summer the debate on conscription raged.

In the hope of deterring Japan from taking advantage of the crisis in Europe it was decided to keep the Pacific Fleet based at Hawaii to where it had already been moved from San Diego in April. Deterring Japan was now the most urgent task, next to making ready herself, that America faced. The task contained an inherently insoluble problem: any action that could effectively deter Japan from expansion would be bound to stimulate action by Japan to forestall it—would, in short, stimulate the aggression it was supposed to deter. This difficulty was to haunt coming developments.

The Japanese Government, unwilling to cut its last moorings to caution, had so far been resisting the pressure of its military members to join the Axis. In alliance with the triumphant Reich the militarists saw themselves freed for action. Germany would keep Russia neutral, freeing Japan to expand southward without worrying about the north. German-Japanese alliance would also, they believed, deter the United States from actively supporting China, allowing Japan finally to conclude the "Incident." "The more effectively we restrain the United States," explained the aggressive War Minister, General Hideki Tojo, to his colleagues, "the more quickly we shall be able to dispose of the Sino-Japanese conflict." Japanese blockade of the British and French Concessions at Tientsin, provocations and pressure on the International Settlement at Shanghai, attacks on American property and the close-shave bombing of another gunboat in the Yangtze were designed to exhibit the democracies' weakness and so eliminate the Government's hesitancy about the Axis alliance.

For Japan too the German triumph over France was a turning point, proving as it seemed that this really *was* the wave of the future. Behind the scenes negotiations with Germany began; publicly the Japanese Foreign Office now associated itself with the militarists' program for a Greater East Asia Co-Prosperity Sphere and agreed that "the uniting of all these regions" was national destiny. The occasion of the Allied extremity in Europe was seized on for a definitive effort to achieve a settlement in China by sealing off China's last avenues of supply from the West.

After three years the end of the "Incident" still eluded the Japanese. Further penetration, bombings, terrorism, overtures, collaborationists— nothing had succeeded. They had intended to control the country by enforced collaboration, but as long as a National Government maintained resistance they had to remain in military occupation. Now in the final hours of the French collapse a Japanese ultimatum required the French to close the railroad from Hanoi into China and to accept a Japanese military base for inspection purposes inside Indochina. At the same time the British were virtually ordered by Japan, to the accompaniment of threats of war, to close the Hong Kong frontier and the Burma Road. The Chinese were not bringing in supplies in any very important amount over that clogged and mismanaged highway, but the Road, scratched out of the mountainsides by the hand labor of 200,000 men, women and children, was now their last channel to the West. The act of closing by a friendly state would be certain to turn sentiment against the democracies and lend weight to the arguments of those advocating a settlement with Japan.

The British Empire and the United States between them could not summon the collective strength to withstand the demand. Britain, now alone against the Axis, asked the United States for joint action in the event that war with Japan followed refusal. The United States, having scraped the bottom of her military warehouse to send arms to Britain in her naked emergency after Dunkirk, was in poor shape to fight, and in any case could not commit herself to belligerency if the *casus belli* were attack on European imperial possessions. She could give no promise of joint action. Britain submitted and on July 12 closed the Burma Road, though with the proviso that it was to be for three months to allow for a further effort to conclude peace between Japan and China.

A wave of pessimism did indeed sweep through Chungking but not enough to recommend peace terms with Japan. The Pan-Asian, anti-Western theme of the Co-Prosperity Sphere appealed to many Chinese but the aroused spirit of patriotism rejected its Japanese sponsors. Wang Ching-wei's puppet government in Nanking failed to win popular support because the Japanese hand pulling its strings was too visible and because Japanese efforts to "pacify" the countryside by force did nothing to make Co-Prosperity attractive.

Chiang Kai-shek did not succumb to the overtures of various emissaries.

He had acted all along in the belief that he would be bailed out when the Western powers inevitably became involved in war with Japan and he was never a man to change his mind, even when the cause of the democracies looked black. Besides, if he dealt with Japan, as one of his countrymen said, "he would be ruined in any case." But from this time forward, his increasingly exigent demands for American aid were accompanied by hints that he might have to come to terms with Japan because Chinese morale was at the point of collapse or because resistance could not be sustained. China did not conceal her bitterness at the powers' failure either to help her or more actively to restrain Japan. The desperate query that Stilwell shared—why cannot America see that the time to stop Japan is *now?*— sounded through the flow of Chinese demands for loans, arms, credit, planes, sanctions or declarations of war and other advice offered by the Generalissimo to Washington.

The President feared that an embargo would have the effect of pushing Japan into the rumored alliance with the Axis, adding to Britain's danger. Yet some gesture to encourage China and warn Japan was essential: on July 26 the United States proclaimed a limited embargo on scrap iron and steel and certain grades of aviation fuel, but not on oil for fear of touching off a Japanese advance to the Indies.

On July 1, 1940, Stilwell attained the goal of every officer's desire— command of a division. He was named Commanding General of the 7th Division and of its base, Camp Ord at Monterey, close by his home at Carmel. The 7th was a new triangular division requiring training in every element. The camp, soon renamed Fort Ord, was in a fever of preparation for the influx of draftees expected in October if the Draft Bill should become law. Men lived in tents while barracks, mess halls, administration buildings and all the quarters for 15,000 men were being hammered together within a few weeks.

Stilwell was busy 16 hours a day, planning, supervising, inspecting, training men, training officers and training officers to train the men. He at once established a school under the command of Colonel Thomas Arms for company officers coming in from the Reserves and National Guard. "Be ready to start a week from today," he told Arms, to give a short course in tactics, demonstration and practice, and a field problem every morning and afternoon. Stilwell spent three or four days a week watching the school exercises with squad and platoon, often himself coaching green officers through an attack problem. Carefully and patiently he would explain the five-paragraph field order and the reason for orders in fixed sequence so that in the heat of action none would be forgotten. He had a habit of appearing from behind a bush and making a critique on the spot;

no one knew where he might turn up. He drove his senior officers without let-up, allowing wide freedom of action but expecting dedication and performance at his own level. "If you didn't deliver you didn't last long," said Arms; "he was cold-blooded, very cold-blooded." Stilwell's leadership was exciting because it was not "book-bound," but it was unsparing of the officers. Some were antagonized; the majority admired and some worshipped him. "You had to," according to one 7th Division colonel, "he had it."

After Congress in September enacted compulsory military service (for men between twenty-one and thirty-five, who could not be required to serve outside the Western Hemisphere or for more than one year), the 7th was filled with 85 percent draftees. Tanks, trucks, mortars, guns, vehicles, ammunition, all the tools of soldiering, were scarce. Men trained with wooden rifles and fired TNT for artillery shells. True battle training was unattainable because the public and the draftees had not accepted the reality of the urgency. Press and parents objected to exposing the draftees to rough conditions. The mood was reflected in the OHIO movement—Over the Hill in October—which infected the one-year men. Stilwell's program allowed little time for that sentiment. He held battle maneuvers and parades to foster pride in the Division and often led marches himself to instill morale. Through his training and tactical skill he forged a division that was to excel in the great maneuvers of 1941.

He was never happier than when making soldiers and would often sit at ease among the enlisted men discussing tactical problems with characteristic quick turns of the head and fleeting wisps of smile. The General in battered hat, hiking boots and lumberman's sweater, almost indistinguishable from civilian workers around the post, was soon being referred to as Uncle Joe, or Galloping Joe in tribute to his walking capacity. He walked all over the hills and dunes of Fort Ord Reservation and often covered half the twelve-mile distance from his home to Headquarters on foot. In September 1940, on news of his promotion to major general, he was greeted at the post by artillery lined up for a thirteen-gun salute, a Cavalry guard of honor with band and a massed group of staff officers, arranged by Dorn not without mischief. "Who the hell planned this?" the General growled in furious embarrassment as he climbed out of his car to receive the salute.

Addressing the assembled troops he was purposely brief. He did not believe in long speeches on occasions of promotion, he said, on the principle that "the higher a monkey climbs a pole, the more you see of his behind."

In a "black cat" or off-the-record talk to the San Francisco Press Club at this time Stilwell said that war with the Japanese was certain; that the United States should have slapped them down in the case of the *Panay;*

that procrastination was giving them choice of time and place for battle. He said that given command of a properly armed and equipped Chinese army with two American divisions to act as spearheads he could run the Japanese out of China in six months because the Japanese were efficient but unimaginative and rigid. They worked by the rules, becoming confused by unorthodox tactics.

This low opinion was universally shared by foreign military observers who watched the Japanese performance in China. Falkenhausen and the other German advisers who were frequently at the front, and from whom Stilwell collected much information on Japanese tactics, used to tell him how easily Japanese officers could be identified because they could always be seen peering through glasses or looking at a map or wearing swords, and that proper marksmanship could have reaped a harvest among them. Captain Carlson, after observing the battle of Shanghai in 1937, wrote that the Japanese war machine was "revealed as a third rate army." He described them as lacking initiative and resourcefulness, trained by rote and doing everything by formula, and when the formula did not work, knowing no alternative. Because of their dependence on heavy equipment and air and artillery support, their forces were "cumbersome on the march and expensive to maintain." After further observation in 1938 he reported "inferiority of striking power, poor coordination of transport, poor coordination of airforce and ground troops, inferiority of weapons, poor direction of artillery fire and lack of imagination and initiative on the part of leaders." Significantly Carlson acknowledged that "many of the errors they are making in this war will not be repeated."

The judgments of Stilwell and Carlson and others, though exaggerated by antipathy to the Japanese, were not invalid for the performance in China and were to have unfortunate effect. They reflected the general tendency of Westerners to assume that because the Japanese were imitative they were not to be feared. "There is little to learn from Japan in the domain of military implements or inventions, and less in what concerns strategy or the art of war," pronounced Colonel Bentley Mott, the dean of American Military Attachés in 1937. It was his complacent judgment that in these matters Japan was simply an imitator and "continues to follow in the wake of Western progress." No awakening was ever to be more painful.

In September 1940, the month of Stilwell's promotion, Japan joined the Axis, officially aligning herself, in Ambassador Grew's phrase, as one of the "predatory powers." From this time on, the President and his advisers believed, as recorded by Secretary Stimson, that the United States "would be drawn into the war eventually," and were reinforced in their conviction of the necessity of sending aid to Britain and by some means or other to China. A loan of $50 million to China was quickly approved in

November less than two months after one of $25 million in September. Joint staff talks were arranged to be held with the British as soon as the Presidential election would be over in November.

The fundamental decision from which all else followed was taken at this time, more than a year before the United States became a belligerent. The President in conference with the two service Secretaries, Stimson and Knox, and the two service chiefs, Marshall and Admiral Harold Stark, agreed, in the event of the United States being drawn into the war, on a basic strategy of primary action in Europe while maintaining the defensive in the Pacific. This "Europe first" strategy reflected the recognition that Europe was the site of world power and the belief that it always would be. It was to determine the shape of the war including Stilwell's role and profoundly affect the relation with China.

On the understanding that there must be no commitment to offensive action by the Army until it should be prepared to take it, Anglo-American staff talks began in January 1941. ABDA (American-British-Dutch-Australian) staff talks on cooperation in the Far East were held at Singapore in April. Since the United States could give no promise of joint action the conversations were less effective than they might have been.

Britain repeatedly asked what the United States would do if Japan attacked Singapore or the Netherlands Indies. The Americans could give no answer. They believed as did the British that if Japan attacked anyone it would be one of the European nations already fighting against Germany. At a meeting of Marshall and Stark with the two service Secretaries in December, "all four agreed" that the war could not be won without the United States becoming involved but they had no idea how this would be brought about. The Japanese too were considering the problem. The Navy, having come to the conclusion, as stated by Admiral Yamamoto, that "We will have no hope of winning unless the U.S. fleet in Hawaiian waters can be destroyed," began that winter to work on the planning operations for attack on Pearl Harbor.

The Chinese in October 1940 presented America with a new request that was to have enormous sequel. They asked for an air force of 500 American planes manned by American pilots who would fly in the service of China, together with a large loan to finance the project. Chiang Kai-shek presented the need as dire and urgent and offered alluring promise of a large return. Speaking the mind of his air adviser, Colonel Chennault, he argued that American planes manned by American pilots could effect a "fundamental solution" by destroying the Japanese Navy in its own bases. Long-range bombers could "carry the war into Japan proper"; medium bombers and fighters by harassing the sea-lanes could forestall a Japanese attack on Singapore, prevent Japan from exercising control of the Chinese coast and from bombing the Burma Road which had just been reopened by the British. Chiang stated that China's economy and morale were on the verge of collapse and that if the planes did not come in time, that is before Japan bombed the Road or closed the sea-lanes by taking Singapore, "it would be too late and China's position would be extremely if not hopelessly critical."

Chiang Kai-shek saw the aid for which he had so persistently asked going to Britain. He was determined that China which had been fighting when Britain was still appeasing ought to have first consideration once the bounties started to flow. While Chennault was pursuing brilliant visions of sinking the Japanese Navy, Chiang was interested in the strengthening of his own position that an air force with all its war material would provide. He admitted to Ambassador Johnson that he was more anxious about the Communists who, he feared, were "taking advantage" of the situation, than about the Japanese.

The Communists had in fact renewed action against the invader in recent months. The war against Japan was both their safeguard against the Kuomintang and their avenue of appeal to the people. They needed it. Fearing defeatism after the fall of France and the possibility of Chiang making a settlement with Japan in terms certain to involve an anti-Communist crusade, they launched a "100 regiments offensive" by the 8th Route Army in Hopei and Shansi to keep the war alive. The guerilla attacks provoked a campaign of terrible retaliation by the Japanese on a newly devised *Senko-seisaku* ("three all") principle—kill all, burn all, destroy all—which left provinces blackened and massacred.*

Renewed Communist activity was not welcomed by Chiang Kai-shek any more than by the Japanese and was soon to move him to action. Disliking especially the presence of the Communist New Fourth Army south of the Yangtze, he ordered them back across the river to the north and in the course of this operation, in January 1941, executed a surprise attack on the New Fourth which recalled his coup in Shanghai in 1926. Thereafter the united front was only a facade for underlying enmity.

The quest for an air force was vigorously pursued in Washington in person by its progenitor, Colonel Chennault, in company with T. V. Soong, the envoy charged with satisfying China's needs in the United States. Chennault was a fighter pilot by choice and temperament, a fanatic of aerial pursuit who had studied his subject to its last turn and twist, applied imagination and daring, and contributed new skills, maneuvers and cap-

---

* The method was to surround a given area and destroy everything in it to make it uninhabitable. Based on Japanese records, a two-month "mopping-up" campaign in one district of Hopei resulted in 4,500 killed, 15,000 houses burned and 17,000 persons deported to Manchuria.

abilities. Fifty years old in 1940, he had started life as a high-school teacher in Texas, took officer's training in 1917 after the United States entered the war, was commissioned in the Infantry Reserve but transferred to the aviation section of the Signal Corps and served without going overseas in the war. Joining the Army Air Corps after 1920 he experimented and tested fighting tactics of his own devising and taught them at Flying School and at the Air Corps Tactical School as well as in a textbook he wrote entitled *The Role of Defensive Pursuit*. He hectored the Air Corps on his dogma of the value and importance of pursuit aviation and the necessity of fighter escort. Since the Air Corps had adopted the contrary Douhet theory which assumed that successive waves of bombers would be self-protecting against pursuit attack, Chennault was not popular. Grounded by deafness and feeling the sense of persecution that afflicts men with a mission when they are not listened to, he retired in 1936. Disciples who had flown for China recommended him and he was snapped up by Chiang Kai-shek in the following year.

Hard, wiry and weathered like Stilwell and about his size with a face scarred from the windstream of open cockpits, Chennault combined great professional skill with a touch of megalomania. He was given to extremes. His meeting with Mme. Chiang Kai-shek in 1937 "was an encounter from which I never recovered." When she "tripped into the room bubbling with energy and enthusiasm" he was "completely captivated" and wrote in his diary that night, "She will always be a princess to me." As a boy of fifteen he had developed a similar crush on his stepmother and never afterwards found "another companion whom I could so completely admire, respect and love." His interest was not China per se but air power. Moving over the country by air to Hankow or Chungking or Kunming, he knew little of the ground—the rivers, the wheelbarrow tracks, the walled villages, the grave-marked countryside or the life of "Old Hundred Names." He worked with the G–mo's entourage, and being unhampered by ideology was not troubled by, if even aware of, the betrayal of origins and decline into despotism of the regime.

Despite his efforts and those of the Russians at Lanchow he had not succeeded in the short time since 1937 in training a group of Chinese combat pilots numerous or effective enough to dispute the skies with the enemy as the RAF was doing over England. His great contribution was the organization of an air warning system by radio manned by spotters in the occupied area, which was so efficient that Chinese headquarters were often warned of raids while Japanese bombers were still warming up at their bases. It gave some protection to the cities but it did not fight back. In default of readiness to take the offensive on the ground, which Stilwell so often complained was not "in" the Chinese, Chennault's proposal of an

American-manned air force offered a magic substitute. Air power was the philosopher's stone, the Aladdin's lamp that could make wishes come true. As conceived by Chennault it offered Chiang a marvelous short cut, an instrument of power without effort, an accretion of war material in his hands, and a sword in other hands to strike the Japanese. As the Aladdin of this operation, Chennault was a favored associate.

The list of requirements brought by Soong to Washington included American ground crews, training planes, parts, field equipment and various schemes for credits, purchase of arms and aircraft, and exchange of military missions. Suggested financial assistance was now enlarged to a request for a joint Anglo-American loan of $200-$300 million. Besides the B-17 heavy bombers to sink the Japanese Navy, Chennault's program asked in Chiang's name for a proportionate number of medium bombers and fighters to make up an air force which could "also support the counter-offensive I am preparing with a view to retaking Canton and Hankow." The quality of fantasy in his proposals was present from the start.

Asking for 500 planes was "like asking for 500 stars," Soong was told by Secretary Morgenthau, the main mover of money and arms to supply America's friends during this period. The United States did not have on hand enough planes to meet its own minimum requirements. Shortages in all branches of matériel were such, according to a War Department survey in September, that the Army could not activate and maintain in the field a combat-ready force of more than 55,000, and then only at the cost of depriving the rest of training equipment. Present production rates gave no hope of equipping the expanded Army, Navy and air arm, while at the same time filling British needs, before April 1942. Even that dateline could only be achieved by increased rate of output and longer working hours.

Yet everyone—the President, Morgenthau, Stimson, Hull and the Joint Board of the armed services—favored planes for China, less for China's sake than to buy time for America to arm. The governing object of American policy was to keep Japan from provoking conflict by southward expansion at least until April 1942. Chennault's plan of offensive operations by a pseudo-Chinese air force using American men and materials promised to perform this service. The presence of air power over her sea-lanes would deter Japan, it was believed, from embarking on the fatal drive to the south.

The strategic object was uppermost but there was also an undertow of desire to help China from natural sympathy and conscience. A company of sympathizers in the White House, State, Treasury, Army, Navy and other agencies "have proposed, pushed, pulled, pounded, sweated and sworn," wrote Stanley Hornbeck, in their efforts to promote American aid to China. "I wanted so much to give these poor men who have been fighting so hard for four years everything we can," as Secretary Stimson expressed it on a later occasion. Roosevelt's view was rather more hard-boiled. "Is he still willing to fight?" he asked when a message came from Chiang Kai-shek in the course of negotiations about the airplanes. Told that this was the purport of the message, he exclaimed, "Wonderful! That's what I have been talking about for four years." He was impressed too by the threat of collapse. "I have real fear that the domestic situation in Free China will deteriorate unless we do something fast," he told Sumner Welles.

But more alluring than either strategy or sympathy was the prospect of American-flown B-17s actually hitting Japan. The Generalissimo's proposal advocated the air raids on the theory that the experience of being bombed might cause the Japanese people "to demand an end to aggression." Since he could hardly have believed in this fanciful notion himself he may have thought it would appeal to the Americans, which it did. It supplied the rationale for a natural instinct to deliver a punch in the eye from which Cabinet members are not immune. Exasperation had been building up under the necessity of swallowing provocations politely ever since the sinking of the *Panay*. China's inability to retaliate while her country was ravaged and cities bombed with impunity had denied Americans even vicarious release. Astonishingly, Secretary Hull proved "a bundle of fervor and vitality" on the bombing project. His Tennessee mountain blood was fired. "What we have got to do, Henry," he told Morgenthau, "is to get 500 planes to start from the Aleutian Islands and fly over Japan just once. . . . That will teach them a lesson. . . . If only we could find some way to have them drop some bombs on Tokyo," he added, leaving Morgenthau speechless. The Secretary of the Treasury too was very taken with the idea, believing that "overnight it would change the whole picture in the Far East." T. V. Soong had persuaded him of the G—mo's thesis that it "would have a very decided effect on the Japanese population."

Soong himself was enthusiastic, and when Morgenthau asked about the danger of bringing retaliatory bombing on China he replied, "They are doing it anyway. . . . This would give us the chance to hit back." Even Lord Lothian, the British Ambassador, shared the enthusiasm. Informed by Morgenthau that he was going to try to get four-engined bombers and crews for the Chinese "with the understanding that these bombers are to be used to bomb Tokyo and other big cities," Lothian agreed "that it might change everything."

Discussion of ways and means began at once but came up against a barrier of caution in Secretary Stimson who thought the idea "rather half-baked" and more representative of Chinese strategy than American. When the requisitions were submitted to General Marshall he declared the whole 500-plane program including the heavy bombers to be "impractical" because aircraft and trained men were simply not available. All that could be scraped together for China was 100 P-40 fighters taken from the number designated for Britain, which they released in the hope of deterring attack on Singapore. With these and with the President's and armed services' backing, the nucleus of Chennault's program went forward.

T. V. Soong and a group of American associates borrowed from the Government organized China Defense Supplies Inc. to conduct all matters of purchase and finance for the hired air force. Regarded by the President as a means of helping a beleaguered democracy, the group had his help and blessing. One of his two closest assistants, Tom Corcoran, was released to the private practice of law and immediately retained by Soong as counsel for China Defense Supplies and contact man with the White House. At the President's suggestion the purchasing group was headed by another Government lawyer, William Youngman, released from the Federal Power Commission. Recruitment of 100 pilots from the Army and Navy air forces was encouraged by the attraction of salaries up to $750 a month and a bonus of $500 for every Japanese plane shot down. Release of the pilots for enlistment as mercenaries in the service of China was authorized by Executive Order in April 1941. Despite official support progress was slowed by difficulties, delays and shortages. The American Volunteer Group (AVG) did not reach Burma to begin Chennault's rigorous course of training until November 1941, too late to deter, though not to fight.

The move that opened the faucet of real aid to China was passage of the Lend-Lease Act in March 1941. Thereafter the flow of aid became an investment, and the need to protect the investment increased the flow until it became a silver cord attaching America to the Nationalist Government. There is no more entangling alliance than aid to indigent friends.

To compensate for the drain on British credit Roosevelt had asked Congress for a program to lend or lease arms and matériel to "the government of any country whose defense the President deems vital to the United States." Since the plan gave promise of keeping the war away from American shores by financing and supplying others to fight while Americans remained nonbelligerent, it had attractions for the isolationists. Providing $700 million worth of war material to begin with, the bill passed by the comfortable margin of 317-71 in the House. China was at once declared eligible. Thereafter Lend-Lease became the core and foundation and, from the Chinese point of view, the most important aspect of the Sino-American relationship. They no longer had to beg; it was now America's obligation to supply their needs. Their appetite swelled to the colossal. Demands for everything an army could use—rifles, howitzers, trench mortars, machine guns, field guns, antitank guns, tanks, ammunition, vehicles and loans to pay for them—poured in. The problem was the same that Stilwell had met in the case of Feng Yu-hsiang: amounts and types of weapons were unrealistic. Thirteen-ton tanks too heavy for Chinese bridges and other unusable weapons appeared on the lists.

The business generated by Lend-Lease through China Defense Supplies was even more lucrative than most military procurement operations. It made the fortunes of the Americans involved in the group and added to Soong's, which through his previous tenure as Minister of Finance and chairman of the Bank of China was already considerable. Soong went in and out of the revolving door of Chiang Kai-shek's favor in rivalry with his other brother-in-law, H. H. Kung, who currently enjoyed the Ministry of Finance owing to the backing of the sisters, Mme. Kung and Mme. Chiang, who made common cause. Though temporarily out of the favored spot, Soong was never out of influence. Endowed with business and political acumen equal to his patriotism, he built up for China Defense Supplies a staff of ability and contacts and access to the right doors, especially to Harry Hopkins and to the Lend-Lease Administrator for China, Lauchlin Currie.

The American aim which had its own element of unreality was "Chinese military self-sufficiency" based on the assumption that the Chinese armies, given arms and equipment and reorganization and training under American advisers, could move to the offensive and cause enough diversion to deter the Japanese from other adventures. A program for arming 30 Chinese divisions (out of an approximate total of 300) with full equipment of divisional weapons was submitted by T. V. Soong. When supplied with artillery and other weapons and trained in their use by American officers, the selected 30 were to become special assault divisions, if and when the Generalissimo and National Military Council could agree on which divisions to designate. Since a division or higher unit was a commander's property and since the whole structure of Chinese politics depended on the relationships of those who disposed of military strength and on the intricate balance the G–mo could maintain among them, this question was to remain one of extreme and continuing difficulty. To carry out the Thirty Division and AVG programs, as well as to organize and supervise the whole Lend-Lease operation, an American Military Mission to China (AMMISCA) was appointed under General John Magruder, who had been both predecessor and successor to Stilwell as Military Attaché. Staffed by a number of former language officers, AMMISCA was also to serve in the event of war as liaison for strategic planning and cooperation and in general to shore up the morale of the Chinese Government.

The program was not philanthropy but intended as a means of enabling the Chinese to keep the Japanese occupied. Through all changing circumstances and conditions in the coming period this remained the purpose of American aid and it retained the original flaw: the American purpose was not the Chinese purpose. China's primary interest was not to keep the Japanese actively occupied burning and terrorizing in China in order to keep them off American backs. The Nationalist Government wanted American money and arms mainly in order to strengthen itself. Unlike Britain which had only a foreign foe, Chungking could always hear at its back the internal enemy hurrying near. Pure acquisitiveness was also a factor. Possession of arms even without use gave the reassurance of power.

This became clear as soon as the AMMISCA officers went to work beginning in October 1941. The mission's artillery expert, Colonel George Sliney, confirmed after an inspection tour what Stilwell had reported as Attaché, that the will to fight an aggressive action "does not yet exist in the Chinese army." Their demand for war material was not "for the purpose of pressing the war against Japan but was to make the Central Government safe against insurrection" after other nations had forced Japan out of China. "The general idea in the U.S. that China has fought Japan to a standstill and has had many glorious victories," he discovered, "is a delusion."

The central idea of American policy, which was essentially to empower Chinese to fight Japanese, was founded on this delusion, though not without warnings. Reading a statement by Senator Austin of Vermont urging the United States to redouble efforts to send arms to China as the quickest means of striking the Axis, the Naval Attaché in Chungking, Captain R. E. Schuirmann, was moved to write that the many such statements made lately by prominent people showed a widespread belief in the potentiality of China as an active military factor in defeating Japan. "If such conception is seriously held by those controlling high strategy," he warned, "it is fatally defective."

Once ingrained, however, and fostered by China's friends and propagandists, the delusion was difficult to eradicate. The press assisted the delusion by its tendency to print what it decided the public wanted to hear about China. One free-lance correspondent tried in vain to make clear how damaging to China was the closing of the railway to Hanoi. Every time she wrote a story pointing out that, no matter how magnificent was the human endeavor that made the Burma Road, nevertheless the loss of the railway was critical, her story, after treatment by editors, would emerge as a eulogy of the Road.

A report on the Burma Road by Daniel Arnstein, a transport expert and taxi-fleet owner, disturbed some illusions. The President's all-purpose agent Harry Hopkins had sent Arnstein to investigate why "not a god damn thing was moving over the Burma Road." Goods shipped under Lend-Lease were piling up on the docks of Rangoon and at Lashio, terminus of the railway that connected with the Road. At the current rate of transport it

Major General Stilwell as Commanding General of the 7th Division (125) at its base, Camp Ord, at Monterey, California (124). Dr. T. V. Soong, Foreign Minister of China, signing Lend-Lease agreement with U.S. Secretary of State Cordell Hull in March 1941 (126). General George C. Marshall and Secretary of War Henry L. Stimson conferring on war strategy (127).

124

125

126

127

128

129

130

131

would take eight months to move the backlog. Arnstein discovered corruption, inefficiency and incompetence amounting to an "impossible situation" which could not be improved, in his opinion, unless management was taken out of the hands of the Government and given to someone competent, "with authority" to correct conditions.

The situation on the nine-foot-wide single-lane highway, 715 miles from Kunming to Lashio, was "appalling." At Kunming, the starting point in China, truck drivers had to pass through eight Customs desks, which sometimes occupied the whole day, before obtaining permission to proceed. At a dozen more checkpoints along the way provincial officials took their toll for permits to pass. At Wanting on the China-Burma border 250 trucks were waiting anywhere from 24 hours to two weeks for customs clearance. The use of grease being apparently unknown or too costly, hundreds of burned-out trucks were stranded along the way. Stolen spare parts were a regular item on the black market. Fifteen official agencies, transport companies and control boards representing—and passing on squeeze to—variour ministries of the Government operated on the Road. Six thousand tons per month were limping through when the total should have been 30,000.

Arnstein wrote a report recommending obvious measures which could bring the traffic to 8,000 trucks operating at a time. Presented to the G–mo in Chinese and indexed, it elicited his delight and a prompt invitation to Arnstein and his two assistants to take over management of the Road as a private concession at so much percentage per truck. This being declined, authority was reshuffled among more commissions and control boards. Though little was changed at the top, traffic was lubricated by an American Technical Group of 46 civilian mechanics despatched by Lend-Lease who set up motor pools and maintenance shops along the way and trained the Chinese in the art of greasing.

The world and the war were suddenly heaved out of balance by the German invasion of Russia in June 1941. Like that startling anomaly, the Nazi-Soviet Pact of 1939, the new reversal changed everything, inserting Germany by choice into a two-front war, the situation that had defeated her the last time, and aligning Russia, now Communist instead of Czarist but still a cuckoo in the nest, with the democracies. The strategic advantage was not appreciated at the time. On the contrary the vaunted German armies were expected to defeat the Russians, as Marshall and Stimson and the brains of the War Department agreed, "in a minimum of one month and a maximum of three months." Elsewhere the outlook was no less dark. Germany had smashed resistance in Greece and Yugoslavia, U-boat "wolf packs" were attacking British shipping in the Atlantic, and Rommel launched a counteroffensive in North Africa. The trend galvanized Japan

Conditions on the Burma Road were "appalling." As U.S. Army engineers worked on the road in difficult terrain (128), supply trucks were backlogged at its beginning (129). A caterpillar pulls out a bogged-down truck (130), and American and Indian engineers build a bridge (131).

to take the fateful decision to move south with southern Indochina as the target. On July 24 under legal cover of agreement with the Vichy regime which was in no position to refuse, Japan acquired use of eight airfields and a naval base at Camranh Bay and Saigon, putting her within striking distance of Malaya, the Indies and the Philippines. The agreement included unlimited access for Japanese troops which were to be used, as the United States learned through its breaking of the Japanese code, for penetration of Siam.

The time for oil embargo—the last deterrent available—had come. Stimson believed it would deter rather than provoke on the theory that the Japanese, however wicked, would have the good sense not to commit suicide in a war with the United States. The freezing of Japanese assets in America, amounting in effect to oil embargo, was ordered on July 26 on the ground that Japan's move into Indochina constituted notice of intent "to pursue a policy of force and conquest" and a step prior to "the seizure of additional territories."

Simultaneously a new possibility opened for American strategy. General MacArthur who had been serving in the Philippines for the past five years recommended in July putting in enough force to defend and hold the Islands, hitherto considered indefensible. The B-17s made the difference. From a base in the Philippines the Flying Fortresses could attack Japanese naval operations. To gain time to equip the base and to build and bring in enough of the big bombers it was now vital to postpone conflict until the last possible minute. The Army and Navy insisted on delay. Talks between Secretary Hull and Ambassador Nomura of Japan in search of terms for a basic settlement had been opened some months before and these were kept going more as "rearguard diplomatic action," in Hull's words, than in real hope of a solution. The stumbling block, as it had always been, was China. Japan could not consent to a settlement that did not recognize her colonial control of China; the United States would not consent to one that did. At bottom there was no area of bargaining.

With October and the end of the one-year draft approaching, the Army faced the loss of men and Reserve officers on whom a year's training had been spent. To create a combat-ready force from men newly trained each year was impossible, and though the President was extremely reluctant to test the temper of Congress, Marshall and Stimson insisted on extension of the Draft. Once more the great debate thundered on Capitol Hill. Against charges of "militarism" and "warmongering" only Marshall's careful, tactful but relentless pressure coaxed the bill through Congress by the margin of a single vote in the House, 203-202. So thin was the victory that it revealed the strength of opposition to the idea that the war was America's affair.

While Congress was debating, the Army in the summer of 1941 held nation-wide maneuvers with over half a million troops of each of the four armies successively engaged over a period of four months. The first to begin was the Fourth Army on the West coast which included Stilwell's 7th Division, now "California's Own." He took the part as usual of the enemy Red force. Supported by other units of the IIIrd Corps, the 7th Division attacked northward from a Los Angeles base against two divisions of the IXth Corps representing the Blues who were defending San Francisco. The "Battle of California" was fought out for five weeks from the end of May through June at the Hunter Liggett military reservation in the area of the Hearst ranch 120 miles south of Monterey.

Stilwell planned a blitzkrieg attack by mechanized battalions up the San Antonio valley with an even chance to break through and capture the Blue headquarters, leaving the way to San Francisco open. He gained surprise by a night start, but the Blues, outnumbering him two to one, simultaneously launched attack on both Red flanks and were able to roll back his offensive. Nevertheless as the maneuvers continued Stilwell clinched his reputation. He toured the entire front making personally sure that everyone knew his duties, observed every emplacement, slept on the ground three hours a night and outwalked his staff, of whom one complained, "My God, the Old Man is all over the place like a herd of sheep!" The 7th became imbued with such fighting spirit that some troops threw away their blank-cartridge rifles and fought with fists. At the end one unit, the 32nd Infantry, in order to be the first to reach camp, still had the vigor to strike out on an unscheduled 17-mile hike in which Stilwell joined for the last eight miles.

The Blues won the war which ended in an armistice on June 30 but the performance of the Red 7th earned Stilwell promotion to command of the IIIrd Corps. The promotion was part of a thorough shake-up affecting 20 generals which Marshall put into effect in the effort to revitalize the high command and replace older by younger generals. Stilwell was now rated by the outgoing head of the IIIrd Corps, Major General Walter K. Wilson, as No. 1 of the 47 major generals in the United States Army.

He was not content with laurels. "I was impressed by the air of calm confidence on the part of our officers," Stilwell said in his critique of the war games. "Nobody was worried which means that everybody was sitting on his fanny." Calm confidence, he suggested, "comes either from ignorance or long experience and in this case I leave it to you to decide which." He ordered the troops back into the field for four more days of exercises to correct deficiencies. In August at Fort Lewis in Washington he commanded the IIIrd Corps against the IXth in renewed maneuvers designed to test the handling of large units and the functioning of the high command in meeting tactical problems set by the umpires. Both the Chief of Staff and the Secretary of War came to observe and Stilwell met Stimson on this occasion, although without recorded comment.

By now the Administration had to face the truth that the country was not going to escape from war. The Joint Board headed by General Marshall and Admiral Stark gave its official opinion in September that Germany could not be defeated by the present coalition against her without the participation of the United States and that the British and Dutch "probably could not successfully withstand" a Japanese attack on Malaya or the Indies without active American military aid. Therefore the United States faced war "simultaneously against Germany and Japan" and must organize a production program to match the problem. The Board reaffirmed the strategic decision to defeat Germany first while maintaining a strong defense against Japan. The main element of this defense should be material support for "Chinese offensives against Japanese forces of occupation."

The formulation of strategy was shared by Britain but not China. Owing to a reputation for leaks China was not included in the military discussions nor, much to the resentment of Chiang Kai-shek, in the top-level Atlantic Conference held by Roosevelt and Churchill in August. After his long wait for the foreign powers Chiang found himself not made an ally by any of the belligerents—Britain, Holland or Russia—not invited to the ABDA staff talks at Singapore and not, as he could sense from the feel of things, occupying first place in American strategy. To improve his access to Washington he had asked at the beginning of Lend-Lease for the traditional political "adviser." Roosevelt, anxious to do the best for China in at least this respect, sent him the man most highly recommended, Owen Lattimore, who had been active in China as businessman, newspaperman, traveler and scholar since 1920 and was the author of books on Mongolia, Manchuria and China's outer provinces. Admiral Yarnell described him as "the greatest authority in America on China and Manchuria" which was the right qualification from the point of view of the sponsor if not the client: when the Chinese asked for an "adviser" what they wanted was advice on America, not China. Lattimore reported at the time of the Atlantic Conference that the Chinese felt politically isolated with growing apprehension that after the war they would not be given "equal status and fair treatment." He urged a formal alliance to encourage them but neither he nor anyone could solve the essential difficulty: that equal status is achieved only by the exercise of equal weight.

Lattimore's report gave a revealing view of China's resentments. The Chinese noticed that Britain and the United States were warning Japan off in all directions—from Indochina, the Indies, Siam and even Siberia—but not from Yunnan where a threatened drive on Kunming might close the Burma Road. Their suspicion was growing that the Western nations, to gain time, might be tacitly encouraging the Japanese "to make a little war on us because we are able to stand such a lot." They believed that American effort to improve transport over the Burma Road was not to help China per se but to keep China fighting Japan so that America and Britain would not have to fight her. "They consider they have been fighting our battle for four years and it's about time we got involved and started fighting their battle for them." They resented all the pacts and commitments being made on all sides with everyone but them and deduced from these the "Europe first" strategy which they considered ominous for China. It indicated that the democracies believed the war could be won in Europe which would leave China nowhere at the peace table and would restore the British Empire at its heart "enabling it to reach out and rebuild its peripheries." The Chinese wanted the war won first in Asia. This would give them time, while the Allies then pursued victory in Europe, to improve their position for the peace conference.

It was the old problem of 1919, of the whole century since the First Opium War—the impotence of the Middle Kingdom in an era dominated by the West, the galling fact that the sense of cultural superiority did not translate itself into power, that China somehow could not harness the capacity to substantiate her due place in the world.

If the Chinese had more confidence in themselves, Lattimore reported, they would "start winning for themselves the victory they want in the East. They would abandon their present insistence that they haven't the artillery and planes," and start working out less orthodox methods, concentrating on guerilla warfare. "But they don't have that confidence." The political and military high command did not trust the people and were afraid to let go their monopoly of power. They had been building up political machines in order to be ready to extend their control over occupied China when it should be liberated from the Japanese. But in the end, he predicted, they would be at a disadvantage if "victory in the East were won primarily by the Great Powers, not by China herself."

Chiang Kai-shek did not see it that way. Trying to make himself heard, his voice rose to a shriek about the threatened Japanese drive on Kunming which he now insisted was the key to the Pacific and could not be defended without air power. The 100 fliers and P-40s of the AVG had just reached a British training base in Burma at this time and were barely ready for action. Chiang called urgently for the British Air Force from Singapore to lend them support and for the United States to add airplanes from the Philippines. His argument and appeal were endorsed by General Magruder.

In a telegram to Churchill and Roosevelt on November 2 Chiang raised the cry that if Kunming were lost and China cut off, the morale of the Chinese Army and people would be "shaken to its foundation" and "for the first time in this long war a real collapse of resistance would be possible."

Worried by the Hull-Nomura talks in Washington, he enlarged his prophecies of doom to instill the fear that China's collapse would lead the rest of Asia to succumb to Japan. Any compromise by the United States with Japan or relaxation of the embargo, he warned, would cause the Chinese people to feel that they had been "completely sacrificed" by the United States with the result that the morale of the entire people would collapse and "every Asiatic nation will lose faith, and indeed suffer such a shock in their faith in democracy that a most tragic epoch in the world will be opened." Thus the collapse of China's resistance could be an "unparalleled catastrophe to the world and I do not indeed know how history in future will record this episode."

This prospect was the President's greatest worry even though it was never clear to Washington how seriously Chiang Kai-shek's frenzied cries should be taken. In the opinion of Ambassador Gauss, who had replaced Johnson, "the continuance indefinitely of China's resistance to Japan must not be taken for granted."

In the tortured councils of the Japanese Government November was the last hour of decision. The talks in Washington offered no realistic hope of breakthrough toward an acceptable settlement in China or even a compromise *modus vivendi* with the United States. Without new sources Japanese oil stocks could not be stretched beyond two years. Germany had already gone far toward establishing leadership of her sphere; if Japan did not move now to gain control of Asia, the wave of the future might leave her behind. If action were postponed until spring, the United States would be that much better prepared. On November 5 the Privy Council met for five hours in the presence of the Emperor and agreed that the negotiations in Washington should continue and preparation of the military arm be completed at the same time; if the one produced no results by the end of the month, the other would be ready to act.

With proposals and counterproposals, with American and still some Japanese efforts to stave off the inevitable, with warnings and readings of the "Magic" code and knowledge of Japanese intentions up to a point, the days of November unrolled toward the most premonitored surprise attack in history.

10

"I'll Go Where I'm Sent"

DECEMBER 1941-FEBRUARY 1942

I N Carmel on a sunny Sunday morning, warm for December, General
and Mrs. Stilwell were holding open house for new junior officers from
Fort Ord. Doors onto the garden were open, and viewed from windows of the upstairs living room, the surf of the sparkling Pacific rolled
and crashed majestically upon the beach. Guests were in civilian clothes
because military uniform was not worn off post; Sunday comics were scattered about the house. The telephone rang. Answering it, Mrs. Stilwell
heard the excited voice of a friend cry, "Win, turn on your radio! Pearl
Harbor is being attacked!" A frantic search for a radio followed; one was
found and plugged in while everyone crowded around to listen, stunned.
The realization flooded over them: out there, on the immense blue ocean
beyond the window, war had begun.

Attack had been expected in Southeast Asia. No one had expected the
Japanese to fling themselves upon the American battle fleet 3,300 miles
across the Pacific in an act of such extraordinary daring. The boldness of
the offensive and its awful success was as astonishing as it was frightening.
The Japanese, hitherto consistently underestimated, were now suddenly
credited with awesome and fearsome capacities and expected to descend
upon the United States at any moment. Within hours the panic rumors were
being telephoned to Fort Ord: the Japanese fleet was ten miles out of
Monterey; San Francisco was expecting an air raid; a periscope had been
sighted off Cliff House, another off Point Lobos.

Stilwell was responsible, under Lieutenant General John L. De Witt, commander of the Fourth Army, for the Southern Sector of the Western Defense Command covering the California coast down to the Mexican border. This was the area where invasion could come, whose defense, owing to the naval losses at Pearl Harbor, now depended on the unready Army. Besides a population of 5 million, the region contained 80 percent of the nation's aviation industry, all of it within naval gun range of ships at sea. Stilwell himself believed California beyond Japan's reach but the weight of his responsibility caused a recurring "sinking feeling" at least once a day. Alarm and confusion were all around him, Fourth Army Headquarters in San Francisco suffered periodic fits of extreme "jitters" on the telephone and he was conscious of the inadequacy of his forces, especially of ammunition.

Sitting at his desk in San Bernardino, headquarters of the Southern Sector, biting his cigaret holder almost in two, he told the War Department he had enough small arms ammunition for a few hours of combat and practically none for artillery. When the officer at the Washington end promised to do "the best we can," Stilwell roared, "The best you can! Good God, what the hell am I supposed to do? Fight 'em off with oranges?" On the news that the Japanese had attacked Guam, Wake Island, Hong Kong, the Philippines and Malaya on the same day as Pearl Harbor, and Midway on the day after, California's alarm mounted. Frantic demands for guards were coming in from aviation plants, radio stations, railroad bridges and tunnels, dams, power plants, aqueducts, reservoirs, oil wells, hospitals, shipbuilding docks and harbor defenses—with each installation making a crucial case of its own need. So many units went out on guard duty that training had to be halted.

Stilwell's days were a succession of tours up and down the coast, conferring with mayors and the Marines and Navy, investigating rumors, protecting airfields, organizing warning procedures, answering queries, arranging billets for extra units sent from the East, trying to locate additional ammunition, while alarms and rumors continued. A Japanese fleet of 34 ships was reported somewhere between San Francisco and Los Angeles on December 9. After anxious hours Stilwell recorded, "Not authentic (sinking feeling is growing)." The enemy ships had been identified as 14 trawlers of the Monterey fishing fleet speeding home for shelter. On December 10 came the incredible news that Britain's newest battleship, the *Prince of Wales,* and the battle cruiser *Repulse,* sent to the Far East in November to deter attack on Singapore, had been sunk by Japanese aerial attack off the coast of Malaya, losing Britain command of the sea in those waters. ("My God, worse and worse.") On December 11 Germany and Italy, in fulfillment of the Axis Pact and at the request of Japan, declared war on the

United States. Another alarm, this time from Fourth Army Headquarters itself, reported, "The main Japanese battle fleet 164 miles off San Francisco. General alert of all units." After sickening hours, this too proved unchecked. ("Good Christ! They'll kill me.")

On December 13 Western Defense Command reported air attack on Los Angeles to be imminent and a general alarm to the population was being considered. Concluding that the casualties and panic resulting from a "general alarm" would be as serious as from air raid, Stilwell decided to disbelieve the report. "Ammunition a little better. . . . The 125th due in 24 hours. . . . Two battalions ready and two in reserve for 175 miles of coast. (The old sinking feeling.) Six tanks coming from Ord (the others won't run). . . . A division coming from somewhere—ten *days*. Sent out an air recon. . . . AA [antiaircraft] coming in. . . . Lingayen landing repulsed . . . Dec. 14. One week of war. Wake and Midway holding. . . . Philippine divisions shot 'em up at Lingayen. . . . Good job. In fact most of the *despised* people (Chinese, Russians, Greeks, Filipinos) are doing the best work for civilization."

Nerves were taut and some broke. "R—— wants to resign—just can't bear it." The commander of an Air Corps bombing range in the south California desert feared a parachute attack from carriers or from a secret base in Lower California that would murder his whole outfit. Scare stories of sabotage, radio spies, submarines and secret airfields proliferated and had to be investigated. Stilwell was urged to move under constant attendance by guards to prevent Japanese agents from killing him.

Suddenly he was summoned out of the frenzy. A call from Fourth Army woke him at 6:30 on the morning of December 22 to say he was ordered to Washington at once "to work on a war plan for some expeditionary force which [the caller] implied I was to command." He was told he would be away for some time. His staff buzzed with excitement. "They think it's big stuff." After a hasty winding up of affairs he went home for a farewell visit and a premature Christmas with his family. "Talked and talked. All composed mentally, thank God." With Dorn he left next morning by plane and reached Washington on the afternoon of the following day, December 24, two days after Churchill and his chiefs of staff arrived for the series of staff talks known as the ARCADIA Conference.

Going straight to the War Plans Division Stilwell was given stunning news of his new assignment: he had been chosen to command the first American offensive of the war in the form of Plan Black, a landing in French West Africa. His informant was the Division's Deputy Chief, his former classmate at Leavenworth, Dwight Eisenhower, freshly wearing his first star. For once Stilwell was conscious that he should have felt something appropriate to the occasion but "it didn't make me feel any different from before, somehow." Marshall had selected him for this, the number-one combat assignment, because he had been impressed, as he afterwards said, by Stilwell's training and handling of the 7th Division in maneuvers and considered him a masterly tactician, fertile, ingenious and confident; a student of military history, and excellent in training. His opinion was confirmed by a survey of general officers he had ordered made by Mark Clark. It placed Stilwell's name first on a list of the Army's nine corps commanders arranged in order of merit.

At the War College Stilwell learned his objective was to be Dakar which had long figured in American planning as the jumping-off place of a German attack across the narrow South Atlantic on South America. The next day this proved far from definitive. "Nobody knows where I am going. This a.m. it was Dakar, this p.m. it is Casablanca." The opening decision of the ARCADIA Conference had been to confirm the Europe-first strategy, and the plan to land at Casablanca on the Atlantic coast of Morocco was designed to secure a base from which to prevent enemy control of the Mediterranean and eventually seize the initiative in the European theater. The code name for the Casablanca operation was GYMNAST. Stilwell found there was "uncertainty about the whole show," a condition which did not improve during the three weeks of the ARCADIA staff talks. Through eight major policy meetings at the White House and twelve meetings of the newly organized Combined (British and American) Chiefs of Staff the conferees struggled to work out agreed war aims, organization of command, a plan of action, and above all, the means of action. GYMNAST bobbed like a cork on a sea of pros and cons.

When war had come to Moscow six months earlier, "No one knew what to do," according to an observer inside the Kremlin, and now the same condition prevailed in Washington. Stilwell, joined by his staff chiefs from the IIIrd Corps, worked on a plan of operations with its objective changing hourly. Was it to be Casablanca or Dakar? Iceland or the Canary Islands? What strength? What prospects? What support? What arms? What anticipated enemy action? All was uncertain and arguable. Alternates and variants were seized and discarded. Stilwell was surrounded, as he wrote his wife, by "clerks rushing in and out of swinging doors, people with papers rushing after other people with papers, groups in corners whispering in huddles, everybody jumping up just as you start to talk, buzzers ringing, telephones ringing, rooms crowded, clerks banging away at typewriters. 'Give me 10 copies of this AT ONCE.' 'Get that secret file out of the safe.' 'Where the hell is the Yellow Plan (Blue, Green Plan, Orange Plan, etc.)?' Everybody furiously smoking cigarettes, everybody passing you on to someone else. Someone with a loud voice and a mean look and a big stick ought to appear and yell, 'HALT! you crazy bastards. SILENCE! you imitation ants.

Now half of you get the hell out of town before dark and the other half sit down and don't move for one hour.' Then they could burn up all the papers and start fresh."

While wrestling with GYMNAST Stilwell worried about the Far East and wondered when the Navy would ever get into action. He had learned by now the extent of the disaster at Pearl Harbor—eight or nearly half America's capital ships sunk or put out of action, 177 planes destroyed and close to 4,000 casualties, more than half of them killed. There had been equal disaster at Clark Field in the Philippines, where several hours after news of the strike at Pearl Harbor, half of General MacArthur's 35 heavy bombers and a third of his fighters were caught and destroyed on the ground. Western entry into the war against Japan—the consummation so long awaited by China—had brought debacle instead of encouragement.

The Japanese had started the war with a Navy approximately equal to the combined American, British and Dutch naval forces in the Far East and Pacific. Japan still had ten battleships and ten carriers with approximately 500 first-line naval planes against a total in capital ships for the Allies of one undamaged and two slightly damaged American battleships and three American carriers. In destroyers, cruisers and submarines the belligerents were about equal. On land the Japanese had an Army of 51 divisions of which 21 were in China, 13 in Manchuria holding the front against Russia, leaving, aside from home defense, 11 active divisions and some 700 Army aircraft assigned to the operations in Southeast Asia and the Southwest Pacific.

These were now crashing through in one astounding victory after another. Guam and Wake fell on December 23. On Christmas day, after a hundred years as a British stronghold, Hong Kong surrendered. In the Philippines, belying first reports, the Japanese had made good their landing and with 200,000 troops ashore were driving the American-Filipino force into the bottleneck of the Bataan peninsula. On January 2 they captured Manila. Parachute troops had invaded the Netherlands Indies, Thailand was occupied and Indochina was opened up by the acquiescent Vichy regime, bringing the Japanese forward to the eastern frontier of Burma. They had also landed on the Malay peninsula at its waist, seized the British airfield there and were advancing southward toward Singapore through the jungle. On land and sea their dive bombers and torpedo planes had air superiority. Under the "hideous efficiency" of the Japanese war machine, as Churchill called it, white prestige in Asia was crumbling in ruins.

In China the news of Pearl Harbor had been greeted as the herald of salvation. "Kuomintang officials went about congratulating each other as if a great victory had been won," wrote Han Suyin. Crowds rejoiced in the streets of Chungking. In cities of the interior celebrants were under the impression that Tokyo was in flames; news of a great far-off air strike came through as a report that 500 American planes had bombed Tokyo, but the error was irrelevant. What was cause for celebration was that China had allies at last. The United States had entered the fight against Japan and could be counted on to finish it off. China had no further duty but to hold out and emerge on the winning side. "Pearl Harbor day in America," commented one American watching the rejoicing in Chungking, "was Armistice Day out here."

As soon as he heard the news Chiang Kai-shek took steps to play a great power's role in the grand alliance and to confirm China's presence in global strategy. On the day of the attack he summoned a conference of British and American representatives in Chungking at which he proposed that all the enemies of the Axis in Asia—America, Britain, China, the Netherlands and Russia (which he then expected to enter the war against Japan)—should join in a military pact for mutual assistance and should establish a war council in Chungking under United States leadership to coordinate their war effort. While he left it to the United States to offer a "comprehensive plan" of strategy, Chiang already had a clear idea of what the strategy should be. He proposed that the Allies including Russia should make their main effort in Asia and defeat Japan in 1942 by air power operating from the South Pacific, Alaska, the Maritime Province of Siberia and the China coast. After air attack had isolated Japanese forces on the Asiatic mainland by severing their supply lines, the Chinese armies would destroy them.

Chiang did not forget to add that the proposed war council in Chungking should "control priorities and supplies." This concerned him as much if not more than strategy because he instantly and correctly perceived that the British would seek to preempt the Lend-Lease arms that were piling up in Burma on consignment to China. He wanted American leadership of the war council to keep the British from taking his goods.

His strategy, aside from being visionary in regard to available air power, did not fit in with the Europe-first strategy to which the United States and Britain were already committed. Chiang was not invited to the ARCADIA Conference although China was included as one of the four major signatories of the joint declaration by the United Nations issued on New Year's Day, 1942. (A list in Roosevelt's handwriting initially placed China second after the United States, followed by the U.S.S.R. and the United Kingdom; he afterwards revised it to place the U.K. second and China fourth, followed by the rest of the 26 nations in alphabetical order.) Chiang was, however, as a matter of protocol, asked to send a preliminary plan of campaign after meeting with Sir Archibald Wavell who had been named Supreme Commander of the ABDA nations' front in the Far East. This meeting in Chungking on December 23, China's first with the long-awaited Western

Allies, was almost as calamitous as Pearl Harbor. It brought to the surface, and augmented, the hostility between two of the three major Allies.

China feared and disliked Britain as the dominant imperial power, the original penetrator of her sovereignty and founder of the unequal treaties. The temporary closing of the Burma Road was still bitterly resented. Britain in turn had little respect for China's Government or military capacity. A British Economic Mission under Sir Otto Niemeyer which had visited China a month before Pearl Harbor reported that the Government was incapable of coping with its manifold problems, that its measures were inept and haphazard and that a loan would not help because it could not be effectively utilized in the face of the real trouble, which was an acute shortage of goods. Chiang Kai-shek, Niemeyer told a State Department official, "did not have an intelligent grasp of the situation." These conclusions were accepted philosophically by Britain which as an imperial state did not share the American interest in a strong China after the war. In the desperate hours of December with every bastion falling, Britain's immediate concern was to hold Burma if possible as the last barrier before India, but if this were lost there was no other thought than that the imperial territories in Asia would be regained after ultimate victory.

China was equally interested in the defense of Burma in order to keep open the flow of Lend-Lease supplies coming through Rangoon, not to mention to keep possession of the thousands of tons already piled up there. A primary concern of the conference in Chungking was a struggle for the Lend-Lease stockpiles and for control of Chennault's newly arrived American Volunteer Group (AVG) based in Burma. China held title to both but the British in dire need considered they could make better use of them.

General Wavell, the sturdy one-eyed soldier of formidable silences who made the confrontation explicit, was fated to exercise command against odds. Born in the same year as Stilwell, he had lost his eye at Ypres in the First World War. This time, after initial victory and then misfortune in the Middle East, he had been transferred to India as Commander-in-Chief in an exchange of places with General Auchinleck. Now, as a result of Marshall's insistence at ARCADIA on unity of command in each theater, he had been assigned the dubious defense of 2,000 miles of front from Java to Burma. The British chiefs suspected an American trick to escape a command doomed to defeat and protested that it would "be fatal to have a British commander responsible for the disasters that are coming to the Americans as well as ourselves." Churchill angrily rejected the imputation and allowed Wavell to assume the theater command in Southeast Asia where he was left to brace a set of soft and rotting posts under the impeccably planned blows of the Japanese.

Struggles over areas of command continued throughout the war to absorb

as much attention as plans for action. Ever since the invention of the
General Staff in the nineteenth century the paper arrangements of warfare
had assumed an importance happily unknown to Caesar, Genghis Khan or
Napoleon. War was now regarded by staff professionals no longer as the
province of Great Captains but as an exercise in "command problems."
Having learned the lesson of World War I, all the conductors of World War
II were so intent on achieving unity of direction for each theater that what
happened in the field seemed almost secondary.

Wavell came to the meeting with Chiang Kai-shek in Chungking prepared to discuss if not to welcome the participation of Chinese troops in
the defense of Burma. On the day after Pearl Harbor Chiang had asked the
British Military Attaché, General Dennys, what Chinese troops would be
needed. All too obviously putting little value on the offer, Dennys had suggested one regiment, possibly a division later. The Generalissimo replied
that he was thinking in terms of two armies* with additional troops to as
many as 80,000 on condition of a total plan of joint strategy. Dennys did
not pursue the subject, with perhaps some excuse, since Chiang Kai-shek
a few weeks earlier had evidently not thought these troops capable of defending Kunming.

When Wavell reached Chungking Burma's danger was more apparent.
The suddenly revealed feebleness of British positions was in the nature of
empire which had hitherto not needed more than the show of power to rule.
A gunboat here and there, the smart slap of rifles at drill on the Bund, a
parade of scarlet uniforms, imposing bearded Sikhs as police, had sufficed
to govern Asia without serious challenge. Pukkah complacency, now undercut by emergency in Europe, had nothing on hand to meet the calculated
assault of Japan. Nevertheless the British had no desire to see Chinese
troops enter Burma, to which China had vague traditional claims never
renounced. Once over the border they might remain, besides causing trouble with the local population who had no love for the Chinese. Wavell was
expecting a reinforcement of Indian troops and naturally preferred that "a
country of the British Empire should be defended by Imperial troops rather
than foreign." Further he was advised that Burma could not feed or transport a large influx of Chinese. He therefore accepted only one Chinese division on condition that it be supplied from China.† His American partner,
General George Brett, an Air Corps officer sent to China to survey possible
bases for heavy bombers, concurred, having been appalled by what he had

---

* A Chinese army, analogous to but smaller than the American Army corps, consisted of three divisions, each with a nominal strength of 9,000 but in practice
averaging from 6,000 to 7,000.
† Later he claimed to have accepted two but this was not what was understood by
those present.

seen so far of Chinese military methods. Wavell's rejection, as General Magruder reported in nervous understatement to Washington, was "somewhat displeasing" to the Generalissimo who was in fact infuriated. Another mark was made in the long track of insult left by the British east of Suez.

On top of this a quarrel flared over use of Lend-Lease arms at Rangoon. Wharves were piled high, warehouses bulged with munitions, and hundreds of trucks stood inanimate in long rows. Meanwhile bombing of the docks was expected and stevedores were deserting. Chinese ability to move the stockpiles was limited and logic suggested that Allied strategic purpose was best served by immediate allocation of the matériel for the defense of Rangoon, which was as vital to China as to her allies. But it was not easy for Chinese supply officers in Burma headed by the Generalissimo's cousin, General Yu Fei-p'eng, to hand over such a wealth of stores, with all their lucrative possibilities, to the British, whose ability to hold the city in any case did not inspire confidence. The Chinese appetite for matériel combined with their inability to utilize it exasperated the Westerners. With time pressing and nerves harried, the Governor-General hinted at confiscation; 150 trucks and a cargo of munitions were taken and other stockpiles impounded by American Lend-Lease officers until their destiny could be settled. When the dispute reached Chungking the Generalissimo, in a nicely studied retaliation for Wavell's slight, offered to release 20 machine guns for the defense of Burma. He subsequently refused to see the British Ambassador and threatened to stop all cooperation between China and Britain.

Waves from the episode hit the ARCADIA Conference with effect that emphasized the divergence between the American and British policies toward China. The British in the midst of their fight for survival did not really want to be bothered about China. America wore China like an albatross around her neck: Shantung, the unfulfilled Nine-Power guarantee, the impotent Stimson Doctrine, the scrap sold to Japan, the "special" American relationship, the return of the Boxer indemnities, the theory of a strong China after the war—all were part of the burden; a compound of guilt, guardianship and illusion. The American leaders at once reacted to Chiang's possibly calculated bad temper with renewed anxiety that he might drop out of the coalition. Since China had every intention of coming through on the winning side and nothing to gain from Japan, the chronic American fear of the Chinese making a separate peace contained an element of unreality. But Chiang's constant cries of impending collapse, and dread of all the Japanese divisions that this might release, kept the fear alive.

Japanese triumphs lent force to the fear. As General Marshall pointed out in an anxious message to Wavell, Japan was mounting a tremendous propaganda drive to capitalize on the loss of Western prestige involved in the fall of Hong Kong and Manila in the hope of bringing about a collapse of Chinese resistance. He urged the necessity of building up China's "faith and confidence in British-American joint purposes in the Far East." Apart from defeating Japan, he might have been hard put to define what the joint purposes were.

Chiefly because of diversion of interests the Allies had no agreed plan for resistance to Japan and had reached no decision at the earlier staff talks in Singapore on how to use available forces or what to defend first. The conference at Chungking agreed it was "a first essential" to secure Rangoon and Burma "which are vital for China's continued resistance," but almost at once the faith and confidence that Marshall mentioned as desirable had begun to erode. Allied reversals caused a "severe shock" to the Chinese, reported Gauss, and public references to the policy of defeating Hitler first caused "indignation." Secretary Stimson was especially worried by the trend. He thought Wavell had been "rather peremptory and tactless and has acted in an old-fashioned British way towards China." More than anyone Stimson felt the obligation of guardianship. He would have preferred a stronger effort in the Far East than allowed by the Europe-first strategy, because he believed it essential to prevent Japan from consolidating control and to keep China from collapsing from discouragement.

Roosevelt was deeply disturbed by the Wavell incident. He was beset by the fear, if Chiang's Government should give up resistance, of all Asia gravitating to Japan. Anything was dangerous that upset the Generalissimo's morale, considered the most delicate of barometers in Washington. "If China goes under," FDR said to his son Elliott, "how many divisions of Japanese troops do you think will be freed—to do what? Take Australia, take India—and it's as ripe as a plum for the picking. Move straight on to the Middle East . . . a giant pincer movement by the Japanese and Nazis, meeting somewhere in the Near East, cutting the Russians off completely, slicing off Egypt, slashing all communication lines through the Mediterranean?" He told Churchill during the ARCADIA Conference that it was particularly important to restore the Generalissimo to a good frame of mind and asked that Wavell be ordered to go out of his way to placate him.

To give Chiang formal status the Allies invited him to serve as Supreme Commander of Allied forces in a separate China theater. But as there was so far no plan to send Allied forces to China this amounted to notification that his sphere of operations was being limited to his own country. The form may have been pleasing but the reality was made plain by the fact that for security reasons the Chinese were not included in the Combined Chiefs of Staff. In compensation Roosevelt was all the more anxious to arrange some sort of inter-Allied military committee in Chungking.

Roosevelt's governing idea was that China should be one of the great powers after the war to fill the vacuum left by Japan. He was not unaware of shortcomings for he once acknowledged to his son that China "was still in the eighteenth century." Nevertheless that great and ancient country with its 500 million enduring people, however frustrated by endless misgovernment, was a geopolitical fact. Roosevelt wanted it on America's side in the future. When Churchill during the ARCADIA visit told him how much he thought American opinion overestimated the contribution which China could make to the war, the President "differed strongly." What would happen, he asked, if China's "enormous population developed in the same way as Japan had done in the last century and got hold of modern weapons?" Churchill replied that he was speaking of the present war "which was quite enough to go on for the time being." The intransigence of the present expressed by Churchill and the shadow of the future by Roosevelt met in this exchange.

If, as Roosevelt believed, China was to function as a great power, she must be treated like one. Chiang Kai-shek could not be spoken to like a "barbarian chieftain," he said to Edgar Snow, author of *Red Star Over China,* in a conversation shortly after Pearl Harbor. Then, in a revealing question, he asked Snow whether the Chinese "like us? Do they think well of us over there?" He went on to talk about his family's Chinese connections and how in 1933 he had wanted to renounce extrality, and although Hull had agreed, State Department advisers (whom Roosevelt disliked and distrusted as a species) had been opposed. Despite the source of the Delano family fortune, Roosevelt disapproved of the foreign penetration of China. He was convinced, as he wrote in a letter of 1934, in one of the soundest policy statements ever formulated and never adopted, that it was better to hasten the crisis in China and "compel the Chinese people more and more to stand on their own feet" than to continue an unsound position for a generation to come.

The evolution of the President's thinking about China, apart from Grandfather Delano and the clipper trade, was something of a hidden process. "At the White House," according to one of his close associates, Judge Rosenman, "the making of FDR's China policy was almost as great a secret as the atom bomb." When General Marshall was asked by Army historians after the war, "What was the President's policy toward China? Did he ever explain it to you?" he could only say that it was "to treat China as a great power." This was more than just a slogan to fill a vacuum. Though it was a policy of make-believe it grew out of genuine conviction. Roosevelt believed that the day of colonial empires was past and that the Western world for its own safety's sake must give up treating the peoples of Asia as inferior. Treating China as an equal, as he told Under Secretary Welles, was the best means of preventing "a fundamental cleavage between the West and East in the years to come."

Here was the ground of cleavage with Churchill who, in his own words, had not taken office to preside over the liquidation of the British Empire. The *status quo ante* was Britain's war aim in the Far East but it was not Roosevelt's. He believed the British Empire was finished and that the surge toward independence in Indochina, Malaya, and the Netherlands Indies would expel the white nations in the long run. His similar view of India, discussed during Churchill's visit, caused the first serious rift between them. "I reacted so strongly and at such length," Churchill wrote, "that he never raised it verbally again."

When ultimate aims diverged they necessarily affected strategy. For the Americans China was the focus; for the British the focus was Singapore and in the background India. Lying between India and China, Burma was seen strategically from two different angles of view and the split focus was never to be resolved.

The American General Staff was as persuaded as the President of the need to support China and for that reason of the vital importance of holding Burma. To the British, support for China was a waste and a strange American aberration, but the need to arrive at a joint strategy was imperative. Churchill agreed that Roosevelt should assume primary responsibility for "dealing with the Chinese in all cases." At American insistence, in order to emphasize the strategic relation to China, Burma was separated from the India command and put under Wavell's Southeast Asia command, a disruption of regular logistic channels regarded with extreme distaste by the British Staff. "The whole scheme wild and half-baked," fumed General Sir Alan Brooke, Marshall's opposite number, the Chief of Imperial General Staff, in London.

Explaining the arrangement to Wavell, Churchill wrote, "I must enlighten you about the American view. China bulks as large in the minds of many of them as Great Britain." The American Chiefs of Staff had put Burma under his command for the sole reason that they considered the linking up with China and the opening of the Burma Road "indispensable to world victory. And never forget that behind all looms the shadow of Asiatic solidarity." He concluded, "If I can epitomise in one word the lesson I learned in the United States, it was 'China.' "

On January 1, 1942, Stilwell recorded in his diary, "George sent for me— with him for over an hour. All about troubles in the Orient." Marshall described the circumstances of the Anglo-Chinese quarrel and said he was looking for a high-ranking American officer to send to Chungking to keep the peace. The name of Lieutenant General Hugh A. Drum, the Army's senior ranking officer and currently commander of the First Army, was discussed, possibly at Stilwell's suggestion. At some point previously

Marshall may have asked him to come armed with a name, for Stilwell had talked the matter over with Dorn who proposed Drum. "The G–mo's a stuffed shirt; let's send him the biggest stuffed shirt we have," was the way he put it.

Drum was a pompous man of large pretensions and self-importance who had been Chief of Staff of the First Army in the AEF and subsequently Pershing's Chief of Staff. He expected to command the next American expeditionary force when war came. Marshall, whom Drum had angered during the past summer's maneuvers by lordly behavior and some scathing remarks, had his own candidates for active command and welcomed a way of disposing of Drum's senior claims. His rank would be a compliment to the Chinese though he had no experience of China. General Magruder, already in China as chief of AMMISCA, would not carry enough cachet; besides he was tired and disillusioned about the Chinese. The only alternative was all too obvious to Stilwell: "Me? No, thank you. They remember me as a small-fry colonel that they kicked around. They saw me on foot in the mud, consorting with coolies, riding soldier trains. Drum will be ponderous and take time through interpreters; he will decide slowly and insist on his dignity. Drum by all means."

GYMNAST at this time was running into deepening confusion of plans and concern about resources. There were doubts about Spain, air cover, submarines, shipping and the general advisability of getting into "a rathole that is under the guns, sure of punishment and hard to supply." Stilwell learned that he had been picked for "initiative, quick thinking and determination" and that the first American attack *must* succeed. "That's O.K. But who wants to be the token?" After long conferences with Marshall and others, he wrote, "All against . . . all agree that means are meager, transport uncertain, the complications numerous, the main facts unknown, the consequences serious." Nevertheless planning continued because, as Stilwell saw it, "the Limeys want us committed" and had "completely hypnotized" Roosevelt who "has acquired this same itch to *do* something. . . . 'Why, rubbish, we can do that.' Our Boy thinks it very queer that ships cannot be unloaded more promptly. 'Two weeks seems a long time to a man in a hurry,' says he." Stilwell put Roosevelt down as a "rank amateur in all military matters" subject to "whims, fancy and sudden childish notions" and "sucked in by the British." In addition, "The Navy is the apple of his eye and the Army is the stepchild."

By January 10 GYMNAST was "getting hot . . . everybody sure it's a crazy gamble. . . . The whole god-damned thing is cockeyed. We should clean the Pacific FIRST and then face east." On January 14, after three weeks wasted in "making a plan that we can prove won't work," the final presentation was made at the last full meeting of ARCADIA. By this time the British had cooled in view of a possible setback in Libya and it was agreed that GYMNAST should be put off.

On the evening of the same day Stilwell was invited to the home of the Secretary of War where he learned, in Stimson's words, that "the finger of destiny is pointing at you," and that its direction was China. While he had been engrossed in GYMNAST, General Drum had been summoned to Washington, and thinking this was the call to greatness, had arrived with an entourage of 40 to 50 staff officers. Instead of appointment as Pershing's successor, he found himself scheduled to go to China with no troops to command and an even greater confusion of objectives and directives than afflicted GYMNAST.

America's wartime policy toward China began to emerge in the discussions with Drum. According to what Stimson told him, the purpose of the mission was to secure China as a base for early operations and eventually for "development of an effective ultimate counter-offensive by or from China proper against Japan." Secondly, the objective was to keep China, which he said was in bad shape and might make a separate peace, in the war. Stimson specified three main duties: "entire disposition" of Lend-Lease, overall command of American air operations in China and probably command of Chinese troops at the suggestion of Chiang Kai-shek who had offered to "turn over one or two of his armies."

Marshall's version had a different emphasis. Besides conserving China as an air base and building up the AVG, the primary objective was to "arm, equip and train the Chinese forces in China" in order that they might operate more effectively against the Japanese and restrain their activities in the Pacific. This was what Lend-Lease was for, as the War Department saw it. Marshall, as a result of his own experience in China, had absorbed Stilwell's view of the Chinese soldier's potential. He knew their endurance and willingness to die, and during a visit to Feng Yu-hsiang's domain, had been impressed by the discipline of his troops. This led him to believe that given competent leadership a force could be developed that would be "unbeatable." Chinese leadership from the company level up he considered incompetent and in need of replacement and retraining.

The mission did not appeal to General Drum who saw it as "nebulous," distant from the main effort and, since Marshall disclaimed any intention of sending American ground troops to the theater, a waste of an officer of his rank and combat experience. While he demurred and debated, Chiang Kai-shek accepted the title of Supreme Commander China Theater with what dignity he could and asked for a high-ranking U.S. officer to serve as chief of his Allied staff who "need not be an expert on the Far East. On the contrary, military men who have a knowledge of Chinese armies when China was under the warlords operate at a disadvantage when they think of the present national armies in terms of the armies of the war lords." This interesting qualification was probably a reference to General Magruder.

The implication of Chiang's message was obvious. What he wanted was someone amenable, of imposing rank and influence at home, and not so knowledgeable as to be critical of Chinese requisitions—in short, a General Drum. But cooled by Drum's disrelish for the task, Stimson ruled him out. With GYMNAST postponed, the finger of destiny swung like a compass needle to Stilwell. Marshall, who wanted him for a field command no less than Stilwell wanted it for himself, tried to avert the sacrifice. "Joe, you have 24 hours to think up a better candidate, otherwise it's you." The first American combat command of the war and of his career had been in Stilwell's grasp and he could fairly expect to lead whatever action replaced GYMNAST. "For God's sake, think hard or we're hooked," he urged Dorn, but he knew the hook was lodged.

In Stimson's eighteenth-century house on its own 20 acres overlooking Rock Creek Park he found himself the only guest. They talked for an hour and a half in front of the fire in the library. "Secwar" asked him how he felt about the mission. "I told him I'd go where I was sent." Stimson too kept a diary and wrote afterwards, "I was very favorably impressed by him. He knows China thoroughly and in half an hour gave me a better first hand picture of the valor of the Chinese armies than I had ever received before. Of this valor he has a very high opinion." Stilwell told him that the whole success of the mission depended on whether Chiang Kai-shek would turn over any part of his Army to American command, which he had always refused to do hitherto. The Secretary assured him that Chiang had suggested it himself and T. V. Soong had promised it. Stilwell expressed doubts but, as recorded by Stimson, said that given such command, the possibilities of the mission were "unbounded and he was very enthusiastic about it." Some of the enthusiasm was certainly Stimson's own for to him the mission represented "fulfillment of a policy and principles which I believed in for many years." Enthusiasm was what he was looking for and Stilwell's feeling for China encouraged him. He went to bed feeling that "I had discovered a man who will be very useful to us in the problems that are coming." He was to remain Stilwell's warmest and steadiest supporter from that day to the end.

Stilwell thrashed out the mission in a long conference with Marshall two days later. He learned that Stimson had at first not wanted to consider him because at a GYMNAST conference he had sat with his head held down. "George told him I was getting ready to butt." Marshall asked Stilwell if he thought the chances of tangible results from the China mission were good. "Yes, if I were given COMMAND." Marshall asked how he thought that could be arranged. "I said, 'Ask CKS if he will.' George said, write the question. So I did and he's sending it to Soong." Marshall told him he would be made a lieutenant general but events were moving fast and "by the time you get there you may be in command in Australia."

There seemed to be no stiffening anywhere from the Indian Ocean to the Southwest Pacific. The Japanese had now made landings in Borneo and the Celebes. On the Malay peninsula two British divisions, unable to get a grip, were retreating toward the strait that guarded Singapore. Incredibly it appeared that the greatest naval base east of Gibraltar, the anchor of the Malay Barrier, might not hold. The Barrier was the chain of land and islands stretching from Burma through Malaya, Sumatra and Java to Australia that protected the Indian Ocean. On January 15 Burma itself, northern anchor of the Barrier, was penetrated in the south by an advance party of Japanese who came from Thailand over mountain passes once used by foot soldiers and elephants of former emperors but supposedly impassable to troops with modern transport and guns. Guided by dissident Burmese nationalists, they advanced on Moulmein.

Suddenly the Chinese divisions, once rejected, appeared desirable. The British now asked for them to take up the defense of the Shan states on Burma's eastern border in order to relieve the 1st Burma Division from that area for the defense of Rangoon. Churchill on returning to London from ARCADIA, faced with a choice of sending the only available reinforcements to Burma or to Singapore, made the rather astonishing statement to his Chiefs of Staff that "as a strategic object I regard keeping the Burma Road open as more important than the retention of Singapore." Its loss would be "very grievous. It would cut us off from the Chinese." For the first time maintaining contact with China seemed important. But the reinforcements in the end went to Singapore because Australia, which had sent its best divisions to fight for Britain in the Middle East, warned that abandonment of Singapore would be an "inexcusable betrayal."

On January 19 Stimson took up with Soong the question of obtaining the Generalissimo's promise of command for the American as yet unnamed "of some of the Chinese troops, particularly those who are to operate in Burma." Chiang's reply was affirmative if not foolproof. He agreed to "executive control" of Chinese units in Burma (the wording in which Soong had relayed the question) and specified a lieutenant general, not to be Magruder. T. V. Soong who had been named Foreign Minister on December 23 interpreted his chief to the Americans and vice versa as he saw fit in the interests of smoothness. A man of strong character and immense ambition, brusque and able, he was thoroughly Westernized in thought and speech and equally Chinese in a quality of bland arrogance. He had small respect for the regime he represented and no reservoir of mutual trust with the leader and brother-in-law whose place he desired to fill. Stimson understood from him that there was "one matter in regard to Burma which still must be straightened out" but this cryptic reference was not clarified. Soong said there was no need to send another radio as his okay was sufficient. He had found out the identity of the nominee, had investigated Stilwell's record, was perfectly satisfied and knew Chiang would be likewise. He thought "the best man in the Army for the job had been chosen." The Generalissimo subsequently approved in a message stating, "General Stilwell's coming to China and assuming duty here is most welcome."

On this basis on January 23 Marshall told Stilwell he appeared to be "it." "Will you go?" he asked. "I'll go where I'm sent," Stilwell answered, as he had to Stimson. He accepted the duty without further remark though not without recording in his diary that "the blow fell" and adding a reference to the goat sacrificed as a burnt offering. His staff took the news in "stunned silence." At the War Department a colleague commented that Marshall had thought "to get rid of Drum in a clever way and all he's accomplished is to lose his best corps commander."

The next days were spent in study of the China files, assembling a staff, preparing requisitions and conferring at length with Soong ("devious and slippery") and the China Defense Supplies group ("usual froth about transport planes, big guns, dive bombers"). He met with Lauchlin Currie, administrator of Lend-Lease to China, and with the Navy, which at about this time was despatching Commander Milton E. Miles, a veteran of the China station, with instructions "to prepare the China coast in any way you can for U.S. Navy landings in three or four years" and meanwhile "to find out what's going on there."

While Stilwell prepared, the enemy progressed. On the day he was named "it" the Japanese landed at Rabaul on the Bismarck archipelago and three days later in the nearby Solomons in their first step toward cutting the United States' line to Australia. In Burma they were closing in on Moulmein where, in the words of a British historian, they "did not come down the road in a straightforward manner" but infiltrated through the jungle in small parties. Here as in Malaya their mobility and progress were astonishing. Lightly equipped, using bicycles or animals for transport, carrying their own ammunition for small-caliber weapons, they were not road-bound. They wore sneakers and shorts and gym shirts and were trained to live on restricted rations of which they could carry enough in their packs for four days. The British, though using troops native to the area, moved in trucks with full equipment of large weapons, tinned foods, helmets, gas masks and heavy boots and suffered the same disadvantages as had General Braddock's Redcoats in the forests of North America.

Marshall was not encouraging. He doubted if the British could hold

Singapore or Rangoon, admitted the China mission was a gamble and re-iterated his warning that Stilwell might end up in Australia. Stilwell was hardly more optimistic. "Will the Chinese play ball? Or will they sit back and let us do it? Will the Limeys cooperate? Will we arrive to find Rangoon gone?"

In a memorandum for Marshall on strategy he saw the Southwest Pacific as a defensive theater and China as the place where "maximum offensive power," involving at least one U.S. Army corps, should be developed for carrying the war to Japan. His final instructions, the first addressed to him as Lieutenant General ("no thrill whatsoever") did not include this concept. They designated him Commanding General of U.S. Army Forces* in the China–Burma–India theater, Chief of Staff to the Supreme Commander China Theater, supervisor of Lend-Lease and U.S. representative on any Allied war council. His functions and purposes were to maintain the Burma Road, "command such Chinese forces as may be assigned to him," "assist in improving the combat efficiency of the Chinese Army" and "increase the effectiveness of U.S. assistance to the Chinese Government for the prosecu-tion of the war"—a phrase carefully drafted to specify the purpose of the assistance. Trying to reduce his tasks to a list, Stilwell found a mixture of eight positions and functions.

Two more tasks of awful proportions, the "Hump" and the Ledo Road, were already taking shape, to counteract the foreseeable loss of Rangoon. When on January 30 the Japanese took Moulmein the threat to Rangoon sharpened. The Chinese, with their faith in Western strength shattered, foresaw the port city lost and themselves isolated once more unless an alternate supply route could be developed. Roosevelt was equally worried and at a Cabinet meeting on January 30 suggested the possibility of opening an air freight route and also an alternate land route which, as Stimson recorded, "He said existed north of the present road through a pass that didn't go over 6,000 feet." Soong, who was consulted at the President's request by Averell Harriman, produced a map with a route marked in red extending from the Persian Gulf by railroad to the Caspian Sea, thence by boat to the railroad across Russian Turkestan as far as the Chinese border, and from there some 2,000 miles by motor road to Chungking, for a total distance of 5,000 miles.

Understandably Soong thought an airline would be more effective. "Mi-raculously enough," as he wrote to Roosevelt on January 31 in a letter that defies comment, one lay "conveniently at hand." It covered only 700 miles of "flying over comparatively level stretches" between Sadiya at the top of

---

* At this stage, staff, technicians and air force.

Assam in northeast India to Kunming in China. He did not mention that between these two points rose the Himalayas, providing probably the most hazardous flight route in the world. He estimated that 100 DC-3 transports could fly 12,000 tons a month into China. The port of entry for supplies would be Calcutta, from where a railroad led north to Assam. Harriman endorsed the proposal in a covering letter which took the precaution to mention the mountains. Within nine days of the request and with quick "can do" confidence in any problem of mere logistics, the President gave Chiang Kai-shek "definite assurance . . . that the supply route to China via India can be maintained by air." Airfields, planes, ground crews, fuel and servicing for an air freight route over the top of the world would have to be called into existence and the task was included under Stilwell's mission before he left. He believed in its necessity. "Events are forcing all concerned to see the vital importance of Burma. We must get the airline going at once and also build the back-country road."

The "back-country road" from India to China that was to be inseparably connected with Stilwell—named as his monument and denounced as his folly—was a proposal initiated by the Chinese on January 1, 1942, two weeks before he was considered for the China mission and three weeks before he was appointed to it. Anticipating even then the loss of lower Burma, even before the Japanese had crossed the border, the Chinese formally requested Lend-Lease material to construct a road from Ledo in Assam across the mountains, forests and rivers of north Burma to tie in with the Burma Road on the Chinese side at Lungling. Over a route unknown by wheeled vehicles, it was an engineering project even more extravagantly difficult than the air route. The Generalissimo suggested that it could be built in five months; AMMISCA officers, after a month's survey of the problems, estimated that it would take two and a half years. The War Plans Division recommended it as an "urgent military necessity." As such it was approved, before Stilwell ever reached China or Burma, by everyone concerned with forwarding aid to China: by the War Department and the President, by T. V. Soong and China Defense Supplies, by Lauchlin Currie for Lend-Lease, and naturally by the Generalissimo, who on a visit to India in February personally undertook to obtain the approval of the Government of India.

When Stilwell returned to Carmel to spend four days with his family before departure he did not express any disappointment he may have felt about giving up the combat command. He seemed glad of the opportunity to fight the Japanese and help the nation he knew in a situation he understood. The mission had now been shaped to his own desire: to enable the Chinese soldier to fight effectively. Besides a staff of 35 officers and five enlisted men who would accompany him by air, the War Department was sending by ship 400 technicians and instructors to aid in training the Chinese in the use of American equipment and tactics.

Stilwell's staff was a combination of the "China gang" and officers from the IIIrd Corps. Colonel Dorn continued as aide and as chief assistant with experience of China. Colonel Frank Roberts, the former language officer whose fate on the *Panay* had caused so much anxiety, now head of the China section of MID, rejoined Stilwell as G-2. Two other former language officers, Colonel Willard Wyman and Colonel Haydon Boatner, who had also served with the 15th Infantry, were recruited, as well as a younger aide, Captain Dick Young, a Hawaiian-born Chinese. Maxwell Taylor, eager to put his knowledge of Japanese to use, was as anxious to go as Stilwell was to have him, but found his name removed from the list by Marshall who wanted him for Europe. As political officer Stilwell borrowed John Paton Davies whom he had known in 1938 on the Embassy staff in Hankow. Born in Szechwan of missionary parents, Davies was knowledgeable, keen and Chinese-speaking, with a talent for informative reports. Chiang Kai-shek was not getting a mission of amiable ignorance. The rest of the staff were drawn mainly from the IIIrd Corps at Fort Ord headed by Brigadier Generals Franklin Sibert as chief Infantry officer and "Long Tom" Hearn, a slow tall southerner, steady but not inspired, as Chief of Staff.

Two men who were decisively to affect the mission were encountered on the last day before Stilwell left. The first, at long distance, was Chennault, the brilliant fighter and agitator of the theater. In the course of negotiations with Chiang Kai-shek over reabsorption of the AVG into the American Army, Marshall had promised him that Chennault would be the ranking air commander in China. But with the development of a strategic air plan for the CBI theater, the structure of command required that Chennault's pursuit group be included in the projected air force for China-based operations. Soong had agreed to the change but, as was his way with problems that promised trouble, failed to inform Chiang Kai-shek. Chennault was now raising loud objections on grounds of the broken promise although his real objection was to serving under the officer designated to be his superior, Colonel Clayton L. Bissell, with whom he had an old feud. Everyone entered the quarrel: Stimson was "quite concerned," Stilwell was sent for, Currie intervened on Chennault's behalf and the Air Force chief, General Hap Arnold, who shared the conventional officer's dislike of Chennault as a black sheep, "hit the ceiling." Though originally nicknamed Happy and known for an expression of amused benignity, General Arnold could throw a temper and on occasion a full inkwell. As overall commander of Americans in the theater, Stilwell insisted that Bissell rank Chennault, and Arnold so ordered. As regards discipline, Stilwell's opinion of Chennault "dropped a lot" as a result of the episode.

The second encounter was with Roosevelt. On a farewell visit to the Secretary of War Stilwell asked, for the sake of enhancing his prestige with the G–mo, if he could carry a personal message from the President. Stimson arranged a meeting, explaining the purpose, and at noon on February 9 Stilwell went to the White House for his first interview with his Commander-in-Chief. It lasted 20 minutes and produced no such rapport as the quiet fireside talk with Stimson. Considering the prejudgments that Stilwell brought with him and Roosevelt's habit of bright monologues, it was not likely to. At home Stilwell was a conventional Republican who shared the sentiments and adopted the tone of the Roosevelt-haters, in which he was influenced by his brother John, an extremist of the species. If he used a cigaret holder "cocked upward at a Rooseveltian angle," as an observer noticed, the similarity was certainly accidental. Yet in their hopes for China there was ground on which they could have met, if either had given the other a chance. The President might have learned more about the real China and Stilwell might have learned something of the President's real aims.

Roosevelt's verbal monopolizing of conversation was so inveterate that his regular associates had to devise special methods to make themselves heard, such as speaking to him at mealtimes when he had his mouth full or timing him for exactly five minutes and then cutting in ruthlessly. On the telephone Secretary Stimson had been known to hang up on him. He was good-humored, intuitive, experimental, calculating, changeable, devious, compromising and given to leaps of thought without discernible coherence. He usually had several lines out and his motives were often mixed. The coherence that guided him, in a phrase used by his daughter, was "his sense of the future." As a British observer said, "He blazed with faith in the future of democracy." His dominant characteristic was confidence—over-confidence as some thought—perhaps the result of his own conquest of paralysis which may have left him with a sense that there was no problem that could not be solved.

He often sounded more frivolous than he was and could obscure his thought by chatter as Stilwell obscured his by silence. Behind the chatter about his ancestors in the China trade he had somehow arrived at the most important thing necessary for the chief of a Western state to know about China: that, as he wrote to a friend in a letter of 1935, "There are forces there which neither you nor I understand, but at least I know that they are almost incomprehensible to us Westerners. Do not let so-called facts or figures lead you to believe that any Western civilization's action can ever affect the people of China very deeply."

Stilwell found him "cordial and pleasant—and frothy. *Un*impressive. Acted as if I were a voter calling on a Congressman. Rambled on about his idea of the war—'a 29,000 mile front is *my* conception,' etc., etc. Just a lot of wind." Among the et ceteras the President said he expected the war to be over in 1943, that "one year from now" would see the turn, that 2,000 planes would go to Australia, that Chiang was not to suppose that Hitler was the one enemy, that all enemies were equal and all the allies in the same boat, and he did not want Mme. Chiang to come on a visit. "After I had enough, I broke in and asked him if he had a message for CKS. He very obviously had not and talked for five minutes hunting around for something world shaking to say. Finally he had it—'Tell him we are in this thing for keeps, and we intend to keep at it until China gets back ALL her lost territory."

This remarkable aim became in fact American policy although it may not have been tossed off as casually as Stilwell thought. As in the case of unconditional surrender at Casablanca a year later, Roosevelt sometimes announced extraordinary decisions seemingly off the top of his head which reflected basic convictions if not prior consultation. Although it was never officially reported, he had enunciated to Stilwell a departure in policy which became a commitment when Stilwell duly conveyed it to Chiang Kai-shek. One country does not usually undertake to win back the lost territories of another, even of an ally, and in 1944 Roosevelt was to state, "I do not want the United States to have the post-war burden of reconstituting France, Italy and the Balkans." Yet he somehow felt an obligation to China.

In the public mind China was the favorite ally. When in his message to Congress on January 6 Roosevelt listed the Allies whom the United States had joined in war, his reference to the "brave people of China" drew the loudest and most spontaneous applause. "Those millions," the President went on, "who for four and a half years have withstood bombs and starvation and have whipped the invaders time and again in spite of superior Japanese equipment and arms." The enduring courage of the Chinese was associated with a mystique about "whipping" the Japanese which the military communiqués of Chungking did everything to elaborate. In one case after Pearl Harbor, the Chinese Government announced the despatch of two armies against the rear of the Japanese who were attacking Hong Kong. Although no such movement took place, a Chinese communiqué reported on December 15 that these forces had engaged the enemy and inflicted 15,000 casualties. In the same fairy-tale spirit in January Chiang Kai-shek informed the American Government of his intention to launch an offensive to drive the Japanese out of Indochina.

The Chinese are "great believers in the world of make-believe," General

Magruder reported to the War Department at this time. They shut their eyes to unpleasant actualities, preferring "flattering but fictitious symbols which they regard as more real than cold facts." He cited the communiqués as an example. Because correspondents from goodwill or laziness reported these fairy tales uncritically, the effect was to create a propaganda about Chinese "victories" that led to misconception.

There were other fictions. As America's ally China could not be admitted to be other than a democratic power. It was impossible to acknowledge that Chiang Kai-shek's Government was what the historian Whitney Griswold, future president of Yale, named it in 1938, "a fascist dictatorship," though a slovenly and ineffectual one. Correspondents, even when outside the country and free of censorship, refrained from reporting the worst of the Kuomintang, on the theory that to do so would be to help the Japanese and besides would ensure that the correspondents could not return. Out of friendship for China they exaggerated her military resistance. It became an established tradition that no journalist "wishing well to China," as one of them wrote, could visit Chungking "without going into ecstasies over the beauty of Madame, the heroic determination of the G–mo, the prowess of the Chinese armies and the general nobility of all hands."

When China in January requested an unrestricted loan of $500 million, Ambassador Gauss, who represented the informed if sour view, cautioned against an unrestricted loan that could be poorly used by "the retrogressive, self-seeking and, I fear, fickle elements" in Chinese ruling circles. The loan was declared necessary by Chungking to support the Government against darkly hinted forces of defeatism. "Nothing but blackmail," Ambassador Litvinov of Russia said privately to Secretary Morgenthau, but the War and State Departments believed that the loan was necessary to encourage the regime and keep China in the war. It was a political and military, not a financial, venture. Morgenthau was exceedingly uncomfortable about fathering a loan without security or controls and proposed a scheme for monthly payments in a special currency directly to the Chinese troops, "so that while the boys fight they get their money, and if they don't fight, no money." This being firmly rejected by the client, Morgenthau continued to struggle to retain for the United States some form of control or supervision or at least right of consultation as to the use of the money. To every such suggestion the Generalissimo said no. He advised Washington that the loan should be regarded as an advance to an ally fighting against a common enemy, "thus requiring no security or other pre-arranged terms as to its use and as regards means of repayment."

This remarkable proposition was allowed to prevail because the real purpose of the loan was to please Chiang Kai-shek and keep him interested in the Allied cause. The motive was the persistent fear, as Morgenthau himself expressed it, that without significant aid, China might move closer to the Japanese and others of the "yellow races." Required to defend the unsecured loan to committees of the House and Senate, he admitted that it was not a banking proposition and that there was a good chance the United States might not get its money back, and he did not deny the imputation of a questioner that the loan was an attempt to outbid the Japanese and prove to Chiang where his interest lay.

Secretary Stimson presented it as a means of mobilizing China's military effort. Quoting what Stilwell had told him of the potential of the Chinese soldier, he testified for the loan before the House Foreign Affairs Committee on February 3 in a speech "as eloquent, as moving and as convincing" as one listener had ever heard. He told the members of China's strategic position and of her "unique relations with us and her unique attitude and confidence towards our government," of Japanese efforts to pull down Chiang Kai-shek "upon whose character and influence rested the Chinese defense," of Chiang's promise to make an American his Chief of Staff and of Stilwell's belief that he could mobilize a fighting capacity. He said the loan was a chance "to play for the highest stakes for the Far East. . . . If America refused to take this chance she would not deserve to win the war." The Committee was so impressed that they did not put a single question and the loan was passed by the House the next day by a voice vote without debate. The Senate, equally favorable, voted unanimously for the loan on the same day that Stimson testified before its Foreign Relations Committee. Congress attached no strings. For the first time, commented the State Department in some awe, a substantial political loan had been made by the United States "without security, without interest, and without retention of control by the U.S. of the expenditure thereof." It was testimony, Roosevelt informed Chiang Kai-shek, of the "wholehearted respect and admiration which the Government and the people of this country have for China."

Like others before and after it, the loan was promised on the necessity of sustaining Chiang Kai-shek in power, whatever his shortcomings, for the sake of maintaining a front in China against Japan. If he should fall, it was feared that collapse of resistance or the outbreak of civil strife would follow, and on that point virtually everyone, whether partisan or detractor, was agreed. Magruder put the case for Lend-Lease on that basis. China had no intention of undertaking any offensive and "will never be a great military asset," he wired on the same day that the Secretary of War was speaking so eloquently to Congress, "but her collapse and loss of her territory for our use would be a liability."

Somewhere between the cold pragmatism of Magruder and the optimism

The U.S. battleship Arizona *crumples under Japanese bombing attack, Pearl Harbor, December 7, 1941 (132).*

133

135

134

136

of Roosevelt, without the romanticism of Carlson or the illusion of Stimson, Stilwell, who knew China, prepared to return.

One of his last interviews was with Harry Hopkins whom he saw at the White House after seeing the President. The record illustrates Stilwell's way of developing his commentary. In his pocket diary he wrote of Hopkins, "Queer gnome." In his expanded notes this becomes "a strange gnomelike creature (stomach ulcers). . . . He had on an old red sweater and crossroads store shoes, and no garters and his hair hadn't been cut for 8 weeks." In a letter to Win the following day Hopkins appears as a "very pleasant old farmer."

Thrust into global problems and newly discovering China, Hopkins was eager to help, if not very precise. "You are going to command troops, I believe," he said, adding that he would not be surprised if Chiang Kai-shek offered Stilwell command of the "whole Chinese Army." He pronounced Chiang to rhyme with bang. He said FDR was "vitally interested" and ready to pull 100 passenger planes off the airlines if needed. He enthused his visitor by a proposal to use the huge *Normandie* as a transport for the theater. "Great stuff," wrote Stilwell who was concerned that shipping was going to be the great problem. Hardly had he left the White House when news came, too pat not to seem an omen, that the *Normandie,* a victim of accident multiplied by monumental incompetence, was burning at her docks in New York. "Is that fate?" Stilwell wondered.

He was heading into a collapsing situation. On the same day, February 9, the Japanese, after a pause at Moulmein to bring up a force of two divisions totaling 18,000 men, crossed the Salween. They were now about 100 miles from the Sittang River, the last natural obstacle before Rangoon. The British had a division of two brigades of Indian and Burmese troops in lower Burma, both of which had been badly mauled by the Japanese on the way to Moulmein. Together forming the 17th Division of about 7,000 men and reinforced by a newly arrived Indian brigade, they abandoned defense of the Salween and withdrew to a position in front of the Sittang. Drawn up behind the river they might have had a chance to fight a delaying action, but an inferior force with its back to a river is in a classic position from which not to fight.

Fifty miles behind them across the plain, Rangoon, though reinforced by another Indian brigade, was emptying in panic. The Indian population, which accounted for half the inhabitants of Rangoon and made up the minor civil service and merchant and urban labor force, were streaming out without adequate food or transport in a desperate trek for home. There were altogether a million Indians in Burma, imported to occupy the ranks between British executive and Burmese peasant, and hated by the native population. Shops and public services were closing, food was short, gov-

Stilwell first met FDR (135) in February 1942 before flying to New Delhi to meet with Sir Archibald Wavell, Supreme Commander in Southeast Asia (133). Stilwell was to be Chief of Staff to Chiang Kai-shek (134). Meanwhile, Soong and Secretary Morgenthau had signed a $500,000,000 loan agreement (136).

ernment bureaus were evacuating to the summer capital at Maymyo in upper Burma, cholera was reported among the refugees. As authority disintegrated, the complex hostilities of various Burmese groups, against the Indians, the British and each other, were breaking out.

The British were anxiously waiting for the two Chinese armies who had not yet begun to move. On February 2 the British commander, Lieutenant General Sir Thomas Hutton, flew to Lashio to meet Chiang Kai-shek who was on his way to India to urge him to hasten the despatch of his armies. The G–mo promised to oblige. On February 5 Wavell flew to Rangoon from his headquarters 2,000 miles away in Java to see what might be done to bolster one more sinking position. The 7th Armored Brigade on its way from the Middle East to reinforce Singapore was now diverted to try to save Rangoon, for more troops could not help Singapore. British forces had evacuated the Malay peninsula and were now collected on Singapore Island where they amounted to four divisions. Morale was low and arrangements muddled and Wavell reported an "inferiority complex which bold and skilful Japanese tactics and their command of the air have caused." He himself while returning from Singapore had fallen from a quay in the dark and injured his back.

On every front the enemy held the initiative. The only pebble of retaliation America could lay hands on, as Stilwell learned before he left, was a daring plan to bomb Tokyo as a means of demonstrating, in this most humiliating hour of Western history, intention and capacity to fight. The President had suggested a raid from Outer Mongolia if it could be done without involving the Russians but General Arnold had another plan in progress.

Stilwell and his staff flew to Miami on February 11 and after two false starts finally succeeded in leaving the United States on the third attempt on Friday the 13th. He was somewhat taken aback to find his plane host to a female civilian, Clare Boothe Luce, on assignment for *Life*. She proved a good sport on the uncomfortable trip and not long afterwards was to write one of the first major articles making Stilwell a character to the American public. "1942 will be a mess," Joe wrote to his wife just before the plane took off for its third start, "but if we can keep it rolling for a year, we'll begin to hand it back."

The journey by Pan American seaplane and DC-3 transport took twelve days in a series of short flights via the Caribbean to South America, across to Africa, north to Cairo ("compared with Peking—phooey") and east over Palestine, Iraq and Persia to New Delhi in the center of India. During this period, February 13-25, one disaster after another in appalling torrent struck the Far Eastern front. On February 15 when a failing water supply climaxed a disheartened and mismanaged campaign, Singapore yielded in unconditional surrender. Eighty thousand troops, about half of them English and Australians, and the rest Indians, went into Japanese prison camps. It was the "worst disaster and largest capitulation of British history" in the words of Churchill's somber acknowledgment. "Christ, what the hell is the matter?" Stilwell asked in angry puzzlement on hearing the news in the middle of Africa.

The dreaded prospect of a joining of Germans and Japanese, if the one should break through the Middle East and the other through India, now appeared possible. Burma was crucial. On February 20 Churchill tried to divert toward Rangoon two Australian divisions which were en route from the Middle East to defend their homeland. "There is nothing else in the world," he wired Prime Minister Curtin of Australia, "that can fill the gap." Curtin, who saw his own country's outer defenses "gone or going," and one Australian division already lost at Singapore and another involved in the British military disaster in Greece, and who had little cause to feel confidence in British conduct of the war, refused to permit the diversion.

On February 23 the British Indian brigades in Burma were defeated in a shambles in front of the Sittang River. To enable retreat, they blew up the bridge, leaving one of their brigades still on the far side. Nothing but a broken army now remained between the Japanese and Rangoon. ("The world is crashing," wrote Stilwell in Cairo.) In Java, in view of Japanese air and sea power dominating the Indies, the ABDA command was dissolved on the same day as the loss of the Sittang, and Wavell returned to India, arriving within a day of Stilwell. From February 26 to 28 the Battle of the Java Sea was fought, ending in defeat for the ABDA naval forces. The loss of Java was now inevitable and the coast of Australia exposed.

"They are very jumpy here," Stilwell wrote home from India in understatement designed for the censor; "there may be trouble ahead."

11

"A Hell of a Beating"

MARCH–MAY 1942

W HETHER Burma could be held to keep open the door to China or whether it would go the way of Singapore was now the crucial question. Events were offering Stilwell a second chance at combat command. Although this was not the original or even primary purpose of his mission, and his command of the two Chinese armies in Burma was intended by Chiang Kai-shek to be no more than a complimentary gesture, the opportunity was one Stilwell was anxious to seize. He knew the Chinese would not take the necessary offensive action in Burma if left to themselves. He did not yet know if his command would be verified.

In New Delhi, India's grandly spacious, tree-shaded new capital built in the 1920s as an imposing setting for the British Raj, he attended a conference at GHQ, "an enormous affair, big enough to run our War Department." The room was full of lieutenant generals, major generals and brigadiers in abundance that seemed disproportionate to the three brigades at the front. He suspected, not without reason, that the meeting was assembled to put him on the spot, for the British were amused at the mission of a high-ranking American general with no troops to command. He began asking questions about the situation in Burma and found that "nobody but the quartermaster knew anything at all." The staff appeared to have no plan of campaign, no coordinate strategy with the Chinese and no intelligence of the enemy's strength or intentions. "The British haven't taken a single prisoner yet."

Stilwell continued east to Calcutta, the teeming, squalid former capital and the takeoff point for Burma on India's east coast. Here he waited for Wavell who flew in from fallen Java on February 28, "a tired depressed man pretty well beaten down." Over dinner in the gloomy dining hall of Calcutta's old Government House he gave Stilwell the story of the three months of defeat. Accompanying him was Major General Lewis Brereton of the American Air Force who had served in Java and was now scheduled to lead the Tenth Air Force based in India under Stilwell's command. He wore an important air and carried a riding crop. "Why the hell does an Air Corps officer need a riding crop?" Stilwell muttered to Dorn; "to beat off the birds maybe?" Some months later on entering General Brereton's plane he stared in unbelief to see it carpeted with a fine Persian rug cut down to fit.

Across the Bay of Bengal in Burma, on the day Wavell and Stilwell met, the civil government was evacuating Rangoon. It had become urgent to move north before the Japanese, advancing from the Sittang, should reach and cut the railroad, isolating the city. The military, who had never prepared for serious defense of the country in which they were stationed, gave little hope of stopping the enemy. Wearily in London, three days after the fall of Singapore, Alan Brooke had acknowledged, "Burma news bad. If the Army cannot fight better than it is doing at present we shall deserve to lose our Empire." Five days later that process had been advanced by the debacle at the Sittang Bridge. The 17th Indian Division had staggered back with one brigade virtually amputated and with survivors, now weaponless, who had forded the river after the bridge was blown.

The Empire was organized to serve the metropolis, not vice versa. Indian troops, like the two brigades hastily sent back to Burma from the Middle East, were trained and used for the desert war against Germany, rather than for service in their own area where they might become contaminated by dangerous ideas of Asian nationalism. Training in jungle warfare was not undertaken because British military planning did not expect a land attack on Malaya or Burma. The troops, like the Americans in the Louisiana maneuvers who could not "de-truck," were tied to their transport and to roads, and helpless against the Japanese tactic of roadblocks. They could not be reinforced or supplied by land because no motor roads existed connecting Burma with India. Roadlessness served the purpose both of the powerful Burma-India Steam Navigation Company which was interested in preserving its monopoly of the carrying trade between Calcutta and Rangoon, and of the British Army in India, which conceived of Burma as a buffer. The Army's view was that "the disease-ridden, jungle-covered mountain ranges of Burma formed an impenetrable barrier, and that an offensive campaign across them was a military impossibility."

In Rangoon the murky smell of burning rubber marked the destruction of Lend-Lease stores including 972 unassembled trucks and 5,000 tires. AMMISCA personnel had moved out as much matériel as possible after the battle of the Sittang, but to the agony of the Chinese more than 900 trucks and jeeps and 1,000 machine guns and other arms had been transferred to the British forces. Government bureaus had departed for upper Burma, Indians of the police and clerical staffs were fleeing, Burmese employees melted into the population. Fires and looting, fifth-column groups and night-roaming marauders took over. All that remained of the civil administration were demolition squads awaiting the Governor-General's last-minute order to blow up the docks.

On the last night at Government House, the Governor, Sir Reginald Dorman-Smith, and a residue of his staff dined in lonely finality with only the cook and butler left out of 110 servants. The halls were emptied of the tall Chaprassis, Indian attendants in long white coats and scarlet and gold waistcoats whose only duty was to stand and wait as silent statues of imperial rule. After dinner the Governor and his aide and one or two others played billiards under the portraits of past Governors of Burma. The portraits' calm, indifferent gaze seemed to irritate the aide, who took up a billiard ball saying, "Don't you think, Sir, that we ought to deny them also to the Japs?" and let fly. The others joined in, hurling balls wildly into ripping canvas, perhaps in frustration, perhaps in some dim recognition that their rule was passing. "It was a massacre," the Governor said afterwards, meaning the portraits, but the Empire too, which had ruled by prestige, was in tatters.

In Burma the British could count on no general support from the population. Although the actively pro-Japanese group was not more than 10 percent, there was an undercurrent of admiration for the Japanese as an Asiatic race who were standing up to the Westerners at last. As the Burmese Premier, U Saw, said, "We Asiatics have had a bad time since Vasco da Gama rounded the Cape." As distinct from the hill tribes—Chins, Kachins and Karens—who were friendly and good fighters, the Burmese of lower Burma were on the whole apathetic, wishing only to keep out of the way of the guns. The nationalist movement had forced some concessions toward Burmese participation in government but the British had refused to promise independence or even Dominion status after the war. As they saw it there was no point in fighting Japan if they had to give up the Empire to do it.

In India agitation for independence, taking advantage of the Japanese menace, was rising to one of its peaks. Roosevelt was so concerned by the idea of the populace opening the door to the Japanese that, despite Churchill's angry reaction in December, he again urged some concession to Indian demands. At the same time, Chiang Kai-shek, eager to play an international role, visited India in February, just before Stilwell's arrival, to rally the Indians against Japan. Results were not altogether as planned. India's Congress Party, instead of being persuaded by Chiang, used him to bring pressure on Britain, and Gandhi pointedly suggested that Chiang's own treatment by Allies did not favor his argument. "They will never voluntarily treat us Indians as equals," he said; "why, they do not even admit your country to their talks." Chiang was stung because he was particularly concerned at this time by China's nonadmission to the Munitions Control Board in Washington which allocated arms and supplies. He promptly quoted Gandhi in a letter to Soong for the benefit of the President, adding, "If we are thus treated during the stress of war, what becomes of our position at the peace conference?" The question was not persuasive for the President's philosophical desire to treat Chiang as an equal stopped short of the Munitions Control Board.

As regards India, Chiang instructed his Ambassador in London to inform Churchill that "I am personally shocked by the Indian military and political situation," and that if it was not "immediately and urgently solved," the danger of a Japanese invasion would daily increase. This might be prevented, he advised, by voluntary concession of real power to the Indians. The advice was not welcomed by Mr. Churchill.

Stilwell and his party left Calcutta on March 3 to complete the last stage of the journey to Chungking where he would establish headquarters, report to Chiang Kai-shek and, he hoped, clarify the question of his command of the Chinese Fifth and Sixth Armies in Burma. The Sixth, a second-rate unit of understrength divisions, had been slowly moving down and on March 1 was not yet fully in position in the Shan states when the 1st Burma Division, which it was to relieve, moved out. The Chinese Fifth Army was a much stronger unit with one full-strength motorized division plus artillery which Chiang was reluctant to let go no matter how urgent was China's interest in holding Burma. He had stalled throughout February and not until March 1 did he order one division of the Fifth to move while holding back the other two.

The first stage of Stilwell's trip took him in a four-and-a-half-hour flight over the wide dun-colored water-streaked Brahmaputra delta and the green hills of Assam and up over the dark mountain ridges of Burma into Lashio. At Porter House, the ample missionary establishment which served for foreign gatherings, he encountered Chiang Kai-shek, accompanied by Madame, who had come down to give directions for the campaign in Burma. The Generalissimo was cordial and welcoming but talked only briefly with Stilwell on this occasion. He looked the same as when Stilwell had last seen him with the same hard, smooth exterior like polished stone, showing no visible evidence of trials or anxieties, and the same forced half-smile that belied his eyes. He wore the neat high-buttoned khaki uniform which he only varied at home with a plain black Chinese gown and his head was shaved close to conceal gray hair. Stilwell watched while Chiang, with a dictator's instinct for balconies, made a speech from the upper porch of Porter House to the commanders and staffs of the Fifth and Sixth Armies who stood in hushed quiet below, listening with strained attention to the sharp, clipped staccato voice of their chief.

In the Generalissimo's entourage Stilwell found his old friend General Shang Chen who, as Director of the Foreign Affairs Bureau of the General Staff, was now in charge of military liaison with China's allies. This was an asset for Shang was a direct and likable man whom Stilwell could talk to without circumlocution. He was not, however, one of the Generalissimo's intimates; in fact they had no love for each other or background in common. Shang, who came from an old official family, had not joined the regime until after the march to the north in 1927 and remained sufficiently detached to label the Generalissimo to Stilwell as *T'ai tzu hsin*, "too self-interested." He owed what influence he had to his being the only one of the upper rank of generals who was fluent in English. All the others used interpreters. Another old acquaintance in the company was Hollington Tong, Vice-Minister of Information and a graduate of the Columbia School of Journalism, who conducted relations with the press, authored China's Munchausen-style communiqués and was detested by Stilwell. "Oily and false," he noted, "mouthing delight at my arrival."

After an hour's stopover he continued on to China via CNAC (China National Aviation Corporation), the well-established commercial line flying DC-3 transports and operated by Americans with only one qualified Chinese pilot among the personnel. The first leg was a two-hour flight over the route of the Burma Road to Kunming where Stilwell stayed overnight in Chennault's quarters. He tackled his first command problem when Chennault flew in next morning. "Had a long talk with him and got him calmed down. He agreed to induction [of the AVG into the American Air Force] and said he'd be glad to serve under me. That's a big relief. . . . He'll be okay." It was not to work out that easily, for the pilots rather than their commander proved to be the first source of trouble when they rebelled against induction.

A rough flight of another two hours with "Chinese passengers all puking" brought the party into Chungking. They came down onto the 2,000-foot concrete landing strip on the edge of the Yangtze. Stilwell took the "same old tough climb" up 365 stone steps to the residence assigned to him, a Western-style house built by T. V. Soong, formerly occupied by Lattimore who had now gone home. Chungking occupied a rocky promontory jutting into the junction of the Yangtze and Chialing rivers and Stilwell's house was on the Chialing side with one story at street level and three stories overlooking the river, like a house in San Francisco. It had a roof terrace with dusty flowers and a pool, a magnificent view of the busy river, and came equipped with servants supplied by Tai Li, China's combination of Himmler and J. Edgar Hoover.

Chungking had a heroic legend earned through three seasons of relentless bombing with no RAF to defend its citizens or to punish the enemy. All that the people had were bomb shelters dug in rock caves and the warning system relayed by watchers stationed along the edges of Free China. They held out during the years in which they fought alone with pride in resistance, but miseries and weariness were mounting. With its extra wartime population stuffed into meager overstrained facilities, Chungking was more uncomfortable, unsanitary and ill provisioned than ever—and the climate was still the same: humid heat in summer, rain and mud the rest of the time. Bomb-shattered houses were leaky and shaky, filth and smells were increased by the crowding, rats came out at night, clerks and workers were underpaid and undernourished, giving rise to the article of belief among American correspondents that "no one ever saw a fat Chinese under the rank of Minister of Finance." Inflation was soaring ("coolies go around with $50 bills," Stilwell noted), officials were eating well and making fortunes while the Government operated by issuing bank notes without controls or a plan. Beaten by circumstance, long since helpless to accomplish its original purpose, the Kuomintang like the last Manchus had settled for one thing—retention of power—without the strength or capacity to cope with multiplying troubles.

Loss of the chief cities and the industrial base to the Japanese had ruined many of the business class, including the most modern and Western-oriented group, who had been strong supporters of the regime. As their influence waned, that of the extreme right wing within the Kuomintang Party grew. Loss of capital and the means of production produced the inflation that ruined the salaried class and drew them into a swelling contagion of black markets and graft in order to live. The long string of defeats and retreats left the army weakened in morale and leadership as well as in arms and equipment, and ate into popular support for the regime. Unrelenting rents, taxes and conscription pauperized the countryside. Armed outbreaks against landlords and officials were increasing. First signs of what was to become a devastating famine appeared in Honan. Discontent provoked repression and repression more discontent, nourishing opposition and turning many minds toward the Communists. The regime was haunted by a sense of insecurity. Concrete machine-gun emplacements on street corners in Chungking and Kunming were not designed for use against the Japanese. The great patriotic surge of 1937-38 that had frustrated the Japanese had petered out in fatigue, oppression and profiteering. Held together by Chiang Kai-shek's aura and his superlative political skill ("The most astute politician of the 20th century" was one of Stilwell's dicta; "he must be or he wouldn't be alive."), the Kuomintang carried on by ignoring spreading sores and sheltering in escapism.

Some Americans in Chungking, especially those who had shared the hopes of the early days, developed, in the words of one, "an intense distaste, even hatred," for Chiang Kai-shek and his Government. Others, like Ambassador Gauss, as Stilwell found when he called on him, were merely "fed up." Formerly Consul-General in Shanghai where he had made a reputation for standing up to the Japanese, Gauss after 30 years of consular service in the country was not a Sinophile with strong feelings one way or another. By virtue of a staff many of whom spoke and read Chinese, traveled widely and often, and had many contacts, he made his Embassy the best informed in China—and was regularly bypassed by policy-makers and special envoys from Washington. He had none of the diplomat's professional suavity and cheer, and owing to his consular background and not very agreeable personality, lacked the entree to the White House of ambassadors like William Bullitt and Joseph Grew. He was businesslike, unremarkable in appearance, a chain smoker of cigars, impatient of the indirect ingratiating methods of the Orient, "hard to fool, hard-thinking, straight-speaking." His persistent refrain was that China "is only a minor asset to us" but could become a "major liability." The Chinese, who found this Westerner inscrutable, called him the Honest Buddha and were not happy with him, as a colleague said, "because he is cold and says No."

Stilwell found old acquaintances in Chungking including Jack Belden, who accompanied him back to Burma as correspondent for *Time,* and General Ho Ying-chin, the Minister of War and Chief of Staff on whom he paid a formal call. Ho had accompanied Chiang from the time they had been fellow students at the military academy in Tokyo before the Revolution, had served with him at Whampoa and had been his Chief of Staff in the Northern Expedition (during which he was nicknamed Grandma by the troops) and ever since. Short and stocky, smooth in manner, with a smiling round face, a small round mouth and round glasses, he was loyal only to Chiang and considered his task as Chief of Staff to be a matter of keeping the army loyal through manipulation of cliques and control of supplies and funds. Having concentrated his energies on this occupation for 15 years with considerable success, he had not acquired much modern military knowledge, in the Western sense, to put at the disposal of his chief. Conferences with him, which were necessarily to be many, were a round of "double talk and tea," as described by Dorn, against a blank wall of courtesy, protocol and delay. Stilwell on March 5 found him "very pleasant" and they talked in Chinese.

Carrying a "hell of a mental load" about the question of command, he reported to Chiang Kai-shek on March 6. He believed Burma could be saved by offensive action and he saw the campaign as a chance to restore Chinese confidence in themselves and make good his own lost command of GYMNAST as well as accomplish an essential military objective. He discovered to his relief that Chiang did intend to give him command in Burma and that he seemed willing to fight. Chiang was "extremely suspicious" of British motives and intentions and "fed up with British retreat and lethargy." Stilwell told him that "we were his gang and would do what he said." He likewise assured Madame that Chennault would not be pushed aside. She was anxious about Chennault's status and told Stilwell that he resigned regularly. The conference ended with Chiang's promise to set up a joint staff for the Burma command the next day; Stilwell left believing he could go back to Burma and fight. "Now I don't have to wake up in a blue funk every morning and wonder what the hell I can do to justify my existence. . . . I'm still not sure what I am but Shang Chen says it's No. 2 in China."

But the next day and the day after were blank, summed up in the word which in one exasperated form or another was to follow every conference with the Chinese—"waiting." While waiting Stilwell wrote down his own plan for strategy in Burma and activity in China. If Rangoon were lost (on the day he wrote, March 7, the Japanese entered the city), he contemplated a strong counterattack by the Chinese Fifth Army combined with British forces to recapture it. In the event of failure, the Allies should fall back on the high ground east of Mandalay from where they could threaten the flank of any Japanese drive to the north and could hold upper Burma. The important thing was to "formulate plans that the British will accept" but the difficulty was that plans were being made in the dark. No one knew what forces the Japanese had committed to Burma, whether they were building for an offensive or were too weak to launch one. Estimates were mere guesses.

In China the main endeavor should be to get the Thirty Division program under way for which the divisions were still not designated. After Burma was made safe Stilwell wanted an offensive to be launched in China to clear the Hankow area and "put us within striking distance of Japan." He planned to take Hankow by a double envelopment with American air power acting in support of Chinese ground troops. His plan for long-range strategy, deposited with Marshall before he left, stated, "First priority, prompt build-up of air support." An equal priority was the need to create an effective military arm on the ground.

To weld a fighting force from the sprawling feeble collection of Chinese armies was a task which had only the uncomplaining hardihood of the men in its favor. Every other factor in the Chinese military system was resistant. The country was divided into twelve war zones with control decentralized so that the Japanese could not finish off the war at one blow. The result was to augment local power and perpetuate use of the armies as political counters and as virtually the property of the area commander. It also caused dispersion of the best divisions leaving no strong force available for use against the Japanese, even had the will to action been present. The will was lacking partly because the Chinese believed they had fought the Japanese long enough and it was now someone else's turn; partly because of the tendency to hoard the armies for local power, or in the case of the Central Government, for use against the Communists; and finally because of lack of confidence. "Chinese could not believe Chinese troops could fight the Japanese," Stilwell wrote.

A total of just under three million men were nominally under arms, organized in some 300 divisions and other formations. Organization was based on multiples of three, with three regiments to a division, three divisions to an army, three armies to a Group Army and usually three Group Armies to a war zone. Divisions varied widely in quality, with those favored by the Generalissimo given the best in arms and equipment and uniforms. These units had boots and leg wrappings, but the Central Government supply system did not reach to all and the average Chinese soldier marched in straw sandals and slept under one blanket for every five men. He carried two grenades in his belt and a long blue stocking around his neck stuffed with dry rice, his only field ration. Recruitment was by press gang, draining the villages and farms of their manpower. Men could escape induction by payment of CN (Chinese Nationalist) $100 and rice contributions at regular intervals. In the march to the base camp recruits were tied by rope. Basic training was three weeks. Divisions were generally understrength because payment was made by lump sum to the commanding general and the fewer troops he had to pay—up to a certain self-limiting point—the greater his profit. A division's manpower did not represent all armed strength because a large proportion was coolie labor necessary for transport.

Losses due to malnutrition and disease were high, sometimes reaching 40 percent or more in a year, so that a division of about 7,000 might require 3,000 new recruits annually. Due to low and irregular pay officer desertions were frequent. The food ration was 25 ounces of rice per day plus some pickled vegetables with salt or red pepper, but the nutritive value was even less than supposedly supplied because pickling destroyed vitamins and both vitamins and proteins were absent from the two-to-three-year-old rice normally issued. Average pay for the men was CN $16-$18 a month from which $8-$10 was deducted for food. Rising inflation made what cash was left over valueless for purchasing the bean curd, fats, green vegetables or occasional fish or meat by which soldiers had formerly supplemented their diet. Even captains and majors at CN $145-$175 a month could not afford adequate nutrition. The men ate their two meals a day from a common pot, often with only three minutes allowed for eating. Food was bolted and ill digested, and the stronger individuals took the most while the weaker grew weaker. Hunger edema along with other complaints afflicted 60 to 70 percent of patients in military hospitals, and deaths from starvation, especially in the transport companies, were frequent. "I have no pain but I have no strength," was the usual complaint. The worst cases were generally hidden before inspection tours. When a unit moved, the roads were lined with bodies along the way.

Epidemics of dysentery and smallpox and louse-borne relapsing fever and typhus recurred. Though delousing stations for recruits were mandatory, commanders often dispensed with them because the fuel, and the extra time requiring extra food, was an added expense. For the same reason the order to cultivate vegetable plots was often ignored because a commander was unwilling to spend money to plant for another unit to harvest in case he had to move. Medical care organized by the Chinese Red Cross under one of China's great men, Dr. Robert K. S. Lim—who was to be forced out by political pressure in 1943—could barely treat the surface of the problem. Most of the men had never practiced sanitation or hygiene and together with many of the noncoms and even officers were unaware of the connection between sanitation and disease. The reason for digging latrines was not understood; fuel for boiling water was just another expense.

Military hospitals were understaffed and ill equipped. In the absence of roads and ambulances the wounded were carried from the scene of combat by stretcher-bearers, to the extent of their capacity, or left to fend for themselves or die where they fell. Red Cross medical units served with divisions in the field, often having to battle the ignorance or resistance of commanders who saw no urgency about saving men when, as one expressed it, "The one thing we have plenty of in China is men." This was the comforting myth but in fact the "plenty" was not enough to serve both the insatiable maw of the armies and the labor needed for agriculture. Some commanders were genuinely concerned for the welfare of their units. A certain General Lo of the 18th Division on the Ichang front discovered that his losses in four years without fighting had amounted to the full strength of his division and decided that he did not want the parents of the men who had died without meeting the Japanese to "curse me as an enemy." He summoned medical help and gradually reduced his death and disease rate by 60 to 75 percent. When he began he had not known that relapsing fever, a scourge in his area, was louse-borne. It was this kind of effort plus increased food, regular pay and provision of arms and training that Stilwell wanted for the Thirty Divisions.

At the end of the third day of waiting in Chungking the plan of command was delivered and proved to be "just stooge stuff, no authority." It put Stilwell on a level with the Chinese commanders. From that moment a struggle began that was never to be resolved until the final crisis. The staff plan seemed to indicate Chiang Kai-shek's real intentions, yet at the same time he talked as if Stilwell's command of the Chinese expeditionary force was understood. Stilwell acted on the verbal evidence, although doubt of its reliability lurked in a corner of his mind.

Discussion continued at a dinner in his honor at the Generalissimo's residence at Huang Shan, a wooded height ten miles to the south with a view over the city and the two river valleys. Among the guests besides Shang Chen and Ho were Yü Ta-wei, the cultivated and thoughtful graduate of Harvard and Heidelberg who was Minister of Ordnance, and Li Tsung-jen and Pai Ch'ung-hsi, the two Kwangsi Generals whose allegiance to Chiang Kai-shek had been variable for many years. They were "very quiet, thinking their own thoughts." Pai was now Deputy Chief of Staff in charge of training, and as a general without an army was increasingly identified with Chiang Kai-shek, but the antagonism between Chiang and Li endured. The guests sat stiffly on the edges of their chairs, talking in whispers and avoiding the glimpse of secret-service boots peeking below red curtains. After the Generalissimo and Madame made a formal entrance, toasts were drunk and Stilwell replied in Chinese, repeating President Roosevelt's message.

During a two-hour discussion of the campaign after dinner Stilwell listened with inner contempt to a discourse of "amateur tactics by CKS" of which the gist was "caution." It was clear that Chiang regarded the Fifth and Sixth Armies as his best divisions and hesitated to risk them because the British might "run away." Further, he said, it required three Chinese to one Japanese division to hold a defense and five to one for attack and he wanted no attack until it was known whether the Japanese were reinforcing. "Let's go before they build up," Stilwell proposed but this was vetoed. Let the enemy take the initiative; if "the Japanese do not move, we can move." Concentration of forces must be avoided because several divisions might be defeated at once, but if only one is wiped out the others remain. Maintain *chung shen p'ei pei* ("defense in depth"), meaning a column of divisions strung out 50 miles apart. These were Chiang's principles, exactly contrary to Stilwell's.

Chiang insisted that he would not take British orders and that he was going to wire Roosevelt to tell Churchill that Stilwell must command the Allied forces. Stilwell reminded him that it was in "our" interest to regain Rangoon whereas "all the British need is a wall in front of India," but Chiang refused to be hurried. He wanted Stilwell to return to Burma, ascertain British intentions, study terrain and rely on *chung shen p'ei pei*.

"What a directive. What a mess. How they hate the Limeys and what a sucker I am," Stilwell wrote, and added with some foresight, "Maybe the Japs will go at us and solve it for us." In a further talk next day he acknowledged that Chiang made "a lot of good sense" on the subject of Chinese temperament and military limitations. Stilwell did his best to be diplomatic: "I repeated instructions and went over all the points he made." In spite of restrictions he felt the Chinese were "doing a big thing from their point of view in handing over this force to a *lao mao tze* they don't know very well." Chiang did in fact on the day after the dinner telegraph Roosevelt proposing Stilwell as Allied Commander in Burma. Caught between the Chinese and British, Roosevelt replied that it was a matter of "extreme delicacy" and suggested the possibility of dividing command between Stilwell in north Burma and the British defense further south.

On March 11, the day Stilwell left, Chiang assured him verbally that "this morning I have issued orders to place the Fifth and Sixth Armies under your command." Their commanders, Generals Tu Li-ming and Kan Li-chu, and General Lin Wei representing the General Staff, had been told "to take orders from you absolutely." Stilwell realized that his command was "under wraps, of course, which I may or may not be able to cast off. In all probability not." It was his habit to write down the most pessimistic case but, like most of humanity, not to believe it.

By the time he returned to Burma the crippled 17th Indian Division had withdrawn from Rangoon toward Prome on the Irrawaddy. At the same time the leading division of the Chinese Fifth Army, the motorized 200th, had come down about level with the British to Toungoo on the Sittang.

The Allied idea, hardly firm enough to be called a plan, was to hold a line across lower Burma through Prome and Toungoo about 150 miles north of Rangoon. Joint operations on a horizontal line presented a certain difficulty because all communications in Burma ran longitudinally along three main river valleys. These were formed by the Irrawaddy and Chindwin on the west, by the Sittang and upper Irrawaddy in the center, and on the east by the great Salween, rising like the Yangtze in remotest uplands behind Tibet. Mandalay, the ancient capital, stood roughly in the center of the country on the banks of the Irrawaddy and at a fork in the railroad

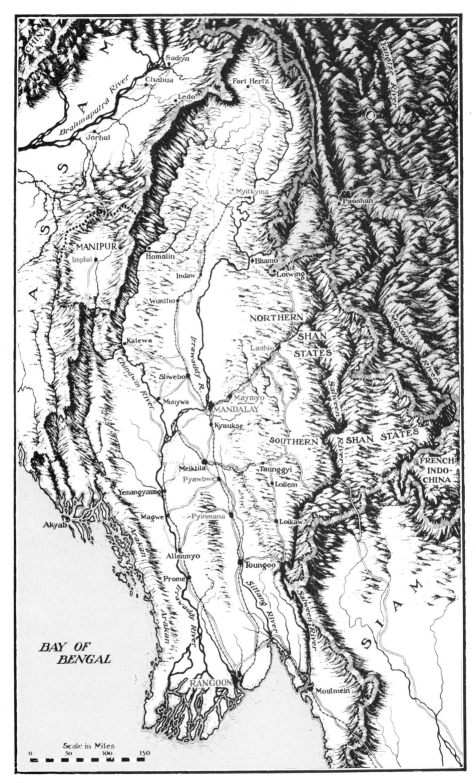

Burma, 1942

of which the western branch led to Myitkyina and the eastern to Maymyo and Lashio where it connected with the Burma Road. Chiang had not yet released the other two divisions of the Fifth Army, the 22nd and 96th, although Stilwell had obtained his promise to send them as far as Mandalay as soon as food supply could be arranged.

Stilwell established headquarters at Maymyo, the hill station and summer capital with dusty streets and lawns and gardens in the English manner where the British Government had now removed. The quarters for himself and his staff were in a red-brick Baptist mission house hung with purple bougainvillea and planted with roses, eucalyptus and honeysuckle.

The history of campaigns tends to be told in terms of the commanding officer, but he does not operate without a staff. Stilwell's was mixed in capacity; as in any operation some were competent, some not. It was said of General Hearn, who was to remain Stilwell's Chief of Staff until the end, that if you wanted something done you went to someone else, but his loyalty and dependability were compensating virtues. Among the line officers who served as tactical advisers and liaison with the Fifth and Sixth Armies was Colonel George Sliney whom a British colleague pronounced "one of the best artillery officers any army has produced." The several graduates of the Chinese language program were invaluable and they were supplemented by Colonel Tseng Shih-kwei as chief interpreter. A graduate of VMI who had fought with bravery and distinction at Shanghai in 1937, he was endowed with the peculiar Chinese combination of worldly charm and strong character and was to remain a close and valued adjutant to Stilwell throughout his mission. None of the staff had prior experience of Burma—its food, roads, currency, transportation, politics or other components of the sea in which they swam. On the whole, given the circumstances, Stilwell did not have a staff adequate to the task confronting them. Too many, in the opinion of one observer, reflected "the influence of two decades of easygoing Army posts and country club porches." The British, who were responsible for supply and transport for the Chinese, considered the American staff, with some justice, pitifully inadequate to handle the six (later nine) Chinese divisions. Stilwell in turn considered the British incapable of working with the Chinese "because they looked down on them."

At Flagstaff House, the Victorian pile on the hill where beer in a silver mug was always ready for guests, British Headquarters consisted of one full general, one lieutenant general, five major generals, 18 brigadiers and 250 staff officers. They served a dwindled field army of less than 15,000, all that was left active of what had been two divisions plus the Armored Brigade. They wore shorts and insisted on writing what Stilwell called "Leavenworth orders" even when the sky was falling.

Stilwell paid a courtesy call at Flagstaff House on the Governor-General (Doormat-Smith in his diary), who was astonished to hear an American announce himself as commander of the Chinese armies in Burma. Puzzlement grew when General Tu Li-ming of the Fifth Army presented himself shortly afterwards in the same capacity. "Ah, Your Excellency," he replied smiling, when Dorman-Smith asked how two men could hold the same position, "the American General only thinks that he is commanding. In fact he is doing no such thing. You see, we Chinese think that the only way to keep the Americans in the war is to give them a few commands on paper. They will not do much harm as long as we do the work."

Tu's version of the situation posed a recurring question between East and West: which face of a mutual situation was the reality? Who was keeping whom in the war? What was the truth of Stilwell's position? The problem caused his command in Burma to take on the complications of a Pirandello play.

While he was establishing relations with the Chinese generals a new commander appeared in Maymyo—the hero of Dunkirk, the very pattern of a gallant British Guards officer, the younger son of an earl, the man originally intended to lead the British share of GYMNAST, General the Right Honourable Sir Harold Alexander. He had come to take over command of Burma from Wavell who reverted to Commander-in-Chief in India. "If we could not send an army," wrote Churchill, "we could at any rate send a man" although "never have I taken the responsibility of sending a general on a more forlorn hope." Wavell had already reported that he had "grave doubts" of holding Burma. Alexander had a reputation for imperturbable cheer in peril and stress, gained under fire as a young lieutenant in World War I and confirmed in the desperate hours when he brought the British out at Dunkirk. He was said to have commented favorably on the marmalade while breakfasting in his "shiniest boots and best breeches" amid fear and fire on the beach. "Confidence spread around him," according to Churchill, but to instill confidence into the defense of Burma at this stage was impossible.

Without roads or Rangoon no reinforcement in arms or men could be brought in even if they had been available. The day after the fall of Rangoon, March 8, Java surrendered, yielding 13,000 more Allied soldiers into prison camps or forced labor. Japanese broadcasts proclaimed the coming invasion of India. The date rounded out, since Pearl Harbor, the three most humiliating months of Western history in relation to the East. To the public in America the reality was obscured by grandiloquent pronouncements and drumbeating headlines, but not to soldiers bombed and wounded and retreating on the spot. They lost confidence in their leaders, in themselves and in a cause that for most of them was not their own. Men will fight in their homeland with no thought of giving up, but in Burma motive was lacking. Burma was the last ditch for no one except the Burmese, who only wanted the belligerents to go away. The despatch of Alexander was an empty gesture.

Stilwell met him with every anti-Limey antenna quivering on the alert. He saw a slight figure, a long, sharp nose, protuberant eyes, a Guardsman's mustache and what he took to be a condescending stare. Alexander "let me stand around outside till Shang Chen came. . . . Astonished to find ME—mere me, a goddam American—in command of Chinese troops. 'Extrawdinery!' Looked me over as if I had just crawled from under a rock." When it came to a discussion of the channels of command, Alexander "just looked blankly at me." Not to be gorgonized by a stony British stare, Stilwell gave him a "dirty look" in return. In the meantime he had radioed Chiang Kai-shek to send the 22nd and 96th Divisions to Pyinmana, 130 miles south of Mandalay, to back up the 200th which was under attack at Toungoo. While waiting for an answer he decided to act and told Lin Wei to start the movements. The British staff, informed of the move, were "pleased, trying to be friendlier," and Alexander was "a new man, all smiles and jokes about how I'd gotten his Chinese troops away from him." Relations improved except with Alexander's Chief of Staff, a haughty character named Major General T. J. W. Winterton whom Stilwell dubbed "Plushbottom" from the Moon Mullins comic strip. He wired Marshall that cooperation had been arranged and "matter of command need not affect conduct of operations." Stilwell believed Pershing had been right in insisting that national units be kept intact but he also believed in unity of command and was perfectly willing, if not happy, to serve under Alexander.

Action made everyone look better. Tu is "O.K. Solid on tactics. Ready to fight." Lin and Hsiao and Shang Chen all agreed that a fight should be made at Toungoo. Stilwell was "amazed at the way the Chinese accept me"—a judgment that proved superficial—and decided that "the only trouble is up top."

Deficiencies were making themselves felt. Radios were few, communications poor, medical facilities lacking, malaria and blackwater fever appearing, his own staff not the most adequate to the circumstances and Japanese bombing steadily blasting one Burmese town after another. The enemy was able to put an average of 260 planes a day in the air against an Allied average of about 45, consisting of one RAF squadron and the dogged AVG fighters who accounted for a remarkable rate of kills despite a chronic shortage of fuel, planes, parts and pilots.

In the cool and pleasant surroundings of Maymyo the top-heavy British staff milled in confusion and planlessness for which Stilwell had the same remedy as in Washington: "The whole mob should sit down, say nothing for two hours and try to think." But they could not think purposefully because they had no clear directive as to their objective after the fall of Rangoon: whether to hold as much of Burma as possible or to withdraw slowly while the defense of India was prepared. The one clear objective that received urgent attention was the building of an escape route over the long-unused road through the Tamu Pass in the Chin Hills to Imphal in India. In the back of every mind was the monsoon coming in the middle of May which would turn trails into mud slides and make Burma a trap unless there were egress by road. The hordes of Indians streaming out of cholera-ridden refugee camps at Mandalay toward the Tamu Pass were limited by the Army to 500 a day over the road so as not to interrupt construction.

Major Frank Merrill, a former Japanese-language officer who had come from the Philippines after Pearl Harbor to act as liaison with the British, told Stilwell the story of the Burma campaign up to now: "no plan, no reconnaissance, no security, no intelligence, no prisoners," in contrast to the Japanese who had excellent communication, great aggressiveness and high mobility. In Merrill who was to play a leading role in Burma Stilwell found a valuable associate. He was a shrewd and genial soldier, tall, heavyset and shortsighted, with glasses perched on a sunburned peeling nose, who had enlisted in the Army at eighteen and afterwards taken the examination for West Point six times before the Academy decided to over-look his astigmatism and accept him.

Another remarkable man, Dr. Gordon Seagrave, appeared at Maymyo at this time to offer his services. An American Baptist missionary surgeon of long experience in Burma, he was unorthodox, uncompromising, out-spoken and dedicated, with something of Stilwell's caustic character and hatred of pretensions. He had organized a hospital in the Shan states and trained a staff of Burmese nurses and now came to offer his unit to serve the Chinese Fifth Army at Toungoo, preferring to serve under American Army leadership than under the British. Seagrave expected to be thrown out since he considered that Stilwell had never heard of him and would probably be prejudiced against missionaries and Burmese nurses. To his surprise the General and his medical officer, Colonel Robert Williams, agreed to his proposal and even asked for his ideas and suggestions on supplies needed for the Chinese troops. At the quickened pace of war he and Stilwell reached mutual understanding and respect with few words exchanged. It was apparent to Seagrave at once that bootlickers "didn't even get a 'good morning' " from the General and that he was best "when you are talking business with him for he gets the point before you are half through and his decision is quick as lightning."

To persuade Chiang Kai-shek to unleash the Chinese divisions Stilwell flew back to Chungking on March 17 and with Shang Chen at his side battled with the Generalissimo for two days. "Every point he set up I knocked down. Just kept at it and at it. . . . Exhausted." Shang Chen conferred with Ho Ying-chin and Pai Ch'ung-hsi and two other members of the General Staff and to Stilwell's astonishment reported that all four agreed on the need for action and would urge the Generalissimo to consent. Repeated arguments were even shaking Madame; "In fact she told me to keep it up." Encouraged and relieved, Stilwell believed the Chinese were accepting his status "which is close to a miracle. At least I know now there are Chinese officers who would agree if they dared." This knowledge gave him the first good night's sleep since Calcutta, for he was becoming increasingly disenchanted with the G–mo's military ideas. He woke up on his fifty-ninth birthday without feeling for the first time in months that "all was lost." At his first press conference since the announcement of his mission he professed his faith in "my troops"—the Chinese—and told the press that "the happiest day of our lives will be when Chinese and American troops together enter Tokyo."

He received a birthday telegram from Marshall saying, "Your presence in China is a tremendous reassurance to the President, to Colonel Stimson and to me." Conscious of the forlorn position to which he had delivered his best corps commander, Marshall continually sent him messages of appreciation in lieu of reinforcements. In response to Stilwell's report of Chiang Kai-shek's refusal to take orders from the British, Marshall dropped his insistence on unity of command and urged the British to permit a duality between Alexander and Stilwell if they wanted to make sure of the participation of the Chinese. Alexander appreciated the point and was agreeable. Roosevelt carried the matter to Churchill, who acquiesced.

In Chungking Chiang Kai-shek was yielding a little on the question of using the Chinese troops. Stilwell secured a promise that the 22nd Division could go down to the level of Pyinmana to support the 200th and could even help the British in case of danger at Prome, but only under Stilwell's command and "only in an emergency." Chiang insisted the 96th must stay at Mandalay. Whether the Japanese had the forces for an offensive toward the north was not yet clear. If nothing happened in a month, Chiang said, maybe the Chinese could attack ("He wants it to be easy"). He repeated that the Fifth and Sixth Armies must not be defeated, "so I told him to send someone who could guarantee that because I couldn't." Next day Chiang vacillated saying he would pull out entirely if the British gave up Prome. "He can't make up his mind. Changeable." Before Chiang could renege further Stilwell flew back to Burma and immediately on reaching

Lashio signed the orders for movement of the Chinese divisions. He hastened on by car to the Fifth Army at Pyawbwe. The Japanese offensive had started and Toungoo was being attacked. Tu was worried. He agreed to hurry down the 22nd to support the 200th and to hurry over a division of the Sixth Army to back up the 22nd. Stilwell rushed back to Maymyo to arrange the movements. "The suspense till the 22nd gets going is bad."

On that day calamity struck at Magwe, the airfield on the Irrawaddy 100 miles above Prome. A bombing raid by 200 Japanese planes caught the RAF and AVG by surprise on the ground. They retreated with what they had left to Loiwing in China, an AVG base just over the Burma border north of Lashio. After two or three halfhearted engagements with disproportionately heavy losses, the RAF squadron withdrew to India without informing General Alexander and did not participate further in combat or reconnaissance. By patching up and cannibalizing their damaged planes the AVG continued for a while to keep a small fighting force in the air. The pilots, forced to fly at a constant disadvantage, were growing bitter and mutinous and resentful of the failure to receive the comparatively small reinforcements with which they believed they could have achieved ascendancy over the enemy. Reinforcements in the form of the planes of the supersecret mission to bomb Tokyo were in fact scheduled to fly on to join Chennault, but the Tokyo mission was still four weeks off. Stilwell's diary was terse on March 23: "No air support left now."

This was the crux of the situation, he wrote to Stimson that night. The opportunity for "what might have been effective opposition has been definitely lost." It had already taken so much time to get the G–mo to move his armies that the delay had "fatally compromised any chance we might have had here in Burma." The Fifth and Sixth Armies had been sent in without any services at all: their rations, rail transport and fuel for trucks were supplied by the British. "As far as I can see, the staff of the Chinese Army did not interest—or bother—themselves in any way about this expedition." He had had to go personally to dig out the Surgeon General. The discipline and spirit of the troops was excellent but the Generalissimo's "tactical ideas are fantastic." He was obsessed by Mandalay and believed "the only way to defend it is to sit on it."

Habitually Stilwell anticipated the worst and went on making the strongest effort he could. During the week of March 24-31 a frantic endeavor was made to bring the 22nd Division into position to launch a counter-attack at Toungoo in order to break through the threatened encirclement of the 200th which was defending the town, and to hold firm the flank of the British at Prome. Four days passed, marked by long and mysterious delays on the railroad—arranged, as Stilwell began to suspect, from Chungking—before the 22nd was even brought into position. Twice

Stilwell ordered the offensive, twice General Tu and his subordinates, after arguments, analyses, excuses and promises, agreed to perform, and twice the 22nd failed to move.

The edge of war moved north with incessant air raids, villages in flames, more and more refugees choking the roads in a long frieze of bullock carts, heat and thirst and dust. "Hell to pay on the railroad. Crews running away. No trains below Pyinmana. No trucks." When Stilwell demanded 150 trucks, he was sent 50 by General Yu Fei-p'eng, the fat chief of supply who controlled 700 trucks at Lashio and was using them for the transport of military supplies to private warehouses in China. All Stilwell's orders had to be relayed through General Tu to Lin Wei to still another liaison figure, General Hou, who had a secret radio set connecting with Chiang Kai-shek, for confirmation at the top; then relayed back down again before they could be acted on. At the same time Madame communicated the Generalissimo's wishes to Stilwell in letters that arrived in a special letter-box by every plane on the Chungking-Lashio run. This procedure was followed because it was believed the Japanese could break the radio codes. The letters were full of warnings, admonitions and Chiang's favorite piece of tactical advice: "He wishes to emphasize again to you the necessity of following the principle of 'deep column tactics.' " Three letters came in one day with several changes of mind ending with renewed permission to move the 22nd Division which Stilwell had already ordered. "Christ, the mental load on a commander who has strings tied to him."

With a few of his staff Stilwell set up personal headquarters with the Fifth Army at Pyawbwe. His days were spent in rough dirty drives back and forth to Maymyo and Pyinmana, often through air raids, and in endless sessions over a map spread out on the table, arguing the advantages of the offensive with Tu and the commander of the 22nd, General Liao Yao-hsiang. Once as four enemy fighters flew over in a low pass to strafe the bungalow, Major Merrill while firing at them with a Bren gun heard the General shout from the bathroom, "The bastards have caught me with my pants down but I'll be down to help you by the time they get back."

At Prome the British forces were assembled as Ist Burma Corps under a new corps commander, Lieutenant General William J. Slim, who had been transferred from the Middle East in the same infusion from the top that brought Alexander. He was a man of fighting temperament who had enlisted as a private in World War I. When Merrill who conducted Stilwell's liaison with the British went to see him to ask if he would join in the counterattack, Slim asked, "What is Stilwell's objective?"

"Rangoon," Merrill replied with a straight face.

"Tell Stilwell he can count me in," said Slim.

Later in the course of shared misfortunes when he came to know Stilwell in person, he found him sometimes "obstinate as a whole team of mules," sometimes deliberately rude, but possessed of a major military virtue: he was "constantly on lookout for an aggressive counterstroke." Slim too believed there was a chance for just that at Toungoo but he had little to work with. Burmese soldiers, worried about their families, were deserting and there were no replacements, air cover was gone, the Indian Division's field guns and heavy equipment had been lost at the Sittang, troops were dispirited, faith in their officers was minimal, positions were abandoned without battle. The countryside was growing sinister. An aide to Wavell who came on an inspection tour felt "anarchy and menace in the air." Dacoits and Thakins, partisans of the nationalist leader Aung San, stalked the area. Burmese peasants like "malignant nursemaids in their skirts and white caps" carried long sharp knives, actually ordinary agricultural tools but they had a wicked look. British soldiers who drove jeeps with the windshields down were sometimes found decapitated by wires stretched across the roads at neck height.

On March 26 Stilwell learned of a riot among British soldiers at Yenangyaung, 120 miles north of Prome, site of the oil fields which supplied all motor fuel and oil for the campaign. Then worse news. "British destroying *the oil fields.* GOOD GOD. What are we fighting for?" It was hard to tell. No one really cared about Burma. It was the end of the line. The main effort of London and Washington was directed elsewhere. With no reinforcements or help coming in, there was a sense of isolation in CBI. Dr. Seagrave, setting up his medical station at Pyinmana behind the Fifth Army, felt it. The only way to believe the task was important, he thought, was to believe that "everything we are trying to do here is being done for America and, perhaps, for the whole world."

Still the 22nd was not in action. Stilwell battled with the railroad whose Indian personnel, afraid of the hostile Burmans, were departing. "Told Martin to hold a gun on the crews and get the trains through. . . . Last train of the 22nd passed Pyawbwe at 7:00. Looks a bit better." Then General Tu had "one of his depressed fits—everything was against attack. *Mei yu pan fa.* [It's impossible.] Christ, he's terrible when he's like that." Now all depended on the arrival of the 22nd. At 3 A.M. two trains were still at Pyinmana; at 9 o'clock all five trains had cleared ("Some bastard stopped the move for three hours. *Who was it?*"). Conflicting reports came in next morning; then suddenly all three regiments were in position, guns and tanks ready for the jumpoff at 4 P.M.

"Later. It *was* too good." Chinese hesitancy and excuses returned. " 'How can we attack? They have 105s and we only have 75s,' " or " 'They have 49 tanks,' " or " 'The 96th can't get here on time' " (having failed to move it by truck) or there would be Burmese sabotage or a break on the railway line; " 'Maybe tomorrow; must think it over.' " At this point word came that the British were withdrawing from Prome, uncovering the Chinese flank. "Well this will raise hell. *What to do?* Tu is too much for me." Stilwell determined on a showdown. He knew Chiang Kai-shek was communicating directly with Tu and Lin Wei, ordering the movements of units down to the regimental level from 2,000 miles away. He returned to Maymyo to catch Lin Wei who had disappeared from Pyawbwe when he felt the attack by the 22nd was going to be forced. At Maymyo he found to his amazement that Chiang Kai-shek now accepted Alexander, who had been up to Chungking to see him in the meantime, as overall commander of the campaign. This remarkable reversal was never explained; however, since it achieved unity of command Stilwell wasted no time worrying about it.

He sought out Lin Wei, kept at him until he agreed to write orders for attack, then hurried back to Pyawbwe to go over plans with Tu. General Liao, commander of the 22nd, "a colorless bird," who talked a lot at high speed without saying anything, wanted to wait for the 96th. "They are dogging it . . . they'll drag it out and do nothing unless I can somehow kick them into it. . . . Okay I'll try to be patient a bit longer. HOT as hell. All of us dried out and exhausted. I am mentally about shot." He had phoned Maymyo to ask for a supporting British attack and received a promise in the affirmative. "Good old Slim. Maybe he's all right after all." But once more Tu found reasons not to move. While he procrastinated, the enemy encircled Toungoo on three sides, coming up between it and Prome, menacing the inner flanks of both Chinese and British. Slim's Armored Brigade, which had actually advanced and gained ground, had to return to save itself from being cut off from behind. The 22nd fired its guns in a gesture of attack but stood still. By 9:30 on the morning of March 30 Stilwell knew there would be no offensive. They "have dogged it again. The pusillanimous bastards."

The 200th, after its stolid twelve-day stand with losses of 1,000 killed, was left to cut its way out and fall back behind the 22nd to the Pyinmana area 60 miles to the north. The Burma Corps was already retreating, supposedly to hold at Allanmyo on a level with Pyinmana, but the men did not stop, nor pause on the way for demolition of bridges to delay the Japanese, until they had gone 80 miles to the Magwe area in front of the oil fields. By this time even British soldiers were deserting, heading for Mandalay with the vague hope of exit through China. Recriminations flared between the Chinese and British, each blaming the other for exposing their respective flanks. The Chinese accused the British of leaving the 200th to starve, to which the British retorted that General Tai had placed his liaison officers so far to the rear that they were cut off by the Japanese encirclement. General Alexander, having achieved command of all the Allied forces, was later in his official report to call the Chinese "parasites" because "they expected me to feed them."

Stilwell had now trapped himself in the position of conducting a fight with troops who refused to obey his orders. "I can't shoot them; I can't relieve them; and just talking to them does no good." He had pushed Chiang Kai-shek into action more or less against his will, although in China's interest; Chiang was now pulling back on the reins. Stilwell considered the choices open to him: to "let it ride and do nothing," to "resign flatly," or to "ooze out and demand our own force." He left for Chungking to have it out with the Generalissimo. Realizing that his mission was on the way to becoming "a messed up affair," he told Dorn to keep a record of everything.

The problem of exacting obedience from unit commanders was not his alone. Retreat without orders and failure to take or hold a given position were habitual and inherent in the traditional Chinese idea of war as a kind of chess game of cunning and maneuver rather than a physical clash. For a commander to lose his life or his army was not gallant but stupid. Disinclination to risk troops in actual battle was so common in China that it led to the formulation in the sixteenth century of *lien tso fa,* a military rule of collective responsibility providing the death penalty for officers all the way through the chain of command when any unit retreated without orders. Chiang Kai-shek applied the rule in the first campaigns of the Whampoa graduates to assure responsibility both vertically within a unit and horizontally between adjoining army groups.

The practice of offering a monetary reward to unit commanders to hold a given position was another substitute for the missing sense of responsibility to the whole. But promise of neither death nor reward could create in military practice what was not developed in the culture, and Chinese officers on the whole did not regard themselves as responsible for the outcome of the battle. Traditionally the military profession was not highly regarded, the Chinese theory being that "good iron is not used to make nails nor good men to make soldiers." Stilwell himself had noted in one of his jottings that the Chinese officer had "no association with a position of trust in the country" nor tradition of duty to the nation. The Chinese commander was not a member of an institutional army like the Western officer. This led to placing loyalty directly in the person of the leader instead of submitting to obedience in a chain of command, with the result that divisional generals and even regimental colonels would frequently take orders only from Chiang Kai-shek himself instead of from their immediate superior. General Hsueh Yueh, the Tiger of Hunan, at one time became so disgusted with the Generalissimo's orders to his sub-ordinates which resulted in the movement or withdrawal of units without his knowledge that he disobeyed orders himself and withdrew in order to "get beyond the reach of those telephone calls."

The atmosphere at Maymyo after the Prome-Toungoo withdrawals be-gan to turn rancid. The Americans of Stilwell's staff, who had not them-selves been in battle and whose country's military performance so far was less than brilliant, felt contempt for both Chinese and British, and as the campaign went on became convinced, according to one of them, that "the situation in Asia was past redemption except by the employment of ex-clusively American troops." Stilwell's "ooze out and demand our own force" already reflected this desire, never to be fulfilled in CBI. The British at Maymyo, in their turn, treated to sarcastic remarks by Americans and Chinese, openly jeered at "Stilwell's great Chinese offensive." With their empire sliding out from under them they were disposed to consider Amer-ican carelessness in losing its Pacific Fleet at Pearl Harbor after repeated warnings as largely to blame. Even India might be lost in consequence.

"Am I the April Fool?" Stilwell asked himself, writing down an ap-praisal of his situation on April 1 in Chungking. Chiang Kai-shek's inter-ference was the basic trouble. If he had not stopped the 22nd Division, it could have cut off the Japanese when they first went around Toungoo, but "he is *hipped* on holding Mandalay and can't see that the way to hold is to lick the Japs at Toungoo." Stilwell learned from Shang Chen that Chiang himself had ordered the retirement to the Pyinmana line.

At his conference with the Generalissimo he "threw the raw meat on the floor. Pulled no punches and said I'd have to be relieved. Proposed an independent army under my command as an alternative. Told him I could not use the 10th Airforce behind such commanders. . . . In plain words the army and divisional commanders failed to obey and I had insufficient authority to force them to obey."

This was in fact pulling a punch because, as Stilwell acknowledged in his diary, "I have to tell CKS with a straight face that his subordinates are not carrying out his orders, when in all probability they are doing just what he tells them. In justice to all of them, however, it is expecting a great deal to have them turn over a couple of armies to a goddam foreigner that they don't know and in whom they can't have much confidence." Unlike many Americans, he appreciated the deep-rooted antiforeign feeling of the Chinese.

Chiang and Madame appeared worried and anxious to rectify the situa-tion and over the next few days promised to do everything to make Stil-well's authority definitive. At Madame's suggestion Chiang agreed to go in person to Lashio "to make it very plain to the boys that I am the boss."

He seemed sincere and convincing and appointed a new executive officer, Lo Cho-ying, who could more effectively handle General Tu than could Lin Wei. Lo was a forceful energetic Cantonese who had achieved his rise in the Bandit Suppression campaigns against the Communists in the 1930s, had fought at Shanghai and Changsha and impressed Stilwell as a "tough bird" who meant business. In addition, Madame understood the Western viewpoint and the mental reactions of a foreigner to indirect Chinese methods, and "promises to help in any way she can which is a whole lot." Stilwell believed he had gained a major victory. "When you consider their history and experiences with foreigners, this is really a handsome gesture that Chiang Kai-shek is making."

Pursued by journalists in Chungking, he noted that already in the press "a flood of crap is released to justify which I would have to be in Rangoon within a week. What a sucker I'll look like if the Japs run me out of Burma." The American public at this time was reading such headlines as "CHINESE CAVALRY ROUTS JAP PANZERS IN BURMA!" The *Fort Ord Panorama,* founded by Stilwell, blazoned the announcement of his mission under the proud boast, "LOOK OUT HIROHITO!"

He returned to Burma on April 5 in company with the Generalissimo and Madame in whose honor the British, with exemplary protocol, broke out the Burma Rifles with bagpipes. Chiang assured Alexander at Maymyo that "General Stilwell has full powers to handle the Chinese troops" and on the following day assembled the Chinese commanders and told them in Stilwell's presence that they must take his orders without question and that "I had full power to promote, relieve and punish any officer in the Chinese Expeditionary Force. (Jesus.) This is a new note in Chinese history." Smiling pictures for the press were taken arm-in-arm with the Generalissimo and Madame, and confirmation of his authority was promised in the form of the *kuan fang* or seal showing the possessor's official title in a large monogram of archaic characters. Its stamp in red ink was required to make a document effective; without it Stilwell's orders were merely advices. When it arrived a week later the *kuan fang* proved to be significantly modified from what had been promised. The inscription read *Tsung ts'an mou chang* of the *T'ung meng chun* (Chief of Staff of the Allied Armies) instead of *Tsung ssu-ling* of the *Yuan mien chun* (Commander-in-Chief of the Burma Expeditionary Force) and it was not accompanied by a letter of authority to reward and punish. Officers of the 38th Division stated after the war that regardless of the Generalissimo's words at Maymyo, the *ts'an mou* of the seal indicated that Stilwell was "adviser" not commanding officer, and they so regarded him.

Yet, to Stilwell it seemed that Chiang had come around to the view that in order to hold it was necessary to attack and that Lo Cho-ying and

37

38

Stilwell's Western-style house in Chungking (137)
had been built by T. V. Soong. It had one story at
street level and three stories overlooking the Chialing
River. Stilwell's staff in Burma included long-time
aide Colonel Frank Dorn (second from left) and
Major General Thomas G. Hearn (far right), seen
here with General Shang Chen, an old friend of
Stilwell's, who, as director of the Foreign Affairs
Bureau of the General Staff, was now in charge of
military liaison with China's allies (138). Dr. Gordon
Seagrave (139), an American Baptist missionary surgeon of long experience in Burma, offered his services to Stilwell. As the pace of war quickened, "he
and Stilwell reached mutual understanding and respect with few words exchanged."

139

140

141

143

142

Tu Li-ming too were "all for it." He felt encouraged, not without help from Madame who, on departing, left him a jar of marmalade and a letter rippling with charm-talk about the jar's contents representing the bitter and the sweet of life and assuring him that "We are back of you. . . . I am at the other end of the line. . . . You have a man's job ahead of you but you are a man—and shall I add—what a man!" Madame did not think it necessary to be subtle with Westerners.

Mrs. Luce too was at Maymyo and interviewed Stilwell for an article that appeared in *Life* with his picture on the cover two months later. She asked if the talks had been a success. "Yep," he said, according to her version, "Yep, yep, yep. The Gissimo handed it to everybody including his own generals straight. So did Alexander. So did I. And Madame translated it all straight too. Without pulling a punch. Yep. Everybody took it right out of the spoon." He said the correspondent could report home that the situation was well in hand. When asked, "But will it last?" he replied, "Nope. It won't last long. It can't last long." But it bought time and "time, time, time"—that was what he was fighting for. "Every hour that Burma holds saves America an hour in Australia and the Philippines."

Vinegar Joe was becoming a public personality. He made good copy, and the press made the most of it, developing a picturesque stereotype, the crusty cracker-barrel soldiers' soldier, tough, leathery, wiry, down-to-earth, wise-cracking, Chinese-speaking, a disciplinarian loved by the troops, with lack of swank and a warm smile, an American "Chinese Gordon," an "Uncle Joe."

Although the Japanese were methodically bombing every town and village ahead of their advance up the Irrawaddy toward Mandalay, the military situation on the ground had not changed visibly during Stilwell's absence in Chungking. "We *still* have a chance." Actually during this period the Japanese were bringing in two more divisions and two tank regiments of which the Allies, owing to poor reconnaissance, were unaware. The Japanese plan was a three-column drive up the three valleys to envelop and destroy the Allies between Lashio and the Chindwin before the monsoon came in mid-May. In conformity with his theory of attack in order to hold, Stilwell believed a counteroffensive could still be launched from the Pyinmana line sufficient to set the enemy back and permit the Allies to consolidate a position in central Burma. In order to hold Mandalay Chiang Kai-shek had sent in a new division, the 38th, commanded by the alert and vigorous General Sun Li-jen, a graduate like George Marshall of VMI, who was to prove himself an able tactician, cool and aggressive in battle, and to become the outstanding Chinese commander in the Burma campaign. Fluency in English assisted both his operations and his reputa-

Generalissimo and Mme. Chiang pose with Stilwell at Maymyo, April 1942 (140). In the Northern Burma jungle Stilwell confers with Chinese officers in his command (141) and with General Sun Li-jen (143). Japanese soldiers support a bridge to assist their troops' advance (142).

tion. A major source of trouble with the other divisions was lack of enough able interpreters.

On April 3 the track of the bombing that left thatch and bamboo villages flaming in the hot midday wind reached Mandalay. Four hundred were killed, the railroad station and hospital destroyed, acres of streets burned out, telephone wires dragging in the ashes, debris and corpses of men and animals lying about, many of them blown into the moat under the huge stone walls of the eighteenth-century palace. The many-towered city was still burning when Stilwell came there on April 8 to confer with Sun Li-jen. With police and civil servants and most of the population having fled, the British authorities had difficulty restoring services and collecting the dead. The stench was appalling. Bloated bodies floated in pink water amid stagnant green scum. Dogs and pigs rooted among decaying corpses in the streets and crows pecked out dead eyes. Replete on the necrophilic diet the birds staggered like drunkards from body to body. Chiang Kai-shek and Madame who came to Mandalay on the same day as Stilwell seized on the horrors to scold the British and vent the angry disillusion in the West which had been mounting among the Chinese since Pearl Harbor. "In all my life of long military experience," Chiang wrote to Churchill, "I have seen nothing to compare with the deplorable unprepared state, confusion and degradation of the war area in Burma."

Armed, as he thought, with new authority, Stilwell hastened once more on the rounds of divisional headquarters in the effort to concentrate the Fifth Army for a fight in the Pyinmana area and the Sixth Army on the Chinese left to guard approaches in the Loikaw area on the Salween front. Nothing went right. The Japanese kept advancing and cutting off Allied positions in short quick hooks that seemed to come out of nowhere. Air raids persisted, disintegration of order and services accelerated, and the flow of the Generalissimo's letters continued. He reversed himself three times on whether, where, when and which Chinese units could be used to reinforce the British sector, causing redeployment on the inadequate transportation system. One letter ordered the bodies of all Chinese dead to be shipped back home in pine coffins so that they could be buried with their ancestors.

At Pyinmana where Stilwell went to show himself to the troops of the 200th, "a fine looking lot of soldiers," the earth rocked under the concussion of Japanese bombs, while over the crackle of burning houses, smoke and flames rolled skyward, spreading in a vast dark umbrella as if to emphasize the darkness in which he fought. Without aerial reconnaissance it was impossible to learn the enemy's lines of approach. "God, I feel like a blind man," he told Dorn. The AVG pilots were refusing to fly at low levels they considered death traps, and an urgent request to the RAF for two reconnaissance planes produced no response. The American Tenth Air Force in India, which had eight bombers at the time with 17 more on the way, sent no support despite Stilwell's demand, because according to Brereton who came to see Stilwell on March 24, his gunners had no gunnery training and the force would not be ready to go into action until May 1. Although he was officially under Stilwell's command, Brereton preferred to consider himself under Wavell and had imbibed in Delhi the spirit that accounted Burma a lost cause.

Stilwell prayed for the monsoon, hoping to be able to hold until the rains came and bogged down the Japanese. On his rounds he would stop to visit Seagrave and his nurses working tirelessly in sweat and blood over the wounded. Looking up, the doctor would find Stilwell watching silently and they would smile grimly at one another. "He always had time," Seagrave wrote, "for someone who was trying to do a good job." Some among the American staff were no longer trying but turning sour, becoming jittery and criticizing the General for stubborn persistence in a campaign in which neither British nor Chinese had any faith, as they had none in themselves or in each other.

Suddenly, like secret ink becoming visible, the easternmost prong of the three Japanese drives came into view. Piecing together scattered reports from the Sixth Army of contacts with enemy detachments, Colonel Roberts at G-2 realized that these represented the probing spearhead of a drive on Lashio where the road to China could be cut. He reported urgently to Stilwell who went off to inspect the disposition of the Sixth Army front and found this discouraging in the extreme. Units had been moved without orders to defensive positions, command posts were lax, General Kan Li-chu, the Army commander, was careless, uninformed and unable to control his divisional generals of whom one, General Chen Li-wu, commander of the 55th Division, had given up vital ground by a needless withdrawal before an inferior Japanese force. He had also failed to carry out strict orders to retake a given position. Villages here were still peaceful in beautiful highland country rich in pine and cedar trees. "Well, whaddya know," Stilwell remarked to Dorn, "pine for the Peanut's coffins." Starting as a code name, Peanut was coming into regular use as his name for the Generalissimo.* On his return to Headquarters he could leave orders with Lo for General Kan to be reprimanded, and General Chen to be relieved of

---

*The military habit of giving code names to people and projects partly accounts for the prevalence if not the nature of the nicknames Stilwell used.

his command and for the lost positions to be regained, but he could not ensure the orders being carried out. Except for the first, none was.

On the Irrawaddy front three days later the Japanese broke through, bypassing the 1st Burma Division and heading for the oil fields at Yenang-yaung. General Slim could get no effective action out of demoralized troops and gave the order to destroy the oil fields on April 15. Stilwell, hastily summoned by Alexander to Maymyo, found "disaster and gloom." Alexander confessed to him that his men were "simply afraid of the Japs," and in his anxiety "calls me Joe now."

In this hour he found too a letter from Chiang Kai-shek ordering the issue of a watermelon to every four men. Nothing in the course of Stilwell's theater command was to have a more baleful effect. Coming at the darkest time in Allied fortunes, when Burma was crashing about his ears—due in large part, as he believed, to the G–mo's other interferences—the watermelon order clinched his contempt for Chiang Kai-shek, and since this ultimately became known, it in turn angered the Generalissimo. The mutual effect was far-reaching.

By previous arrangement with the Generalissimo, Sun Li-jen's 38th Division had been moved down to the Irrawaddy front to strengthen the link with the British and was now thrown in to stem the Japanese for long enough to save the 1st Burma Division. Through three days of desperate battle at Yenangyaung the Chinese of the 38th Division held ground and counterattacked along with the British Armored Brigade in the strongest fighting of the campaign, exhibiting the qualities Stilwell always said they would under determined leadership. The Chinese action permitted the escape of the 1st Burma Division—although with loss of most of its motor transport, mortars, field and antiaircraft guns, and 20 percent casualties—and incidentally saved the 17th Indian Division further to the east, which could have been overrun if the Japanese had destroyed its companion.

Fear spread after the battle, fanned by the same savagery the enemy had practiced in China. Indian prisoners were tied by the Japanese in bamboo houses and set afire or soaked in gasoline and burned alive. More shocking and frightening to Westerners in Burma was the fact that captured British officers were used no better; in some cases they were stripped and tied to trees for bayonet practice. Until now every Westerner who ever entered Asia had taken it for granted that he would receive different treatment than a native.

Before the battle was joined, on April 15, Stilwell radioed a pessimistic summary of the situation to Marshall. He expressed his belief that the British had written off Burma for some time. He was convinced there were enough troops in India to have saved Burma and they "could have been marched in long ago had they meant business." In his own mind he concluded from what he considered Alexander's unwillingness to commit his forces that he was under orders from London to make a token resistance and withdraw from Burma. This was a view gaining wide credibility among Americans, not only on Stilwell's staff. "Sir Childe Harold Alexander has small intention of holding the Dark Tower he has come to, if it proves too painful," wrote Mrs. Luce privately to Stilwell on April 10 after a conversation with Alexander. (He had added a "priceless" remark: "I do hope Joe doesn't leave. I would find it very difficult to command the Chinese without him.") Colonel Louis Johnson, the rather bellicose former Assistant Secretary of War whom Roosevelt had despatched as his special envoy to India, gained the same impression. The British preferred to give up Burma, he reported, rather than be indebted to the Chinese or make concessions to Burmese nationalists in order to retain it. They intended to regain it at the peace table in any event and wanted it free of any commitments as to future form of government.

Burma was last on everybody's priority list. When a Japanese fleet of six carriers entered the Bay of Bengal in the first week of April, Wavell's alarm for Calcutta was so great that it inspired Brereton to send his eight bombers on a not too effective raid of Rangoon and the Andaman Islands where the Japanese were accumulating shipping. Occurring within a week of the time he had denied support for Burma, the action infuriated Stilwell and even more Chiang Kai-shek who had been assured that the Tenth Air Force was under Stilwell's command and took Brereton's raid as proof that the United States would sacrifice China's interest to Britain's whenever necessary. Chiang's experience of allies was intensifying his anti-Western sentiments rather than the contrary. He let it be known that such diversions from the China theater coupled with further Allied war reverses could make China go "completely antiforeign overnight"* and quit the war.

Nevertheless, when it came to a choice between West and East, Marshall did not waver. When planes from the Japanese carriers attacked Ceylon on April 9, justifying Wavell's alarm, he agreed to assign the Tenth Air Force to the defense of India. This was the price of Britain's agreement to begin the buildup of forces in the British Isles for the cross-Channel invasion of Europe. The Americans led by Marshall were bent on the invasion; the British were reluctant and made their agreement conditional on defense of the Middle East and India. Marshall was reminded by his staff that

---

*The wording was that of the American Naval Attaché, Colonel James McHugh, who was on close personal terms with Chiang and Madame and often served as mouthpiece for their views.

his decision would "adversely affect the Chinese situation and Stilwell's operations," but China's interests were in fact secondary. In extenuation he informed the Generalissimo and Stilwell that the threat to Calcutta and the east coast of India was "critical not only to India itself but to our future ability to assist China."

Stilwell had to make do with moral, in place of air, support. "I assure you that in the world wide picture your efforts assume a clear cut and definite importance," Marshall told him, which did not help to stop the Japanese. With not enough planes to go around it was all Marshall could offer.

"We are about to take a beating, I think," Stilwell wrote to his wife on April 16. To be defeated in his first active command was a bitter prospect that filled him with rage for revenge and vindication. He was already planning a campaign to recapture Burma. Whatever it was to the English, Burma in his mind was still the essential corridor to China where he believed the eventual campaign against Japan would be fought, with American troops, as he hoped, joining Chinese under his command.

In the midst of catastrophe he drew up the plan that was to be his vehicle of return. It called for the transfer of Chinese troops to India where they could be trained and equipped under American direction as the task force for reconquest. He never proclaimed to the public, "I shall return," but this became a determination fixed in iron. He intended to beat the enemy who was now beating him and prove that the Chinese, properly led, could do it and become their own saviors. On April 16 he sent the plan by one of his staff to Chungking for the Generalissimo's approval.

As Chiang's Chief of Staff he advised that the supply route to China by road and air across north Burma would probably become interrupted by Japanese air power. Therefore the Chinese forces must go to the weapons if the weapons could not come to them. He proposed a force to be organized and trained in India of two corps, each of three divisions with Chinese officers up to the grade of regimental commander. Higher commanders and principal staff officers were initially to be American until Chinese could be substituted. He took the crucial question—how were the troops to reach India?—in a wild leap, proposing that they should march across north Burma from Myitkyina via Mogaung and Shingbwiyang (names that were to acquire a terrible familiarity) over the trace of the Ledo Road to the railhead in Assam "with such assistance from the U.S. Air Freight Line as may be practicable." He had been notified that 25 transport planes had been assembled or were on their way to Assam and ready to begin operations. He wanted the movement of Chinese troops to begin May 15, which meant during the monsoon. Since he knew this was the worst time, it can only be supposed that he named a date as early as possible on the assumption that Chiang would not meet it anyway.

Stilwell specified "Recapture Burma" as the plan's objective with the decisive effort to be made from India and a supplementary effort by other Chinese divisions from Yunnan. From this plan he never varied. Chiang Kai-shek gave his approval "in general" two weeks later on condition that the Chinese should not be used in support of the British against the Indians in case of an uprising. The War Department also gave its approval since the plan fitted the American concept of fighting the war on the mainland of Asia with local troops.

In the faint hope that Burma's northern tier might still be held, Stilwell was trying, futilely as it proved, to move the 200th Division by truck and train to fill a gap that had opened between the Chinese and British. At this moment news reached Headquarters of the Doolittle raid on Tokyo, the wildly adventurous mission that was to have brought 16 B-25s to join Chennault's air force. Every one of the 16 was lost. Owing to enforced takeoff from the aircraft carriers at a greater distance than planned, the planes ran out of fuel and crashed in China in or near the occupied zone. The Japanese swept over the districts where Chinese had succored American crews in a brutal punitive campaign and sent a force of 53 battalions to destroy the airfields from which bombers might again strike at Japan. Although it caused some diversion of forces by the enemy, the brave Doolittle blow was designed primarily to pierce the discouragement and sluggish production of the American people, and carry promise of ultimate victory amid the general Allied gloom. It achieved its result at the cost of death and ruin to many Chinese and the increased resentment of Chiang Kai-shek. Because of the security problem Chiang was not informed of the operation to be carried out on his territory until about a week before the date. He objected strenuously, fearing loss of certain airfields in Chekiang through enemy action. He was informed, however, that the mission was too far advanced for cancellation. The episode did not help to persuade him that China was being treated as an equal much less a great power. In Burma it enhanced the isolation of men and officers who already had ceased to look skyward to identify a plane because it was certain to be Japanese.

On April 20 came the decisive stroke: the Japanese end run for Lashio broke through on the eastern flank, scattering the 55th Division. "Disaster at Loikaw. 55th completely smashed . . . Kan terrified . . . Jesus. This may screw us completely." In the gap on the central front the enemy outflanked the 96th Division. "Looks like a collapse here too. Jesus again. Sent Sibert to find out. . . . Phone wires all cut. Are the British going to run out on us? *Yes*. The outcome is becoming apparent."

Days followed of frantic effort to plug holes, to regroup, to agree on plans and try to deploy tangled divisions to conform to them, but the crumbling could not be arrested. Few of the Chinese units were where they were supposed to be and could not be moved into position because trucks could not be obtained; "65,000 gallons of gas and 850 trucks at Lashio about April 18," Stilwell noted in passing, but they were too busy hauling goods to China to haul soldiers. Trains were blocked or stalled, commanders were out of touch, military discipline was dissolving. Liaison officers brought "tales of disobedience and absence." (In an aside Stilwell noted "the way the boys look at me in the jams, dead-pan, to see how I take it: 'Will it break you down I wonder?' ")

Generals Tu and Kan, gripped by fear of losing their armies, kept units from advancing or ordered withdrawals, on one occasion against the wish of a divisional commander who wanted to fight. To recapture Taunggyi, a key point reached by an advance column of Japanese, Stilwell personally took command of a Chinese company under intense fire and ordered it to stand fast until reinforcements arrived. Then, at Lo's suggestion, he offered a reward of 50,000 rupees if Taunggyi were taken by 5 o'clock. The goal was promptly accomplished with an hour to spare but the reverse method—a demand for the execution or court-martial of General Chen of the 55th whose division simply vanished into the hills—failed. Stilwell's demand for punishment was ignored. As for the 55th, he said in awe to Belden, "There's not a trace of it. It's the god-damnedest thing I ever saw. Last night I had a division, and today there isn't any."

"It is an impossible situation," he concluded in one of his periodic summaries, "which I will have to see through as best I may. CKS has made it impossible for me to do anything, and I might as well acknowledge it now." The Generalissimo's trip to Lashio had been a farce; "it fooled me completely, sap that I was. . . . But I thought he was being sincere. . . ." The higher commanders were impossible to control and, with exceptions like Sun Li-jen and some others, were "saturated" with the Generalissimo's doctrine that it took three to one for defense and five to one for attack. Stilwell thought with envy of the 8th Route Army and wished, as he often told his staff, that he could "get those Communists down here to fight."

Chinese hoarding of resources for some yet greater emergency was another hindrance to fighting. To the Chinese, chronically short as they were of everything, it was a cultural imperative. From Chungking the Generalissimo personally doled out the movement of the Fifth Army's nine tanks one by one so that what usefulness they might have had as a group was destroyed. At Toungoo Alexander asked General Tu what had happened to his field guns which he had seen the day before, expertly dug in, well-sited and carefully camouflaged. Tu said he had withdrawn them to safety.

"Then you mean that they will take no part in the battle?"

"Exactly."

"But then what use are they?"

"General, the Fifth Army is our best army because it is the only one which has any field guns, and I cannot afford to risk those guns. If I lose them the Fifth Army will no longer be our best."

The turning of the Allied east flank by the Japanese drive on Lashio ended any hope of prolonging the campaign. With unbelievable speed the Japanese, using motorized transport, had already bypassed Taunggyi and were well north of it on the road to Lashio. Every effort to concentrate the Sixth Army failed. Summoned to send 150 trucks, the Chinese Service of Supply at Lashio delivered 22. On the central front the Fifth Army was being heavily attacked, and further west the Japanese were advancing toward the Chindwin in a drive to come up between the Allies and India. Envelopment threatened on both sides.

Stilwell and Alexander held a conference with Lo and Tu at Kyaukse, 25 miles south of Mandalay, on the night of April 25. Stilwell in his World War I campaign hat and government-issue khakis which, in a kind of inverse snobbery he wore without insignia or decorations, looked "terribly tired" to Seagrave who caught a glimpse of him. Lo looked "plump and unhappy" and Tu "uncertain and sulky." It was agreed that a general retreat was the only course, and once this had been acknowledged the campaign now became a race to withdraw before being trapped. In the east the fragmented Sixth Army plus the 200th Division at Taunggyi and two new Chinese divisions, which were just then entering via the Burma Road, could retreat toward the Chinese border. The main problem for Alexander and Stilwell was to get the Burma Corps and the 38th, 22nd and 96th Chinese Divisions out through Mandalay and over to the west bank of the Irrawaddy from where the British could retreat to India and the Chinese northward via Myitkyina. The only place where tanks and large numbers of troops could cross the river was the Ava rail and highway bridge at Mandalay. When all were across, the bridge was to be destroyed. The British had prepared it for demolition as long ago as February.

As he watched Alexander dictate the general order for retreat, Stilwell recalled a Chinese saying about "eating bitterness." The only shred of consolation was that the orders did not call for surrender, as at Singapore and Java. Underlining defeat, six enemy bombers roared over the site of the conference. While officers scrambled for cover, a 500-pounder hit with a deafening blast within 100 yards. Through the raid Alexander, performing the commander's role, stood stiff and defiant in the garden and Stilwell, not to be outdone, leaned against the porch railing with his amber cigaret holder cocked at its Rooseveltian angle.

Headquarters was moved 50 miles north of Mandalay to Shwebo, where the Japanese planes pursued. Among the staffs a sense was rising not only of military disaster but of personal danger. Some self-reportedly were in "a state of funk," others relapsed into passivity, not knowing what to do. The railroad was the worst problem. Stilwell was determined to get troop trains down to bring out the 22nd Division but Chinese organization was lax or nonfunctioning. Because none of his staff was technically authorized to issue orders to the Chinese he went back to Mandalay himself to try to stir up action. He returned over the bridge among the stream of retiring troops while below in the river others were crossing in ferry boats. On the road to Shwebo, clogged with trucks and caissons and the piled carts of refugees, the mass of retreat moved in dust and heat and the sour smell of fear. Once-proud Sikhs were dirty and disheveled in ragged turbans. Chinese soldiers marched with frightened eyes in a strange land where they could not shed uniforms and slip away into the countryside. Yellow-robed bodies of Buddhist monks lay on the ground, shot by the Chinese who believed them to be spies in disguise. Japanese Zeros flew over, strafing the road with machine-gun fire. Chinese generals in their cars, and British officers conscious of the "natives," were concerned not to lose face, but everyone was conscious that all had lost face, in the eyes of Asia, the world, and "worst of all" as Dorn wrote, "in our own."

On April 29 the trap narrowed: on the east the Japanese took Lashio, cutting the Burma Road, and on the west they took Monywa on the Chindwin, only 60 miles below Shwebo, endangering the path of the British retreat to India. It was now urgent for the British to reach the crossing of the Chindwin at Kalewa before the Japanese. Last-minute efforts to stock the lines of retreat with food and water had to be cut short. The blowing up of the Ava bridge was set for midnight on April 30. Stilwell had intended to move his headquarters to Myitkyina in order to stay in contact with the Chinese as long as possible, but the fall of Lashio, opening the Japanese way to Myitkyina over the hills, made this impossible. He decided to send the bulk of his staff out to India by plane while he would go to Loiwing on the Lashio front taking General Lo with him. He radioed for a plane to take him out on May 1. His staff, sweltering in the heat and eating boiled rice because canned goods were being saved for an unpredictable future, were growling restlessly. Angry at the repeated Chinese failure to fulfill agreements and carry out orders, they agreed that "The Boss should tell the Chinese to go to hell and get out while the getting was good."

Heat, defeat and fear, disgust with allies and a general sense of desertion were not bringing out the best in them.

A message came through on April 29 reporting Chiang Kai-shek's approval in principle of the training program in India. Stilwell's mind was now fixed on this like a mariner's on the North Star. "God, if we can only get those 100,000 Chinese to India, *we'll have something.*" He at once wired Marshall for assurance of support and matériel, otherwise the plan would have to depend on British support "which would be fatal." While everyone around him wanted only to see the last of Burma, he sat under a tattered punkah telling Darrell Berrigan of the United Press about his strategy for return and for reopening the door to China—the springboard, he said, from which the Allies could strike Japan. Marshall passed his telegram on to the President who, now that the loss of Burma loomed, was once again afflicted by fear that China would withdraw from the war. "Ways will be found," Roosevelt announced on April 28, "to deliver airplanes and munitions of war to the armies of Generalissimo Chiang Kai-shek." As if to reassure himself as much as Chiang, Roosevelt repeated his theme that in the future "an unconquerable China will play its proper role in maintaining peace and prosperity not only in Eastern Asia but in the whole world."

On May 1 Stilwell woke to discover that General Lo Cho-ying, the chief executive officer, had decamped for Myitkyina and its airfield. He had commandeered a locomotive with 17 cars at gunpoint and after proceeding 25 miles had run his unscheduled train into collision with another, blocking the railroad for two days. "Unfortunately he was not killed." His defection soured even Sibert, hitherto a holdout among the disaffected. "Christ, Joe, let's go home," he pleaded. Loiwing was closed down, but Stilwell still felt obliged to do what he could to ensure that the Chinese escape routes were stocked with rice. The staff argued that his place was at Headquarters in Delhi. "No," he said, "and I will tell you why." With one defeat after another, including American defeat in the Philippines, Western prestige had never been so low. It was his job to take care of the Chinese whom he commanded, at least on paper. "If I run out now that will be one more defeat, one more surrender. I could not command the Chinese again."

He sat down to draw up his list of who among the staff was to go to Delhi and who to stay with him. Alexander came in "very worried." It was their last meeting in Burma. The final order for the British retreat was issued the following day and Alexander departed by car on the 107-mile trek to the Chindwin, a six days' march for those on foot. They crossed the Chindwin ahead of the Japanese but with forced abandonment of tanks, guns and many vehicles. Arrangements for transport and food had been made on the other side. Twelve thousand of the Burma Corps straggled into India between May 12 and 20, leaving behind 13,500 casualties in killed, wounded and missing during their four months' campaign. "Of course we shall take Burma back; it's part of the British Empire," Alexander said in farewell on terminating his command on May 20. Shortly afterwards he returned to London and went on to command GYMNAST and win renown in Tunisia. He did not return to Burma.

Alexander and Lo were gone; Stilwell was left. Companions in a gin-rummy game, scattering during an air raid, returned to find him still at the table "resignedly playing solitaire." By now the Japanese had taken and passed beyond Mandalay and the sound of their artillery could be heard. "It's a great May Day," Stilwell said to Belden. "Down with everything. Down with everybody."

Before the day was over, an American transport plane came in, flown by Colonels Caleb Haynes and Robert Scott, Commander and Executive Officer of the new Assam-Burma-China Ferry Command, which had begun operations ten days previously. The transports were unarmed Douglas C-47s (DC-3s) which the pilots, who hated the job and the route, called "gooney birds" for a species said to fly backward to see where they came from. Haynes and Scott had received a message from General Hap Arnold instructing them to "proceed immediately vicinity Shwebo effect evacuation Stilwell and staff most urgent."

Ushered into the tea planter's house where Stilwell had his headquarters, they found the General in his ancient hat, writing at a desk. Scott, a heroic type who was later to join Chennault's pursuit group and claim a notable score of Japanese kills, announced with fitting drama if not tact, "General Arnold sent us to rescue you, Sir." Gaunt and haggard from the strain of the last days, Stilwell looked through his rimless glasses at the "fly boys" and declined the privilege. The aviators gaped. They told him they had sighted enemy units within 20 miles of Shwebo on the way in. Stilwell was not to be shaken. From the beginning of the collapse his sole idea was to go out with the Chinese troops. This was his duty as commander which, for him, allowed no deviation. He welcomed the plane to take out the staff but he himself intended to reach Myitkyina, by train or truck or jeep or whatever means possible, where he expected to make contact with the Chinese.

He offered no reasons for his decision, a kind of negation that was part of his temperament, like not wearing insignia. As a three-star general he felt no obligation to explain himself to a couple of Air Force colonels, but more than that, he had no wish to talk of what he felt deeply to brash and uncomprehending strangers. To the aviators this refusal to be rescued by the air arm, this absurd preference for the ground, expressed by an old man in a battered World War I hat sitting behind a desk within 20 miles of the enemy, was virtually an insult. Richly elaborated by Scott, it was to become evidence for the future contention of the Chennault cult that "Walking Joe" did not understand air power.

Stilwell sent out his headquarters group on the plane with orders to Roberts "to find me a place to train the Chinese. You know what I want." With the remainder of his staff he moved 60 miles north to Wuntho, hoping to get past the block on the railroad. Every American was now thinking of his own chances of escape and survival. Their vehicles, overheating and breaking down, struggled over the rutted cart track through dry, desolate, burning hot country, past overloaded Chinese Army trucks with men clinging to them like swarmed bees. At Wuntho Paul Jones, the transportation officer, who had been devoted to Stilwell ever since training under him with the Reserves at San Diego in 1934, went out on the tracks to try personally with a crowbar to move stalled cars. Stilwell went to "talk supply" to a Fifth Army commander who had no plan and was not interested. Three garbled radio messages from Chiang Kai-shek were no help. Lo was found but he asked if Stilwell would return to see him at 8 P.M. At the appointed time Stilwell found the house dark and everybody gone. He realized he could keep trying too long. "It is now apparent that we can no longer be of much use." He decided the time had come to go—by train to Myitkyina, if possible; if not, west across country to India. "Chinese control very weak. Believe collapse near," he radioed Marshall and gave his plans.

He had with him now a collection of tatterdemalion vehicles and a party of about 100 consisting of 18 American officers and six enlisted men, Seagrave's unit of two doctors and 19 Burmese nurses, an escort of 16 Chinese guards, a British Quaker ambulance unit of seven members, nine Indian, Malayan and Burmese cooks and porters, several stray British officers and civilian refugees, an American missionary, Mr. Case, president of the Agricultural College at Pyinmana who spoke the dialects of the hill tribes, Jack Belden, who had refused to leave when all other correspondents were ordered out by the British, and assorted stragglers. Among the American officers were Merrill, Sibert, Sliney, McCabe, Wyman, Ferris, Williams the medical officer, Dorn and Young the two aides, Paul Jones and another reserve officer, Fred Eldridge, formerly a police reporter who had served as public relations officer at Fort Ord and accompanied the unit in the same capacity.

Sent ahead to reconnoiter, Jones reported the railroad hopelessly jammed. Stilwell determined to continue north, parallel to the railway, for one more day, then turn west and head overland, not toward the Tamu Pass but by a more northerly route in order to cross the Chindwin as far ahead of the Japanese as possible. The party would go by road as far as it lasted, then by trail to the Uyu, a tributary of the Chindwin, then by raft downstream to the confluence.* After crossing the Chindwin at Homalin they would continue over the mountains to Imphal in India. Stilwell had been warned that this route was little used and difficult and he chose it for that reason— to avoid the stream of refugees and the escaping Chinese. Shortage of food was the overriding fear which made fellow refugees as great a danger as the enemy. Three divisions of Chinese would be making for the escape routes west of the Irrawaddy in addition to the fleeing population. A million Indians had left or were trying to leave Burma, many of them already out or dead of privation along the way. Thousands were still pushing toward the mountains and the whitened bones of those who failed were to be found beside the trails at the time of the return. Two British brigadiers leading a party of twelve tried strenuously to persuade Stilwell to join them on the more direct route but he refused and was to learn weeks later that their party had been ambushed by Japanese and several of them killed.

Burned-out motors, flat tires and reports of the enemy in the vicinity harassed progress on May 4-5. Stilwell agonized at every delay. The coming monsoon—once prayed for, now a menace—added to the need for haste. The mood of the group was growing mean. Seagrave overheard talk of "paying the nurses off and leaving them so they wouldn't be a drag on the party." On being informed, Stilwell "squelched it at once." "Everyone is losing faith in himself," Belden recorded. "The defeat is producing an enormous impression." General Lo reappeared, having failed to make it to Myitkyina, and dejectedly joined a Chinese party of refugees. At Indaw a last grasp for a train proved futile. In the town all vestige of order was gone, soldiers were looting, civilians dying; a few dazed British officials helplessly witnessed the end of empire. Chinese soldiers in trucks beat off the clutching hands of their fellows with rifle butts. Stilwell said afterwards the chaos in Indaw was the worst sight he had ever seen in the Far East. He warned his group they might have to fight for it. "Keep moving. Don't stop for anything."

At this point the turn away from the railway line into the unknown forest was made. Except for one radio sending-set, communications with the outside world were severed; isolation was closing in. Stilwell did not know where the enemy was and for one dreadful moment thought a column of soldiers coming down the road was Japanese. "God, I was never so scared in my life." After continuing delays ("Christ, if I can only get them *around the corner*") the party was assembled by evening. Seagrave led the nurses in singing "Onward Christian Soldiers." At the sound of their pure, thin voices everyone fell still; cursing and griping stopped. Stilwell, about to climb into a jeep, stood motionless. After a silence the convoy

* For route of the walkout, see map on page 417.

headed west in the darkness under huge trees. Elephants trumpeted in the woods. At a ford when trucks stuck in the mud a group of Chinese "went right through us like Red Grange." Desperate to keep going, Stilwell ordered the stalled trucks abandoned. He made camp at 11 P.M., "I think still ahead of the deluge."

Assembling the group on the morning of May 6 he discovered a party of 15 newcomers, British commandos, unshaven, dirty, half-starved, led by an officer, Colonel Davidson-Houston. "Where'd you come from?" he snarled. "Got any rations?" They shook their heads. He glared, and agreed to let them stay. They included a useful addition, Major Barton, who had lived most of his life in the jungle areas and many years in Burma. The party now numbered 114. At the end of that day's trek the road gave out and all vehicles, except jeeps for carrying supplies, had to be abandoned, including the radio truck and the radio set itself which weighed 200 pounds. Last messages were sent. The sergeant bent to his work, tapping, listening anxiously and tapping again. The message to Brereton in India advised him of the route and stated "we are running low on food with none in sight." He was asked to send food and bearers and medicines to meet the party at Homalin and to alert the Indian Government that tens of thousands of refugees and Chinese troops were heading for India along the various trails as far north as the Hukawng valley and that it was urgent to stock the trails with rice and to send police and doctors "or thousands will die. . . . Large numbers on way. All control gone. Catastrophe possible." The Stilwell party should reach the Uyu in three days. "This is our last message." To the War Department via Chungking Stilwell did not admit the worst since they could not help anyway. "We are armed have food and map and are now on foot 50 miles west of Indaw. No occasion for worry. Chinese troops coming to India this general route. . . . Believe this is probably our last message for a while. Cheerio. Stilwell." The radio was then smashed with an axe and codes and file copies burned.

That evening the first piece of good luck appeared in the shape of a Chinese pack train of 20 tiny mules and two raffish and ruffianly drivers who were on their way unloaded from the "northern mountains" to India, probably, Stilwell suspected, to smuggle opium back into China. They were hired and arrangements were also made with the local head man at a nearby village for 60 carriers (the local people were "good eggs").

Standing on a truck at daylight to address the company, Stilwell explained the plan of march and laid down his rules. All food was to be pooled and all personal belongings discarded except for what each person could carry in addition to weapon and ammunition. A journey of some 140 miles lay ahead with a river and mountain range to cross. The pass lay at 7,000 feet. They must make 14 miles a day; any slowing of progress would require more food than they had and would risk being caught by the rains. He warned that the party could only survive through discipline. Anyone who did not wish to accept his orders could leave now with a week's rations and make his own way. He looked around; no one moved. "By the time we get out of here," he finished, "many of you will hate my guts but I'll tell you one thing: you'll all get out."

At the head of the column he set the pace at the regulation Army rate of 105 steps a minute. The ghost of General Castner walked with him but Stilwell himself was the only veteran of those long-ago forced marches of the 15th Infantry. From the first day many among the Americans lagged and fell out, suffering from heat exhaustion. May in Burma, just before the monsoon, was the hottest time of year. Stilwell raged at the softness and the "damn poor show of physique." He allowed a five-minute rest every hour but otherwise would not slow or stop. Coming to a river he plunged in without a break in his stride, "obstinately scrutinizing his watch and counting out 105 steps to the minute" while he slogged steadily through the water with the long column stretching out behind in a single file. As malaria and dysentery attacked the marchers, weakness spread and slowed the pace. Stilwell had to increase the rest to ten minutes, conscious that every extra hour lengthened the odds. Two officers collapsed from sunstroke and had to be loaded onto the overburdened pack mules. Colonel Williams' box of medicines was stolen at one encampment, "a terrible loss." Ants, thorns, broken packs, vanishing bearers, a rogue elephant, insects, leeches, leg sores, blisters, infections and the blazing sun plagued the march and shredded what was left of goodwill and fellowship. One officer was discovered to have added a bedroll containing a mattress and all his clothing to the porters' loads. Without mentioning the individual by name, Stilwell excoriated him among the whole company for taking up the space that might have carried one of the sick. His voice shook with rage and his eyes filled with tears. "Jesus, even his campaign hat looks madder than hell," whispered one awed listener.

Merrill fainted in the river from a sunstroke complicated by a weak heart and had to be pulled over on an air mattress and afterwards carried by bearers. He was unconscious for two hours. Others faltered and dropped. Williams pleaded for halts for the sick. "This column can't stop," Stilwell answered. "Dammit, Williams, you and I can stand it. We're both older than any of them. Why *can't* they take it?" He kept them moving by tongue-lashing and implacable example. In constant anxiety about the food supply for over 100 people, he ordered half-rations and appointed Dorn mess officer to prevent cheating. He himself insisted on standing last in the chow line. He required the men to take turns standing guard every night and forming vanguards by day to guard against Japanese ambush.

The Uyu was reached in the three days he had allowed. Rafts, ordered by messengers sent ahead, were ready. The mule train escorted by an American officer and a group of the Chinese guards went ahead by land. Seagrave's nurses, "always willing," made roofs of leaves to shield the rafts against the sun and a hospital shelter of grass matting for Merrill and other invalids. As the convoy moved out to pole downstream toward the Chindwin an unspoken fear of their destination was in many minds. "Could this be an appointment in Samarra?" asked Paul Jones. Progress was "too damn slow" and Stilwell kept them poling and pushing all night. Ominous rain showers fell the next day. A bomber flew over, passed up-river, circled and came back. Everyone cowered; then, as they saw the red and blue markings of the RAF, broke into cheers and frantic waving. Circling in three low sweeps, the plane opened its bomb bays to drop food sacks on the beach. Half-naked dark mountain people rushed from the jungle to seize the first drops before the raft contingent, howling with wrath, could reach the banks and collect the rest. The drop included a sack of medical supplies enabling Colonel Williams to start quinine doses. This sudden recognition from outside of their plight raised hopes that rescue would be waiting at Homalin. On his raft Stilwell discoursed to Belden of his plan for reconquest: if the United States provided planes and supplies—, if the British could reorganize—, if the Chinese would cooperate—. "We've got to get out first," said Belden. Again they poled through the night. The rafts were hitting snags and breaking up and Stilwell was "dead beat all night."

Hiking into Homalin from the river they met a shock of disappointment: no one waiting for them, no food, no messages. The failure strained Stilwell's leadership thin; murmurs of anger and criticism grew audible and some members began to scheme for private survival. Preparing for the crossing of the Chindwin and a possible meeting with the enemy next day, Stilwell ordered an arms inspection. At the Chindwin no Japanese were met and the party crossed safely in dugouts and freight boats.

Shan and Kachin bearers were now exchanged for dark unkempt Nagas and Tangkhuls with a crest of hair down the middle of their shaved heads like Iroquois, and pierced ears holding cartridges or cigarets or flowers. They were good-humored and friendly, drank rice beer and could carry 50-pound loads on wooden back-packs. As the party dragged itself up a climb of 3,000 feet on May 14 the rains came down heavily, almost cause for despair. But that day they were met by the help which had failed at Homalin in the person of a British district official named Sharpe with a supply of live pigs for a roast dinner and the announcement that ponies, food, a doctor, whiskey, cigarets, and 400 porters were just behind him. "Quite a relief," Stilwell recorded mildly. Sharpe was to guide the party

Now which way will we go?

Don hangs it up. AGAIN

That God damn bridge that nearly made a maniac out of me

The bridge south of Indaw. This damn near stymied us.

There go ALL of our G-2 & G-4 records!

CHUNGKING
AMMISCA FOR ~~AQWAR~~.

HEADING FOR HOMALIN AND IM
PHAL WITH PARTY OF ONE HU
DRED. INCLUDES H.Q. GROUP, SE
GRAVES SURGICAL UNIT AND STR
WE ARE ARMED, HAVE FOOD AN
MAP, AND ARE NOW ON FOOT FIFT
MILES WEST OF ~~INDAW~~. NO OC
SION FOR WORRY. CHINESE TROO
COMING TO INDIA ON THIS GENE
AL ROUTE. ~~ES~~ CONTROL HAS EN
TIRELY PASSED TO SMALL UNIT
IN THIS AREA. HOPELESS TO TR
TO HANDLE THE MOB. WILL E
DEAVOR TO CARRY RADIO FARTH
BUT BELIEVE THIS IS PROBABL
LAST MESSAGE FOR A WHILE
CHEERIO.   ① May 6   STILWE

Together, boys, or we'll walk from ...

Sample of highway near Indaw.

Sorting out bearers & loads.
Mr. Case, Paul Jones, & ole Turkey Neck.

End of the motor transport.
Threw away all our stuff here
(Mansi, Burma)

The trail was damp at times.

Salvaging food dropped from plane
on Uyu River.

well kept a large group of U.S. Army photographs documenting the walkout from Burma in 1942
inscribed them with his inimitable captions. Many are reproduced on these four pages from
Stilwell Collection at the Hoover Institution Archives. On May 6 he sent a last radio message
Chungking (153) stating that there was "no occasion for worry" (144–166).

The Burmese nurses making
shelters for the rafts.

Paul is puzzled. How do you do

Dr Seagrave's medical unit.

Stilwell preceded by a guide, leading the c

Cleaning up at HOMALIN.

Sibert offers advice on how to
clean a Tommy gun.

Our rafts on the UYU.

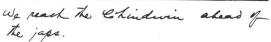

Sibley, Merrill, & Strwatowski soaking out.

We reach the Chindwin ahead of the japs.

the Uyu.

must be about time to rest. Let's pee.

In the Naga hills, towards the end.

into Imphal. The message to expect him had been enclosed in the lost RAF food sacks. Asked by Stilwell how he had known on which of four routes through the mountains to find the party, Sharpe replied, "I called Delhi to find out what kind of man you were. Delhi said you were very intelligent. This is the only trail it makes common sense to take so I figured you would be on it." He assured Stilwell that the other trails were being stocked and he brought sad word too of the surrender of Corregidor.

Five more days of continued climbing followed, with the pace pushed to 15 and 16 miles a day and on the downhill side to 17 and more in a race against the monsoon. Preliminary rains had already begun, making the trails so slippery that men fell repeatedly, stumbling and cursing, and often had to climb sideways, edging their feet into the hill. Seagrave, suffering from leg infections, was so worn at the end of a day that he could do nothing "but roll up in my blanket and pray for a sudden and easy death." But the party now had food and the invalids could ride except for one who was too ill with malaria to sit a pony and had to be carried in a sedan chair by shifts of bearers. The "cream puffs" and "sissies" were doing better and the unfaltering nurses sang Christian hymns and American popular songs. "What a picture . . . Chinese soldiers, Burmese girls, Americans and Limeys, all in the brook washing and shaving and soaking feet." A local head man in a brilliant red blanket presented Stilwell with a goat and welcoming Nagas offered rice wine and chickens.

Imphal was reached on May 20. Through careful planning and relentless leadership Stilwell had brought his party out without a single person missing—the only group, military or civilian, to reach India without loss of life. Many of those who walked out under his command did hate his guts but all 114 knew they owed him their lives. He came out, reported a correspondent, "looking like the wrath of God and cursing like a fallen angel." He had lost 20 pounds. His already spare frame was worn down to a minimum, his hands trembled, his skin was yellowish with jaundice, his eyes sunk in their sockets. Dorn had lost 32 pounds, Colonel Holcombe, one of those invalided most of the way, was "emaciated, resembles Gandhi." The Chinese troops had not been heard from.

Stilwell found a "nice message" from George Marshall waiting for him, expressing the commendation of "Secwar, President and entire War Department." Conscious only of the defeat of all his purposes, he wrote the one-word comment, "Why?" Humiliation as a soldier required justification and his subsequent report to the War Department on the campaign (written by Dorn with Stilwell's additions) was so blistering with regard to British and Chinese failures that all copies were ordered destroyed—with the incomplete success that such orders naturally attain. The implication of his report was that the British performance allowed only one interpretation:

that they had never intended from the beginning to hold Burma and had deliberately scuttled it in order to weaken China. What is true in history is often less important than what people believe to be true.

Elsewhere Stilwell summarized the causes of defeat as technical inferiority—in air force, tanks, artillery, machine guns, trench mortars, ammunition and transport—hostile population, Japanese initiative and "stupid gutless command, interference by CKS, Br. mess on RR, rotten communications, Br. defeatist attitude, vulnerable tactical situation." The list gave too little credit to the enemy for whom the physical difficulties of campaigning in Burma were no less and the tactical difficulties greater. The essential difference was one of intent, as between the invader who had planned, prepared and moved under his own power, and the defenders who had neither planned nor prepared nor were determined in purpose.

While Stilwell was walking out, the Japanese invaded China along the Burma Road. After badly defeating the incoming 29th Division they took Wanting on May 8 and reached the deep gorge of the Salween just after the retreating Chinese destroyed the bridge. The Chinese armies in Yunnan, strongly supported by the AVG, fought in real alarm to stem the invasion. Here in the southern mountains, having run out of momentum and accomplished the main object of blockading China from the south, the Japanese came to a halt.

Anxiety in Washington about the attitude of China, now isolated, was extreme. Marshall on May 9 despatched a stern instruction to AMMISCA in Stilwell's absence, warning all officers on duty in China to maintain an "attitude of calm optimism with respect to Chinese future." Plans and conversations must not "imply any thought of helplessness in situation." Movements must be so regulated "that they cannot possibly be construed as an evacuation by Americans."

The fate of the Chinese units in Burma varied. Sun Li-jen brought the 38th Division out through great hardships but in good order by a route somewhat to the south of Stilwell's, reaching India May 25-30. The 200th Division of the Fifth Army fought its way out, along with the remnants of the Sixth Army, to Yunnan. The 22nd and 96th Divisions of the Fifth Army struggled northward in veering directions and redoubled traces because of changing orders from Chiang Kai-shek. Caught by the monsoon in the high jungle of the northwest, they were kept alive on food drops by the RAF and American Air Force. Survivors of the 22nd reached India through Ledo in July and August, while those of the 96th after an epic of endurance eventually made their way over mountains to China via Fort Hertz.

Chinese communiqués reported the last days of the Burma campaign

in characteristic style, duly elaborated by American correspondents in
Chungking and rewrite men at home. For May 10-11 the Chungking communiqué reported one Japanese column in Yunnan "completely wiped
out," another "also annihilated" and the invasion force "trapped" from
behind by the Chinese in Burma who had "recaptured" Maymyo and were
"closing in on Mandalay from east and west with the object of recapture."
The AP correspondent transmitted this as a "smashing defeat" of the
Japanese invasion force, while his UP colleague even more vigorously
described Japanese "reeling" back from China, "liquidated . . . fleeing in
disorder." Desk editors in America, on the patriotic assumption that all
Chinese were under Stilwell's command, presented these despatches to their
readers under such headlines as "INVADING JAP FORCE CRUSHED BY STIL-
WELL," or on May 11, "STILWELL'S CHINA TROOPS TRAP JAPS, Invasion
Army in Full Retreat. Enemy Cut Off as 'Uncle Joe' Slams China's Back
Door. Bulletin!!!" On that day Uncle Joe was on a raft on the Uyu.

From the hill station at Imphal Stilwell and his party traveled by truck
to the Assam railroad and by train past the endless rows of glossy tea
shrubs to Dinjan and Tinsukia where the airfields of the Air Transport
Command were located. Wavell and Alexander, Brereton and Bissell of the
Tenth Air Force, and officers of his own staff in New Delhi came up to talk
to him. In Brereton's plane with the Persian rug he flew to Delhi and fame
on May 24. Followed from the airport to the Imperial Hotel (whose tele-
graphic address, he noted, was "Comfort") by a crowd of newspapermen,
he agreed to hold a press conference. After an hour's questions and answers
about the campaign in which he stressed Japanese air superiority as the
most damaging factor, he concluded with one of the historic statements of
the war: "I claim we got a hell of a beating. We got run out of Burma and
it is humiliating as hell. I think we ought to find out what caused it, go back
and retake it."

The impact of the words was clean and hard. Stilwell's honesty cut
through the pap and plush prose of Army public relations, as the *San
Francisco Chronicle* recalled at a later time, like "a sharp salt wind." *The
New York Times* in a lead editorial stated that Churchill and Roosevelt,
for all their magnificent rhetoric, "each of them could learn something
from General Stilwell," and lesser officialdom could heed him "both as to
diction and as to policy." His statement became synonymous with his
name, quoted thereafter every time he made news. He had chosen to do
a simple thing: tell the public the truth.

12

The Client

JUNE–OCTOBER 1942

THE loss of Burma, completing the blockade of China, raised the fear in American minds that China's will to resist would not survive her isolation. She clearly required encouragement in the form of tangible support. The question was how to deliver it. With the Japanese in Myitkyina forcing the flight northward, the air transport route was aggravated in danger and difficulty. Priorities in any case were assigned to Europe. Strategy in Asia was still uncertain. All that could be envisaged so far was the necessity of keeping China in the war as a base for air operations against Japan's sea-lanes and ultimate springboard for invasion. "Keeping China in the War," the title of a War Department plan at this time, meant in effect sending her enough supplies to keep her operational, and that meant in effect the reconquest of Burma.

Stilwell had a plan for the reconquest ready to commit to paper by the time he reached Delhi. Inevitably, after his experience in Burma, it called for American divisions. "My belief in decisive strategic importance of China is so strong," he wired the War Department on May 25, "that I feel certain a serious mistake is being made in not sending American combat units into this theater." Marshall could not be persuaded to divert any strength from full commitment to a Second Front in Europe. All he could offer was to return the Tenth Air Force to Stilwell's command. The outlook for CBI was not encouraging and made Stilwell more than ever determined to carry out his project for training a Chinese task force in India.

He had little support. The miasma of defeat and the sense of being in a low-priority theater had permeated many of the Americans on duty in CBI. One after another of the staff in Delhi asked to be relieved, some pleading illness, some ambitious for a more promising assignment. "Christ, isn't there one of them that puts the war first and himself second?" Stilwell himself was suffering from jaundice contracted from defective yellow fever serum, but though feeling "weak as a rag" and confined to bed off and on for the next several weeks, his idea of duty allowed him little sympathy for anyone who wanted relief. Stilwell could not understand a soldier who did not put duty to the mission first. He had "an exalted concept of true soldiering and an impossible ideal of what a true soldier should be," wrote the journalist Eric Sevareid after serving in CBI.

After conferring with Wavell who "mumbled" an assurance, "WILL go back for Burma," Stilwell departed for Chungking, arriving on June 3 after a five-day stopover in Kunming because of bad weather. The journey between his two headquarters, which he was to make seven times in the next seven months, covered 1,100 miles from Delhi to the Assam airfields, 550 over the Hump to Kunming, and 450 from Kunming to Chungking, a total of 2,100. The Hump portion, over 15,000-foot mountains, was flown at twice normal altitudes, often through air currents so turbulent they could break up an airplane. Flying at 17,000-20,000 feet it was necessary to take oxygen. The old slow transports, not designed for such conditions, flew without aids to navigation or arms against Japanese pursuit. On this occasion Stilwell rode a B-25 bomber at 250 miles an hour, "not so comfortable but fast as hell. Beat the transport in."

Stilwell found his reception by the Generalissimo and Madame surprisingly cordial, considering the fiasco in Burma. He was invited to the Chiangs' home at Huang Shan for the weekend, though too ill to accept. Despite the surface cordiality, Chiang was thoroughly disenchanted with his allies, especially Britain; for the sake of Lend-Lease, of which Stilwell held the key, he could not afford to be too disenchanted with the United States. From the Chinese point of view, the campaign under Stilwell's leadership, despite Chiang's strenuous efforts to contain it, had ended in the loss not only of Burma but also of the motorized Fifth Army with its artillery. This was what came of the "ill-fated strategy of attack," as it was called by a Chinese military historian. The result confirmed the Generalissimo in his mistrust of the offensive. "A hundred victories in a hundred battles is not the best of the best," according to a Chinese proverb; "the best of the best is to subdue the enemy without fighting." It was equally best, when defeat loomed, to succumb to the enemy without fighting. The crippling of two of his best armies, as Chiang considered them, was not what he had planned when he conferred their command on a foreigner. He had made the gesture to please the United States and to enhance China's claim to Lend-Lease and in any event had not intended it to be real. Stilwell's command was a case of *yu ming wu shih,* "having the name without the reality," as distinguished from *yu shih wu ming,* "reality without the name."

China's causes for disenchantment were real enough. After the great hopes of relief by the Allies, she was now worse off than before: the Burma Road lost, Yunnan invaded, and as a result of the Doolittle raid, the Japanese rampaging through Chekiang on a renewed offensive which the Chinese feared might expand into another drive on Changsha, perhaps even on Chungking. In addition to their military failures the Allies failed to treat China as an equal. The Chinese resented their failure to match the Atlantic Charter by a Pacific Charter of anticolonial principles. They resented the emphasis on a Second Front in Europe, implying neglect of their own situation. This was already evident in China's exclusion from Allied conferences on the occasion of Churchill's second visit to Washington in June. More damaging was continued exclusion from the Munitions Control Board: China's direct request for admission to the Combined Chiefs, which would have carried membership on the Munitions Board, was turned down because of the security risk on June 13.

Cynicism about the war and a lapse into increasing passivity was the result. An attitude of "Let the Allies do it" prevailed in the teahouses of Chungking after the fall of Burma. To use barbarians to fight other barbarians was a traditional principle of Chinese statecraft which now more than ever appeared not only advisable but justified. Chinese opinion, according to a foreign resident, held that not only was China justified in remaining passive after five years of resistance; "it was her right to get as much as possible out of her allies while they fought." The exercise of this right became the Government's chief war effort. The long endeavor to shake off the foreigners and emerge from dependence had not succeeded; China's problems had been too great. With dwindling capacity to cope with its own circumstances, the Kuomintang applied all its energy to making dependence pay.

Chiang Kai-shek raised the alarm at once. Unless the Chinese saw visible evidence of help from their allies, he warned the United States on May 25, "Chinese confidence in their Allies will be completely shaken" and this could presage "total collapse of Chinese resistance." The advance of the Japanese in Chekiang lent force to his warning. Morale was "never lower," Madame wrote to the Lend-Lease Administrator, Lauchlin Currie, on May 23, adding that the Generalissimo was for the "first time" pessimistic. Chiang followed with a letter to Roosevelt asking him to send Harry Hopkins to China in lieu of coming himself because the situation was at a "crucial stage such as I have never experienced before." Other messages warned of the rise of defeatists prepared to overthrow Chiang Kai-shek and come to terms with the Japanese. Already exceedingly worried, Roosevelt on May 5 had asked General Arnold to "explore every possibility" of flying freight to China for it was "essential that our route be kept open no matter how difficult." Ambassador Gauss, though not impressed by the threat of a separate peace, believed that prolonged passivity in the form of an "undeclared peace involving virtual cessation of hostilities" was not unlikely.

This was exactly the opposite of what Stilwell had been sent to achieve. The rationale of Lend-Lease was essentially the utilization of Allied manpower to fight the common enemy, and the object of Stilwell's mission was to see that Lend-Lease was used for its purpose. The obstacle that now rose in his way was the passivity, for understandable reasons, of the client. The Generalissimo would fight only in so far as failure to do so might cut off the flow of supplies. He could not by negative threat alone obtain enough; he had to promise military performance in order to commit America to supply the necessary matériel. Stilwell had the power of decision in this process. As the Generalissimo's Chief of Staff, his function, as the Generalissimo saw it, was to obtain for him what he wanted.

Stilwell did not see himself in the role of purveyor, nor even "adviser" in the sense of an instrument to be used for Chinese purposes. He saw himself as a soldier whose function and objective was to defeat the enemy and for this he needed an army. With or without a spearhead of American troops, the bulk of the fighting force would have to be Chinese, and to be effective the existing Chinese Army, or whatever part of it was made available for fighting, would have to be reformed. If he was to be an adviser, he intended, like so many others before him, to bring about fundamental change. Whether in currency or judiciary or customs collection or political structure or agriculture, the long train of China's advisers had in common a determination to reform. No one assigned to work in China under the conditions of 1942 could want less, unless he were of the Old China Hand variety, convinced the Chinese were "like that" and reform was futile.

Stilwell was the opposite of a cynic—a believer and a doer. When he saw something wrong, as Maxwell Taylor had observed in Peking, he wanted to correct it. "Every American has his own solution for China," a Chinese observer has said. Stilwell's, for China's sake, the war's sake, and his own, was reform of the army. He saw the 300 divisions, "sprawled all over China," on the average 40 percent understrength, with commanders drawing pay for full strength and "officers getting rich, men dying of malnutrition, malaria, dysentery, cholera, the sick simply turned loose. Ammo and weapons being sold. Open traffic with the enemy on all 'fronts.' . . . Transport being used for smuggling. None to move troops." Chiang Kaishek "never goes to look at his Army" and his constant talk about trucks, planes and guns "only reveals his complete ignorance of the necessity for training, replacements, leadership, medical care, SOS, etc. etc." Stilwell knew the scope for reform was so great as likely to be self-defeating, but he believed that with Lend-Lease as his quid pro quo he could require reform, at least beginning with the Thirty Divisions.

While still in Delhi he had drawn up a statement of military failings and needs which he took with him on his first day in Chungking when he went to report to the Generalissimo on the late campaign. Though ill at the time, he was seething with what he had to say and pulled himself out of bed to keep the appointment. He had hopes that telling the Generalissimo the truth about the performance in Burma might "scare him into real reorganization of his army," as he wrote to Stimson. "Quite a few of the Chinese high command should be shot," and he was making that recommendation for the Sixth Army commander, Kan Li-chu, as well as for two divisional commanders and one of a regiment.

Although Chiang had been sending orders to the armies in Burma every day from Chungking he knew little at first hand of current conditions or performance in military or other matters. In the Byzantine atmosphere of his court no one was anxious to inform him of deteriorating realities, and the worse these became, the less he was told. This stemmed not merely from fear or servility but from a basic philosophic preference of the Chinese for preserving appearances. "Forgetting evil and speaking only good," according to a Chinese precept, "helps to hold society together and preserve men's dignity with one another." The result was to leave the Generalissimo in what Stilwell called "ignorance and fatuous complacency," making it that much more difficult to convince him of the need for military reform.

On this occasion he told Chiang and Madame the "whole truth" of the campaign, "Naming names . . . and it was like kicking an old lady in the stomach." But "NO ONE else dares to tell him, so it's up to me all the more." Facing a man, especially a Chinese, with the failings under his leadership was not the best way to make him amenable to improvement, but Stilwell was bent on obtaining action against the enemy and felt he had no other choice. He then presented his program for military reorganization, for which the primary need was to reduce the total number of divisions and concentrate the available arms and equipment. It was the old problem of disbandment which had defeated Chiang's efforts in 1928-30. Since

then he had been doing his best by a tactic of nonsupply and nonreplace-
ment to eliminate the unattached provincial units, with little success.
Stilwell now recommended "the merging of divisions to bring all units
up to full strength and the assignment of all available weapons to these
divisions as far as they will go. . . . A few dependable, well-equipped, well-
supported divisions would be worth far more than double the number of
the present average . . . as well as more efficient and easier to supply and
handle." Even with present meager resources China could produce an
effective striking force that would be "usable, as it is not now" to hold the
Japanese off until Allied offensive power turned the scales toward victory.

He also recommended a thorough sifting of the officer corps on the basis
of merit with promotions for the able and a "rigid purge of inefficient high
commanders," failing which "the Army will continue to go downhill no matter how much material is supplied for it." He concluded on a sensitive point,
urging that for Commander-in-Chief in the field, the Generalissimo must
pick a man in whom he has confidence, "give him a general directive and
then let him handle the troops without interference from anyone whomso-
ever." He left the paper with Madame who took a quick look and said,
"Why, that's what the German advisers told him!"*

The Generalissimo did not answer the memorandum. At a second meeting ten days later to discuss the promised assignment of troops for training
in India he reverted to matériel. "The same old complex—planes, tanks,
guns, etc. will win the war. I got a bit hot and told him that the only way
to do it was to thoroughly reorganize the ground forces." At this point
Madame interjected that the Generalissimo had to consider "certain influences."

Stilwell knew well enough from the time of his own comments on disbandment in 1929 that Chiang was a prisoner of the complex of private
interests in the military structure of his country. He could not be too free
with the armies under the war zone commanders and he exercised undisputed control only over the ten armies belonging to the Central Government. Under the heading "Troubles of a Peanut dictator," Stilwell analyzed the factors that limited Chiang's freedom of action. He had allowed
too many of his lieutenants to combine the political functions of governor
and the military authority of commander in one person. *"Now he finds it
makes the boys too powerful and he's been trying for a year to shake*

---

* General Hans von Seeckt, former chief of the Reichswehr in the 1920s, when
military adviser to China in 1934 presented a program in which he stressed quality
as against size and recommended the training and equipment of 20, later enlarged to
60, divisions and a purge of the officer corps. A chief failure, he noted, was the
choosing of officer candidates for patronage value without reference to merit, record,
ability or leadership.

them loose, without success. . . . The way it works is by threat. The Peanut wants to shake Hsueh Yueh loose. If he pulls out troops, Hsueh squawks, 'I cannot be responsible for the security of my area,' and he might even arrange for a Jap reaction. The understrappers are told to pressurize and a flood of protest reaches various officials of the Central Government. They then tell the Peanut the opposition is very strong, and that forcing the issue might cause dirty work. So the Peanut lays off and waits. The plain fact is he doesn't *dare* to take vigorous action."

Yet a compact, effective, "usable" army seemed so obviously in the regime's interests that Stilwell could not believe that "with the U.S. on his side and backing him," Chiang should fail to grasp "the big opportunity of his life." Even apart from military performance, it was essential to the welfare of China to reduce the terrible drain of the press gang on the peasantry. But Chiang was exhibiting a client's most exasperating quality —nonrecognition of enlightened self-interest; or what seemed to an American his self-interest. In his frustration Stilwell thought that only some influence outside the Government could help China. "Either enemy action will smash her" or, he wrote in one of his peculiarly clarifying phrases, "some regenerative idea must be formed and put into effect at once."

Chiang's resistance to Stilwell's proposals was never fixed or solid but changeable and vacillating in proportion to what he thought Stilwell could obtain for him from America. He had to give in enough to keep American aid coming. The War Department at this time drew plans for a campaign to reopen the Burma Road using 45,000 tons of Chinese Lend-Lease material which had piled up in India, unable to be delivered. (Another 149,000 tons choking the wharves at Newport News was repossessed by the United States.) A renewed land campaign did not appeal to Chiang. He wanted the United States to concentrate on increasing the capacity of air transport over the Hump for two main purposes: to keep war material coming in for his own uses and to fuel and maintain Chennault's air force which, on Chennault's assurance, would take care of fighting the Japanese.

Air Transport Command (ATC) was operating with barely 25 planes, far from the 100 Roosevelt had promised. China's insistent demands for more transports were not being satisfied by the Munitions Control Board because of a general shortage of planes and crews. Nor was full satisfaction given to China's requests for war material, which continued as gargantuan as ever regardless of the blockade. The fault lay in the competing priorities of BOLERO* and the Russians, but T. V. Soong ascribed it to

* The buildup in England for the Second Front.

Stilwell. "In the absence of supporting telegram from you," he wired, the War Department was acting on China's requests "rather slowly." He urged Stilwell to realize the "miraculous hold" he had in the United States, from President, Secretary and Chief of Staff downward and "that any request from you will be supported." Stripped of the flattery, the last phrase in Soong's statement was something the Chinese believed. Because of their total disinterest in the war in Europe they were convinced there was unlimited matériel and that the short supply to them was simply owed to Stilwell's failure to ask for it.

Prodded by Soong, the Generalissimo became more responsive to Stilwell and the shift was reflected in gradual assent to the program for training troops in India. At a conference on June 24, with Madame urging each of his points on the Generalissimo, Stilwell obtained most of his terms. After he refused to accept Tu Li-ming as commander, it was finally agreed that Stilwell himself should have command and control of training if he would accept Lo Cho-ying as vice-commander in charge of administration and discipline. Chiang even agreed to send 50,000 troops by air. "It was one of those sudden turn-arounds" that marked negotiations. The bait was the "Big Picture"—the plan to arm China for counteroffensive operations on the basis of 5,000 tons a month over the Hump and 500 combat planes.

The endless torturing problem of tonnage over the Hump had become the fulcrum of the theater. Since April, owing to interruptions by the monsoon and by airdrops to the refugees, the transports had managed to make an average of only two round trips each a month, resulting in delivery to China of a monthly average of less than 100 tons. Despite all the promises, crews and equipment were short, maintenance poor, airfields in Assam shoddy and inadequate, and the weather treacherous. The United States was now operating seven Air Force commands overseas and four at home and their requirements were summed up by a commander in Alaska who wrote, "I need everything!" The Hump needed the most and the equipment it received had to travel 12,000 miles from the United States to west coast Indian ports, another 1,500 miles over Indian railways to Calcutta, and from there over the narrow-gauge Assam-Bengal Railway to the airfields.

Originally built to haul the Assam tea crop, this railway was a bottleneck that drove men to despair. It switched to different railbeds three times between Calcutta and Ledo and included a crossing of the unbridged Brahmaputra by barge. British management operated with the habits and tempo of a less exigent time. Labor conditions in India were disrupted by the strikes and national movement of "noncooperation" called by the Congress Party in the summer of 1942. Tonnage delivered over the

Assam-Bengal line was persistently short of agreed estimates and the rigidity of its managers defied even the competence and courtesy of General "Speck" Wheeler, chief of SOS for the theater. The problem choked the supply effort and was to continue for nearly two years until agreement was finally reached in February 1944 to militarize the line and operate it with American railway battalions.

On the other side of the Hump in China, fuel and parts for Chennault's air force had to be carted by road and river several hundred miles beyond Kunming to the several air bases, the journey often taking as much as eight weeks. The ATC burned one gallon of fuel for every gallon it delivered in China, and had to deliver 18 tons of supplies to enable Chennault's air force to drop one ton of bombs on the Japanese. A single cargo plane could carry approximately four to five tons, and under optimum conditions could make one round trip per day. But rarely more than 60-70 percent of assigned planes were in operation at any one time, and weather and other failures reduced the flights. Losses over the route were heavy. In three years of operation the ATC was to lose 468 planes, an average of 13 a month. Sometimes the crew were able to parachute to safety and be guided out by Kachin rescue teams organized by OSS agents in Burma. Others died in the jungle or were captured by the Japanese or in some cases were caught in the tree tops and their corpses found hanging long afterwards, eaten by ants.

Chronically short of everything an air force needed, Chennault could have used every ton the ATC could carry. His normal state was exasperation like Stilwell's or almost anybody's in CBI. While his men patched planes and scavenged parts and filtered engine oil to use twice, the sight of American staff officers, he wrote, "scuttling pompously about India and China with brief cases infuriated us all." Crossing the Hump, passengers took up room that could have been filled by fuel, tires, spark plugs, carburetors, tools, overalls, cigarets, soap and everything else the AVG was not receiving. When induction into the American Air Force took effect on July 4, 1942, the unit, now designated China Air Task Force with Chennault as commander, became a component of the Tenth Air Force, which was the overall air unit for CBI. Chennault was promoted to brigadier general, but Bissell, his *bête noir*, was promoted a day earlier and named air commander for the theater. The bypassing of his candidate was taken by Chiang Kai-shek as "a direct kick in the teeth" (according to McHugh), indicating that China would not be given the air strength he wanted, whereas in fact it reflected General Arnold's distaste for Chennault. Chinese influence was put to work toward the removal of Bissell and the elevation of Chennault and was ultimately to succeed in the first aim, if not in the second.

Even Chennault, though a favorite, had his troubles with Chiang Kai-shek, not unlike Stilwell's. When Madame on one occasion told him he must in future communicate directly with the Generalissimo rather than through her, he replied that without her as intermediary, interested persons were able to persuade the Generalissimo to "issue unacceptable orders." He expressed such manifest panic at the prospect that he was granted permission to continue as before. Chinese pilots, whose training Chennault supervised, presented the same problems as Stilwell found in the officer corps. The situation, Chennault complained to Madame in May 1942, "has grown from bad to worse and is now almost hopeless." The worst pilots were transferred to instructorships and were "incapable" of teaching or maintaining discipline. They ignored American recommendations and were "resentful of American influence." He had found it impossible to rectify these conditions over the past four years and now could not certify the pilots for completion of their training in the United States. He felt obliged to report to the War Department that "flying training methods in China are hopelessly deficient." If expected to continue he must have "full authority" over schools and personnel. Later when pursuing the thesis that Stilwell's personal faults caused his clash with the Generalissimo, Chennault left his own difficulties unmentioned.

Deficiencies of supply were the more maddening to Chennault because he was supremely confident that if given the tools his air force alone could knock out Japan by obstructing the flow of her war materials through the South China seas. The lure of the single solution was powerful. "We should always examine the optimums," Chennault wrote, "and forget about feasibility; it will compromise us soon enough. Let's look at what might be and be invigorated by it." He was himself over-invigorated by this admirable principle. What was needed in Pacific war strategy, he wrote to Stilwell that summer, was to cut Japan's sea-lanes, inspire Chinese ground forces to action against Japanese-occupied areas, neutralize Japanese air efforts in Burma and Indochina, relieve the Japanese threat to India, safeguard the Hump route to China, and "supply a successful offensive to inspire all Allied powers." If provided with 500 combat planes and 100 transports plus "complete authority in this theater," he would attain all of these objectives.

To Chiang Kai-shek and Madame the thesis was compelling. If 500 combat planes and 100 transports and "full authority" for Chennault could win the war, there was no need to reform the army and disturb the dangerously delicate balance of cliques and persons and war zone commanders which constituted Chiang's teetering seat of power. Air power required no Chinese effort; besides, it looked so easy. "If we destroy 15 Nippon planes every day," wrote Madame to Chennault in reply to one of his weekly combat reports, "soon there will be no more left." It became the Chiangs' fixed goal to induce the United States to provide the 500-plane air force and to send over the Hump the supplies to operate and maintain it.

Chiang Kai-shek's resentment at unfulfilled promises was growing. HALPRO, a plan to bomb Japan with China-based B-24s, in which he was much interested, was canceled and the B-24s held up in Egypt, at Stilwell's recommendation, because the loss of the Chekiang bases and the inadequate ATC supply made the project impossible. The 100 transports promised for the ATC were cut to 75 and then to 57 because of requirements elsewhere. Stilwell was obliged to inform the Generalissimo that under present conditions the ATC could not deliver a tenth of the 5,000 tons a month originally estimated. In the manner of ancient kings, Chiang blamed bad tidings on the bearer, the more so as he had been told by T. V. Soong that Stilwell was not pressing China's demands with sufficient vigor.

To the Generalissimo this represented a dereliction of Stilwell's duty as his Chief of Staff. As he saw it, failure by a foreigner to obtain what was needed from his own country was simply a failure of influence. That supplies had to travel an immense journey by ship and rail and plane to reach China did not concern him. He was not impressed by the physical facts of logistics, of which his knowledge was vague. If Stilwell could not produce, it meant only that he was either not sufficiently influential or not acting wholeheartedly in China's behalf. Madame had a remedy for the former and an inducement to the latter. "We're going to see that you are made a *full general,*" she told Stilwell. "The hell they are," he muttered in his diary, outraged. He considered it, as he told his staff, an attempted bribe to gain his compliance in recommending all Chinese requisitions, which indeed it was.

The issue of supply came to a head in the crisis of the Three Demands at the end of June. The trigger was Rommel's capture of Tobruk on June 21, sweeping the British back into Egypt and raising once more the threat of a German breakthrough into the Middle East. In the emergency Brereton's heavy bombers of the Tenth Air Force, together with transports and crews of the ATC, were ordered to Egypt and a force of B-24 heavy bombers on its way to China was halted at Khartoum for diversion to the British. It was left to Stilwell to convey these tidings to the Generalissimo whose predictable reaction he shared. "We fail in *all* our commitments and blithely tell him just to carry on, old top."

Chiang Kai-shek and Madame used the occasion for a spectacular explosion. Every time the British suffered a defeat, China's equipment was taken away, raged Madame, "and such being the case there is no need for

China to continue in the war." The Generalissimo claimed that China was "lightly regarded" and demanded a "clear cut answer" as to whether America and Britain "considered it as one of the Allied theaters." He came at once to the point that really interested him: Lend-Lease. Less than 10 percent of the war material promised by Roosevelt was being delivered, he said, which amounted to "disobedience" of the President's orders. "As Chief of Staff to me, you are responsible for seeing to it that the promised material is forthcoming." Madame concluded in a tone of ultimatum, "The Generalissimo wants a yes or no answer whether the Allies consider this theater necessary and will support it."

Stilwell was inclined to sympathize since he wanted more support for the theater no less than they. But he was angered by the charge of failure on his part and "threw it right back at them, telling them what I had asked for." He thought their outburst had been calculated by the Chiangs on the theory that "violent protests" gave them the upper hand. This was very likely. Beneath all courtesies, conferences, services, friendships or other relationships, the Chinese regarded Westerners fundamentally as adversaries to be got the better of in any exchange. Underlying that level, the deep cause of Chiang's resentment was not being able to control allotments of Lend-Lease within his country as the British controlled theirs. The reason for the difference was the common knowledge that if supplies were turned over freely to China, a large part would never see use against Japan, but it appeared clearly discriminatory to the Chinese. To Chiang it was an unforgivable face-losing and the foundation of his dislike for Stilwell who as controller of Lend-Lease was its visible representative.

The verbal ultimatum was followed three days later by formal presentation of the Three Demands with a time deadline. The demands were:

1. Three American divisions to arrive in India between August and September to restore communication to China through Burma.

2. 500 combat airplanes to operate from China beginning in August and to be maintained continuously at that strength.

3. Delivery of 5,000 tons a month to be maintained by the ATC beginning in August.

If these "minimum requirements" were not met, the Chiangs stated, the alternative would be "liquidation" of the China theater and a "re-adjustment" of their position requiring "other arrangements."

Stilwell was more than willing to forward the demands since, apart from the number of planes and the time limit, they were close to what he had asked Marshall for himself, but he refused Madame's subsequent demand that he forward them with his recommendation. He would not, he told her, support an ultimatum to his own Government. Madame "got hot . . . and started to bawl me out," brought in her secretary and "took down everything I said. Obviously mad as *hell*. She had snapped the whip and the stooge had not come across." Stilwell took the occasion to point out his dual status. Though Chief of Staff to the Generalissimo, he could not be called in and given orders with regard to his own Government. He spelled out his other capacities as Commanding General of American forces in CBI, representative of his Government on Allied war councils, and on Lend-Lease matters, and "a U.S. Army officer sworn to uphold the interests of the U.S. . . . If she doesn't get the point she's dumber than I think she is."

He also explained to Madame the logistics of what it took to deliver 5,000 tons a month over the Hump: 304 planes, 275 men in flight crews, 3,400 men on the ground, and five airfields at each end, each field capable of handling 50 transports. "She began to get some light." He told her finally that he thought the Generalissimo "wanted a soldier and not a rubber stamp or a transmitting agency," which was disingenuous, considering that the reverse was the case.

To give credence to the threat of a separate peace, which was all that the Chinese had to make the Three Demands an ultimatum, rumors were set afloat in Chungking that a Japanese envoy and representatives of Nanking had arrived to bargain on peace terms. Stilwell was not impressed because he felt sure that China had too much to gain from the United States and "nothing to gain and everything to lose by making peace with Japan." Ambassador Gauss, with whom he discussed the matter, agreed with him and informed Washington the threat was a "bluff" although the need was real. According to Chou En-lai, interviewed by an OSS agent, there was no danger at all of a separate peace; on the contrary, "resistance has become a good business since help is easy to get." Kuomintang officials, he said, were proud of their diplomatic skill in playing on American nerves; they maintained contact with Japanese in Shanghai "in order to excite fears in Washington."

The United States could not afford to take chances on losing China as a base of operations. The answer to the Three Demands depended on disposable resources, which in turn depended on conflicts and bargains with the British about the Second Front in Europe. Pending a decision, the President wrote Chiang a soothing letter promising a settlement in the near future.

Angered by a dispute with Stilwell over the disposition of two transport planes, the Generalissimo launched an attempt to divest him of control of Lend-Lease that was to have accidental but important consequence. As he put it to Roosevelt, Stilwell's dual responsibility to the American and Chinese Governments appeared to conflict in the matter of Lend-Lease and had to be resolved. In a reply, drafted by Marshall who was aware that Lend-Lease was Stilwell's only lever, the President emphatically refused to divide Stilwell's functions and explicitly affirmed his primary responsibility to the United States. It was "not practical for all of General Stilwell's duties to be subject to orders from you." Any successor, Roosevelt added, would carry the same powers.

The letter violated the main principle of Chinese intercourse which is to preserve a man's dignity by not confronting him with direct denials. Since the White House and War Department appeared to lack an amanuensis learned in Chinese custom, T. V. Soong undertook to fill the vacuum. In the interest of a quiet life he altered the letter both as to sense and language before forwarding it to the Generalissimo. Meanwhile Marshall had sent an information copy of the original to Stilwell, who thus saw his position confirmed while Chiang Kai-shek thought otherwise. Several weeks' tangle ensued, during which their mutual dissatisfaction mounted, before the truth came out. Chiang was predictably insulted when he read the genuine text and staged another protest about liquidating the China theater. Soong was summoned to the White House and told in person that Stilwell's status remained unaltered. Not wishing any more than Chiang's other ministers and officials to be a messenger of unpleasantness, he continued to expurgate messages as he saw fit. Two years later, after further experience of altered messages, the President ordered that all communications from himself to the Generalissimo should be delivered in person by the senior American officer in Chungking.

While an answer to the Three Demands was awaited Stilwell continued to press for the training program in India, the Thirty Division program and the reconquest of Burma. Relations with the Generalissimo were maintained at surface propriety, alternating with neglect, and conferences with the War Ministry always produced promises of cooperation. "No" was not a word used by the Chinese. It was always possible for Stilwell to believe that he was about to accomplish something. He was aware of a whispering campaign, which he believed planted by Soong, to the effect that he had sabotaged an offensive by the Fifth and Sixth Armies in Burma and had then "run away." But there were always Chinese friends who wanted him to succeed in his plans for reform and who encouraged his hopes. Tseng Shih-kwei, chief interpreter in the Burma campaign who continued as liaison officer, came in for a talk and "really seems to believe I can work up enough influence to have a vital effect on the situation."

Life was not enjoyable during these months. When jaundice was succeeded by "gut ache," finally diagnosed as worms in his system, he found himself taking eight different medicines in 36 hours and recording afterwards, to his astonishment, "feeling better!" He was saddened by news of the death of his mother in June and worried by trouble with his eyesight which had been poor for years, depending almost entirely on the use of one eye. The discomfort of air raids and the heat of Chungking were unpleasant and he thought longingly of Carmel and his family. He was reassured by a message from Marshall and Stimson promising that if efforts to secure more active cooperation from the Generalissimo proved unsuccessful, they would transfer him to another theater where he could be more useful.

There were some encouragements. After prolonged negotiations, and over the extreme reluctance of the Government of India, he had secured Wavell's assignment of Ramgarh, a former camp for 20,000 Italian prisoners of war, about 200 miles west of Calcutta, as a base for the Chinese troop training program. The British were afraid of the effect of a body of armed Chinese on the Indian rebellion and had no wish to employ them for the recapture of Burma. Eight thousand Chinese of the 38th and 22nd Divisions were in India, however, and the United States, which was not planning to send its own infantry to CBI, pressed strongly for Stilwell's program, and prevailed. An agreement was reached by which the British housed, fed and paid the troops as reverse Lend-Lease and America equipped and trained them. The program began with an initial 8,000. After three months' delay, the additional troops, which Chiang had promised on June 24, were despatched by airlift beginning in October.

Obstacles in the way of army reform were greater. The military establishment was split between the party of military bureaucrats led by the War Minister, Ho Ying-chin, and the Whampoa clique which held most of the active commands. Ho's party was tied to the existing system of organization, which was why a general like Tu Li-ming, as Stilwell noted, could be "so independent." Ho Ying-chin firmly opposed any spending of the Central Government's military power and could be expected to discover objections and deterrents to any program requiring either change or action.

The Whampoa group, led by two veterans of Whampoa's first class, Generals Ch'en Ch'eng and Hu Tsung-nan, was more open to improvement. General Ch'en, the Governor and commander of Hupeh, was the man Stilwell had considered "the most powerful and most interesting" of the generals in 1938 and whom he now had in mind as a possible Commander-in-Chief or, hopefully, a replacement for Ho. As a close associate of the Generalissimo, regarded as his interim heir until Chiang's son was ready, Ch'en enjoyed the necessary favor; there was no use in considering anyone who did not. He was believed to aspire to the succession in his own right. He resembled the Generalissimo physically, cultivated the same shaved head and small mustache, and spoke in the same shrill voice, giving rise to stories that they were half-brothers. Despite this association, he had worked with Chou En-lai and the Communists during the period of the united front to establish a political bureau in each division of the army and to apply their methods of organizing popular resistance to the Japanese.

Hu Tsung-nan, the other Whampoa leader, also a trusted intimate of the Generalissimo, held the quarantine line against the Communists from headquarters in Sian. He commanded a force of 400,000, the largest and best-equipped body of soldiers in China. He was a close associate of Tai Li, another Whampoa man.

Many other figures of varying loyalty and connections had to be taken into account. There was Chang Fa-kwei, allied with the southern clique, former commander of the old Ironsides Army, "who has made money and gone soft" but was still a personage of influence. There were at least seven war zone commanders including Ch'en Ch'eng who combined the political and military posts. Among them was the Tiger of Changsha, Hsueh Yueh, of the proverbially bellicose province of Hunan, "the only tough guy in the Army," who, when Chiang sent him interfering messages, "howls for relief." Others of the seven off in the wings were semifeudal overlords like Yen Hsi-shan in Shansi and the virtually autonomous Governor of Yunnan, Lung Yun, a tiny man with vast wealth of opium origins, who issued his own currency and maintained his own army. His relations with Chiang Kai-shek were such that on an occasion of political crisis when Lung Yun was needed in Chungking, he did not go until Madame had arrived in Yunnanfu to remain as a hostage during his absence.

Another of the seven was Ku Chu-tung, the commander in Chekiang who during the action against the Japanese "was fifty or more miles in the rear and never went up." Colonel Barrett, Stilwell's former assistant in Peking, now Military Attaché, came back from a personal survey of the front with a report of a "bitched-up action" at Ch'u Hsien, the big bomber airfield which the Generalissimo had been particularly anxious not to lose when he protested the Doolittle raid. It was now lost as a result of that action. According to Barrett's findings, Chiang had again directed operations from Chungking "with the usual brilliant result. . . . Peanut ordered two armies to hide in the mountains and attack on the flank when the Japanese passed. The Japs simply blocked the exit roads and went on. . . . The troops had only the poorest equipment. No medical attention. No transport. Many sick. Most recruits were conscripts, delivered tied up. Conscription is a scandal. Only the unfortunates without money or influence are grabbed. . . . Why doesn't the little dummy realize that his only hope

167

169

168

Stilwell greets Chennault; in the background, members of the American Volunteer Group, or AGV (167). Major Emmet J. Theissen piloted "Uncle Joe's Chariot" on Stilwell business (168), and occasionally gave war correspondents a hitch (169): (left to right) Robert Martin of UP, Stilwell, Brooks Atkinson, Brigadier General William Bergin, Theodore White (on floor), Norman Soong.

170

171

172

173

At the Chinese troop training camp at Ra
garh, India, Stilwell checks students on a r
range (170) and inspects their uniforms (17
Three soldiers of the 38th Division look ov
a U.S. Army maintenance manual (172), a
Stilwell addresses his students from a ma
shift platform (173).

is the 30 Division plan, and the creation of a separate, well-equipped, and well-trained force?"

The answer to this exasperating question was to unfold only gradually. It was a long time before Stilwell could bring himself to admit that Chiang did not really want a well-trained, well-equipped fighting force; that such a force represented to him less a boon than a threat; that he feared that an effective 30 divisions might come under a new leader or group, undermining or challenging his own control, and that Stilwell's proposal to remove incompetent commanders would remove those loyal and beholden to him; that he was not interested in an army that could fight the Japanese but only in one that could sustain him internally; that for this he believed it sufficed to have more divisions and more guns, planes and tanks than the Communists.

Stilwell kept on trying. He was moved by the conviction of a man with a "regenerative idea" and he believed that the enormous bargaining power of American aid could exact army reform and overcome political obstacles. He envisaged a force squeezed down ultimately to about 100 full-strength divisions. The nucleus of the first 30, after being trained and armed in the area of Kunming, would provide the troops for the Y-force, that is, the eastern prong of the double invasion of Burma. (In American planning this operation was known as the X-Y plan, with X representing the force invading from India.) Stilwell planned a system of training by cadres which in turn would train their fellows, rather than the training of whole divisions. The Chinese War Ministry agreed on the "general outline" but evaded a firm date to begin the training.

In a new memorandum to bestir the Generalissimo, Stilwell strongly argued the philosophy behind his efforts. China must not think, he urged, in terms of military power she did not possess—a large air force and heavy artillery—but make use of what she had, "a large reservoir of manpower armed fairly well with rifles, machine guns and mortars." With the number of divisions reduced by 50 percent and those remaining brought up to full strength, each unit could have a normal complement of these weapons plus improved artillery support. "I realize and appreciate the objections that are raised when changes in command are advocated," he concluded, and refrained from making any specific suggestions on that score.

To this memorandum, as to five others which Stilwell had submitted in the past month, the Generalissimo gave no reply. A request for an interview had gone unanswered for a week. "This is the most dreary type of maneuvering I've ever done," Stilwell wrote home, "trying to guide and influence a stubborn, ignorant, prejudiced, conceited despot who never hears the truth except from me and finds it hard to believe." He thought, as he explained to Stimson, that by telling him the "unvarnished truth, to establish a gradual growth of confidence on his part," which was a naive expectation. "In searching this man for his good points," he continued to Stimson, "his environment and experience must be taken into account. . . . He has no sound education. . . . He has no friends at all, only servants who are without exception ill at ease in his presence." His wife was his only real friend. "Actually she is very much afraid of him and she subsides at once when his anger flares up. She considers her job to be the fight to make China great," and if she could be the G–mo, "progress would be five times faster than it is."

Stilwell's overall objective was to force into existence the campaign that nobody wanted—the recovery of Burma. He would offer the campaign to Chiang as a way out of his ultimatum to Washington. By "showing his willingness to cooperate," the Generalissimo would get the American supplies, and the Americans would have to supply and support the campaign on an adequate scale once the Chinese were committed. The British would have to be pushed into it by pressure from Washington. Stilwell still hoped for one or more American divisions and believed that if Chinese and American units were ready to move, "the British could hardly fail to act to regain their own territory."

On that basis on July 19 he submitted to Chiang Kai-shek a four-point military plan following his original conception of the two-pronged offensive. It called for participation by "20 picked divisions" on the Chinese side. The lure was the reopening of Rangoon to shipping which would permit the War Department, Stilwell estimated, to allot to China a renewed flow of 30,000 tons a month for six months. Simultaneous with the land offensive, the plan called for the British to reestablish naval control of the Bay of Bengal, retake the Andaman Islands and carry out a landing at Rangoon.

On the arrival of Lauchlin Currie the next day as the President's emissary in lieu of Harry Hopkins, Stilwell learned that no American divisions would be assigned: "too much tonnage." Although this was one of the Three Demands, Currie was nevertheless "all pepped up" after initial talks with the Generalissimo, and "thinks he smoothed it all out." Currie was a man of small stature and compensating self-esteem whom Roosevelt had first sent to Chungking as his personal representative in the spring of 1940 and who had been in charge of Lend-Lease dealings with China at the Washington end since then. He soon appeared in Stilwell's diary as "Currie Comb" and "Cutie Currie." He did not believe in requiring performance as a quid pro quo for Lend-Lease. "In view of the dependence by China on us for continued aid, it is not anticipated that any difficulty of noncooperation will be experienced," he informed Marshall in a classic misjudgment. He underestimated China's ability to make use of her users for her own ends.

In conferences with Currie the Generalissimo expressed his dissatisfaction with Stilwell in a renewed effort to have him removed, or at least separated from control of Lend-Lease. At any time in the course of his mission, Stilwell could have made himself agreeable to Chiang Kai-shek if he had been more amenable in the matter of matériel, had recommended the G–mo's requisitions and not concerned himself too strictly about their use. Nothing would have been easier. Having very soon discovered that Stilwell was not prepared to be cooperative in this sense, Chiang thereafter never gave up for long the effort to replace him. When Currie relayed the substance of Chiang's complaints, Stilwell wrote in rebuttal that he had told the G–mo the truth about situations because he believed he wanted the truth. "I cannot continue on any other basis."

On August 1 Chiang Kai-shek took the "out" Stilwell had offered and accepted the Burma plan of campaign on two shrewd conditions: full British participation by land and sea, and the effective support of an adequate air force. The campaign depended, he pointed out, on first ascertaining the intentions of the British Government. John Davies, Stilwell's political adviser, had just assessed these. For the same reasons that the British had not aggressively defended Burma to begin with, he wrote on July 31, they now "have no intention of attempting to retake Burma in the foreseeable future." Since this was what Chiang suspected, he felt reasonably safe in agreeing to the offensive, even going so far as to designate 15 of the 20 divisions which would take part. A decision on the campaign was now up to the Combined Chiefs of Staff in Washington.

American aid to China, whatever its military intent, was in effect going to a regime, not to a war effort. "Until we re-take Burma," wrote Colonel Dorn to the War Department on August 4, "all talk and planning to aid China are utterly meaningless. But all aid to China must have a string which demands action from them." Otherwise "the present regime will do nothing but hoard the material in order to perpetuate itself after the war." Almost casually he glanced at the core of the problem: "They expect an upheaval or revolution of some sort. In fact T. V. Soong in Washington expressed the opinion that the present regime would be out of a job six months after the war. He ought to know. . . ."

The domestic issue was central and pervaded the air. Except for friendly recollections of conversations with Chou En-lai and Yeh Chien-ying in 1938, Stilwell had little direct knowledge of the Communists. He knew the 8th Route Army was said to number 500,000 and that Communist strength was spreading in the north. According to some reports, only one district in Shantung remained under Central Government control. His only encounter with the Communists since his return was second hand in a remark by Chou En-lai, who was still in Chungking, to John Davies in June. Half laughing, half seriously, he had said that if the Generalissimo would permit, he would lead the Communist troops in a campaign to retake Burma and "*I* would obey General Stilwell's orders!" Though he stored up the remark, Stilwell spared little attention to the Communists; he was absorbed by the problem of Chiang Kai-shek who was in the foreground.

Though a conservative Republican at home, Stilwell was bothered, like many other Americans in Chungking, by the incompatibility of the ally he was charged with supporting. The problem occupied his pen on the hot summer nights. He wrote of the United States "forced into partnership with a gang of fascists under a one-party government similar in many respects to our German enemy." This was partly the result of the "silly, gullible and false propaganda" about the gallant six-year fight of the Chinese under the dauntless leadership of Chiang Kai-shek. There was "sympathy here for the Nazis. Same type of government, same outlook, same gangsterism," except that it was neither forceful nor efficient. Chiang "is not taking a single step forward or doing anything concrete to improve the position of China." Like Hitler he believed himself "infallible" and worked by "intuition." "How do you move a guy like that? How do you get his point of view?"

Foreseeing a civil war with the "Reds" after the war, Stilwell asked himself, "What can we do to help the Chinese people? Stop the silly propaganda. . . . Where is the gallant resistance? Where is the great guerilla warfare? Where is reform or even elementary understanding of the problem?"

Stilwell thought Chiang was "as intensely pro-Chinese, i.e. contemptuous of everyone else, as the Ch'ings* were," and haunted by the fear of being thought pro-American and of acknowledging his dependence on the United States. He might have carried the thought further for it was relevant to his own situation. Though Chiang had used many foreigners including his long-time political adviser, W. H. Donald; his chief of bodyguard, the German Walther Stennes; his financial adviser, Arthur Young; his pilot, Royal Leonard—nevertheless his attitude underneath was xenophobic. Hating the British and Americans as imperialists, he felt humiliated by his relationship with Stilwell.

As his troubles waxed, he had become increasingly authoritarian and unapproachable, content to be set apart. Stilwell was not the only one

---

* The Manchu dynasty.

who had difficulty obtaining an appointment. Officials waited weeks to see him and often could make their problems known only through Madame, which they resented. By keeping rivals off balance through a technique of "fear and favor," in Stilwell's phrase, he appeared strong and indispensable but he did not know how to make a government. Though long on experience, his mind was narrow and his education limited. His most serious handicap was the lack of competent government servants. He never allowed a really able man to reach an important post lest he become too strong. Because he made loyalty rather than ability the criterion of service he was surrounded by mediocrities. His brother-in-law H. H. Kung, who as vice-president of the Executive Yuan headed the civil government and usually served as Finance Minister, was described by Cyril Rogers, representative of the Bank of England in China, as having "the mentality of a child of 12. If I were to record his conversations with me about banking and play it back, nobody would ever take Chiang's government seriously again." Kung nevertheless excelled at private finance and his family was the favorite subject of Chungking gossip of which it was said that "90 percent is untrue but ten percent is even worse than the gossip." The Kungs and Soongs and various brothers and nephews and nieces made up the palace clique under the matriarchal control of Mme. Kung who dominated her sister, Mme. Chiang, and reached through her to the Generalissimo. Mme. Chiang's influence on the Generalissimo had limitations, which she ascribed to her failure to bear him children.

Government resided in the Legislative, Judicial and Executive Yuans as a matter of form. The real power was exercised by the Kuomintang Party under the chairmanship of Chiang Kai-shek. Among its factions the strongest was the right-wing CC clique of the brothers Chen, two fossils of the Revolution who were nephews of Chiang Kai-shek's first patron, Chen Chi-mei and leaders of the group which founded the Blue Shirts, the Kuomintang's stormtroopers, in 1932. The younger brother, Chen Li-fu, who had been Chiang's personal secretary during the Northern Expedition of 1927, was now the Kuomintang Party boss. Party cells existed in every village district and army unit, with representatives appointed to a one-party National Congress which met at long intervals of three or four years. No elections to the Congress had been held since 1935 and none of the progressive groups had any vote or voice. Between sessions the Central Executive Committee (CEC) was the governing body of the country; its Standing Committee, which met every two weeks, made the decisions. Though sensitive to Party pressures, Chiang in practice gave orders to the Standing Committee.

His outlook was basically Confucian. The easy victory of 1927, confirmed by his success in maintaining himself at the top for 15 years, suggested that the mandate of heaven had passed to him. In recognition thereof, his manner, apart from periodic temper tantrums, was composed and enameled. He took for granted that the first requirement of all subordinates—including Stilwell as his Chief of Staff—was obedience. The disobedience of the Communists, their defiance of his authority, was what made them in his eyes more criminal than the Japanese. His other opponents, among the disgruntled intellectuals and provincial leaders, could not coalesce. Sun Fo, the son of Sun Yat-sen, enjoyed wide support and was one of the few who could speak bluntly to the Generalissimo, but like his father he had no power base. Li Tsung-jen, as potential leader of the southern coalition, remained a threat. The Kuomintang had never succeeded in really uniting the country. Aware that the past had left too many pockets of doubtful loyalty, Chiang could not trust all his armies. The opportunity for social change had passed him by. Dependent more than ever on the right wing since the loss of the modernist and business community of the coastal cities, he could not afford to antagonize them by reform measures. He governed for survival and ignored what he wanted to ignore. As chief of a system without an exit, he was, as Stilwell wrote, "in a hell of a fix."

The American public, blanketed under the active propaganda of China's friends, partisans and church groups, knew nothing of actual conditions. State Department officials like Maxwell Hamilton, chief of the Far East Division, and his predecessor Stanley Hornbeck, now shunted to the post of Political Adviser, remained fixed in the positions they had staked out. Modern China, wrote Hamilton in a policy statement of February 1942, represents "a mass movement of people led by a great leader. It is on this that the United States should build." Chiang Kai-shek's "determination, persistence and on the whole broad gauge outlook constitute perhaps the most important element in China as a fighting ally." At approximately the same time Ambassador Gauss reported, in reference to the concept of Chiang as a great leader directing the "energetic resistance" of China to Japan, that "looking the cold facts in the face one could only dismiss this as rot."

The President could see no alternative to support for the Generalissimo. Fearing a vacuum after the defeat of Japan and repeatedly advised that only Chiang could hold China together, he gave him support in the form of a blank check. He was continually warned by China's friends, who from sincere or self-interested motives wanted to get aid to China, that any slackening of support would lead to collapse of the Chungking Government. In a typical alarm of this kind, Dr. Donald Van Slyke of the Rockefeller Institute, president of the American Bureau for Medical Aid to China, informed the President that China's morale was "deteriorating rapidly," the "defeatist element was gaining face," and the "danger grows of [Chiang Kai-shek's] losing power and of a compromise between China and Japan." He enclosed a cable from "eight responsible Americans in West China" as the source of his information. Gauss in his reports did not exclude the possibility that some provincial generals like Lung Yun in Yunnan might come to terms with the Japanese, giving them a chance to move in, in which case Chiang's Government "might readily fall" or be forced to evacuate beyond reach of help to Shansi or Kansu. "Of course," Gauss added in a prediction which the future was to validate, "if anything happens he will gladly blame everything on the failure to receive American aid."

Temperamentally Roosevelt was predisposed against the quid pro quo management of Lend-Lease although the War Department, at Stilwell's urging, favored it. Roosevelt did not like haggling and thought it would be ungenerous to exact terms from a beleaguered ally. In August he received the War Department's recommendation that the Burma campaign be undertaken in the coming spring and that Lend-Lease be allocated on the basis of China's participation and on the introduction of army reforms as recommended by Stilwell. Meanwhile Currie on his return early in August had supported Stilwell's policies, but without the teeth. "I do not think we need to lay down any conditions or tie any strings to our support," he told the President. He also reported on the "personal" difficulties between Stilwell and the Generalissimo which he ascribed to Stilwell's unconcealed resentment of Chiang's interference in Burma and Chiang's resentment of Stilwell's refusal to obey his orders. In a bold sweep he suggested the replacement of Stilwell, Gauss and T. V. Soong (failing which he recommended as a precaution that Stilwell in the future receive a copy of all the President's communications to the Generalissimo).

Roosevelt seized on Currie's explanation as an easy or at least feasible solution for the nagging problems of China. "I cannot help feeling that the whole situation depends largely on the problem of personalities rather than on strategic plans or even on Sino-British relations or on the Indian situation," he wrote to Currie in a characteristic flight of optimism. He agreed to consider a number of changes, "until we get the right people." Stilwell's noticeable personality with its rasping edges was an obvious place to begin, but Roosevelt's feelers were rejected by Marshall and Stimson. They insisted that Stilwell was the necessary man to reopen Burma and obtain military action from the Chinese.

A limited campaign in Burma, in the north only, with the object of pushing a road through from Ledo in Assam to reconnect with the Burma Road was agreed on by the Allied planners in September. The full campaign that Stilwell had proposed with Rangoon as objective and with naval support—called ANAKIM in Allied planning—was put aside. In competition with North Africa and the Second Front and Russia's demands, the resources were considered not available. The British, who throughout the war were to spend enormous effort on planning ANAKIM and even more on avoiding it, undertook instead to launch a small operation to regain Akyab on the strip of Burma coast called the Arakan for the purpose of establishing a fighter base for a future campaign. They agreed to join the north Burma campaign, but without enthusiasm since they did not share the American sense of urgency about the need to funnel aid to China. In a "reappraisal" of the situation, the British took the view that China could go on for another year without further aid.

The United States, however, agreed to satisfy a modified version of the Generalissimo's Three Demands, but without American divisions. Roosevelt informed Chiang Kai-shek in October that beginning in 1943, 100 transport planes would be assigned to deliver 5,000 tons a month over the Hump and 265 combat planes would be assigned to China. No quid pro quo was required of him, although the President's message urged that military reorganization "would be of the greatest importance in obtaining our mutual objectives."

Before the final reply Roosevelt approached Marshall again with the suggestion "to recall General Stilwell leaving General Wheeler as acting chief." He used Currie as his messenger. "A little gnome-like man," as Marshall later recalled, came into his office, curled one leg under him and said the President wanted Stilwell relieved. "He does, does he?" said Marshall. Currie replied yes, he did.

"Is he sending you around to tell me?" asked Marshall. Currie agreed he was.

"How long were you in China?" asked Marshall.

"Three weeks, Sir," replied Currie, and, facing the bleak silence of the Chief of Staff, departed.

Roosevelt did not give up. "What is the situation with regard to Stilwell in China?" he wrote to Marshall directly. "Apparently the matter is so involved between him and the Generalissimo that I suppose Stilwell would be more effective in some other field." Marshall and Stimson persuaded him that it would be impossible to find anyone better than Stilwell as replacement. The person to carry out the reopening of Burma must be an American and a troop leader, Marshall wrote, rather than a negotiator or supply man "who would only serve to promote harmony in Chungking."

Marshall's phrase fixed on the theme that was to pursue Stilwell during his tenure in China and his reputation thereafter. "Harmony in Chungking" would have made all the problems less obtrusive. It could have been achieved by a more gracious and less exacting personality who did not insist on raising the problems that threatened the Generalissimo and on telling him truths he preferred not to hear and requiring performance in which he preferred not to engage. Stilwell himself was aware of the problem when, bogged down in delays and jockeyings with the Generalissimo, he wrote to his wife in August, "It's a hell of a way to fight a war from my point of view, and makes me feel like a complete slacker. Now if I were in addition a slicker, I might make some headway." A slicker might indeed have obtained harmony in Chungking, but harmony was not the purpose of Stilwell's mission.

13

"Peanut and I on a Raft"
AUGUST 1942–JANUARY 1943

T HE one place where Stilwell had control and was free to train Chinese soldiers for the return to Burma was at Ramgarh. Here he had the beginnings of the task force which he had begun to plan for even in the midst of defeat, and here he could put into operation the methods which he had always claimed would give the Chinese a combat efficiency equal to any. When the endless objections and disapprovals of the Government of India were finally overcome ("The bastards will sabotage the scheme yet"), the program at Ramgarh was officially inaugurated in August with about 9,000 survivors of the Burma campaign who had walked out to India as the initial group. A large proportion of them were in the hospital. The remnants of the 22nd Division, slowed by the vacillating orders of the Generalissimo, had failed to keep ahead of the monsoon and had straggled out of Burma in pitiful condition, ragged and half-starved, with ruined and rusty rifles, weak from malaria and dysentery and with flesh rotted by Naga sores. Caused by infected leech bites or leech heads left under the skin, the Naga sores were often fatal. The sick were treated at the Ramgarh hospital, staffed at the outset by Seagrave's unit, later supplemented by an American Station Hospital. Vaccinated against cholera, typhoid and smallpox, fed three meals a day (which produced an average weight gain in the first months of 21 pounds per man), outfitted with new uniforms, helmets, boots, packs, rifles, bayonets, trucks, artillery and all the lavish American equipment, the Chinese were physically quickly transformed.

Stilwell came down to India for three weeks in August and again in October when the airlift of the additional Chinese divisions at last got under way. Despite the promise to send troops in good physical condition, American medical officers at the China end rejected an average of 40 percent for underweight and disease over the next two years. Sometimes, for a particularly sorry group, the rate reached 89 percent in one month. More were rejected than flown over. Disapproving the wasteful habits of the West, the Chinese passed on the rejectees to the Y-force. For the airlift to India, the meager bodies were packed 35 to 40 in a cargo plane; some planes which had been used for airdrops lacked doors. Lo Cho-ying, full of enthusiasm, said, "Put 50 in a plane naked. It's only three hours!" This was done by the Chinese command on the theory that it would be foolish to waste uniforms if the men were to be given new ones anyway. The squads were flown from Kunming in nothing but a pair of shorts with a paper bag in case of airsickness as their only baggage. Several died of the cold. The Ramgarh staff asked that quilted cotton jackets be provided on the planes for the successive use of each load like coats on a ski-tow, but the Chinese authorities did not think this necessary. The arrivals deplaned chilled and airsick but after an hour of sitting in the Indian sun usually recovered quickly.

Stilwell specified an initial transportation of 400 a day and this figure was met in October and surpassed in November when 16 planeloads brought in 650 a day, causing the usual glut on the languid Assam-Bengal Railway. It found itself unable to move the troops down to Calcutta by rail at the rate the airlift could fly them over the Hump. By the end of December 32,000 were in training at Ramgarh. Stilwell's object was to create a force of two full-strength divisions plus three artillery regiments and other auxiliaries to be ready for combat by February 1943 when the campaign to regain Burma was to begin. He wanted also to keep replacements coming in and to train 1,500 Chinese instructors for the Thirty Division program in China. Altogether over the next two years a total of 53,000 were to pass through the Ramgarh schools.

Distinct from the British system of white officers in command of native troops, Stilwell as adviser to a sovereign nation planned a system of American liaison teams or single officers acting in advisory capacity alongside Chinese commanders at each level. Based on his experience in Burma, this was chiefly designed to ensure that a unit was where it said it was and would move into action or into a given position as ordered. His method was the intensive training of small units in accordance with his belief that if two platoons could be well trained individually, when put together they would know what to do. Films taken at Ramgarh show a scrawny figure in shorts, open-collared tunic and stiff-brimmed World War I hat moving along a row of prone Chinese soldiers, patiently lying down next to each to demonstrate or correct the sighting of each rifle. He worked personally among the soldiers with more than one purpose in mind. An American sergeant who was amazed to watch the General down in the dust at rifle practice only realized afterwards that what Stilwell was trying to do was not only to teach, but to set an example to Americans of how to teach.

Because of the language barrier and paucity of interpreters, training was largely by demonstration. The Chinese knack for imitation made it effective. "Thank God we don't speak Chinese and don't have enough interpreters," said General Sliney. "We demonstrate and they copy. They are the greatest mimics in the world and are learning very, very fast." Peasants from the fields who had never seen a machine mastered the use of the pack howitzer and machine gun in a week and learned with delight to operate field telephones and radios. Later, in combat, individuals were decorated, the first decorations Chinese enlisted men had ever received. "The limies are watching us with considerable interest," Stilwell wrote to Win. "It's something brand new to them to see colonels actually working."

Colonel McCabe, who had been chief of Operations at Fort Ord, served as commandant of the training center. Colonel Boatner, with the experience of a former Chinese-language officer and veteran of the 15th Infantry, became chief of staff of the task force, called *Chih Hui Pu*. The name, which meant literally Command Headquarters, was understood to stand for the Chinese Army in India. Colonel Arms, who had planned the training course at Ford Ord and had since organized training for the National Guard, was summoned from America to join the staff.

Chinese officers at Ramgarh were trained in tactics and combat techniques and the men in the handling of rifles, machine guns, mortars, rocketlaunchers, antitank guns and other equipment for specialized combat duties. After mastering the weapons they were given an eight-day course in jungle warfare. The six-week artillery course taught the handling of pack artillery and the use of howitzers and assault guns in jungle conditions. Line officers and noncoms were trained in field sanitation and medical care and colonels and generals of the Thirty Division program were flown to Ramgarh for a six-week staff and command course modeled on the wartime course at Leavenworth. Spirit, especially in the new artillery units, was strong. One of Stilwell's primary concerns was to increase the ratio of artillery to infantry from one company in nine to one in three. Spurred by the knowledge that they would now have firepower equal to that of the Japanese, the Chinese worked eagerly at the task of transforming infantrymen into artillerymen in four months.

Ramgarh was not a cozy paternalistic family; cultural clash was sharp and quarrels frequent, especially with the Chinese officers. They resented criticism by Americans who had never been under fire and insisted that, since they themselves had to give orders in the field, they could not allow their authority to be undermined in the course of training. The Americans in their turn believed that the Chinese officers, being imbued with the spirit of the defensive, would impede training for the attack, and so tended to bypass them. More disruptive was the American endeavor to bypass the private arrangements for squeeze involved in Chinese military organization by distributing pay individually to the men by public roll call instead of by lump sum to the commanding officer. This quarrel reached its peak in a prolonged dispute with General Lo over pay and the assignment of replacements. Lo had not expected to be number two in fact as well as name. "He was counting on the old by-pass game—I to be *ts'an mou chang* [Chief of Staff] again." Not to be caught twice in the same mistake, Stilwell had taken care this time to have his authority made explicit. In negotiations with the War Ministry he had insisted on authority to shoot officers up to the rank of major for disobedience of orders and to relieve officers above that rank. In the end, since General Lo refused to adapt to American interference with his administrative authority which was believed to be netting him 100,000 rupees a month at Ramgarh, he parted company with *Chih Hui Pu.*

Stilwell's strict orders against any American laying hands on a Chinese soldier caused considerable griping when it proved not reciprocal. In sudden eruptions Chinese soldiers more than once drew their guns. The Americans were also under orders not to interfere in discipline and were often sickened or enraged to see a Chinese soldier casually shot for using a hand grenade to catch fish, or another beaten with 125 strokes of a pole until the muscles were torn and the bone exposed as punishment for losing his blanket. At staff meetings Boatner was shocked when he handed over reports to the Chinese commanders of the number of soldiers who had died on the way to Ramgarh to see them tossed into the wastebasket while meticulous accounting of supply lists continued.

General Sun Li-jen, lean and handsome and slow of speech with a slight stutter, and General Liao Yao-hsiang, short, stocky, bespectacled and loquacious, remained in charge of their respective divisions, the 38th and 22nd. Liao turned out to be better than he had appeared in Burma although he lacked the drive and character of Sun who was stubborn and assured and would stand up to anyone, including Stilwell. Working and planning with them on his visits, inspecting motor school, drum corps, hospital and firing ranges, Stilwell was satisfied once more to be making soldiers.

Standing under the Chinese flag on August 23, and again on October 25 at a Sun Yat-sen memorial service, he addressed the troops in Chinese, impressing them immensely by talking in their language and telling stories from their own history. He flavored his speech with appropriate quotations of *Ch'eng-yu,* the classical proverbs, invoking for instance, when he spoke of loyalty to country, the example of Yüeh Fei, a Sung dynasty official proverbial for resistance to the invading Mongols, or citing the King of Wu who slept on boards and ate poor food to remind himself of humiliating defeat. He told the troops he was representing Chiang Kai-shek and they must fight well, otherwise he would lose face with the Generalissimo who had honored him by the appointment. He reminded them what they had to do for their country and promised that they need have no worry about weapons and equipment as he would personally guarantee them equipment as good as the Japanese.

"I'm too busy to mope," he wrote home and reported that he was feeling better and putting on some weight. "If I could get some new teeth and eyes and some hair dye, I wouldn't look a day over 70." Though a doctor in Calcutta diagnosed his eye trouble as a mild cataract in one eye, his sight was still sharp enough to notice details. He saw a movie in which Lewis Stone played an Army officer "with stomach sticking out. Why don't they catch such things?"

In New Delhi, where he went for conferences and "poisonous paper work," he was "oppressed by the magnificence and grandiose style" of Headquarters, both American and British. The gleam of brass hats in Delhi, it was said, lit the way for airplanes to land in a fog. Stilwell found himself bogged in all the administrative and personnel problems of the theater whose American forces he commanded. There were jealousies, resignations, "jaundice campaign ribbons, booze parties," participation in smuggling over the Hump, various peculations and other scandals which required the visit of an Inspector General from Washington to investigate. Bored by inactivity, the staff kept office hours from 9 A.M. till noon, griped about sacrificing their military careers and in many cases criticized Stilwell for pursuing a hopeless mission from what they could only see as personal ambition to create for himself a bigger command. Not everything was negative. Wheeler, chief of the American Service of Supply (SOS), "is a joy," and *CBI Roundup,* the theater newspaper, was functioning without inhibitions. Founded by Stilwell with "If you can prove it, print it" as his only instruction, and with Fred Eldridge as editor, *Roundup* was the first Army paper overseas and because of its freedom to criticize remained one of the liveliest.

"I have now arrived at the pinnacle of social success," Stilwell wrote home on August 30, "having been entertained at lunch by the Viceroy himself. I am all in a dither about it." The Viceroy was Lord Linlithgow, a six-foot-six Scot, austere and grand and perfectly housed in the majestic

Viceroy's Palace that was the architectural apotheosis of the British Empire. A huge complex of reddish sandstone, reminiscent of Egypt with Roman overtones, the Palace and Government Building stood together on a rise of ground above massive foundations approached by ramps. The Rajpath, an immense tree-lined avenue without buildings, like a naked Champs-Elysées, led up to it from the India Gate at the far end. Inside the Palace in the circular domed Durbar Hall two thrones stood under a towering canopy of crimson velvet. Reception rooms were of splendid proportions with 18-foot windows and glowing Oriental carpeting. Ceilings were painted with the pageantry of moghuls and rajahs, the Banquet Hall held a single table seating 108, the terraces overlooked vast formal gardens with topiary and fountains; the whole required 300 softly padding white-robed Indian servants to operate it. Like the monuments of the Pharaohs or the Sun King at Versailles, it belonged among those edifices raised by rulers to portray their permanence and grandeur, and it announced, with no room for doubt, that its builders considered themselves in India to stay.

Back in Chungking Stilwell brought photographs of Ramgarh to show Chiang Kai-shek, with happy effect. After weeks of stalling, the additional divisions for the airlift were approved all at once. In the photographs Chiang could actually see the training and the artillery and was obviously pleased. "Why shouldn't he be, the little jackass? We are doing our damnedest to help him and he makes his approval look like a tremendous concession." The result, Stilwell noted wryly, "after being blocked and double-crossed endlessly," was such a feeling of relief on being given the go-ahead signal, "that you are almost grateful to the very guy you are trying to help in spite of himself." He could not help but believe that Chiang, "unless he is terribly dumb, will want to go on with this kind of business."

On October 1, 1942, Chungking was girding to impress a very important American visitor in the person of Wendell Willkie, the most memorable defeated candidate for the Presidency since William Jennings Bryan. As advocate of a "one-world" philosophy of international relations, Willkie shared Roosevelt's view of foreign if not domestic policy and was traveling on a 49-day round-the-world tour as the special envoy of his successful rival. He was regarded by the Chinese, according to a statement by the Generalissimo, as the first American of "highest rank" to visit China since ex-President Ulysses S. Grant came in 1879. A more practical reason for Chinese interest in Willkie was the expectation that he might very well be the next President. A large, exuberant, expansive individual, he was still in the flush of the popularity and influence won by his campaign. The Chinese were prepared to spend a major effort upon him with the general object of strengthening American support for the Kuomintang Government and the immediate object of obtaining a greater investment of American air power. This had come to mean in Chiang's mind replacing Stilwell with Chennault, a problem in the judicious exercise of influence which was a Chinese specialty.

In the manipulation of foreigners every Chinese from amah and house-boy to the Generalissimo and Madame considered himself expert. In this matter Chinese confidence in themselves was supreme and their skills un-surpassed. They were adept, unrelenting, smooth and more often than not successful. Unlike the Japanese who had set out to use Western tech-niques to outdo the West, the Chinese never attempted to outdo the West because they already considered themselves superior. For all their experi-ence in the hundred years since the Opium Wars, they were unshaken in the conviction that they had to do with barbarians who *ipso facto* could be manipulated. "Let me see the British officials," said General Hsiung, chief of a Chinese military mission, to a colleague on arriving in London, "and I will turn them around my little finger."

Willkie's visit supremely illustrated the Chinese process of influencing American public opinion. "He's to be smothered," Stilwell wrote. There was to be an unbroken schedule of banquets, receptions, reviews, dinners, visits to schools, factories, girl scouts, arsenals. He was to be installed in a Chinese guest house as the guest of the Chinese Government rather than in the American Embassy, much to the annoyance and disapproval of Ambassador Gauss. The arrangement ensured that Willkie would see and hear only what his hosts wanted him to, and would be kept, as Stilwell wrote, "well insulated from pollution by Americans. The idea is to get him so exhausted and keep him so torpid with food and drink that his faculties will be dulled and he'll be stuffed with the right doctrines."

In a spasm of face-making for the occasion, the police of Chungking tore down paupers' shacks, herded the more wretched beggars beyond city limits and ordered the poorest and shabbiest shops to close during the visit. Streets were decked with banners and welcoming wall slogans; schoolchildren, waving and shouting, lined the eleven-mile route from the airport; and the populace was ordered to buy Chinese and American paper flags from the police. Willkie did not fail to recognize that what he saw was an organized demonstration but being an open-hearted generous man he was nevertheless moved by it as "an impressive show of the simple strength in people and emotions which is China's great resource." In this kind of large goodwill based on large generalities his progress continued.

Two Chinese escorts were closely attached to him throughout his visit —the glib American-educated Hollington Tong and General Chu Shao-liang, a trusted associate of the Generalissimo who was Commander-in-

Chief of the Eighth War Zone in the northwest. Though General Chu spoke no English he made up for it, according to Willkie, by "one of the most endearing personalities I have ever known"—which was doubtless why he was chosen. Willkie never ended a speech or conference or banquet "without seeing him smiling at me in the friendliest possible way," a smile that made him feel that China was a "warmhearted hospitable land filled with friends of America."

Willkie's impressions were notable for his capacity to accept what he was told or shown at face value. He was to pass them on to the American public in ten newspaper installments and a book called *One World* which was an instant bestseller on an unprecedented scale. Booksellers' orders were 200,000 in the first four days and sales reached one million copies in eight weeks. The Chinese could not have made a better investment.

In China a military review was staged for him on a wide parade ground bordered by foreign-style buildings. Attending dignitaries were richly dressed, guards and police were white-gloved, and the military units who marched past in perfect formation and modified German goose-step were superbly equipped helmeted squads bristling with weapons and followed by tanks, armored cars and cavalry with pennants. It was an exhibition army. The distinguished visitor also watched "exciting" maneuvers by thousands of officer cadets of the Chengtu Military Academy who swam a swift river holding rifles over their heads, crawled up a hill through the smoke of mortar fire and cut their way through barbed wire. He saw no recruits tied with ropes or soldiers sent to the front after three weeks' training or the skinny, diseased collection offered to fill the ranks at Ramgarh. He was able to report, "Military China is united; its leaders are trained and able generals; its armies are tough fighting organizations of men who know both what they are fighting for and how to fight for it." So high was motivation and morale that "Even the sons of high estate enlist as privates in the army," a statement doubtless owed to the creative imagination of Hollington Tong.

Stilwell sourly watched Willkie absorbing the propaganda that obscured the need for reform of the army. At a cocktail reception for Willkie given by the War Ministry at a Chinese military club with the Generalissimo present, General Ho Ying-chin proposed a visit to the "front," in the bend of the Yellow River near Sian, the area of Stilwell's road-building 20 years before. There were a number of these show fronts marking the edges of Japanese-occupied China to which visitors were customarily escorted. "Certainly Mr. Willkie must go," said General Stilwell aloud in a roomful of high-ranking Chinese officers. "He mustn't miss it. It's the biggest market in China. It's where the Japanese and Chinese meet to trade all the goods they need from each other." Stilwell was rarely impolite except on purpose and the remark was another way of saying his usual phrase when impatient with polite pretenses, "Aw, cut it out."

The visit to the front, which Willkie thought was his own idea, arranged only after overcoming the Generalissimo's "solicitude for my safety," duly took place. The party went from Sian to the Yellow River by train and handcar over the same route Stilwell had once walked with Feng Yu-hsiang's troops. The front was the river itself, 1,200 yards wide at this point, and Willkie was a little disappointed to find "less physical danger than we expected." However, it was satisfactory to "look down the muzzle of Japanese guns" through telescopes. His escort, Chiang Wego Wei-kuo, the Generalissimo's adopted son, demonstrated to Willkie's satisfaction that the front was more than a showplace. He came into the dining car of the train on the return with his arms full of Japanese cavalry swords as presents for the visitors, as well as bottles of excellent French wine. Both had been captured, he said, by raiding parties which crossed the river by night and returned with this and other booty, including "prisoners and military plans." Willkie was not shown any prisoners.

Resident correspondents were accustomed to such tours of "cold battle-fields" where they were regularly shown stacks of Japanese guns, helmets and other equipment. To test the theory that the material was transferred from one place to another for their benefit, one newspaperman claimed he had scratched his initials on a helmet and saw it again a few months later on another tour.

Except for the galloping inflation and its train of ruin which could not be ignored, Willkie treated any imperfections of Chiang Kai-shek's rule with the loyal reticence required by the Allied cause and the customary idealization of China. Evidence of totalitarian rule uncomfortably reminiscent of Fascism he delicately referred to as "centralized control" of Chinese life necessary to the "tutelary stage" of development. If teachers or editors or university presidents told him of corruption or oppression or trading with the enemy, he was always assured by the faithful Tong, and in turn assured his American audience, that the forces of good combating these evils had in the Generalissimo "a firm and steadfast friend." Chiang Kai-shek with his poise and dignity and appearance of a "scholar" in his Chinese gown, appeared to Willkie "even bigger than his legendary reputation," an impression warmly assisted by Madame who lavished her charms on the potential next President of the United States. Willkie succumbed with ripe ardor and conceived of a happy means of continuing the acquaintance. He suggested that she undertake a goodwill tour of the United States. This would accomplish the double purpose of promoting his quite genuine conviction that it was "vital for my fellow-countrymen to understand the problem of Asia." With "brains, persuasiveness and moral force

... with wit and charm, a generous and understanding heart, a gracious and a beautiful manner and appearance, and a burning conviction ... Madame would be the perfect ambassador ... we would listen to her as to no one else"—a prediction soon to prove correct. Willkie was so enthused by his idea that he kept telling Madame during his last interview that she must come on the plane with him "tomorrow" and that he would see to it that Roosevelt would give her all the planes she wanted.

The Generalissimo understood little if any English. To him, according to John Carter Vincent of the Embassy, who had long served in China and was present at these interviews, the hearty, broad-chested, tousled Willkie was the kind of foreigner who smelled like raw beef to a Chinese and caused Chiang to order the windows opened after the visitor had left "to let the smell of the foreigner out."

Though Stilwell hated the business of trying to influence anyone, he felt the necessity because of a discouraging report from Washington brought by Davies who had just returned. "This theater kaput. No help coming ... Currie appears to be trying to cut my throat. Not much hope for CBI. 'Major strategic effort is elsewhere.' Chief of Staff says no ground troops." At the same time he was alerted that "CKS is planning skullduggery and double-crossing on command." He tried to prime Willkie on basic facts before he saw the Generalissimo, but Willkie was tired out and sleepy and did not appear to take in what was being said. Stilwell talked with him again the next day. "Nothin'. He didn't ask a question. Completely sold on CKS and Mme. Advised me to put it on with a trowel. To hell with that stuff." Again the day after he recorded that Willkie was "either worn out or very indifferent to me. Practically nothing to say or ask about. Almost pointed."

By contrast, responding to the desire of Chiang and Madame, Willkie was very receptive to Chennault who saw an opportunity to put over his program for the defeat of Japan by a China-based air force. Chennault had come to the conclusion, in concert with the Chiangs, that the necessary support for this could only be obtained through himself as commander in the theater in place of Stilwell. So long as Stilwell was in control he would insist that a major share of the supply effort over the Hump be channeled to the Chinese infantry for laborious ground campaigns for which Chiang had no taste and Chennault had contempt. Their interests coincided. The Generalissimo wanted to satisfy the active belligerency which was required of him as an Allied power by air action to which his contribution would be the airfields. Chennault, with the bitter intensity of a man who has fallen out with the establishment, wanted to prove his theories of air fighting and gain immortal vindication by winning the war alone with his Flying Tigers. Each for his own reasons wanted belligerency by American air power. For the future of China a Chinese air force would have had more validity than an American one but, as Chennault had already discovered, the spirit for this was lacking.

The reputation of his air fighters by now was great. He himself was led to overestimate what they could do because he believed their performance had prevented the Japanese from crossing the Salween when they broke into Yunnan from Burma in May. Trained in swift and supple tactics, his fighter pilots had established superiority over the Japanese in repeated aerial combat which their leader equated with stopping troops on the ground. Elsewhere they had deterred the Japanese terror-bombing of cities in east China, and by reputation, plus convincing rows of dummy planes on the ground, saved Chungking from a fourth season of merciless raids. Their prowess spread over the grapevines of China with the result that Chennault was the American most widely known and admired and a hero to the Chinese.

It was natural that air power should appear as the winning weapon. Few stopped to consider that an airplane was as dependent on a landing field as a fish on water. Once on an inspection tour Stilwell growled to Colonel Henry Byroade, an Engineer officer, "What the hell are you building this airfield for?"

"Well, Chennault says he needs it."

"How's he going to defend it?"

This was the essence of the problem. Chennault and his disciples, with their eyes fixed on the "optimums," assumed that defense would be taken care of by the Chinese armies, of which they knew little. The "fly boys" tended by the nature of their calling to forget the ground and rely on the assumption of Colonel Scott, the pilot who had come to rescue Stilwell in Burma, that "God Is My Co-Pilot." The aviator's view of China was expressed by Scott when he wrote that "Sian is to the north of Kunming," which was information about as helpful as saying that Boston is to the north of Mexico City.

With his stubborn drudgery on the ground, Stilwell appeared to Chennault and the passionate devotees he inspired as an antediluvian, foot-slogging diehard who was obstructing victory by air power. Whatever means could be used to remove him, including political influence, wire-pulling and the arts of publicity, were justified. Willkie offered a means of direct access to the President.

Chennault could not officially approach Willkie without Stilwell's permission which, rather to his surprise since he was conscious of no friendly intention, he received. Stilwell told him he was free to tell Willkie anything he chose and even escorted Willkie to Pai Shih Yi, the airfield outside Chungking where Chennault was found standing picturesquely against a line of his P-40 fighters with their snouts painted to resemble sharks. Stilwell left the two men to talk in privacy in Chennault's office for two hours. Willkie came away with a letter dated October 8, 1942, for transmittal to the President, which is one of the extraordinary documents of the war.

In this letter Chennault claimed that with only 105 modern fighters and 30 medium and 12 heavy bombers, maintained at that level by replacements, he could "accomplish the downfall of Japan . . . probably within six months, within one year at the outside."* This, he informed the President, was his "professional opinion" as a professional air fighter. The military task was "a simple one" with only one catch. Chennault did not sidle up to his point but presented it boldly: he would require "full authority as the American military commander in China." Given that, he was prepared to offer Roosevelt more than mere military victory. Operating on the statesman's level, he was "confident . . . that I can not only bring about the downfall of Japan but I can make the Chinese lasting friends of the United States" and "I can create such goodwill that China will be a great and friendly trade market for generations." Refraining, perhaps wisely, from explaining the mechanics of this promise, Chennault returned to the subject of his military strategy. It was based on the premise that "Japan can be defeated in China" and that he could destroy the Japanese Air Force which had only a limited production of aircraft by forcing it to "fight me in a position of my own selection." While the Japanese Air Force was thus occupied, the American offensive in the Southwest Pacific could be pushed forward "at will," and meanwhile "I will guarantee to destroy the principal industrial centers of Japan."

To enable him to carry out this program the air transport line from India over the Hump would have to be built up and defended, but not, he added with obvious reference to Stilwell, according to present methods which "show a complete lack of conception of the true use of air power or even of basic military strategy." Rather, given "full authority," Chennault said he would defend the Hump as Scipio Africanus had defended Rome by striking at Carthage (that is, the Japanese home islands), or as Grant had defeated the South by cutting Lee off from his line of communications. The entire program was "simple," a word repeated four times in the letter, as was the claim that "I have no doubts of my success," and that if given real authority, "I can cause the collapse of Japan." The prerequisite was that

* The downfall of Japan, which Chennault was prepared to accomplish in six months with one air force of 147 combat aircraft, was to require three more years of war and the efforts, in air power alone, not counting combat on land and sea, of nine Army air forces operating from India, China, the Pacific and Alaska, a Naval air force which amounted in 1945 to 90 carriers and 14,847 combat aircraft, and ultimately two atom bombs. In early August 1945, a force of 801 B-29s attacked Japan in a single operation.

"I be given complete freedom of fighting action" and freedom to deal directly with the Generalissimo. The only reference to ground action in the document was to the effect that his program would "enable the Chinese ground forces to operate successfully."

The letter was the self-annunciation of a military messiah. As such it explains the intensity of Chennault's desire for the top command without which his messiahship could not function. It explains too why his resentment of Stilwell as the man in his way was to grow into venomous hatred. Militarily Chennault's proposals had a certain "simple" logic which might have been operational if nothing else had been happening in the war. Given the various realities which he overlooked, his views, as Marshall said afterwards, were "just nonsense; not bad strategy, just nonsense." To Roosevelt, however, this was not so clear. Chennault's letter, which might otherwise have been dismissed as megalomania, carried the authority of a brilliant fighter of proven performance. His feeling for the upright pronoun echoed the self-assurance of General MacArthur, which in that time of gloom and confusion was almost welcome. Chennault merited attention not because the President believed he could bring about "the downfall of Japan" but because if he could accomplish even a portion of what he promised, it would be worth giving him the means.

Following the despatch of Chennault's letter, the Generalissimo mobilized further pressure for Stilwell's recall through his American confidant, Colonel McHugh, the Naval Attaché. A former language officer and author of a Chinese-language textbook, McHugh in the 1930s had been a close friend and golfing companion of the Generalissimo's then-adviser, W. H. Donald, and in those days used to lunch three or four times a week at the Chiangs'. As an intimate of the palace circle, he served as Ambassador Johnson's eyes and ears, much to the irritation of his fellow Attaché at that time, Colonel Stilwell, who saw McHugh always bustling with private knowledge and whispering to the Ambassador.

Chiang Kai-shek and Madame now summoned McHugh to lunch and emphasized the benefits to the Allied cause of replacing Stilwell with Chennault. McHugh heartily endorsed the suggestion in a report to Secretary Knox in which he stated that Stilwell's insistence on the recapture of Burma was a personal ambition resulting from his defeat and represented a dissipation of strength preventing the effective employment of air power in accordance with Chennault's program. The Generalissimo would be encouraged and "the war in this theater would be materially aided by the removal of both Generals Stilwell and Bissell and their huge staffs," especially if "the baton were passed to Chennault." The Generalissimo wanted Chennault in full control. Neither Bissell nor Brereton nor any of Stilwell's air staff understood the basic principles of air strategy and Stilwell himself "does not even visualize the damage that could be done to Japan" by air attack.

Secretary Knox passed the report on to Secretary Stimson who showed it to Marshall who was infuriated, the more so when he learned that McHugh had repeated his thesis to Wavell in Delhi. Marshall believed this intervention caused "irreparable harm" to the American war effort in CBI and angrily required of the Navy that McHugh, who was then on his way home, should not be allowed to serve again in China. Meantime a copy of the document reached the President who read it, according to report, "with much interest."

Already prepared to let Stilwell go, Roosevelt was receptive to the pressures on behalf of Chennault and to the idea of concentrating on air power. But he faced the opposition of the Secretary of War and the Chief of Staff who considered the reopening of Burma essential, not in opposition to air power but in support of it. A dependable supply route was necessary to meet the needs of both ground and air forces operating in China. Stilwell himself mistakenly believed, as he wrote to Stimson at this time, that the ATC "will never be able to do more than supply very small quantities of important materials." Less pessimistic, the War Department made the essential point, in commenting on Chennault's plan and McHugh's report, that even if the ATC could be built up to lift the necessary supplies, both the route and its terminal in Assam remained vulnerable to attack as long as the Japanese occupied north Burma. To save the air freight route it was necessary to move forces into Burma. To deliver combat materials to the Chinese ground forces a land route to supplement the air route was essential. These purposes could be attained, the Operations Division stated, "only by a fight to regain Burma."

Uninterested in logistics or in the ground foundations of air power, Chiang Kai-shek never accepted this proposition. No more did Chennault and his many partisans.

At the War Department Chennault's bid for the top command had no chance of being considered seriously. He was regarded as a maverick by the military establishment and had made matters worse by committing the unpardonable sin of going "outside channels" in appealing directly to the President and in continuing to mobilize the lobbying of his apostles. But the dynamics of a messiah complex do not admit of the impossible, and Chennault, fanatically supported by his public relations aide, Joseph Alsop, believed the command should and could be his. Assisted by the ceaseless efforts of Chiang and Madame who took for granted that anything was possible by political influence, and of Harry Hopkins who listened to Alsop, his cause was pressed with growing effect.

Marshall and Stimson separately and explicitly reaffirmed their support of Stilwell in interviews with T. V. Soong, who was leaving on October 10 to return to Chungking. They made it plain that the support had a purpose —the expectation of military action. As Stimson put it, the problem of supplying China depended on reopening ground communication, and that depended on military action, and that depended, since the British and Chinese admittedly did not get on well together, on the American representative being a "fighting military leader," not just a smooth and diplomatic person. He asked Soong to tell Chiang Kai-shek that "pepper was required more than molasses."

Privately Marshall informed Stilwell of the efforts through Currie and McHugh to have him recalled, assured him of support and advised him to "develop more of patience and tolerance than is ordinarily expected of a man, and much more than is your constituent portion."

In Chungking winter weather had set in, bringing rain, fog, mud and slime, but at least better than the terrible muggy heat of the last few months. Ho Ying-chin was in one of his cooperative phases. Prodded by Stilwell's insistence that China must show action on the Thirty Division program to justify continuance of Lend-Lease aid, he offered to "settle everything." "My God, can it be possible?" Stilwell asked himself. Each recurrent promise encouraged him to believe he was making headway.

To prepare the ground in Burma the Office of Strategic Services (OSS) despatched a mission headed by a former Treasury agent, Colonel Carl F. Eifler, with the principal object of denying use of the Myitkyina airfield to the Japanese. It was to organize sabotage of railroad tracks, bridges, rolling stock and river tankers in order to reduce shipments of fuel to the air base. Stilwell's parting instruction was, "Eifler, I don't want to see you again until I hear a boom from Burma!"

Given an assistant of ability and initiative, he was prompt to delegate authority. "He never told me what to do," recalled General Wheeler who handled the vast logistic problems for the theater; "he just told me what he wanted." While malcontents from time to time wanted to transfer to a theater of greater opportunity, the "old reliables" remained: Bill Bergin the Adjutant and "mainstay" of his headquarters staff, Carl Arnold, the senior aide in place of Dorn, who was now named Artillery officer; Powell, the Operations officer; Williams, the medical officer; Merrill; and Paul Jones. Stilwell had sent for his son, Joe Jr., then a lieutenant colonel, who arrived in November to serve as G-2, as well as his son-in-law, Colonel Ernest Easterbrook, who came with Colonel Arms to join the Ramgarh staff. He brought Jones up from Delhi because he liked to have an old friend around with whom he could talk about the family, and Jones was in any case invaluable. "Paul makes good wherever you put him—running a railroad, warehousing supplies, driving coolies or repairing trucks. I wish I had a hundred like him." For those "who ran out on us," Stilwell designed with the help of Pinky Dorn an Order of the Rat to be hung from a Double Cross. "Pinky is going strong—mad at lots of people. . . . He keeps up a healthy hate for all hypocrites and stuffed shirts."

On October 14 after receiving the American reply to the Three Demands, Chiang Kai-shek undertook to engage in the offensive in Burma. He presented Stilwell with a Chinese plan of campaign (in fact Stilwell's own plan) which again insisted, as a prerequisite for the participation of 15 to 20 Chinese divisions, on the British and Americans sending enough naval and carrier units to establish sea and air superiority in the Bay of Bengal and on an amphibious landing at Rangoon. The problem now was to commit the British. Stilwell left for India on that errand on October 15. To bring the two unwilling allies to the point of action he employed what he called his "sleeve-jerking" technique. "Hell, I'm nothing but an errand boy," he explained. "I run up to Chungking and jerk the Gimo's sleeve. I tell him he better get ready to move down the Salween because the British are planning to move into Burma from the south . . . and the Chinese are going to lose a lot of face if the British do it alone. Then I fly down to India and jerk Archie's sleeve" and tell him, "The Gimo is going to move down the Salween and you better get going too. You Limeys are going to have a hell of a time with the white man's burden if the Chinese have nerve enough to fight and you haven't."

The British were already making difficulties about the increase of Chinese troops at Ramgarh. Although Wavell had approved the increase, Lord Linlithgow, the Viceroy, referred the matter to London. Stilwell's quills instantly went up. "So they are determined to bitch it. Sent George a hot radio asking for help." If the British stopped the entry of Chinese, the insult to Chiang might cause him to "pull out of the whole show." The British motive, Stilwell recognized, was "long-range policy: fear of Chinese-Indian cooperation." Long-range policy—with reference to the Empire in the case of the British and with reference to domestic survival in the case of the Chinese—in fact governed the conduct of the war by both allies. Their concern was not simply how to win but how to emerge from the war with existing interests enhanced or at least preserved. The United States had not yet adopted the Clausewitz concept of war as a continuation of policy. War was still considered an aberration, something to be finished off as quickly as possible so that society could go about its regular business.

In Delhi Wavell raised all sorts of difficulties to make it plain that the incoming two divisions for Ramgarh were not welcome: the railroads were congested, 200 troops a day would have to be the upper limit, there was a shortage of trucks and animal transport, it was a diversion of resources from the Indian Army. "They don't want Chinese troops participating in the retaking of Burma. That's all." Wavell wanted to know how many Chinese troops were still to come and what for. "WHAT FOR? My God! I told them to help our allies retake Burma."

The British fear was not without basis. Some months later, in July 1943, the Chinese Ministry of Information published a map which revived ancient claims to include all north Burma as Chinese territory.

On the third day of talks with Wavell Stilwell found a remarkable change. "They will give us a sector at Ledo. They will supply us. . . . Everything is lovely again, so obviously George has turned on the heat." Wavell agreed in general to the ANAKIM plan for retaking all of Burma including Rangoon "as a basis for planning." The slot assigned to Stilwell for the advance of the Chinese forces from Ramgarh was the Hukawng valley of north Burma, which the British were confident he would never get through. Myitkyina and its airfield and a junction with the Yunnan force was the objective. A joint planning staff was set up with Merrill acting as Stilwell's representative. To move the Chinese from Ramgarh to Ledo and from there into north Burma and sustain them in the field would require, it was calculated, 800 trucks and 200 tons of supplies a day delivered over a 350-mile line of communications. The British offered 500 trucks plus animal transport for pack artillery and suggested, with some foresight, that air supply should be considered. A million Indian laborers were at that time engaged in construction of airfields. It was further agreed that the Americans would assume responsibility for building a road from Ledo through the Hukawng valley to supply the offensive as it advanced and eventually to link up with the Burma Road.

The Ledo Road was yet another project of the American "Support China" policy which was unwanted and disliked by the British. They would have preferred to maintain the roadlessness of the frontier in the interests of the shipping monopoly, and even more because they wanted no access to India for the Chinese. They agreed to the road on paper because of Washington's insistence and because open refusal would have antagonized the Chinese more than ever, but they never ceased to oppose and obstruct it behind the scenes. Although British engineers had built a road through the Tamu Pass in country almost as difficult, they claimed the Ledo trace was impossible; it could not be done, it was a waste of effort, a drain on available resources. The reason they agreed to the Rangoon operation was in the hope of avoiding a completed road, but since what they really intended was to wait until they could go to Singapore, not Rangoon, this commitment was not very firm.

"It is no fun bucking two nationalities to get at the Japs," Stilwell wrote home, but the prospects now seemed to him improved. He found "some good eggs" among the Limeys and he dined again with Lord Linlithgow who pumped him about probable Chinese action after the war and earned the comment, "He has done some thinking on his own." Eldridge, the *Roundup* editor, wrote to the Stilwell family that Uncle Joe was still "hopping all over the place like a cricket . . . sticking his nose into everything" and violating all uniform regulations. The last to adopt the wearing of shorts, "he now wears them to *dinner*" although they were supposed to be barred after sundown. The old campaign hat, which proved airy and practical in the tropics, was held on by a shoelace instead of a leather strap.

The Generalissimo in a new turn-about was now all willingness and co-operation. At a conference on November 3 he agreed to put 15 divisions on the Yunnan side, to put his available artillery with them and to be ready by February 15. When Stilwell said 15 would be plenty if they were good troops, properly led, Chiang quickly agreed, at Madame's suggestion, to let him pick the divisions and name the commanders. As Stilwell recognized when he thought it over, this would have left him no excuse in the event of failure—had the offer been carried out, which it never was. Chiang agreed that Stilwell was to command the Ramgarh force and could fire Lo at any time and reiterated his insistence on naval and air domination "or he wouldn't move."

"Something has happened. If they mean what they said, it's grand. The biggest step forward we have taken." The unexpected agent of change was T. V. Soong, who had arrived in Chungking and was present at the conference. His own position depended on how much Lend-Lease he could produce. After his talks with Stimson and Marshall he had concluded that he could do better working with Stilwell than against him. He arrived with a gift of a watch and a cigaret lighter for Stilwell and had obviously persuaded the Generalissimo that he could get more matériel from the United States by agreeing to military action than by resisting it. "Teevy" now became an active ally and intermediary with the Generalissimo, replacing Madame, who was shortly to leave for the United States. As measured by the absence of an uncomplimentary nickname, Stilwell's appreciation of his help was genuine. Conferences with the War Ministry began to produce results. "Well this begins to look like something. Actually accepting an offensive operation. Actually assigning troops, reducing number of divisions, filling to strength, adding weapons, and attaching artillery. . . . The word has passed that I cut ice here now; it is obvious in their treatment of me."

At Stilwell's insistence Teevy even obtained the promised removal of Yu

Fei-p'eng, supply chief of the first Burma campaign, and of Tu Li-ming, former commander of the Fifth Army, from any connection with the Y-force—or so it appeared at the time. But in the case of Tu Li-ming, the inner obligations of Chinese relationships were stronger than promises, and each time Stilwell thought he was rid of him, Tu reappeared in another capacity.

Supply and transport for the reorganized 30 divisions from which the Y-force would be drawn were planned in discussions between the Operations staff of the Chinese War Ministry and General Wheeler who came up from Delhi. Depots and traffic control, medical, signal and engineer service, and equipment from mosquito nets to howitzers filled the agenda. The exact requirements in personnel and matériel needed to bring a reorganized Chinese regiment up to strength, and the percentage of the Lend-Lease contribution in each category had been worked out in detail by the American staff working with the Chinese Operations Division over the past months. For the initial operations of the Y-force it was calculated that 4,300 tons would need to be brought over the Hump in the three months before February 15. Since this cut into the cargo space for fuel for Chennault, he protested vigorously. Stilwell regarded him at this stage more or less tolerantly as an ill-disciplined prima donna rather than as a major rival. "Chennault with his squawk" he noted on the occasion of an earlier protest. "He's a pain in the neck. Still sore at Bissell. Told him to shut up and take orders." That was not going to suffice. The requirements of the Y-force, and Stilwell's calculation of a continuing need of 3,500 tons a month for the Chinese ground forces, were soon to bring the issue to a head.

He already had in mind a retraining program for a second 30 divisions for the coming year, and ultimately a third 30, toward his goal of a reorganized Chinese Army of 100 full-strength divisions. He continued to plan on a campaign for Hankow to follow the retaking of Burma, and after Hankow an attack on Hsuchow, scene of his eventful mission in 1927, from where an air offensive could be mounted against Japan. Far from ignoring air power, he urged in a memo to Soong that "A large increase of aviation should be secured to support the operation, and at once capitalize on it by starting an intensive and continuous bombing of Japan."

Support for the Burma campaign was growing among the Chinese military. They felt, according to Teevy, that Stilwell was the only one who had any faith in the Chinese Army. At the National Military Council with the big table full, Stilwell was asked serious and practical questions: "We actually did business." Ordnance was asking for orders, divisions were being consolidated, artillery being made available, SOS taking advice. Yü Ta-wei, the chief of Ordnance, was "with us 100 percent." Li Tsung-jen was "most complimentary and friendly . . . all these birds are now sold on getting Burma back." On November 19 he wrote, "We're rolling," adding a knock on wood, "If we can keep a fire lit under Wavell. . . ."

Within two days the fire flickered. "Ominous stuff from India. Limeys thinking on limited lines. Their objective is a joke—Arakan Hills, Chin Hills, Kalewa." Their Admiral, Sir James Somerville, and the RAF were hedging. "On the whole, they want to dig in in north Burma and wait till next fall before going after it seriously." This renewed hesitancy reflected the uncertain progress in North Africa where Allied forces had landed on November 8 and jerked through a series of snafus, of which the only sure outcome was that the campaign would be prolonged and would preclude a major operation in CBI until late in 1943. In the Pacific two American carriers had been sunk in the struggle to hold Guadalcanal, leaving the Pacific Fleet down to its last carrier. In the Atlantic, shipping losses, especially on the Murmansk run, were heavy, with as many as 13 out of 40 ships sunk in one convoy. When every front called for strength, CBI, where strategy and aims were most at odds, was not a place where the Allies could agree to divert resources.

The condition was made plain to Stilwell by a message from Marshall, appropriately received on Thanksgiving Day. Stilwell summarized, "For our 'war,' we are graciously allotted, 1) the Lend-Lease stuff we already have, 2) the personnel for training, 3) some engineer equipment, how much not known, 4) the 'increasing effectiveness of the ferry line.' My God. So that's the support we get to put on a campaign. I wonder what they gave them in Africa. Am I to comfort the Chinese with this prospect?" To his wife that night he wrote, "Peanut and I are on a raft, with one sandwich between us, and the rescue ship is heading away from the scene."

In a wrathful reply to the War Department, intended for if not addressed to Marshall, he said he wanted no more expressions of support if this was what they came to in practice. "I read your profane message," Marshall acknowledged by letter, "and I sympathize with you in your reaction."

On December 7, the first anniversary of Pearl Harbor, Wavell suggested "eliminating" the north Burma offensive. This was the campaign's quietus although it took a month to die. Wavell's move came just as Stilwell received word from Marshall that it had been decided to increase American support for the offensive on the basis that the reopened land route through Burma would permit greater air power to operate from China. Stilwell's requirements were to be given a priority immediately after Eisenhower's in North Africa, including, as evidence of serious intent, 6,000 American service troops for road-building and other tasks.

Stilwell hurried to India. British Headquarters was "extremely pessimistic and obstructionist." Wavell mumbled every kind of obstacle: "Everything is *very* difficult. . . . Can't supply the boys during the monsoon. Japs have the road net on interior lines. . . . Very skeptical about Chinese action of the Y-force. Wants to wait till November, 1943, before doing anything serious." For the present Wavell had cut his original seven-division plan down to three and could promise nothing more than to take Akyab and form a line on the Chindwin.

This time pressure by Washington on London had no effect. "They will by one means or another do everything possible to block any Chinese forces from operating in Burma," advised Colonel Roberts, Stilwell's former G-2 who was now at the War Department. The British maintained they lacked the naval resources to control the Bay of Bengal and support a landing at Rangoon. Since this was Chiang's condition of action, failure to fulfill it was bound to make him withdraw. Stilwell on his return could feel a slow chill begin to numb the preparations in Chungking. Ho Ying-chin returned to the tactics of deliberately delaying and then pleading lack of time as an excuse. In the course of discussions Stilwell received a long letter from him "telling me some boxes had been broken and also *a bottle of iodine*! Explained the procedure he would like us to follow in such cases." Here was a man, Stilwell raged, who combined the offices of Stimson and Marshall and "gets eloquent because a bottle of iodine is spilled in India." It was the same order of triviality as Chiang's call for watermelons in the midst of debacle in Burma. At the peak of his exasperation Stilwell concluded, "There must be tremendous cohesion in the Chinese people for them to survive the terrible neglect and maladministration of their so-called leaders." It was this knowledge that kept him trying until the end of his mission.

On December 28 Chiang Kai-shek notified Roosevelt that his original condition of sea and air superiority in the Bay of Bengal was not being met. Roosevelt, stressing the need to reopen the land supply line, urged him not to make a negative decision until he, the President, could shortly consult Churchill.* Marshall in anxiety radioed Stilwell that "means must be found" to enable the attack to jump off, but he had none to offer. Stilwell rained memoranda on T. V. Soong, mustering every argument of China's self-interest, future strategy, and the possible effect of cancellation on further aid. Failing Chinese action, he tried to suggest, his Government would be bound to ask, "Under the existing conditions in China, with the present personnel, organization and policy, is it worthwhile for the U.S. to put further effort and resources into the China theater?" The weakness of Stilwell's position was that he had no authority to presume a negative answer.

* At the forthcoming conference at Casablanca scheduled for January 14-23.

As Chinese laborers hauled a primitive stone roller to level a runway for planes such as the American bomber flying overhead (174), the Army Air Force dropped supplies to American and Chinese troops in the Burmese jungles (175) and transported Chinese troops over the Hump to India (176).

174

175

176

A C-46 carrying four tons of cargo flies over the Hump to deliver supplies to the Chinese (177).

Stilwell, in conference with Chinese generals during the action at Taunggyi (178), received the DS for heroism there. He waited with Ambassador Gauss to greet Wendell Willkie at his Chungking stopover (179), where Willkie was given royal treatment by Chiang and Madame (180).

On January 8 the Generalissimo formally declined to undertake the offensive. He did not need to wait until Roosevelt consulted Churchill. It was evident enough that they were not going to fulfill his condition and he was determined not to be pushed into fighting for Burma, even in China's interest, unless the Allies were fully committed to the campaign. "If the navy is unable to control the Burma seas," he informed Roosevelt, the campaign had better be postponed until autumn. Another failure in Burma would be a disaster for China and "under the circumstances, the most cautious course appears the only one open to me." He proposed instead what he had wanted all along—emphasis on American air power according to Chennault's thesis, almost in Chennault's words, citing "the remarkable potentialities of an air offensive," and the promise of a return "out of all proportion to the investment."

Stilwell put the date down as Black Friday. He was disgusted but not inclined to give up. There had been so many delays and frustrations already that he doubted if the target date could have been met. He recognized that Chiang Kai-shek had lined himself up behind Chennault but he evidently felt that with the War Department's backing, confirmed by a warm letter from Stimson, his own position was stronger; and that with the heartening alliance of T. V. Soong and encouragement inside the Chinese military establishment, even the Peanut was not beyond all control. He supposed the Chinese would have to buy back American favor in order to keep up the flow of supplies and that he could use this situation to further his program for army reform and for the 30 divisions. He thought an ultimatum to Chiang Kai-shek might still be possible and drafted one "to be sent from Washington if George agrees"—without reference to the Presidency. He continued exerting pressure to build up the X-force (at Ramgarh) and the Y-force. Tseng Shih-kwei came in with "The old story: 'Stick it out for the sake of the 400,000,000.'"

On January 16 in a surprise ceremony Stilwell received the DSC for heroism under fire during the action at Taunggyi in the previous April. Met by Dorn at the entrance to his headquarters, he found the staff lined up in the courtyard in an attitude of awful solemnity. General Bergin stepped forward to shake his hand and say, "Stand about there, Sir, if you please."

"What is this, an execution?" the victim muttered.

Bergin read the citation describing how his "presence and personal example in the front lines of a Chinese division" had inspired the unit to the renewed effort which resulted in the capture of Taunggyi, and citing other occasions at the front. "Who brought up all this bunk?" Stilwell whispered, fidgeting. Joe Jr. stepped forward, hissed "Stand still," and pinned the medal. Brooks Atkinson of *The New York Times* and Theodore White of

Time reported the ceremony in the tone of dry affection accorded by the press to Stilwell, and the *Times* added an editorial on "Decorating Uncle Joe." The recipient was unimpressed. "The whole thing is bunk, pumped up out of a very minor incident and entirely undeserved," he wrote to Win. "It is embarrassing but luckily time moves on and such things are forgotten."

181

182

When Stilwell received the DSC in a surprise ceremony on January 16, 1943, the citation was read by General Bergin in front of his staff (181). His son Joe Jr. pinned on the medal (182).

14

The President's Policy

JANUARY–MAY 1943

AMONG the gifts sent to Mme. Chiang in care of the White House when she came to the United States in November 1942 was a letter from Mrs. Cathleen Quinn of East Orange, New Jersey, enclosing a $3 money order and a clipping of the news picture of 1937 showing the crying baby sitting on the railroad tracks in the aftermath of air attack on Shanghai. The writer asked the President to present the money order to Mme. Chiang; "It is from my three daughters and it is for the little guy on the railroad tracks somewhere in China."

In the public appearances during her lengthy visit, which lasted until May 1943, Madame aroused a greater outpouring of admiration and welcome than anyone since Lindbergh flew the Atlantic. As Willkie had predicted, Americans listened to her "as to no one else." When she addressed Congress on February 18 she enraptured her audience. "Goddam it," said a Congressman, "I never saw anything like it. Mme. Chiang had me on the verge of bursting into tears." Dressed in black in the seductive Chinese *chongsam,* small, slender and calmly assured, speaking perfect English in her lovely voice and exquisite diction, she made Congress feel itself "in the presence of one of the world's great personalities." Members were "captivated . . . amazed . . . dizzied" by her "grace, charm and intelligence," according to a dazzled or well-instructed reporter for *Life.* The burden of her speech, after a four-minute standing ovation, was that the defeat of Japan was more important than that of Germany and that the United

States should enable her countrymen to fight the war in China rather than spend so much effort in the Pacific. The applause reached its height when she said that after five and a half years of resistance the Chinese were convinced that it was better "not to accept failure ignominiously but to risk it gloriously." That Chiang Kai-shek had just opted not to risk it gloriously in Burma was, of course, not public knowledge.

Editorial comment on the occasion stressed the friendship between two great peoples and was glad of the fact that "in the difficult present and perhaps even more difficult future" this relationship could be counted upon. Lord Halifax, the British Ambassador, reported to London in some anxiety that there was a risk of Congress being swept on a wave of public emotion into making promises to China which as he put it, "would be difficult to fulfill." He meant a promise to return *all* China's territory.

Educated in the United States from the age of ten to nineteen and thoroughly Westernized in thought and speech, Madame conveyed to the average American a sense of China's similarity to themselves rather than a sense of difference. She addressed a rally of 20,000 in Madison Square Garden with Willkie as a fellow speaker, and 30,000 in the Hollywood Bowl, and spoke at meetings in Chicago and San Francisco on a cross-country fund-raising tour, and in broadcasts over major networks. She received hundreds of letters a day from the American public and once, on passing through a whistle stop in the Middle West, a box of home-made cookies from the station master's wife. Notified at 3 A.M. that the train was coming through at 8 A.M., the station master had waked his wife to tell her the news and she, wanting to show her feelings, did what she knew best. Madame touched off an immense desire in people to express goodwill and a feeling that she was somehow the symbol of this universal desire; that, as Carl Sandburg wrote in the Washington *Post,* "What she wants, she wants for the Family of Man over the entire earth."

The private scene was somewhat different. The prospect of her visit had alarmed the Combined Chiefs who feared she would bewitch the President into altering the strategy of defeating Germany first. She immediately set about the attempt, beginning with Harry Hopkins who met her when she arrived in an American plane provided by the War Department on November 27. Suffering from a periodic skin trouble, she had asked to come to the United States for treatment in a hospital and, accompanied by Hollington Tong and a nephew and niece of the Kung family, was driven by Hopkins to the Harkness Pavilion in New York where the entire twelfth floor was put at her disposal. In her talk with Hopkins she was uninterested in the war in Europe or the Pacific and "confined her interest entirely to what we are doing in China proper." She clearly "does not like Stilwell and expressed the greatest admiration for Chennault." She told Hopkins that Stilwell "does not understand the Chinese people and that he made a tragic mistake in forcing Chiang Kai-shek to put one of his best divisions in Burma where it was later lost." Pursuing her second objective, the recognition of China as one of the four great powers, she discoursed at length on her views about the peace table and the postwar world, urging an immediate move by the United States to initiate talks by the "four great powers" on postwar affairs.

Mrs. Roosevelt visited her in the hospital where she seemed so "small and delicate" that "I had a desire to help her and take care of her as if she had been my own daughter." Madame moved into the White House early in January with two nurses and the two Kungs. The niece regularly wore men's clothes, causing Roosevelt to address her as "my boy." Madame brought her own silk sheets which were changed daily, or twice a day if she napped in the afternoon. She took most of her meals in her suite and angered the White House staff by clapping her hands for their attention although all the rooms were equipped with bells and telephones. When she was staying at the Waldorf in New York, the Secret Service detail, on being notified by her nephew when she was going out, would clear the corridor between her suite and the elevator and between the landing and exit, after which she would more often than not change her mind and not go out until several hours later, or not at all. When the Secret Service chief asked her to be more firm in her arrangements she demanded his removal. The two young Kungs with far less prerogative behaved with equal arrogance.

As a ruling Soong and the partner of an autocrat, Madame had leanings toward royalty. Once she asked Colonel Dorn rather grumpily why he and his colleagues addressed her as *Ma*dam instead of *Madame* when it was known that the former was used in the United States to refer to the proprietress of a house of prostitution. Quick thinking inspired the reply that the Queen of England was customarily addressed as "Madam" and the usage by the American officers was intended to suggest a quality of majesty. "You never saw a facial expression change so fast in your life." From a complaining look her face broke into a burst of delighted sunshine and for the rest of the visitor's errand she was on her most gracious and queenly behavior.

Apprised of the famous charm, the President when preparing for his first interview discarded the usual arrangement of seating his guest on the sofa next to him, and had a card table placed in front of him with a chair on its far side. He just didn't want his visitor "too close," he explained to his daughter. On extended acquaintance, he discovered in Madame a determination "as hard as steel," not entirely consistent with the sweet and gentle figure described by his wife. At dinner one evening, apropos of a miners' strike called by John L. Lewis, Roosevelt asked Madame what her

Government would do in such circumstances in wartime, and when she drew a finger across her throat he threw his head back and laughed aloud and called across the table to his wife, "Eleanor, did you see *that*?"

Madame took up the same themes with the President as with Hopkins, and in the course of her discussion of Stilwell and Chennault ascribed Stilwell's bad relations with the Generalissimo to the watermelon incident. Stilwell's reply to the Generalissimo on receipt of this order was, according to her, "bitterly and openly contemptuous" and this, she said, played a part in all their relations thereafter.

She invited the President to come back to China with her as she did each of the top men in the Administration whom she set about "vamping," to use Roosevelt's word. Admiral Leahy, who served as chairman of the Joint Chiefs, was invited up to her suite in the White House, though he was afterwards "never quite certain of the purpose of this interview." Secretary Stimson found her "a most attractive and beguiling little lady" who "commented on the beauty of my hands" but he warned McCloy, his Assistant Secretary whom she also invited to visit her, "to watch out sharply for what she said." She importuned all of them for more planes for the Air Transport Command with such insistence that Roosevelt ordered the immediate delivery of Curtiss Wright's new C-46s before their performance was tested. When they were put into use, the structural flaws brought out by the rough flight over the Hump proved lethal for many fliers, further embittering the already sour morale of the ATC.

Roosevelt respected Mme. Chiang as a real power in the Chinese Government but did not trust her and grew less beguiled the longer she stayed. Her tact did not match her charm. When he held a press conference for her at the White House attended by 172 reporters she yielded to him a question on how the United States could get supplies into China. When the President answered we would get them there as fast as the Lord would let us, she pointedly suggested that "the Lord helps those who help themselves." Roosevelt's face was seen to redden but whether from embarrassment or anger is moot.

Late in February the chief usher at the White House telephoned Morgenthau's personal secretary on behalf of Madame to ask that the Treasury instruct the Collector of Customs to release a shipment of a special brand of English cigarets which had just arrived for her in New York. When it was discovered that the cigarets were still on board ship, the calls on behalf of Madame persisted all day until the Treasury in desperation instructed an agent to "get them off the boat and fly them down here." Like the watermelons, the English cigarets were a petty matter with large implications. Madame's behavior did not suggest a leader who was guiding her country toward a democratic future. "The President . . . is just crazy to get her out of the country," Morgenthau told his staff. Roosevelt's reason was not so much personal irritation as a growing concern that Madame's private manners might gain unfavorable publicity to spoil her public image—and with it his policy.

Besides his fixed intent that China should be one of the four major powers in the postwar structure, Roosevelt's main objectives were to keep China in the war for the present and aligned with the United States in the future. He believed that no other country was so likely to be the source of postwar trouble. His four principles for the underpinning of China's future stability, according to Sumner Welles, the person best qualified to know, were: first, that China should come to an agreement with Russia to prevent Russia from interfering after the war; second, that China should get back all her territories taken by Japan and other powers, including Hong Kong; third, that the Nationalist Government should be supported as the only regime capable of unifying China; and finally, that American foreign policy in the Far East should be predicated on a close working relation between China and the United States.

Roosevelt had already taken a notable step toward implementing China's equality among nations by negotiating repeal of the unequal treaties and all remaining extraterritorial rights, privileges and concessions of the United States, and by prevailing upon Britain to do likewise, short of Hong Kong. The American action, announced on China's Independence Day, October 10 of 1942, was formalized along with the British in separate treaties signed January 11, 1943, ending the century of intrusions on China's sovereignty since the First Opium War. Chiang Kai-shek hailed the event as marking a "new epoch in Chinese history" and placing an independent China "on equal footing with Great Britain and the United States."

All of Roosevelt's principles and the success of his China policy depended on the assumption that the Kuomintang was a viable government, which was already questionable. No well-informed observer by 1943 believed the Kuomintang could escape a major civil challenge after the war and few were sure of the outcome. Nevertheless, for the sake of the great-power concept, the Kuomintang had to be treated with full respect, which meant that policy was conducted through the veils of a conscious illusion. The information available to Washington was not at fault. Foreign service reports were knowledgeable and sound. The consensus of most American officials and correspondents working in China was that the Kuomintang was incompetent, corrupt, oppressive, unrepresentative, riddled by internal weakness and unlikely to last. George Atcheson, a diplomat of 20 years' experience in China, on arriving as Chargé d'Affaires in Chungking in May 1943, reported that the situation was "seriously deteriorating in practically all aspects" and economic deterioration was "leading toward something that may eventually spell ruin." Chinese leaders were "helpless" and escaped realities by concerning themselves with postwar problems. His report did not sink into oblivion in Department files; it went to Admiral Leahy's office in the White House. Pearl Buck made the same point in a letter to Mrs. Roosevelt, written to pierce the clouds of glory surrounding the visit of Mme. Chiang. Describing the Government of Chiang and the Soongs as a clique with no claim to be representative, she wrote, "It is a peculiar and interesting situation. It cannot of course last. I fear an outbreak from the people immediately after the war, or at least as soon as the people can recuperate sufficiently to make it." Currie, another with direct access to the President, received the uncensored text of Theodore White's outraged eyewitness account for *Time* of the terrible Honan famine of 1942-43. He reported the "stupidity and inefficiency" of the relief effort, the continued collection of taxes from starving peasants by local officials, the "bland equanimity" of Chungking because officially all taxes had been remitted, and finally the conviction of the writer that the loyalty of the peasants of Honan had been "hollowed to nothingness by the extortions of their governments."*

Between policy-makers in the capital and realities in the field lies an eternal gap whitened by the bones of failed and futile efforts. Washington's China policy of 1943 was not made in terms of current information but in terms of the accumulated notions of a lifetime by which minds had already been formed. It was conditioned, not by Atcheson's report or Pearl Buck's letter, but by the Congressional Resolution of 1912 welcoming China into the company of the democracies and firmly congratulating her people on "successfully asserting . . . the powers, duties and responsibilities of self-government," and by all the ensuing ideas and images of the 30 years that followed. Information coming from the field had to battle against this accumulated weight, besides succeeding in its other struggle to gain the eye and penetrate the mind of the chief of state. When informed advice succeeded in reaching him, it could still be ignored if it discommoded a wishful policy already determined. This was the most formidable barrier of all. To halt the momentum of an accepted idea, to reexamine assumptions, is a disturbing process and requires more courage than governments can generally summon. The State Department in the case of China drew no inference from the reports of its own envoys that a fresh look was called for. The President preferred not to look at the weaknesses of the regime to which

---

* *Time* published the report on March 22, 1943, in a version cut to 750 words with all mention of officials' failures, corruption, profiteering, continued tax collecting and rising hatred of the regime omitted.

he was committed because he was intent on China as the fourth corner of a stable world order. If there was no alternative to Chiang Kai-shek capable of holding China united, then Chiang had to be supported regardless of weakness.

The need of a "regenerative idea" to strengthen or invigorate the Chinese Government occurred to others beside Stilwell. Faced with the passivity and deterioration of China and the loss of war potential which this meant to the Allies, such men were consumed with a desire to find some way to improve matters. Foreign loans could no longer help, reported Atcheson, but if the Central Government could retake Ichang and the hinterland leading to southern Hupeh and Hunan, the flow of cotton and produce would bring a reduction of 50 percent in the cost of food and clothing, as he had been told by the Minister of Economic Affairs, Wong Wen Hao, one of the finest and most respected of China's public officials. Atcheson wondered if the Allies could help the Chinese to undertake a "determined offensive action to attack and recapture . . . points such as Hankow, Ichang and others." He was moved by "the necessity of doing something." The necessity of "doing something" was the cry of Chinese like Wong Wen Hao as well as Americans, but like the effort of the reformers in the last years of the Manchus, it beat against a government too feeble and too fearful of change to act.

The American public all this time heard and accepted on faith only the version of China transmitted through such reports as Willkie's. Correspondents were hampered because they had to have War Department credentials, for which they had to sign an agreement to submit everything they wrote to censorship; violation risked loss of the credentials. Owing partly to censorship but more to voluntary reticence, the press up to 1943 published nothing realistic about the brave and favorite ally. Probably never before had the people of one country viewed the government of another under misapprehension so complete.

On the agenda of the Casablanca conference in January 1943 was the question of reviving the ANAKIM campaign for the overall reconquest of Burma including amphibious action to take Rangoon. With initiative now beginning to swing to the Allies, both American service chiefs, General Marshall and Admiral King, were strongly in favor of ANAKIM as the prerequisite for establishing effective bases in China for air operations against Japanese industry and Japanese sea-lanes. Reopening access to China also offered the possibility that Japanese forces could be put on the defensive on the main foothold of their empire, that is, if the Chinese armies could be equipped and energized to fight. This was much more desirable from the American point of view than using American manpower to fight the slow, difficult, piecemeal, costly struggle up through the humid island jungles of the Southwest Pacific. Japanese counterattack in the islands was fierce, and America, as Marshall said, "could not stand another Bataan." By putting the Japanese on the defensive in China we could "reduce our hazards in the Pacific and thus undertake the campaigns against Germany." Marshall was not averse to blackmail. Unless ANAKIM were undertaken, he said to the British at Casablanca, "a situation might arise in the Pacific at any time that would necessitate the U.S. regretfully withdrawing from the commitments in the European theater."

British reasons for dislike of the campaign had not changed. They too could use blackmail. The landing craft required to take Rangoon, they said, must necessarily reduce Britain's share in the cross-Channel attack in Europe. This was disposed of by Admiral King, a man like an axe who made Marshall seem gentle, who offered to supply the landing craft for Rangoon from the Pacific. On that basis it was agreed that ANAKIM, which had to be completed in one combat season, that is, between November and May, would be planned for launching on a target date of November 15, 1943, and with a final decision to be made no later than July.

To obtain Chiang Kai-shek's agreement to participate, and to smooth over the fact of Chinese absence from Casablanca, so embarrassing to the concept of China as one of the big four, a high-level mission was sent to confer with him composed of General Arnold of the Air Force, General Brehon B. Somervell, chief of American SOS, and Sir John Dill, British representative of the Combined Chiefs.

Behind the mission was the issue of air versus ground strategy. Under the influence of the Chiang-Chennault pressures, Roosevelt was already beginning to have doubts about ANAKIM and to favor air warfare as the quickest and cheapest way of damaging the enemy. He proposed sending Arnold to China as a proponent of air war who was eager to "get at the bombing of Japan as soon as possible." Somervell, who represented the War Department doctrine that the Hump could never supply as much as the Road, was sent along by Marshall as a counterweight.

The mission was a revelation to its members both of the realities and of the flights from reality in CBI. In Delhi it seemed to Arnold that Wavell's plan of campaign was not a plan at all but "several pages of well written paragraphs, telling why the mission could not be accomplished." On reaching China on February 4, he found Chennault not "realistic" about the logistics of his operations and Chiang Kai-shek even less so. Accompanied by Stilwell to a series of conferences at the Chiangs' hilltop residence (named "Peanut's Berchtesgaden" by his guide), Arnold found that the Generalissimo "would not listen to logic or reason." Chiang was not mollified by the promise Arnold brought of 137 transports for the Hump, the number necessary to deliver 5,000 tons a month, nor by the promise of a group of B-24 bombers to come. Far from feeling it necessary to buy himself back into American favor as Stilwell had supposed, Chiang now had three new demands: an independent command for Chennault, 10,000 tons a month over the Hump and 500 combat planes for China by November.

One reason behind the demands was need for the defense of Chungking by Chennault's Air Task Force in default of the Chinese Air Force. Chinese air corps cadets trained in the United States "do not go on to actual battle experience," reported Gauss, "and apparently have been lost to the war effort." The Russian training effort at Lanchow had proved equally futile. The Russians discovered the aircraft they delivered were misused or cracked up by inexperienced personnel, and the other matériel seemed scarcely ever to find its way into combat against the Japanese. "It disappeared and no accounting was given," they stated. Having failed in its training program, ruined most of its Lend-Lease aircraft and disdained operational control by a foreigner, the Chinese Air Force was in no shape to protect Chungking when the Japanese bombers should return with spring.

When it came to the necessities required for building and maintaining airfields and supplying fuel, Arnold found that Chiang and Chennault "glossed over these things with a wave of their hands. They could not or would not be bothered with logistics." To the Generalissimo all explanations of the practical difficulties were "excuses, excuses." He wanted 5,000 tons a month right away; "There are ways and means of doing things and they must be done." He resorted again to ultimatum: "Tell your President that unless I get these three things I cannot fight this war and he cannot count on me to have our Army participate in the campaign."

"I'll be damned if I take any such message back to the President," Arnold said to Stilwell afterwards. Ignoring the ultimatum, he returned to the talks and promised increased tonnage but nothing more, leaving it to the tactful Dill to "smoke out" the Generalissimo on whether he would or would not take the offensive in November. Chiang said he would, although without the 10,000 tons and 500 planes he could offer no assurance of success. Not content with this, Stilwell asked whether he would participate if naval support were limited. "He got mad as hell and said, 'Didn't I say I would?' He sent word by T.V. that I had embarrassed him publicly. He can go to hell. I have him on that point." Chiang repeated his promise along with his three new demands in a letter to Roosevelt of February 7, stating that "the Chinese army will be in readiness to perform its assigned task at the specified time without fail." The November campaign was confirmed by all parties at a conference in Calcutta on February 9 attended by Ho Ying-chin and T. V. Soong for China, Dill and Wavell for Britain, and Arnold, Somervell, Bissell and Stilwell for the United States. "All were in agreement," according to Wavell's summary, and it only remained to press on "with the greatest possible energy" to prepare for the battle immediately after the monsoon.

Stilwell was pleased that his visitors had had a look for themselves at the "machinery of Chinese government" and at the personalities—meaning Chiang and Ho Ying-chin—with whom he had to deal. Arnold had said to him on leaving, "You ought to get a laurel wreath," and wrote afterwards, "Dear Joe: You have one S.O.B. of a job. . . . If at any time you think I can help, just yell."

The yells came instead from Chennault whose operations continued to be limited by the inexorable mathematics of tonnages over the Hump. The ATC was flying in about 3,000 tons a month at this time, of which Stilwell allotted the major share to train and equip the Y-force for the Burma campaign and the minor share to the Air Force. Chennault's objections were loudly voiced, publicly by articles planted in the press to force the issue, and privately to Hopkins' office in the White House by the agency of Alsop, a journalist with a tendency to cataclysmic opinions. A relative of the Roosevelts and well known around Washington as a political columnist, Alsop was a devotee of the airplane as the definitive weapon and had found his idol in Chennault whom he had joined as public relations aide in 1941. Captured a few months later in Hong Kong by the Japanese and repatriated to the United States, he had since arranged through Hopkins to have himself appointed Lend-Lease representative in Chungking and had departed for China in December 1942. Roosevelt had written to him at that time saying he wished he could go with him to see Chennault and suggesting as an alternative that Chennault come to Washington. The President tended to trust the reports of private envoys more than those of officials and Alsop qualified for that advantage. He was literate, excitable and persuasive with just enough superficial acquaintance with the situation to be opinionated and to appear knowledgeable. Hopkins, according to his biographer, was "unquestionably influenced" by Alsop's flood of letters.

His reports were alarming. Before even reaching China he melodramatically informed Hopkins on the basis of talks with returned fliers that the American Air Force situation in China was "a national tragedy . . . a national scandal . . . grossly dishonoring to President, Army and country." He begged to be recalled within two months to report in person. On arriving in Chungking, he went to see Stilwell, becoming, after one interview, "Alslop" in the diary. He was back in Washington in less than two months with the solution for the war in CBI, presented to Hopkins in 21 passionate and plausible pages. The gist was that in adopting the Burma campaign we had embarked on "grandiose, dangerous and doubtfully

fruitful" ground operations while neglecting the "brilliant and easy opportunity in the air."

The solution was the removal of Stilwell, "a conventional infantryman
of the high, narrow, old school" who "does not understand and grossly
underestimates" air power and whose ground approach to the problem "can
only end in something very close to disaster for all of us." Stilwell's attitude
toward the Chinese was described as condescending. His training program
was represented with total inaccuracy as designed "to substitute American
for Chinese command in the field." Alsop was correct, however, in reporting
that Stilwell's contemptuous remarks were carried back to the Generalissimo
by Tai Li's agents. He concluded that since Stilwell was holding down the
air effort and had made it plain that he would keep control of supplies
as long as Marshall was Chief of Staff, he should be transferred.

Events reinforced the argument against ground operations when the
British effort to take Akyab on Burma's west coast was beaten back by the
Japanese and petered out in a series of inglorious reverses and damaged
morale. The result dimmed the prospects for ANAKIM. To Churchill the
reconquest of Burma appeared like "munching a porcupine quill by quill."
Roosevelt was beginning to agree with him and suggested to Marshall that
ANAKIM ought perhaps to be abandoned as conflicting with preparations
for the Second Front in Europe. This would leave all the more reason for
transferring the burden of activity to Chennault, with enough support to
enable him to operate effectively. The idea appealed to Roosevelt as the
easiest and most immediate way of showing activity in the China theater,
to make up for having promised the major American effort against Germany.
It was in any case his habit to give advisers with strong views their head
and see what came of it. He was prepared to overlook Arnold's restrained
enthusiasm for Chennault and overrule the War Department's demand for
a quid pro quo approach to the Chinese, though not prepared to insist on
the transfer of Stilwell or to divest him of control of Lend-Lease.

His decision, like so many others in the complicated conduct of the
war, was a compromise. On March 8 he ordered a separate air force for
Chennault independent of the Tenth Air Force under Bissell though not
independent of Stilwell. He assured Chiang Kai-shek of intention to build
up toward 500 combat planes and 10,000 tons a month without a quid
pro quo. At the insistence of the War Department, however, Chiang was
reminded that air transport could never supply enough and that ground
communications would have to be opened. Roosevelt made it clear to
Marshall that while "still hopeful of the Burma operation," he wanted
emphasis on Chennault's air operations in 1943. Construction and improvement of airfields was to be "pushed to the limit"; Chennault was to have

a share of supplies "that will really keep his force operating," at least 1,500 tons out of 4,000 and anything over 4,000 up to 2,500. He was to have "complete control" over his own operations and tactics, "with Stilwell's approval," an obviously inoperable condition.

What motivated the President in his decision was policy not strategy. He was not concerned with making some historic choice between air and ground action but with pursuing his concept of China's status as a great power. Support for Chennault was what China's Chief Executive wanted, whereas Stilwell's insistence on reforming the Chinese Army detracted from the great-power image. Roosevelt was basically not interested in the mission to "increase the combat efficiency of the Chinese Army" because, like most Americans accustomed to the victorious Chinese communiqués, he did not recognize the need, and even more because army reorganization was something Stilwell was pushing against the Generalissimo's will. In this respect the President's instinct was right, if not for the right reasons. In any fundamental sense the army could not be reformed against the will of the ruler; it could not be reshaped without reshaping the society of which it was the product. More disturbing, however, were things like "Peanut" which offended Roosevelt as a fellow-ruler. He felt that Chiang was entitled to the same dignity as himself, if not a little extra to make up for his difficult position.

He made the point clear in a notable letter to Marshall explaining his reasons for overruling the War Department. Citing a message from Stilwell about the need for a sterner tone to, and a commitment from, Chiang Kai-shek, the President said this was going about it in "just the wrong way." The Generalissimo was chief of state as well as Commander-in-Chief and "one cannot speak sternly to a man like that or exact commitments from him as we might do from the Sultan of Morocco." Chiang had come up the hard way to become "undisputed leader of 400,000,000 people . . . and to create in a very short time throughout China what it took us a couple of centuries to attain."

Not intended as rhetoric for public consumption, this was a clear statement of the American illusion. Although the Chinese people, as Stilwell had said, had a "tremendous cohesion" that enabled them to withstand bad government, and a cultural unity older and stronger than anything in the United States, the idea that the Kuomintang in only 15 harassed and embattled years had obtained the same degree of national cohesion as the United States was a fantasy and not a harmless one. It allowed America to rest policy on a collapsible base.

Stilwell fumed constantly at the comparable illusion about China's military performance. Stolid Chinese troops were in fact defending their country as well as they were allowed to, but the daily communiqués reporting "furious Chinese counterattacks" on the Salween front and "heavy enemy losses" were, he estimated, at least 90 percent false; nevertheless they were given wide publicity in the United States. "This makes my job more difficult, of course," he wrote to Marshall. "If the Chinese Army is so full of fight and so well led, what am I here for?" He continued to believe that he could require reform of the army if only he were given the authority to exact a quid pro quo for Lend-Lease weapons. This to him was the crux and he pleaded the point unceasingly. He never doubted the power of American matériel and know-how, directed by himself as one of the superlative professionals of military training, to accomplish the desired result. He too had illusions.

Marshall's reply to the President's letter was a basic statement of Stilwell's case for reform and supply of the ground forces. He defined the dependence of air power on the ground, and the consequent necessity of Stilwell's program to raise Chinese combat efficiency. "As soon as our air effort hurts the Japs they will move in on us" and then protection for the airfields would have to come from the Chinese Army. *"Here is the most serious consideration . . .* we must build for that now." He pointed out that the bases in Chekiang from which it had been hoped to bomb Tokyo had already been destroyed by Japanese ground action and had not been repaired. In order to increase air action against the Japanese a land supply route through Burma was necessary, and this too required Chinese ground forces. He became emphatic: "The present low combat worth of the Chinese Army must be reversed before we can fully realize the Chinese potential in this war. To correct this must be the primary objective of any representative dispatched to this theater to represent American interests."

In his last sentence Marshall was entering the sphere of policy and his version was not the President's policy. Roosevelt did not want to insist on mobilizing China's forces against the will of China's leader. He opposed the quid pro quo approach because he believed that any promise extracted from the Chinese on that basis would not be kept. He preferred to go along with Chiang Kai-shek's clear preference for Chennault's program, especially as it fitted with his own belief that Japanese merchant shipping was the vulnerable point. Defense of the airfields could be allowed to rest on Chennault's various assurances that 50 or 100 or 150 airplanes would enable Chinese ground forces to fight successfully.

At the President's order, the Fourteenth Air Force under Chennault was duly activated on March 11 and its commander promoted to major general. The War Department, having been overruled, reacted promptly. Fearing that Chennault's promotion would lower Stilwell's influence in

Chinese eyes, OPD (Operations Division) proposed to award Stilwell the Legion of Merit in the degree of Chief Commander* so that "Nothing should be left undone to convince China that General Stilwell enjoys full American confidence" and that we look to him in Chinese matters as "chief arbiter." Although Marshall approved the award for Stilwell on March 16, it came to an end there (though not permanently) because Roosevelt wanted to make Chiang Kai-shek the first foreign recipient of the award and it was thought his appreciation might be marred if Stilwell received it in the same degree at the same time.

Marshall duly conveyed to Stilwell Roosevelt's implied rebuke about not treating Chiang Kai-shek like the Sultan of Morocco (cautiously altered for radio purposes to "tribal chieftain"). Mutterings about "tribal chieftain" periodically appeared thereafter in the diary.

Since the Black Friday in December when Chiang Kai-shek called off the Burma campaign, Stilwell had concentrated on trying to assemble, train and equip the Yoke force in preparation for renewal of the campaign in the coming November. The program had two parts: bringing the divisions up to full strength and training the officer cadres. General Ch'en Ch'eng, Stilwell's candidate, had been named commander of the Y-force, a Chinese staff and American instructors appointed, the 30 divisions designated, physical arrangements for the training school established at Kunming, consent of Lung Yun, Governor of Yunnan, obtained, and an opening date for the schools set for April 1. Actual progress in carrying out the program was slow and discouraging but Ramgarh was evidence of what could be done. One regiment of the 38th Division from Ramgarh had already reentered north Burma to patrol ahead of the road-builders. John Davies predicted in March that Stilwell "may yet perform what has seemed impossible—cause the launching of a Chinese offensive against the Japanese."

The material was not promising. The eleven armies selected to provide the 30 divisions were all under strength, to a total deficiency of 185,000 men. They had only 50 percent of the normal requirement of weapons and half of those they had were unserviceable for lack of critical parts. Fillers repeatedly promised by the War Ministry, according to a definite schedule negotiated with Stilwell, never appeared, or straggled in prodded by bayonets in such sorry shape that it required a special program of five or six weeks with three meals a day, and mainly sleep and short walks the first

---

* The Legion of Merit, created by George Washington, had been reestablished in 1942. The degree of Chief Commander, specified for heads of state and high-ranking military, was intended as the highest decoration the United States could give to foreigners.

week, to make them fit for duty. On the way to the depots recruits were not fed; they lived on what they could snatch from the villages at gun point, adding to the anger and misery of the country people. Surplus drafts were always ordered on the basis of expected loss. "Ho expects one third of replacements to die or desert en route," Stilwell wrote. "And he calmly accepts the situation." The rate of loss by death or desertion of all Chinese conscripts in 1943 was 44 percent, or 750,000 out of a total of 1,670,000 —a "terrible indictment of China's leaders."

Bursts of encouragement occasionally broke through the frustrations. "V FOR VICTORY," Stilwell recorded on March 23. "Orders are out for fillers to report. All drafts start by end of April and should join units by end of May. . . . March 24. Honeymoon continues. Dorn saw the T/O boys and everything is just the way we want it . . . 100 per cent agreement . . . Pai Ch'ung-hsi reported in yesterday, offering to help. *He* wants to see Ramgarh now. Ho making speeches about Ramgarh and how wonderful it is!" To Stimson Stilwell wrote that he was getting "excellent cooperation" from the Chinese Ordnance and Communication departments. "The medical set-up should be the best the Chinese have ever had by far."

The Kunming Training Center was organized at the outset to give six-week courses to 450 officers in the Infantry classes, 300 in Artillery and 150 each in Signal and Medical services. Colonel Dorn was Chief of Staff with Colonel (shortly afterwards General) Arms as head of the training program, Colonel Barrett as executive officer of the center and Colonel Tseng Shih-kwei, who had been Stilwell's liaison officer since the beginning of the Burma campaign, as executive officer of the Chinese administration. The center possessed buildings, firing ranges, faculty and equipment but never enough students because of the failure of the Chinese Army to fill the places. The Artillery class opened with 87 officers instead of 300; through 1943 it operated at about 25 percent of capacity and the Infantry center at about 60 percent of capacity. Of those who did come, many were of disappointing quality as officer material but many were eager and quick to learn. "They were really taking it in fast," according to one American instructor. "It was a wonderful experience. I never got a response like that from Americans."

A strike was called soon after the opening by the 23 interpreters, who as members of the scholar class suffered severely from the inflation. Colonel Tseng demonstrated to an American friend how these matters were settled in China. He issued ammunition to a platoon of school troops whom he assigned to guard the interpreters' barracks with orders to shoot anyone leaving, even for meals. When the interpreters sent word the next day that they were willing to negotiate, he had them brought to his office under armed guard, placing a loaded pistol and a prepared statement on his desk, and ordered each to sign the paper stating they were satisfied with their pay, otherwise "I will shoot you dead." When they had returned to work he explained to the American that during the battle of Shanghai he had been forced to shoot nine officers for "so grossly exaggerating the tactical and logistical situation that I couldn't make sound decisions." Their replacements had then been "motivated to do a good job." He was not proud of such measures but under the current conditions in the Chinese Army, he said, it was the only way to get results.

Backstage the struggle continued. General Ch'en Ch'eng, Stilwell believed, was genuinely cooperating but the War Minister was dragging his feet. "Ho Ying-chin realizes that if Ch'en succeeds he'll be a big name, and Ho will slide down into the discard. So Ho will accept the failure of the effort with great equanimity and will perhaps actively try to sabotage it." In addition, Ho was afraid of arousing the animosity of Lung Yun by the concentration of Central Government divisions in his province. The opium traffic in Yunnan was still active, Stilwell wrote, and "our presence here threatens to affect the enormous smuggling racket." Lung Yun's resources for raising money were infinite. In one case he ordered that all two-wheeled carts, the common vehicle of the area, must be equipped with rubber tires. He then opened his warehouses to sell the tires he had confiscated during the days of traffic on the Burma Road. After that he passed a new law taxing all carts with rubber tires.

At Ledo, on the other side of Burma, work on the Road inched forward against obstacles of terrain and climate as drastic as those of the Hump. Mountains, canyons and torrential streams marked the path, the thick cover of trees and vines made accurate survey of the ground impossible, the annual rainfall amounted to 150 inches with an intensity at times during the monsoon of 14 inches in 24 hours; mud, leeches and malaria were daily hazards. Explorations and experiments over the past year of alternative routes to China through Iran, Afghanistan and Tibet had proved these impractical, leaving the Hukawng valley route the only choice. The Japanese had not occupied the extreme northwestern corner of Burma but rumors and alarms of their presence were frequent. General Wheeler as an Engineer disapproved of the road project but nevertheless laid out the trace with 13 culverts to a mile to carry the runoff of heavy rains. U.S. Army Engineers including a battalion of Negro troops began the work along with Indian contract labor furnished by the British. Ultimately 80,000 men, of whom 50,000 were Americans and the rest Chinese and Indians, were to share in the work. The trace as far as Shingbwiyang in the Hukawng valley, where combat could be expected to begin, covered a distance of 103 miles which Wheeler hoped to complete by June. The con-

183

Mme. Chiang Kai-shek made a lengthy visit to the United States that lasted from November 1942 to May 1943. She was personally welcomed at the Washington railroad station by FDR and rode with him to the White House (184). On January 18 she addressed a joint session of Congress (183).

184

185

186

struction rate during good weather was three quarters of a mile a day of single-track roadway with turnouts. Forward units crossed the frontier 43 miles from Ledo on February 28, 1943, and erected a sign saying, "Welcome to Burma! This way to Tokyo!" Dr. Seagrave and his staff, who accompanied the Chinese patrol units from Ramgarh, hiked back over the refugee trail past skeletons lying in groups around every waterhole and at the foot of every ascent. Tattered remnants of clothing, civilian and military, English, Indian and Burmese, clung to the bones, witness of the awful exodus of the year before.

Work slowed after the frontier had been crossed owing to a variety of troubles. Only four miles beyond the frontier had been completed by the time the rains came on May 11 to add to the difficulties.

From February to April Stilwell was constantly moving from Kunming to Ledo to Chabua in Assam (Headquarters of the ATC), to Ramgarh, to Delhi and back to Chungking, inspecting, conferring, hearing complaints, dealing out priorities, negotiating with and prodding his allies. At Chabua he arrived unheralded to test reports of foul conditions at the Polo Ground Mess, one more affliction of the ATC. Conditions had become an open scandal which senior officers, who could eat elsewhere, had done little to remedy. After going through the mess line with the GIs and sitting at filthy benches to share the "slop," Stilwell announced, "All right boys, let 'em have it." The place exploded in a flying melee of food, tin plates and over-turned tables. Stilwell then called in the base commander, said, "There's your mess," and told him that unless he found decent conditions at his next unscheduled visit, the commander would be relieved and sent home.

Return to Chungking brought "papers and grief" and a dinner at the Chiangs': "Very simple food and little ritual or ceremony, but oh! the atmosphere. In the presence of the Most High no one dares to make a re-mark or venture an opinion. . . . You can see from the rigid postures and strained expressions that the sweat is running down the boys' backs." On March 19, his sixtieth birthday, he let "the terrible date ooze by" without writing home.

At all times and hours and places Stilwell scribbled his notes and memos, the tracks of a mind constantly twisting and turning in search of a solution. "Take a port and put a U.S. force in south China? Amalgamate with the south Chinese. Invite the Reds to join. . . . Am I through in China?"

"CKS is blind. . . . Solution—Open the Road? For What? If CKS handles supply, this means only hoarding for maintenance of KMT."

"CKS not a free agent: zone commanders, political influences, Red obsession. Won't (can't) reorganize."

There was a note on his own situation: "No strings to pull." There were notes on his reading: Walter Lippmann's *Foreign Policy,* Lattimore's book

Stilwell, photographed between Ho Ying-chin, the Chinese Minister of War (left), and Lung Yun, the Yunnan warlord (185). On the back of one picture (186), Stilwell scribbled: "A little exercise in stream crossing. Two stuck out of four. We made it." Work on the Ledo Road inched forward; here trucks bring gravel for resurfacing (187).

and a list of books on China. There was a five-page essay on China's situation, an essay on "The Problem of India," notes on the Oriental, on Lend-Lease, on the Russian soldier, on the Taoist doctrine of nonresistance to events and external forces, on the dangers of a too-close tie with Britain, on the United States and Russia as the two great postwar powers.

Beginning in March the Japanese launched a renewed offensive up the Yangtze into the Hupeh-Hunan rice-bowl area of central China. The military purpose was uncertain but the objective appeared to be Ichang where the Yangtze gorges form a natural barrier on the way to Chungking. Ho Ying-chin insisted the drive was designed to capture Chungking and forestall the Allies' Burma campaign. He wanted to withdraw the Y-force troops to defend Chungking, which was exactly what Stilwell believed the Japanese intended him to do because they were becoming concerned about the presence of this force in Yunnan. On April 19 Stilwell had "a hell of a session with the Gmo . . . sneers and complaints. . . . Talks of a counter-offensive and 'morale at low ebb.' Acts scared." Later Ho Ying-chin did divert two armies and 70,000 fillers from the Y-force, further delaying the training program. A greater loss was the recall of Ch'en Ch'eng, zone commander of Hupeh, whom the Generalissimo ordered back to Hupeh to defend his province against the Japanese.

In April came "the famous call to Washington," as Stilwell afterwards described it. The call was a direct if unintended result of action by the Generalissimo who "has had a brainstorm with the help of Chennault." Independence had not solved Chennault's problem. He was not getting the priority in supplies which the President had ordered for him but had left operationally ambivalent. Stilwell still had control of Hump tonnage, and since he was still committed to preparing the Y-force for the Burma campaign on which all parties had agreed, he continued to allot three eighths of supplies to aviation and five eighths to the ground forces and all other purposes. These included material for China's small-arms arsenals as well as tons of paper money which, owing to shortages of mills and materials in China, had to be printed abroad and flown in to meet the appetite of the inflation.

Frightened by the Japanese drive, the Generalissimo determined that a major offensive must be launched by the Fourteenth Air Force and he asked Roosevelt to call Chennault back to Washington for consultation over Stilwell's head. Roosevelt was willing since he had had the same idea himself, but Marshall, who in his turn had been considering bringing Stilwell home to argue with the President, instantly warned that interference by an ally in the chain of American command could set a dangerous precedent. He suggested that the difficulty could be met by calling Stilwell back at the same time, permitting both Generals to be present for the forthcoming conference with Churchill and the Combined Chiefs in May. Accordingly Stilwell and Chennault left China together on April 23 and arrived in Washington on April 28. The determined euphoria of the press concerning anything to do with China was extended to the return of Uncle Joe, whom *The New York Times* editorialized as a diplomat beloved in Chungking: "From the Generalissimo down they all like him."

After a reunion with Win who came to Washington to join him, Stilwell's first visit was to Marshall and Stimson who informed him he had an appointment at the White House for the following day where he was expected to present the arguments to the President against the major air offensive wanted by Chiang Kai-shek and Chennault. The plan brought to Washington by Chennault called for a six-month program of combat action to wrest air superiority from the Japanese, and of bombing action against river and coastal shipping gradually extended over the South China Sea and by the end of the year to Japan itself. To supply the program he wanted the entire air transport tonnage for May and June, 4,700 tons a month from July through September and just over 7,000 tons a month thereafter.

The War Department opposed the plan as premature because unless accompanied by a ground offensive in Burma it would provoke the Japanese to wipe out the airfields in China and attack the Assam bases as well. Chiang Kai-shek gave his "personal assurance" to Roosevelt at this time that if the enemy moved against the air bases, such action could "be halted by the existing Chinese ground forces."

Stilwell prepared a memorandum of what he wanted to say to the President. In addition to all the basic arguments made in Marshall's letter for reopening Burma and raising the combat efficiency of the Chinese Army, it fastened on the great empty space in the direction of the war in Asia and urged that a "general strategic plan" be prepared to tie in future operations in China with the campaign in the Southwest Pacific. It repeated his hope, never relinquished, of a U.S. Army corps for action in China. It stated the case against the air offensive and predicted that if the Japanese launched a systematic attack against the air bases as they had in Chekiang, the Chinese would be no better able to stop them than they had been then. This was why his program for preparing 60 divisions was necessary and why it needed a land supply route through Burma. It was a cogent and forceful brief which was to be fumbled in argument.

At the White House on the following day, April 30, Stilwell was unable to speak his thesis effectively to Roosevelt; instead, according to Marshall, he sat humped over with his head down and "muttered something about China not fighting." Roosevelt seized on his attitude to wonder if he were ill and to ask Marshall if a sick man should not be relieved. Marshall replied that the "sick man" could put on a better physical performance than any two men in the White House; nevertheless he was chagrined and disappointed. Stilwell afterwards said he realized he had let him down.

What blocked him may have been the feeling that in arguing for his own program he would be promoting himself. This was something Stilwell constitutionally could not do. His entry for *Who's Who* at this time was stated in six terse lines (in comparison with 15 for Eisenhower, 33 for Patton and 55 for MacArthur). The recapture of Burma and the commitment to enable the Chinese soldier to fight effectively had a profound personal meaning for him which in effect closed his lips, the more so as the importance of both seemed to him obvious. Like Cordelia he would not speak what should have needed no explaining. His own hostility to the President, and the knowledge that it was to some extent returned, played a part. Roosevelt's pronounced inclination to gratify the Generalissimo's wishes, his glossy view of Chiang and Chennault, his obvious intention to try out the air force no matter what, all combined to make Stilwell inarticulate. He did not have the tact or capacity to deal with opinions which he held in contempt, and contempt came to him easily. He might have but did not try to explain to Roosevelt that Chiang's "personal assurance" was hardly more than a Chinese formality. He was unable to say what he had put so well in writing: that the creation of an effective ground force would be of far more lasting and effective benefit to China than "increased air activity without a foundation. . . . Air coverage over nothing is in my opinion of little value."

He had no difficulty in putting the case to Secretary Stimson that evening when he and Win and the McCloys were invited to dinner. While talking of the last war the three men discovered that they had all been at Langres at about the same time. In an effort to help put across Stilwell's argument, which was that of the War Department, Stimson telephoned Roosevelt to tell him "how strongly I admired Stilwell and thus to answer the evident doubt he had of him." He embroidered a little to say he had known Stilwell since the last war "when he and I were classmates at Langres" and followed the call with a letter recalling his responsibility in selecting Stilwell for China. "We knowingly gave him the toughest task in this war. . . . He has convinced me in the last few days that he is the only man I know who can carry that big job through."

It did not help, for Roosevelt had already on May 2 informed Marshall of his decision that nothing must be allowed to delay the proposed air offensive. The Japanese drive up the Yangtze had raised once again the nine-lived specter of China's collapse, dramatized by the Generalissimo's evidently genuine fright. At a meeting with Hopkins and the Joint Chiefs Roosevelt said the "situation of Chiang Kai-shek was critical and there was a possibility of the collapse of his whole government." He was determined to give Chiang Kai-shek as far as possible what he wanted, without a quid pro quo, and on this issue, despite his great reliance on and trust in Marshall, he was prepared to overrule his military advisers. He told Marshall that "politically he must support Chiang Kai-shek," that he agreed on the necessity of supplying the Y-force and would "handle Chiang Kai-shek on that," but that otherwise Chennault must have first priority. He favored a modified ANAKIM in north Burma only, without the Rangoon objective, but this too must take second place to the air offensive.

Informed by Marshall, Stilwell summed up the decision as based on "total misapprehension of the character, intentions, authority and ability of Chiang Kai-shek." Privately he thought Madame had "put it over FDR like a tent." Chiang's Government was "a one-man joke. The KMT is his tool. Madame is his front. The silly U.S. propaganda is his lever. We are his suckers."

The fate of ANAKIM and the future strategy of the war in the Far East were still to be settled at the full-dress conference code-named TRIDENT which was about to convene. It was the largest of the strategic meetings held so far and the first one at which field commanders from CBI appeared. Wavell, Stilwell and Chennault were the center of interest although the European theater supplied the principal issue. This was the choice between a Mediterranean approach favored by the British and a cross-Channel attack by the Americans. To gain their way the Americans periodically threatened a "Pacific alternative" to Europe. In the Far East Churchill had as always the political end in view and wished frankly to "by-pass" Burma in favor of operations leading eventually to Singapore, "the only prize that will restore British prestige in this region." This was not an American aim. Both Roosevelt and the military, though disagreeing as to means, wanted action leading to China as a base of operations against Japan.

A fundamental divergence underlay the strategic issue: the United States for reasons of policy as well as strategy wished to aid China; Britain did not. The vision of China as one of the four great postwar powers had no appeal for the British. They were not anxious to see the war end with China in the strong position once held by Japan. The British flag in that event would not fly for long over Hong Kong. Nor did they agree with Roosevelt's view that China had no aggressive or imperialistic ambitions. She claimed Tibet (thereby posing a threat to India), as well as Mongolia and unofficially north Burma. As Anthony Eden put it to Roosevelt during a visit preparatory to TRIDENT, he "did not much like the idea of the Chinese running up and down the Pacific." On the other hand he expected

China to undergo revolution after the war, a development which the British regarded with equanimity as it was expected to leave China divided and weak.

In the face of American insistence at TRIDENT on lifting the siege of China, Wavell and his staff were as pessimistic as ever. But rather than commit their resources to ANAKIM and the opening of a land route to China, they took Roosevelt's side against the War Department in favor of putting greater effort into support of the Hump and air supply. The Navy led by Admiral King sided with Marshall. When King's formidable temper was aroused, according to an associate, "he could even raise holy hell with FDR." King felt strongly that China's manpower, given munitions and equipment, could be applied against Japan and this was his reason for favoring the recapture of Burma and, in his words, for "unceasing endeavor to reach China by sea." Holding these views, he "always believed in Stilwell and trusted him."

Marshall was angered by Roosevelt's decision in favor of the Chiang-Chennault strategy. In his dealings with the President he took pains to be formal and official, would not let himself smile when Roosevelt cracked jokes and sat frozen-faced when others laughed. His conscious purpose was to avoid an easy relationship in order that any agreement reached between them should be an official War Department commitment that could not be overturned "with a wave of the cigarette holder." Marshall was a formal person even when he was not trying—Stilwell was said to be the only officer ever heard to call him George—and when annoyed he was icy. His annoyance in the matter of China extended to Hopkins, with whom on every other issue he was on terms of mutual respect. By the time of TRIDENT, as far as China policy was concerned, their quarrel was such that they had ceased to speak to each other. The Chennault affair, Marshall said afterwards, caused the only serious dispute he ever had with Hopkins. Marshall considered Chennault unfitted for independent command because, as he told Roosevelt, though "probably a tactical genius" he knew nothing of logistics and had been "for many years a paid employee of the Chinese Government and hence under the undue influence of the G–mo." He despised Chennault's machinations and told him to his face that he did not trust him. When he spoke of him to Army historians after the war, "down would come that VMI ring on the desk." His especial anathema was Alsop whom he knew to have tried to persuade T. V. Soong to have the Chinese withdraw from their share of the Burma campaign and who not unnaturally earned some of Marshall's harshest remarks. As a consequence of these divisions the President's two most important advisers—Hopkins on policy and Marshall on strategy—were too far apart on China to discuss it, with the result that the President was left to settle matters his own way.

After a flying five-day holiday at home ("Better an hour of Carmel than a cycle of Cathay") Stilwell returned to Washington for the opening discussion of ANAKIM on May 14. The refrain of the imposing array of British brass at the long table was "can't—can't—can't." The visitors were headed by the Chief of Imperial General Staff, Sir Alan Brooke, a small, dark, unamiable man who disliked Americans and vice versa. He was the kind to stimulate Stilwell, who recorded with pleasure that he had "locked horns with Brooke to King's delight," but this was on specifics rather than general policy. When the conference moved to the White House in the presence of President and Prime Minister he failed again to summon any eloquence. Marshall was more than ever irritated. "Apparently Stilwell shut up like a clam and made therefore an unfavorable impression," Stimson sadly recorded after hearing Marshall's report. "Hard to say my piece," Stilwell's diary acknowledged.

If he had been Cicero it would not have made much difference, for both Roosevelt and Churchill were opposed to putting the major effort into Burma that ANAKIM would require. King tried to insist that it was indispensable. Churchill said he was not going to do anything "silly" just to pacify the Chinese. Stilwell became vocal enough to say that Britain and the United States were pledged in good faith to the north Burma campaign in the current year. At one point in discussions after the formal session the President, who was intensely interested in the character of Chiang Kai-shek, asked Stilwell and Chennault for their opinions. "He's a vacillating tricky undependable old scoundrel who never keeps his word," Stilwell replied. Chennault nobly offered, "Sir, I think the Generalissimo is one of the two or three greatest military and political leaders in the world today. He has never broken a commitment or promise made to me."

While the conferees continued to argue for another week, the Chinese agitated. Madame, who to Roosevelt's vexation had resumed residence in the White House for the period of the conference, called in McCloy, the highest official she could reach, to insist on full compliance with the Generalissimo's demands. He was, after all, she said, Supreme Commander of the China theater. T. V. Soong, now back in Washington, made the same point when called in to present China's views to TRIDENT. He also stated specifically that Chiang would not enter the Burma campaign unless Rangoon were included and would make a separate peace with Japan unless wholehearted operations for the relief of China were undertaken. Roosevelt told the conference he did not think this was crying wolf and that the Allies "must not be put into the position of being responsible for the collapse of China."

After heated discussion over what form military action should take, Roosevelt's view, supported by the British military, prevailed in favor of putting the major effort into increased and enlarged service over the Hump. In the end ANAKIM was put aside without a decision; it remained on the books, to be resurrected and reinterred at each future conference. At the insistence of the War Department, which claimed that the Hump route could not deliver more unless Myitkyina were retaken to shorten the flight and that a land route to China was in any case essential, the north Burma campaign was saved and given a code name of its own—SAUCY. The War Department agreed to invest the effort required to deliver 7,000 tons a month over the Hump beginning in July and 10,000 by September. The President specifically ordered that starting July 1 Chennault was to have the first 4,700 tons a month flown into China, with the next 2,000 tons going to "all other purposes including the ground forces," and the next 300 again to the air force.

The 2,000 tons spared for "all other purposes" meant in effect only 500 tons a month for the Y-force after the "other purposes" were filled. "They made it practically impossible for me to prepare the Y-force," Stilwell summed up, "and then ordered it used in an offensive . . .", in north Burma. Yet he did not ask to be relieved after TRIDENT or at any other time. In spite of every denial of the means, and every argument running against him, he never really gave up the belief that somehow he could bring off the comeback through Burma. His theater had the lowest priority of any and though, as Robert Sherwood wrote, every commander except Eisenhower and Nimitz felt himself the most neglected, abused and cheated of them all, "none had as much right to feel this way as did Stilwell." He had to work against defeatism in the India command and passive resistance in China; his own Commander-in-Chief as well as the Commander to whom he was accredited wanted him recalled; his requests for American troops and for authority to exact a quid pro quo had been denied and his means of supply now diverted to the air force. His customary description of his mission in Chungking was "shovelling the manure pile." Yet, whether from duty or a desire for vindication or both, he left no indication that he ever considered not returning.

As the "MacArthur of China" he was much interviewed by the press and consulted by officialdom while in Washington. He had conferences with Secretary Hull and Hornbeck and Currie and Colonel Donovan of OSS and two "very satisfactory" sessions with Senators La Follette, Connally, Douglas and others on the Hill. He tried to use the opportunity as far as he could to get the truth to Americans about the problems of China. Davies arranged for Eugene Meyer, publisher of the Washington *Post,* to give a dinner for him with six or eight leading correspondents; 20 or more other guests came in after the dinner to listen. Articulate when facing an audience who wanted to hear, Stilwell spoke bluntly and frankly of the situation he faced and asked Davies to speak afterwards on its political aspects. From about this time on, cracks began to appear in the idealized press treatment of China. Afterwards Stilwell sent Davies back to the United States several times to orient the press on developments.

One person who was interested to hear more from him while in Washington was Churchill, who invited him for a talk at the British Embassy, "to get acquainted," as he said. One of the points that had been brought out at TRIDENT was Wavell's defeatism and the lethargy of the India command, which Secretary Stimson had frankly told Churchill needed attention. Before Stilwell had his encounter with the Prime Minister, Stimson coached him "so as to get some punch into his remarks and not be afraid of him." At the interview Stilwell felt he was being listened to sympathetically with the result that he talked well and, being thoroughly knowledgeable, impressed his listener. To his surprise Churchill thoroughly agreed with him on the lack of energy in India and had in fact already made up his mind to replace Wavell and his senior commanders. He formed the beginnings of "great respect and liking for General Stilwell."

In China panic had seized the Government as the Japanese drive progressed during April and May, and the Generalissimo in one of his celebrated tantrums reportedly threw teapots at the bearers of bad tidings. From his staff in China Stilwell learned "there was hell to pay at Ichang" and he ordered Hearn to "prepare for the worst" and Bissell to send 40 pursuit planes from India to the Fourteenth Air Force to aid in the defense and to prepare to send a squadron of medium bombers. Throughout this time Chinese communiqués reported heavy and continuous fighting, with the Japanese several times said to be "collapsing under Chinese counterthrusts" and suffering "heavy losses," "encirclement" and "annihilation." Eventually in June the Japanese withdrew without pursuit from what appeared to have been a training and foraging offensive to collect rice and river shipping. The result was announced by the Chinese, and willingly reported by American correspondents, as a major Chinese victory.

Stilwell returned to China via London and Cairo, stopping en route to call on fellow-commanders in North Africa, as he told reporters, to "check on their tactics." After the Hump, "crossing the Atlantic is *nothing*. You don't know you're doing it." In London he engaged on a round of high-level visits (arranged on instructions from Marshall to enhance his prestige) culminating in a state luncheon in his honor with a speech by Mr. Attlee, the Deputy Prime Minister, and a response by himself. Although he wrote that this was "making much of the country boy," he was perhaps not entirely indifferent to the occupations of the past month. His diary for the two days in London included the cryptic note, "High time I retired the other me."

15

Stilwell Must Go

JUNE-OCTOBER 1943

T HE effort to supply China, and the air and ground forces in China, presented the greatest logistic challenge of the war, probably of any war. If natural obstacles of terrain and climate were extreme, human obstacles raised by the mutual antagonisms and soured morale of reluctant cobelligerents were no less so, and the monsoon of the summer months thickened the misery. To raise the Hump's deliveries to 10,000 tons a month under these conditions, as directed by TRIDENT, was a struggle.

"The C-46 is full of bugs," Stilwell noted worriedly on one of his inspection tours. "Carburetor ices up. We have lost six over the Hump and the boys' morale is lower and lower." Crews were rebellious and often bailed out as soon as an engine missed once, or refused to fly if there was a cloud in the sky. Convinced that the "slopeys" were not fighting and that black markets awaited the cargo destined for the ground forces, the fliers did not want to risk their lives to fill private godowns, although they would take any risk to fly supplies to the Fourteenth Air Force. Defense against Japanese fighters was poor because the Japanese concealed their airfields from aerial photography and even from Kachin scouts by hiding their planes in holes in the ground covered with sod. The OSS unit rescued 125 ATC crew members in 1943 but this represented less than a third of all who went down, the rest to death or capture. Nevertheless, with reinforcements, a new ATC commander and new energizing after TRIDENT, and gradual ironing out of the C-46 faults, morale and flying conditions improved, and tonnages rose from 3,000 in May to 5,500 in July to 8,000 in September, and, after the rains ended, to an unbelievable 13,000 in November.

But the results were gained at the expense of the Road because many bulldozers, trucks, graders and shovels as well as men were diverted to build up the Assam airfields. The effort to bring supplies to men who were left at the roadhead bogged down in mud during the monsoon. Vehicles could not get through; elephants and Naga porters could not deliver the necessary amounts of food, fuel and equipment; earth slides destroyed a day's work in an hour; bulldozers were lost over banks when the ground gave way; everything—men, machines, tents and terrain—was sodden with rain; food was inadequate and malaria chronic. Burma was even ready with a new and unprepared-for disease, scrub typhus, which produced skin lesions, high fever, internal hemorrhage, confusion, delirium and all too frequently death.

While the ATC expanded, the Road progressed only three miles from May to August. It came to be identified in the theater with Stilwell because of his insistence on the recovery of north Burma, and it was generally regarded as Stilwell's folly. The British were forever saying it was an impossibility because there never had been a lateral road across the mountains of Burma; nature arranged that communications ran north and south in line with the river valleys. This was true though not necessarily conclusive. Few thought the Road could ever deliver enough to make it worth the expenditure in resources, men and misery. Only Stilwell, according to General Slim, believed it was "both possible and worth the resources it would demand," whereas he himself would have used the resources required for the Road to launch a full-scale offensive to retake all Burma from Rangoon up, thus supplying China with far more than the Road could carry. That much was obvious, and what Stilwell heartily wanted far more than Slim. The only difficulty was that Slim's chiefs, as he well knew, unrelentingly refused from first to last to launch any such full-scale offensive. Stilwell did not choose the Ledo Road as preferable but as a poor alternative, necessary first of all to supply the campaign in north Burma and ultimately operations in China. He could say with Hannibal, "I will find a way or make one."

By August the difficulties made it apparent that Road and Hump together would not suffice both to carry themselves and deliver enough fuel for expanded air operations from China. Facing the stark fact that it required a ton of gasoline to deliver a ton of cargo to China, the planners at the Quebec Conference in August decided that the situation required a pipeline. Another wild leap of engineering, stretching 1,800 miles from Calcutta to Kunming, laid across mountains and canyons, through streams and river beds, carried by wooden trestles and suspension bridges built without steel, it was to be the longest pipeline through the worst territory in the world and was naturally christened Pipe Dream by its builders. Like the Road, it would have to follow in the track of the offensive, and neither pipeline nor road could reach China unless the campaign succeeded.

Underlying all the physical disabilities of CBI was the lack of an agreed upon goal to fight for and to generate enthusiasm. The average American in China, without his usual beer and PX supplies for which ATC space could not be spared, disgusted by the surrounding squalor and filth which afflicted him with diarrhea, worms and every variety of intestinal disease, alienated by the callous cruelties of Chinese life, and with little understanding of the long deprivation and hunger for goods that led Chinese theft and graft to flourish, did not, as the romanticists like to believe, learn through contact that all men are brothers. On the contrary, he came to regard all Chinese as corrupt, inefficient, unreliable, triple-damned, steal-you-blind, hopeless, slopey sons-of-bitches. In and around the supply bases the hostility on the whole was returned. The average Chinese found the Americans stupidly profligate, coarse, contemptuous, often brutal and easily corruptible. The "better class of people" in China, according to Embassy reports, were "surprised and shocked" by the rowdiness of American troops on leave and the "boorish" manners and "unkempt and disreputable" appearance of Fourteenth Air Force personnel.

Lend-Lease provided limitless opportunity for mutual antipathies. No item, from medicine to half-ton trucks, was not for sale on the black markets of Kunming. Even the Fourteenth Air Force reported that "the Chinese are caching gasoline and charging it to our planes." One plane was listed as having been refueled eight times in one day for a total of 700 gallons when it had actually flown a total of four hours, an arrangement that could hardly have been accomplished without American connivance. In the atmosphere of CBI Americans were not slow to share the graft. Smuggling of gold, sulfa drugs, foreign currency, cigarets, gems and PX supplies was carried on by American Air Force, Army, Red Cross and civilian personnel for an estimated take of over $4,000,000 by the end of 1944. Investigators of the Army CID had 300 cases under charge at one time, of which the most notable was the "Bordello Affair" of the Fourteenth Air Force. Besides its primary purpose involving girls imported from Kweilin, the glamour city of south China, and from India over the Hump, the place was also used as a smuggling center and this, on being reported, required Stilwell to take official action. "Officers pimping. Hauling whores in our planes. Sent for Chennault. He *knew*. . . . More dope on gas-stealing ring." The affair generated investigation by the theater Inspector General, and because of the involvement of Chennault, which proved deeper than just knowing, created further ill feeling. Chennault's various financial operations in China were one cause of General Arnold's disfavor.

India, the Rear Echelon, was exasperating both for its British imperialists and supine "wogs," as Americans called the Indians. Americans tended to associate the British in India with George III, and the Indian uprising of 1942 with Lexington, Concord and Bunker Hill, but their initial sympathy with the Indians soon faded into impatience and contempt. There were so many of them, so apparently habituated to servility. They lacked the vitality and laughter and inner self-assurance of the Chinese. Americans quickly assimilated the British attitude toward the natives without ceasing to castigate imperialism. Not without reason the initials CBI were said to represent Confused Bastards in India. Its members wore on their sleeves the shield-shaped CBI patch with the star of India and sun of China surmounting the stripes of the United States. This was intended to distinguish Americans from British and to show that they were in Asia as Allies to defeat the Japanese, not to restore the British Empire. But the three parts of the emblem could not make a whole. With the kudos and promotions going elsewhere, ridden by discontent, scandals, frustrations and complex animosities, CBI was an unhappy theater, at odds within itself.

Deprived of leverage, Stilwell had now to obtain Chiang Kai-shek's consent to participate in a Burma campaign that did not include Rangoon. As consolation or perhaps bribe, it was going to be his happy duty to confer Roosevelt's proposed award of the Legion of Merit on Chiang and also on Ho Ying-chin, the man he believed more than anyone responsible for the debility of the Chinese Army and for whose removal he never ceased agitating. "It will make me want to throw up," he wrote to Win. (By way of compensation the medal was also going to his friend Shang Chen, to Dr. Robert K. S. Lim of the Red Cross and to the generally admired Yü Ta-wei, chief of Ordnance.)

Stilwell's disgust was more than just personal. He felt there was something fundamentally wrong about America's having maneuvered herself "into the position of having to support this rotten regime"; one that so curiously mirrored what she was fighting against in Germany—in both cases, as he saw it, "a one-party government, supported by a Gestapo [Tai Li's organization] and headed by an unbalanced man with little education." He tried at times to recapture understanding. He wrote down at length a talk with his friend and adviser Chiang Monlin, the leading academic figure in China, who reminded him that while Europe had been working through the process of political education for centuries, China had had only 50 years and was working on an imported civilization, not a domestic one. Though the Generalissimo, he said, was handicapped by lack of education, "even now there is no one better in sight." It was not surprising, as Stilwell knew from his experience of the 1920s and 30s, that the Kuomintang governed the country so badly because the concept of civic as distinct from family responsibility had not developed in China and the mandarinate which had performed civic functions had been destroyed.

But Stilwell's own frustrations were uppermost. Roosevelt's decision in favor of Chennault had obviously reduced his influence and confirmed the Generalissimo in his resolve neither to fight nor reform. "I have been ignored, slighted, blocked, delayed, double-crossed, lied to and about. . . ." He had lost tolerance.

After three weeks of waiting for a reply from Chiang, he discovered that Ho, although War Minister and Chief of Staff, knew nothing about the TRIDENT proposal; he had not been told. To Stilwell's rage he was trying to divert arms from the Y-force for use in Hupeh. Delays and postponements in assignment of divisions for the Y-force, all of which had been promised for March 1 at the latest, continued. Ch'en Ch'eng was refusing to return to the command until they were in position. One of the missing divisions, promised "positively" for May 20, still had not arrived by June; in July a token of 1,200 men appeared. Fillers for Ramgarh presented the same problem. Of 4,500 promised for March, not one had appeared by July. Of 200 men promised for the heavy artillery, all but 65 were rejected by Chinese doctors and 30 more by American doctors; 35 reached Ramgarh. Later, under pressure of the actual campaign, boys of twelve to fourteen were sent as replacements. After a meeting with Ho taken up with a dispute about trucks, Stilwell's endless persistence nearly gave out. "I struck a new low after this conference. It seems absolutely impossible to do anything."

He ascribed Ho's developing resistance to Ramgarh to the loss of face its methods reflected on Ho's own management of the Chinese Army. He overlooked the fact that in direct pay of the troops and in raised expectations of food and medical care, Ramgarh was in effect subversive. With regard to the Y-force Stilwell felt the Chinese were resisting every attempt to help them get ready to fight. "That's the crux of it— they just don't want to get ready to fight." This was indeed the crux. It was not the Chinese way to seek solutions through decisive battle. The one occasion when they had sought battle, at Shanghai in 1937, had not been for a military purpose but for its effect on national and foreign opinion. The promises made to Stilwell about the Y-force were made to obtain matériel, not with intention to carry them out. In Chinese practice a promise was a method of getting on with people, not the equivalent of intended performance. Stilwell knew this well enough yet he continually counted on the promises made to him

—and wrote down angry lists of nonfulfillment—because he could not escape his inborn assumption that a promise represented intention.

There were Chinese who wanted a reformed army. Many of the officers at the Kunming schools were hard-working and eager for instruction. Pai Ch'ung-hsi, appointed Director of Training, was enthusiastic when he became the first Chinese officer from the capital to inspect the schools; neither the Generalissimo nor anyone from the War Ministry had come. Pai visited each course, asked for the field manuals, made speeches to the officers about American methods and was ready to start the school for the second 30 divisions at Kweilin, the capital of Kwangsi province. His enthusiasm was not disinterested, for the program would mean an accrual of strength to the Kwangsi faction of which he was one of the leaders. It was just such a development that Chiang Kai-shek feared. To Stilwell, ever ready to seize on encouragement, Pai's support appeared as a "major victory" and Pai "perhaps the best man in China."

Yet he ached to have "real authority" to carry out the consolidation and training of 60 divisions for a combat-worthy Chinese Army; otherwise Lend-Lease would never be used for its intended purpose—to arm Chinese to fight Japanese. He came to the conclusion about this time that he could never accomplish his aim and the original purpose of his mission without a more definite form of command within the Chinese Army than his purely advisory post as Chief of Staff to Chiang Kai-shek. He conceived of a position as "Field Chief of Staff" which he believed the United States could obtain for him if they were willing to tell China that loss of Lend-Lease was the alternative. This plan, which took shape in his notes of June 1943, was the genesis of the proposal that a year later was to enclose his fate. As Stilwell conceived it, the United States would require the Generalissimo to appoint him to the post with accompanying orders to the War Ministry to implement his decisions. If Chiang refused, the United States should "stop all supply to China. . . . He can't refuse. It's his neck if we turn him loose. $500,000,000 talks here."

He drafted messages to Marshall at this time proposing that his plan be implemented. The drafts testify almost to agony at the failure of his Government to use the bargaining power of Lend-Lease. "Our policy is wrong. Our conception of Oriental policy is wrong." Because of the President's refusal to demand a quid pro quo for American aid, Stilwell held him responsible for the failure to reform the Chinese Army. He exaggerated the power of the quid pro quo because he did not have it, although it was plain that in face of an ultimatum Chiang would always have found a way to avoid introducing reforms he dared not make. Underneath Stilwell knew the bargaining power of Lend-Lease was no magic wand to transform the nature of the Chinese system: in one of his random essays on the general derelictions of the regime he wrote, "To reform such a system, it must be torn to pieces."

Radios from Marshall prodded him on the Legion of Merit. "Cooperate, damn you," as Stilwell recorded them, "FDR wants a date!" Stilwell had raised the rather naive objection that Chiang had not earned the Legion of Merit. Chiang in his turn, presumably none too pleased to receive the medal from Stilwell, had proposed that it be delivered to him by messenger, which Stilwell took as an insult to the highest award America could give a foreigner. In this mood the ceremony duly took place on July 7, immortalized by film. With both principals dead-pan, Stilwell read the citation in Chinese to the "champion of liberty and freedom" for his "noble and inspiring achievements," and pinned on the medal at arm's length while Chiang gazed into the distance and Madame, looking chic in a sleeveless print but for her inevitable butterfly-bowed open-toed shoes, watched benevolently. "Peanut was half an hour late. . . . Everyone anywhere near him turned to stone. . . . When I grabbed his coat and pinned it on, he jumped as if he was afraid I was going to stab him."

Five days later on July 12 Chiang agreed to take part in the Burma campaign, this time in writing and signed. Stilwell's pen, as had now become habitual, ran down the long list of obstructions, skullduggery and "general cussedness" it had taken to reach this point. "Holy Christ, I was just about at the end of my rope." He was in no mood to remember how much of the backing and filling on Burma had been Anglo-American. He went off at once to India for a stay of six weeks to prepare for the campaign. After a surfeit of Chungking, he looked forward to commanding the Ramgarh force in action himself. Ch'en Ch'eng, who was said to be suffering from ulcers, had not returned but whether from illness or reluctance or the inner workings of Chinese politics, was uncertain. While the Y-force was in far from satisfactory condition, Stilwell believed there was little more he could do. The training program would continue under Dorn's command, but as to obtaining divisions and replacements he felt he had used up his resources.

By this midsummer of 1943 he was forced to recognize that what he, the American, had come to bring—fighting effectiveness—was not wanted. What had seemed Chiang's inexplicable resistance to his own best interests Stilwell now realized was rooted in his fear that "it would be risky to have an efficient trained ground force come under the command of a possible rival." He acknowledged the reason to Marshall in a letter of July 23 and wrestled with the problem further in his notes. The recurring obstructions that had plagued and puzzled him all along he now saw as stemming from Chiang's "fear of a challenge to his authority, as well as to his belief that air power is decisive and there is no use putting any time on ground troops. Otherwise he could not complacently take the terrible risk of leaving his army in its deplorable condition." There was one other possible explanation: that "he really thought the Army was in excellent shape and only in need of weapons to make it formidable. It is hard to imagine a military man as dumb as this. . . ." The truth of the matter was that Chiang was not so much dumb as uninformed because he refused to listen to anything but favorable reports. As Chiang Monlin had said, "He does not know what is going on. He writes orders by the thousand—like snowflakes—and everybody says, 'yes, yes,' and he never knows what has been done." He seemed the reincarnation of Yeh Ming-ch'en, Governor-General of Canton in the Second Opium War, who refused either to negotiate or surrender when bombarded by British naval forces, and was celebrated in a Cantonese topical ballad: "He would not fight, he would not make peace and he would not make a defense. He would not die, he would not surrender and he would not run away."

At this point, in an effort to put a new face on the discontents and divisions of the theater, CBI was broken up under a major realignment of command. All through the summer between TRIDENT and the next conference at Quebec the variance between the British and American evaluation of the importance of keeping China in the war stunted the strategic planning for CBI. Although Wavell had been elevated to Viceroy and replaced as Commander-in-Chief India by General Sir Claude Auchinleck, former commander of the British Eighth Army in North Africa, the recommendations of Auchinleck and his staff proved as pessimistic as his predecessor's. The basic reason was that the British no longer trusted the will of the Indian Army to fight for the Empire. Under the circumstances they did not want to undertake the major effort and risk of a campaign through the wastes of north Burma merely to assist the Chinese whose role in the war they claimed was "generally worthless" and whose future stability they were not concerned to support. When, during staff discussions in London, American planning officers argued that failure to open a supply route through Burma might cause the collapse of China and with it the loss of the Allied assault base, Ambassador John Winant commented to John Davies that "the PM was quite willing to see China collapse." Churchill had not for a moment changed his belief that Japan would be defeated from the perimeter, leaving China out of the strategic plan.

Roosevelt was as determined as ever on having China as the fourth cornerstone of the postwar world order, and to promote the cause had suggested in June a meeting between himself and Chiang Kai-shek for later in the year. He was strongly dissatisfied "with the way our whole show is running in China." The Generalissimo and Chennault complained of unkept promises and the President continued to lay the blame on personalities. At a conference with Hopkins, Marshall, Leahy and Somervell on July 15 he stated that "Stilwell obviously hated the Chinese," that his telegrams were sarcastic, that this feeling was undoubtedly known to the Chinese and the Generalissimo, and furthermore "that it is quite clear the Generalissimo does not like Stilwell." Marshall admitted that Stilwell was indiscreet but distinguished between his feeling about Chinese officialdom and "his great regard for the Chinese people" and continued to maintain that he was indispensable.

Churchill's proposal that a new Southeast Asia Command (SEAC) be established separate from the existing India command appeared to offer a prospect of settling some of the difficulties. Since there were no American combat troops in the area and none contemplated, it being American principle not to fight to restore imperial territory, the commander of SEAC would have to be British. At Quebec a Supreme Allied Commander (SAC) was finally agreed upon in the handsome, gallant and pleasing person of forty-three-year-old Vice-Admiral Lord Louis Mountbatten, a cousin of the King with the permanent rank of Captain who as Chief of Combined Operations had led the ill-fated raid on Dieppe.

Stilwell was to be Deputy SAC while retaining his other positions as commander of Americans in CBI and as Chief of Staff to the Generalissimo. He was thus made responsible simultaneously and severally to three sets of command: through Mountbatten to the Allied Combined Chiefs, through Marshall to the American Joint Chiefs, and to the Generalissimo. In addition he held operational command of the Ramgarh force, now renamed, for proper military suitability and added confusion, Northern Combat Area Command (NCAC). The interlocking and overlapping areas of command, geographically, operationally and nationally under these arrangements, were of such tangled complexity that no one then or since has been able to sort them into a logical pattern. Mountbatten and even Marshall were a bit dazed by them; Churchill confessed they were incomprehensible. Stilwell, the chief victim, not being the kind to take tables of organization more seriously than the tasks they cover, was content to describe his fate rather mildly as "a Chinese puzzle with Wavell, Auk, Mountbatten, Peanut, Alexander [the ATC commander] and me all interwoven and mixed beyond recognition."

The British motive behind SEAC, as Davies analyzed it for Stilwell, hinged on the reconquest of their possessions in Southeast Asia which was an essential undertaking if Britain was to be fully restored to the position of a first-class power. The American presence in India and Burma was an embarrassment, but since they had to bear with it, their aim was "to effect the partnership and then dominate it . . . so as to bring us into line with their policy and action." This, he suggested, was the role of Mountbatten who might or might not carry confidential orders from Churchill "designed to inhibit his natural vigor."

Britain knew, Davies continued, that to whatever degree she joined the United States in actions designed to help China she would be acting contrary to her own interests, while the United States should know that to whatever degree she joined Britain in helping to restore colonial rule and white supremacy would be acting contrary to American policy, sentiment and future relations with the countries of Asia. A State Department official on reading the report wrote in the margin, "I am extremely glad we have in our service a man capable of producing it. But how depressing the future is!"

China was predicated by the planners at Quebec as the base for future long-range bombing of Japan. But the shadow of an alternative was cast by a significant decision to advance through the central Pacific to the Gilbert and Marshall Islands. These were still 2,500 miles from Japan and the strategic concept of long-range bombing from a Pacific base was barely more than a gleam in the Air Force eye. The long step forward to Saipan in the Marianas, 1,450 miles from Japan, was still far ahead and the capabilities of the B-29, designed to have a radius of 1,500 miles, were not fully known. The Americans at Quebec held to the view of the indispensability of China without persuading the British. All the old disputes were reargued. Apart from the north Burma campaign, no firm overall strategy for SEAC to match the handsome new command structure was reached. The projected defeat of Japan was put four years ahead in 1947 or, at the most optimistic, twelve months after the defeat of Germany which was envisaged for 1944.

The only step taken beyond TRIDENT for CBI was one Stilwell had long desired, the introduction of American combat troops, but only in the form of a small commando force of 3,000 assigned to north Burma under the code name GALAHAD. The model—so far not very successful—was Wingate's Raiders whose remarkable leader, a genius of unorthodox warfare, Churchill had brought with him to Quebec. After an innovative military career in Abyssinia and Palestine, Brigadier Orde Wingate had evolved a theory of Long Range Penetration (LRP) tactics based on the establishment of scattered small strong points in occupied territory from which commando parties would fan out behind the enemy to cut his line of communications. His scheme offered the same lure as did Chennault's of a quick cheap way to destroy the enemy. When the campaign for the previous spring had been canceled, Wingate's group, trained by him to an

extreme of readiness, had been allowed to go into action in Burma anyway, though without a strategic objective, except possibly to exhibit British
activity. Dramatic publicity attended the operation, though not its results
which were a disastrous 800 killed or missing out of 3,000. Nevertheless
the methods were considered valid and a renewed effort was planned in
concert with the coming campaign.

Marshall, impressed by the potential of LRP to shorten the campaign,
agreed to add an American unit. He was anxious to limit American action
in Asia and to get the war over quickly. Prolongation, he believed, held
dangers for the institutions of society. Because of the unpleasant fate of
Wingate's wounded, left to become prisoners of the Japanese, Marshall
and Arnold conceived of LRP as entirely dependent on air support for
supply, evacuation and reinforcement. Though the GALAHAD contingent
was to be under Stilwell's overall command, Marshall agreed to let it
serve under Wingate's direction.

Stilwell's reaction was predictable. "After a long struggle we get a handful of U.S. troops and by God they tell us they are going to operate under
WINGATE! We don't know how to handle them but that exhibitionist does!
He has done nothing but make an abortive jaunt to Katha, cutting some
railroad that our people had already cut, get caught east of the Irrawaddy
and come out with a loss of 40 percent. Now he's the expert. That is
enough to *discourage Christ.*" Marshall calmed him with a reminder that
"We must all eat some crow if we are to fight the same war together. The
impact on the Jap is the pay-off." Earlier he had sent Stilwell a message
urging an effort at genuine cooperation with the British; General Handy,
chief of OPD, suggested as an addendum that when the British played
"God Save the King," Stilwell did not have to join in the singing but he
might at least stand up.

Other discontents flourished besides his own: Chennault's were louder
than ever and found sardonic echo in Stilwell's diary. "He has been
screaming for help. 'The Japs are going to run us out of China!' It is to
laugh. Six months ago he was going to run them out." Chennault was
asking for reinforcements from the Tenth Air Force because his attacks
on merchant shipping had provoked sharp Japanese reaction against his
air bases. Since this is what he had always claimed would give his fighters
the opportunity to knock the Japanese out of the sky, Stilwell was dis-
inclined to divert planes from their primary duty of protecting the Hump
route to help him.

In the anterooms of Quebec the ubiquitous T. V. Soong in his black hat,
black-rimmed spectacles and cane exerted himself to find out what deci-

sions had been made affecting China. By this time the Americans had
learned through their access to the Japanese code that the Japanese in their
turn had broken the Chinese code. Chinese security, already a sieve, now
had large holes in it, making admission of China to the Combined Chiefs
foolhardy. The British were adamant against informing Soong of decisions
but it was impossible to tell him why, because if the information became
known to the Japanese, they would know that their own code had been
broken. Marshall, who never lost his iron tact or steel finesse, undertook
to handle the situation. He called Soong in, swore him to secrecy with
upraised hand, informed him of the Quebec decisions and of the fact that
the Chinese code had been broken, and said that if he violated his oath
and relayed the information by radio, the War Department would know
of it and that would be the end of him. He would have to return to Chungking and convey the information orally.

Simultaneously with Quebec the first honest statement appeared in the
American press of China's military incapacity and its corollary: that it
would be "calamitous" if the American people expected the Chinese to
play the main or a decisive part in the ultimate defeat of Japan. Hanson
Baldwin, military correspondent of *The New York Times,* had to go outside his own journal to tell the public (through the *Reader's Digest* of
August) that there had been "Too Much Wishful Thinking About China"—
the title of his article. "Missionaries, war relief drives, able ambassadors and
the movies have oversold us," he wrote. China "is not—in our sense—winning
battles, but losing them." Her great contribution lay in holding down 15-
22 Japanese divisions but "She has no real army as we understand the
term" and her communiqués were "almost worthless." Drawing on his
connections in the War Department, he described all the inadequacies of
health, training, equipment and defensive spirit in words Stilwell might
have used himself, but Baldwin came to different conclusions. Neither the
Hump nor the Road, he wrote, could supply enough for a major campaign
in China nor could ports be recaptured without a tremendous amphibious
campaign. Baldwin's conclusion, significant because it reflected the new
thinking in the War Department, was that Japan would have to be beaten
at sea, and on the mainland only in Manchuria where Russian power could
be applied.

Stilwell, who had to believe in his own mission, continued to see China
as indispensable. He drew up his own long-range plan for the defeat of
Japan involving a land offensive toward the coast at Canton of which the
spearhead would be three American divisions moved into China from
India after the reopening of Burma. This would be coordinated with
MacArthur's drive toward the same point through the Philippines and
Formosa, and with China-based air attack on the enemy's sea-lanes. The

final phase was to be a land offensive toward Shanghai along with long-range bombing of the Japanese home islands. He believed this design would cut down on the Quebec time table by one or two years. It depended on a vanguard of American troops and, in Stilwell's mind, on an American being in command of the joint Chinese-American forces. Often urged by his staff to lobby for his needs like other theater commanders, or to use the press like MacArthur or Chennault, he refused. "I will not bring any pressure on George Marshall. He's running a war all over the world. It's up to him to determine who should get what."

Stilwell did his best, however, to open the eyes of a group of five Senators on a tour of Allied countries who reached China in August. He kept telling himself that if the truth about the Kuomintang regime were made known, the resulting disillusion in America would frighten Chungking into taking action for fear of losing American aid. He escorted the Senators through Kunming and Chungking and "poisoned their minds as much as possible in the brief time I had but May [Mme. Chiang] turned on the glamor and I don't know who won." He believed that "at least they learned enough to be suspicious" and left "with their assurance shaken." When the Senators returned to the United States they reported that the British were using Lend-Lease to promote imperial interests, but at the urging of the State Department they said nothing openly critical of China. When Senator Lodge in a talk to the National Press Club went so far as to say that it was time "this sugary propaganda about China" was stopped, his remarks were filed by Hornbeck at the State Department under the title "Belittling China."

Talk was circulating in Washington to justify this title. Through enforced cooperation Americans were discovering how little China matched her myth. The new appreciation was reflected in the planning and strategy section of the War Department which began to reexamine the role of China in the overall strategy for the defeat of Japan. In comparison with developing prospects in the Pacific, the effort that would be required to utilize China's potential appeared not worth the expenditure. The cost of keeping China in the war for use against Japan, reckoned in the number of air force and service troops in CBI, had increased 500 percent in 1943 to a total of 95,500. Although these were few in comparison to 700,000 in the Pacific and 1,400,000 in Europe, they were where tradition was against putting them—on the mainland of Asia. In a paper entitled "Re-Analysis of our Strategic Policy in Asia," OPD put forward in October a tentative thesis: that little more be spent in China than was necessary to keep her in the war, that the bomber offensive base be limited, that only 30 divisions be trained, that Burma be bypassed and that excess service troops be withdrawn from CBI and used in other theaters. This drastic proposal, virtually embracing the British position, was not adopted, but the idea that China was strategically—if not politically—dispensable had been implanted.

On his return to Chungking from India at the end of August, Stilwell suddenly found himself the object of a peculiar tug-of-war that was to last through two months of mysteriously motivated maneuvers. It began with his first proposal involving the Communists. After consulting with a Kuomintang General, Teng Pao-shan, commander of the 22nd Army in the north, and with Davies and John Service of the Embassy, on the possibility of cooperating with the Communist 18th Group Army (formerly the 8th Route Army), he submitted a plan for a joint Kuomintang-Communist military action in the north as a diversion to forestall any plan the Japanese might have to renew the campaign up the Yangtze or the threat to Changsha. He suspected the enemy was contemplating such a move as a diversion to upset concentration of the Y-force. As Chief of Staff to the Generalissimo he advised that it was better to seize the initative and keep the Japs guessing rather than let them "throw *us* off balance by just such a diversionary attack as the one proposed against them." He outlined a precise plan of action "based entirely on military considerations," urging as an added argument that it would provide a test case of the Communists' professed willingness to operate under the Generalissimo's orders against Japan. "It will be ignored," he wrote in his diary.

Stilwell had made no contact with Chou En-lai or other Communists and, except for Davies, had not allowed any of his staff to meet with them. "Don't let me hear of your trying it," he warned when Dorn suggested it; "we're here with the Government." Six months earlier Chou En-lai had reiterated his invitation to American military observers to come to north China to study the ground for future operations at first hand, but the suggestion was not pursued.

During the summer in the course of reopened negotiations between Chungking and Yenan, Chiang had made it a condition of legal status for the Communists that they give up separate government in the north and put their armies under Central control. This was refused. A section of China's Central Executive Committee was pressing for a showdown now with the Communists, while Russia was still occupied against Germany, and the rumor spread that Chiang was planning an attack in September. Stilwell suspected this might be Chiang's diversion to avoid participating in the Burma campaign. He heard reports of Kuomintang troop movements to the north and asked Marshall to consider a directive on the role of U.S. forces in the event of civil war. His own advice was a strictly hands-off policy. The Embassy too grew alarmed by the reports. Setting foot on what was to be a long and tortured road, American diplomacy began exerting pressure for

In 1943 Stilwell conferred Roosevelt's award of the Legion of Merit on Chiang Kai-shek (188). He wrote on the picture of Madame admiring the medal: "May being coy" (189). Mme. Chiang and her sister Mme. Kung (190) later involved Stilwell in an intrafamily power struggle.

188

189

190

191

a coalition. For the time being the crisis lapsed. In a statement to the Central Executive Committee on September 13, Chiang Kai-shek disavowed the intention to use force against the Communists and affirmed that the problem was a political one to be settled by political means.

On the day of this announcement Stilwell was surprised to find himself invited by Mme. Chiang to a meeting at her home with herself and her sister, Mme. Kung. It was the beginning of a puzzling alliance with conspiratorial overtones promoted by the sisters through many meetings thereafter. Ella and May (for Ei-ling and Mei-ling) told Stilwell they were alarmed about the state of military preparations and anxious to do something about Chinese inaction. They agreed with him that Ho Ying-chin was the main obstacle and even that he must be removed. It was pathetic evidence of how restricted was the Generalissimo's area of trust, or how scant the supply of talent, or both, that the replacement for Ho suggested by the sisters was Madame herself. They urged Stilwell to keep up his pressure and promised to work on the Generalissimo in behalf of his efforts. "We signed an offensive and defensive alliance," Stilwell wrote without being too sure what it meant, but whatever the cause of this strange development, he believed his new allies meant business. "Isn't it a hell of a way to fight a war?" he wrote to Win.

The sisters told him that a campaign for his removal was under way (which he attributed to Ho Ying-chin) and of the grounds of complaint against him: that he had called Yu Fei-p'eng "that bandit"; that he signed memoranda as "Lieut.-Gen. USA" instead of "Chief of Staff to the Generalissimo"; that "I am 'haughty' and anti-Chinese . . . and say the Chinese are no good and look upon them with contempt." By now there was just enough half-truth to the complaint to give it life. In his diary, and doubtless in occasional speech, Stilwell was in the habit of referring to Yu Fei-p'eng and his kind as "tramps" if not "gangsters." It was undeniable that he regarded the military bureaucrats with contempt, though no more so than did many Chinese. As Gauss reported, they were a group renowned for "mismanagement and corruption." Stilwell's fault was his usual one of dispensing with euphemisms. He had been assigned to, and insisted on carrying out, a mission which its clients were doing their best to resist and the effect of being consistently thwarted did not improve a disposition difficult to begin with.

Stilwell imagined that the sisters' advocacy was owed to T. V. Soong who, he supposed, as a result of Marshall's prodding, must have told them "they had better get behind me and cooperate." The reverse was the case. The overture by Ella and May was a direct rebuttal of their brother who had initiated in Washington the campaign for Stilwell's recall, with the same vigor he had previously invested in his support. Claiming that Mountbatten's appointment eliminated the need for Stilwell's command, he submitted to

Brigadier Orde Wingate, who led the Raiders, also known as Chindits (191), and Lord Louis Mountbatten, Supreme Allied Commander in Southeast Asia (192), were two of Stilwell's dynamic English colleagues. In a group photo of Chinese officers (193), General Ho Ying-chin stands on Stilwell's right.

Roosevelt on September 15 a new plan for CBI involving the replacement of Stilwell by a Chinese who should have authority over the ATC as well as over all other military units of whatever nationality operating in the China theater. This was accompanied by a renewed demand for placing China on the Combined Chiefs and Munitions Control Board. Soong's motive was the primary urge for control of Lend-Lease. His influence was high so long as he could produce American aid for China's purposes, but Stilwell's insistence on making the Burma campaign a reality, thus absorbing supplies, threatened his position; hence Stilwell must go.

The sisters' counteroffensive reflected the fierce Soong family feud which was essentially a struggle for position and power. T.V.'s ultimate ambition was to lead China in Chiang's place. He represented the choice Emperor Meiji had made for Japan—adaptation of the techniques of the modern Western world to needs of his country—and as China's would-be Meiji he hoped to forge a power base from which to oust his brother-in-law, sweep out the reactionary faction and install a government that could modernize the country. Chiang Kai-shek had been turned back, by circumstance and a sea of troubles and disillusion with the West, more and more upon the past, to the values of Confucius and the mood of the Boxers. Palace rivalries, however, were more concerned with status than ideology. Ella and May were fighting for their husbands' and therefore their own positions against the challenge of their brother—the same grim in-fighting of a reigning family that led to murdered heirs and poisoned nephews in the days of the dynasties.

Stilwell's position carrying with it control of Lend-Lease became for a while the focus of this struggle—for reasons not entirely clear. Doubtless with Stilwell gone, T.V. expected to gain greater control of Lend-Lease; perhaps, by accomplishing for the G–mo the removal of his bane, he intended to demonstrate his own influence and move himself up the rungs of power closer to his target. This was what the sisters were determined to block.

T.V. was the most unembarrrassed and untiring lobbyist of his time. He used every conceivable channel to the President including James Roosevelt, Archibald MacLeish and innumerable others who, moved by his impressive powers of persuasion, undertook to convey his letters on the desperateness of every situation under the Presidential eye. Suffering from the family weakness for royal privilege, he asked in July for a White House No. 1 priority to fly to England and return with seven additional people and 500 pounds of excess baggage. (The answer is not on record.) In September when Soong presented his request for Stilwell's recall, the President, who had attempted it often enough himself, turned the matter over to Marshall with a note, "Dear George, will you talk to Dr. Soong about this? FDR."

The repeated maneuvers to remove Stilwell whether by the White House or Chungking or the Chennault claque or now Soong infuriated Marshall who felt they were in a sense a reflection on himself. He had selected Stilwell for the post and felt responsible for having consigned him to an ill-supported mission* and wasted the talents of an officer he respected as one of America's ablest field commanders. In his remote way he liked Stilwell and wrote to him some of his rare personal letters, with a note of muted banter missing from his other correspondence. He informed T. V. Soong that no change in the command structure was contemplated. Undeterred, Soong thereupon left for China with intent to accomplish his purpose another way. According to what he told associates, he had the President's promise (probably in the form of an assurance received from Hopkins) that if the Generalissimo officially requested it, Stilwell would be recalled.

Marshall and Secretary Stimson considered at this time whether it might not be advisable, after all, to withdraw Stilwell and offer him (as Stimson was later to write him) "some less impossible task." Marshall thought of giving him command of the Fourth Army, in which he had been serving at the time of Pearl Harbor. It was now in Alaska, with Stilwell's own 7th Division designated for the Marshall Islands operation. To replace Stilwell, General Marshall contemplated sacrificing the invaluable Somervell, then en route to China as a troubleshooter. But the change was not made, perhaps because the problems of China were too intractable. The Assam line of communications was clogged as usual, the ATC was hampered in consequence, Chennault's damage to the enemy was disappointing. Roosevelt was now less interested in Chennault than in the plan to mount long-range bombers in China, and this too was suffering the delays and obstacles that afflicted every effort in the theater. "Everything seems to go wrong," the President complained to Marshall in disgust. It was the classic complaint of CBI.

Each time the Chinese agreed to consolidate divisions, Stilwell was unfailingly encouraged. "VICTORY," he wrote on September 1 when he received a list of divisions for the second 30 which were to go into training as the Z-force at Kweilin. Taking this to mean that he was at last making headway, and encouraged by Ella and May who appeared genuinely to want action, he once more presented to Chiang Kai-shek a formal eight-point program for reform of the army over his signature as "Joint Chief of Staff for the Generalissimo." To meet the real cause of the Generalissimo's fears he urged that two 30-division groups properly constituted and trained would "assure the Central Government of obedience to its orders" and enable China to "emerge

---

* In his Third Biennial Report Marshall described it as "one of the most difficult of the war . . . at the end of the thinnest supply line of all."

at the end of the war with the means of assuring her stability." He did not really expect an answer and none was vouchsafed. Madame warned at this juncture that he was in trouble with the Generalissimo because of his proposal about the Communists, and he left for a week to inspect his forces and meet Mountbatten who had now arrived in India.

In obedience to Marshall, Stilwell meant to be agreeable and nobody made this easier than Mountbatten whose notable charm was expected to be a tonic for a dispirited theater. Encouragingly he had chosen a phoenix rising from the ashes as his emblem for SEAC and by way of a cheerful start brought a bevy of WRENS in his entourage and even persuaded Marshall to send 50 WACS despite Stilwell's rule of no women in the theater. He was anxious for success but the pessimism and inertia he met in India would have been enough to discourage Candide. Staff and line officers of his new command had no faith in offensive action in Burma and regarded the promised junction with the Y-force as Stilwell's hallucination. Mountbatten was told by General Irwin, retiring chief of the ground forces, that he was taking over a hopeless command and that morale among soldiers and airmen was so low that they could not fight again without two years of rehabilitation. Snubbing his rank, the air, naval and ground chiefs of SEAC (Air Marshal Peirse, Admiral Somerville and General Giffard) communicated over his head to London. Mountbatten impressed Stilwell as "a good egg" who was "energetic and willing to do anything to make it go" and "a nice informal guy." "This fellow seems all right," Stilwell said to Wedemeyer, who was to be Mountbatten's American Chief of Staff. "I think he's fair and I think he wants to do something." But he finished warily, "You watch him, Wedemeyer, keep your eye on him."

Characteristically, though senior in age and rank, Stilwell felt no resentment at serving under Mountbatten. This was not something that ever bothered him, perhaps because in his heart he was not ambitious or desirous of the top command; even, in his inmost heart, did not think he deserved it. Stilwell had many small ways of denigrating himself: in frequently not wearing medals or insignia of rank, in standing in line for mess or the barber's chair, in never using rank to obtain even normal privilege, in his living arrangements at the front in Burma which seemed to General Slim "unnecessarily primitive." A friend once overheard him in Washington as a four-star general telephoning for a pullman reservation without giving his name and meekly accepting an upper. He was one of those individuals who, though conscious of their quick intelligence and superior ability, for some reason do not think highly of themselves and even more lowly of most other people. This makes for being cantankerous. Yet Stilwell was basically optimistic and cheerful and happy when with his family or people he trusted.

Omens were somber as the Ramgarh force prepared to reenter Burma. A new fracas arose when Sun Li-jen, commander of the 38th Division, demanded the removal of General Boatner, Stilwell's deputy in command of the Forward Echelon, and his replacement by a Chinese. Sun had been claiming for weeks that Boatner underestimated Japanese strength in the Hukawng valley and was ordering Chinese patrols forward to certain disaster. Though himself one of the more aggressive Chinese commanders, Sun had no wish to suffer losses in his division which would cause his own position to dwindle in proportion; or it may have been that Chiang Kai-shek did not want losses and was acting behind Sun to hoard the now valuable Ramgarh force for purposes after the war. In any event Chiang supported Sun's demand for the removal of Boatner. As events were to prove, Boatner's estimate of Japanese strength in the valley was seriously at fault, but Stilwell took Sun Li-jen's maneuver as one more example of Chinese reluctance for the offensive. He wanted a Chinese-speaking officer (which Boatner was) to command the NCAC, and he felt a debt of loyalty to those of his officers like Boatner who had stuck by him and not run off to the richer opportunities of the European theater. In a decision that was to have unfortunate consequences all around, he refused to relieve Boatner on the ground that his post included command of American service forces supporting the offensive, and that there was no Chinese officer qualified to fill this position. Sun Li-jen and the Generalissimo had to acquiesce, with no accretion of good feeling.

Facing return to the cabals of Chungking, Stilwell had reached a low point and hated the prospect of going back to the begging and endless run-arounds. "If things don't look up in the next few months," he wrote to Win on October 15, "I'll be tempted to ask for a division or a regiment or even a squad somewhere else where the mental wear and tear is less." He longed for escape to action in the Hukawng valley. Reporting to Stimson all the failed promises to make ready the Y-force, he finished with profound sincerity, "I am awaiting impatiently the beginning of operations. It will be a heavenly surcease to get out with the troops and have a part in shooting at someone."

Stilwell returned to Chungking on October 15 to find himself a target. Within hours of his arrival he was stunned by an explicit demand for his recall from the Generalissimo himself on the ground that he had "lost the confidence of the troops." It was voiced through T. V. Soong acting as the Generalissimo's interpreter in an interview with General Somervell who had just arrived. Soong had already told Somervell that Roosevelt had agreed to the recall and he had told Mountbatten on his way through Delhi that Stilwell's relations with the Chinese troops were very bad and that his appointment as Deputy SAC would have "disastrous irrevocable repercussions."

The affair of Sun Li-jen, with whom Soong had been in correspondence, provided a basis. Somervell broke the news of the Generalissimo's demand to Stilwell to whom it seemed definitive: "Here go 20 months of struggle."

He knew the real reason for Chiang's antagonism was annoyance at being pushed into action and goaded to reform. In one of his earlier summaries of frustration he had written, "I have told him the truth. I have brought all deficiencies to his notice. I have warned him about the condition of his army. I have demonstrated to him how these things can be corrected. All of this he ignores and shuts his eyes to the deplorable condition of his army which is a terrible indictment of him, his War Ministry and his General Staff." This was exactly Stilwell's crime. His constant reminders of the regime's deficiencies caused Chiang to lose face, especially as they concerned his own sphere of military affairs. Stilwell's presence itself had become the "terrible indictment."

The sisters at once moved to the counteroffensive. Frenzied conferences ensued. Ho Ying-chin, pursuing his own interests, appeared in the astonishing role of Stilwell's advocate. The reason for this was that Ho's rival, Ch'en Ch'eng, who represented the forward group among the military, figured as an ally in T.V.'s plans. Since Ch'en Ch'eng was also Stilwell's favorite and had always been his candidate to replace Ho, this aspect of T.V.'s scheme becomes something of a Chinese puzzle.

On the day of the crisis, Mountbatten arrived in Chungking to discover that his Deputy, the man most versed—however unhappily—in relations with China, was about to be snatched from under him. New to the theater and in need of collaborators, he was alarmed for his own sake and went at once to tell Stilwell, "If you want your job back, I'll get it for you." Stilwell had no doubts as to the reason. "He is burned up because he'll have to work with a new man. Wants me to wait over and break him in." Convinced himself that he was through, he doubted that Mountbatten could bring about a reversal and drew back from the doorway on his arrival saying, "You should not be seen shaking hands with me; it will be bad for you." But Mountbatten was confident and sure-footed. Before going to meet the Generalissimo he sent word through Somervell that he could not proceed with plans for using the Chinese forces if the man who had commanded them for nearly two years was to be removed. However little Chiang wished to share in the campaign, to have his forces formally rejected would be an unacceptable loss of face.

He was now open to pressure. Somervell exerted all his tact and persuasions and May and Ella their various and evidently vigorous arguments. By evening they were able to tell Stilwell that the act could be undone if he would go to see Chiang and say that he had only one aim, the good of China, that if he had made mistakes they were from misunderstanding not intent, and that he was ready to cooperate fully. They argued persuasively that if this could be put over, his position would be much stronger than before; his "star was rising." To avoid dismissal, Stilwell with rage in his heart swallowed the necessity. He "put on the act" and found the Generalissimo—trapped by the internal power struggle complicated by the intervention of Mountbatten—"doing his best to be conciliatory." Reconciliation was effected and the crisis settled within 24 hours of its eruption. Visibly, if not in the recesses of the Generalissimo's spirit, Stilwell's position was reinforced, and the episode had undoubtedly ended, as he wrote, in a "terrific loss of face for Peanut."

That Chiang should have let himself be caught in a situation that required him to back down after officially making the request to Somervell was the strangest aspect of the whole strange affair. He had clearly been persuaded by T.V., who had failed to count on Mountbatten's reaction or on the strength of the influences his sisters were able to mobilize. In penalty Soong was ordered in effect to sweep the tombs of his ancestors and disappeared from the scenes of power for nearly a year. For Stilwell it had been a "nasty damn experience" that left him with "a dark brown taste" in his mouth and a "dark brown outlook" in his mind. He had no generosity left for the Generalissimo (he did not know until later of the role played by T.V.) and the simile that occurred to him was of a rattlesnake that had struck without rattling.

Mountbatten could now proceed to open official relations which he did by presenting Madame with a Cartier vanity case set with her initials in diamonds and by introducing himself to Chiang Kai-shek as a young and relatively inexperienced officer for such a high command who was ready to "lean on his vast experience for help and advice." This line, he reported to Roosevelt, "went down very well with him," and he had separately taken a similar approach to Madame with equal success. They had presented him in turn with the most charming carved Chinese jade seals for himself and his wife, enabling him to depart feeling he had made two real friends and "they were good enough to express the same views to me." Now the "only difficulty" that remained was the line of communications and the airlift to China, and "if we can only get our logistics to come out right," the future could be looked to with confidence. Roosevelt replied that he was "really thrilled over the fact that for the first time in two years I have confidence in the personality problems in the China and Burma fields—and you personally are largely responsible for this."

A little tact, a Cartier compact, a gracious personality—harmony in Chungking at last.

16

China's Hour at Cairo
NOVEMBER-DECEMBER 1943

For a while the harmony seemed real. The Generalissimo became astonishingly amiable and in conferences on the campaign was willing and cooperative. Somervell returned to Washington with an encouraging report and Mountbatten returned to India very satisfied; fooled, Stilwell thought, by Chinese politeness: "He thinks they will do everything." Assent to his own demands by Chinese War Ministry officials was now ungrudging and even respectful. May and Ella promised to push through all his proposals and opened the exhilarating possibility of replacing Ho Ying-chin by Shang Chen. "May calls me Uncle Joe now"—the name by which he was generally known in the theater. ("Vinegar Joe" was used chiefly by the press.) The sisters wished him to speak for China at the coming inter-Allied conference at Cairo, the first at which China was to be present as a full partner. They wanted him "to put China right with the powers."

This was the clue. The Chinese saw Cairo as their major opportunity for status as well as more tangible acquisitions; Stilwell was needed to underwrite their requirements by a convincing presentation of China's military role in the defeat of Japan. Chiang Kai-shek was prepared to be "very friendly," according to Ella, and so he proved when Stilwell went to confer with him on November 6. The meeting was "Reconciliation Day! Love Feast Day!" and "the rattlesnake was affable as hell." He began by promising the long-sought 50,000 troops for fillers (if Stilwell supplied the gasoline to move them) and agreeing to feed them and even to supply extra rations.

Was there anything else Stilwell wanted? No? "Well, then, I officially request you to make the report for China at Cairo." Ella reported afterwards that Chiang was in a "jubilant" mood and "not only pleased but happy" over the talk with Stilwell which he considered to be "the most satisfactory we had ever had."

Formal recognition of China as a great power at the Foreign Ministers' conference at Moscow in the last week of October was behind all the good cheer. At American insistence, against the stiff opposition of the Soviets, China had been included as a signatory of a Four-Power Declaration pledging united action after the war to establish "a general international organization . . . for the maintenance of international peace and security." Chiang Kai-shek was thus at last the acknowledged equal of Churchill, Roosevelt and Stalin, and his status was about to be made visible by his presence at Cairo. His affability extended to Stilwell because he needed him to carry the burden of military plans and logistics before the Combined Chiefs—a task for which the Chinese staff was not adequate.

A special Presidential envoy in the person of Major General Patrick J. Hurley, who was to play a role in Stilwell's future, arrived in Chungking on November 7. His task was to complete the protocol—under negotiation ever since June—for Chiang's meeting with the other heads of state. Since the Soviet Union was not a cobelligerent against Japan, there could be no four-power meeting. The hoped-for entry of the Soviets was a crucial if muffled problem, and it was a part of Hurley's mission to ascertain China's attitude toward that event. Chiang expressed willingness to cooperate with Russia but stipulated for dignity's sake that Roosevelt must meet with him before meeting with Stalin. It was so arranged: after conferring with Chiang at Cairo, Roosevelt and Churchill would move on to meet with Stalin just outside his own borders at Tehran.

Hurley was a breezy Oklahoman who had risen from log-cabin origins via the law, overseas service in World War I and impressive talents as a wire-puller, to become Hoover's Secretary of War. A tall, handsome man of flashy appearance with a pointed gray mustache and an important air, he inspired Colonel Barrett's memorable if irreverent greeting in Chungking, "General, I see you have every campaign ribbon but Shay's Rebellion." The reasons for Roosevelt's choice of Hurley as a diplomatic legman were probably mixed. A President usually has more than one object to accomplish with every appointment and, with next year's election in mind, Hurley as a "tame Republican" might be useful. To Stilwell he appeared as "a breath of fresh air, a real American." Coming from Delhi, Hurley told Stilwell that Mountbatten wanted to get rid of him because he, Mountbatten, was playing the Empire game and did not want risks but only "something that could be labelled a victory." Hurley was full of praise for Stilwell's efforts, told him he was regarded in the United States as the "Savior of China," laid it on thick and "says he is in my corner." Stilwell admitted enjoying his company because "the scarcity and unexpectedness of such an attitude is overwhelming."

He was especially irritated at this time by the President who, he felt, gave away every opportunity to drive a bargain with Chiang Kai-shek for Chinese military performance. "FDR has undercut me again" he wrote when the President informed Chiang of the project to base long-range B-29 bombers in China, "so I can't bargain on that." He allowed himself on November 9 the term "Rubberlegs" in referring to the President, a horrid mockery of Roosevelt's infirmity that appeared only once or twice again in the diary.

Elements of the 38th Division had by now advanced ahead of the Ledo Road to Shingbwiyang on the edge of the Hukawng valley. Without formal authorization, or certainty of support, or declared commitment to the offensive by the Combined Chiefs, Stilwell had launched a none-too-eager vanguard on the return to Burma. He conceived of it as a jerk to the sleeves of his allies that could not be ignored. Once committed to Burma, the Ledo force would draw in support after them and shame the British and Chungking into joining the campaign. The immediate objective was to occupy land for an airstrip. Thereafter, supplied by airdrop plus pack train and porters, the advance would cover the forward movement of the Road until it reached the Tarung River, takeoff line for the main thrust which was expected to begin about December 1. The overall plan called for a three-phase advance through the Hukawng and Mogaung valleys to Myitkyina, to be coordinated with a still uncertain British offensive further south from Imphal across the Chindwin to Indaw. The opening move into the Hukawng was based on an erroneous estimate of NCAC Intelligence that no enemy would be encountered in the first phase except some scattered Burman conscripts. In fact Japanese jungle fighters, veterans of Singapore, had established bridgeheads across the Tarung in preparation for their own offensive into India.

In Chungking the Generalissimo's promise of 50,000 replacements shrank the day afterwards, in the course of a conference between Stilwell and Ho Ying-chin, to 25,000 trained men and the rest recruits. "While we were talking the 25,000 became 20,000 and then, when pushed to state what units they were and when available, the 20,000 became 18 battalions which at full strength will be 14,000." Ch'en Ch'eng, the "Man of Genius" as Stilwell sometimes called him, on whom he had placed such hopes, had now joined T. V. Soong in eclipse and was definitely retired from command of the Y-force. He had been replaced by Wei Li-huang, Commander of the First War Zone and known as "Hundred Victories Wei." In Stilwell's records as Military Attaché he had rated Wei as the ablest of the war zone commanders, known for a driving personality, but now he was doubtful. To cross the Salween into Burma, "the Y-force needs a pusher and I doubt if this is it."

On the eve of his departure for Cairo the prognosis for an effective 30 divisions as reported by Dorn was bleak. The trouble was everywhere, in the elusive and pervasive absence of responsible agencies to deal with. Dorn recognized that the army could be made no better than its Government when he wrote in desperate jest, "The obvious remedy is to clear out the entire Chinese Government and start afresh." Otherwise, assuming continued intention to utilize the Y-force, the only alternative was to insist on absolute American control of all training, command and distribution without reference to Chungking "except for their information only." This was much the same conclusion Stilwell had reached in his plan to have himself appointed "Field Chief of Staff" with absolute authority. Dorn had worked out his proposal in concert with "serious-thinking" Chinese officers who were very worried about the trend of events and did not think effective reorganization could be accomplished without a "decided change" at the top. Beyond Chungking, they said, the Generalissimo's control was shaky; Yunnan was virtually independent, Kweichow had been seething in rebellion for the past six months and a threatened outbreak in Szechwan had been settled after a three-day battle between provincial and Central Government troops only by the Government's promise to remit taxes. In their view the Central Government "will be overthrown within six months after the war has been completed."

On November 13 the ruler over this thin ice accepted the proposals Stilwell had drawn up for China to present at Cairo. They were divided into two parts, stating what the Generalissimo was prepared to do and what he expected his allies to do. In the first half he was committed to a program for bringing 90 divisions, in three groups of 30 each, to effective combat strength. The first group was to be ready for the field by January 1, the second group, reequipped after opening of the Road from India, by August 1944, and the third group by January 1945. Stilwell's paper further committed China "to participate according to the agreed plan in the recapture of Burma" with combined attacks from Ledo and Yunnan. Following the opening of Burma, "an operation will be conducted to seize the Canton-Hong Kong area and open communication by sea." The Generalissimo's expectations were listed as an "all-out" Allied effort early in 1944 to reopen communications to China through Burma, using land, air and naval forces; American equipment of the 90 divisions; maintenance of the Fourteenth Air Force, the Chinese Air Force and the ATC at 10,000 tons a month; future operation of China-based long-range bombers; and finally Stilwell's dream, a U.S. force of ten Infantry and three Armored divisions to be landed after the reopening of Canton for operations against central and north China, with American command of the Chinese-American forces engaged in this operation.

The program was a statement of the maximum. How seriously Stilwell believed in it, despite all he had learned of the physical, political and philosophical limitations of Chinese military performance, is impossible to say. Certainly he saw himself as the commander-designate of the Chinese-American ground force. Though deeply distrustful of Chiang's intentions, he believed himself now in a strengthened position from which the goal seemed not impossible. He recorded the Generalissimo's specific acceptance of a future American commander with his ever-confident "VICTORY!"

Relations with Peanut were "cozy as can be," as each departed for Cairo.

The site of the Conference was the handsome Mena House hotel on the edge of the desert in view of the pyramids. The gathering was the largest yet with "all the British and American officers of whom one had ever heard," according to one awed participant,* plus the President and Prime Minister, attended by Hopkins and Anthony Eden and various ambassadors and civilian advisers. Stilwell recorded "a scramble for bathrooms." The strategic purpose with regard to the war in Asia was to decide what degree of investment to make in China, in combination with the Pacific, as the approach to Japan. The apparent reconciliation of Chiang Kai-shek and Stilwell revived the American concept of using Chinese troops, properly trained and led, once supplies could be got to them. Chiang's burst of cooperativeness appeared to Marshall and his staff as evidence of willingness at last to join in action against the Japanese.

At the same time a trend of opinion that now discounted Chinese capacity and recognized reliance on it as wishful thinking was running in favor of the Pacific. China remained essential as a base for the B-29s but the supposed advantage of Chinese manpower was beginning to appear nullified by the agonies of trying to mobilize it. Islands and aircraft carriers, now increasingly available, offered to replace the Chinese mainland and promise a shorter and faster campaign. The Pacific strategy was seen as combining eventually with use of Russian air bases and a Russian land offensive in Manchuria.

The Conference also had a political purpose. Roosevelt was determined that it should be a success from the Chinese point of view. He wanted to lay the ground for settlement of Sino-Soviet relations and of the Kuomintang-Communist schism, so likely to disturb the postwar order. The future of colonies was on his mind and the reassignment of Japan's territorial conquests was on the agenda. Although Roosevelt's strong anticolonial convic-

* Harold Macmillan, the future Prime Minister of Britain.

tions ran against a stone wall in Churchill, he looked forward to meeting Chiang Kai-shek and Stalin and was confident he could arrange matters with goodwill at the personal level. He considered it a "great triumph" to be assured by the Moscow Four-Power Declaration that hundreds of millions of Chinese would be on the Allied side in the postwar period.

For the present he considered that the job in China could be boiled down to one essential: "to keep China in the war tying up Japanese soldiers." At Tehran he told Stalin this was "our one great objective." The chronic fear of China's collapse obscured the fact that self-interest would keep her in the war under any circumstances. She could only regain Manchuria, Formosa and other possessions seized by Japan, as proposed at the Moscow Conference, if she emerged as one of the Allied team on the winning side.

Roosevelt's confidence in Chiang Kai-shek was not quite what it had been. He complained to Sumner Welles of the "innumerable difficulties" he had experienced over the past year with the Generalissimo whom he now classified, closer to Stilwell's version than Chennault's, as "highly temperamental." He spoke feelingly of the "corruption and inefficiency" that characterized Chiang's administration and said he had "no patience with the regime's apparent lack of sympathy for the abject misery of the masses of the Chinese people." Nevertheless, however "limited" the Generalissimo's military vision and "badly as his troops were fighting"—a new admission for Roosevelt—he was the only one who after the war would be able to hold the Chinese people together. "With all their shortcomings," he told his son, "we've got to depend on the Chiangs."

Accompanied by John Davies and Colonel Merrill, Stilwell arrived in Cairo on November 20. Seven thousand miles to the east on that day the U.S. Marines landed on the Gilbert Islands, the step that in ultimate effect was to cancel the need for China. Were it given to man to see over the horizon of time, the deliberations at Cairo could have been shorter and certainly simpler; as it was, the conferees proceeded as planned in the known terms of the moment. Everyone looked forward with open curiosity to seeing Chiang Kai-shek. His arrival at the airport, unannounced for security reasons, was not met by Roosevelt or Churchill, with wounding result to the Generalissimo's pride.

Roosevelt saw in him "the first real Oriental" he had met, unlike the Western-educated variety whom he knew. Sir Alan Brooke, unfriendly throughout, saw "a shrewd foxy face" like a ferret's and a leader "with no grasp of war in its larger aspects but determined to get the best of all bargains." Churchill was impressed by the Generalissimo's "calm, reserved and efficient personality" but irritated by the exaggerated attention given by the Americans to China's problems. Roosevelt was

The Cairo Conference, 1943. Standing behind the four principals are General Shan, Chen, Lieutenant General Liu Wei, General Somervell, Stilwell, General Arnold

ield Marshal Dill, Admiral Mountbatten and Major General Carton de Wiart (194).

"soon closeted in long conferences with the Generalissimo" and insisted on Chiang being present at the opening session of the Conference, thus preventing prior consultation between British and Americans. As a result, Chinese business which in Churchill's opinion was "lengthy, complicated and minor . . . occupied first instead of last place at Cairo."

China's aim was acquisition, while the opportunity lasted, of arms and title to former territories, including a bonus in the form of the Bonin Islands east of Japan. The return of Manchuria and Formosa, already agreed on by the Allies, was incorporated in a Cairo Declaration held in abeyance until Stalin could be consulted. More delicate questions concerning Dairen and other former Russian concessions, Hong Kong and relations with Britain, and the problem of the Communists were discussed in Roosevelt's talks with Chiang and Madame, of which no minutes were kept. Ever since the threatened clash with the Communists in September, American advisers had been anxious to avert Chinese civil war. Some thought that further American aid should be made contingent on a domestic settlement in China on the hopeful theory that pasting over the schism would somehow bring irreconcilable opponents into a workable coalition.

The military discussions occupied three days and the fate of the Burma offensive was darker at the end than at the beginning. The plan drawn by SEAC for the naval and amphibious action that Chiang insisted on (because he believed it would draw off the Japanese from heavy reaction to the land offensive) provided for capture of the Andaman Islands off the Burma coast. Its code name was BUCCANEER. The land offensive proposed for the British called for establishment of a bridgehead over the Chindwin and an airborne landing at Indaw on the railway to Myitkyina without further specified objective. Large numbers of troops and landing craft were scheduled to ensure the guaranteed victory that Mountbatten believed the theater required.

Stilwell summarized both operations as "abortions." They did not go anywhere or lead anywhere. They would show activity, satisfy Chiang's naval requirement and engage the enemy up to a point. Chiang was not told the actual objective of the Bay of Bengal operation, only that there would be one. Apart from leading nowhere, the main flaw of BUCCANEER was the disinclination of the British chiefs, especially Churchill, to undertake it, for reasons tangled in the dispute over the Second Front in Europe. Churchill did not want to do OVERLORD—the cross-Channel attack— either, preferring the peripheral approach through the Mediterranean aimed at the soft underbelly. He wanted to use the landing craft necessary for BUCCANEER for an attack on Rhodes with the object of bringing Turkey into the war. He always had on hand an option that could be proposed to avoid another course of action he did not like. Marshall intensely disliked the Rhodes proposal which would "burn up our logistics right down the line" and detract from OVERLORD on which American sights were fixed. The American chiefs were determined to carry out BUCCANEER in order to fulfill the promise to Chiang Kai-shek and thus bring in the troops from Yunnan without whom Stilwell's campaign could not open the back door to China. Marshall and King had been deeply impressed by Chiang's approval of Stilwell's program; they believed it represented a change of attitude that ought in no event to be discouraged.

Marshall's advocacy was bruised by the Chinese performance. Chiang Kai-shek was grasping and alienated sentiment in spite of the efforts of Madame who, not satisfied that the official interpreter conveyed "the full meaning of the thoughts the Generalissimo wishes to express," retranslated every statement made by or to him. He kept insisting that simultaneously with the campaign in Burma, and regardless of conflicting logistics, deliveries over the Hump must be maintained at 10,000 tons a month, and he insisted on an increased number of transports to assure this. Marshall, who considered the transports already assigned to the Hump as harmful to operations in Europe, reminded the Generalissimo in an angry outburst that these were American planes, personnel and matériel, that China must fight to reopen the Road if she wanted more matériel, and that there would be no further increase in transports: "There must be no misunderstanding about this."

At the session of November 23, when Stilwell was about to make China's presentation, he received a message from the Generalissimo telling him not to do so, that Chiang himself was coming, which was followed by several more messages canceling and reinstating his intentions. Meanwhile Anglo-American discussions of the Burma campaign, with Sir Alan Brooke in the chair, grew acrimonious. "Brooke got nasty and King got good and sore. King almost climbed over the table at Brooke. God, he was mad. I wish he had socked him."

In the afternoon Chiang and his generals came. "Terrible performance. They couldn't ask a question. Brooke was insulting. I helped them out." When, in the presence of the three chiefs of state, the Chinese were asked questions about the Yunnan force which they could not answer, Stilwell replied for them. Madame, the only feminine presence among all the uniforms, dressed in clinging black satin printed in golden chrysanthemums, with black tulle bows in her hair and on her open-toed shoes, did her best to distract attention with movements of studied gracefulness and glimpses through the slit skirt of a shapely leg. Brooke, the type of Englishman who considered a foreigner something to be snubbed and if nonwhite to be stepped on, pressed the embarrassed Chinese further, asking for their view of the plan of campaign which had previously been given them to read. There ensued, according to his account, "the most ghastly silence," followed by the Chinese "whispering together in a state of excitement," after which a spokesman announced, "We wish to listen to your deliberations." As the first such meeting the Chinese had attended, one in an alien context and language and overwhelming in gold braid and brass, it was not an experience in which they could easily shine.

When the session had been brought to an unhappy close, Brooke sneered to Marshall, "That was a ghastly waste of time," and afterwards recorded that it was "thanks to him and the American outlook that we had to suffer this depressing interlude."

Stilwell spent the evening helping the Chinese to prepare questions for the next day and briefing Madame for a lunch meeting she was to have with Marshall. He wrote out notes for her to use in arguing the case for American divisions. Before the afternoon meeting, the Generalissimo again changed his mind twice about attending; he came but asked Stilwell to present his views. Understandably dissatisfied with the short objectives of the SEAC campaign, he vacillated about committing the Y-force on this basis, while at the same time insisting on increased ATC deliveries.

In this impasse Roosevelt sent Mountbatten, the charmer, to try to explain realities to Chiang and secure his promise to cross the Salween; "a welcome change," as Stilwell wrote, "from me trying to fix it up." Through Madame as interpreter, Mountbatten worked hard to convince the Generalissimo that extra planes were simply not available. Chiang maintained a bland insistence on 535 transports. "The President will refuse me nothing," he told Mountbatten. "Anything I ask, he will do." In a last effort Mountbatten said that even if that many planes could be found, it would be impossible to meet the Generalissimo's demands for the Hump and at the same time mount the airborne assault on Mandalay that he wanted before the monsoon. At this point a prolonged colloquy ensued between Chiang and his wife until, responding to the query in Mountbatten's raised eyebrows, Madame turned to him and said, "Believe it or not, he does not know about the monsoon."

It was an enlightening proof of some of Stilwell's difficulties with the G–mo. The monsoon was the governing fact of life and of war in Southeast Asia. But Chiang Kai-shek was ruler of the Middle Kingdom and Chinese in his Middle-Kingdomness. China has no monsoon; ergo, he knew nothing of it.

On the afternoon of Thanksgiving day, November 25, Stilwell, escorted by Marshall went to see Roosevelt to present his argument for American troops and an American command in China. First on his mind was the post of "Field Chief of Staff," the source of future crisis. This appeared first in the notes he prepared for the interview under the heading "Ask FDR." He listed five components of the post: manpower, executive authority, U.S. troops, Chinese-American command and retention of command over the X-force with addition of one corps. In the notes he wrote, "No matter what Peanut agrees to, if something is not done about the Chinese high command the effort is wasted." He planned to tell the President of the need for a new War Minister to replace Ho Ying-chin or a "thorough reorganization" of his department or, echoing Dorn's last cry, underlined, *"Americans take over the first 30 complete and operate them."*

This time he made a genuine effort to explain the needs of the situation as he saw it. He felt the President heard him with "little attention." He broke into Stilwell's discourse to talk about the Andaman Islands, and in reply to the request for U.S. troops he offered to send a brigade of Marines to Chungking because, as he said, "Marines are well known. They've been all over China, to Peking and Shanghai and everywhere. The Army has only been in Tientsin." This remarkable irrelevancy, almost on a level with Chiang Kai-shek's ignorance of the monsoon, suggests there may be a special failure of communication in dealing with heads of state. Or perhaps it was the President's circuitous way of denying American combat troops for China. He did, however, agree, without a definite target date, to equip the 90 divisions, more from a desire to give Chiang Kai-shek something to show for his journey than from belief in a reformed Chinese Army. Stilwell considered this one of the "sure" commitments of Cairo. The Chinese, without ever producing 90 consolidated divisions, were to pursue it as a commitment for years.

Roosevelt did have positive ideas about the future. Stilwell recorded the President's plan for Indochina after the war: three commissioners, British, Chinese, American; "NOT TO GO BACK TO FRANCE!" As to his own proposals he drew a heavy line through them in his notebook and wrote, "N.B. *FDR is not interested.*"

During the interview the President reported that the Generalissimo after a private talk had now accepted the SEAC plan of campaign for Burma and agreed to send in the Y-force. At 9:00 that evening Stilwell received a call from Hopkins summoning him back to the residence where he learned that as of two hours ago Chiang had withdrawn his consent. "My God. He's off again."

The next morning a body of generals consisting of Mountbatten, Stilwell, Arnold, Somervell, Wheeler, Stratemeyer (the new Air Force commander for CBI) and Chennault descended upon the Generalissimo. "John Liu green with fright because we were three minutes late. Shang Chen peering out the door with ashen face and trembling knees. What a life for those boys. Scared witless all the time." Chiang went back to insisting on his 10,000 tons a month but was talked into again agreeing to the campaign by his assembled visitors—or so they thought. Before leaving for China the following day he reversed himself once more and told Stilwell to stay and protest and hold out for the airborne assault on Mandalay and 10,000 tons. Meanwhile Roosevelt and Churchill and the European contingent had left for Tehran while Stilwell was to wait for their return and a final decision. "So where are we?" he wondered, and concluded that War by Committee left the executors out on a limb. "Louis [Mountbatten] is fed up on Peanut," he noted, "As who is not?"

That was a fair summary, confirmed by Mountbatten's diary. The Conference, he wrote, was the first experience for Roosevelt, Churchill and the Combined Chiefs of negotiating with Chiang Kai-shek, and "They have been driven absolutely mad." The Generalissimo had cause to feel the same way, for in fact the British and Americans had never reached a firm decision or even agreement on the campaign they expected him to join. He had all along insisted he would not reenter Burma without a major amphibious campaign to commit the British, and from past experience Chinese trust in the word of the Western nations was small. He had reason for his doubts for in fact Churchill considered that the President had promised an amphibious operation in the Bay of Bengal over his objections, and recorded in his own minutes that he did not consider himself obligated.

In private conversation Marshall told Stilwell at Cairo how in September he had been ready to offer him the choice of giving up China and taking the Fourth Army and asked him what his decision would have been. Stilwell recorded no reply except the private one, "I've got to shovel." He accepted a scolding for the scathing language he used at his headquarters in referring to the Generalissimo, which his staff officers promptly peddled all over China. Stilwell promised to reform and two weeks later, as Marshall afterwards said, had gone back to his old ways.

While the Tehran meeting was in progress he plunged into sightseeing, flying to Jerusalem and also up the Nile to Luxor, site of ancient Thebes, visiting the tombs of Rameses and Tutankhamen and the temples of Karnak and recording with absorbed interest all he saw, at greater length in his diary than he gave to the Conference. "I am a sucker for antiquities and this is where they are," he wrote to Win. "I could spend months wandering around here. . . . If it hadn't been for this stupid conference I probably never would have seen these things"—on balance a not unreasonable order of priorities.

Two developments at Tehran crystalized the results of Cairo. These were Stalin's insistence on OVERLORD plus ANVIL (the coordinated landing in southern France) as soon as possible and his reiteration of the statement made earlier to Harriman and Hull at Moscow in October, that Russia would join the war against Japan as soon as Germany was defeated. Although Churchill fought hard for Rhodes and Turkey, American and Russian support of OVERLORD carried the day.* This promptly supplied Churchill with the excuse to cancel BUCCANEER and use its landing craft for southern France. He refused positively to do both, especially since, in his view, the Russian promise to enter the war against Japan eliminated the need for a campaign in China or a major effort to support China. BUCCANEER would be wasted. The prospect of Russia's entry, he maintained, changed everything.

Roosevelt was no less impressed by the promise which, though known before Cairo, evidently carried more weight when repeated at the summit by Stalin in person. Coming on top of the discouraging encounter with the Chinese, it raised the possibility of a substitute for China both as wartime partner and afterwards. Fresh from disappointment in Chiang Kai-shek, Roosevelt was the more anxious to find in Stalin a strong fourth corner of his postwar design. He once said to Ambassador Bullitt, "I think that if I give him everything I possibly can and ask nothing of him in return, noblesse oblige, he won't try to annex anything and will work with me for a world of democracy and peace." He believed that by cooperating fully and amicably with Stalin on such matters as OVERLORD, and meeting legitimate demands such as access to a warm-water port like Dairen, he could bring the Soviet Union wholeheartedly into the planned league of united nations. In the cordial mood of a historic meeting he formed the conclusion that Stalin was "getatable" and could be drawn into postwar cooperation for common aims. Responding to toasts at Churchill's birthday dinner on November 30, he said, "We have proved here at Tehran that the varying ideals of our nations can come together in a harmonious whole." In this presumed harmony the problem of China began to seem less urgent.

Casually Stalin contributed his bit to the decline. When Roosevelt told him about the Burma offensive and the role of the Yunnan force he remarked that the fighting capacity of the Chinese troops was low owing to "poor leadership." He made no objections to the proposed Declaration on the return of China's territories and future independence for Korea, merely commenting that "the Chinese must be made to fight which thus far they had not done."

On December 1 the Cairo Declaration, signed by Britain, China and the United States, was made public, stamping the seal of international recogni-

---

* Stilwell's terse summary of the Tehran Conference was: "Churchill wanted to poop around the periphery and take Rhodes but Stalin said No and that was that. . . . OVERLORD is on. Joe will hop the Japs as soon as Hitler folds."

tion on China's status as a great power, and accomplishing the aim of Roosevelt's policy just at the time he began to have doubts. The Declaration promised the return "of all the territories Japan has stolen from the Chinese" and committed the signatories to fight until the unconditional surrender of Japan. China was now precluded officially as well as by self-interest from a separate peace and her threats to withdraw consequently reduced in value. But there is often a time lag before the actors in events appreciate a change they themselves have wrought, and the toothlessness of China's only means of blackmail was not immediately apparent, except to those who already appreciated it.

Upon the return to Cairo BUCCANEER became the crux of an intense struggle. The American Joint Chiefs vigorously opposed its abandonment. They denied that it was a diversion from OVERLORD or that ANVIL needed its landing craft, and insisted that nonfulfillment would allow the Generalissimo to withhold the Y-force, thus causing the failure of the Burma campaign. Without that campaign Marshall and King feared the Japanese would be able to resist the Pacific advance more forcefully. Admiral Leahy was still in the grip of the fear that "Chiang might drop out of the war." Roosevelt argued that he had a moral obligation to Chiang Kai-shek who had left Cairo with the definite understanding that there would be an amphibious operation, even though uncommitted himself. Churchill remained adamant in refusal. His argument that BUCCANEER's resources could be put to better use was aided by Mountbatten's inflated requirement of 50,000 men for the action. Queried on alternatives, the SEAC staff asserted that without the Yunnan force the land route to China could not be reopened. The dispute raged for three days. At no conference before or after, according to Admiral Leahy, was there such "determined opposition" to an American proposal.

An unkind accident aided the British when a radiogram from General Boatner reported that the forward elements of the Chinese 38th Division in the Hukawng valley, on meeting unexpected Japanese reaction, had dug in and despite all orders to advance refused to budge. The message addressed to Stilwell was delivered by mischance to Wedemeyer on the SEAC staff, thus becoming known to his British colleagues who seized with glee on this evidence from Stilwell's own command that the Chinese would not fight. Within hours it had circulated throughout the Conference as proof of the fantasy of his proposed juncture with the Y-force. What had in fact happened in the Hukawng was that Boatner, who from old experience automatically discounted Chinese intelligence by 20 percent, had refused to send in the artillery the Chinese officers demanded and failed to visit the front himself to ascertain the facts.

On December 5 Roosevelt yielded in a laconic three-word message to

Churchill, "BUCCANEER is off." Thus ended the two weeks of Cairo-Tehran. In those two weeks China moved into the shadow. At the beginning Roosevelt was determined to make the occasion a Chinese success; at the end he sacrificed Chiang Kai-shek to Stalin. He had found a new partner at the dance. His three words marked a turning point, though not then recognized, in relations with China. The President was not conscious of doing anything definitive; the definitive was not his habit. He knew in general the direction he wanted to follow but his decisions en route were empiric. His way of fighting the enemy on a given day, said his friend Averell Harriman, was "to weigh the evidence on his desk that morning." A choice had to be made and Roosevelt made it in conformity with the choice from the beginning in favor of Europe first. Strategically it was the right decision because BUCCANEER was essentially a gesture.

The upshot of Cairo was not what had been intended. No sooner was China recognized as a great power than the promise to Chiang Kai-shek was broken just as if he had been the Sultan of Morocco after all. China's mistrust of the West deepened and Western confidence in Chiang plummeted as a result of their mutual contact.

Chiang was informed of the reversal by a telegram from Roosevelt asking whether he would go ahead with the north Burma campaign without the amphibious action or wait for a year until after the next monsoon when the Allies could mount a major seaborne operation, meanwhile maintaining Hump deliveries to the utmost. Though Stilwell was not obliged to be bearer of the news, Roosevelt and Marshall recognized that the situation left him once again the victim. To return to Chungking empty-handed was likely to make his position difficult. Marshall offered to transfer him to another theater where he would have American troops to command and scope for his talents. Stilwell declined to be rescued. He had never thought much of BUCCANEER and its cancellation did not disturb him except as it might affect the Y-force. Chiang's reluctance was so basic that a further excuse did not change the situation radically. Besides, Stilwell believed that when it came to the point, the Chinese would have to enter the fight to open their own communications. And though he never put it on record it is probable that from the day he walked out of Burma nothing could have altered his determination to lead the way back.

Before he left Cairo he required to know from the President whether the BUCCANEER decision reflected a change in policy and how he was expected to deal with the Generalissimo in the new situation. Accompanied by Davies he went to the residence for another interview with Roosevelt and Hopkins, of which his record—in dialogue without comment—is as vivid a reproduction of Roosevelt talking as anything extant.

"Well, Joe, what do you think of the bad news?" the President began, and proceeded through America's friendship with China, the missionaries, the Delanos in Canton, a plan for curtailing Chinese inflation, a plan to make Hong Kong a free port ("But let's raise the Chinese flag there first, and then Chiang can next day make a grand gesture and make it a free port. That's the way to handle that! Same way in Dairen!"), a plan for trusteeship for Indochina and Korea for 25 years or so (". . . till we get them on their feet. Just like the Philippines. I asked Chiang point-blank if he wanted Indochina and he said, 'Under no circumstances!' Just like that—'Under no circumstances!' ") and a variety of other subjects ending with an account of a long conversation with H. H. Kung about a $50-million loan for developing transportation. Despite several attempts by Stilwell and Davies to turn the flow toward current policy they could obtain no practical guidance.

The President dropped a hint of his new doubts. "How long," he asked, "do you think Chiang can last?" Stilwell replied that the situation was serious and a repetition of last summer's Japanese offensive might overturn him. "Well then," Roosevelt said, "we should look for some other man or group of men to carry on." Stilwell suggested that any such candidates "would probably be looking for us," and the matter was left at that. He came away unrelenting in his opinion: "The man is a flighty fool. . . . Hopeless outlook." It was one of history's cruel tricks that between these two who cared so much to make the relationship with China work, there should be dislike and a total mutual absence of understanding. Hopkins, however, throwing a strand across the information gap, asked in future to see copies of Davies' reports and from time to time thereafter passed them on to the President.

Chiang Kai-shek was hardly home from Cairo bearing the proud certificate of great-power status and telling everyone that he had an assurance of action in the Bay of Bengal when the telegram announcing its cancellation was delivered. He instantly put a high price on his humiliation. He asked for a loan of $1 billion on the ground that his task in rallying his nation to continued resistance had now been made "infinitely more difficult," and that China's military and economic weakness made it "impossible" to hold on for six months, much less another year, and that collapse of the China theater would have "grave consequences on the global war." He also asked for an increase of at least double the number of aircraft for the Fourteenth Air Force and the Chinese Air Force and, in order to make their operations effective, an increase in the Hump airlift to 20,000 tons a month.

Stilwell's first thought on his return to Chungking had been to advise Madame against blackmail, warning that "our people are fed up." But of this the Generalissimo was not to be persuaded. He summoned Gauss to impress upon him how crucial was the need to support the currency while Madame spoke bitterly of how much it was costing China to maintain the American air effort. Gauss was hard to impress, which was why the Generalissimo had long been as desirous of his recall as of Stilwell's. A loan could not help, Gauss advised Washington, because China's military and economic conditions "are deteriorating so fast" that in order to prevent collapse, "military measures to restore the Burma Road and reopen land transportation to China are imperative at an early date."

Chiang Kai-shek's action in virtually putting a monetary price on his continuing in the war aided the increasing disenchantment with China in Washington. Morgenthau opposed the loan for the same reason as Gauss, because, as he told the President, China had no way of using it and it would be ineffective to control inflation. The Chinese had made a fiasco of the loan of 1942; moreover they still had $460 million of unpledged funds in the United States. Their refusal to fix a realistic rate of exchange and insistence on maintaining an artificial rate of 20 to 1, six times the actual value (which by November 1943 had reached 120 to 1), was causing increasing resentment among all Government and private agencies dealing with China. Chinese officials exploited the situation, according to Gauss, to accumulate "large reserves of U.S. dollars out of our expenditure for the war effort." The Treasury knew that $867,000 of Chinese Government funds had been turned over to the young Kung, Madame's nephew, and to Dr. S. C. Wu, another member of her party.

In a memorandum of "unvarnished truth" Morgenthau advised rejection of the loan with a detailed explanation showing that what China needed was food, goods, machines and arms in amounts which could only be brought in by land or sea. For the reopening of these doors, he suggested, China herself should share the fight. To his astonishment, and the distress of Secretary Hull, the President proposed to send the whole memorandum verbatim to Chiang Kai-shek and, with the insertion of some placating assurances of goodwill, actually did so.

In Chungking Stilwell was endeavoring to nudge the Generalissimo into Burma regardless of the Allies' broken commitment. Through two long sessions Chiang kept insisting that there were eight Japanese divisions in Burma, not five, that SEAC's plans were inadequate, that despite the buildup of Allied forces and air cover there was even less chance of winning now than there had been in 1942, that it was better to stay on the defensive and let the Japanese attack, that he must not risk defeat because the effect on the Chinese people would be too serious. Stilwell rebutted every argument with little effect. "He's just plain crazy. . . . Even at the expense of being cut off—still he won't risk defeat." May and Ella were frantic and could not sleep from worry. "May *prayed* with Peanut. Told me she'd done everything except murder him." Chiang agreed, however, to let the Ledo force fight as planned and to give Stilwell in writing full command without interference and with "full power to fire any and all officers." He said it was Stilwell's army and, except for a caution against sacrificing it in British interests, that Stilwell could use it as he saw fit. In reply to further urging from Roosevelt, instigated by Stilwell at Madame's suggestion, he refused to use the Y-force in Burma unless the Allies took the Andaman Islands or Rangoon or Moulmein to cut off the Japanese rear.

Chiang's response to the rejection of the billion-dollar loan was a new demand of drastic proportions: that the United States should pay at the official rate the cost of constructing the airfields in the Chengtu area for the B-29 bombing program decided upon at Cairo. If the United States felt itself unable to do this, the Chinese Government regretted that it "would have no means at its disposal to meet the requirements of United States forces in China . . . and could not make any further material or financial contribution, including the construction of works for military use." Work on the fields, scheduled to begin January 15, was held up.

"My God," wrote Stilwell, "50 million gold to build the fields and 50 million gold squeeze!" In Washington Morgenthau was outraged. "They are just a bunch of damn crooks," he stormed. "I am not going up on the Hill . . . and ask for one nickel." He proposed "we tell them to go jump in the Yangtze" and build and pay for the fields ourselves by operating through the black market; he would send "a million dollars worth of gold in jewelers' bars every day to General Somervell." Calming down, he discussed alternatives with his staff and was advised that to pay for the fields at the official rate of 20 to 1 would be prohibitive; the cost was estimated at $800 million. It was becoming apparent that even the United States was not rich enough to fight in China.

To Americans there was a kind of insanity, an infuriating absence of conscience, in the demand that the United States pay the costs, at six times real value, of defeating the occupier of China's territory. But the conscience stemming from the Judaeo-Christian tradition takes different forms from the Confucian. It may be that all the slights and disillusions that China had stored up against the West were being balanced for payment in Chiang's demand. His basic xenophobia had every reason to be exacerbated by the results of Cairo and he deeply resented the greater portion of Lend-Lease being given to Britain and Russia.

Like all money quarrels, this one left a rancid taste. "Maybe we don't need them, by God—" said Morgenthau. He would find some military way to do it. He called Somervell to ask how it might be accomplished. "I am mad as hell. Is this something I have got to stomach and vomit and take it, or have you got some way to wiggle out and do something else?" After conferring with Marshall and Stimson, Somervell reported that the Army was "very dissatisfied" and prepared to "get tough" even up to and including the Secretary of War, once China's most ardent partisan. "I do not fear that the Chinese are going to drop out of the war now that we are so close," Stimson wrote sensibly in his diary that day.

Meeting with Morgenthau on January 20, Somervell said the Army was prepared to stop building the airfields and "approach Japan from another direction." He offered another and more startling idea: the United States "could break Chiang Kai-shek by withdrawing American support" or, if they wanted to, by "buying one of his competitors with an expenditure of $100 million"; there were lots of candidates. General Lucius Clay suggested sending no more Lend-Lease or diverting some of it to provincial generals, "or, if necessary even pull out of China, or just do nothing and continue at a slow pace."

From this meeting on, it could be said, American support of the Generalissimo's Government was invested with little conviction or faith. Nevertheless it was continued, with no effort by the United States to broaden its options. To deal with the incumbent in power is the easiest course and the inertia of policy in foreign affairs resists the effort to change or take chances. All in Washington were agreed that the United States could not and would not accept the official rate, but the State Department was anxious not to weaken, and Roosevelt not prepared to drop, Chiang Kai-shek. Compromise proposals for a rate of 40 to 1 were made, and H. H. Kung was invited to Washington to carry on further discussions. The Chinese continued to demand either the billion-dollar loan or the rate of 20 to 1. In an interview with Ambassador Gauss before leaving, Kung, referring to the possibility of China's collapse, remarked that Japan had been making "some very good offers."

By February American advances in the Pacific raised the possibility of speeding up by several months the approach to a port in China, a prospect which made the airfields more necessary to assist the attack. The military vision of doing without China passed; the money-grubbing battle went on. Nearly a year later at Bretton Woods Dr. Kung was still smilingly insisting on 20 to 1.

Meanwhile under various interim financial compromises the Chinese people built the fields and the B-29s flew. In Szechwan 450,000 workmen were assembled from local *hsien,* or districts. Each *hsien* provided its quota of men, women and children with tools and food for 90 days' work. They came on foot, bringing their materials in wheelbarrows. Nine fields, four of them with 9,000-foot runways, were constructed without trucks, steam shovels or concrete. Topsoil, laboriously preserved for thousands of years for growing rice, was cleared off in wicker baskets carried on shoulder poles, and the subsoil flattened by men pulling huge rollers back and forth. A cobblestone base was laid from stones hauled from stream beds in an endless train of wheelbarrows. This was covered by layers of soil mixed with mud slurry alternating with layers of crushed rock made by women and girls sitting all day and hammering. The topsoil was then hauled back and rerolled. Foremen with pennants representing each village directed the work of their own townspeople, under orders of the engineers, of whom all but 14 Americans were Chinese. The first B-29 landed after 60 days; in 90 days all the fields were completed.

The first counteroffer to Chiang Kai-shek before the Kung mission was proposed had suggested an American expenditure of $25 million a month on terms to be negotiated jointly by Ambassador Gauss and General Stilwell. By the time this lethal fate was arranged for him, Stilwell was no longer in Chungking nor planning soon to return. He left for the front in Burma on December 20, the day after Chiang confirmed his command of the Ramgarh force, now called the New First Army, in writing. With the none-too-confident question in his diary, "CAN WE PUT IT OVER?", he escaped to the "heavenly surcease" of action in Burma.

Hundreds of Chinese working on the Laohwangping airfield with virtually no modern equipment. Airfields could be made ready for B-29s in sixty days (195).

17

The Road Back

DECEMBER 1943–JULY 1944

A headquarters general and theater commander is not supposed to operate at the front at divisional much less regimental or battalion level. Stilwell headed back into Burma on this unorthodox course, not simply from a surfeit of the higher echelons nor a pure desire for combat, but from a practical recognition that only his personal leadership could bring the Chinese to the offensive and give the campaign any chance of succeeding.

Disregarding criticism of his absence from Headquarters and gibes about "the best three-star company commander in the U.S. Army" or the "platoon war in Burma," he remained in the jungle, except for one or two quick flights to Delhi and Chungking, for seven months, from the end of December to July. His principle was the same as Pershing's, when as a General and Governor of a province in the Philippines in 1913 he took the place of a captain killed in action and led the company himself in assault on a Moro fort for which he was proposed for the Congressional Medal of Honor. He rejected the honor, in a letter to the War Department, for the simplest of reasons: "I went to that part of the line because my presence there was necessary."

The important thing in Stilwell's mind when he started was to open the land route to China for the sake of eventual meeting with U.S. forces on the China coast, and in so doing to prove his old contention that the

Chinese soldier, properly armed, trained and led, was the equal of any in the world. He had the Generalissimo's assurance that Chinese divisions of the NCAC were "his" army to command free of interference, and while profoundly skeptical by now of all Chinese promises, he assumed the purpose of the expedition was not one that Chiang would want to thwart. He had no authority to bring in the Y-force ahead of him or the British behind him to fulfill their planned part in the campaign; this would have to be left to prevailing pressures from higher up. In any event he saw no point in wrestling any longer with endless evasions in Chungking and Delhi; the only course was to force the issue by opening military action forthwith. His goal was Myitkyina* before the monsoon.

According to the plan code-named CAPITAL approved by the Combined Chiefs, north Burma was to be pinched off by the Y-force crossing the Salween to engage the enemy on the east, and by the British IVth Corps advancing to the Chindwin to engage the Japanese divisions on the west, thus preventing their interfering with Stilwell's advance. Meanwhile his army like an apple-corer would be penetrating upper Burma as vanguard for the Road.

His plan of campaign was succinct: "We have to go in through a rat hole and dig the hole as we go." The rat hole was a series of three valleys: the Hukawng, terminating in a ridge called the Jambu Bum; next the Mogaung valley leading to the main north-south railroad; and on the other side of the railroad the broad Irrawaddy valley, Burma's central corridor. Myitkyina, the northernmost major Japanese garrison and air base, lay on the railroad and river 40 miles below Mogaung; from here a road descended southward to connect with the old Burma Road into China. The slot assigned to the NCAC, thick with jungle growth and threaded by overgrown trails which allowed progress of sometimes as little as a mile an hour, and edged by mountain ranges carved in directionless ridges by the run offs from heavy rains, was as forbidding fighting country as any in the world.

The enemy facing the NCAC was the renowned 18th Division, veteran of the first Burma campaign and the conquest of Singapore, considered one of the ablest and best-trained divisions in the Japanese Army. Its commander, General Shinichi Tanaka, a plump comfortable-looking officer in a topee, was a soldier of outstanding capacity who maneuvered his resources superbly and knew how to make the best of what he had. Altogether the Japanese had five divisions in Burma at this time, reinforced to eight within the next two months, plus four Thai divisions, service

_____
* Pronounced Mit-chi-nah.

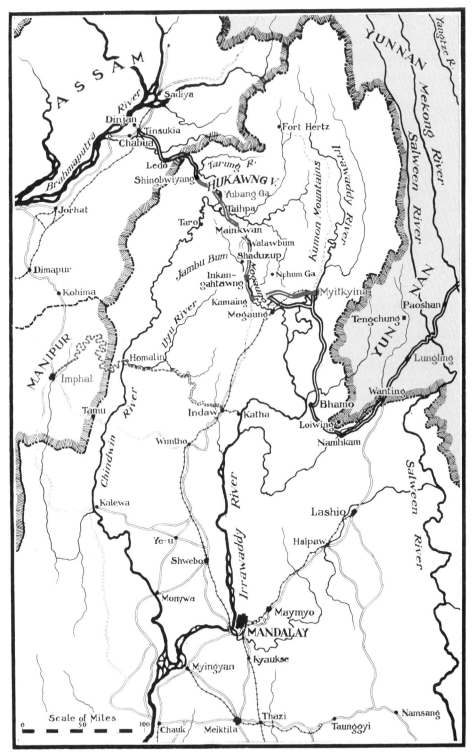

North Burma, 1944
Ledo Road and Burma Road =====
Route of the walkout in 1942: by road ·······; *by foot trail* ------

troops and some collaborationist Indian and Burmese units that were not much use to them.

The Allies outnumbered them in available if not active forces: Stilwell commanded three divisions of 12,000 each—the 22nd and 38th, which had been reconstituted at Ramgarh, and the 30th Division, extracted from Ho Ying-chin bit by bit and flown to India over the past months, of which one regiment was now in reserve at Ledo and one was still in training at Ramgarh ("We will never get the third"). Altogether the NCAC numbered at the start between 30,000 and 35,000 men.

The British had six divisions (five Indian and one West African) organized in two corps, IVth and XVth, plus the three brigades of Wingate's Raiders, called the Chindits, plus a variety of other regiments and auxiliary units. Their main base was at Imphal about 200 miles south of Ledo in the province of Manipur on the Burma border. Divisions of the Indian Army were generally composed of two-thirds Indians and Gurkhas and one-third British, organized by regiments or battalions that were racially homogeneous. All senior and some junior officers were British while the NCOs were Indian. In January soon after Stilwell entered Burma the XVth Corps was launched into action in the Arakan against one Japanese division in an effort to push southward down the coast toward the port and airfields of Akyab. Divorced from BUCCANEER and from a campaign for lower Burma, this was an objective of no compelling necessity except to give SEAC a sure success—which proved elusive.

On the other side of Burma in Yunnan were the eleven still-immobile divisions of the Y-force.

Besides being superior in numbers and equipment if not in unity or purpose, the Allies now had command of the air, not only in combat strength but in ability to supply, reinforce, evacuate and provide mobility to the ground troops. This was the enabling factor of the campaign. The NCAC, with units spread out on separate paths in advance of the Road, "had to have the air to eat," as one of its officers put it. Airlift also made possible action behind enemy lines and the transfer of troops at critical moments. The new uses of air power and methods of delivery developed in north Burma were later to be used in France and the Battle of the Bulge.

Stilwell's tactics employed the same hook the Japanese had used in 1942 combined with the wide end-run envelopment which he had made his specialty in the maneuvers of 1940-41. His design was to engage the enemy frontally while launching the real attack through the jungle from the flank, and at the same time despatching an enveloping arm through the hills aimed at a point behind the enemy with the object of establishing a roadblock to cut off his retreat. The 18th Division was thus to be netted and annihilated in sections as NCAC advanced. Owing to a variety of malign and unexpected obstacles, practice frequently failed to live up to the design, the more so as the Chinese, inheritors of Sun Tzu's dictum, "To a surrounded enemy you must leave a way of escape," were averse to closing the net. They preferred a U-shaped ambush with a well-advertised escape route to avoid a savage fight to the death by trapped Japanese. Repeatedly the enemy succeeded in withdrawing from an engagement which Stilwell had planned to be conclusive, and though yielding ground, remained to fight again further down. As a result, pressures of time built up in the race against the monsoon that were to demand desperate expedients.

Not all the training and new equipment of Ramgarh could dispel the Chinese sense of military inferiority to the Japanese; they did not believe they could defeat them—a factor which for a commander put a drag on impetus. To prove they could, Stilwell took care to give them numerical superiority in every contest; if a Japanese company was to be destroyed, he assigned a Chinese regiment to the task. He bullied, flattered and shamed, cajoled, bribed, goaded and pushed, rewarded with decorations, unit citations, press photos and every device of public relations, and kept the offensive going by the unrelieved pressure of his physical presence. Many times, in General Slim's opinion, this "was the only thing that would impart real drive to his troops."

For intelligence he relied on the Kachin guerillas organized by Detachment 101 of the OSS. A friendly, smiling, brave people, violently anti-Japanese and quick to learn the handling of radios, they located the enemy, guided the NCAC, blew up trains and bridges, and wiped out isolated Japanese patrols. For no less necessary information about his own troops Stilwell relied on American liaison officers who were attached, nominally as "advisers," to each Chinese regiment and in some cases to battalions. They carried their own radios and reported to him daily in code on action and progress, often in contrast to the version he received from the Chinese commanding officer. Although enjoined from command, and under strict orders in any conflict of judgment to respect the Chinese decision, they could exercise influence through the power to relay—or veto—supply requisitions. Here at least Stilwell could exercise the quid pro quo. The adviser system produced Sino-American quarrels as well as enduring friendships, and on the whole proved not as effective as had been hoped in maintaining the battle order or instilling the offensive spirit.

On December 21 when Stilwell arrived in the Hukawng valley, the NCAC offensive, which was supposed to have taken off from the line of the river Tarung, was already a month behind schedule. Japanese units, probing for positions for an offensive which they too were planning, held Yubang Ga, key to the river crossing and the point where the Ledo Road was supposed to cross the river. Three battalions of General Sun Li-jen's 38th Division, coming under fire from this unexpected presence, had dug in and were now separately surrounded by the enemy, supplied by inadequate airdrops and unable to advance or retreat. Attempts to relieve them had failed. Generals Sun and Boatner were at angry odds over questions of supply and demands for artillery. On his way home from Cairo, the Generalissimo, with his instinct for hoarding, had cautioned against deploying more than one regiment on the Tarung, "because we had only six regiments and if two were used and cut off by the enemy we would have only four regiments left."

Stilwell established headquarters for the first phase of the campaign at Shingbwiyang, which was reached by the Road a week after his arrival, enabling trucks and jeeps to bring up supplies. He worked out plans for a serious attack on Yubang Ga with Sun and the regimental commander, arranged for artillery barrage and flank attacks and made a speech to the troops saying this was an important attack that must succeed. "Wherever Stilwell went something happened," noticed Seagrave who was serving with the forward troops. The attack opened on December 24. Stilwell went forward at 6:30, hiking two hours over trails to the command post and staying throughout the day to observe. The opening artillery barrage, fired at a range of 30 yards ahead of the attacking troops, was followed by an awful hesitation of five minutes, then the sound of the Chinese bugle and the infantry's advance. To clear the Japanese out of jungle pockets and gain the river against land mines and concealed machine guns proved difficult. Wearing a steel helmet and unconcerned by the fire of a concealed machine-gun sniper probing for the range of the command post, Stilwell caused intense discomfort to Sun Li-jen and his officers who feared he might be hit and they be held responsible.

The Chinese attack, though too cautious for Stilwell's taste, did not let up. Sun "swears they are trying to do a good job for the *lao hsien sheng* [Old Man] and the troops are all bucked up to have me with them." The Japanese resisted fiercely from foxholes and dugouts; when one lone machine-gunner was killed, another man rushed from the woods to man the isolated weapon. It took a week before Yubang Ga was secured and all pockets cleared out. By the end of December the 38th Division had suffered casualties of 315 killed and 429 wounded but it had overcome the enemy for the first time in Burma. As the first test of American training the outcome was critical: it proved to the Chinese that they could actually defeat Japanese. A company of the 22nd Division after its first victory staged a parade with the heads of Japanese stuck on bamboo poles, to the horror of the American liaison officer who demanded to resign from his assignment. From the quality of the fighting and the equipment and air-drops, the Japanese too recognized that they confronted a new enemy.

Stilwell's presence at the front and his living close to the men made a strong impression on Chinese officers. To avoid headquarters routine and the mass of papers, messages and envoys from the Rear Echelon that pursued him, he often moved out of Shingbwiyang and subsequent base head-quarters to stay at a private combat headquarters of his own in a clearing in the woods. He lived with his aide Dick Young in a *basha* or bamboo hut or sometimes a tent, with an underground dugout for shelter, a packing case for a desk and only the luxury of two wicker chairs as a concession to rank. Here he slept on a cot or in a hammock stretched between two trees, shaved and washed from a helmet, stood in line for chow and ate C-rations from a mess kit. At base camp his meals were cooked for him by Sergeant Jules Raynaud, called Gus, former chef of the Stork Club, who complained that the Boss ate "like the birds": for dinner usually only a couple of pieces of raisin bread which Gus baked for him, with butter and jam and a cup of coffee. Gus foraged for vegetables to take the curse off Spam and stood over the Boss till he ate them. The family, always Stil-well's main anchor in life, was represented by his son Joe Jr. serving as G-2 for NCAC, and his sons-in-law Colonel Ernest Easterbrook and Major Ellis Cox, serving as liaison officers with the Chinese divisions.

On the march when he saw Chinese soldiers smoking rolled-up leaves, Stilwell would take out his own cigarets and hand them out and he made an extra effort to have cigarets flown in. He paid "special attention to people at the bottom," said a Chinese officer, and when the soldiers saw him they would crowd around "our Commander" and want to talk to him. The most important morale factor was his insistence on the wounded being carried back to the field hospitals and flown if necessary to the 20th General Hospital at Ledo. He brought relentless pressure until an airfield was built for the hospital and supported every demand of its chief, Colonel Isidor Ravdin, a surgeon from civilian life who on Stilwell's recommendation was to become the first Medical Reserve officer promoted to brigadier general. When Ravdin complained that the hospital had no fans, urgently needed for the typhus wards, Stilwell radioed General Dan Sultan, his deputy in Delhi, "Dig up 150 ceiling fans, 160 standing fans and 11 air-conditioning units. . . . You and I both know where a lot of it can be dug up." The Imperial Hotel where the American staff of SEAC lodged was duly stripped of its fans for the hospital at Ledo. On Sunday morning Stilwell usually flew in to visit the patients who had been injured the previous week. His order that no Chinese soldiers were to be searched on leaving the hospital resulted in a steady disappearance of medicines, blankets, pajamas and equipment, but it was issued in that expectation for Stilwell also took care to order that Ravdin should not be held responsible for anything missing.

The combined efforts of American medics, from stretcher teams and field hospitals to the 20th General, reduced the death rate from wounds, ordinarily a limitless figure in the Chinese Army, to 3.5 percent. Chinese soldiers were not afraid of being killed in battle, they used to say, but only of being left wounded on the battlefield to die, which was the usual fate in China for those who could not walk away from combat. The feeling that they were being looked out for in the NCAC gave the soldiers a new-found pride and confidence. In the knowledge, too, that planes would keep them supplied with ammunition, they were not afraid to shoot what they had as in the first Burma campaign.

They were a young army, many as young as fifteen, and if not robust in body, yet as brothers of the Communists who had trudged the 6,000 miles of the Long March, they were the sturdiest walkers of any army in the world. They had in large measure the good soldier's qualities of courage, stamina, willingness and an eye for the country, and their dominant characteristic, as Wingate observed, was cheerfulness. "Under conditions which would reduce Europeans to gloomy despair, smiles of pure joy break out constantly over the Chinese face." Measured time was of no concern to them and no plan based on accurate timing had a hope of success. Nor could any plan succeed that ignored consideration of face. Familiar with the absence in the home army of any supply, transport or medical organization worth the name, they were accustomed to keeping themselves alive by scavenging and would take or steal any object of any kind that lay loose.

At dawn Stilwell would set out regularly to hike three to five miles, often taking two or more hours, to the regimental command post, trailed by his aide, bodyguard and two or three of the hardier correspondents. On the way he studied and remembered the trails and terrain features and villages, and at night sketched his situation maps by candlelight, recording in marginal comments every move and engagement of the troops. At the command posts he would observe and advise without exercising direct command. His presence at the front became known to the Japanese who broadcast from Rangoon their intention to capture him alive, adding im-measurably to the uneasiness of whatever Chinese commanders he chose to visit. They feared execution if the Commanding General was shot or ambushed by a patrol and captured while in their vicinity. Taking advan-tage of this anxiety, in the case of a commander who delayed or stalled,

Stilwell would hang around his command post and refuse to go away until the order to move was given.

The difficulty of inculcating aggressive spirit in the Chinese superior officers persisted. The Artillery, trained by General Sliney and led by able and energetic Chinese officers, was vigorous and reliable, but all the efforts at Ramgarh could not eliminate characters like one Major Ch'en, a battalion commander of the 38th Division, who, during the month before Stilwell came to the Hukawng, failed to occupy his given post, remained four weeks without doing any offensive patrolling, failed to issue supplies to a special patrol unit and could provide no record of what had been done with 31,000 rations and 28 tons of ammunition dropped to him during this period.

Friction over supply was constant. On the one hand Chinese requisitions were usually double what a unit needed or could use; on the other hand units were sometimes left close to starvation when pilots in bad weather were less than aggressive about flying in airdrops. Stilwell remedied this situation by requiring air crews to exchange places with men on the ground and live in the mud on Spam and hot water for a few days. "After the air boys learned what it was like down there," recalled Paul Jones, "they flew in every day, flew when you thought no one could, when clouds were on the tree tops."

All the while messages from Chungking or Delhi, buzzing with "Z-Z-Z-Z" for urgent, poured into Stilwell's command post, "screaming for me to come to both places and decide on this or that." His deputy in Delhi, General Sultan, the ranking major general in the Army whom Marshall had sent to help Stilwell in 1943, was dependable and excellent —"Dan Sultan is the best thing that ever happened to the theater" in his chief's opinion—but it is the nature of miltary channels that everything, however petty, is passed on to the top, with exasperating effect if the occupant of the top is not by temperament an administrator. The problem is not unknown in civil government. Roosevelt, complained Secretary Stimson, was "the poorest administrator I have ever worked under." One issue that Stilwell could not avoid, involving as it did the military's most absorbing concern, was his place in the chain of command. He made a quick overnight jump to Delhi on December 31 to settle it.

As operational chief of NCAC he held a temporary corps command within the SEAC structure of which, under another hat, he was Deputy Supreme Allied Commander. The situation was like that of the Lord Chancellor in *Iolanthe* who tangled with himself as suitor to his own ward and wondered whether he could give his consent to his own marriage, or marry without his own consent, and in that case could he cite himself for contempt of his own court? But no glimmer of inherent absurdity lightened the problem at SEAC headquarters. The Supremo, as Mountbatten was called, wanted Stilwell to serve along with Slim, who commanded the Fourteenth Army comprising the two British corps, under General Sir George Giffard, commander of the ground forces of SEAC. Stilwell despised Giffard whom he called the Ho Ying-chin of Burma and who was reputed among Americans to have been given his job because "he was the kind of man who would ensure that there would be no fighting." Believing that Giffard would contrive to hold back his progress, Stilwell refused utterly to come under his control. Putting on his hat as Deputy SAC he said he was superior to Giffard, and in another guise as Commanding General of American forces in CBI he said he did not have Presidential authority to put himself under Giffard. The adroit way he shifted from one to another of his various offices (in the theater's table of organization he occupied no less than five boxes at various levels) was, according to Slim, "a lesson in the mobile offensive-defensive." The more Mountbatten reasoned with him the more stubbornly he resisted, exhibiting, Slim thought, "a surly obstinacy that showed him at his worst."

Matters were at a deadlock until suddenly he astonished everybody by announcing, "I am prepared to come under General Slim's operational control until I get to Kamaing," that is, to the midpoint of the Mogaung valley, about halfway to Myitkyina. Having confidence in Slim's fighting intentions, Stilwell knew that under this arrangement he would not be hampered. Slim's junior rank was immaterial: "I would fight under a corporal as long as he would let me fight," he said.

Slim believed Stilwell to be "two people," one when talked to alone and another in front of an audience when he adopted the "Vinegar Joe" attitude. "He had courage to an extent few people have and a determination which, as he usually concentrated it along narrow lines, had a dynamic force. . . . He was undoubtedly the most colorful character in South-East Asia—and I liked him." That Stilwell put on an act in front of a certain kind of audience was true. With friends he could be unaffected and easy, and at home he loved to joke, but with people of whom he was suspicious for one reason or another, whether from a sense of difference or inferiority or impatience or contempt, he could undoubtedly be rude or caustic or sometimes coarse and deliberately boorish, as his way of thumbing his nose. During the second campaign in Burma this attitude became more pronounced with regard to the Rear Echelon when, after sleeping in his clothes and coming under fire and suffering the companionship of fly-eggs in his blanket and scorpions in his dugout, he came out to the overstuffed conferences of Delhi. He tended to feel for the desk generals and colonels the sentiments of Hotspur in his favorite passage from Shakespeare who, when "dry with rage and extreme toil" after battle, raged against the popinjay from head-quarters.

In Marshall's opinion Stilwell was "his own worst enemy" who poisoned his relations with the British and Chinese by making no effort to conceal his contempt for their "do-nothing" attitudes. While he had ample cause for impatience, his personality faults, Marshall thought, thwarted Mount-batten's effort to get along with him. Stilwell certainly lacked the iron control over his feelings that characterized Marshall but the underlying source of the poison was his belief that both British and Chinese had been cowardly in the first Burma campaign and had devoted their energies to nonperformance in Burma ever since. He never had any trouble getting along with either British or Chinese who in his opinion were doers and fighters. This was the reason why he often wished he could command the Communists who seemed to be both, and why he admired the Russians for their stunning resistance at Leningrad and fight at Stalingrad. He sent congratulations to the Red Army on the occasion of its twenty-sixth birth-day and received a message from Stalin in reply.

"You will find, if you get below the surface," Marshall wrote to Mount-batten on learning of Stilwell's consent to serve under Slim, "that he wants merely to get things done without delays. . . . He will provide tremendous energy, courage and unlimited ingenuity and imagination to any aggressive proposals and operations. His mind is far more alert than almost any of our generals and his training and understanding are on an unusually high level. Impatience with conservatism and slow motion is his weakness—but a damned good one in this emergency."

After hurried conference with his staff chiefs, including Colonel Merrill whom he wanted to command the GALAHAD force, Stilwell was back at Shingbwiyang within 24 hours. One gain from the trip was victory in his obstinate struggle to have GALAHAD reassigned to his control, as a result of the canceling of the larger plans for Burma. Wingate's angry com-ment on being informed was, "'You can tell General Stilwell he can take his Americans and —." But military action requires even the most ill-disposed allies to coordinate plans, and Wingate came to Shingbwiyang to confer on January 3. The meeting was recorded by one of his officers, Brigadier Bernard Fergusson, who attended rather nervously, knowing that the two principals "could both display atrocious manners and were not prepared to be thwarted by anybody."

Wingate at forty, handsome, bearded, strong-bodied, with heavy brows over piercing blue eyes and the look, manner and passion of a prophet, was a notable contrast to Stilwell at sixty, wiry and gaunt, with a quizzical eye behind his steel-rimmed spectacles and the shrewd, skeptical, speculative look of a down-east Yankee farmer. Fergusson thought both had the characteristics of prophets, "vision, intolerance, energy, ruthless courage," but this was romanticizing Stilwell. Though he possessed the last three qualities in eminent degree, he was no prophet but a practical man whose motivating principle was "get on with it." What was rare was the matchless driving spirit he put behind a mission and the degree of devotion he was willing to invest until it was accomplished. Wingate was both doer and fighter and the fact that he disliked and was thoroughly disliked by the average British officer of the Indian Army was no lack of recommendation to Stilwell. The meeting passed off amicably. Wingate agreed to send in the Americans soon and to deploy his own LRP force around Indaw to draw off enemy attention from the NCAC.

Stilwell was anxious for the advent of the Americans to invigorate the Chinese who were starting to stall again in the Hukawng. "Sun not moving," he noted on January 2. "Preposterous demands for air support, ammo and artillery." The Chinese soldiers were doing well; "it's only the higher-ups who are weak. . . . If I could just have a couple of U.S. divisions!" He worried constantly about replacements, and his hikes to the forward command and observation posts were growing more tiring. On one occasion he trudged 18 miles up and back, on another it took three and a half hours to cover three miles, "tripping and cursing at every step," on another his party came under the concentrated shell fire with which the Japanese often raked the trails in the hope of catching a mule train or a file of troops, and a shell burst within ten yards of him. He was proud of a regiment that made a good crossing of the river, "no fuss, good discipline, no grenade fishing . . . high class work." Colonel Fu, their commander, "asserts this is the first time in his experience he has seen a real envelopment like this— *na ko shao chien* [something rarely seen]." But Sun's unaccountable hesitation "will now cost lives."

All of January was consumed in effort to clear the enemy from the Taro plain, a valley lying parallel to and south of the Hukawng, so that no Japanese would be left in the rear of the main advance. A suspicious pattern of reluctance was becoming evident. The battalion of the laggard Major Ch'en, assigned to the Taro mission, had not moved from the edge of the plain, and Sun, his divisional commander, was "slow and sulky." Stilwell argued and pleaded with him on the importance of the action and the consequences of failure and warned against giving the Japanese time. A few days later he found that another battalion of the 38th had not taken up its position and "raised hell" with the regimental commander, "told him by god to get it back and find out who had disobeyed orders." When this happened a third time Stilwell suspected that Sun must be receiving messages from the Generalissimo to slow down for fear of losses, in fatal repetition of the first Burma campaign. He warned Sun explicitly with no tactful circumlocutions that if his orders as Commanding General were not carried out he would resign and report the circumstances to Washington with a recommendation of "very radical measures"—meaning cessation of U.S. aid.

The 22nd was doing better. Li Hung, a battalion commander, was pleased, "says I bring him luck. . . . Fu of the 65th will go anywhere if he has rations." But five days later the 65th was stalled in a "sad fizzle" and Fu relieved of command. Every order for combat involved a struggle. Finally the 65th moved. The tank battalion of 60 light tanks under Colonel Rothwell Brown, the only Chinese unit under direct American command, did "a fine job under terrible conditions." On January 28 the 65th cleared a pocket accounting for 250 Japanese dead; two days later, "65th got to TARO!", clearing the way for the main advance.

Far from joining the action, Mountbatten was backing out. On January 8 SEAC produced a revised plan of campaign called AXIOM proposing a halt to the Road and to Stilwell's effort to reopen north Burma, which was declared to be impossible before the rains in view of Chiang Kai-shek's refusal to commit the Y-force. Instead Mountbatten proposed a return to the sea strategy via Malaya and Sumatra and the significant inclusion of Hong Kong within SEAC boundaries. "Louis welshes on entire program," was Stilwell's summary. He sent a radio to Marshall urging efforts to prod the Generalissimo into Burma so that the British would have no excuse, and despatched one of his staff, Colonel John Cleveland, to Chungking on the same errand. Cleveland returned with bad news: the Generalissimo still insisted on British landings and commitment to a major campaign in lower Burma before he would move. "We are out on a limb," Stilwell recorded.

Chiang's withholding of the Y-force coupled with his extreme monetary demands reinforced the impression in Washington that he was asking in effect to be paid to fight in Burma. Since the campaign was designed to lift the siege of China and since the Y-force had been American-equipped for that purpose, the obvious course in view of Chiang's unwillingness to assist in his own rescue would have been to call off the effort. This, however, the United States was not prepared to do because of the need for China in American strategy and the persistent fear of a Chinese collapse. Allowing a note of anger to creep into his tone, Roosevelt all but reached the demand to fish-or-we-shall-cut-bait that Stilwell longed for. "If the Y forces cannot be employed," Roosevelt telegraphed Chiang on January 14, "it would appear that we should avoid for the present the movement of critical materials to them . . . and curtail the continuing build-up of stock piles in India." Convinced of his indispensability, Chiang was not frightened and the Y-force did not move.

Stilwell did not intend to stay out on a limb. On learning that Mountbatten was sending Wedemeyer at the head of an Anglo-American mission of no less than 17 staff officers including three generals to London and Washington to persuade the Combined Chiefs to adopt AXIOM, he decided to send a delegation of his own to Washington to "checkmate the limies." Boatner and Davies were selected to go. In the theater Mountbatten summoned a high-level strategy conference to consider his new plan but it had to wait for Stilwell until after Taro had been taken. He emerged on January 31 to go to Delhi for the conference which, however negative from his point of view, at least provided the occasion for his first bath in twenty-nine days. "He damn near went to sleep in the tub," his son wrote home.

The sea strategy of AXIOM, of which Wedemeyer had become the leading advocate on the SEAC staff, was a concerted effort by all the antagonists of Stilwell's road strategy to pull away from a fight in the dangerous, difficult and altogether disagreeable conditions of Burma. The argument of all was that Stilwell was wasting Allied energy and resources on an effort that could not succeed in the current combat season, and if it ever did, could not deliver enough to China to be worth its cost. The British interest was best expressed by Churchill who, as always, was thinking ahead. He disliked intensely the prospect of a large-scale campaign in north Burma, than which it was impossible to choose a worse place for fighting the Japanese. To become "sidetracked and entangled" there, or even in lower Burma, "would deny us our rightful share in a Far East victory"—meaning that the imperial trail lay through Singapore to Hong Kong and he wanted these well in hand before coming to the peace table. Burma, though part of the Empire, led nowhere, except to China which was the wrong place from Britain's point of view. The British intended to reach Hong Kong by sea before the Chinese were able to reach it by land. "I liked Mountbatten's new plan," Churchill finished sweetly.

The ever-active cohorts of Chennault also opposed the NCAC campaign because they wanted its resources, although how they expected the pipeline, which they also wanted, to get through to China without the campaign is a military mystery. "I warn you solemnly," intoned the untiring Alsop in his flow of letters to Hopkins, that Stilwell is "arrogantly courting disaster" by forcing a march through a "trackless, foodless, mountainous waste." Voicing Chiang Kai-shek's theme, of which Alsop considered himself the spokesman, he predicted Stilwell would be defeated, in which case the Japanese "will cut off China at last from the outside world and then the Chinese resistance will surely collapse and the Chinese base will be lost to us." Stilwell "is playing soldiers at Ledo," he wrote again in January. He hopes to "breathe life into the Burma campaign's corpse. . . . In my opinion he has no more chance of doing so than of flying over the moon."

It was also his opinion that the VLR* B-29 bomber program which threatened to take priority in resources away from Chennault was "dangerously theoretical" and the choice of Chengtu as its base was a mistaken concession "to General Stilwell's oft-repeated theory that the Japanese can capture the forward airbases in East China whenever they have a mind to." The easiest way to improve the situation, he urged, would be to "confide the top command to General Wedemeyer who knows how to work with everyone," besides being young and efficient.

Enjoying, unlike Chennault, the favor of the War Department, Wedemeyer, aged forty-six, was the new candidate of Stilwell's opponents. He was an ornament of the General Staff who had served with 15th Infantry at Tientsin in 1930-32. After graduating with honors from Leavenworth he took another General Staff course at the *Kriegsakademie* (the German War College) in 1936-38 under the Nazi regime, returning from the experience, according to an observer, "with a suggestion of the monocled aplomb which distinguishes the best of the German General Staff." Tall and imposing, smooth, able and ambitious, he went on to an impressive career in the Planning Division of the War Department and was making an equal impression at SEAC. Not given, as he climbed, to reticence about his virtues, he subsequently vindicated his career in a book which bore his own name and an exclamation point in the title. "Thinks well of himself, that young man," Stilwell had noted mildly once or twice, feeling as yet no need for a caustic nickname, although inspiration did not fail when the time came.

As presented at the conference of January 31, AXIOM proposed to keep the British forces out of Burma, conserving them until the next dry season, that is, the winter of 1944-45, for the assault on Sumatra and Malaya. By that time it was expected that landing craft would be released from Europe, and the next stage would be advance to the China coast. SEAC claimed that Myitkyina could not be taken in time to bring up the Road before the monsoon, nor could the Road be reopened from there to Kunming before 1946, too late to support a Pacific offensive to the China coast. The goal of Myitkyina, it was argued, should be abandoned and Stilwell should content himself with reaching the Mogaung valley from where he could offer security to the air transport route, while the resources gathered for his campaign and for building the Road could be devoted to expanding the capacity of the Hump.

---

* Very Long Range.

Presented in full panoply of maps and planning papers, all this meant to Stilwell was "fancy charts, false figures, and dirty intentions." He expressed as much to the conference. He said that if the British divisions and the Y-force helped as originally planned, China could be reached more quickly by land than by sea. Why wait six months to do what could be done at once? The difficulties of the Burma campaign were known whereas those of Malaya and Sumatra were still to be learned. He did not believe the Allies could bank on the defeat of Germany in 1944 and long-term operations were better recommended on the basis of resources in hand than on those yet to be acquired. The way to defeat the Japanese in CBI was to build a strong army and drive to the sea. Wedemeyer rose to explain that this depended on installing and maintaining lines of communication to the interior of China and "our technical experts tell us that we cannot do that for at least two years."* Stilwell's reply to Wedemeyer, according to reports, was vintage vinegar. His answer to all alleged impossibles was a sarcastic reminder that Clive had conquered India with 123 men. Since the SEAC staff alone numbered ten times as many, this shaft was received, not surprisingly, in dead silence.

The decision was up to Washington and London. Boatner and Davies left at once for the United States, five days ahead of the Wedemeyer mission, much to the wrath of Mountbatten who considered that Stilwell's move in sending his own delegates was disloyal to him as Supreme Commander. On arrival the two delegates found their persuasions were hardly needed; AXIOM did not have a chance in Washington. Roosevelt did not like the plan at all as being both peripheral and neocolonial, and it made no appeal to the Joint Chiefs. Pacific strategy was now aimed at seizing the Luzon (Philippines)-Formosa-Canton triangle and progress had been made by a landing on Kwajalein in the Marshall Islands (by the Stilwell-trained 7th Division) on January 31, the same day as the conference in Delhi. It was the American intent that the assault on Japan should be an American war. The Navy especially wanted to keep the British out of it, partly because interests were divergent but mainly because the Navy with its new carriers did not want to be hampered by the older and slower British warships. Stilwell's campaign was strongly favored by the Joint Chiefs because the elimination of Myitkyina was considered essential to the VLR bombing program which in turn was needed to assist operations in the Luzon-Formosa-Canton triangle. Boatner found his way cleared to go straight to the President.

"Tell me about Burma, young man," said Roosevelt, all charm and wel-

---

* The first convoy over the completed Road was to enter China on January 28, 1945, exactly one year minus three days from the day Wedemeyer made his prediction.

come. Having provided himself with a magnificent topographical map in full color ranging from the dark red of the Himalayas to the pale green of the Irrawaddy plains, Boatner spread it out on the floor beside the President's chair and was soon down on his hands and knees pointing out places as he talked. Two or three times Pa Watson, Roosevelt's military aide, came in to shepherd him away in an effort to keep the Presidential schedule, but Roosevelt waved him off saying, "I am having the time of my life." His enthusiasm nerved Boatner to urge him to "put pressure on Mr. Churchill so he will put pressure on the British in India to help and not hinder General Stilwell."

"All right," Roosevelt agreed, "let's you and I send him a radio." Stunned but willing, Boatner found himself dictating while the President took down his suggestions in pencil on a pad. As Boatner was about to leave, the President said, "Young man, give me your ideas about the future of French Indo-China," and without pausing proceeded to give his own. As often happened, these varied from listener to listener. "I have told Chiang," he said this time, "to be ready to take it over at the end of the war. The French have forfeited their right to it by neglect."

The telegram to Churchill, after polishing by the Joint Chiefs, stated all the compelling arguments for the taking of Myitkyina in the current season, cited Stilwell's confidence that he could take it if the British did their part, and "urgently" hoped "that you will back to the maximum a vigorous and immediate campaign in Upper Burma." Churchill was not prepared to be persuaded. The Joint Chiefs in their turn formally rejected AXIOM when presented by Wedemeyer.

Another impasse would have ensued, leaving Stilwell out on his limb, but for the intervention of the enemy. As at Pearl Harbor the Japanese resolved their opponents' difficulty. On March 7 they launched their long-planned attack on the Imphal plain, forcing the British to fight on, and eventually over, the border. Thus were the British to come back to Burma. By provoking the Japanese offensive, Stilwell's march had succeeded, if not in the way he planned, in engaging his ally. The battle was to be decisive though not of Britain's choice, and Mountbatten, in the final irony, would emerge after the war as Viscount Mountbatten of Burma.

While these events were in the making, Stilwell was straining to trap a large part of the 18th Division at Mainkwan, the main Japanese base in the center of the Hukawng valley. He planned an enveloping hook by the 65th Regiment from the Taro plain on the right, and a wide-end run over obscure trails by the American commando force on the left to come out at Walawbum below Mainkwan where they would place themselves across the single main road to block the Japanese retreat. Through the center of the

Hukawng five Chinese regiments and the tank corps would advance in parallel drives toward Mainkwan. The Road and pipeline were progressing steadily close behind. General Lewis Pick, designer of the Missouri River dam system, the dynamic commander of the Road, locally called Pick's Pike, came in to see Stilwell on February 5. He promised to have gravel as far as Taihpa, the new headquarters, by the 20th and an airfield for transports in three days. Three days later the field was laid, "a dandy, 4600' and smooth, built in 14 hours under fire."

"Just a matter now of weather," Stilwell wrote on February 1. "God give us a few dry days and we can go." Rain poured down heavily on two of the next four days and began again the following week. So far there had been twelve days of rain in January and there were to be 18 in February, ten in March and ten in April although this was the "dry" season. In this of all years an abnormal 175 inches of rain fell in north Burma.

A planned maneuver by the 66th failed when the regiment was discovered to be "way off course" and could not be located. Liaison officers were bewildered, patrols threshed about in vain for two days ("I sat around and went crazy"). Dragging Liao, the divisional commander, with him on the third day, Stilwell set out in person with his aide and bodyguard and one or two American and Chinese officers to find the missing battalions. Marching by compass in uncertain proximity to the enemy, over ridges and through elephant grass ten feet tall which made visibility near zero and ambush a possibility, they found the lost 66th by evening. Stilwell listened to an unacceptable explanation by the commanding officer, ordered him relieved, instructed his successor how to reach the objective and went to bed in a dugout. The hike back next day, "tough as hell," exhausted him. On one steep grade he turned around and said to Colonel McCabe, "If I had a pack I'd fall down on the trail." It was the first time, McCabe reported, he ever heard the Boss admit he was in trouble. The party had to be helped off with their packs when they staggered into 22nd Division's headquarters. If the 66th had been in place, it was to have closed off a retreat of the Japanese who, in the event, escaped.

At this time, on February 19, the American commando force entered the Hukawng under Merrill, now a brigadier general. Officially designated the 5307th Provisional Regiment, which one soldier disgustedly said "sounds like a street address in Los Angeles," the unit on arrival in the Hukawng was more handsomely named Merrill's Marauders by the correspondents attached to NCAC. As the first and only American ground combat force in the theater (and America's answer to the Chindits whose exploits at Churchill's insistence the British were heavily publicizing), the Marauders attracted a greater share of attention from the press and from history than a similar-

Stilwell returned to Burma in December 1943 (196). Here he opens a can of C-rations for his breakfast on Christmas morning at Ningan Sekan (197). The importance of mail to morale was clearly evident in the jungle (198). A rare moment of relaxation for Stilwell at Taihpa Ga in February 1944 (199).

197

198

199

sized unit merited anywhere else. As a result their ultimate tragedy loomed large, reaching the point of a Congressional hearing.

To condition the men they had been marched in from Ledo, a distance of 130 miles over the Naga range, against the advice of a Burma veteran who warned it was better to conserve strength. Merrill, described by a colleague as a "born leader" who never exposed his troops to more risk than he was willing to take himself, had his reasons. GALAHAD was not the physically superior force of tough and adventurous volunteers that had been intended. To obtain men with jungle experience the three battalions of a thousand men each were raised from units in the Southwest Pacific and Caribbean. One group from New Caledonia included many already subject to malaria. Another group was raised from the 33rd Infantry in Trinidad, a regiment suffering from the discomfort and boredom of jungle training far from the front. It produced many genuine volunteers anxious not to miss the real war but not enough to make up the quota of one thousand. The balance, pushed forward by one means or another, included many who should not have been taken. On the whole, the call for a hazardous mission with promise of contact with the enemy brought to GALAHAD many brave and aggressive men including veterans of action in the Pacific, as well as many rough characters, misfits and malcontents. During the three months of training in India they had proved raw and ill disciplined, despising the accommodations and rations provided by the British, but gradually developing pride of unit and daredevil spirit and loyalty to their commander, Colonel Charles Hunter, who remained to serve under Merrill. On the way to Ledo by train some of the men were discovered by a horrified officer to be shooting out the windows at the "wogs" and their cows in the fields.

Meeting his first American combat troops after two years of war, Stilwell spoke to them, as one recalled, "simply and quietly," saying there had been two very encouraging developments: the appearance of aggressive spirit among the Chinese, and their own arrival which he and everyone had been waiting for—a hard-hitting American unit which would "get things done."

In his *basha* afterwards the staff gathered around Merrill to discuss the terms of a written directive. "Aw, to hell with this," Stilwell broke in suddenly. "Come on outside, Frank, and let's get this thing settled." They squatted on their heels under a tree examining a map. Pointing to Walawbum, about ten miles below Mainkwan, Stilwell said, "I want you to hit there on March 3." Like Pershing who, when he took over the French directives for reducing the St. Mihiel salient, reduced them from two

Jungle conferences with divisional commander Liao Yao-hsiang (200) and Colonel Rothwell Brown (201). Stilwell sent Win this picture of himself with his son and sons-in-law (202), labeling it "Your quota for the war effort." From left: Stilwell, Ernest Easterbrook, Joe Jr., Ellis Cox.

volumes to fourteen pages, Stilwell believed in stating the objective and the major lines of approach without tying down each mile of progress to a rigid schedule. Once when asked for a directive by Sun Li-jen, he replied, "Very simple. Keep going." As one of the master tacticians of the Army, he knew exactly, from studying and memorizing the terrain and geography, where and how to proceed. "When he told you what to do in Burma," General Arms said, "you had confidence that was the right thing to do. That is what a soldier wants to know."

Rain and snafus harassed the advance toward Mainkwan. Fighter planes flew ahead to hit roads and bridges and block Japanese movements, but air support in the jungle was none too effective because the pilots could not see their targets. News from the Arakan reported that a British division had been surprised by a strong Japanese attack, its headquarters overrun and its positions besieged and surrounded. This assault was a Japanese diversion to draw attention away from their preparations for the Imphal front. Though they had three divisions in the Arakan to the Japanese one, the British hastily airlifted a division from Imphal as reinforcements. Planes from the ATC had to be diverted as troop carriers, evoking angry comments by Stilwell although it had been agreed that Mountbatten could call upon the ATC to move troops in an emergency.

Worst was the rain; rain that made life in the jungle even less bearable than normal and kept the supply planes from coming in to reach the units ahead of the Road. Until the Road was surfaced by gravel, rain made a quagmire of the trace; even jeeps became stuck and trucks could bring only enough supplies forward to keep the road-builders alive. Combat troops needed the air, not only to eat but to evacuate the wounded. When it rained at night Stilwell lay awake, listening and cursing; "every drop hurt me." Peering at the leaden sky one morning outside his *basha* he said to Paul Jones, "I don't know what we're going to do," and there were tears in his eyes. Then came the sound of motors and the planes slid in.

After a 60-mile trek through the jungle which took them eight days, GALAHAD came out to meet their airdrop and seize the road at Walawbum on schedule but were heavily counterattacked the next day. Joined by a regiment of the 38th Division, they fought a fierce five-day engagement, the first occasion in which Chinese and Americans fought side by side. As a result of various foul-ups and confusions and a too-cautious advance by one Chinese regiment, the main body of the Japanese got away, though 1,500 had died and the area was left to the Allies. Booty taken at Walawbum included a number of Lend-Lease jeeps and trucks that the Japanese had captured at Rangoon. Stilwell recorded with grim satisfaction that an enemy broadcast described the fighting in the Hukawng, though not on a large scale, as "probably the fiercest in Asia." His loathing of the Japanese

was intense. When a frightened prisoner surrounded by interrogators attempted to shake hands with him, he snatched his hand away and snarled,
"Not with you, you dirty bastard."

In the Arakan with the aid of the airlifted division the British had
broken the Japanese offensive and retrieved the situation. General Slim,
"jubilant" at the result, flew in to confer with Stilwell about the launching
of Wingate's airborne brigades into the area south of the NCAC advance.
Their object was to disrupt Japanese communication so as to prevent
attack on the NCAC flank and reinforcement of the garrison at Myitkyina.
One brigade marched in from Ledo to Indaw covering 250 miles on
foot; the other two, airborne by 250 troop carriers and gliders of the
American Air Commando force under Colonel Philip Cochran, were
flown in to prepared landing strips during the period March 5-11. Despite
crashes and accidents, 9,000 men and 1,300 mules were landed in 650
sorties in six days. "All our columns are inserted in the enemy's guts,"
declared Wingate in his Order of the Day, in the rhetoric that made correct
British officers wince. "We will oppose him with resolve to reconquer our
territory of Northern Burma. Let us . . . press forward with our sword
in the enemy's ribs. . . . This is a moment to live in history."

Up to this time the Generalissimo, whatever his private messages to Sun
Li-jen, had inflicted no advice upon Stilwell; now he suddenly came to life.
Evidently suspicious of events in the Arakan, or angry that planes from the
Hump had been diverted once again from supplying China to rescuing the
British, he radioed Stilwell on March 6 that until the British advanced in
the Arakan, "our army should stop at the present position so that we will
not be attacked individually." Like MID of old, he requested Stilwell to
report his operational plans in advance. "O Jesus, now *that* starts," Stilwell
moaned, with no intention of complying.

However deep in the jungle, Stilwell could not escape politics. A radio
from Marshall regretted that "discord and suspicion" had arisen between
him and Mountbatten as a result of quarrels over Boatner's mission to
Washington and diversion of the Hump transports, and ordered him to
reestablish cordial relations. Stilwell felt himself the aggrieved party but
the Supremo spared him the trouble of coming out by coming up himself to
the Hukawng. Stilwell's descent to a field command, however deplorable
from a Headquarters point of view, had an attraction for the press which
put Mountbatten at something of a disadvantage. One of the sources of their
discord was his complaint that Stilwell made statements to the press which
gave the impression that he was the only person in SEAC fighting a war.
The public-relations war was in fact the most active front in Asia. The main
purpose of Mountbatten's visit, apart from attracting the spotlight, was to

adjust the relative credit in communiqués and press coverage and "harmonize" Anglo-American public relations in his theater, a matter of extreme importance and sensitivity to the British Empire.

No nation has ever produced a military history of such verbal nobility as the British. Retreat or advance, win or lose, blunder or bravery, murderous folly or unyielding resolution, all emerge alike clothed in dignity and touched with glory. Every engagement is gallant, every battle a decisive action. There is no shrinking from superlatives: every campaign produces a general or generalship hailed as the most brilliant of the war. Everyone is splendid: soldiers are staunch, commanders cool, the fighting magnificent. Whatever the fiasco, aplomb is unbroken. Mistakes, failures, stupidities or other causes of disaster mysteriously vanish. Disasters are recorded with care and pride and become transmuted into things of beauty. Official histories record every move in monumental and infinite detail but the details serve to obscure. Why Singapore fell or how the Sittang happened remains shrouded. Other nations attempt but never quite achieve the same self-esteem. It was not by might but by the power of her self-image that Britain in her century dominated the world. That this was irrecoverable (and that no successor would inherit it) was not yet clear in 1944.

Churchill was intensely concerned with the publicity emanating from SEAC; no less than an Air Chief Marshal and hero of the First World War, Sir Philip Joubert de la Ferté, was in charge of it. As to Mountbatten, "There was never any nonsense about his hiding his light under a bushel," according to a member of his public-relations staff. He took an intense interest in everything to do with publicity, especially his own. Too much of the wrong kind embarrassed him and too little upset him. He read every public-relations message that came in or went out of Headquarters and redrafted many of them. When he visited the troops he liked to give an impression of "spontaneous vitality." Printed orders would precede him prescribing procedures in detail, such as that troops were to sit on the ground with their backs to the sun when he addressed them so that they might see him without the sun in their eyes. He would drive up in his jeep, vault nimbly out, jump agilely onto a packing case carefully placed in advance, and deliver "an absolutely first class and apparently impromptu speech—simple, direct and genuinely inspiring. The men loved it."

He arrived at Taihpa to review the NCAC on March 6 escorted by 16 fighter planes, using up enough aviation gasoline, according to Stilwell, to "keep my campaign going for a week. . . . We had four fighters working on the battle." In knife-edged, impeccable tan tropical uniform with three rows of campaign ribbons and six-inch gold shoulder bars encrusted with stars, crowns, crossed sword and baton and royal initials, the Supremo was as elegant in the Hukawng as he would have been in Mayfair. "Old Turkey

Neck," as Stilwell called himself, greeted him in GI pants and field jacket without decorations or insignia of rank. He removed these in combat areas because he liked to talk to the men unrecognized, which frequently occurred. Once riding in a jeep wearing his long-visored Chinese soldier's cap like a hunter's and holding a carbine across his knees, he passed a group of Marauders of whom one, bitter against anyone on wheels, looked up and growled, "Christ, a goddamn duck-hunter." A GI belonging to an Engineer unit on the Road was more sympathetic. "Look at that poor old man," he said, "some draft boards will do anything." Later when Dorn told Stilwell he ought not to remove his insignia—that the men in that godforsaken area needed to see the Commanding General for their morale, that it gave them a thrill and something to write home about—he thought it over and wore them thereafter.

He and the Supremo managed a personal if not a strategic rapprochement and got along "famously," as he wrote to Win. He "ate crow" and apologized for not telling Mountbatten about his mission to Washington. This caused him no pain to do since his views had prevailed, and it pleased the Supremo very much.

In Mountbatten's view Stilwell had "fire in his belly" in his desire to come to grips with the enemy but no understanding of global strategy—the planner's crown of thorns—and he could not be made to take the least interest in administrative matters. "He is really a grand old warrior," he reported to Dill, but "only the Trinity" could be in Delhi, Chungking and Burma simultaneously. Because Mountbatten was trying to build a smooth-working happy team, he felt Stilwell's scathing remarks and unveiled criticisms were disruptive and harmful to the Allied cause. He wanted Stilwell to be eased out of SEAC and his command confined to China while Wedemeyer or Sultan replaced him at Delhi.

Escorted on a tour of the battlefield at Walawbum, he was upset by the smell of the corpses and remarked that sea battle was much cleaner. Regardless of their show of Allied cordiality, the fundamental dichotomy between the two commanders, in style, method and purpose, as in national interests, was felt by everyone in the theater. When Mountbatten a day later on the tour ran a bamboo splinter into his eye and had to be operated on at the 20th General, the version that circulated among the GIs was that Uncle Joe had "busted the Limey in the eye."

At this juncture, while the Supreme Commander was *hors de combat,* the Japanese in a gamble that could have been as devastating in effect as Pearl Harbor, launched their offensive toward Imphal and the Assam-Bengal Railway.

Ever since their surge of conquest in 1942 had netted Burma even sooner than anticipated, Japanese field generals and the Burma Area Command and Imperial Headquarters in Tokyo had been at odds whether to attempt the invasion of India, if only as far as Manipur and Assam, in order to wipe out the base of any possible Allied return. The forbidding, roadless, mountainous, disease-ridden country of Stilwell's walkout, which the British had so long counted on as a barrier to India, seemed no less so—in the opposite direction—to many of the Japanese. Opponents of the offensive argued it was not feasible to lead an army in strength across the Naga hills or to expect an Allied counteroffensive. The Japanese decided to stay where they were and consolidate gains. But in 1943 the assembling of the Yunnan and Ramgarh divisions, Wingate's first penetration which appeared to be reconnaissance for a coming offensive, and the growing action from the Assam air bases, all seemed to suggest aggressive Allied intentions and gave force to other arguments in favor of the Imphal campaign.

Planning began in the summer of 1943, energized by General Mutaguchi, commander of the Japanese Fifteenth Army in Burma, a heavy-bodied, bullet-headed officer with hard eyes and thick lips who fiercely overrode the intractable problem of supply and whose wrath was so feared by his staff that they did not press their doubts. Mutaguchi's plan allowed his men a month to reach their goal, during which they were to carry enough rice to live on together with what food they could forage and what could be piled in forward dumps. When the month was up they were expected to have captured the British stores at Imphal. According to plan, they would move on Kohima and be in Dimapur astride the railway in time to establish a firm position before the monsoon. To support the effort a road was pushed through to Homalin on the Chindwin, while debate and dispute persisted at Headquarters. It was not until January 19 when the loss of the Taro plain to the NCAC was imminent, presaging the loss of north Burma to the Japanese, that the order to execute the Imphal plan was given.

Although the British knew an attack was forming, and air reconnaissance continually reported signs of enemy movement and had sighted the road to Homalin as well as the assembly of rafts on the Uyu River, nevertheless they were unprepared. Within a week Mutaguchi's columns had crossed the Chindwin, in another week had scrambled over the mountains to the outskirts of Ukhrul, 35 miles from Imphal, and in the third week, on March 29, they cut the Imphal-Kohima road, leaving Imphal isolated except by air. Radio Tokyo blared the invasion and coming conquest of India, and *"Banzai!"* resounded through the Empire. Actually the offensive was not intended to go beyond Manipur although its commanders hoped that success would lead it forward.

Genuine and major catastrophe threatened the entire Southeast Asia Command. If, after two years' preparation and the attainment of air superiority, the British Fourteenth Army fell back now from Imphal leaving the frontier provinces to the enemy, the moral effect on India would have been incalculable, Assam would have been cut off from Calcutta, and retrieval of the will if not the military means to regain the position doubtful. Reacting vigorously to rally the defense, General Slim asked for the immediate return of the division that had been sent to reinforce the Arakan, which meant another call on the services of the ATC. Roosevelt, always nervous about China, had told Mountbatten that he was not to ask for the planes again, but the new emergency was decisive and Mountbatten, emerging from the hospital on March 14, gave the order.

General Sultan asked him the unavoidable question: how was it possible that three Japanese divisions could come through the mountains in sufficient strength to endanger Imphal when the British staff had been claiming for two years that to send an expedition in the opposite direction through the same country was impossible? Mountbatten offered the usual SEAC explanation of resources and logistics and this and that, but the real reason was will. In military as in other human affairs will is what makes things happen. There are circumstances that can modify or nullify it, but for offense or defense its presence is essential and its absence fatal. In India the will to hold was firm, withdrawal was unallowable, and the British fought in that spirit. After the transfer of the division from the Arakan had been completed, the ATC planes were kept in service on the British front for another two and a half months to keep Imphal and the besieged garrison at Kohima alive by air. Together with the RAF they ferried in supplies to 153,000 people and brought out the wounded and noncombatants.

For Stilwell the prospect during the first month of the offensive was appalling. If the British retreated and the Japanese cut the Assam-Bengal Railway, the NCAC would be isolated in Burma, all his effort and his hopes brought to nought, with no outlook but another humiliation and no escape but another walkout, over the Hump itself to China. "This about ruins everything," he wrote on the first news of the Japanese attack. When in addition it rained that night his sad short summary was "God is mad at me." He radioed Marshall that now was the time he needed help; the Generalissimo must be made to enter the Y-force.

The need for a second front on the Salween was now crucial, and Mountbatten, like Wavell waking to his extremity in 1942, was suddenly pleading for the despised Chinese. He asked both the President and Prime Minister to make personal appeals to Chiang Kai-shek with "great urgency." In reply to Roosevelt's immediate message, Chiang maintained that China was too weak and her economy too damaged to undertake a major campaign; the Communists threatened to rise in the north and the

Japanese were preparing an offensive north of the Yangtze; under these circumstances it was "impossible" to take the offensive from Yunnan. Since Chiang already had 450,000 troops quarantining the Communists, the troops in Yunnan, especially given China's transportation difficulties, were hardly relevant to that situation. His answer annoyed Roosevelt who could see the positions marked by pins in his map room. He saw only one Japanese division facing the Chinese across the Salween, and was moved to prepare a sharp reply

Stilwell went on pushing in a renewed effort to get below and envelop the 18th Division. His object now was to get across the Jambu Bum and engage the enemy in the Shaduzup area while he sent another enveloping arm around behind them to cut off their retreat to Kamaing, the central Japanese position in the Mogaung valley. GALAHAD and a regiment of the 38th Division were sent on this errand, involving a march of 85 miles, while Stilwell pressed the Chinese on the frontal route. "Item: it pays to go up to push. At least it's a coincidence that every time I do, they spurt a bit."

The 66th Regiment took the Jambu Bum on March 19, his sixty-first birthday. By some miracle in the woods, a large chocolate cake inscribed in icing "Happy Birthday Uncle Joe" graced the occasion, served from a makeshift camp table under tall trees. Wearing an old sweater, Stilwell cut the cake with a bolo knife and handed out pieces to officers and enlisted men as they filed past. His face had changed in two years. In contrast to the hard healthy look at the start of the war, he appeared old and worn with deep lines around mouth and eyes and a white patch in the middle of his hair. He was suffering from a liver ailment but, bent on reaching his goal in time, he refused to be hospitalized. A birthday telegram from Marshall assured him that "your work may well be of historic importance in this war and the future of China" and his staff in Chungking radioed, "You have the admiration, affection and loyalty of every individual in your command." *Roundup* published an analysis of CBI's controversial commander which concluded, "Someday when the war is only a filthy memory the whole story of Stilwell in Asia will be told, the epic of an unpretentious man who went forth sword in hand and slew the dragons of adversity in their dens."

The dragons were crowding him now. "Japs in UKRUHL. My God," he wrote on March 23. A plea from Slim urged him "to get Yoke in," as if he could have done so for the asking, and Intelligence reported a thousand Japanese on the route of GALAHAD's march ("My nerves are taking a beating"). It was like "the old sinking feeling" in the days after Pearl Harbor. He tried to be patient "at a terrific price in repressed fury and high blood pressure. . . . Some day I expect to burst into a thousand pieces. . . . I'm a worrier and I just can't help it." But when others worried about the Imphal offensive he would say, "If the Japs are behind us, we are also behind them."

Davies came in on his return from Washington to report that AXIOM was licked but he thought "FDR has gone his limit" with regard to the Generalissimo. Stilwell determined to try his own hand. "If I can't move Peanut the jig is up for the season." He flew to Chungking on March 27 for a conference with the Generalissimo from which he obtained, if not the Y-force, at least the promise of two divisions to reinforce the NCAC for the final drive on Myitkyina. This promise was kept a month later when the 14th and 50th Divisions were airlifted in a record eight days to Assam where they were armed and refitted and flown to staging areas in Hukawng. Back at the front on March 30 Stilwell found that Merrill, long a sufferer from heart trouble, was so weak that he had to be ordered out over his protests to the Ledo hospital. The weather was now wet five days out of six, and worse, it looked as if the Japanese were about to break through between Imphal and Kohima and reach the road and railway.

Stilwell was in an agonizing position. He could not move ahead without making sure of the rear. He had to find out if the British could hold and he determined on a maneuver of some risk to test the situation. Asking Mountbatten and Slim to meet him at Jorhat, one of the Assam air bases, on April 3, he offered to pull out the 38th Division, of which two regiments were then in reserve, and assign it to Slim to help stem the Japanese advance. Airlift of the 14th and 50th Divisions from China had begun that same day—April 3. Even so, to give up the hardened 38th might have slowed if not halted his entire campaign and cost the hope of taking Myitkyina, but it is doubtful if he expected the British to accept Chinese assistance. He was frequently caustic on the subject of the Indian Army divisions kept to guard India's Northwest Frontier and his offer may have been conceived as a form of smoking these out. If Slim had accepted the offer, the necessity would have allowed Stilwell no choice, for a Japanese breakthrough behind him would have ended his campaign in any event.

Though "obviously bitter and disappointed he made no criticisms and uttered no reproaches," according to Slim, while Slim himself, in his rather too noble account, realizing that advance now was Stilwell's great opportunity, rose to the occasion and refused the offer. In fact, to have called on the Chinese to help defend British positions in India would have been almost as damaging as to lose those positions to the Japanese. Though "nervous and concerned" as he appeared to Stilwell, Slim was confident he could stop the Japanese and he guaranteed that NCAC's line of communications would not be interrupted for more than ten days. The battle for Imphal would be decisive, he said, and promised the British would not lose.

Enormously relieved, Stilwell returned to headquarters at Shaduzup, assembled a conference of the major Chinese and American officers, and ordered "Speed to Kamaing." Thirty miles beyond Kamaing lay the railroad running through Mogaung and Myitkyina along the edge of the broad Irrawaddy valley. To prevent the NCAC from reaching the railroad the Japanese had orders to hold Kamaing at all costs. When two battalions of GALAHAD emerged on March 23 from a grueling march and several skirmishes with the Japanese, to block the road behind the enemy at Inkangahtawng about 20 miles above Kamaing, they were counterattacked and forced back into the hills. Taking up a hilltop position at Nphum Ga they held it through eleven days of savage siege until the Japanese, threatened from behind by the advance of the Chinese plus the third battalion of GALAHAD, themselves withdrew on April 8. Once more the net had not closed.

To the south the Chindits' operations were effectively preventing attack on Stilwell's flank. On March 24 Wingate was killed when his plane crashed into a mountainside. At his last meeting with Slim shortly before his death he had turned back from the door as he was about to leave and said, "You are the only senior officer in Southeast Asia who doesn't wish me dead!" His loss drained much of the effectiveness of the LRP force. "He had created it, inspired, defended it, given it confidence," Slim wrote. "It was the offspring of his vivid imagination and ruthless energy. It had no other parent." One of the brigade commanders, Brigadier William Lentaigne, with whom Stilwell was to enter into strenuous quarrel, was named to succeed Wingate, and in consideration of the fact that NCAC was diverting Japanese strength from Imphal, the Chindits were given the sole task of supporting Stilwell's operations and placed under his overall command. "If it had not been for NCAC," in the opinion of Colonel George Demetriadi, Slim's liaison officer with Stilwell, "the Japs would have succeeded at Imphal."

In the continuing effort to close in on Kamaing, Sun and Liao were unmistakably dragging their feet, on orders, as Stilwell was now sure, from Chiang Kai-shek. Repeatedly his own orders to advance were not obeyed and Chinese officers of the tank corps informed Colonel Brown that Liao was not going to attack until the Generalissimo thought it was safe and gave permission. Confronted by Stilwell on this issue, Liao admitted that the Generalissimo communicated with him directly but had ordered him to obey Stilwell "even when I'm wrong." Liao continued to stall nevertheless, convincing Stilwell that Chiang, with a wary eye on Imphal, was ordering caution.

Stilwell's absence was causing mounting confusion and irritation at various headquarters. The air was thick with radio messages to and from and between Chungking, Kunming and Delhi. Sultan told Stilwell that none of his deputies could take intelligent action and pleaded for a conference in Assam where he could make known his intentions and "put us all on the same beam." Stilwell summoned them to a conference at Mainkwan instead. Listening to the rain and counting the days, he would not leave for fear of relaxing pressures for a day. Alone of all commanders, Allied or enemy in any theater on any front, he could not count on field commanders who would carry out his directions as a matter of course. Obedience to orders depends in the end on fear of sanctions, and Sun and Liao were well aware that it was from Chiang Kai-shek not Stilwell that sanctions would flow.

The passivity of the Y-force in the midst of the publicized fighting in Burma was causing unfavorable comment in Chungking and discomfort to many Chinese who were not satisfied with the Generalissimo's explanations. He remained unaffected. Renewed urging came from Roosevelt who had moved—or let himself be carried by the War Department—a long way toward taking the Sultan-of-Morocco tone he had once deplored to Chiang Kai-shek. "It is inconceivable to me," he radioed on April 3, "that your Yoke forces with their American equipment would be unable to advance against the Japanese 56th Division in its present depleted strength. To me the time is ripe for . . . advance without further delay. . . . A shell of a division opposes you on the Salween. . . . To take advantage of just such an opportunity we have during the past year been equipping and training your Yoke forces. If they are not to be used in the common cause our most strenuous and extensive efforts to fly in equipment and furnish instructional personnel have not been justified. . . . I do hope you can act." This was tough but without teeth; it contained no or-else. Chiang was reported by Madame to be very annoyed at the tone and likely to leave the message unanswered as his way of not accepting the loss of face it conveyed.

At this point American impatience at last reached the point of quid pro quo, although, as sometimes happens at historic moments, the originating authority for the decision is not clear cut. Roosevelt was absent in Warm Springs. Stilwell communicated with Marshall and received assurance that unless the Y-force moved, its Lend-Lease supplies should end. Stilwell so instructed General Hearn, his Chief of Staff in Chungking, in a message reading, "I agree fully with George. If the Gmo won't fight, in spite of all his promises and all our efforts, I can see no reason for our wasting another ton. I recommend diversion to air activities of all tonnage being delivered to any Chinese agency." To avoid another issue of face with Chiang Kai-shek the ensuing negotiations were carried on by Hearn with Ho Ying-chin at the working level below the throne. Ho was informed that unless the Y-force moved, its Hump tonnage for the current month would be diverted to the Fourteenth Air Force. The Generalissimo was shocked into action though spared the necessity of a personal concession. Within two days of Hearn's notice, on April 14, Ho Ying-chin stamped the official seal on the order to the Yoke divsons to cross the Salween. He took care to inform Marshall that the decision "was made on initiative of Chinese without influence of outside pressure."

"Wish to God he had three months ago," wrote Dorn, American Chief of Staff to the Y-force. Divisions had still not been brought up to strength, he reported to Stilwell, but officers were eager to accomplish the mission. Hsiao I-shu, Chief of Staff to Wei Li-huang, was highly competent and all for action and General Lu Tze, in charge of supply, "is a ball of fire. When he says trucks will be there, they are there a day ahead of time." Even Ho Ying-chin was coming down for the jumpoff. The jumpoff immediately showed symptoms of the endemic postponement disease. "My God repeat God," Stilwell radioed Dorn, "so that begins again. Do not shoot yourself before notifying me three days in advance."

Stilwell now staged the final dash for Myitkyina. Given the delays and slowdowns already experienced and the several failures to eliminate the 18th Division in battle, and with Sun and Liao deliberately stalling, there was no chance left but a desperate gamble. As of April 21 he determined on a rapid secret penetration across the mountains by a striking force of GALAHAD and Chinese to seize the Myitkyina airstrip, permitting reinforcements and heavy weapons to be flown in to complete capture of the town. The Kachins warned that the steep Kumon mountain range could not be crossed by pack animals except in dry weather but Stilwell was determined to make the attempt. Except for a battery of 22nd Division artillery, the Chinese selected for the march were not of Sun's or Liao's men but one regiment of the 30th and one of the newly arrived 50th Division. Even so Stilwell believed he could not count on their impetus without an American vanguard, which made it necessary to send the battered remnant of GALAHAD out once again.

This was a grave choice because the Americans were sick, dazed and exhausted from their marches and battles and believed themselves used up, in rightful need of evacuation and rest. More than half by now had already been evacuated, chiefly because of disease; 1,400 were left of the original 3,000. Though sunk in misery and wrath they were the only force at Stilwell's disposal that he could count on to do as it was told. Colonel Hunter, though he came to hate Stilwell, was schooled in the West Point creed of obedience and Merrill was ready to resume overall command. The 90 days of GALAHAD's mission would be up on May 7, but 90 days or not, as Stilwell saw it, the campaign required them, and their officers declared them fit to go.

The men thought otherwise. In their three treks so far they had covered nearly 300 miles, slipping and stumbling, battling jungle growth and struggling with fallen mules, waiting for airdrops, eating cold K-rations, sleeping on wet ground, suffering hunger, fever, thirst and above all, as every step took them deeper into hostile land and nearer to a dismaying enemy, fear. It was the sense of "danger—above everything," according to the account of Lieutenant Charles Ogburn, that was the worst. Morale was not helped by their sense of being unappreciated and by their resentment of what they considered Stilwell's exaggerated rewards and recognition of the Chinese. Much of the sullenness, even given the hardships, might have been dispelled by personal encouragement from the Commanding General, by citations, promotions, medals and just such evidence of appreciation as he was giving the Chinese. Stilwell had congratulated the unit after the fight at Walawbum, but in Pershing's tradition he took a puritan view of decorations for his countrymen. Neither he nor Merrill were men who spared themselves and he believed that Americans should fight without needing to be "patted on the back or have their hands held," as he put it in the bitter aftermath.

When, after the bloodshed and casualties of the fight at Nphum Ga, orders came *not* to return to India but for yet another march over a 6,000-foot mountain pass and rougher territory than before, the GALAHAD survivors heard it in consternation. They could hardly believe it when "our own battalion commander and our own column commanders and our regimental and battalion surgeons all collaborated in the fanciful idea that the majority of the outfit was in condition to continue. . . ." They felt they were being sent to their deaths like the Light Brigade because someone had blundered, or because Stilwell had determined to make a record for the Chinese "if necessary at the expense of the one American infantry unit in the theater."

Stilwell told Merrill that he knew he was calling on the men for more effort than could fairly be expected but that he had no other option. Once the airstrip was taken he authorized Merrill to begin evacuating the Marauders "without further order if everything worked out as expected." The task force of 1,400 Americans, 4,000 Chinese and 600 Kachin Rangers moved out on April 28. At the same time, as if released by invisible reins, Sun and Liao moved forward in a renewed drive on Kamaing. Perhaps encouraged by the British relief of Kohima on April 20, Chiang Kai-shek had presumably given permission.

Now the swollen clouds spilled their burden and the trails became torrents. Stilwell was tormented by anxiety. He had organized and despatched the task force to Myitkyina in great secrecy without telling Mountbatten for fear of the gloating triumph of SEAC if it should fail. Whenever on earlier occasions he would talk of the goal to Slim he always insisted that Slim speak of it to no one else. That Myitkyina was the ultimate object and crowning purpose of Stilwell's campaign was hardly a secret in the theater—indeed had been specifically stated as such in Roosevelt's message to Churchill of February 25—but Mountbatten's staff had so convinced him that Myitkyina could not be taken, or if taken could not be held, or if held was not worth it, that he never believed Stilwell could achieve more than a rainy-season anchorage in the Mogaung valley. In April SEAC was not yet thinking in terms of exploiting success at Imphal, when won, into reconquest of north Burma, but rather was still pulling away toward the sea in favor of assault on Rangoon if not Sumatra. In response to urging by the Joint Chiefs to fulfill the agreed plan for north Burma, Mountbatten replied on April 14 that conquest of that area by the given dates was "impossible" and even by a later date "unsound and should not be attempted."

On April 14 SEAC moved physically in the direction of the sea strategy by transferring its headquarters 1,500 miles southward from Delhi to Kandy in Ceylon. Providing a fleet base in the Indian Ocean, Ceylon was that much nearer to Malaya and Sumatra and even further than Delhi from land operations in Burma.

A decisive move in American strategy followed. The Joint Chiefs affirmed on May 4 the intention to land on the Philippines, Formosa and the China coast, the last for the purpose, as Admiral King wrote with undeterred faith, of supplying and "utilizing Chinese manpower as the ultimate land force in defeating the Japanese on the continent of Asia." Much had been learned in the course of the last two years to suggest that to induce China's leaders to carry out America's fighting plans was not as easy as blowing a whistle, but old ideas die hard. The Navy was especially eager. Admiral Nimitz, Commander-in-Chief in the Pacific, thought the process might be foreshortened by bypassing the Philippines if the enemy's deteriorating strength permitted, except that a mere mention of this possibility, as he wrote to King, caused General MacArthur to "blow up" and deliver an oration on his "sacred obligation—redemption of 17 million people—blood on his soul—etc., etc." Nimitz and King agreed that Stilwell should name the best place on the coast from the point of view of meeting with the Chinese forces, and that early consultations with him should be sought as to ultimate Chinese operations.

The Army was thinking more in terms of China as a base of heavy bombers than of utilizing China's manpower to fight. Stilwell was notified that supply of the air effort under his command for the purpose of assisting the assaults on the Philippines in November and on Formosa in February was to have first priority. With this intent the Joint Chiefs on May 3 gave his mission a new directive: Myitkyina was to be his primary goal, independent of SEAC, and the new purpose of his overall mission was to be the development of overland communications to China and the conduct of such operations in China as would most effectively support the effort in the Pacific.

In effect, though unacknowledged, this marked the silent separation of Anglo-American effort in Asia. No one said as much in so many words. The American staff of SEAC moved with their British colleagues to Kandy and continued to function as before. But the direct thrust through the Pacific, with Stilwell's spearhead through Burma to China in its support, were now fixed policy regardless of imperial pulls toward the periphery.

It had been arranged that the Myitkyina task force would signal to alert the troop carriers when they believed themselves within 48 hours of their goal. While the force struggled painfully over the mountains at a crawl of four to five miles a day, Stilwell pushed on through the Mogaung and waited in suspense for the signal. Perversely the weather now provided several clear days, but he was blocked by stalling tactics again. Against growing fatigue ("Fell up the hill into CP, exhausted.... No wind, no legs.... Felt like an old man when I staggered in") he forced himself forward to the command posts to drag action from the Chinese by the face-losing method. "Told them to fight or I would go stand in the trail up front. This makes them move and is the only thing that does." But combat casualties were causing concern. "The 22nd Division has had 57 company officers killed. Can't push them under the circumstances. . . . Christ but I feel helpless."

Clambering and crawling over the mountains, sometimes on hands and knees, or cutting steps into the muddy inclines, while half their pack mules died from exhaustion or slipped and fell into the gorges, the Myitkyina task force crept forward. A Japanese-held village was surrounded and taken after a sharp fight en route. Colonel Kinnison, commander of one of the three combat teams, and several of the men died of mite typhus. Two of the combat teams at the end of their rations halted at prearranged clearings to wait for airdrops. Colonel Hunter's team kept going and on May 14 sent the 48-hour signal. In the Mogaung Stilwell was joined in his tense wait by General Old, commander of troop carriers for the Tenth Air Force. On May 15 the 24-hour signal came in. On May 16 Colonel Hunter's team moved to a bivouac within two miles of the Myitkyina airstrip to ensure a quick springboard for surprise attack. It was feared that skirmishes with Japanese patrols en route might have forewarned the garrison, but Kachin scouts found no signs of alert and reported the airstrip lightly held. There were in fact no more than 700 active Japanese troops holding Myitkyina at that moment.

At 10 o'clock on the morning of May 17 the attack on the airstrip was launched by the 150th Regiment of the 50th Division while the GALAHAD 1st Battalion was assigned to take a nearby ferry terminal on the Irrawaddy. Surprise was complete and the airstrip quickly seized and surrounded. At 10:50 Stilwell received from Merrill, who was at task force headquarters at Nawbum, the prearranged signal "In the Ring" meaning "At the Field." Colonel Hunter wanted to make sure his hold was secure before sending the conclusive signal. As soon as "In the Ring" was received, General Old flew a reconnaissance plane over the Myitkyina airstrip but reported on his return that he could see nothing. "We'll just have to sweat it out," Stilwell recorded, periodically venting his anxiety in his pocket diary during this day. The wait lasted four hours. At 3:30 the message came, MERCHANT OF VENICE! meaning "Transports can land." With a single "WHOOPS!" in the diary, Stilwell ordered guns and reinforcements started on their way; "first ones over at 4 . . . told them to keep going all night . . . WILL THIS BURN UP THE LIMIES!"

It did. The first important Japanese position to be recaptured in Southeast Asia had been taken by Stilwell's task force while the British had not yet succeeded in taking even Akyab. It was brutally embarrassing for the Supreme Allied Commander to wake up and discover a component of his forces in Myitkyina when he had not known the expedition was on its way, though in view of the Joint Chiefs' directive of May 4 his unawareness could only have come from looking in the other direction. Mountbatten was outraged that he had not been informed, and further discomfited by a sharp query from Churchill who wanted an explanation for how "the Americans by a brilliant feat of arms have landed us in Myitkyina." Public relations was unprepared for the coup, but after a day and a half of internal stress produced a very handsome Order of the Day addressed to Stilwell in Mountbatten's name. "By the boldness of your leadership," it read, "backed by the courage and endurance of your American and Chinese troops, you have taken the enemy completely by surprise and achieved a most outstanding success by seizing the Myitkyina airfield." The crossing of the Kumon range was declared to be "a feat which will live in military

Troops of the 38th Division after fording the river at Taihpa Ga, February 1944 (203). Lieutenant General Sir William Slim addresses troops of the 20th Division (204). Reinforcements move up the Ledo Road during a monsoon in 1944 (205).

203

204

205

208

On May 17, 1944, Stilwell launched the attack on the Myitkyina air-strip. Chinese troops of the 14th Division were flown in by C-47 (208) as GALAHAD forces fought for a nearby ferry terminal on the Irra-waddy (207). The message, "Transports can land," came in the after-noon, and the airstrip was then open for Allied planes (206).

206

207

2

21

Stilwell confers with Colonel Charles Hunter of Mer
rill's Marauders after successful attack at Myitkyin.
(210). The Chinese continue the pursuit of the Japa
nese, crossing the Salween River in rubber boa.
(209), and an artillery pack train of the 22nd Div.
sion moves up a trail near Warazup (211).

history" and care was taken to bring in the Chindits "who have been severing Japanese communications between Myitkyina and the south" for a share of the credit. Global strategists including Wedemeyer flew all the way up to the muddy clearing in the woods to share in the occasion they had declared to be impossible.

The triumph, Stilwell's first in two years of ceaseless frustration, was nectar to a parched soul, but unfinished. It was beset at once by misadventure and threat of reverse. Everyone at NCAC expected the opening of the airstrip, giving access to reinforcements, to lead to the quick fall of Myitkyina proper. Stilwell decided the honor should go to the Chinese; two battalions of the 150th Regiment advanced on the town on the afternoon of May 17, but coming under Japanese sniper fire at dusk, fell into confusion, fired on each other in error and continued shooting and killing each other in uncontrollable response until they were pulled out. This was matched by an American snafu when the Tenth Air Force Headquarters sent an antiaircraft battery on the first transports instead of the infantry and food preordered by Merrill and Hunter.

The full effect of these errors was not yet realized and expectations were still high when Stilwell (with no less than twelve correspondents) reached the airstrip the next morning. Greeted by Merrill who had flown in to take command, the two men were caught by the camera as Stilwell stepped from the plane, hugging and laughing for joy. But the day ended badly. A second foray by the 150th Regiment resulted in the same confusion as before. The Marauders, sustained on their march only by the belief that they would be flown out to Ledo as soon as the airstrip was taken, were now asked for further effort. Hunter hurriedly summoned the two lagging combat teams whose airdrops in some cases had missed or gone astray. Many men had not eaten in several days, many limped from Naga sores, others suffering from dysentery had cut away the seats of their pants so as not to be hampered in combat and were in Merrill's words, "a pitiful but still splendid sight." Merrill himself was felled by another heart attack on May 19 and had to be evacuated.

The Japanese rushed reinforcements from other garrisons and outposts in north, east and west. Within a week, despite the Chindit block to the south, they had 3,000 men in Myitkyina and 5,000 within two weeks. They fought the same suicidal defense as they did on the Pacific islands. After the failure to take Myitkyina immediately, the monsoon closed in and the situation congealed in a deadly slough of troubles, quarrels and failures of all kinds. "Good God, what goes on at Mitch?" Stilwell asked himself, tortured with worry. In order to keep pressure on Sun and Liao to clear the Mogaung valley so the Road could go through, he remained with the NCAC. "Rain—if we can't land planes we can't land troops . . .

this is one of those terrible worry days when you wish you were dead." June was an uninterrupted month of such days. Even when the ceiling was zero the transports flew in men and supplies to Myitkyina, seeming to "smell their way to the field," in the phrase of Seagrave who was serving as ever at the front. But G-2 seriously underestimated the number of Japanese in the garrison and the Chinese, though reinforced by fresh regiments, could not prevail over the entrenched defenders. And as Stilwell had to admit on one of his visits, "GALAHAD is shot."

Bitter with a sense of betrayal and broken promises, without will to fight and only mistrust and hatred of the theater commander in its place, they were a ruined unit with no thought but to get out of Myitkyina and out of Burma. The sick were being evacuated at the rate of 75-100 a day, the criterion being a fever of 102 for three consecutive days, but a shell of the unit was held in place. As an Allied commander Stilwell felt he could not withdraw the Americans while keeping the Chinese and Chindits in the fight. He was engaged in a fierce broil with Lentaigne throughout this period because the Chindit units, dwindled to exhausted remnants like GALAHAD, were insisting on withdrawal and in one case had given up a position Stilwell considered essential. While angrily refusing to let them withdraw, he could not treat the Americans differently. The last of GALAHAD, called to stem a Japanese counterattack, fell asleep under fire and Colonel McGee, their commander, fainted three times while directing the engagement. When Stilwell came to investigate, one enlisted man said regretfully afterwards, "I had him in my rifle sights. I coulda squeezed one off and no one woulda known it wasn't a Jap that got the son of a bitch."

At one time or another Stilwell tried three different American commanders as successor to Merrill. For most of the time General Boatner was in charge. Food and supplies during June were down to a minimum because Japanese mortars, pounding the field, interrupted the flights of the transports. At times no more than a day's rations were on hand. For a period of crisis early in the month it appeared that the Japanese might even recapture the airfield. Stilwell called in Generals Hu Su and Pan Yu-kan, commanders of the units from the 30th and 50th Divisions, and told them "under no circumstances would they retreat one step." To lose Myitkyina now would have been unendurable. Reluctant to ask for more Chinese casualties, he ordered in two battalions of Engineers from the Road, following the Leavenworth principle that recognizes Combat Engineers as Infantry reserve in emergency. Though nominally Combat Engineers, the road-builders had not held a rifle since basic training and proved initially worthless. Two battalions of replacements for GALAHAD, just arrived in India from the United States and rushed to Myitkyina without training, were no better. "They are in many cases simply terrified of the Japs," reported Boatner; they would not follow their officers, refused to attack and ran under fire.

To Stilwell, out at the end of the line in CBI, U.S. troops had seemed to promise reliable action. "Terrible letter from Boatner," he wrote, and added one of the most poignant lines of the diary: "US troops shaky. Hard to believe." To maintain an American presence, and conscious that the Chinese had taken a far higher rate of direct combat casualties than the Americans, he now gave orders for return to the front of all GALA-HAD convalescents fit for field duty. This was the last whiplash. To everyone in the 5307th his name by now, according to Ogburn, was "as a red flag to a bull" and to Ogburn himself Stilwell seemed "bloodless and utterly coldhearted, without a drop of human kindness." Understandable from the GALAHAD point of view, it was a judgment, considering Stilwell's real nature, that can only be reckoned as one more of the tragedies of CBI. Ravdin of the 20th General Hospital, though he disputed Stilwell's order to return the GALAHAD evacuees to duty, nevertheless considered him a commander who "thought more of his men than any commanding general I have ever known." In *Yank,* the soldiers' newspaper, he appeared within four months of GALAHAD's agony as "The GI's Favorite" who had canceled the rule against pets for GIs in his theater ("It's unnatural for a soldier not to have pets") and banned the "officers only" signs from restaurants and cafes and forbidden officers to date enlisted WACS in order to give GIs a chance. His record was too plain to make him out a Patton.

In China the situation looked ominous under the impact of a new and menacing Japanese offensive. The Generalissimo, still thoroughly persuaded of Chennault's thesis that the air force could fight his war and defend the air bases, summoned Stilwell "immediately" to Chungking on June 3 to demand more planes, supplies and fuel for the Fourteenth Air Force. Required to face the danger that was soon to become enveloping, Stilwell hurried to the capital for two days, June 4-5, and returned as soon as he could to Burma's portion of "worry, worry, worry." General Arms, hurriedly summoned from Kunming, organized basic training behind the lines for the Engineers and GALAHAD replacements. Worked in three shifts of eight hours each to train, fight and sleep, they were pulled together and hardened. The grip on Myitkyina was holding but "The wear and tear on the nerves continues. Are we attempting too much? Can they hold us? Is there a surprise ready? Counterattack? Will our people stick it out? Casualties too heavy? I can tell I've nearly had enough of this. . . ."

It was in the midst of these concerns that Mountbatten raised the affair of Noel Coward, which if not quite on the global strategy level was evidently a matter of serious portent. Coward was making a tour of the Burma front and the Supremo with the kindest intent wanted to share his entertainments with the U.S. forces. A request for transportation for the actor and his troupe to the Ledo front had been refused by Stilwell, either from simple prejudice or perhaps on the theory that Coward's talents would not be appreciated by Chinese and American GIs, but in any case with wounding effect on Mountbatten. "I consider this a slam in the face," he complained to General Wheeler and expressed his resentment in a letter to Stilwell. Wheeler suggested an expression of regret from Stilwell and messages thickened between Kandy and Shaduzup. In the end Coward made his way to Ledo where the reception of his first performance was reportedly "completely flat"; the audience for the second at the 20th General Hospital was "directed to show expressions of approval." "If any more piano players start this way," Stilwell radioed to Sultan, "you know what to do with the piano."

In final unbelievable reality the Y-force had jumped off on May 11 and was inching its way over 10,000-foot mountains and the gorges of the Salween toward Japanese-occupied Lungling on the old Burma Road. The route lay along a spur of the Himalayan range, the highest battleground in the world. The campaign was a mixture of extraordinary human exertion and the manifold debilities and overcaution of the Chinese Army. All the energy and endlessly compliant endurance of the men and the vigor and boldness of many of the officers were vitiated by the inertia and unwillingness that seeped down from the top. All the reluctance, delays and passivity could be crystallized in the unending problem of replacements. Ninety-five thousand had been promised by the spring of 1944; up to May 23,000 had been furnished and then replacements stopped. When the Chinese Exeditionary Force, as the Y-force was now called, went into action it was 115,000 under its table-of-organization strength and was to suffer an attrition rate during the campaign of over 5,000 a month.

"They've done well at last," Dorn wrote to Stilwell when after the long postponement the CEF, accompanied by American liaison officers and medical teams, crossed the rushing Salween on bamboo rafts and rubber boats. The river was 60 feet deep at the two crossings and full of whirlpools. In a thousand years of occupation, Hsiao I-shu said, the Chinese had never been able to cross the river with troops at these two places. Gaining surprise, the Force was out of the gorge and had climbed the cold cloud-covered mountains before the Japanese knew of their advent.

"There was even enthusiasm," Dorn wrote. Wei Li-huang, the Commanding General, "pounded the table and Hsiao yelled at the commanders . . . and is doing his damndest." But even Wei and Hsiao "cannot inject what it takes into some of these birds." He reported 32,000 men across the river on the first day, moving thousands of pack horses, pack cows, mules and transport coolies up the fearful incline in pouring rain. "I have never seen such a cheerful bunch of men." Wherever he passed, "the whole mob started yelling Ting-hao, Hello, Okay, and other Americanized expressions which have become passwords in the CEF." Troops who could be cheerful under such conditions and march and keep marching over the damned mountains, "can do anything if only given the breaks in leadership and equipment."

Once more, however, results were dispiriting. The Chinese took Lungling on June 10 and a week later were driven out by a determined Japanese counterattack more successful than that at Myitkyina. Forces were reassembled for another attempt. Possession of Lungling was essential to open the passage from Burma to China and permit Stilwell's troops to come through once Myitkyina was taken. Although the CEF outnumbered the enemy by about ten to one it was two months before Lungling was reentered.

Chiang Kai-shek had been sufficiently impressed by the coup at Myitkyina to loosen the reins in Burma. Sun Li-jen suddenly bounded forward and led his troops through a month of hard aggressive fighting to the capture of Kamaing on June 16. "Took a nap," Stilwell recorded for the first time. "I needed it. . . . We are just making the grade, everytime and by an eyelash." Ten days later, with Stilwell viciously prodding the worn remnant of the 77th Chindit Brigade into simultaneous advance from the south, Mogaung was taken, causing a renewed outburst of the public-relations war over rival claims for credit.

The NCAC stood at last astride the railroad at the entrance to the Irrawaddy valley. Crippled by 50 percent casualties, the Japanese 18th Division was reduced to a shattered 3,000 who, with some 2,000 more from other regiments, succeeded in withdrawing toward Mandalay. Except for the short gap between Mogaung and Myitkyina, north Burma as far as the Irrawaddy was now regained with the Ledo Road following on the heels of the advance. Closure of the remaining gap between the NCAC and the CEF was still to be achieved and depended on whether offensive impetus could be maintained.

At Myitkyina attrition was slowly weakening the Japanese defense and the Allied grasp was gradually being extended. On the borders of India the Japanese gamble had failed—although the fight went on—when Kohima was relieved and communications restored between Imphal and the Dimapur Road at the end of April. General Mutaguchi's troops were left at the end of jungle trails without supply arrangements and with the monsoon pouring down. They fought on while they died of starvation and disease. By the end of June the fanatic offensive had crumbled into rain-soaked and putrefying chaos. When retreat was finally ordered in mid-July Japanese casualties including ill and wounded had reached 85 to 90 percent and the dead numbered 65,000 out of the original 155,000. On these same trails the refugees of the exodus of 1942 had dropped and died, now to be covered by the rotting corpses of their conquerors. The senseless tides of war rolled and receded impersonally over the shadowed uplands of Burma.

In China the thrust of the Japanese offensive was strong: Changsha which had three times withstood attack in the past fell without a fight on June 18; Hengyang, first in the chain of American air bases, was under siege. Washington was alarmed. A "message from George" with a proposal of unusual dimensions reached Stilwell on July 2. His new task was at hand.

Stilwell at Myitkyina looking at aerial photographs (212).

18

"The Future of All Asia Is at Stake"

JUNE–SEPTEMBER 1944

URING the months when Stilwell was in Burma, China's situation
had degenerated alarmingly from the effects of civic and economic paralysis, renewed Japanese penetration, and rising disunity
and discontent. Dissatisfaction with the regime had erupted in the previous December, when Chiang Kai-shek was in Cairo, in a conspiracy of
younger officers to enforce the removal, not of Chiang himself, but of
Ho Ying-chin, Tai Li, Dr. Kung, the Chen brothers and senior civil and
military officials considered guilty of corruption and inefficiency. Uncovered
by Tai Li's agents before it could accomplish anything, the Young Generals'
Plot, as it became known, was said to have involved between 200 and 600
officers and to have resulted in the execution of 16 generals. Trapped in
the narrow circle of the very few figures whom he trusted, of whom Kung
and Ho were the two most important, Chiang took no measures to respond
to the grievances expressed by the movement.

From January to June reports from American foreign service officers
in posts from Kunming and Kweilin to Sian and Lanchow were filled with
mounting evidence of deterioration and dissidence. Their burden was that
China was becoming progressively demoralized, official life infected by
unprecedented corruption, the army ineffective and the Government engaged
in a prolonged suicide in which the only hold on life was preparation for
civil war against the Communists. Under the long strains of war and occupation, the paste of unity was cracking and the pattern of warlord separatism reappearing. The Kwangsi-Kwangtung faction had revived under

455

the leadership of two early Kuomintang leaders of always uncertain allegiance, Yu Han-mou and Chang Fa-kwei, joined or possibly exceeded in discontent by a figure of great influence in the southern provinces, Marshal Li Chi-shen. Provincial factions of Szechwan and Yunnan were said to be drawing together with the Kwangsi-Kwangtung group toward a possible autonomous regime in the event of collapse at Chungking. Disaffection was openly expressed at the headquarters of Hsueh Yueh, Commander of the Ninth War Zone in the rice-bowl region of Hunan. Groups in Chengtu were agitating for reform of the Central Government along democratic lines. In Yunnan the Government was denounced, according to a consular report, as "a clique almost completely lacking in popular support." In the north restlessness was reported among former warlords who had been insurgents before and could be again, among them the "Model Governor," Yen Hsi-shan, for whom Stilwell had built his first road in 1921.

The dismal chorus of the American foreign service reports showed the economy to be stagnating owing to the Government's effort to control inflation by a policy of forced purchase at prices barely one-third the cost of production. Seven out of every eight mines in Kwangsi had closed down as had 14 out of 18 iron foundries in Chungking. Little effort had been made to organize workable transportation, to carry out rationing, or to regulate tax collecting which through corruption and inefficiency now delivered no more than one third of its revenues to the Central Government. Conscription pressed as heavily as ever upon the peasant, trees and livestock were confiscated, and enforced grain quotas added to the limitless burden of legal and illegal taxes. Derelict soldiers, too starved or ill to keep up with their units and too far from home to find succor, could be seen along the roads hunched over their begging bowls in silent misery. Laborers impressed to build the airfields worked under armed guard, were seldom paid and ate only if their families lived near enough to bring them food. Many were soldiers from provincial armies scheduled for reduction and were fed so little that they usually died. On the sick body of the economy officials profiteered luxuriously through an unimaginable variety of grafts and rackets. After six months in Chengtu an American captain confessed, "I'd like to get a year's leave of absence from the Army to organize a really efficient revolution in this country."

Foreign correspondents in their chronic feud with the censorship felt the same way. In April they addressed a joint protest to Chiang Kai-shek stating that although permitted to send stories that created an idealized portrait of China, they were prevented from writing anything that implied criticism of the Government or that disclosed "the full gravity of China's economic situation" or that questioned in any way "the direction, condition or use of the Chinese armies," and that it was impossible to function as responsible journalists unless the policy were liberalized. Chiang's answer was merely that reports that were not detrimental to China's resistance would be given every consideration.

In Chungking discontent was surfacing through the crust of official suppression. Chang Lan, former Governor of Szechwan and President of the Federation of Democratic Parties, boldly published a pamphlet protesting the Government's dictatorship. Mme. Sun Yat-sen, always a political foe of her family, was now outspoken in criticism, and even the approved newspapers were calling for democratic reforms. The same call was loud in Kunming where slogans of dissent appeared on the walls and students paraded with placards and petitions. Through it all Chiang's unresponsiveness appeared baffling and incredible. His failure at the 12th Plenary Session of the Central Executive Committee in May to take any reform measures was considered by many Chinese to mark the "turning point in the situation in China," according to a report by Gauss on June 8. From here on, the Ambassador warned, the tide of political unrest could be expected to rise.

Into this situation the new Japanese offensive, code-named ICHIGO, brought havoc. The war by now had turned against Japan. Her Western enemy was advancing implacably toward her across the Pacific. The hubris that had struck at Pearl Harbor and seized an empire from Mukden to Singapore was meeting its classic fate. Japan's reach had exceeded her grasp, but though the edges crumbled, she was not going to let go in China. The overall aim of ICHIGO was to consolidate Japan's position on the mainland by fusing a solid line of communications from Tientsin to Canton, and by eliminating the American air bases. Indirectly it may have represented one last effort to bring about a surrender of the Chinese Government.

The first phase began in April in a drive down from the Yellow River against the gap in the Peking-Hankow Railway which the Japanese had so far not occupied. The 34 Chinese divisions in Honan, including some reputed to be among the Government's best, showed little evidence, according to a Fourteenth Air Force intelligence report, "of either plan or capability to hamper Japanese movement." They melted away before the enemy, leaving Honan in chaos with homes looted down to their last cooking pots by bands of wandering soldiers, and peasants turned bandit with captured arms as in the days of the Red Spears of 1927. In the wake of the collapse Communist units from neighboring Shansi filtered in. An Embassy observer in Sian reported that the inhabitants expected the

Communists to be in control by the time the Japanese were expelled and "It would not seem strange if they turned out to be right."

ICHIGO's second phase, in the form of a southward drive from Hankow toward the chain of Fourteenth Air Force bases in east China, opened in June with every sign of duplicating the earlier success. The Chinese General Staff had drawn up no plans for defense of the airfields and the centers adjoining them. When Changsha, capital of the rice-bowl region, fell on June 18, resentment of the Government's laxity, rising out of the ravages of Honan, spread to the south. The domestic prospect, quite aside from the military, was dismaying: loss of food stocks, disruption of trade, influx of refugees into the unoccupied zone, a reduced area of Free China, causing increase of conscription and taxes. Summarized by an American report, it meant lowered morale, weakening of the Central Government, proportionate strengthening of the provincial cliques, continued inflation and economic crisis. In short, how long could the Central Government survive? The author of the report, John Service, thought it could survive for a while but its weaknesses would grow and its collapse in the long run would be only a matter of time.

Service was another China-born member of the Embassy's staff, "the ablest group of young diplomats," according to Eric Sevareid, "I had ever seen in a single American mission abroad. They were the best informed foreigners in China." Along with two other second secretaries, Raymond Ludden and John Emmerson, Service had recently been recruited, much to the Ambassador's annoyance, as political adviser by Stilwell's headquarters in Chungking.

The emergency brought on by the Japanese drive in the south precipitated the bitterest phase of the Chennault-Stilwell dispute and the long train of rancor and abuse by Chennault and his associates that was to follow after the war. The issue of the effectiveness of Chennault's air arm occupied a far larger place in everyone's mind at the time than it retains in historical perspective, and was a determining factor in attitudes and decisions.

By persistent and damaging attacks on Japanese supply lines the Fourteenth Air Force succeeded in hampering but not halting the offensive. As it became apparent that the fliers alone could not stop the march toward the air bases, Chennault hammered at Stilwell for more planes, supplies and fuel and even for arms for the defending forces on the ground. He claimed his means were "hopelessly inadequate" and insisted he must have 10,000 tons. Stilwell regarded this as a campaign "to duck the consequences of having sold the wrong bill of goods." Having assured the Generalissimo that the Fourteenth Air Force, if supported effectively, could hold the Japanese and now finding that it could not be done,

Chennault was "trying to prepare an out for himself by claiming that with a little more, which we won't give him, he can still do it." The extra tonnage would have to come from the B-29 allotments and Stilwell believed it would be wasted because of weakness on the ground. Air cover over nothing, as he had said at TRIDENT, was valueless.

This dispute was the reason for his being summoned from Burma by the Generalissimo on June 4. Under Chiang's extreme pressure Stilwell agreed to divert 1,500 tons from the B-29s to make up Chennault's 10,000 if the War Department consented. Marshall refused. He had come to the conclusion that the huge effort to supply Chennault's air offensive had not been worth the cost and he was bitter at the delay caused to success in Europe for lack of air transport absorbed by the Hump. "It has been bleeding us white in transport airplanes," Stimson complained. On June 6, the day before Marshall's reply to Stilwell, Rome fell and the Allies landed in Normandy. Marshall believed that more rapid progress could have been made in Italy and France if the transport planes then in the China theater had been available for air support.

Furthermore military thinking now heavily favored long-range strategic bombing of enemy industry. In his telegram turning down a diversion of the long-range bombers' supplies to Chennault, Marshall stated that nothing must interfere with the launching of the B-29 assault on Japan. This, he claimed, would be of greater service to China in the long run than the transfer of its stocks to Chennault. He also pointed out, for Chiang Kai-shek's benefit, that experience in Europe proved the limitations of "a purely air resistance" to a ground offensive.

Like an emperor's thumbs-down signal in the gladiatorial arena, Marshall's reply marked the definite rejection by the Joint Chiefs of Chennault's claim. The flaw in the rejection was that Chennault and his protagonists never understood what had happened to them with the result that their enduring rage was directed against Stilwell. He, of course, was left in no doubt. "Instructions understood," he replied to Marshall, "and exactly what I had hoped for." Stilwell's seeming indifference to the fate of east China was based on his belief that the Japanese would eventually outrun their supply lines and come to a natural stop; meantime it was too late to save the first airfields in their path. His plan, after he had succeeded in reopening the Burma Road, was to bring the Y divisions and the NCAC back into southwest China and together with the Z divisions and an American Army corps, for which he was still hoping, collect a force of 250,000 with which to clear a path to the coast and seize a port.

To keep the condition of China smothered under benevolent fictions in the American press was no longer possible. Articles critical of the regime were appearing and even the Luce publications had to make the best of a bad situation by admitting China's ills and deficiencies and blaming them on the blockade which the United States had failed in its duty to break. *Life* on May 1 published a report of excoriating frankness by Theodore White who described the Kuomintang as a "corrupt political clique that combines some of the worst features of Tammany Hall and the Spanish Inquisition" and declared that "progressive deterioration" within the Nationalist Party left the future outcome of civil war with the Communists uncertain. The slightly askew conclusion (possibly drawn by the editorial hand of the home office) was that it was the "obligation" of America to assist this antidemocratic and losing regime "with force at the present moment on a scale far greater than we have done for the past two years."

There were those who doubted that this would solve the problem; who wondered, like Graham Peck, an officer of OWI in China, whether the blank check of American aid, by encouraging the Kuomintang to be dependent rather than self-strengthening, might not represent "a prolonged kiss of death."

For a hundred years the Chinese had struggled to unburden themselves of misgovernment only to have each effort of reform or revolution turn itself back into oppression and corruption, as if the magic prince were bewitched in reverse to turn back into a toad. China's misgovernment was not so much a case of absolute as of ineffective rule. If power corrupts, weakness in the seat of power, with its constant necessity of deals and bribes and compromising arrangements, corrupts even more. For 30 years Ambassador Gauss had watched the process and wearily in June 1944 recognized the limits of American instrumentality to affect it. "I confess," he wrote the State Department, "there is nothing I can suggest that we might do."

Counsels of incapacity are not welcome to the American spirit. One thing that it was believed America could do would be to push, persuade or force China into directing her whole available military strength against Japan and, to that end, into closing the rift with the Communists that paralyzed her war efforts. Ambassador Gauss was instructed on June 15 to make this clear to Chiang Kai-shek. He was to urge Chiang to reach an agreement with the Communists that would permit the quarantine to be ended so that troops of both sides might be released to fight the Japanese. In reply to recent Chinese requests for more aid and for continuation of Lend-Lease after the war, he was to inform Chiang that because of commitments in Europe the United States could not increase military aid to China for the present. That was as far as he could go.

Chiang was dependent but not compliant. He and his associates did not believe that the United States would ever take the risk of withdrawing support from him. Yet in May the State Department in a policy advice circulated to its own officers stated that the United States was "not committed to support the Nationalist Government in any and all circumstances." This astonishing burst of independence could have been useful had Gauss been empowered to convey it to Chiang Kai-shek, but there is no evidence that he was. The persuasions and connections of the Soongs, the influence of church bodies and United China Relief, the ramifications of China Defense Supplies—nucleus of what was to become the China Lobby—and the underlying inertia of government all operated to maintain the tie. Occasionally, as in the State Department's May policy advice, the United States thrashed about in the Chinese cobweb, but the threads held.

In the summer of 1944 growing impatience with the paralysis of Chungking turned American military interest toward the war potential of the Communists. They were reported to be aggressively engaged in guerilla warfare against the enemy in the provinces of Shantung, Hopei, Shansi and north Kiangsu, although direct evidence was lacking because no foreigner accredited to Chungking was allowed to visit the area north of the quarantine line. They were established in north China in a region crucial for the final defeat of Japan which contained the largest concentration of Japanese troops and Japanese industry on the mainland apart from Manchuria. It was also the area that would be contiguous to Russian operations if and when Russia joined the war in the Far East.

Since 1937 the remnant that survived the Long March to reach Yenan had become the government of a region the size of Japan. In these seven years the area under Communist control was estimated to have increased from 35,000 to 155,000 square miles, the population from 1,500,000 to 54,000,000, and the armed forces from 100,000 to 475,000. Communist enclaves were held behind Japanese lines in parts of north Kiangsu and Hupeh and also in the south around Canton and on the island of Hainan. The spread had been achieved by infiltration behind Japanese advances which often left large areas behind without adequate garrison. Moving in with effective political and military organization, offering tax reduction and elimination of rent to landlords who had joined the puppet regime, the Communists gained the support of the populace. Given protection from extortion and the press gang, the peasants felt for the first time they were getting something in return for their taxes. As the Communist base expanded, their position relative to the Central Government was strengthened and their confidence grew, and when Kuomintang weakness was revealed by the debacle in Honan, it grew apace.

American interest was concerned as much with averting the disintegration of China in a civil war as with gaining Communist military cooperation against Japan. Civil war, besides destroying any hope of the stable China that was needed to keep the future peace, might lead to American-Soviet conflict. For political as well as military reasons it appeared essential to bring the contenders into some form of coalition. Both Communists and Kuomintang gave lip service to the idea of coalition government and had opened negotiations in 1943 for a political settlement, probably less from conviction than because neither side wished to appear to be pursuing civil war as a policy. American hope of coalition was based on the prevailing belief that the Communist aim was not to dominate China but to arrive at a political settlement with Chungking permitting a national effort against Japan. It was assumed, as Stalin personally assured Ambassador Harriman, that the Chinese Communists were not really Communists at all but a "margarine" imitation of the real thing, or alternatively, a "radish" variety —red outside and white inside.

An additional motive from the American point of view was that the Communists as the more dynamic force might actually win a civil war. It was not part of the American war aim to have a hostile ideology, radish or not, govern China after the war and it seemed advisable to achieve a coalition government before the Soviet Union moved onto the scene. That event was an even greater worry to Chiang Kai-shek. He was reported to be strengthening the quarantine line by troops withdrawn from Honan and to be preparing to attack the Communists while the Allies were still occupied in Europe, and before either the Soviets could move in the Far East or the Americans land in China.

Both the foreign press and the American Government had been pressing for months for permission to visit the Communist zone. A promise given to the press in November 1943 was pursued through half a year of evasions until a selected group of three correspondents, representing a pool of English, American and other publications,* was finally allowed to go in May. Washington's effort to send a Military Observers Mission continued to meet polite assent without fulfillment.

The mission and the opening of a consulate in Yenan were first suggested by Davies in a report to Stilwell of June 1943 which argued the

---

* The three were Harrison Forman, representing the *New York Herald-Tribune,* UP and London *Times;* Guenther Stein, representing the *Christian Science Monitor,* AP and London *News-Chronicle;* and Israel Epstein, representing *The New York Times,* Time-Life, *Allied Labor News* and Sydney *Morning-Herald.* Other members of the party were Father Shanahan, representing American Catholic publications, and Maurice Votaw, an employee of the Chinese Information Ministry, denounced by the other correspondents as a "Kuomintang stooge" and attached to the party as nominal representative of the *Baltimore Sun.* After heavy pressure by the correspondents a second group consisting of Brooks Atkinson, Theodore White and Harold Isaacs of *Newsweek* was permitted to go in September.

military importance of the area and its relation to future Soviet entry and pointed out that the only official American observer to have visited the Communist region was Captain Carlson in 1938. Davies and General Timberman of the General Staff, another veteran of the 15th Infantry now attached to CBI Headquarters in Chungking, persuaded Marshall of the need for the mission, and a second report by Davies in January 1944 reached Hopkins in the White House. In February Roosevelt formally requested Chiang Kai-shek to permit military observers to go "immediately" to Shansi and Shensi, tactfully omitting to specify the region as Communist. Chiang gracefully agreed to "facilitate" the mission which, he added, could of course visit only those areas under the Central Government's control.

On the basis of his consent CBI Headquarters organized the project while ignoring for the time being the restriction that made nonsense of it. To ensure observers who would not be at the mercy of their hosts, Stilwell looked for candidates who had knowledge of the language and acquaintance with China. As chief of mission he named Colonel Barrett, said to be the only American who could tell jokes convincingly in Chinese to Chinese, with John Service as his political assistant.

Stilwell's own interest in the matter was a natural craving for a junction with what he believed to be vigorous, motivated troops. He remembered the Communists in terms of their startling if limited defeat of the Japanese at the pass of Pinghsingkwan in 1937, and like everyone else he had an impression of successful and energetic guerilla warfare ever since. He had been favorably impressed in 1938 by Yeh Chien-ying, the Communist Chief of Staff, and his associates, and he had not forgotten the word passed to him from Chou En-lai after the defeat in Burma: "I would serve under General Stilwell and *I* would obey." It took on an exaggerated significance in his mind as he struggled against the frustrations of the Kuomintang military system. At one time he thought of using Communists to make up the desperately needed replacements for the Y-force on the basis of 20 to a company of 100. The idea was dropped after Dorn discussed it with Hsiao I-shu, the Y-force Chief of Staff, who said that on a 20 percent basis the newcomers would have the whole company Communist within two weeks. Stilwell knew by now that as long as Chiang Kai-shek remained, reform of the army and combat efficiency would never be achieved, and that knowledge made the idea of contact with the far-off unseen fighters of the Communist zone more compelling. For the present what was needed was first-hand information.

Under the name DIXIE for the rebel side, and for the song "Is It True What They Say About Dixie?", the Military Observers Mission was ready to go in March but the Generalissimo continued to stall. The President renewed his request in April, without success, and at that point the matter passed into the hands of yet another special envoy, Vice-President Henry Wallace.

The purpose of the Wallace mission, if any, was to persuade Chiang to negotiate with the Communists. It is a feature of government that the more important the problem, the further it tends to be removed from handling by anyone well acquainted with the subject. The President, deeply concerned about China, casting about for solutions, anxious to do something without knowing what, fell back on the device of a personal envoy. To a man like Roosevelt it always seemed that if only he could go in person, he could arrange matters; the next best thing was a surrogate for himself, and who more natural than the Vice-President?

Actually the selection of Wallace had more to do with domestic politics than with China. Preparing for a fourth term, Roosevelt knew the delegates to the Democratic Convention in July would balk at renominating Wallace who had made many enemies. The President was anxious to avoid a fight that would divide the Party. Remembering Woodrow Wilson's experience he wanted to cement his support in Congress in order to create the United Nations which he saw as the main task ahead. He was considering dumping Wallace in favor of some more generally acceptable running mate, and it was a natural instinct under the circumstances to want him out of sight. Hence the mission to China. When CBI Headquarters was notified of his coming, they asked that he be empowered to "insist" to Chiang Kai-shek that the Military Mission be allowed to visit Communist areas. This, as it turned out, proved to be the one accomplishment of Wallace's eight days in China. Otherwise the main result was one more recommendation for Stilwell's removal.

In the course of four long conversations with Wallace on June 21-24 Chiang Kai-shek rejected the prevalent notion that the Communists were "agrarian democrats" and said they definitely wanted to seize power in China and were in fact "more communistic than the Russian communists." When it came to permission for the Military Mission to visit Yenan, he at first refused and then surprisingly reversed himself the next day, perhaps in the hope of a reciprocal favor from Roosevelt. Chiang had long wished to divest himself of both Stilwell and Gauss, the two unillusioned men who controlled his channels to the United States, but after his many failures in the case of Stilwell he did not this time ask directly for his relief but rather for a personal emissary from the President who could give him access to the White House without having to go through the State or War Departments. With T. V. Soong, now back in favor, as interpreter, he gave a moving account of Stilwell's failure to respond to the needs of the Fourteenth Air Force and of his "lack of confidence in General Stilwell's judgment."

Although Wallace did not find himself in sympathy with the Generalissimo, he felt this was one area in which he might be of use. "I was deeply moved by the cry of a man in distress," as he put it later.

This impression was given every nourishment by Chennault who was on hand to greet Wallace in Chungking and assigned Lieutenant Alsop to him as "air aide." Afterwards they were Wallace's hosts in Kunming. Unaware that their day was over, Chennault and Alsop were convinced that if they could only get rid of Stilwell, air war in China would prevail. They had a persuasive ally in T. V. Soong whose interest in removing Stilwell, after the bungle of his last attempt, was greater than ever. Under their auspices Wallace not surprisingly concluded that Stilwell must go. Though favoring Chennault as successor, he was advised that Wedemeyer would be a more realistic candidate. Gauss too, when consulted, stated his opinion that the Generalissimo could no longer effectively cooperate with Stilwell.

Gauss was of course right. Stilwell might as well have been withdrawn, not for the suspect reasons of Chennault and Soong, but because his mission to mobilize the war effort of China could not overcome the unwillingness of Chiang Kai-shek to let it be mobilized. This American *non possumus*—a "We cannot" that contradicted the "Can Do" of the 15th Infantry—was something that neither Stilwell nor Marshall nor the bulk of their countrymen was prepared to recognize.

In a telegram which Alsop later claimed credit for composing, Wallace strongly recommended to the President the adoption of Chiang Kai-shek's request for "a personal representative to serve as liaison between you and him." In addition, or alternatively, he urged the replacement of Stilwell by a general officer of the highest caliber, such as Wedemeyer, who could win the Generalissimo's confidence which Chiang had informed him "bluntly" General Stilwell did not enjoy. The telegram went on to relay the assurance always given to visiting Americans, that "with the right man to do the job it should be possible to induce the Generalissimo to reform his regime." He was represented as anxious for aid and "even guidance" and ready to make "relatively drastic changes if wisely approached."

Wallace did not extend himself to obtain the views of the theater commander whose removal he recommended, nor did Stilwell extend himself to give them. Occupied in his desperate struggle to hold Myitkyina and take Mogaung, he refused to leave Burma. He sent Davies and Jones to represent him and invite Wallace to meet with him in the Mogaung valley but the invitation was not accepted.

As far as they concerned Stilwell, Wallace's recommendations were, of course, blocked by Marshall who was well informed of their source and described them to Stimson as the product of Alsop's "usual poison." They were in addition out of date for Wallace's persuaders did not know that while they were endeavoring to maneuver Stilwell out of China, heavier British pressures were being brought to move him out of SEAC *into* China.

In another report written after his return Wallace urged that the United States should try to influence the Generalissimo in every possible way to adopt progressive policies so as to inspire popular support and instill new vitality into China's war effort.

This was a plea that was rising insistently in reports from China. In Kunming, where the American presence was strong, Chinese liberals pleaded with the Consul-General, William Langdon, for American pressure to be brought on the Kuomintang to widen its political base; otherwise, they said, American military and financial aid would serve only to strengthen a reactionary regime. Through the official detachment of Langdon's report their despairing voices spoke: Chiang and his clique were "incapable of building a modern nation in China" and had "no rational plans" for postwar reconstruction. Chiang himself was a man of limited ability and vision and the future of China was "dark under his leadership." Langdon's own conclusion, as radical as Stilwell's, was that nothing much could help China without a change at the top. "Present trends," he wrote, "can be changed only through the death of Chiang or by successful revolution."

So long as American policy could not detach itself from the incumbent, Langdon's statement of the case posed a fundamental problem. What was to be done, as one foreign service officer put it in later testimony, when "we were stuck with a regime that was losing power"? That was the crux. Was there any answer to Gauss' hopeless shrug: "I can think of nothing. . . ."? In a brief prepared for Wallace, John Service suggested the answer lay in broadening American options not only by support of liberal elements but also by withdrawing unconditional support for a government which in any free election would be rejected by 80 percent of the voters. A United States policy that could find no other option, he suggested, was one of "indolent short-term expediency."

The Joint Chiefs were not concerned with solving China's problems but with winning the war. Their proposal in China's crisis was the exact opposite of Wallace's: to enlarge rather than terminate Stilwell's authority in China—in short, to put him in command of the Chinese armed forces.

The success of ICHIGO was the determining factor, but not because of the approaching loss of the east China air bases. Strategic weight had shifted definitely to the Pacific on June 15 when Saipan in the Marianas, within bombing distance of Japan, was invaded. After a fierce three-week struggle the island was secured and construction of airfields for the B-29s begun. This reduced the importance of China as an air base, but another problem remained.

The success of ICHIGO and the Chinese military passivity in the face of it raised the fear that the Japanese army in China might root itself into the mainland and continue to fight even after defeat of the home islands, prolonging the war perhaps for years before it could be conquered. In that event, Russia's entry into the war would take on added importance and give her added opportunity in Manchuria, not altogether a welcome prospect. Even less welcome in Washington was the thought of transferring GIs to Asia after the war in Europe was won, to the accompanying howl of the American public. Stilwell made the danger of a Japanese prolongation the basis for one of his periodic pleas for American divisions, arguing that if China were bypassed, the Japanese on the mainland would not surrender and the Chinese alone would be too weak to cope with them.

The Joint Chiefs' recipe for China's paralysis was to use Stilwell himself in lieu of American divisions. Thus was born the plan to put him in command of the Chinese armed forces with authority to energize and direct a Chinese military effort. It had the added advantage of satisfying the British insistence that he be moved out of SEAC into China. This had now reached the status of an official demand. When Marshall visited London in June he was told by his opposite number, Sir Alan Brooke, that Stilwell would have to be relieved as Deputy to Mountbatten because he could not get on with the three service chiefs. Offense at his handling of the Chindits and his freedom of expression as a limey-hater were added factors.* Marshall's anger flared: "Brooke, you have three CinCs in India; none of them will fight. We have one man who will fight and you want him taken out. What the hell kind of business is this?" Though Brooke was "enraged" by this attitude, his acknowledgment that the three service chiefs were all being recalled, at Mountbatten's insistence, deprived Marshall of an issue.

China's situation was pulling and the British pushing toward a common solution and Marshall seized it. The idea originated in Stilwell's own concept of a "Field Chief of Staff" with power to coordinate, which he had discussed with Marshall at Cairo. To go with the enlarged command Marshall proposed to promote him to full general. On June 30 the War Department drew up an eloquent statement of the case for promotion and the new command pointing out that Stilwell had "welded an effective Chinese army in Burma" against every kind of obstacle including the

---

* In November 1944, in view of Stilwell's reported remarks to the effect that the Indian Army was inert and its officers lethargic, a Conservative M.P., Mr. Reginald Purbrick, asked in the House of Commons that Stilwell be declared *persona non grata* in any area where British troops were engaged. Several years after the war, General Alexander remarked in conversation with General Boatner, "Dear old Joe—he could be mighty naughty at times."

apathy of his allies, and in the drive for Myitkyina had "staged a campaign that history will call brilliant."

By this time there had been two and a half years' experience of China's lack of interest in taking aggressive action against the Japanese. What made the War Department suppose that Chiang Kai-shek's fixed intent could be altered and performance somehow dragged from him? One answer was the self-confidence of the American military. In CBI, for all its miseries, they had already accomplished extraordinary feats—the Ledo Road, the Hump, the pipeline, the "impossible" return through north Burma. Why should the Generalissimo prove more formidable? It always seemed possible that with sufficient pressure he could be made to do what Americans wanted him to do. Besides, with the enlarged capacity of the Hump and the imminent opening of the pipeline and Road to carry forward the now enormously increased capacity of the Assam-Bengal Railway, the logistical means at hand were very much greater. And Chiang's ability to resist American pressure in his current situation was considered to be very much reduced. In any event the alternative to a step-up for Stilwell would sooner or later have been his withdrawal and the succumbing to his enemies that Marshall had so long and so resolutely resisted. In putting the question to Stilwell on July 1 he did not mention the promotion so that it could not influence his decision.

Was it, he asked, in Stilwell's opinion worthwhile, once Myitkyina had been secured, to transfer his principal efforts to the "rehabilitation and in effect the direction" of the Chinese forces in China proper? He told him tactfully that the British were pressing for a "readjustment of command relationships." He acknowledged that Stilwell had already had more than his share of complications "which beset you in a degree I do not believe any other commander of modern times has experienced." Clearly aware that he was offering no prize, he finished, "Don't let the humidity and difficulties of the day culminate in an explosion."

Stilwell's answer was not a simple "I'll go where I'm sent." If he felt any relish at the personal challenge to the Generalissimo, it was outweighed by the difficulties and calamities of the situation he was being called upon to save. He put these in the bleakest, most unmistakable terms to Marshall:

. . . If the President were to send him a very stiff message, emphasizing our investment and interest in China, and also the serious pass to which China has come due to neglect of the Army, and insisting that desperate cases require desperate remedies, the G–mo might be forced to give me a command job. I believe the Chinese Army would accept me. Ho Ying-chin would have to step out as Chief of Staff, or if he kept the title, give up the power. Without complete authority over the Army, I would not attempt the job. Even with complete authority the damage done is so tremendous that I can see only one chance to repair it. This is to stage a counter-offensive from Shansi. . . . The Communists should also participate in Shansi, but unless the G–mo makes an agreement with them, they won't. Two years ago they offered to fight with me. They might listen now. . . . Outside of this one shot I see no chance to save the situation. . . . To sum up, there is still a faint chance to salvage something in China but action must be quick and radical and the G–mo must give one commander full powers. . . . The chances are definitely not good, but I can see no other solution at the moment.

This was anything but an eager acceptance, but Marshall gave him no leeway. Within 24 hours he submitted to the President, in the name of the Joint Chiefs, his proposal for Stilwell's promotion and appointment to command the Chinese armed forces and also the text of the message—incorporating much of Stilwell's advice and some of his wording—that was to inform Chiang Kai-shek. To allow Roosevelt no room to refuse he prefaced it by a harsh summary of results since TRIDENT which rather rudely reminded the Commander-in-Chief that the immense effort in transportation to supply Chennault had proved a "poorly directed and possibly completely wasteful procedure," and that Stilwell had been right all along in predicting that the effectiveness of the Fourteenth Air Force would only provoke counterattack on the airfields and that their necessary defense lay in building up combat efficiency on the ground.

For Roosevelt the proposal meant a complete about-face in his view of how the Generalissimo should be treated, but after Cairo he was more ready to make it. Bewildered by the problem of China, and backed into a corner by Marshall, he accepted the recommendation in toto. As a pragmatist, he was now willing to try Stilwell as he had once tried Chennault. Whether he believed that Chiang Kai-shek could be made to consent is impossible to say. The Generalissimo's constant cries of weakness may have suggested that he could not afford to refuse; in any event Roosevelt had come to recognize that militarily nothing could be expected of Chiang. "What I am trying to find out," he had said to Kung a few days earlier, "is where is the Chinese army and why aren't they fighting because the Japanese seem to be able to push them in any direction they want to." Since neither he nor the Joint Chiefs knew what else to try, the assignment was handed to Stilwell. As the climax of the wartime effort in China, the proposal to put an American in command of China's armed forces represented in part a profound faith in the efficacy of American influence and in part a last resort.

The "very stiff message" that Stilwell wanted, signed by the President without change from the War Department's draft, was forthwith despatched to the Generalissimo on July 6:

... The critical situation which now exists in my opinion calls for the delegation to one individual of the power to coordinate all Allied military resources in China, including the Communist forces.

I think I am fully aware of your feelings regarding General Stilwell, nevertheless ... I know of no other man who has the ability, the force and the determination to offset the disaster which now threatens China and our over-all plans for the conquest of Japan. I am promoting Stilwell to the rank of full General and I recommend for your most urgent consideration that you recall him from Burma and place him directly under you in command of all Chinese and American forces and that you charge him with full responsibility and authority for the coordination and direction of the operations required to stem the tide of the enemy's advances. I feel that the case of China is so desperate that if radical and properly applied remedies are not immediately effected, our common cause will suffer a serious setback.

... I assure you there is no intent on my part to dictate to you in matters concerning China; however, the future of all Asia is at stake along with the tremendous effort which America has expended in that region. Therefore I have reason for a profound interest in the matter.

Please have in mind that it has clearly been demonstrated in Italy, in France, and in the Pacific that air power alone cannot stop a determined enemy.

The President's message made no attempt to spare the Generalissimo's feelings or avoid the frankness so distasteful to the Chinese. It bluntly rejected the known policies of Chiang Kai-shek: it asked for power within the Chinese state for an American whom he had repeatedly tried to remove; it discarded the Chiang-Chennault thesis of reliance on air warfare which Roosevelt had gone to such lengths to uphold the year before; and it specifically proposed to bring within the scope of American aid Chiang's feared internal enemies, the Communists. In tone it was rough and in substance it was an invasion of sovereignty that denied Roosevelt's own concept of China as a great power and accepted Stilwell's view of Chiang as incapable of managing his country's role in the war. It called him Peanut by implication.

Lest there be any softening of the terms in transmission, after the habit of T. V. Soong, Roosevelt's message was delivered to Chiang in person by General Ferris, then senior officer in Chungking, with Service accompanying him as translator. This procedure, which was to figure in the final clash, had been ordered by the President in May when it had been noticed that Chiang's replies to Roosevelt's telegrams urging action by the Y-force were not fitting the messages.

Stilwell was now informed by Marshall of his promotion and the terms of the President's message, coupled with a stern warning to avoid further offense to the Generalissimo.

What Chiang's emotions were on receiving Roosevelt's demand are not a matter of historical record, but it can be said that regardless of Stilwell's faults and offenses, even had he had the tongue of angels, the temperament of a saint and the professional charm of a Japanese geisha, the Generalissimo would still have had no more intention of giving him command of his armed forces than of giving it to Mao Tse-tung. "Today a fateful decision is again being made in Washington," T. V. Soong telegraphed Hopkins. "The War Department wants to force General Stilwell down his [Chiang Kai-shek's] throat . . . I personally assure you without qualification that on this point the Generalissimo will not and cannot yield."*

In view of his dependence on American aid, however, Chiang had to move carefully. His reply was soft, even deferential and appeared to be an acceptance except in the matter of urgency. He suggested a "preparatory period in order to enable General Stilwell to have absolute command of the Chinese troops without any hindrance." He repeated his request for an intermediary who would have "full power" and "could adjust the relations between me and General Stilwell." As Soong frankly explained to Gauss, this meant someone empowered to give Stilwell orders. Chiang allowed himself only one hint of displeasure—with regard to the method of delivery. He suggested that if the President had any messages for him in future they could be given to Dr. Kung to transmit.

The idea of a personal emissary was agreeable to Roosevelt, if not at all to Marshall, and while this matter was under discussion Chiang's qualifications began to come in. On July 23 he attached three conditions: the Communists were not to come under Stilwell's command until they accepted the authority of the Central Government; the limits of Stilwell's position in relation to himself were to be clearly defined; Lend-Lease was to be "entirely under the authority of the Chinese Government." A further limitation emerged from talks held with Kung in Washington from which it appeared that Chiang conceived of the command as confined to those Chinese divisions actually engaged against the Japanese, not those in reserve.

The question must be asked whether Stilwell himself, after all he had experienced, believed the position would offer any possibility of exercising real command. Part of the answer lies in the officer's code in which he was schooled which does not allow a mission to be considered impossible until a total effort has been made to accomplish it. Like everyone else, he considered China's situation so alarming as to leave Chiang Kai-shek little choice. He had given up hope of consolidation of divisions and reform of the army but his continuing hope was to obtain some sort of tacit consent

---

* The existing copy of this message is undated and may have been sent at some other time in the ensuing crisis but the principle remains the same.

for the position of overall commander with power to coordinate all units, which had never existed in China. He thought it would be worth establishing as at least better than the existing situation. He knew that his orders in such a post would be blocked or undercut or passively resisted but he believed that if he could cut the channels of command from Chungking to the field he might be able to function effectively. "We will only have real command in the field," Pai Ch'ung-hsi once said to him, "when all the telephone lines to Chungking are cut."

In Hengyang the army of Hsueh Yueh, aided by the strenuous efforts of the Fourteenth Air Force, held off the Japanese through July but no help was sent or diversionary attack mounted by the Central Government. Stilwell, who was still in Burma, authorized one shipment of arms to Hsueh Yueh's forces, which was protested by Central Government representatives in Kweilin as likely to fall into the hands of "bandits." Thereafter, despite the insistent demands of Chennault and the pleas of his own deputy, General Hearn, in Chungking, Stilwell refused to send more. He maintained, in reply to Hearn, that the decision was up to the Generalissimo who for two years had insisted that everything go to Chennault. If Chennault, who had received 12,000 tons in June, now realized that he could not stop the Japanese, he should so inform the Generalissimo "who can make any proposition he sees fit."

Governed by doubts of Hsueh Yueh's loyalty, Chiang made no proposition. In his turn Hsueh Yueh would make no request of the Central Government because, according to the American staff in Kweilin, "he states it will be refused." He was now reported to be associated with Chang Fa-kwei, Li Chi-shen and others in the plan for an autonomous government if cut off from Chungking. Hengyang fell on August 8. The sad eternal trek of refugees, with bundles and babies and cooking pots and old people in wheelbarrows and swarms clinging to the last train, moved westward once more. The Japanese, suffering from Fourteenth Air Force attacks on their communications, halted for a month to bring up supplies and then moved on against the next air base in the chain, only 100 miles from Kweilin.

In desperation Chennault now offered to turn over 1,000 tons of his allotment to arms and ammunition for Hsueh Yueh, but not through the medium of the Central Government. He knew as well as anyone that the defender of the east China air bases was not being supported by the Generalissimo. "I would not be interested in turning this over to the Minister of War," he acknowledged realistically to Hearn, "because the chances are great that it would never reach Hsueh Yueh." This notable admission left something of a hole in his thesis that Stilwell was responsible for the disaster in east China through his failure to supply arms. But a bold polemicist is a disregarder of holes. Chennault, assisted by the excited voice of Alsop, continued to pursue his theme which, when the time came, provided the Generalissimo with his official excuse.

Stilwell gave them every help. For a year his efforts to equip the Y-force and prepare an effective 30 divisions on the ground had been sacrificed, at Chiang's insistence implemented by Roosevelt, to Chennault's priority. He was not now, when Chennault's claims were proved vain, going to allot arms in order to cover up the Chennault-Chiang error; he wanted the error to be made plain. He did not believe in any case, though Hsueh Yueh was a genuine fighter, that help to him now would be effective. If Hsueh had not been able to hold Changsha, there was no reason to suppose he would do better at Hengyang, especially under the overall direction of Chiang Kai-shek. Stilwell had no trust whatever in Chiang's generalship which he considered politically motivated and militarily contemptible and he was determined that American arms should be used for fighting the Japanese only where there was some American control. He rejected Chennault's proposal to turn over 1,000 tons to Hsueh Yueh. Until a proposition came from the Generalissimo, he told Hearn harshly, "let them stew."

On July 30, in what was to prove a final departure, he left Burma for Kandy. While the question of his appointment to command in China hung fire, he was to take command of SEAC during the absence of the Supremo in London. No one had expected Stilwell to accept the official invitation to assume his place as Deputy SAC ("Sad Sac" as of course he called it), and the announcement that he actually intended to do so aroused in Kandy the emotions of Rome awaiting Alaric the Goth. Stilwell knew that one of Mountbatten's objectives in London was to replace him as Deputy but this did not worry him unduly. "At one time or another all the Best People have attempted to get the can attached, but have somehow slipped up on it—up to now anyway." His purpose in going among the "Kandy Kids" was no more sinister than the need for a rest which he would not get in Chungking. Knowing from Japanese prisoners that the defense of Myitkyina was nearing its end, with the remnant of defenders living on half a bowl of rice a day, he could go in good conscience.

Met at the airfield by the Supremo's black Cadillac with Allied flags flying, he said, "Get me a jeep." With his leg hanging over the side in what seemed to some a petty and unnecessary show of disdain, he drove up the mountain road to Kandy preceded by the Cadillac with the luggage. He joined Mountbatten at his residence, the King's Pavilion, for a farewell lunch, remarking afterwards, "I've got to quit eating with Louis. I actually like those rum cocktails." Two days later at 3:45 on the afternoon of August 3 Myitkyina fell after a siege of 78 days. "Over at last," Stilwell wrote next morning. "Thank God. Not a worry in the world this a.m. For five minutes anyway."

Of all the comments on the event the most interesting was that of Brooke in London: "It is clear, now that Stilwell has led us down to Myitkyina, we shall have to go on fighting in Burma."

After north Burma Stilwell found Ceylon a paradise. Kandy was 2,000 feet up and beyond it at 7,000 feet was the summer hill station of Newara Eliya in clean and bracing air that reminded him of Yellowstone, with waterfalls everywhere, deep and distant views, cypress trees, a lake and Easter lilies growing wild. Avoiding the King's Pavilion—a miniature white palace set among lily ponds, hibiscus trees, an orchid garden with parading white peacocks, and a nine-hole golf course—Stilwell made his residence in an American officers' bungalow. Apart from the physical comforts, he did not find his new command congenial. The SEAC staff numbered 3,000 including a band of 30 musicians and motorcycle outriders for the Cadillac. The Officers' Club provided comfortable leather chairs, a good library with the English newspapers, and ubiquitous barefooted servants. Staff officers looked "sleek, smart and prosperous" to an English former civilian, but he too found "something wrong with Headquarters at Kandy . . . I always felt half asleep."

Every afternoon a full-dress meeting was held of heads of departments and sections with a situation report on every theater of the war. Until Imphal and Myitkyina tumbled the British into Burma, the theme had been global strategy which meant fighting somewhere else next year. Now the meetings concerned the enlarged campaign in Burma, directed southward toward Mandalay. With the prospect of ever-lengthening lines of supply, Mountbatten did not think he could advance beyond Mandalay and so proposed an amphibious assault on Rangoon (BUCCANEER revived) which should then extend northward to join the other forces in the center. To obtain the necessary landing craft and other means was the main purpose of his journey to London. Churchill was now willing to abandon all thought of Sumatra and turn his ever-fresh enthusiasm back to Rangoon as a preliminary to attack on Singapore, "the supreme British objective."

Stilwell took no interest in staff planning. Logistics were for others to take care of. When a campaign or operation was in question he would dash off a rapid tactical plan without charts or appendices on the theory "that we all know where we want to go anyway." At Kandy he made no effort to conceal his boredom and impatience with the endless conferences over which he was supposed to preside. They appeared in his diary as "terrible" or "dumb" or "sad" or "crappier than usual" or "zero." "I never felt at ease in such make-believe acts." He took an impish pleasure, however, in the concept of himself as military governor of a British colony (Burma) and enjoyed contemplating all kinds of orders he might issue—"freeing the Kachins, etc."

On August 7 his promotion to full general became official, with the fourth star pinned on him by Merrill. "I never signed a commission which has given me greater satisfaction," Stimson wrote. Congratulations from a regiment of the NCAC said there was nothing comparable to "your consumate achievement in this theater which was taken for granted impossible," except in the Iliad.

In July when developments in China looked "very black," Stilwell wrote that if the crisis "were just sufficient to get rid of Peanut without entirely wrecking the ship, it would be worth it." For a brief moment after the fall of Hengyang there appeared to be a chance. On August 9 Li Chi-shen sent an emissary to Arthur Ringwalt, the American Consul in Kweilin, to say he intended to set up an independent government in Kwangtung and Fukien accompanied by a public demand for the resignation of Chiang Kai-shek. Claiming to dispose of a force of six to eight divisions, he wished to open negotiations toward cooperation with a U.S. landing on the China coast. Ringwalt believed the message should be given serious consideration for if Li's group were to gain the support of the Communist and democratic parties, and the Central Government were to collapse in consequence, "the result may not be an unmitigated evil to China and to the cause of the allied nations."

"Hooray for crime!" Stilwell commented on being notified of this development, but long acquaintance with the luckless southern secessionist efforts warned against raising his hopes or leaping in to offer encouragement. He sent Timberman to Kweilin to investigate under instructions that gave no room for adventure: "Our policy is to lay off the internal affairs of China. . . . Listen to any proposition that may be made but do not make any commitments nor even express any opinion. Just say you will forward any messages proposed." Equally cautious, Gauss believed the Li Chi-shen inquiry was a feeler to find out whether the United States would support such a movement. He advised Ringwalt to stay aloof.

The question in all minds was how extensive was Li's support and whether the local Communists were likely to join him. Though it represented "genuine bitter opposition," according to Consul Langdon in Kunming, the effort lacked cohesion, leadership and sufficient military power and he did not think it would have "any noticeable effect on the Generalissimo's willingness to reform his Government." The non-Communist opposition of provincial warlords and democratic groups was unlikely, he thought, to succeed and even if it did it would be in a "Kerensky" position and soon overthrown by the Communists. Timberman came to much the same conclusion. He found the Communists were not involved, nor was Pai Ch'ung-hsi who remained loyal to the Central Government and had already moved his family out of Kweilin to the west "with several freight-car loads of personal effects." He judged Li Chi-shen's movement "too small for us to do more than continue our present policy of receptive observation." Gauss in his report concurred in this estimate. The flare in the south offered the United States no option.

At this time the reports of the first foreigners to visit the Communist region since the war were made known. They were enthusiastic. The journalists were disposed to be friendly because they were so thoroughly disgusted with the frustration of their profession in Chungking: the auto-cratic censorship, the endless promises and evasions, and the most exas-perating Chinese habit of all—the bland declaration as fact of what both the declarer and listener know to be nonsense. Released from the miasma of Kuomintang China, they were in a mood to find a new world and they did. They were struck first by the physical appearance of the people, "better fed, huskier and more energetic than in other parts of China," and by their transformation of the once barren land of north Shensi into an area of intensive cultivation and stockbreeding. By this reclamation process the Communist soldiery made themselves self-supporting, with no need to live off the peasantry. As the strongest single factor in their favor in local eyes, this was a point stressed by all the correspondents.

Industrial achievement through the organization of handicrafts and workshops was no less impressive. With its home-made products and in-dependent subsistence, Yenan appeared as a "magnificent symbol of the tenacity and determination" of its people. The correspondents all bought new coats and suits tailored for them from locally woven tweeds, discov-ering afterwards that their tailor was a member of the Supreme People's Council. Members of the Military Observers Mission which reached Yenan on July 23 had their pictures taken in the heavy, substantial made-to-order uniforms of the 8th Route Army whose soldiers, according to the *Times,* were "among the best-clothed and best-fed the writer has seen anywhere in China." Hard evidence of guerilla warfare was found in the presence of several hundred Japanese prisoners. No one had ever seen the prisoners claimed by the Kuomintang except for a token group which was always the same, like the captured helmets. It seemed obvious to the visitors that the Communist armies, like the Yugoslav partisans, would be "valuable allies" in the war whose proper use would speed up victory. Any Allied commander, declared Stein in the *Monitor,* "would be proud to command those tough, well-fed, hardened troops."

Although the reports were heavily censored in Chungking and in some

Vice President Henry Wallace was sent to China in June 1944 (213) to persuade Chiang to negotiate with the Communists. Hsueh Yueh (214), the "Tiger of Hunan," struggled to hold off the Japanese with the help of the Fourteenth Air Force. On August 7 Stilwell received his fourth star (215).

213

214

215

2

2

Yenan, 1944: Colonel David Barrett (top right) and John Service (second from left) with Chu Teh and Mao Tse-tung (216). The American Military Mission in "Chung-shan" suits of native homespun presented to them by the Communists to show the success of their production drive (217).

cases killed in toto, the tone of enthusiasm could not be squeezed out. The correspondents humanized the Communist leaders for their readers, telling how Mao had worked his way through school; how Kao Kang, chief of the Party's Northwest Bureau, was the son of a poor peasant beaten to death by the bailiffs of a Shensi militarist because he had failed to pay the tax on his donkey; how Wang Chen, a "dashing brilliant" brigade commander, had once been a fireman on the Peking-Hankow Railway. They told of doctors, students, university teachers and former YMCA secretaries all working "at a high pitch for their country with the conviction that the ways adopted here are right." In the fall when a second group of journalists came, they reported plentiful harvests and fruit in abundance, pears and grapes, pumpkins and tomatoes, buckwheat, millet, cotton and tobacco. Brooks Atkinson happily described local theatricals and unrationed gasoline for the ten trucks of Yenan and the *Times* obliged him with a friendly headline, "YENAN, A CHINESE WONDERLAND CITY." The journalists reported what they saw and heard and the saddest thing about it, in the long, cruel light of history, was that it was all true.

Reporting for the DIXIE Mission, Service was no less impressed. He found morale high and the people serious with a sense of mission and a purposeful program under competent leadership. Coolies read newspapers, recruits marched without escort, there were no gendarmes, no bureaucracy, none of the "clap-trap of Chungking" and none of its defeatism. There was a certain smugness and self-righteous consciousness of a cause but no feeling of restraint or suppression. There was self-confidence, self-respect, an emphasis on relations with the common people and such impetus to the program, tied so closely to the people, "that it will not easily be killed."

The DIXIE Mission, which consisted of nine members representing the Air Corps, Medical Corps, Signal Corps and Infantry and was followed a month later by a second contingent, was sent to observe with a purpose: to evaluate the Communist potential for military collaboration against the Japanese. They were also instructed to assess "the most effective means of assisting the Communists to increase the value of their war effort." This meant American aid and an American relationship, which was exactly what Chiang Kai-shek feared and the reason he had done his best to obstruct the mission.

Mao Tse-tung was also thinking of American aid. He made it plain that he looked forward to American landings in China. If the Americans failed to land, it would be unfortunate for China, he said. "The Kuomintang will continue as the Government—without being able to be the Government."

In the talks of Barrett and Service with Mao, Chou En-lai, Lin Piao, Yeh Chien-ying and Chu Teh, the Communists' theme was that the Kuomintang was in the "dying throes" of incapacity while the Communists had established a viable government and could propose useful cooperation with the Americans under an "Allied" command rather than under a "bankrupt" Kuomintang command. They made no reference to fighting under Stilwell's command nor asked that any such proposal be conveyed to him; indeed it was Colonel Barrett's impression that "they never seemed much interested in General Stilwell."

They talked in terms of coalition not revolution. Their stated aim at this time was a return to the united front with representation on a national council, release of the blockade and freedom to maintain their own regime in their own areas while engaged in a common if not a joint effort against Japan. This concept did not include allegiance to the Central Government nor acceptance of its authority as stipulated by Chiang Kai-shek.

The Chinese Communists of 1944 did not appear alarming, but on the contrary, like most challengers who have yet to succeed, rather attractive. In their rough and rumpled clothes, their earnest talk, their hard work and simple life, their energy, vitality and sincerity, they were a refreshing contrast to the world of the Kuomintang. That was their chief charm. In the absence of war effort by the Central Government especially after ICHIGO, it began to be taken for granted by Americans that the United States would have to cooperate with the Communists. As soldiers they looked useful. They were "better men physically," as General Dorn later testified, "better fed, better clothed . . . with better morale than the Nationalist troops." Their leaders on the whole appeared more able, less corrupt, fundamentally stronger men than those of the Kuomintang.

Chiang Kai-shek was well aware that if Stilwell or any American, no matter who, was given military authority in China, he, the Generalissimo, could not control the degree of aid or cooperation given to the Communists. He needed no other reason to determine his attitude. On August 9 Washington offered him General Hurley as intermediary and pressed hard for "immediate action" on Stilwell's appointment, "otherwise it may be too late." Chiang continued evasive. While pleased to accept Hurley, he replied that the command problem required thorough preparation and "mature consideration."

The choice of Hurley, ultimately unfortunate, was haphazard, though made with confidence. Marshall was responsible. He had steadily opposed the idea of an agent between the President and Generalissimo, but on learning that Hopkins was about to take action, he moved quickly to head him off. He wanted to ensure an appointee friendly to Stilwell and feared Hopkins would be influenced by the Soong-Chennault axis. When Stimson mentioned that he was looking for "an adequate job for Pat Hurley," Marshall seized on the name as someone who would be accepted by Stilwell and who would be able to smooth over the strained relations resulting from Stilwell's "extreme tactlessness." He sounded out Hurley the same day and within hours the eager appointee was at the State Department where he informed Under Secretary Stettinius that Marshall was sending him to China and he would like to be made Ambassador. Though discouraged by Stettinius, he insisted that his request should be put to Hull. Meantime as intermediary he seemed a "very fortunate" choice to Stimson. "Hurley is loyal, intelligent and extremely energetic . . . pleasant and diplomatic in his manner" and "the only man that either Marshall or I could think of to revolutionize the situation of backbiting and recrimination and stalemate that has been surrounding poor Stilwell." Queried by Marshall, Stilwell agreed to the choice on the theory that "it takes oil as well as vinegar to make a good dressing."

Roosevelt too was content. Once, in reply to doubts expressed by Morgenthau on the usefulness of personal envoys, he had said, "The only thing that saves the information is that I know my men." He had confidence in Hurley's ability to carry out a mission accurately but he startled Marshall by a telephone call to ask if Donald Nelson, lately chairman of the War Production Board and formerly of Sears, Roebuck, could go too. A horrendous feud between Nelson and his successor, Charles E. Wilson, was currently roiling the Administration. When Marshall asked why Nelson should go to China, Roosevelt replied calmly that he would like to get him out of the country, an aim with which, as Marshall said later, he could sympathize. He consented on condition that Nelson was not to meddle with policy or strategy but confine himself to selling razor blades. For purposes of public announcement this was translated as "studying China's economy."

Nelson's selection was the genesis of a principle of political appointment. "You get three years in Washington to find out whether or not you are a schlemiel," Morgenthau said of him at this time to his assistant Harry Dexter White. "And if you are you get promoted," White replied.

On August 23 the American reply to the Generalissimo's three conditions was delivered in a second message from Roosevelt to Chiang even more imperious than the first. Drafted as usual at the War Department, the message disposed of the three conditions, which to Chiang were of the essence, as "matters of detail." That was the impression gained by Roosevelt and Marshall from a discussion with Kung who doubtless softened the terms after the amiable manner of Chinese intercourse.

With regard to the first condition concerning the Communists, the President stated, "I do not think the forces to come under General Stilwell's command should be limited. . . . When the enemy is pressing us toward possible disaster, it appears unsound to refuse the aid of anyone who will kill Japanese." Intent on the Japanese as the enemy, Roosevelt and his Government assumed the same was true of China. It never seemed quite real to them that the Generalissimo should regard—had always regarded —the Communists as the greater danger and made his decisions accordingly. The same obtuseness about China was shown by Hopkins who could not understand in talking with Davies why Davies should think that Stilwell would be "skeptical" of his proposed command or should suggest that its exercise would "be undercut at every turn." Hopkins thought Stilwell would have "a great deal of power" because he would have the White House behind him.

With regard to the second condition about the command relationship, Roosevelt suggested it should be "that of a head of state with his commander in the field." The title given to Stilwell should imply "that directly under you he commands the armed forces in China."

With regard to Lend-Lease, Chiang was informed that a new arrangement was being worked out in Washington "relieving General Stilwell of his burden" which would be communicated to the Generalissimo later on. In the meantime Chiang was sternly reminded that "extended deliberations and perfection of arrangements may have fateful consequences." He was urged to "take the necessary measures to place General Stilwell in command of the Chinese force, under your direction, at the earliest possible date. . . . With further delay, it may be too late to avert a military catastrophe tragic both to China and to our Allied plans for the early overthrow of Japan."

If Chiang was less impressed by the need of urgency, it was because he was not bothered like Washington by doubts of his own staying power or fears of his own collapse. He thoroughly intended in his own mind to stay out the war, if necessary in the last provinces of the west, no matter how much of east China was lost, until the Allies should defeat Japan and he could emerge on the winning side. However calamitous the situation in the face of ICHIGO, he was probably not entirely unhappy to see it directed against the dissident south. Central Government armies were not engaged.

It was also true that Chiang, as Gauss reported, had withdrawn increasingly from outside contacts and comments, "trusting no one but himself," and was in consequence ignorant of how far the condition of his country and his people had degenerated. Indeed his failure to be more frightened than he was gave rise to reports that he was resting on some arrangement with the Japanese, but it is unlikely that these had any foundation. The condition of his army did not worry him unduly, partly because he never saw starving soldiers, partly because all he wanted was that the army should continue to be armed by the United States and be stronger than the Communist army. He equated strength with armament, ignoring organization, motivation, leadership and simple nutrition. For the rest, he had been convinced by Chennault that the war could be won by the air arm. He was not at all anxious for American landings and joint military operations. He disliked the idea of an immense intrusion of foreigners no less than the court of Peking had disliked it before him. Believing that the war could be won for him without his additional effort, Chiang predicated his policy in so far as he had any, on survival in power while the Japanese were defeated by the Allies *outside* China. As far as the external enemy was concerned, he had made a shrewd, and as it was to prove, a sound calculation.

That the American advent could be other than welcomed was not an idea easily assimilated in Washington—though understood by some Americans in China. In the brief prepared for Wallace in June John Service stated that once it was recognized that the regime did not want to fight the Japanese any more than it could help, "we must go further and recognize that it may even seek to prevent China from becoming the battleground for large-scale campaigns against the Japanese land forces." There is no evidence that this thought penetrated the War Department or the White House. If Stilwell appreciated it, as he could hardly have failed to, it was probably outweighed in his mind by the opportunity to take over military command in China and by belief in himself.

The Lend-Lease arrangement being studied in Washington envisaged a Sino-American committee or board in Chungking to weigh requisitions which, when approved in Washington, would be delivered directly to units at the front; title would not pass until then. The hope was to eliminate the most contentious aspect of Stilwell's functions, especially in expectation of the increased shipments that would follow reopening of the Road. The new arrangement would also put China in a position more like that of the other great powers. In a telegram to Stilwell on this subject Marshall assumed that future aid would go to a Chinese Army which might include the Communists if they were to unite with the Nationalists in fighting Japan. Schemes for resolving the command relationship of Burma to China ended in a decision to split CBI to which Stilwell reluctantly consented.

When Hurley and Nelson arrived in New Delhi where Stilwell met them on September 4, he was much encouraged by their evident intention to "pound the table." Hurley and Nelson, both tall, imposing men, talked even bigger than they looked. They were the apotheosis of American instrumentality. "First we'll tell the G–mo what to do," said Hurley, "and then we'll explain to him what the U.S. will do." Nelson spelled this out. He said they were prepared to face Chiang Kai-shek with two conditions: one, that

China must be a united nation (meaning presumably a settlement with the Communists) and two, that China must prove its desire to help defeat Japan by giving Stilwell command of the Chinese Army. If Chiang refused to cooperate, Nelson said, they would "advise the President to throw her overboard and shift our base to Russia." If Chiang did cooperate, he could expect the United States to help China industrialize after the war and to transfer Japan's business to her. Stilwell could hardly help but feel that he had backing for the quid pro quo at last.

Reaching Chungking on September 6 he was summoned to a meeting with the Generalissimo at 9:30 the next morning while Hurley and Nelson were given an appointment at 11:00. "Why me ahead of them? Love feast." Chiang talked as if the command were a settled matter, just as he had in 1942 before the first campaign in Burma. He said "that up to now my work had been 100 per cent military—now, AS COMMANDER OF THE CHINESE ARMY, it would be 60 per cent military and 40 per cent political. If I used the Reds, they would have to acknowledge the authority of the National Military Council. He would advise me from time to time. . . . He had full confidence in me. Kidded about my saying Chinese commanders were no good. . . . Well here it is. . . . Now what do I do?"

Stilwell, flanked by Donald Nelson and General Hurley, Chungking, 1944 (218).

19

The Limits of "Can Do"

SEPTEMBER– NOVEMBER 1944

T

HE question was premature for Chiang's acceptance was so far only verbal and none of his three conditions had been met. When Hurley opened negotiations on September 8 a new point of dispute emerged. The Generalissimo demanded that the Chinese divisions at Myitkyina should attack southward toward Bhamo to draw off the Japanese from Lungling. Stilwell objected on the ground that the troops needed rest, while the Yoke divisions, which had received no replacements at all since going into action in May, could take Lungling if they were brought up to strength. In any event, he estimated, the Japanese could probably resist an attack at Bhamo without withdrawing troops from Lungling. Officially his refusal was justified because Chiang could not give orders for action in Mountbatten's theater. But in slighting the Generalissimo's judgment, he gave him new cause for resentment that was shortly to have a critical result.

With regard to the Communists Chiang repeated his condition that they must be incorporated into the Chinese Army under his overall authority before Stilwell could take command. As chief of state he could require no less but it was not a condition likely to be fulfilled. The British Ambassador, Sir Horace Seymour, queried by his Government at this time as to whether an effort should be made to bring the two parties in China to a compromise, thought that nothing could come of it. The Kuomintang, he advised, was already discredited, its military command "childishly incompetent" and the high fighting value of the Chinese soldier merely wasted. Knowing this and conscious of the strength of their own position, the Communists would make no vital surrender to the Central Government. If this much was plain to Sir Horace, it could not have been entirely unsuspected by Chiang Kai-shek. His condition was one on which the Stilwell appointment would be certain to founder, if on nothing else.

When it came to Lend-Lease, T. V. Soong made it clear that the Generalissimo must have control. Hurley, as Stilwell recorded, "told him to write down DISAGREED in capital letters. . . . That's what the G-mo is after: just a blank check. Now we come to the showdown." The blank check was now a richer prize than before owing to Stilwell's success in north Burma. The capture of Myitkyina had enabled the ATC to fly a more southerly route without fear of Japanese fighters, thus shortening and flattening the Hump trip with astonishing results. Deliveries jumped to 18,000 tons in June, 25,000 in July, 29,000 in August and were to reach almost 30,000 in September, 35,000 in October and 39,000 in November. In fact there was no Hump after Myitkyina. By the time the Road was reopened in January 1945 the ATC was able to deliver more per month than the land route, causing Stilwell's enemies to gloat at this proof of how stupid and obsolete had been his insistence on the Road all along. But the full result of the flattening of the Hump had not been foreseen; and the man who flattened it was the combat infantryman on the ground.

By now the poverty of his armies was forcing itself on Chiang's notice. Refusing to believe reports that sick and starving conscripts were dying at a staging center in downtown Chungking, he sent his son to investigate, who confirmed the truth. According to the story that was all over town within hours, Chiang went to see for himself, and finding conditions as stated, with two recruits lying dead in a corner, he flew into a rage, beat the Chief of Conscription in the face with his cane and ordered him arrested. A new man was appointed to his post but the system remained unchanged. In the month of August 138 dead soldiers were picked up in the streets of Kunming. Chiang was reported finally to be considering measures to consolidate divisions, as Stilwell had recommended two years before.

In his shaky circumstances Chiang badly needed to control the distribution of war material, and especially to keep it out of the hands of the Communists. At the next conference with Hurley on September 12 he was "very difficult," insisted on control of Lend-Lease and said that Stilwell, presumably because of Lend-Lease, had "more real power in China" than he had. According to the new American proposal, distribution of

Lend-Lease was to be handled by an American commission sitting in Chungking with a Chinese representative, but this was no safeguard to the Generalissimo. His problem was clearly seen and stated by Gauss: with the war approaching the China coast, "it appears that we are to be faced inevitably with the problem of determining whether the Chinese Communists are to be supplied with American arms and equipment in the struggle against Japan." Since this would have to be done against the will of Chiang Kai-shek, Gauss pointed out, the decision could bring about the fall of his regime.

Stilwell stated his position on the Communists flatly and frankly in a memorandum for Hurley. "The 18th Group Army (Reds) will be used. There must be no misunderstanding on this point. They can be brought to bear where there will be no conflict with Central Government troops but they must be accepted as part of the team during the crisis."

This was not exactly a conspirator's undercover plot to use the Communists to overthrow Chiang Kai-shek as was later, in the hysterical days of American anti-Communism, suggested. Hurley, who subsequently joined and largely assisted the hysteria, at this time took Stilwell's proposition for granted and made no demurrer. Stilwell was equally plain with Marshall. "If CKS and Co are allowed to control supplies you know who will get them. You also know who will not get them. Somehow we must get arms to the Communists who will fight." In the last three words lay his interest.

He received a visit on September 13 from two Communist emissaries who brought greetings from Chu Teh and Mao. He did not record what was discussed except to report to Marshall that "They have communicated with me and will fight under my command but not under a Chinese commander designated by CKS." According to his diary he told his visitors he would go to Yenan and they departed much pleased.

The Communists themselves in their discussions with John Service at Yenan gave far more weight than Stilwell to the certain opposition of the Central Government and seemed careful in conversation to recognize its authority. They clearly had no expectation of immediate American support and were extremely cautious about discussing it. Any move toward "active collaboration," Chou En-lai said, would be strongly and obstinately resisted by the Kuomintang. Asked whether the Yenan forces would serve under an American commander, he said yes "if agreed to by the Central Government" but the question could wait until such time as American men and supplies were coming into China in significant quantities and the counteroffensive against the Japanese was actually in sight. For the present he thought there might be a slow and careful course toward "modified collaboration." Service's report suggested this could take the form of furnishing basic military supplies which the Communists "desperately lacked," and training in use of the equipment, leading as the war developed to "actual tactical cooperation."

It did not require anyone to be "pro"-Communist in an ideological sense to advocate American contact with, aid to or tactical collaboration with the Yenan regime. This was a course of military expediency made obvious both by the defaults of the Central Government and the geography of the north. Japan's awesome Kwantung Army loomed ten feet tall in Manchuria and north China and the problem of how to deal with its expected long-drawn-out resistance haunted the American planners. To explore the military potential of Yenan was the official purpose of the DIXIE Mission, conceived without the benefit of Communist cells or secret agents in the American Government. It was equally devoid of ideological content when advocated by Stilwell as when advocated, oddly enough, by Chennault. Chennault thought it expedient to write to the President in September what he would not have said to his patron the Generalissimo, that it had become essential to sponsor "thorough reconstruction at Chungking, followed by true unification between Chungking and Yenan" and this must be given "absolute priority over all other objectives either military or political." To talk of "true unification" was twaddle on a par with his boast to bring about the downfall of Japan but it would not be grounds for calling Chennault pro-Communist.

Advocacy of a relationship with Yenan grew out of the context of 1944. Those who may have looked beyond military expediency to hope that American aid to Yenan might lead to the overthrow of the Kuomintang could do so in the belief that this would only benefit China. A rigid Communism was not seen as the replacement, and the reason why it was not was that few believed the Chinese Communists were "real" Communists. This negative assumption was derived from the syllogism that while Communism was known to be a bad thing, it seemed to operate in many ways as a good thing in China; therefore it could not be orthodox Communism. The difficulty was resolved by referring to its proponents, as did the President and Captain Carlson in an exchange of letters at this time, as "so-called Communists." * This became the routine phrase in official correspondence. Stilwell invariably referred to them, as he had to the Kuomintang in its early days, as Reds (interchanging it with "Rebs" in 1911), signifying revolutionaries. To a man named for a hero of Bunker Hill there was nothing inherently un-American about revolution. China had

---

* Thanking Carlson for enclosing a letter from Chou En-lai about the Military Observers Mission, Roosevelt wrote on November 15, 1944, "I am hoping and praying for a real working out of the situation with the so-called Communists."

been in need of revolution for a long time, and to most Americans sympathetic to that need, the Communists appeared as modern Taipings. They were considered to be an energetic variety of progressives or, in a phrase of the time, "agrarian reformers" (once rendered by Stilwell as "agricultural liberals"), nor was this necessarily naive.

Mao and his group represented the triumph in Chinese Communist development of a peasant-oriented movement while retaining as the less visible part of the iceberg the dogma of Lenin about the role of the Party and its seizure of power. Their aim was to win the peasant mainstay of China by measures meaningful in the agrarian life of the country rather than by the measures prescribed by Marx for revolution in Western industrial society. Agrarian reform was in fact what they were concerned with in the effort to build up their party and army, gain a territorial base and begin the remaking of China. Their future alignment in international affairs was not, in 1944, necessarily fixed. What course Chinese Communism might have taken if an American connection had been brought to bear is a question that lost opportunities have made forever unanswerable. The only certainty is that it could not have been worse.

Stilwell's concept of what his command was to include incorporated his original plan for reform of the army. He embodied it in the draft of a directive from the Generalissimo to himself which was to accompany his commission as Field Commander of the Ground and Air Forces of the Republic of China. The directive authorized him to proceed at once with preparations for a counteroffensive against the Japanese, and with reorganization and relocation of China's forces, including the authority to activate new units, disband old units, transfer personnel from one unit to another and units from one commander or locality to another "without regard to the jurisdiction of commanders or of provincial and war area boundaries." Except for the possible leeway implied here, no reference was made to the Communists. The directive further empowered him to "initiate at once plans to improve the livelihood of officers and soldiers . . . so that it will be at least equal to that of people in the rear areas."

Since it was unrealistic to expect that the Generalissimo would sign such a directive, with its admission of inadequate livelihood, it probably represented Stilwell's maximum position. He may even have allowed himself to believe it could be imposed because of the support of his own Government, which he now supposed was behind him. Hurley naturally saw no objection and presented the proposed commission and directive to the Generalissimo. During the usual wait that followed, Stilwell did battle with Ho for fillers for the Y-force which was now down to an effective combat strength of 14,000. He managed to extract a promise of

10,000 in exchange for some Canadian Bren guns. "They throw away 300,000 men in Honan without batting an eye and I break my back trying to get 10,000 to replace battle casualties."

In east China a second American air base had fallen and the Japanese were bearing down on Kweilin, the Paris of the south, with every indication that the loss of the city was imminent. Tired and disorganized, the defense of east China suffered from the same lack of plan and provisions that had overtaken the hapless Czarist armies of World War I. Units were equipped with old and outmoded arms, in some cases not enough rifles for every man or enough ammunition for every rifle. Although generally well supplied with machine guns, they had meager artillery and insufficient shells or, if a division had enough field guns, these were parceled out for use one by one. Coordinated action was stultified by bickering between field commanders and Chungking, by the uncertain strategy and utter inadequacy of the General Staff, and by the Generalissimo's vacillations and mistrust of the southern commanders which resulted in supplies and reinforcements being doled out piecemeal or too late. Chiang allowed himself the assumption that the defense line in the mountains 70 miles north of Kweilin could be held for three months but the Japanese breached the pass in three days. Efforts by Hsueh and Chang Fa-kwei, War Zone Commander in the Kweilin area, to concentrate strength at any one place were defeated by the Generalissimo's fatal affinity for using one unit and holding back one for fear of losing both. All the while the thin and threadbare troops climbed the hilltops in the heat, held their forlorn positions and died under the enemy's guns.

While the Japanese cut their way into Kwangsi, 16 Chinese armies in the north were held motionless in the quarantine of the Communists. When one relief army, the 93rd, was sent down to Kweilin by the Central Government, the troops, who were strangers to the region, did more looting than fighting. The Commanding General of the 93rd, as reported by Theodore White who covered the campaign, "did not know where his flanks were, did not know the distance to the next unit in line, did not know which villages the enemy held" and abandoned the position he was supposed to hold without firing a shot. In the countryside the uprooted population clogged the roads while fifth columnists working for the Japanese spread fire and panic.

Stilwell flew to Kweilin on September 14 to confer with Chang Fa-kwei and decide on the fate of the extensive American air installations. Chang told him that against his own judgment the Generalissimo's orders were to retire inside Kweilin with the only remaining reliable divisions and defend the city from within, a decision that in Stilwell's opinion would make the place "another rat-trap." Chang Fa-kwei said he could hold Kweilin for two months but he had no forces to protect the airfield except the unreliable 93rd Army. After conferring with Chennault, Stilwell gave the hard order for evacuation of American men and equipment and demolition of all the airstrips except one which could be used up to the last minute to bring in guns and ammunition to the besieged garrison of Kweilin. After he had gone, the cargo planes of the ATC came in to carry away the stocks of bombs, gasoline, spare parts, trucks and repair shops they had brought in ton by ton at such cost over the Hump. They left behind 550 barrels of gasoline for use by the demolition squads to fire the installations. Such was the value of Chiang Kai-shek's "personal assurance" to Roosevelt in 1943 that his armies could defend the air bases.

Two months later at the end of November an American OSS unit discovered a cache of arms hidden in the hills around Tushan, 200 miles west of Kweilin in the province of Kweichow. In 20 or more warehouses each about 200 feet long there was stored 50,000 tons of weapons and ammunition, including 50 new field guns and their shells, which the Central Government had collected over the years for use in case of need in east China. By that time Kweilin and Liuchow had fallen, the Japanese were probing at Kweichow, Chungking was trembling—and the arms were still being stored against a crisis.

Stilwell was in Kweilin no more than 24 hours before he was summoned back to a conference with the Generalissimo. Frightened by the Japanese breakthrough, Chiang delivered what amounted to an ultimatum: either the Burma divisions attacked toward Bhamo within one week to take the pressure off the Chinese at Lungling or he would pull the Y-force back across the Salween to protect Kunming. He was afraid that a defeat at Lungling would be followed by a Japanese attack on Kunming and this prospect, because of the city's position on the same interior line as Chungking, always caused him the greatest alarm. His ultimatum meant in effect terminating the action in north Burma just short of the capstone of the campaign whose capture would have completed the reopening of the road to China.

"The crazy little bastard," wrote Stilwell in a fury. "The little matter of the Ledo Road is forgotten. The only point on the whole trace we do not control is Lungling and he wants to give that up and sabotage the whole God-damn project—men, money, material, time and sweat that we have put on it for two and a half years just to help China. Unthinkable. It does not even enter that hickory nut he uses for a head. . . . Usual cockeyed reasons and idiotic tactical and strategic conceptions. He is impossible." Just at this moment the Y-force succeeded in taking Teng-chung, the walled city controlling a side road to Burma, and with the 10,000 replacements promised by Ho the prospects for taking Lungling looked good.

Stilwell immediately reported the Generalissimo's intention to Marshall, saying that he had been "appalled" and had protested strongly without making any impression on Chiang Kai-shek who "will not listen to reason. ... I am now convinced that he regards the South China catastrophe as of little moment, believing that the Japs will not bother him further in that area, and that he imagines that he can get behind the Salween front and there wait in safety for the U.S. to finish the war." Here was the basis of the fundamental cultural clash between Chiang's and Stilwell's theories of war. Throughout Stilwell's mission every action and decision of the Generalissimo had been molded by the principle of hoarding resources and waiting until one barbarian should defeat the other. From the Chinese point of view this was sensible and justified. From the point of view of the Americans, who were providing the resources and believed in taking action to command fate, it was unacceptable and unjustified. There could be no meeting across this divide.

Stilwell determined to try some "plain talk" with T. V. Soong in the hope of getting through to the Generalissimo. With his Westernized education and familiarity with Western ways, T.V. was the nearest thing to a bridge, although so smooth in manner as to make the footing sometimes slippery. His frankness and friendliness were exceedingly effective with foreigners: Hurley was succumbing and Nelson making promises. T.V.'s restoration was now reinforced by the absence of his sisters. After months of rumor and gossip about Chiang's refusal to banish a concubine from his household, Madame had departed on July 1 to visit with Mme. Kung in Brazil. The Generalissimo had given a farewell party at which he publicly denied infidelity. On Madame's arrival in the United States in September rumors of a marital rift were so current that the Chinese Embassy felt obliged to issue a denial. She remained abroad for over a year until September 1945.

Stilwell's plain talk with T.V., far from bridging the gulf, served rather to make its full extent visible. Both were shocked by the discovery. According to his advance notes, Stilwell was prepared to tell T.V. that the Generalissimo would have to make up his mind "to do things never before done"—that is appoint an overall commander with full power—and that if he were not willing, Stilwell's recommendation to his Government would be "to withdraw entirely from China and India and set up a base elsewhere." He was also prepared to ask for the replacement of Ho as War Minister and Chief of Staff by Ch'en Ch'eng and Pai Ch'ung-hsi, respectively. When he stated these and the conditions outlined in his draft directive, T.V. was "appalled at the gap between our conception of field commander and the Generalissimo's." When T.V. in turn described the Generalissimo's concept of the post, Stilwell indignantly summed it up as that of an "overall stooge."

He had not sought and did not want "the God-awful job," he told T.V., but if he took it he would have to have full authority, otherwise he would not accept the responsibility. And if he got it, "the G–mo would have to keep his fingers out of the pie." He said he had looked forward for 44 years for the chance to command American troops, and could have had it if he had not been a real friend of China.

Like anyone in a dilemma Stilwell was ambivalent. It was true he had given up the first American overseas combat command of the war to come to China but the impossible conditions of GYMNAST when it was first handed to him had certainly made that decision easier. It also was true that common sense told him he did not want the god-awful job now at issue, yet at the same time he did want it and tried his best to obtain it. His sense of responsibility to China was strong. After consulting with Pai Ch'ung-hsi about Kweilin he drew up a plan of action for a more effective defense than the Generalissimo's "Rat Trap Special." Instead of allowing the last remaining units to be surrounded in Kweilin, the plan called for them to be used in a battle of maneuver with specified positions and objectives. If unsuccessful, the units—instead of being completely lost—could at least be withdrawn to join the forces Stilwell planned to collect in Kweichow for the eventual drive to the coast. This plan was submitted to the Generalissimo on September 18.

Chiang's threat to withdraw behind the Salween, as reported by Stilwell to Marshall, lit the final "firecracker." Stilwell's telegram reached Marshall in the midst of the second Quebec Conference where Churchill and Roosevelt were plunged in heated controversy over the future treatment of Germany, and the Combined Chiefs were pursuing new and old disputes of strategy and planning. All these, however acrimonious, at least represented progress. China was the one area of serious disappointment and bewilderment, where neither statesmen nor commanders had a coherent or consistent idea of what course to pursue.

Presiding from depression to war, Roosevelt was in his twelfth year of office and for the last three years had been spending at least sixteen hours a day meeting crises and making decisions. He was too worn to attempt any radical new thought or new effort. Militarily China had proved a losing game and by now was not vitally needed except as a holding theater. The strategic aim that took shape at Quebec was to keep China in the war and not much more. No U.S. units were planned for CBI; Marshall was definite

on that point. Further operations in Burma were to be left as far as possible
to the British so that the United States would not be involved in the reconquest of colonial territory—or such was the intention.

Now, on top of the progressive collapse in east China, came the Generalissimo's grand refusal, or threat of refusal, to take any further part in breaking his own blockade. Marshall presented the gist of Stilwell's telegram to
the Conference in the presence of Roosevelt and Churchill at the session of
September 16. He apparently came furnished with the text of a reply, for the
minutes record, in a paroxysm of understatement, that a "note" was sent by
the President to the Generalissimo pointing out that he must accept full
responsibility for the consequences of his action. This "note," which was to
be the fatal catalyst, was a 600-word telegram drafted by Marshall's staff
at Quebec and bearing in Marshall's handwriting the endorsement, "I
recommend that you send the proposed attached message to the Generalissimo." Roosevelt's long-stroked signature appears at the bottom.

The making of foreign policy in World War II came out of the great
Allied conferences dominated by the military where the military staffs were
the working members, and the civil arm, except for the two chiefs of state,
was represented meagerly, if at all. Pomp and uniforms held the floor and
everyone appeared twice as authoritative as he would have in the two-button
business suit of ordinary life. Human fallibility was concealed by all those
beribboned chests and knife-edged tailoring. By the nature of the message they proposed to send Chiang Kai-shek, the military were conducting
foreign policy but nobody questioned it. Stilwell's colleagues in the War
Department shared his outrage and were prepared to talk tough—not without an element of the white man's superiority; it is doubtful if the note would
have been addressed to the head of any European government. Roosevelt
was either past caring about Chiang Kai-shek's dignity or else signed Marshall's message with little attention, which amounts to the same thing.

The message adopted the tone of a headmaster to a sullen and incorrigible
schoolboy. It repeated all the arguments that Stilwell had tried to get
through the "hickory head": that the courage and sacrifices of the Yoke
forces would be in vain unless they were reinforced and supported and allowed to go on to complete the opening of the Burma Road; that a withdrawal behind the Salween was exactly what the enemy was striving to
cause; that if Chiang broke off the action "we will lose all chance of opening
land communications with China and immediately jeopardize the air route
over the Hump. For this you must yourself be prepared to accept the consequences and assume the personal responsibility." The telegram continued:

I have urged time and again in recent months that you take drastic action to
resist the disaster which has been moving closer to China and to you. Now,
when you have not yet placed General Stilwell in command of all forces in

China, we are faced with the loss of a critical area in east China with possible catastrophic consequences. . . . The advance of our forces across the Pacific is swift. But this advance will be too late for China unless you act now and vigorously . . . to preserve the fruits of your long years of struggle and the effort we have been able to make to support you. . . .

I am certain that the only thing you can now do to prevent the Jap from achieving his objectives in China is to reinforce your Salween armies immediately and press their offensive, while at once placing General Stilwell in unrestricted command of all your forces. The action I am asking you to take will fortify us in our decision and in the continued efforts the United States proposes to take to maintain and increase our aid to you. . . . It appears plainly evident to all of us here that all your and our efforts to save China are to be lost by further delays.

There was nothing in this that was not justified; the fault lay in failure to think through the implications. It made no sense to send a message of implied unfitness to rule to a chief of state unless it was backed by readiness to cease investing support in him. In the absence of such readiness the message was a crippled ultimatum from which the senders must inevitably retreat.

Stilwell, to whom the message was addressed for delivery, not unnaturally took it as evidence of decisive firmness in Washington. It seemed to him that "FDR's eyes have been opened. . . . At very long last he has finally spoken plain words and plenty of them with a firecracker in every sentence. . . . A hot firecracker." As senior officer in Chungking it was his duty to deliver a message from the President to the Generalissimo in person. Had he wished to avoid being the bearer of offense to a head of state whose consent he needed, and with whom he had to collaborate, he could easily have stretched a point and given the message to Hurley to deliver. But the sharp wording in the President's name, so clearly suggesting disrespect, encouraged him to abandon restraint. Moreover the message had been sent to him, not to Hurley, with no accompanying instructions or evidence of desire to cushion the impact. All the anger and contempt he had accumulated through two and a half years of being thwarted in his profession and mission by Chiang Kai-shek's determined nonperformance came to a head when Chiang announced his intention to withdraw from Lungling. When Stilwell read the President's message demanding for him "unrestricted command" of all China's forces, he leapt at the chance to plunge it into the Peanut's heart.

He ordered a Chinese translation made and took it to the Huang Shan residence where Chiang was in conference with Hurley, Soong, Ho Ying-chin, Pai and others on the terms of Stilwell's proposed command. Before entering the conference room he sent for Hurley and showed him the text. Hurley's diplomatic instinct counseled softening and he offered to paraphrase the terms verbally for the Generalissimo. This was just what T. V.

Soong, Madame and other transmitters had been doing in the past and what the personal delivery procedure was designed to prevent. Stilwell refused, took it in himself, and as he wrote afterwards with rather horrid satisfaction, "handed this bundle of paprika to the Peanut and then sank back with a sigh. The harpoon hit the little bugger right in the solar plexus and went right through him." Chiang read the Chinese version with no show of emotion, looked at Stilwell and said, "I understand," and after sitting for a moment in silence, jiggling one foot, closed the meeting. "What! No teapots? No, just a calm silence. I got out promptly and came home. Pretty sight crossing the river: lights all on in Chungking."

Afterwards in a letter to his wife he elaborated his relish in verse of the kind he had once composed about the "Ambastardor." It deserves to be buried but, on the principle of warts-and-all, cannot be.

> I've waited long for vengeance—
> At last I've had my chance,
> I've looked the Peanut in the eye
> And kicked him in the pants.
>
> The old harpoon was ready
> With aim and timing true,
> I sank it to the handle
> And stung him through and through.
>
> The little bastard shivered,
> And lost the power of speech.
> His face turned green and quivered
> As he struggled not to screech.
>
> For all my weary battles,
> For all my hours of woe,
> At last I've had my innings
> And laid the Peanut low.
>
> I know I've still to suffer,
> And run a weary race,
> But oh! the blessed pleasure!
> I've wrecked the Peanut's face.

To Chiang Kai-shek the message was unquestionably a shock. His wrath after the meeting was reported to have been tremendous and it did not take him long to recognize the implications. He knew he could not accept the American demand made in such terms without opening the way to his own discard. If the Americans succeeded in imposing Stilwell on him against his will, they might do likewise in the matter of the Communists. Gauss was not the only one who saw this leading to the possible collapse of the Kuomintang. The issue had to be met. Guided by Soong's realistic advice, Chiang did not think the United States would abandon him and he was prepared to bring it to the test. The message of September 18 gave him the excuse he was waiting for. According to T. V. Soong he said it canceled his promise to give Stilwell the command.

The problem he and Soong now faced was how to formulate the cancellation without seeming to blame the President whom they could not afford to alienate for fear of risking Lend-Lease. While T.V. applied his skills to this task, the Generalissimo, in his unpredictable way, imperturbably accepted Stilwell's plan for the defense of Kweilin. Pai Ch'ung-hsi was delegated to go down to superintend the execution. He brought the good news to Stilwell on September 20 and mentioned, as another sign of progress, that the commander of the 93rd Army had been executed—to "encourage the rest," as Stilwell noted in the words of Voltaire.

He had learned by now of the Generalissimo's wrath but neither he nor, despite his ex post facto explanations, Hurley, considered at the time that this was definitive. The Kweilin development appeared encouraging and Stilwell thought he was in a strong position because he assumed a sticking point had been reached in Washington. To break the deadlock over the appointment he offered a new set of proposals on September 23 in which he undertook to go to Yenan to negotiate the Communists' acceptance of the Central Government's authority and of military command exercised through himself. According to these proposals the Communist troops would be employed north of the Yellow River out of contact with Government troops. American arms and equipment were suggested for only five divisions. "This will knock the persimmons off the trees!" exclaimed Hurley confidently and went off to present the paper to the Generalissimo.

He met with a shock. Chiang presented him not merely with refusal of the command post but with a formal demand for the recall of General Stilwell.

Chiang was a man no less persistent than Stilwell in pursuit of an objective. He had made up his mind to be rid of a presence that was a continuing indictment of himself and his regime. If he was Stilwell's incubus, Stilwell was his goad. Their past as well as future relationship was in the scales. At bottom was the principle contained in the issue between Chennault's program and Stilwell's: one offering to let the American air arm fight for China, the other proposing to enable the Chinese to fight for themselves. Had it been within the Generalissimo's power or philosophy to adopt Stilwell's program for reform of the army, he would have had the combat efficiency available to resist the Japanese offensive of 1944 and, quite possibly, to overcome the Communists in the clash that was to come. That opportunity had now gone by, nor is it likely that the Generalissimo either recognized or regretted it. His concern was to remove the source of a pressure he could not tolerate.

He now felt able to take the risk because the presence of Hurley and Nelson reassured him of continued American support. The Chinese were delighted with Hurley whom they found congenial and amenable and who provided the channel Chiang wanted for communicating his views and desires without going through Stilwell and Gauss. In addition, Nelson had drawn up an impressive program of American support for China's postwar economic reconstruction and had promised the Generalissimo, or, through the hazards of interpreted conversation and wishful listening, had given the impression that he promised him, control of Lend-Lease. This was an important factor in the developments.*

Through two long sessions on the day Chiang voiced his demand for Stilwell's recall, Hurley did his best to dissuade him from a decision that meant a failure in part of his own assignment. But Chiang had found his ground and stood on it with the same granite immovability he had displayed when kidnapped at Sian. The problem of blame was solved by placing it all on Stilwell. By personally delivering the President's message he had put Chiang in the position of his subordinate—according to Chiang. The G–mo said Stilwell had disobeyed him by refusing to order the attack on Bhamo and he would have a mutiny on his hands if he gave Stilwell command of the army. His reasons were elaborated in an aide-memoire which charged that Stilwell "had no intention of cooperating with me but believed that he was in fact appointed to command me," that he was "unfitted for the vast and complex duties which the new command will entail" and that his appointment would do "irreparable injury" to Chinese-American military cooperation. It assured the President that Chiang was still ready to appoint an American to command the Chinese armed forces and to make other important changes that would contribute to "harmonious" operations. "T.V. undoubtedly wrote the thing," was Stilwell's comment.

From this point on, during negotiations that continued for another three weeks, the only person certain of the outcome was Chiang Kai-shek. He was in a weak position but he had absolute firmness of intent while the United States had all the advantages except firmness of intent. To the participants caught in it, the situation was not that clear. Hurley who still wanted to be

---

* Nelson was treated to luscious flattery. Chiang Kai-shek asked him to return to China to take charge of the reconstruction of the country's economy. His acceptance would be a "historic event" that would give China the greatest hope. "If you do not come then it would appear that China is hopeless. . . . I regard you as a Chinese citizen and wish to entrust to you the entire responsibility for China's economic reconstruction. . . . I will unconditionally invest in you all China's economic powers."

Ambassador was inclined to accept the Soong-Chiang thesis that Stilwell's act of delivery was the blameworthy cause and so reported to Roosevelt on September 25. Hurley also listened receptively when Soong expressed his and the Generalissimo's belief that Stilwell himself was the author of the insolent message which, according to this theory, he had suggested to Washington and arranged to have sent back in the President's name. This was an omnipotence Stilwell would have been happy to possess.

It was a measure of his low estimation of Chiang that in the face of an official demand for his recall he went on trying to obtain command of China's armies. He wanted it not as a means of his own aggrandizement but as a means to scourge the enemy. In the midst of war against a still formidable opponent, the defeat of Japan was his primary concern. He was intent on obtaining the authority that would enable him to launch the long-planned counteroffensive toward the coast. As always his mind would not accept an impossibility though he knew it to be one. He explicitly stated to Marshall on September 26 that Chiang had no intention of making further efforts to prosecute the war, and that "Anyone who crowds him toward such action will be blocked or eliminated." Yet he went on trying to crowd him. Chiang had reversed himself backwards and forwards so many times in the past that there was reason to suppose he might do so again. He had not, as Stilwell learned, informed the National Military Council or even Ho Ying-chin of his demand for Stilwell's recall which suggested that he was leaving room for another maneuver depending on Washington's reaction. That this was awaited in obvious anxiety was indicated by Soong's "highly nervous and disturbed condition."

On September 28 Stilwell offered a compromise, suggested by Lin Wei who did not know about the demand for recall but thought that if the issue of Communist participation were dropped the Generalissimo would agree to give Stilwell the command. Stilwell proposed this to Ho Ying-chin, offering to defer the Communist role for the time being and concentrate on organizing and preparing a force drawn from the NCAC, the Y and the Z groups which could "take the offensive within six months." This was exactly the crowding he knew the Generalissimo would not tolerate but it had to be proposed for how else, as he saw it, were the Japanese on the mainland to be defeated?

In Washington the Generalissimo's renewed demand for Stilwell's recall went straight to the weak link in the American position. This lay in the fact that Marshall had pushed the President into taking a position that Roosevelt did not really believe in. Roosevelt had let himself be pushed partly because of his disillusion with Chiang since Cairo and his anger at the long refusal to move the Y-force, partly because Stilwell had proved himself an accomplisher, and finally because he did not know what else to try. There is nothing in wartime like recalcitrant allies for creating quandaries. But he was not now prepared to impose an American commander against the express wishes of a chief of state. That would be impossible to reconcile with his own part in rescinding the unequal treaties and restoring China's sovereignty. Resting on Chiang's stated readiness to appoint another American, the President was willing enough to back down on Stilwell. Marshall definitely was not but while they were struggling over the matter an unofficial version of the President's attitude was conveyed by Hopkins to Kung at a dinner party and immediately telegraphed to Soong on October 1.

Whatever Hopkins may or may not have said, the conclusion Kung telegraphed was that since it concerned the sovereign right of China, the President intended to comply with the request for the recall of Stilwell. As soon as he had discussed it with Marshall and solved the problem of a successor, he would make his reply to the Generalissimo. This was what Chiang and Soong had been waiting for and all that they needed. The Generalissimo at once closed his own lines of retreat by announcing his intention to dismiss Stilwell to the Standing Committee of the CEC.* Proceedings of the Committee, which met regularly Monday afternoons, were strictly secret and usually took from three days to a week to circulate but an account of the session of October 2 was leaked to Gauss on the same day, doubtless on purpose so that it could be reported back to Washington and close off any other lines of retreat.

Speaking heatedly and banging the table the Generalissimo had insisted that General Stilwell "must go" and that all Lend-Lease must come to him for distribution. He said that an American commander, if there was to be any, would be allowed to have contact only with the Chinese forces put at his disposal by the Generalissimo. Although he was grateful for the abolition of extrality and the Exclusion Act, the Americans were now trying to infringe on China's sovereignty in another way. "This is a new form of imperialism; if we agree we should be nothing but puppets; we might as well go over to Wang Ching-wei." He repeated that he was not going to compromise on a matter of sovereign rights. He complained that Stilwell had disobeyed orders in refusing to advance on Bhamo and had boasted that if he went to Yenan he could get the Red Army to cooperate, but he would never be permitted to go to Yenan "until the Communists submit to my orders." The G–mo told the meeting not to fear in case the Americans should now withdraw aid. "We can get along without them . . . we can still stand on our feet in four provinces."

Although there was much murmuring only one member of the Standing Committee ventured a reply. He said Stilwell might be the best man they

* Central Executive Committee.

could get "who understands China and the ways of the people" whereas a new man might be worse "because the usual American is not so considerate and he may want things done quicker and he may be more brusque." That at least was a unique tribute.

As soon as he learned of Chiang's speech to the Standing Committee and of Hopkins' disclosure (which Soong took pains to report to Hurley), Stilwell knew the struggle was close to an end although the official American reply was still awaited. That day he wrote farewell letters to the leading Chinese commanders who had served under him and warned his wife to prepare "to have me thrown out on the garbage pile." The President's yielding was to him the decisive factor. "If Old Softy gives in on this as he apparently has, the Peanut will be out of control from now on."

As if to confirm the sliding of the ground from under him, Merrill came in that night from the Quebec Conference with a summary of disinterest in the China theater. He reported that the statements of Admiral Nimitz and others about the need for bases on the China coast were purely a cover for "our real operations" (the coming assault on the Philippines); that all plans for operations against the Japanese assumed no action by China beyond containing some enemy forces on the mainland; there was no intention "to get mixed up on the Continent with large U.S. forces"; and in final epitaph, that General Handy of OPD admitted that by now the "Stilwell mission was primarily political and that not much in the way of real action by the Chinese was hoped for." In this acknowledgment was the true end of Stilwell's mission; recall was but the form it took.

The drama was not quite played out. Marshall, the initiator of the command crisis, refused to acquiesce in the recall in which his own policy as much as loyalty to Stilwell was involved. He drafted a "sharp rejoinder" to Chiang Kai-shek's charges which this time Roosevelt declined to send.

As seen by Stilwell himself the issue was the combat effort of China. Insistently he repeated to Marshall that if Chiang Kai-shek had his way in this affair no further Chinese action in the war could be expected and future American effort in China would be wasted. If the Generalissimo succeeded both in dismissing Stilwell and keeping American aid and support he would be confirmed in intransigence. With options lost the United States would have tied itself to his chariot for good or ill. This was true but the difficulty was that the issue of Stilwell's command, in so far as it conflicted with sovereignty, made a bad case that could not be sustained.

The option to end support of China was almost taken. More from general dissatisfaction than far-seeing policy, the Joint Chiefs considered the alternative of abandoning the line over the Hump and, as Stimson recorded, giving up for the present "aiding China at all." They were forced to conclude, however, that this would have such a bad effect on China's morale and give the Japanese so much to talk about that the United States could not afford to do it. The decision was bitter because of the feeling that the long effort over the Hump to supply Chennault had been wasted and, as Stimson wrote, was likely "to cost an extra winter in the main theater of the war." All along the front from Cherbourg to Arnhem the thrust of Allied spearheads was slowed for lack of air transport. Stimson was particularly indignant. Although Chennault had been given "almost twice as much in the way of equipment over the Hump as he asked for," he was unable to stop the Japanese while Stilwell who "has proved the only success on the whole horizon" in CBI was being made the victim.

Roosevelt's long-awaited reply to Chiang Kai-shek, dated October 5, acceded to the recall only halfway. Marshall had succeeded in beating out a compromise according to which Stilwell would be relieved as Chief of Staff to Chiang Kai-shek and of responsibility for Lend-Lease but would remain in command of the Chinese forces in Burma and Yunnan. The message informed the Generalissimo that no American would be named to command the Chinese armed forces because the ground situation in China had so deteriorated since the original proposal that the U.S. Government "should not assume the responsibility." That was of course no loss to Chiang. The message was again a harsh one but it did not contain the one thing he feared—discontinuance of supply. On the contrary he was assured that deliveries over the Hump would be maintained because it was "of such tremendous importance to the stability of your Government." The United States too was concerned with face-saving.

The crucial point having been given away, Stimson as an old lawyer felt "pretty sure" Chiang would not accept the compromise—nor did he. Making sovereignty the issue, he addressed to the President a renewed demand for Stilwell's removal from China. "So long as I am Head of State and Supreme Commander in China it seems to me that there can be no question as to my right to request the recall of an officer in whom I can no longer repose confidence." This was accompanied by a massive statement of the case designed to absolve himself of responsibility for the military situation and establish Stilwell as culpable.

Through the Generalissimo's eyes realities were reversed and everything seen upside down, as if his statement had been composed by the Red Queen in *Through the Looking-Glass*. Fresh from adopting Stilwell's plan for the defense of Kweilin, he now declared with impressive tautology that "I not only have no confidence in General Stilwell but also lack confidence in his military judgment." The Burma campaign was the root of the matter. Far from having accomplished anything for China, it was accused of having "drained off most of the properly trained and equipped reserves in China" (without mentioning who had trained and equipped them) and "greatly reduced incoming supply tonnage" (which was the opposite of the case) thus rendering China unable to resist the Japanese offensive. In consequence General Stilwell bore "grave responsibility" for the loss of east China. In a final twist after three years of incessant cries of China's imminent collapse, Chiang now could not agree that "the deterioration is so serious as the President suggests" nor could he "foresee any disaster fundamentally incapacitating China"—though of course continued aid was essential.

The Generalissimo's case for recall was forwarded by Hurley on October 11 and endorsed on the essential basis that Chiang and Stilwell were "fundamentally incompatible," which was true and reason enough. Hurley went on to advise the President that "If you sustain Stilwell in this controversy you will lose Chiang Kai-shek and possibly you will lose China with him." That Chiang was losable by the United States was an unlikely proposition but it did not greatly matter for, though it appeared otherwise to the participants, Hurley's contributions to the affair had no important effect on the outcome one way or another.

Picking out the fallacy at once, Stilwell radioed Marshall, "It is not a choice between throwing me out or losing CKS and possibly China" but of "losing China's potential effort if CKS is allowed to make the rules now." He suggested another last-minute compromise in the form of a Sino-American Council to save the Generalissimo's face while leaving himself in position to ensure that orders were obeyed. Incredibly at this late stage he was still trying; he was a man who never gave up on anything. On October 14 he went down to Liuchow below Kweilin to confer with Chang Fa-kwei and Pai Ch'ung-hsi on plans for counterattack.

From October 6 to 15 Marshall was in France; on his return he went to the White House prepared to renew battle for Stilwell but it was no use. Convinced that the Generalissimo would not tolerate Stilwell, Roosevelt gave "direct and positive" orders to remove him from China without delay. Regardless of rights and wrongs, if America was going to continue to support Chiang Kai-shek's regime, he could have come to no other decision.

The question arises, was there an alternative—or at the top level of Government a search for an alternative—to support for the Kuomintang? The consensus of advice had been for so long that only Chiang Kai-shek could hold China together that policy-making was conditioned by it and by the persistent fear of China falling back into the turmoil and disunity of the warlord years. New voices were now urging that though Chiang was dependent on us, the contrary was not necessarily true; that, as Davies said in one of his reports, "We must not indefinitely underwrite a politically bankrupt regime." But a status quo power, as the United States, the once brave young republic, had now become, tends to stay with another incumbent even if bankrupt. Any other course is awkward and risky and in the case of China would lead to the Communists, the only group sufficiently dynamic and organized to represent a realistic challenge. It was not feasible for the United States to transfer support to Yenan. The available alternative was the endeavor, which American policy was already promoting, to bring the two parties together.

"THE AXE FALLS," Stilwell learned on October 19, warned by an advance radio from Marshall. The President's official reply followed, informing the Generalissimo that instructions had been issued "to recall General Stilwell from the theater immediately." Coldest in all the train of messages, it reminded Chiang that the decision to conduct the Burma campaign was not Stilwell's but the Combined Chiefs' approved by the President and Prime Minister and dictated by the need to supply China. It pointedly drew to his attention the fact that the campaign had already resulted in the low-level flying route and the opening of the pipeline at Myitkyina on September 29. As a change necessitated by Stilwell's recall, it announced the dissolution of the CBI theater and its separation into two theaters, Burma-India and China. General Sultan would succeed Stilwell in the former and General Wedemeyer would succeed him as Chief of Staff to the Generalissimo and commander of American forces in China.* The hope was expressed that the Ramgarh operations would continue, "otherwise the fighting power of these units will inevitably and quickly dwindle away," and that the Y-forces would continue action in Burma.

Thus ended the command crisis and with it Stilwell's mission. Controversy over the Hopkins disclosure or Hurley's role or Stilwell's delivery of the message was largely irrelevant; these were not causes but only mechanisms. The recall was the inevitable outcome of the assumption, growing out of China's dependence and passivity, that an American solution could be imposed on China. Responsibility lay with Marshall for initiating the attempt, with Roosevelt for authorizing it and with Stilwell himself for agreeing to and promoting it. At a deeper level was the incompatibility, superficially of two men, fundamentally of two purposes.

Stilwell remained only 48 hours in Chungking after the notice of recall. The hurry and secrecy of his departure were at the orders of General Marshall who, with reason to fear Stilwell's outspokenness, was anxious to bring him out of the theater and back to Washington before the recall was announced and the press fell upon him. An already slanderous Presidential campaign was reaching its climax and Marshall hoped to avoid any blasts

---

* Stilwell's third position as Deputy Commander of SEAC was filled by General Wheeler.

by Stilwell that might make it difficult to give him another major assignment.

Stilwell's anxiety to tell his side of the story was marked by agonized entries in the diary: "Will a statement be made about the relief?" "Will I be allowed to make a statement?" He called in White and Atkinson to tell them in confidence what had happened and urge that the facts be recorded for history. For the journalists it was a story that would blow the roof at last but it could not be written from Chungking. Atkinson, who was scheduled to leave within a month, determined to go home at once to force publication—an enterprise which shortly came to pass in a mighty explosion.

Also at this time Stilwell ordered the fateful return to Washington of John Service to make the case, so cogently argued in his reports from Yenan, for opening relations with the Communists. Colonel Barrett had recently written to Stilwell that "they want to fight the Japanese and their troops are capable of fighting . . . and they want to fight under you." Though himself out of the picture Stilwell was thinking always of the 24 Japanese divisions still on the mainland, and believed that some military action by the Communists would have to be organized against them. Doubtless also he was animated by no spirit of friendliness to the Kuomintang. He cleared the assignment with Service's superior, Ambassador Gauss, who had long resented the robbing of his best staff by Stilwell's headquarters. Left in no doubt of the motives, Gauss explained to the Department that "some of our Army officers and perhaps Stilwell favor direct aid to Chinese Communist forces" and this was the reason for sending Service to Washington. His mission was to lead to the future tragic and destructive assault on the China foreign service officers.

In the last rushed hours Stilwell finished his farewell messages including a very decent letter to Chennault taking pride in his achievements and acknowledging the admiration in which he was held by the Chinese, and another to Chu Teh in Yenan expressing his "keen disappointment" that he was not to be associated "with you and the excellent troops you have developed" in operations against Japan. The only Englishman to receive other than a formal farewell was General Auchinleck to whom he wrote that he thought of him, he hoped reciprocally, "as a friend." He paid a farewell call on Mme. Sun Yat-sen who cried and wished she could go to the United States and tell the President the facts. He took formal farewell of Ambassador Gauss and learned that he too had reached an end. Bypassed by all the special envoys of whom Hurley and Nelson were the last straw, ignored by Chiang Kai-shek because he was not influential, aware that he was not listened to by the White House and weary of a hopeless task, he had made up his mind to resign at the end of the Presidential term.

There remained one final farewell. A messenger arrived from the Generalissimo with offer of the Special Grand Cordon of the Blue Sky and

A group of Chinese replacements wait to be transported to a hospital in Kweiyang, 1944 (219), w *evacuations begin at Kweilin in September (221) and Liuchow in November (220). General Dorn* *the Y-force was present at the capture of Tengchun which a five-week siege had reduced to rut* *(222). Stilwell, photographed shortly before learning of his dismissal, October 19, 1944 (223).*

221

222

223

White Sun, the highest Chinese decoration for which a foreigner could qualify. Stilwell's refusal was predictable* but he had to steel himself to accept an invitation to tea. Chiang Kai-shek, with T. V. Soong at his elbow, was gracious. He regretted all this very much, it was only due to differences of personality, he hoped Stilwell would continue to be China's friend. He asked for suggestions and criticisms, especially about the situation at Liuchow, and was astonished to find that Stilwell had actually gone down there in person. The guest was laconic. Asking that the Generalissimo remember only that his motives had been for China's good, he gave the war slogan *Tsui hou sheng li* (For the final victory) and departed.

On October 21 under a cold, cloudy, dark gray sky he climbed into his plane accompanied by General Bergin who insisted that if the Boss went he would not remain, and by Hurley's aide, Colonel McNally, who had served in the theater for two years and shared Bergin's sentiments. Unhappy himself, Hurley acknowledged to Stilwell that he had "bitched it up" and Stilwell was inclined to agree. He considered that he had been "Hurleyed out of China" besides being "a fugitive from a Chiang gang." Because of the secrecy only Hurley and T. V. Soong were at the airfield to say goodbye. Atkinson joined the departing party and at the last minute Ho Ying-chin drove up, emerged from his car and saluted. Stilwell returned the salute, looked around, asked, "What are we waiting for?" and took off. He had leeway of only three days for stops at Kunming, at Y-force headquarters at Paoshan, at Myitkyina and at Ramgarh to say goodbye privately to old companions. No formal leave-talking was allowed of the troops and road-builders and air crews who had accomplished the return through Burma under his command, and "that hurt." He reached Delhi on October 24 and two days later, after 32 months of unslackened pursuit of the least attainable American goal of the war, he wrote the last entry of his mission: "Shoved off—last day in CBI."

To the Americans and many of the Chinese who had fought with him— if not to the Fourteenth Air Force which rejoiced at the news—the recall of General Stilwell was a kind of closing, the visible signal that a great endeavor was over. The effort had been made, and as some felt, wasted. If the man who had given it impetus and direction was gone, pulled out with-

---

* The Blue and White was first proposed for Stilwell by the Chinese Government in March 1944. Stilwell told the War Department that in order to keep his complete freedom of action he did not want to accept a decoration from either the Chinese or British and if there was no other way to do this "peacefully," he would take refuge in the War Department rule prohibiting those involved in the allocation of Lend-Lease from accepting foreign orders. This reason was offered by the War Department on his behalf for his final refusal of the Blue and White.

out ceremony or recognition, there seemed to many only futility in remaining. The feeling was summarized in a letter from Dorn to Bergin written from the Salween front. He explained that he could not leave because he felt it would be wrong to desert the Chinese and Americans serving under him in the unfinished campaign but, he wrote, "The more I think of it the more hopeless the future looks. Everything has always been 'in the future' and now there isn't any. . . . I have always believed, even in the usual mess, that we could accomplish things here. Now I do not. . . ."

In Washington, with the campaign in its final week, Stilwell's return was awaited with extreme nervousness. "I foresee an infinite amount of trouble," Stimson wrote; "Stilwell's success has made him very popular with the American people." The election campaign had been in Roosevelt's opinion "the dirtiest in history" and it was likely enough that a popular hero's recall would provoke charges of skullduggery. Blowing with the advance winds of the cold war, the Republican candidate, Governor Dewey, was proclaiming in last-minute orations that Communists had seized control of the New Deal. While no real doubt was felt in the President's circle that he would defeat Dewey, the press predicted a close result and Roosevelt wanted as strong a mandate as he could get. No public announcement of Stilwell's recall had yet been made and extraordinary precautions were taken to keep him out of the hands of the press.

Brooks Atkinson, with his story already written, had left Delhi ahead of Stilwell. At Cairo an M.P. at the runway demanded the submission to censorship of all papers and contents of briefcases but Atkinson's story was fortunately in his pocket. Held up at Tunis, he gave it to John Service, who had a higher travel priority, with instructions to take it straight to the *Times* while he himself would follow on the next available plane. Service delivered it safely but the wartime censorship stopped publication. While the *Times* battled for its scoop for three days, Atkinson arrived in the country circumventing the question of origin. The issue was taken to the President who decided that since the facts were substantially as stated, the *Times* was entitled to publish them. The front-page story appeared on October 31 before Stilwell arrived in the country.

It declared that General Stilwell's recall from China represented the "political triumph of a moribund anti-democratic regime" and had committed the United States to at least passive support of a government which had become "increasingly unpopular and distrusted in China." It described Chiang Kai-shek as "bewildered and alarmed by the rapidity with which China is falling apart." It scorned the decision to appoint another American Chief of Staff to the Generalissimo which "has the effect of making us acquiesce in an unenlightened cold-hearted autocratic political regime . . . unrepresentative of the Chinese people who are good allies." It described

Stilwell as the ablest field commander in China since "Chinese" Gordon who was "personally incapable of assuming a reverential mood toward the Generalissimo," but even had he been otherwise, no diplomatic genius could have overcome the "basic unwillingness" of the Generalissimo to risk his armies in battle with the Japanese.

The floods burst through Atkinson's breach. Gauss' resignation, which was leaked to the press and appeared to be connected with Stilwell's recall, added to the sensation. Every correspondent or former correspondent in CBI wrote all the things he had not been permitted to publish for years. News stories, editorials, columnists and radio commentators contributed to what Joseph C. Harsch of CBS called "the bursting of a great illusion . . . the long-delayed washday for China's dirty linen." Asking the inevitable question, why the American public had not been informed, Thoburn Wiant of AP, who had been in Chungking and Burma, said it was because Washington had kept on hoping that it could clear up the mess but Stilwell's recall was testimony that it could not. Dr. Walter Judd, the Generalissimo's ardent partisan, made the point that no self-respecting head of state could have accepted what was demanded of him. "Stilwell did not make the mistake. . . . We had to back down from an impossible position in which we should never have put ourselves."

Obliged to comment at a press conference, Roosevelt was never more bland. It was all a conflict of personalities. Chiang Kai-shek and General Stilwell had "certain fallings-out—oh, quite a while ago—and it finally ended the other day." No politics were involved, not even Chinese politics; no (in reply to question after question), not strategy, not policy, not Lend-Lease nor the Hump tonnage, nor Hurley-Nelson, nor Gauss' resignation, nor the "so-called Communists" had anything to do with it. It was "just personalities." A *Times* editorial punctured the personality issue with respect to both Stillwell and Gauss. "It is scarcely conceivable that more tactful representatives, if tact was what they lacked, could have overcome the disorganization and corruption which have hamstrung the Chinese war effort."

In the midst of the press furor Stilwell reached home shores at Palm Beach on Thursday November 2, five days before the election, and was smuggled into Washington the next day under security regulations as tight as if he had been Rudolf Hess just defected from the enemy. His wartime mission of little glory and no thanks was matched by his reception at home. There was no welcome appropriate to what Stimson called "the most difficult task assigned to any American in the entire war." Stilwell was an embarrassment to his superiors; the visible symbol of their retreat. In their anxiety to keep attention away from him, the White House and War Department could think only to keep him out of sight. Presumably for fear of attracting the press, neither Marshall nor Stimson came to meet him; in fact Stimson, who knew the time of his arrival, left by plane for his weekend home from the same airport half an hour earlier. Stilwell was met by his wife and by Marshall's aide, Colonel Frank McCarthy, who had instructions to get him off the airplane and out of the airport without being seen. He was escorted to guest quarters at Fort Meyer across the street from Marshall's house where he was greeted by General Handy and General Surles, chief of Army public relations, who warned him not to talk.

Marshall came to see him after nightfall. For the present he had nothing better to offer than command of the Army Ground Forces in charge of training at home, with promise of something indefinite in Europe or the Pacific later. "There is really no job for me," Stilwell recognized. Now a four-star general, he asked to be given a division; Marshall laughed and told him to take a month off. It was clear to Stilwell they wanted him out of the way and muzzled until after the election.

That was his homecoming. The fear of what he might say appears exaggerated. Stilwell was prepared to obey the order not to talk, the more so as he had no desire to be shelved when the war was reaching its climax. But he had a long history of lack of inhibition against giving offense, which may have influenced Marshall who had had to protect him from its results ever since Benning and was anxious to avoid an indiscretion. The M.P.s and protective custody and secrecy accompanied him across the country to California and he continued to be muzzled at home. Followed everywhere by the press ready with notebooks and microphones for anything he wanted to say, and bursting with the need to speak, he telegraphed General Surles to know when the ban would be lifted. The answer was the refuge of the bureaucrat: "The less you say the stronger your position becomes." The excuse for muzzling was no longer valid, if it ever had been, but no one really wanted Stilwell to make it too plain, as he had once before, that what had taken place, this time to American effort, was "a hell of a beating."

Personally he could be consoled—though never for long—by the delight of being at home in Carmel, reunited with his beloved family, free to walk with his dog along the beach. The appreciation he had had to forgo poured in from the theater. "We all felt lost" when the news came, wrote General Pan Yu-kan, commander of the 50th Division, the first into Myitkyina. General Pick, the road-builder, wrote, "I never had a commander before I regretted losing as I do you." The theater's Provost Marshal, Colonel Harry Cooper, asked to be assigned to "go with you wherever you go." In their messages the Chinese felt that what Stilwell had done had been done for China, while the Americans felt that what

224

Stilwell, greeted by his wife and daughters as he arrived home in California in 1944 (224), we directly to his beloved Carmel house (225). He met the press in his garden in November (22 Lieutenant General Albert C. Wedemeyer succeeded him as Chief of Staff to the Generalissimo (22 Many Chinese who fought with Stilwell differed from Chiang in their estimate of the America commander. "Hundred Victories Wei" (228), commander of the Y-forces on the Salween, was o of the many who made their approval known.

they had done had been done for one man: "It was doing a job for Uncle Joe." *CBI Roundup* condensed the sense of loss in a sonnet entitled "Salute." In troubled days ahead, it predicted,

> . . . a spry
> Small ghostly figure will be seen along
> The Ledo Road—his campaign hat awry—
> Roaring in his jeep down toward Mogaung,
> . . . and we shall say
> "You see? He never really went away."

The Chinese who had fought with Stilwell estimated his accomplishment rather differently than did Chiang Kai-shek. "Hundred Victories Wei," commander of the Y-forces on the Salween, recalled that the Government had given him the taxes of four counties in appreciation of his victories in the anti-Communist campaigns and, as he said to Dorn, "For a man like General Stilwell, well, they will surely give him at least ten counties!" The best and final judgment came in a letter from General Tseng Hsi-kwei, colleague since the first Burma campaign, who wrote, "For at least three years you have made things possible out of impossibilities."

Stilwell had always believed that what he called the phony propaganda about China was his worst enemy and at peaks of frustration would ask himself, "What will happen when the American public learns the truth?" Nothing happened. Official policy continued to flow in the channel it had carved for itself. Hurley, of course, was named Ambassador to succeed Gauss, because he was there, because he wanted it, because he was agreeable to the chief of state, although career officers in China considered him 50 percent vapor and pleaded "anyone but Hurley." Wedemeyer, equally polished and *persona grata,* filled the post of American Chief of Staff.

Marked by the naval Battle of Leyte Gulf in the Philippines which opened on the day Stilwell left Chungking, the direction of the war approached China, but American military interest receded except for the trapped effort to shore up Chungking and simply keep China in the war. In mid-November the twin Japanese drives, inward from the coast and southward through Kwangsi, effected a junction at Liuchow, which fell within a few days of Kweilin. Soon afterwards the enemy advance came to an end on the frozen mountain roads of Kweichow, stopped by winter and over-extension. Since April eight provinces, half a million soldiers, a population of 100,000,000 and the last access of the coast had been lost. The credit of the Kuomintang with its people was irreparably damaged. Chiang Kai-shek still stood, confident of American support, "too weak to rule," as a fellow countryman said, "too strong to be overthrown." Four years later S. I. Hsiung, a laudatory biographer of the Generalissimo, obliquely suggested that many great men would be considered greater if they had had the sense to die earlier, for example Napoleon before Waterloo, Wilson before Versailles and "Chiang Kaishek before the recall of General Stilwell."

Stilwell at home in Carmel with Garry (229).

20

"We Ought to Get Out–NOW"

1945-46

B Y a bolt of luck into whose path Stilwell alertly stepped, he was to finish the war in the field as he hoped. In the first months after his return, however, his fate seemed to be a desk. Appointed commander of the Army Ground Forces in the United States on January 23, he had charge of training, but the job had no charm for him while combat mounted overseas. "I will stand it as long as I can and then explode," he wrote Win. Marshall could tell him nothing definite about a possible command in the Pacific and Stilwell thought the President's failure to receive him at all was ominous.

Headquarters of the AGF was in Washington but most of Stilwell's time was spent going from one army camp to another to inspect training and administer the problems of returned soldiers. Unlike the usual general on inspection, he ignored the barracks and, as at Ramgarh, went at once to watch training exercises and firing practice. In between tours he found himself a celebrity attested by the ultimate mark—a police escort that took him all the way from Albany to Washington when a plane was grounded. There were speeches and meetings and testimonials, a special warmth of applause that singled him out at public dinners, an invitation to give the graduating address at West Point, a meeting with Vice-President Truman who "wants to talk," a statement by Judge Vinson, the future Chief Justice, that the "American people think of me as an institution. My God."

A bittersweet honor came when the Ledo Road, pushed through to

China in final actuality, was named for him. The Y-forces and the Burma forces had made their junction early in January. Following closely behind, the Road was cut through to join the old Burma Road at Bhamo and officially opened for through traffic on January 25. "I have a convoy formed," signaled the builder, General Pick, to General Sultan who had succeeded to Stilwell's command in Burma. "I would like your permission to take it through to China." As the first trucks drove into Kunming after 24 rough days on the way from Assam, thousands of ecstatic people waved colored banners inscribed with the Chinese characters for "Welcome First Convoy Over Stilwell Road." Stilwell's picture was carried in the celebrations along with those of Chiang Kai-shek and Roosevelt. "We," proclaimed the Generalissimo, "have broken the siege of China. Let me name this road after General Joseph Stilwell in memory of his distinctive contribution and of the signal part which the Allied and Chinese forces under his direction played in the Burma campaign and in the building of the road." "I wonder who put him up to that?" the title character mused.

U.S. Headquarters for the India-Burma theater confirmed the name in an official order. Stilwell's own statement for the occasion, broadcast over the Army Hour radio program, paid tribute to all the men—infantry, engineers, medics, air crews, truck crews and laborers—"who fought for it and built it," and was as silent about his own role as if he had not been there. Better than all the formalities a private message from Sultan acknowledged that what had opened the road to China was "your indomitable will."

Whatever his resentment of the President's treatment, Stilwell expressed nothing privately or publicly, even by so much as a significant smile or a lifted eyebrow. "The curtain was down right to the floor," said a friend. Inwardly his mind was churning in an agony that poured itself out in notes and reflections on the circumstances of his command and the problem of China. The inescapable conclusion expressed at dinner at Secretary Stimson's house and recorded by his host was that "nothing can be done in China until we get rid of Chiang Kai-shek." Equally inescapable was the obverse: what was the alternative? Because there was no other realistic answer, but more than that, because they were vigorously working for a change, Stilwell was persuaded that the Communists, as the "agricultural liberals" of China might offer the United States a base to build on. In another conversation Senator Morse found him "equally critical" of the Communists as of Chiang. He said China was in for "a long pull of civil war, and there was nothing we could do about it." We would just have to wait until China went through her turmoil. So long as Chiang was at the helm, Stilwell wrote in his notes, there would be no progress toward unity or even working coalition. By backing the reactionary Chungking Government, America was getting a black eye in China and associating herself with the old colonial system. "Unless we stand clear, we will be classed with France, England, Holland and Chungking."

His major outlet was editing and contributing to the massive official record of his command, *History of the CBI Theater,* which his staff was preparing. Including the combat report, the political aspects, sections on each branch of the service and a Master Narrative, the whole was to fill a trunk when completed and delivered to the War Department on March 7. Asked what it contained when he was seen helping to carry the trunk through the Pentagon's corridors, he replied, "a letter for General Handy." Its central thesis, summarized in the concluding chapter, was that in supporting China without exacting a commitment to action in return for Lend-Lease, the United States had conducted a "vacillating policy which drained public funds into a futile transfusion." With regard to his own command in the field, Stilwell's conclusion was that it had been vitiated by lack of the right to "order" his troops, with the result that he could not form strategy nor direct tactics. In criticism of his own country and profession he found that American military education had proved deficient. Lacking knowledge of the methods and characteristics of foreign countries, our men "knew how to deal only in the American way and when this failed to bring results they became confused and lost patience." He believed the educational system would have to take account of this problem if the United States expected to hold a leading place among the international armies of tomorrow.

Challenging American policy, the report closed with a condemnation of Chiang Kai-shek's Government, a reproval of the United States' commitment to its support and a prediction of its downfall. At the bidding of the General Staff the contents were reduced to a manageable volume of under 700 pages, but even then Stilwell was told that if he wanted to have it officially published he would have to cut out his unsparing criticism of Chiang and the British. He refused, effectively assuring the report's suppression.

Stilwell's judgment might have been worth listening to. "There was no American in China at that time, or perhaps ever," wrote A. T. Steele, correspondent in China for the *Chicago Daily News* and other papers from 1932 to 1950, "who was in a better position to observe the Generalissimo at his best and at his worst."

There were others too whose advice was not taken. In anguish at the conduct of policy, the political officers of the Embassy despatched in February an unprecedented joint telegram signed by Atcheson as Chargé d'Affaires in Hurley's absence. They warned that the policy of continued support for Chiang Kai-shek was making him unwilling to compromise;

meanwhile, as witnessed in person by one of their number in a three months' tour of the northern areas, the Communists were increasing in strength and bringing closer the unavoidable dilemma when the United States would have to decide, following a landing in China, whether to accept or refuse cooperation with them. Plans had been drawn by Wedemeyer's command to put U.S. parachute troops into Communist territory to "organize, lead and command," as it was put with combined innocence and arrogance, Communist guerilla troops against the Japanese. No working arrangements could be made, however, until Chiang Kai-shek settled the terms under which the Communists should enter the Government. The Embassy officers argued that the only way to compel Chiang toward unity was to tell him, not ask him. They advised that the American decision to cooperate with the Communists should be made now, with or without the Generalissimo's consent, and he should be so informed. Their telegram was forwarded by Under Secretary Grew with a favorable recommendation to the White House on March 2 in the same week that Stilwell's report was delivered to the Pentagon.

It was no accident that the foreign service officers took this step when Hurley was in Washington, for their advice was in effect and intention a vote of no confidence in the Ambassador. Hurley was under instructions to support the recognized government, keep it from collapse and press for immediate unification of the Nationalist and Communist armed forces. He was to act as go-between to bring the two parties into some form of agreement. Starting with breezy overconfidence, he was soon, for all his native shrewdness, over his depth. Pleased by the flattering attentions showered on him by the Kuomintang, and lacking knowledge of the domestic background or appreciation of the depth of the problem, he listened to the persuasive voices of Chiang Kai-shek's circle and accepted their repeated assurances that everything could be arranged. Yet despite meetings and truces, offers and counteroffers, he was making no real progress toward the coalition for which his Government was pressing. For Washington the urgency was growing. A China on the brink of civil war could not fill the vacuum that would be left by the defeat of Japan. In addition it was feared that if the split were not closed the Soviet Union might reach some arrangement with the Communists for control of Manchuria.

The frustrations and difficulties rattled Hurley who began to exhibit increasingly explosive behavior, raging and cursing, disrupting every Embassy routine and alienating the staff to the point of complete and mutual mistrust. Hurley considered that the reports of Service, Ludden and others urging a realistic policy more independent of the Kuomintang and more cognizant of the Communists were undermining his efforts. Convinced of a conspiracy against him, he conducted complicated negotiations with the Chinese with only a sergeant as stenographer, and reported to Washington without consulting his staff. Their conviction in turn that his reports were dangerously one-sided and misleading led to their filing reports of their own which were not submitted to him as chief of mission, and led finally to the group telegram of February.

Upholding Hurley against the staff, the President ruled that America could not aid the Communists unless Chiang Kai-shek consented. The decision was grounded on the same issue of sovereignty on which he had recalled Stilwell. American policy remained fixed in the proper position of refusing to deal independently with, or aid, a dissident group in domestic conflict with the sovereign government. This was correct but unreal. The sovereignty of the Central Government was a husk, just as its democracy was an illusion. The Communists were not, as Hurley maintained in a statement to Chou En-lai, merely one of the political parties of China different from the rest only because it was armed, but a virtually independent body with the de facto attributes of statehood—political organization, territorial control and an army. The Communist pretense, for the time being, that they were merely an element within the state and willing to negotiate unification on certain terms helped to confuse the issue but not the facts. They were dynamic and growing while the Kuomintang was eroding.

This was not hidden from Washington. Secretary Stettinius (who had succeeded the ailing Hull in November 1944) advised the President in January 1945 that Chiang resisted coalition because it would mean the end of Kuomintang domination and open the way "for the more virile and popular Communists . . . who are daily growing stronger" to extend their influence, possibly to the point of controlling the Government. Failure to settle with them, on the other hand, could invite "the danger of eventual overthrow of the Kuomintang."

The Generalissimo was not that worried. Consistent American support made him feel stronger than he was and defeated its own purpose by assisting him to be adamant instead of moving him toward concessions. He underestimated the strength of the Communists and misunderstood his own situation because, as Stilwell had so often complained, no one told him the truth—or otherwise admitted it. Ho Ying-chin's "ridiculous" estimates of Communist strength, revealing his "utterly unscrupulous disregard of truth," indicated to an exasperated officer of the China desk "the hopelessness of efforts to effect unity in China as long as men of this type exercise important influence."

The American Government, by nature nervous of the new, was unable to summon the resolution to loosen its support of Chiang and risk his fall.

Following the decision to uphold Hurley, the dissenting foreign service officers in fairness to the Ambassador were reassigned to other posts. The Communists drew the indicated conclusion that American policy was not coming their way. They began to move toward suspicion which later events were to deepen into hostility. It lay anyway not far below the surface in basic antiforeignism and in ideological enmity to an "imperialist" state. On the American side the no less intrinsic fear of Communists as property-takers was certainly an element in the making of policy. Whether or not Roosevelt shared it, he was well aware of its dangerous potency in domestic politics. Probably his determining reason above all the rest was fear that he could not afford to let Chiang crumble now although he himself had little illusion left that China under Chiang's Government could fill the role of great power that he had planned.

This was made clear by his disposal without Chiang's knowledge or consent of certain of China's interests to the Soviet Union at Yalta. The Yalta Agreement of February 1945 was a hard-driven bargain to secure Soviet combat—in default of Chinese—against Japan. The concessions to Stalin, apart from issues in Poland, involved Soviet resumption of the old Czarist rights to Dairen and the Chinese Eastern Railway. These were coupled with Soviet acknowledgment of China's "full sovereignty" over Manchuria and of readiness to conclude a pact of friendship and alliance with Chiang Kai-shek as head of the recognized government. It was not the concessions but the invited reappearance of Russia in Manchuria that was to make Yalta a red flag of future controversy.

What determined the need was the Chinese vacuum. It had long been taken for granted that Russian ground forces were required to defeat the Japanese Kwantung Army in Manchuria. This was an absolute for which the President had to rely on the advice of the military. At this time the atomic bomb had not yet been tested, the war in Europe not yet won, and owing to miscalculation by military intelligence of Japan's capacity to prolong resistance, the war against Japan was expected to last for 18 months after the defeat of Germany. Despite some opinion to the contrary, the prevalent view of the strategists was that direct invasion of the Japanese home islands would be necessary, with the possibility of as many as a million American casualties. Beyond that was the fear of the Kwantung Army, an almost self-sustained force, joining with the Japanese armies in China proper to continue the fight and perhaps, as General Deane, chief of the Military Mission in Moscow, envisaged, "set up a new Japanese state."

Roosevelt's concessions at Yalta were reckoned in terms of American lives. He had to give something, for as Stalin frankly said, why should Russia join the war against Japan if she were not to get anything for it?

If the Chinese had been able to play an active military part the need to bring in the Russians would have been correspondingly less. Had Stilwell's program for an effective combat force of 90 divisions been accomplished there might have been no Yalta.

On February 10, 1945, the belated Legion of Merit for "constancy of purpose and untiring zeal" was awarded to Stilwell along with the Oak Leaf cluster of the DSM in recognition of the "tremendous magnitude and complexity" of his achievement in opening the Road. As he pinned on the medals Secretary Stimson said he had never awarded any decorations that gave him more pleasure. They were no compensation to Stilwell for missing action that was taking place elsewhere. He hated Washington which seemed to him "as big a pile of manure as Chungking was." To Win he wrote, "Unless something active comes my way I am going to do what I told you (ask for a division) and put the onus on the W.D."

In the back of his mind was the hope of commanding the eventual landing on the China coast. The triangle Luzon-Formosa-south China still figured in strategic plans. On February 7 he noted a speculative article by the United Press which listed candidates for Commanding General of the China invasion as himself, MacArthur and Nimitz, in that order. Stilwell had never been a man content to wait for fortune to drop in his lap. When Nimitz came to Washington he called on him and whether or not the subject was broached, recorded the meeting as "very cordial." Accompanying a group of soldiers to the White House on March 8, he found no evidence that the President would be an impediment. "FDR held on to me after the session and talked about the shortage of men and seriousness of attack on Japan. Said he was pleased the Ledo Road was named after me. He looked terrible but not as bad as the Yalta pictures." To his aide on the way out Stilwell even expressed a grudging approval as if, now close to the weary end, he had felt for a brief moment a ray of the Roosevelt charm. A little over a month later, on April 12, the President was dead. The most consistent supporter of China as a great power and, whatever his illusions, the most determined to align the China of the future on America's side, he died too soon to know—unless he had a glimmer— what would be the fate of his efforts.

Return to China seemed not impossible to Stilwell. Merrill came in from the theater to report that he was missed, that "not ten people were with CKS in my affair," that Sun Li-jen had proposed a petition to FDR from Chinese officers for his return. According to reports, Wedemeyer and his staff "are making a case that we messed it up so badly that even they will have trouble putting it straight." When, however, a Japanese attack on Kunming seemed imminent, the recourse of the Generalissimo and

Wedemeyer was to demand the recall from Burma of the two original divisions, the 22nd and 38th, which had trained and fought with Stilwell. The 22nd and 14th, another Ramgarh-trained division, were airlifted back to China for the emergency, unnecessarily as it proved. Owing to increased American air attack and the need to protect the Canton-Hankow Railway and guard the coast against a possible American landing, the Japanese offensive in south China was not renewed.

As Stilwell had before him, Wedemeyer planned a drive to the coast at Canton by Chinese divisions, based on resources far greater than had been available to his predecessor. Hump deliveries reached the unprecedented total of 46,000 tons in January 1945, supplemented by the Road and pipeline which Stilwell's campaign had opened. The Generalissimo agreed to the campaign but despite harmony in Chungking performance proved as elusive as it had for Stilwell. Wedemeyer made a handsome show of cordial relations with the Generalissimo and of the ease with which respect for the amenities won his cooperation, but his reports to Marshall had a familiar ring. "If only the Chinese will cooperate!" he wailed. The Generalissimo and his adherents were "impotent and confounded," the high command stultified by "political intrigues and false pride," staff commanders "incompetent to issue directives," the Chinese SOS "terrifyingly inefficient."

Free of these troubles, Stilwell kept alert to the struggle that was taking place over command in the Pacific. A friend in the War Department after a long talk "says it will boil down to me. The Administration can't take Doug." On the contrary, MacArthur like the Himalayas could not be avoided. He considered himself the natural choice for command of the entire war in the Pacific but until now this had been divided on a geographical basis between him and Nimitz. In April as the focus narrowed toward Japan the command was reorganized with MacArthur designated Commander-in-Chief of all U.S. Army forces in the Pacific on a par with Nimitz in command of all naval forces.

On April 1 Okinawa, largest of the Ryukyu chain lying between Formosa and the southern tip of Japan, had been invaded and was currently being fought for in the fiercest, costliest and most savagely defended of all the island battles. Possession of the island 350 miles from the center of Japan would allow the B-29s to mount a more intensive attack on Japanese industry and lines of communication with the mainland than was possible from Guam and Saipan in the Marianas. With their fleet outmatched, the Japanese brought out a last desperate weapon—the kamikaze suicide planes. Day after day the screaming pilots flung themselves in fatal dives upon the assembly of American ships supporting the invasion and achieved fearful destruction. On shore the greatest concentration of artillery the defenders could assemble, in contest against the guns and planes and flame-throwers of the American Tenth Army, tore the island into a chaos of mud and ruins but was unable to throw off the invaders. Since the Japanese could not reinforce, there was little doubt of the outcome.

On May 8 victory was won in Europe. For the last phase against Japan the advocates of direct invasion prevailed over those who argued that bombardment, blockade and encirclement would suffice to bring surrender. The plan now adopted was for a two-phase invasion beginning with attack on Kyushu, southernmost of the home islands, with a target date of November 1, 1945, followed four months later by invasion of Honshu, the main island. The first phase, named OLYMPIC, would be carried out by the Sixth Army consisting of twelve divisions, and the second phase, named CORONET for the crowning attack, by the Eighth and Tenth Armies totaling 25 divisions. The First Army, transferred from Europe, would be in reserve. MacArthur was charged with the conduct of the campaign on land and Nimitz with its naval and amphibious phases.

That Soviet entry into the war would pin down the Japanese armies on the mainland was a precondition assumed by MacArthur notwithstanding the beclouding of this issue in later years by the hot air of the cold war. The expected difficulty of the invasion was reflected by the official estimate, even after V-E Day, despite a body of more optimistic opinion within the War Department, that the defeat of Japan was still 15 months distant.

The capture of Okinawa obviated the need for the China coast. It was expected that the Japanese army in east and south China would probably be withdrawn to hold the Yangtze valley or reinforce the home islands, leaving entrance to the ports of south China unopposed. No plans for a forced landing in China were drawn. That long-expected climax which had shimmered on the horizon throughout Stilwell's years in China faded away. Subsequently in June the Japanese began evacuating the region captured in the east China campaign of 1944. Burning and demolishing Kweilin, Liuchow, Nanning and other cities before they left, they withdrew to the coast and to the north. The Chinese forces were able to reenter the wasted area without a battle.

Stilwell had known MacArthur since cadet days when they were only a class apart at West Point. If there were to be any openings, he judged the source would be where the MacGregor sat and he determined to go to the source if he could. Marshall was cooperative. A mission to the Pacific fronts to survey the needs of Army commanders in relation to the functioning of the Army Ground Forces was arranged. At a final talk on May 10 Marshall "had nothing to offer except that I could go and make my own arrangements. . . . Doug obviously out of control; W.D. afraid of him. So I'll go out and look around. Talked to Dorn, Bergin and Jones about it. They all say GO." Without formal orders Dorn and Bergin arranged to go along as the nucleus of a staff for Stilwell, just in case. He left on May 21 and after tours of the islands en route reached Manila on May 25. MacArthur greeted him cordially and in character: he made a speech. "Says he wants a friend to speak up for him." He urged Stilwell to go everywhere, see everyone, talk to Krueger and Eichelberger, commanders of the Sixth and Eighth Armies, make suggestions and give him ideas.

A month was passed in this occupation including a visit to Okinawa where Stilwell's own 7th Division from Fort Ord was fighting as part of the Tenth Army. Caves, holes and tombs from which the Japanese were flushed by flamethrowers were everywhere. "The poor Okinawans have had even their ancestors blown to pieces." Men were pinned down in mud two feet deep for days under incessant fire. Both sides fought in a daze of death and misery. Ultimate casualties for the 60-mile island were 12,000 Americans killed, 36,000 wounded, over 100,000 Japanese killed and 8,000 prisoners.

On June 18, the day before Stilwell was due to leave, MacArthur asked him if he would serve as his Chief of Staff. "Told him No, I fancied myself as a field commander." MacArthur asked if he would be willing to take an army despite his four stars. Stilwell replied he would take a division to be with troops. "Pooh pooh," said MacArthur, "if you would take an Army I would rather have you than anyone else I know." He discussed the Tenth Army which was an apple of discord between himself and Nimitz who retained command of operations on Okinawa. The commander of the Tenth, General Simon Bolivar Buckner, leaned toward Nimitz. MacArthur said that if he could get the Tenth Army away from the Navy he would like to have Stilwell command it, if Marshall agreed. Stilwell started for home the following day. At Guam, his first stop, he learned that General Buckner had been killed by a shell on Okinawa. He sent a radio to MacArthur telling where he could be reached and continued eastward. On arriving in Honolulu, he found the hoped-for message: "Command Tenth Army. Return to Guam at once."

On June 23 Stilwell took over command of the Army he could expect to lead in the crowning attack on Japan. Ten days earlier the Joint Chiefs had ordered plans to be made for the possible contingency of Japan's sudden collapse or surrender. In New Mexico the operation called Manhattan Project was nearly ready for the first test of its product. What would come of it was unknown nor did commanders in the field know of its existence. Operations in Okinawa had reached the mopping-up stage. The task of developing the island as a base and rehabilitating and preparing the Tenth

Army for the ultimate battle remained. Stilwell found it a high-pressure 24-hours-a-day job hampered by a lack of coordination and drive. "I have got to be an s.o.b. or risk disaster." The greatest compliment he ever received, he said later, was when 7th Division men, looking up from a hole as he passed in a jeep, called "Hey guys, Joe's back!" in voices that sounded pleased.

His notes filled up with plans and ideas for the invasion including the increased use of tactical aviation which, with obvious reference to an old colleague, he wanted under ground control, assuring better teamwork than in the past and worthwhile results "if properly coordinated." On July 6, about the time these remarks were being written, their target, General Chennault, angrily resigned his command of the Fourteenth Air Force. He was pushed by Marshall and Arnold who, in the course of a reorganization, named Stratemeyer over his head as air chief in China. Chennault's energetic fighting record could not cancel the mistrust which his resort to outside channels and pressures induced in his superiors. In a mammoth letter of resignation composed for him by Alsop, whose hyperactivity was part of its cause, Chennault closed his military career "with bitterness" and deposited the blame for all that had gone wrong in China on Stilwell.

On July 16 the atomic bomb was successfully but still secretly tested in New Mexico. From July 17 to August 2 Truman and Churchill met with Stalin at the Potsdam Conference and summoned Japan to surrender unconditionally or face "prompt and utter destruction." The ultimatum was rejected by Japan's military rulers although civilian efforts to reach a negotiated peace through Russia had already been opened with the Emperor's consent. In the meantime the Joint Chiefs warned MacArthur and Nimitz that preparations for a possible Japanese capitulation had become a "pressing necessity." The plan of action in case of surrender, code-named BLACKLIST, which reached Stilwell on August 3 provided for the Tenth Army to occupy Korea. "Manila is optimistic about it," he noted. At the same time planning for the invasion continued. He learned that the British were to participate in CORONET with a corps of one Canadian, one Australian and one Indian division. "To be under my command. My God." The arrangement had been approved by the War Ministry. "They said they knew where they stood with me. . . . Mountbatten has to give up units for this operation! Life is funny."

On August 6 the atomic bomb was dropped on Hiroshima. On August 8 the Russians entered the war. On August 9 a second bomb was dropped on Nagasaki. "Revolutionary all right. Human civilization approaching suicide rapidly. I will now acknowledge that the Japs may quit. Russia plus the bomb should do the trick." An unanticipated result of the bomb was to provide Japan with a face-saving reason for quick surrender and that development now followed more precipitately than foreseen. After an intense struggle over the status of the Emperor, ending in American agreement to his retention, Japan surrendered on August 14.

"SO IT IS OVER," Stilwell recorded as he had once before in 1918. Although it meant that the opportunity to command American troops in battle was gone for good, he shared the immense relief of everyone. No sensible man looked forward to the invasion of Japan. His first thought was for his youngest son just turned eighteen. "I am so thankful we don't have to throw Ben into the pot," he wrote to Win, "that I don't care what they do with the God damn emperor. . . . Hooray, Hooray. We have survived. No blanks in our list. Lucky people."

His own immediate future looked disappointing. As a result of the "Doug-Nimitz hate," the Tenth Army was being torn apart like the baby offered for Solomon's judgment. Except for corps used separately, it appeared to be out of the occupation forces. From MacArthur Stilwell learned of an added complication: Chiang Kai-shek had questioned Washington about a rumor that General Stilwell would be in command of U.S. troops to land on the China coast; Truman had replied that General Stilwell would not land on the China coast. MacArthur professed to believe that a query to Washington asking whether Korea was included in the China coast would undoubtedly be answered "yes." He did not want to risk delay in the movement of his occupation forces. He promised to put the Tenth Army in Japan later if it could be arranged. Stilwell was bitter. "So they cut my throat once more"—in deference to Chiang Kai-shek.

News from the mainland was brought by visiting correspondents. "China in a mess. Danger of U.S. getting embroiled. Reds linking up with Russians." The problem of ensuring the surrender of more than a million Japanese in China proper and almost as many in Manchuria was enormous. Confronted with the overwhelming task, unexpected so soon, of reoccupying the major cities from Canton to Peking, not to mention Manchuria which had been under Japanese rule for 15 years and Formosa for 50, the Central Government had neither plan, organization nor resources equal to the need. Transportation, always China's greatest handicap, was in shreds with 90 percent of railroads out of operation, rolling stock and river shipping destroyed, and roads as inadequate as ever. For ultimate control of the country, the return of Government forces to the key cities of north China and Manchuria before the Communists could gain them was the most urgent concern. American air and sea transport of the troops to Shanghai, Peking, Tientsin, Tsingtao and other places was made available. In the north, clash with Communist units heading for the same ports and cities was inevitable. American aid to one side and not the other in the race made involvement in the civil conflict more than likely, and the added hos-

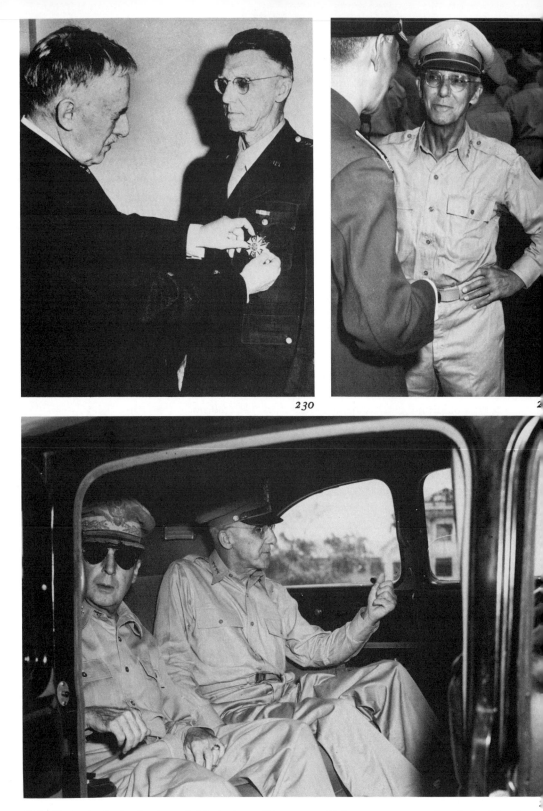

*Stilwell received the Legion of Merit from Stimson on February 10, 1945 (230). In May he w[ ]
to Manila, where MacArthur greeted him cordially (232), and on September 2 he was presen[ ]
the surrender of Japan aboard the* Missouri. *Here he chats with a Chinese general after the cerem[ ]
(231).*

233

234

235

On September 7 Stilwell himself presided at the Ryukyu surrender (233) and signed the surrender document (234). Earlier he had visited Okinawa, where his own 7th Division from Fort Ord was fighting, and where he sloshed through the mud with General "Hap" Arnold (235).

tility of the non-aided side certain. Stilwell could see only one solution. "We ought to get out—*now*," he wrote firmly on August 19.

He was to have the satisfaction, he learned, of taking the formal surrender of the enemy, if not on the grounds of his own battle in Burma at least in the Ryukyus, and of attending the full ceremonial surrender of Japan scheduled for September 2 in Tokyo Bay. With other officers he arrived in the defeated country two days in advance of the ceremony and took a harsh pleasure in touring the gutted and burned-out districts of Yokohama and staring at the once arrogant "buck-toothed bastards," now living in shanties of scrap lumber and tin and scratching in the dirt to plant onions. The helpless rage he had shared in the 1930s at the brutalities inflicted on China and the humiliation of foreigners was revenged. "We gloated over the destruction and came in feeling fine."

Seen through Stilwell's eyes the ceremony on board the *Missouri* had not quite the quality wanted for schoolbooks. Boarding the battleship as the ranking American Army officer in the group, he led the way to the quarter deck where the group took their places and waited. Eleven Japanese representatives, headed by Foreign Minister Shigemitsu for the civilians and General Umezu for the military, climbed on deck and took their places too; "hard cruel hateful faces under excruciating humiliation as we stared at them." Lined up at attention, they stood silently, looking straight ahead. "No one spoke. We just looked at them . . . for well over ten minutes. It must have seemed ten years to them." MacArthur, the designated representative of all the Allies, emerged from the Admiral's cabin, took his place and made his speech with hands and legs trembling noticeably: "Krueger says it is not nervousness but palsy but it looked like hell." Shigemitsu and Umezu then signed the surrender, followed by MacArthur, while Generals Wainwright and Percival who had surrendered at Bataan and Singapore respectively, and had been in Japanese prison camps ever since, stood beside him. Stilwell's comments about Percival, beginning with "the weakest sister I have ever seen, even in the British army," and elaborating, were unnecessarily nasty. When venting certain prejudices the vinegar flowed in excess.

Led by Nimitz for the United States, the Allied representatives then signed individually. Except for the American Admiral and the Chinese, they appeared to Stilwell a "scratchy-looking crowd": the Englishman "a fat red dumpling," the Australian "a tub of guts," the Canadian "an elderly masher of the gigolo type," the Frenchman "rather trim" but with a pair of "dirty-looking apaches" as aides, the Dutchman fat and bald, the New Zealanders amateur-looking. "What a crew of caricatures in the eyes of the Japs. The human race was poorly represented."

On September 7 he himself presided at the Ryukyu surrender at which the Japanese were represented by two generals and an admiral. The painful ten-minute wait standing at attention as the focus of all eyes was repeated before Stilwell made his appearance. GIs yelled, "That's right, Joe, make 'em wait. Keep 'em waiting, Joe." The band struck up the General's march, Stilwell took his place at the table, signed the document, issued instructions through an American Nisei sergeant for the three Japanese to sign and, as a massed group of 100 Navy fighters and 60 B-29s flew past, closed the proceedings. "Just cold hard business." His war was over.

Afterwards on learning that the Tenth Army was not to take part in the occupation but to return to the United States on October 15, he made one more attempt to reenter China. While on a second visit to examine Japan, he radioed Marshall on September 26 for permission to go to Peking to see old friends. After a week's wait while the Generalissimo's reaction was being queried by Stratemeyer, the answer was no. Evidently fearing Stilwell's influence or intentions, Chiang Kai-shek replied that owing to the presence of both Communist and Japanese troops in Peking the situation was "confusing" and pending the entry of Nationalist troops (which six weeks after the surrender had still not arrived) a visit by General Stilwell might be exploited by the Communists. He promised that a formal invitation to visit China would be extended to Stilwell "as soon as the situation of the country becomes normal." Unfortunately the trend of the situation was not toward normality. Stilwell took it as a compliment that "my presence is not desired on the continent of Asia. . . . Maybe CKS thinks I would start a revolution. . . . I would like to do just that." It was done without him. He was not to see China again.

When Stilwell returned home on October 18, 1945, he had a year minus a week left to live. He could normally expect to retire in March 1947 on reaching sixty-four. With the Tenth Army dissolved, he was temporarily assigned to duty in Washington as President of the War Equipment Board, eliciting the comment, "I am eminently suited to something else and would just as lief sit on a tack." Closer to the mark the *Army Times* nominated him to be soldiers' representative at the peace table as the man who "has seen more front line combat than any other top-ranking officer in this war." The world was spared a peace conference and Stilwell's Washington duty fortunately lasted only a few weeks. In January he was happily and fittingly reassigned as Commander of the Sixth Army in charge of the Western Defense Command with headquarters at the Presidio of San Francisco within a few hours of Carmel.

Before he left Washington the American entanglement in China erupted in another furor equal to his own recall. On November 25 Hurley resigned his Ambassadorship with the sensational public charge that "a considerable section of our State Department is endeavoring to support Communism generally as well as specifically in China."

After V-J Day American support for China through the maintenance of Wedemeyer's command and the continuance of Lend-Lease had been prolonged for six months until the Japanese could be repatriated and the threatening specter of civil war somehow suppressed. Nursed by every American agency of persuasion and mediation, the negotiations between Chungking and Yenan were kept alive while their forces were already meeting and firing in sporadic conflicts. Mao Tse-tung and his chief lieutenants, Chou En-lai and Chu Teh, repeatedly protested the lifting of Chiang's armies to the north by American air transport and warships, as well as the landing of Marines to hold cities in advance of the Nationalists' arrival and the continuing supply of arms to Chungking. The rationale for this assistance was the ominous presence of large bodies of armed Japanese. To the Communists, straining to extend their hold in north China and gain Manchuria, it appeared as intervention. It fed their hostility and eroded American influence as mediator since America appeared committed to one side in the mediation.

Risks of American involvement in the civil strife were underfoot at every turn, and explosive incidents often only narrowly avoided. Approaching Chefoo, a strategic port across the bay from Dairen, an American convoy was warned by the Communists not to land because the 8th Route Army already held the port and the region. The American admiral and Marine general in command of the convoy, on ascertaining that this was in fact the case and that conditions were orderly with no Japanese troops or prisoners of war in the area, sensibly reported that there was "no military reason for landing U.S. troops at this time" and withdrew. Coolness and common sense could not be expected always to prevail. Meanwhile the Generalissimo's demands for assistance mounted, including the equipping of 90 divisions through Lend-Lease as rather airily promised by Roosevelt at Cairo. Chiang's organization and resources were proving all too obviously inadequate to establish control. Loyalty at the cost of competence left him with a General Staff and a body of officials at a loss to cope with the enormous problems they faced. They were soon absorbed in the endless opportunities for deals and graft which accompanied the takeover of cities from the former puppet regime. In the north, where the Government lacked any popular support, the situation was especially unpromising. As early as August 15 Colonel Yeaton, new chief of the Military Observers Mission in Yenan, warned that despite Communist numerical inferiority, "over a long period of time as an occupying force the Kuomintang cannot hold out even with U.S. help."

In the painful light of this prospect the State-War-Navy Coordinating

Committee (SWNCC, known to Washington as "Swink") was directed to work out a policy. The best it could offer was a general directive of October 22 stating that America's aim was to see China a friendly, unified, independent nation "with a stable government resting, in so far as practicable, on the freely expressed support of the Chinese people." Under this canopy, acts and decisions in China continued to tie the United States to a government which met none of the criteria.

Nationalist forces lifted into the northern provinces by American agency naturally met and clashed with Communist units. On November 11 the Military Attaché in Chungking reported, "The fighting is becoming more bitter and larger numbers of men are becoming involved." That it would be possible to disarm and evacuate all the Japanese without becoming involved in the civil war seemed less and less likely. The decision was pressing whether to deactivate Wedemeyer's command and close Lend-Lease as scheduled at the end of the year. Was the United States to terminate aid to the Generalissimo and let the situation seek its own level—which meant civil war and defeat of the American purpose—or persist in the effort to help a failing government extend its rule to areas where it was strongly challenged?

The decision to continue that effort was determined by the new world alignment. No sooner was Fascism defeated than Communism loomed as the new enemy. The presence of Soviet armies in Manchuria and the prospect of their making common cause with the Chinese Communists was now America's worry despite a formal accord reached by the Russians with Chiang Kai-shek. The dilemma in China sharpened. The most earnest and anxious consultations of State-War-Navy and the President could recommend no other course than to continue to invest in the Generalissimo while bringing pressure on both sides to make concessions toward a representative government.

The situation had become too much for Hurley. Under the new Administration he again believed himself the victim of a conspiracy in which Truman and Secretary of State Byrnes and Under Secretary Acheson were listening to his critics and preparing to replace him by a "deserving Democrat." Returning to Washington in November, he repeated earlier threats to resign but was persuaded by Truman and Byrnes to go back to China and try again. The next day in a sudden reversal, without informing the President or Secretary, Hurley made his dramatic announcement directly to the press.

His accusation captured the spirit of the time. Since the dissolution of wartime alliance with the Soviet Union, innate fear and hate of Communism reasserted itself in America. On that dark yeast, grudge, ambition and vindictiveness could feed, and demagogues grow fat. Hurley opened the journey toward the tawdry reign of terror soon to be imposed with such astonishing ease by Senator Joe McCarthy. The time of hysterics had arrived. America's China policy was its central issue, the agents and partisans of Chiang Kai-shek, collectively known as the China Lobby, its promoters. A first step had already been taken in June 1945 with a raid on the offices of the pro-Communist magazine *Amerasia* and the resulting arrest along with five others of John Service. Copies of his reports from Yenan were found in the *Amerasia* files. When sent back to Washington by Stilwell the previous autumn, Service had indiscreetly lent the drafts of his reports to the magazine's editor as part of the effort to inform the press. A grand jury found no grounds for indictment in his case and he was reassigned on Stilwell's recommendation to MacArthur's staff in Tokyo. But the hounding of the China foreign service officers through multiplying loyalty investigations and subversion hunts had barely begun. The attacks and savagery that were soon to rage over America's China policy wrecked careers, blasted reputations and by the eventual dismissal of Davies, Service and others cowed the future exercise of independent judgment in the foreign service.

For the present China confronted the American Government with a foreign crisis and domestic hazards both of alarming potential. Truman acted rapidly. In the hope of canceling the effect of Hurley's explosion he asked General Marshall, a figure above politics who commanded national respect, to take up the mission to bring truce and united government to China. Marshall had just retired as Chief of Staff a week previously and was looking forward with his wife to his first relief from the unbroken burden of six years. His sense of duty, in the same tradition as Stilwell's, allowed only one answer when called on by the Commander-in-Chief: he accepted. After his intimate connection with Stilwell's experience in China, he might have hesitated but he felt urgently the need to try to save the purpose for which America had fought in the Far East. As a principal architect of victory he may have felt an extra interest in protecting it.

To compel the parties to an agreement he was instructed to use the movement of troops to north China as his lever. In confirming his instructions Marshall himself determined their crucial point. It was his understanding, he said to Truman and Byrnes, that if the Communists refused to make reasonable concessions, he would move Nationalist troops to north China. On the other hand if the Generalissimo refused to make concessions and this led to a breakdown in the effects for unity, the United States could not abandon him because "there would follow the tragic consequences of a divided China and of a probable Russian resumption of power in Manchuria . . . resulting in the defeat or loss of the major purpose of our war in the Pacific." Under these circumstances he understood that he was to "go ahead and assist the Generalissimo in the movement of troops to North China" at least until the evacuation of Japanese was completed. Truman and Byrnes concurred.

It was essentially a decision for counter-revolution. The same choice was made in former colonial territories where, contrary to the late President's intent, American forces were actively helping to restore French rule in Indochina against a strong movement for independence. In charters and declarations American aims were democratic but in practice the executants opted for the old regime. In China the decision was not merely futile; it aligned America in popular eyes with the oppressor and landlord and tax collector, it disheartened the liberal forces and violently antagonized the future rulers. While many suspected that the effort was misguided, American policy could not readjust. It preferred the status quo even when the status quo was a sinking ship. There seemed to be no feasible alternative. To abandon the legal government for the Communists was not within American capacity and would have meant political suicide at home. The only other possibility was Stilwell's advice to "get out—*now*" and this was ahead of its time by a year and a half.

Stilwell snorted when he learned the terms of Marshall's mission from General Byroade who was to accompany Marshall as his chief assistant. Held by the Pearl Harbor hearings until the last minute before departure, Marshall sent Byroade, a veteran of CBI, to ask Stilwell's advice. Stilwell asked what were Marshall's instructions and concluded that the mission would not succeed. Once Chiang Kai-shek sensed the situation he would merely become more intransigent. "Don't you realize the Chinese respect only power?" he said to Byroade several times in the course of the conversation. Later as he watched the troubles develop, he summed up the Marshall mission in one of his sharp, apt phrases: "But what did they expect? George Marshall can't walk on water."

The comment was written in a letter of April 6, 1946, which by virtue of another remark it contained was to become notorious. "Isn't Manchuria a spectacle?" Stilwell wrote. Then followed the comment about Marshall, and then the sentence, "It makes me itch to throw down my shovel and get over there and shoulder a rifle with Chu Teh." * The itch represented for Stilwell, as for so many others, an inclination toward the Chinese Communists that was simply the obverse of disgust with the Kuomintang. His casual

* The addressee is unknown. The letter in Stilwell's handwriting came into the possession of Johannes Steel, a pro-Communist free-lance journalist. After Stilwell's death he published it in photostat, with the name of the addressee torn out, in the first issue (January 1947) of his newsletter, *Report on World Affairs*. The letter was given notoriety by Joseph Alsop, who made much of Stilwell's reference to Chu Teh in testimony before the Senate Internal Security hearings in 1951.

remark tossed off in a private letter was seized upon by extremists of both left and right and made the foundation of a marvelous ideological structure purporting to demonstrate his allegiance to Yenan. Promoted by Alsop, the structure was to reach a peak of creative imagination in testimony given by General Chennault to a Congressional investigating committee in 1952. He said that in July 1945 Stilwell proposed to take the Tenth Army (scheduled for the invasion of Japan) to "the coast north of Shanghai, north of the Shensi River [*sic*]," where he would arm 200,000 or 300,000 Communists and lead them south to capture Shanghai. In short, in the most immense and fearsome operation of the war, he credited Stilwell with planning all on his own to lead half the invasion fleet to another destination, presumably leaving the attack on Japan to be carried out by the Eighth Army alone. Only the unlimited accusations of the McCarthy era combining with the relentless animus of Alsop and Chennault could have produced this remarkable fiction.

While in command at San Francisco Stilwell kept his connection with the Weapons Board and in this capacity was sent as an observer of the two tests of atomic bomb effects at Bikini in the Marshall Islands in July 1946. On his return after a month's absence Win noticed a physical change in him: he appeared shrunk and unwell and complained of lack of energy. During the remainder of the summer he suffered from chills, occasional dizziness and bouts of exhaustion, several times falling asleep in a chair. Medical tests discovered "something suspicious in my liver." The next day, as if in defiance, he walked miles—for the last time. On September 28 he entered Letterman General Hospital and on October 3 underwent an abdominal operation which disclosed cancer of the stomach with metasteses to the liver in a more advanced stage than suspected. It had obviously been in his system for a long time. He had had no pain, which mystified the doctors.

It was known that although he had the DSC, DSM and Legion of Merit, his one wish was for the Combat Infantryman Badge, a simple pin with a wreathed rifle generally reserved for the enlisted foot soldier who proved himself under fire. Award of the badge to General Stilwell was announced on October 11 by Secretary of War Patterson who had succeeded Stimson. The badge was not, however, pinned on in a bedside ceremony lest Stilwell realize that he was dying. He slept during most of the last two days, woke briefly to ask the nurse, "Say, isn't this Saturday?" (it was), and died in his sleep shortly after noon on October 12, 1946.

According to his wish no public funeral was held; his body was cremated and the ashes scattered over the Pacific. In the flow of comment and tribute, editorials referred again and again to his "I claim we took a hell of a beating" as evidence of "tough-mindedness" and a refusal to pretend. Emphasis was on the "Vinegar Joe" who had captured the public imagination as had only a handful of military men, according to the *Atlanta Constitution,* in the life of the nation. "They'll have a hell of a time replacing him," was General Merrill's succinct summary.

There was little assessment of his role in China where the confusion and flux of the hour allowed no perspective. The nearest was Colonel Carlson's characteristic superlative, "No more devoted friend of the Chinese people has ever appeared on the pages of history." Chiang Kai-shek marked the passing of his great detractor by a very small Christian service in a private home in Nanking with no prior publicity or announcement and only the American Ambassador, John Leighton Stuart, and a few invited Americans, but no Chinese, in attendance. To those present it seemed a sad, mean ceremony for the man who had commanded the American war effort in China, but its very inadequacy suggested that Stilwell's ideas for the army had gathered too strong a following for the Generalissimo's comfort.

Stilwell died too soon to see his prescription to "get out" accepted. Marshall's efforts proved fruitless. He could neither unite the contenders nor, when that failed, sufficiently reinvigorate the Central Government to enable it to take hold. In the year after V-J Day between 400,000 and 500,000 Nationalist troops were ferried by American agency to Shanghai, Nanking and key cities in Manchuria and north China; 50,000 American Marines were landed to hold ports, coal mines and railroad centers; $600,000,000 of Lend-Lease arms and ammunition and other matériel was supplied and economic assistance extended. No infusion was enough because none was used effectively. In the effort to compel Chiang Kai-shek to cease hostilities which he could not win, Marshall shut off the supply of arms to the Nationalists in July 1946, without effect. The Generalissimo, as Marshall said later in echo of a spry small ghost, "simply does not know what is going on." Supported by a "dominant group of reactionaries" in the Kuomintang who frankly stated their belief that cooperation with the Communists was inconceivable and that only force could settle the issue, he remained recalcitrant, counting on American support whatever happened. The dominant group among the Communists was equally unwilling to try for a settlement. Though numerically inferior in armed forces, they counted on economic collapse accelerated by guerilla warfare to bring down the Government. In contrast to the Kuomintang, they were organized, Marshall noticed, from the grass roots up "with the strength that gives them in public support."

On October 1, 1946, Marshall notified the Generalissimo who had launched an offensive toward Kalgan that he would discontinue mediation unless a basis for agreement with the Communists were found without delay. No concessions were proposed. In December Marshall warned Chiang in person that the Communists were too strong to be defeated militarily and that negotiations offered the only way to avert the collapse of China's economy. Chiang was impervious to the advice. That month, after a year in China, Marshall notified Truman that his mission had failed. He was recalled early in January 1947 to become Secretary of State. Washington announced termination of the effort to mediate a settlement and withdrawal of American forces. Within a year and a half of victory in the Far East, the goal it had been meant to achieve had receded beyond reach, in mockery of the American effort.

As Secretary of State, Marshall remained convinced that the Kuomintang could not win the civil war without American military intervention. To this he was steadily and unalterably opposed, nor was there any public sentiment calling for it. Under the rising heat of political pressure, demands for every other kind of help were strident. Arms sales to the Nationalists were resumed, various missions were sent and $400,000,000 of economic assistance was extended by the China Aid Act of 1948. Denounced by the Communists as a useless prolonging of the civil war, this aid was used to generate a wave of anti-American feeling in the weary populace. Chiang's forces under "the world's worst leadership" (in the words of General Barr, chief of a new Army Advisory Group) lost crucial battles; entire divisions defected to the Communists; economic chaos increased popular detestation of the discredited Kuomintang. In October 1948 the Generalissimo declared that the salvation of Asia depended on China and he hoped "the American people and their statesmen will dedicate their lives to this task." Madame came to Washington to ask for a new aid program of $3 billion over three years and a declaration of American determination to defeat Communism.

There was no support now that could have been effective. Born of the imperfect Revolution of 1911, crippled by the Japanese before it was fully established, and renegade to its origins, the Kuomintang had spent its mandate in one generation. In December 1948 the Communists took the crucial city of Hsuchow, the legendary key to control of China. In April 1949 their forces swept across the Yangtze. In ensuing weeks the Generalissimo's Government, followed by some two million adherents, decamped to Formosa where it successfully established itself with American support. The Middle Kingdom was left to the ungentle reign of a new Revolution.

Would the fate of China have been different if Stilwell had been allowed to reform the army and create an effective combat force of 90 divisions? "I myself firmly believe," wrote General William R. Peers, who as a colonel had served as chief of the OSS guerilla unit in Burma, "that had Stilwell's plan for equipping, organizing, and training the Chinese ground forces been carried through to completion, Japanese infantry would not have been able to overrun the air bases in south China in 1944 . . . nor would the Chinese Communist ground troops have achieved their ends after the war against the Japanese was over."

This assumption might have been true if Asia were clay in the hands of the West. But the "regenerative idea," Stilwell's or another's, could not be imposed from outside. The Kuomintang military structure could not be reformed without reform of the system from which it sprang and, as Stilwell himself recognized, to reform such a system "it must be torn to pieces."

In great things, wrote Erasmus, it is enough to have tried. Stilwell's mission was America's supreme try in China. He made the maximum effort because his temperament permitted no less; he never slackened and he never gave up. Yet the mission failed in its ultimate purpose because the goal was unachievable. The impulse was not Chinese. Combat efficiency and the offensive spirit, like the Christianity and democracy offered by missionaries and foreign advisers, were not indigenous demands of the society and culture to which they were brought. Even the Yellow River Road that Stilwell built in 1921 had disappeared twelve years later. China was a problem for which there was no American solution. The American effort to sustain the status quo could not supply an outworn government with strength and stability or popular support. It could not hold up a husk nor long delay the cyclical passing of the mandate of heaven. In the end China went her own way as if the Americans had never come.

The Combat Infantryman Badge awarded to Stilwell in his last days by Under Secretary of War Robert Patterson (236).

Afterword

The question that readers of this book invariably ask is whether the course of events would have been different if the major agent of the United States in China had been a more tactful and diplomatic man than General Stilwell. What other course of events the questioner has in mind is never quite articulated, but the implication seems to be that, given a more suave character as commanding general in the CBI theater and as Chief of Staff to the Generalissimo, we might not have "lost" China.

The answer is of course that *we* did not "lose" China to the Communists; the Kuomintang did.

It is the theme of this book that, whatever the thorns of Stilwell's character, he represented the best instrument in terms of goodwill and military talent that the United States could have employed; no one else could have brought to the task the same knowledge of the country combined with the same steadfast devotion to duty and effective generalship. Further, it is my theme that even with these qualities, American intervention did not and could not have basically directed China's destiny one way or another.

It should also be clear that an American commander more agreeable to Chiang Kai-shek could have had only one effect: to conceal behind a façade of amiability the hollowness of the Generalissimo's rule, thus prolonging for that much longer America's investment in a hollow cause. This would have been the result under Generals Hurley and Wedemeyer. They could have polished the Generalissimo's ego, but they could not have sustained him against the Communist revolution for one more day, nor would continuation of American aid, as Secretary of State George Marshall recognized in 1948, have overcome the corruption and lackadaisical performance of the Nationalist army to transform it into a force capable of effective combat against the Revolutionary army.

Stilwell's inability to conceal his contempt for Chiang Kai-shek, far from losing us a stalwart ally, prevented us from wasting further investment in a bankrupt client and saved us from what would have been a fatal move into active military intervention. Unfortunately, Stilwell's example had no lasting effect. Since Chiang Kai-shek, the United States' choice of clients, from Ngo Dinh Diem of Saigon, to the Shah of Iran, to the recent leaders of Argentina, Chile and Central America, has not been notably perceptive. Tact and diplomacy do not always serve a nation's best interests; thorny characters have their uses.

APPENDIX

Road-Building 1921: Haphazard Conversations

BY MAJOR JOSEPH W. STILWELL

The Messenger

The Messenger has returned from (presumably) delivering a letter.

Q. Did you deliver the letter?

A. Yes.

Q. To whom did you give it?

A. I gave it to Mr. Oleson.

Q. But Mr. Oleson was not there. He is here now. You could not have given it to him.

A. Oh, no. I gave it to the interpreter.

Q. But the interpreter is also here with Mr. Oleson, and says you did NOT give it to him.

A. Oh, yes, I gave it to the cook.

Q. What cook?

A. The cook up there.

Q. Up where?

A. At Hsieh Kung Ling.

Q. But there is no cook, or house, or anything at Hsieh Kung Ling.

A. Yes, I really gave it to the cook.

Q. But listen to me! There IS NO COOK there! To whom did you give the letter?

A. I gave it to the ma-foo [groom].

Q. What ma-foo?

A. Mr. Oleson's ma-foo.

Q. But Mr. Oleson has no ma-foo, so you did not give it to him.

A. Ma-foo?

Q. Yes, ma-foo-ma-foo. Mr. Oleson has no ma-foo.

A. Oh, I gave the letter to the other letter-carrier.

About this time the average foreigner gives it up and either writes another letter, murders the messenger, or goes home by the next boat. The next morning the letter is probably found on the dining-room table.

The Mayor of Ch'i K'ou

The Ch'u Chang, or mayor, of Ch'i K'ou wished to make a decided impression at his first call on the visiting engineers. They might bring the road through his town, and strangely enough, in view of the feeling in other towns, they were most anxious to have it. Probably because if it went to Chun Tu, they realized that Ch'i K'ou's fame as a Yellow River port would sadly dwindle. So behold the Ch'u Chang, five feet two in his stockings, marshalling his body-guard, a six-foot policeman, into position for an imposing entrance. The policeman carries a huge lantern with honorific characters painted on it, and precedes his chief, who smooths down his garments, opens his fan, coughs discreetly, bows three or four times and begins:

The Ch'u Chang: Your honorable name? (He knows, but he has to ask.)

The Eng.: How dare I? My unworthy name is Shih.

C. C.: Your honorable country is America, is it not?

Eng.: Yes, my barren country is America.

C. C.: So. And when will the road reach Ch'i K'ou?

Eng.: Oh, it is not yet determined.

C. C.: Ch'i K'ou is a great port,—all the business of the Yellow River is done here. And Chun Tu is not a very desirable place,—no business, no houses, nothing. It would never do to take the road *there*.

Eng.: But is the route shorter to Ch'i K'ou or to Chun Tu?

The mayor, never having been to Chun Tu or seen the route, turns his head over his shoulder and with a deep frown and in a gruff voice shouts out the question to the policeman.

C. C.: Is the route shorter to Ch'i K'ou or to Chun Tu?

Pol.: (In the timid voice of a three-year-old child) Old Grandfather, it is shorter to Chun Tu.

The answer makes the Ch'u Chang furious, but he controls himself and says mildly to the Engineer who of course has already heard it,—

C. C.: It is shorter to Chun Tu.

Eng.: And is there any other road from Liu Lin direct to Ch'i K'ou?

C. C.: (Shouting to the policeman) Is there any other road from Liu Lin direct to Ch'i K'ou?

Pol.: Old Grandfather, there is a road direct from Liu Lin.

C. C.: (To Eng.) Yes, there is a road direct to Liu Lin.

Eng.: How far is it from Liu Lin to here?

C. C.: (Shouting to policeman) How far is it from Liu Lin to here?

Pol.: Old Grandfather, one hundred li.

C. C.: (To Eng.) It is one hundred li.

Eng.: But is it a good road?

C. C.: (Shouting to the policeman) Is it a good road?

Pol.: It is a good road for camel, not much rock, mostly dirt. . . .

And so the double-relay conversation proceeds.

The Culvert

Enter a coolie, just the usual type, with his pants very evidently cut to fit him in the squatting position, sleeveless vest, straw hat, aimless look. He edges in slowly, as if we had as much time as he has, and after trying to size up the crowd and decide who is boss, gives it up and whispers to the interpreter. The latter, in a stage whisper, says: "There he is—the one with the muddy shoes and no shirt. But don't call him *Mu-shih* (Missionary —the customary salutation). It makes him excited. He is an engineer."

John then shuffles over and addresses the Engineer as *Hsien sheng* or Before Born, an honorific title suggesting that the person addressed is older, hence presumably more learned and entitled to respect on account of seniority.

John: Before Born, the culvert . . .

Eng.: What culvert?

John: Why, *the* culvert, of course.

Eng.: But what about it? WHAT ABOUT IT?

John: Before Born, it is about the culvert.

Eng.: Yes, yes. But what do you *want?* What did you come for?

John: I came about the culvert.

John is now beginning to think that this foreigner must be considerably of an ignoramus. Chief engineer! Why, *any* old engineer should know more than a coolie, and yet, apparently, he doesn't.

Eng.: All *right*. But what do you want of me? What do you want me to *do* with the culvert?

John: I built the culvert.

Eng.: Do you want to get paid for it?

John: What?

Eng.: Do-you-want-to-get-paid-for-it?

John: Paid for what?

Eng.: My God! For the culvert!

John: I do not understand.

The engineer does not bite a radiator, because there are none handy. Instead he swallows four or five times, and then says sweetly,—

Eng.: What stake are you working at?

John: Stake? Stake? *What* stake?

Eng.: (Trying again) Where are you working?

John: I am not working.

   O-H-H-H-H-H-H ! ! !

Eng.: Yes. But where have you been working? (A glimmer, a glimmer, sure!)

John: I have been working Mu Ts'un east side.

Eng.: Ah! ! ! And did you build a culvert?

John: Yes, I built a very fine culvert.

Eng.: And did you get paid?

John: Yes, but it was hardly enough for the men to buy food to eat.

Eng.: Is that why you came? Do you want me to give you more money?

John: Oh, no.

Eng.: What do you want?

John: The culvert. Hsieh Ts'un west side there is also a culvert. (We have it! We have it!)

Eng.: Oh, you mean you want to build another culvert?

John looks at the engineer pityingly, as much as to say, "You poor object, why didn't you get that long ago instead of waving your arms, rolling your eyes, and frothing at the mouth? *I* knew it when I came in!" Then he answers gently: "Yes."

Of course, John gets the job.

BIBLIOGRAPHY
AND
NOTES

Bibliography

AND OTHER SOURCES

Archives and Manuscript Collections

STILWELL, JOSEPH W., Papers, Carmel, California, and Hoover Library, Stanford, California.

General Stilwell's papers, which were naturally my main source, are the extensive collection of a man who wrote constantly and saved everything, including football tickets of 1904. The primary document is the Diary, written in a clear hand in pencil in 50 pocket-size notebooks that cover, though haphazardly, the years 1900 to 1946. Some of these conform to the calendar year, others do not. Some contain consecutive dated entries, others are erratic. Some contain only undated random notes and sketches; others have diary entries and random notes on alternate pages. During periods of more intense activity and interest, or stress, the Diary is supplemented, as I have mentioned in the Foreword, by expanded notes, many undated, which I have called the Supplements. These are written on loose sheets of paper or, for the period from Pearl Harbor to December 1943, in four hard-cover school exercise books (called for convenience the Black and White Books I and II, the Black Book and the Data Book). The Diary, which begins with a few scattered entries in plebe year at West Point, was not continuous; the hiatuses generally coincide with Stilwell's periods of residence in the United States. He made daily entries, however, during both wars and for most of the period of his service in China except for a blank space in his first year with the

543

15th Infantry. During his travel when he was sightseeing the entries became especially copious.

In addition to the Diary and its Supplements, Stilwell kept letters written to him during most of his career, and Mrs. Stilwell kept the letters he wrote to her and to other members of the family during his long absences from home. The Stilwell Papers also include his formal writings—essays, sketches, short stories, articles and speeches—as well as photograph albums of pictures taken by him on his journeys through China, and scrapbooks of newspaper clippings. The contents of both albums and scrapbooks, to the torture of the historian, are undated and unidentified.

The Diary and Supplements from Pearl Harbor to November 1944, as well as a major part, though by no means all, of the correspondence and records of the CBI command, are at the Hoover Library in Stanford. Since inter-Allied World War II documents, especially those pertaining to China, are not yet declassified, the Army has gone through the Hoover collection and removed a considerable portion, politely leaving a white slip in each instance in mute witness of its passage. Fortunately, in many cases copies of the removed documents are available elsewhere.

The main body of the Stilwell Papers remains in Mrs. Stilwell's possession at her home in Carmel (cited in my Notes as "Carmel"). These have been arranged by the family and myself, acting as amateur archivists, in four groups. The A, or career file, folders 1-40, covers the years 1911 to 1946. These contain official orders and correspondence, G-2 reports and other historical material during the tours of duty in China, lectures and tactical studies at Benning, the loose Supplements to the Diary for the 1920s and 30s, and letters received on professional matters or (during World War II) from the public. The B, or personal and family file, folders 1-19, covers the years 1883 (and previous family history) to 1946. This contains school and family records, correspondence to and from parents, wife, children and friends, and domestic records of various kinds. The C, or literary, file, folders 1-4, covering the years 1906-46, contains essays, sketches, poems, speeches, and many notes for or drafts of studies of various kinds. The D file contains photographs and newspaper clippings.

It may be noticed by a close student of the subject that my quotations from the Diary and Supplements do not invariably exactly coincide with those of the same date selected and published by Theodore White in *The Stilwell Papers* and by Romanus and Sunderland in their volumes on the CBI theater in the official series, *The U.S. Army in World War II*. The reason for the discrepancies is that in some cases I have quoted from the daily Diary where they have quoted from the Supplements, or vice versa. Likewise my citations do not necessarily agree with those of Romanus and Sunderland because the papers are no longer in the order in which those editors arranged them.

THE NATIONAL ARCHIVES, Army Records (now Modern Military Records Division), referred to in the Notes as NA. Documents are cited under RG (Record Group), MSO (Military Secretary's Office), AGO (Adjutant General's Office).

OFFICE OF THE CHIEF OF MILITARY HISTORY (OCMH). This is not a repository of documents, but it has on file interviews recorded by its historians (see under ROMANUS and SUNDERLAND). I am indebted to this Office and to the Modern Military Records Division of the National Archives for making available to me on request particular documents from the World War II archives which could be declassified.

BINGHAM, SENATOR HIRAM, Papers, Library of Congress. Senator Bingham, who visited Peking in 1927, appeared from Legation documents to have been escorted by Stilwell for part of his visit. On further investigation, this proved to have been a cover (see Chapter 5); his papers, while containing nothing relevant to Stilwell, include some interesting contemporary material on China.

CHENNAULT, MAJOR GENERAL CLAIRE LEE, Papers, Hoover Library, Stanford, California (and microfilm copy at Library of Congress).

HOPKINS, HARRY, Papers, Franklin D. Roosevelt Library, Hyde Park, New York.

HORNBECK, STANLEY K., Papers, Hoover Library, Stanford, California. (Access to this collection, which occupies an entire loft at the Hoover Library, was kindly made available to me by Dr. Kenneth Glazier when the collection was first acquired, before it had been catalogued or inventoried. I have cited the documents according to the heading on the box or file as Mr. Hornbeck left them.)

JOHNSON, NELSON T., Papers, Library of Congress.

McHUGH, COLONEL JAMES, Papers, Cornell University, Ithaca, New York. (I am indebted to Miss Rebecca Fox for search of this collection.)

ORAL HISTORY PROJECT, Columbia University, New York, New York. See under LI TSUNG-JEN and RAVDIN, DR. ISIDOR.

ROOSEVELT, FRANKLIN D., Papers, Franklin D. Roosevelt Library, Hyde Park, New York. Documents are cited as PSF (President's Secretary's File), PPF (President's Personal File) and OF (Official File).

STIMSON, HENRY L., Papers, Yale University, New Haven, Connecticut.

FILMS: National Archives, Film Division; also Army Pictorial Center, Long Island City, New York. (The Signal Corps, which appears to have been everywhere and never missed anything, provides in its motion-picture film a source of unsurpassed historical value.)

Books, Articles and Individual Manuscripts

ABEND, HALLETT, My Life in China, 1926-41, New York, Harcourt, 1943.

ALEXANDER, FIELD MARSHAL EARL, "Report" in Wavell, Operations in Burma from 15 December 1941 to 20 May 1942, Supplement to the London Gazette, 5 March 1948.

ALSOP, JOSEPH, "Why We Lost China," *Saturday Evening Post*, 7, 14, 21 January 1950.

ANDERS, LESLIE, *The Ledo Road*, Norman, Univ. of Oklahoma Press, 1965.

ARNOLD, GENERAL H. H., *Global Mission*, New York, Harper, 1949.

ARNOLD, RALPH, *A Very Quiet War*, London, Hart-Davis, 1962.

BAILEY, THOMAS A., *Woodrow Wilson and the Great Betrayal*, New York, Macmillan, 1945.

———, *The Man in the Street: The Impact of American Public Opinion on Foreign Policy*, New York, Macmillan, 1948.

BARRETT, COLONEL DAVID D., "Soldiers of Fortune, unpublished manuscript.

———, "The Dixie Mission," unpublished manuscript.

BEALE, HOWARD K., *Theodore Roosevelt and the Rise of America to World Power*, Baltimore, Johns Hopkins, 1956.

BELDEN, JACK, *Retreat with Stilwell*, New York, Knopf, 1943.

———, *Still Time to Die*, New York, Harper, 1944.

BERTRAM, JAMES, *First Act in China: The Story of the Sian Mutiny*, New York, Viking, 1938.

BISSON, T. A., *Japan in China*, New York, Macmillan, 1938.

BLAND, J. O. P., *China: The Pity of It*, New York, Doubleday, 1932.

BLUM, JOHN M., *From the Morgenthau Diaries*, 3 vols., Boston, Houghton Mifflin, 1959-67.

BOOKER, EDNA LEE, *News Is My Job*, New York, Macmillan, 1940.

BORG, DOROTHY, *American Policy and the Chinese Revolution, 1925-28*, New York, American Council, Institute of Pacific Relations, 1947.

———, *The United States and the Far Eastern Crisis of 1933-38*, Cambridge, Harvard Univ. Press, 1964.

BROUN, HEYWOOD, *The A. E. F.*, New York, Appleton, 1918.

BRYANT, SIR ARTHUR, *The Turn of the Tide: A History of the War Years Based on the Diaries of Field Marshal Lord Alanbrooke*, New York, Doubleday, 1957.

———, *Triumph in the West* (continuation of the above), New York, Doubleday, 1959.

BUCK, PEARL S., *My Several Worlds*, New York, John Day, 1954.

BULLARD, MAJOR GENERAL ROBERT LEE, *Personalities and Reminiscences of the War*, New York, Doubleday, 1925.

BURNS, JAMES MACGREGOR, *Roosevelt: Soldier of Freedom*, New York, Harcourt, 1970.

BURR, LIEUTENANT COLONEL JOHN C., *The Framework of Battle*, Philadelphia, Lippincott, 1943.

CARLSON, COLONEL EVANS FORDYCE, *The Chinese Army*, New York, American Council, Institute of Pacific Relations, 1940.

———, *Twin Stars of China*, New York, Dodd Mead, 1940.

CHENNAULT, MAJOR GENERAL CLAIRE LEE, *Way of a Fighter*, New York, Putnam, 1949.

CHIANG MONLIN, *Tides from the West: A Chinese Autobiography*, New Haven, Yale Univ. Press, 1947.

CHURCHILL, WINSTON, *The Second World War*, vol. III, *The Grand Alliance*; vol. IV, *The Hinge of Fate*; vol. V, *Closing the Ring*; Boston, Houghton Mifflin, 1950-51.

CLINE, RAY S., *Washington Command Post: The Operations Division*, Washington, Dept. of the Army, Historical Division, 1951.

CLUBB, O. EDMUND, *Twentieth Century China*, New York, Columbia Univ. Press, 1966 (first published 1964).

COLLIER, BASIL, *The Second World War: A Military History in One Volume* (the British view), New York, Morrow, 1967.

COLLIER, LIEUTENANT COLONEL THOMAS WATTS, "The Chinese Language Officer Program of the U.S. Army, 1919-43," unpublished Ph.D. thesis for Department of History, Duke University, 1966.

COLLIS, MAURICE, *Foreign Mud*, London, Faber, 1946.

————, *Last and First in Burma, 1941-48* (based on Dorman-Smith papers), London, Faber, 1956.

CROW, CARL, *400 Million Customers*, New York, Harper, 1937.

————, *Foreign Devils in the Flowery Kingdom*, New York, Harper, 1940.

CULLUM, GENERAL GEORGE W., *Biographical Register of the Officers and Graduates of the USMA*, New York, Harper, 1940.

DAWSON, RAYMOND, *The Chinese Chameleon*, London, Oxford Univ. Press, 1967.

DEANE, JOHN R., *The Strange Alliance*, New York, Viking, 1947.

DENNETT, TYLER, *Americans in Eastern Asia*, New York, Macmillan, 1922.

DICKMAN, MAJOR GENERAL JOSEPH T. (Commander of the IVth Corps), *The Great Crusade: A Narrative of the World War*, New York, Appleton, 1927.

DORN, BRIGADIER GENERAL FRANK, "Walkout," unpublished manuscript.

DULLES, FOSTER RHEA, *China and America: The Story of Their Relations Since 1784*, Princeton Univ. Press, 1946.

DUPUY, COLONEL R. ERNEST, *The Compact History of the United States Army*, New York, Hawthorn, 1956.

EISENHOWER, DWIGHT D., *Crusade in Europe*, New York, Doubleday, 1948.

ELDRIDGE, FRED, *Wrath in Burma*, New York, Doubleday, 1946.

EPSTEIN, ISRAEL, *The Unfinished Revolution in China*, Boston, Little, Brown, 1947.

EVANS, LIEUTENANT GENERAL SIR GEOFFREY, *Slim, as Military Commander*, London, Batsford, 1969.

FAIRBANK, JOHN K., *The United States and China*, Cambridge, Harvard Univ. Press, 1948.

FAIRBANK, J. K., REISCHAUER, E. O., and CRAIG, A. M., *East Asia: The Modern Transformation*, Boston, Houghton Mifflin, 1965.

FEIS, HERBERT, *The China Tangle*, New York, Atheneum, 1965 (first published by Princeton Univ. Press, 1953).

FERGUSSON, BERNARD, *The Black Watch*, New York, Crowell, 1950.

FERRELL, ROBERT H., *Frank B. Kellogg and Henry L. Stimson*, in *American*

Secretaries of State and Their Diplomacy, vol. XI, New York, Cooper Square, 1963.

FIFTEENTH INFANTRY, *The Fifteenth Infantry Regiment, 1861-1953*, n.p., n.d.

——, *Customs of the Fifteenth Infantry*, Peiyang Press, Tientsin-Peiping. (A facsimile reproduction is published by C. E. Dornbusch at Hope Farm Press, Cornwallville, New York, 1959.)

FINNEY, CHARLES G., *The Old China Hands*, New York, Doubleday, 1961.

FLEMING, D. F., *The United States and the League of Nations, 1918-20*, New York, Putnam, 1932.

FORMAN, HARRISON, *Horizon Hunter*, New York, McBride, 1940.

FRILLMAN, PAUL, and PECK, GRAHAM, *China: The Remembered Life*, Boston, Houghton Mifflin, 1968.

GILBERT, RODNEY, *What's Wrong with China*, London, John Murray, 1926.

GOETTE, JOHN, *Japan Fights for Asia*, New York, Harcourt, 1943.

GREW, JOSEPH C., *Ten Years in Japan*, New York, Simon & Schuster, 1944.

GRIFFITH, GENERAL SAMUEL B., *The People's Liberation Army*, New York, Council on Foreign Relations (McGraw-Hill), 1967.

GRISWOLD, A. WHITNEY, *The Far Eastern Policy of the United States*, New York, Harcourt, 1938.

GUNTHER, JOHN, *Inside Asia*, New York, Harper, 1939.

——, *Roosevelt in Retrospect*, New York, Harper, 1950.

HAHN, EMILY, *The Soong Sisters*, New York, Doubleday, 1943.

HAN SUYIN, *Birdless Summer*, New York, Putnam, 1968.

HARBORD, GENERAL JAMES G., *The American Army in France*, Boston, Little, Brown, 1936.

HO YUNGCHI, *The Big Circle: China's Role in the Burma Campaigns*, New York, Exposition, 1948.

HOLCOMBE, ARTHUR N., *The Spirit of the Chinese Revolution*, New York, Knopf, 1930.

HOSACK, ROBERT E., "The Shantung Question and the Senate," *South Atlantic Quarterly*, April 1944.

HSIUNG, S. I., *The Life of Chiang Kai-shek*, London, Davies, 1948.

HUBBARD, SAMUEL T. (a neighbor of the Stilwells in Yonkers), *Memoirs of a Staff Officer*, Tuckahoe, Cardinal Associates, 1959.

HULL, CORDELL, *Memoirs*, 2 vols., New York, Macmillan, 1948.

HUNT, ELVID, *History of Fort Leavenworth*, General Service Schools Press, Fort Leavenworth, 1926.

HUNTINGTON, SAMUEL, *The Soldier and the State*, Cambridge, Harvard Univ. Press, Belknap Press, 1957.

INFANTRY SCHOOL, FORT BENNING, GEORGIA, *Mailing List,* vols. I-VIII, 1930-34, semi-annual.

IRIYE, AKIRA, *Across the Pacific*, New York, Harcourt, 1967.

ISAACS, HAROLD R., *The Tragedy of the Chinese Revolution*, Stanford Univ. Press, 1938, rev. ed. 1951.

——, *No Peace for Asia*, Cambridge, M.I.T. Press, 1967 (first published 1947).

————, *Scratches on our Minds: American Images of China and India*, New York, John Day, 1958.

JANOWITZ, MORRIS, *The Professional Soldier*, Glencoe, Free Press, 1960.

JAPAN, *Operations of the Japanese Forces in Burma*, documents submitted by HQ Japanese Burma Area Army to HQ (British) Twelfth Army, Rangoon, issued by HQ Twelfth Army, November 1945.

JOHNSON, CHALMERS, *Peasant Nationalism and Communist Power*, Stanford Univ. Press, 1962.

KATES, GEORGE N., *The Years That Were Fat: Peking, 1933-40*, New York, Harper, 1952.

KING, ERNEST J., and WHITEHILL, WALTER MUIR, *Fleet Admiral King*, New York, Norton, 1952.

KIRBY, MAJOR GENERAL S. WOODBURN, *The War Against Japan*, 4 vols. (UK Military Series, History of the Second World War), London, HMSO, 1957-65.

KLEEMAN, RITA HALLE, *Gracious Lady* (Sara Delano Roosevelt), New York, Appleton, 1932.

KOLKO, GABRIEL, *The Politics of War*, New York, Random, 1968.

LANGER, WILLIAM L., and GLEASON, EVERETT, *The Challenge to Isolation, 1937-40*, New York, Harper, 1952.

————, *The Undeclared War, 1940-41*, New York, Harper, 1953.

LEAHY, FLEET ADMIRAL WILLIAM D., *I Was There*, New York, Whittlesey, 1950.

LEONARD, ROYAL, *I Flew for China: Chiang Kai-shek's Personal Pilot*, New York, Doubleday, 1942.

LI TSUNG-JEN, *Reminiscences*, Chinese Oral History Project, East Asian Institute, Columbia University.

LIGGETT, MAJOR GENERAL HUNTER, *A. E. F. Ten Years Ago in France*, New York, Dodd Mead, 1928.

LINEBARGER, PAUL, M. A., *The China of Chiang Kai-shek*, Boston, World Peace Foundation, 1941.

LIU, F. F., *A Military History of Modern China*, Princeton Univ. Press, 1956.

LOHBECK, DON, *Patrick J. Hurley*, Chicago, Regnery, 1956.

MACARTHUR, DOUGLAS, *Reminiscences*, New York, McGraw-Hill, 1964.

MAGRUDER, GENERAL JOHN, "The Chinese as a Fighting Man," *Foreign Affairs*, April 1931.

MALRAUX, ANDRÉ, *Man's Fate* (*La Condition Humaine*), New York, Smith & Haas, 1934.

MARSHALL, GEORGE C., *The War Reports of Marshall, Arnold and King*, Philadelphia, Lippincott, 1947.

MARSHALL, KATHERINE TUPPER, *Together: Annals of an Army Wife*, New York, Tupper & Love, 1946.

MATLOFF, MAURICE, and SNELL, EDWIN, *Strategic Planning for Coalition Warfare, 1941-42*, Washington, Dept. of the Army, Historical Division, 1953.

MATLOFF, MAURICE, *Strategic Planning for Coalition Warfare, 1943-44*, Washington, Dept. of the Army, Historical Division, 1959.

MAY, ERNEST, ed., *Ultimate Decision: The President as Commander in Chief* ("FDR" by William Emerson), New York, Braziller, 1960.

McINTIRE, VICE ADMIRAL ROSS T., *White House Physician*, New York, Putnam, 1946.

MILES, VICE ADMIRAL MILTON E., *A Different Kind of War*, New York, Doubleday, 1967.

MOLEY, RAYMOND, *After Seven Years*, New York, Harper, 1939.

MORGENTHAU, HENRY, JR., *Morgenthau Diary, China*, 2 vols., U.S. Senate, 89th Congress, 1st Session, Committee on the Judiciary, Subcommittee to Investigate the Administration of the Internal Security Laws, Washington, GPO, 1965. (The Subcommittee's staff, on the hunt for subversion, extracted and published in this compilation all the references to China in the Morgenthau Diaries, providing in the process a documentary source of unique and inestimable value.)

MORISON, ELTING E., *Turmoil and Tradition: The Life and Times of Henry L. Stimson,* Boston, Houghton Mifflin, 1960.

MORSE, H. B., and MacNAIR, H. F., *Far Eastern International Relations*, Boston, Houghton Mifflin, 1931.

MORTON, LOUIS, *Strategy and Command: The First Two Years*, Washington, Dept. of the Army, Historical Division, 1962.

MOTT, COLONEL T. BENTLEY, *Twenty Years as a Military Attaché*, Oxford Univ. Press, 1937.

MOUNTBATTEN OF BURMA, VICE ADMIRAL THE EARL, *Report to the Combined Chiefs of Staff by the Supreme Allied Commander, South East Asia, 1943-45,* London, Houghton Mifflin, 1951.

NEVINS, ALLAN, *The United States in a Chaotic World, 1918-33*, New Haven, Yale Univ. Press, 1950.

NIXON, EDGAR B., *Franklin D. Roosevelt and Foreign Affairs* (documents from the Hyde Park Library), 3 vols., Cambridge, Harvard Univ. Press, 1969.

O'CONNOR, RICHARD, *Black Jack Pershing*, New York, Doubleday, 1961.

OGBURN, CHARLTON, JR., *The Marauders*, New York, Harper, 1959.

PECK, GRAHAM, *Two Kinds of Time*, Boston, Houghton Mifflin, 1950.

PEERS, WILLIAM R., and BRELIS, DEAN, *Behind the Burma Road*, Boston, Little, Brown, 1963.

PEFFER, NATHANIEL, *The Far East: A Modern History*, Ann Arbor, Univ. of Michigan Press, 1958.

PELISSIER, ROGER, ed., *The Awakening of China, 1783-1949* (an anthology of contemporary accounts and primary sources), New York, Putnam, 1967.

PERSHING, GENERAL JOHN J., *My Experiences in the World War*, 2 vols., New York, Stokes, 1931.

PHILLIPS, WILLIAM, *Ventures in Diplomacy*, Boston, Beacon, 1952.

POGUE, FORREST C., *George C. Marshall*, vols. I and II, New York, Viking, 1963, 1968.

POWELL, JOHN B., *My 25 Years in China*, New York, Macmillan, 1945.

PRATT, JULIUS, *Cordell Hull*, 2 vols., in *American Secretaries of State and Their Diplomacy*, New York, Cooper Square, 1964.

PUSEY, MERLO J., *Charles Evans Hughes*, 2 vols., New York, Columbia Univ. Press, 1963.

RASMUSSEN, A. H., *China Trader*, New York, Crowell, 1954.

RAVDIN, DR. ISIDOR, *Reminiscences*, Chinese Oral History Project, East Asian Institute, Columbia University.

REINSCH, PAUL S., *An American Diplomat in China, 1913-19*, New York, Doubleday Page, 1922.

RIDGWAY, MATTHEW BUNKER, *Soldier* (memoirs), New York, Harper, 1946.

ROMANUS, CHARLES, and SUNDERLAND, RILEY, *Stilwell's Mission to China* (cited as R&S*), Washington, Dept. of the Army, Historical Division, 1953.

———, *Stilwell's Command Problems* (cited as R&S**), Washington, Dept. of the Army, Historical Division, 1956.

———, *Time Runs Out in CBI* (cited as R&S***), Washington, Dept. of the Army, Historical Division, 1959. The authors of these volumes, with resources open to them which no individual investigation could duplicate, have produced out of the vast mass of military and political records an extraordinarily thorough, detailed, inclusive and eclectic documentation of the war in CBI. In making available these sources in print, they have put everyone who enters the field afterwards in their debt.

ROMANUS, CHARLES, and SUNDERLAND, RILEY, *Two Interviews with General Merrill*, 20 and 28 April 1948; *Three Interviews with General Hearn*, 22 and 28 November 1948, 17 May 1950; *Two Interviews with General Marshall*, 6 and 13 July 1949, unpublished, on file at OCMH.

ROOSEVELT, ELEANOR, *Autobiography*, New York, Harper, 1961.

ROOSEVELT, ELLIOTT, *As He Saw It*, New York, Duell, Sloane & Pearce, 1946.

ROOSEVELT, F. D. (ed. Elliott Roosevelt), *His Personal Letters*, 2 vols., New York, Duell, Sloane & Pearce, 1950.

ROSENMAN, JUDGE SAMUEL, *Working with Roosevelt*, New York, Harper, 1952.

SCOTT, ROBERT LEE, JR., *Flying Tiger: Chennault of China*, New York, Doubleday, 1959.

SEAGRAVE, GORDON, *Burma Surgeon*, New York, Norton, 1943.

———, *Burma Surgeon Returns*, New York, Norton, 1946.

SENTINEL, THE, Tientsin. Journal of the 15th Infantry (files in the New York Public Library).

SELLE, EARL ALBERT, *Donald of China*, New York, Harper, 1948.

SEVAREID, ERIC, *Not So Wild a Dream*, New York, Knopf, 1946.

SHEEAN, VINCENT, *Personal History*, New York, Doubleday, 1935.

———, *Between the Thunder and the Sun*, New York, Random, 1943.

SHERIDAN, JAMES E., *Chinese Warlord: The Career of Feng Yu-hsiang*, Stanford Univ. Press, 1966.

SHERWOOD, ROBERT E., *Roosevelt and Hopkins*, New York, Harper, 1948.

SHIGEMITSU, MAMORU, *Japan and Her Destiny*, New York, Dutton, 1958.

SLIM, FIELD MARSHAL THE VISCOUNT, *Defeat Into Victory*, New York, McKay, 1961.

SMEDLEY, AGNES, *Battle Hymn of China*, New York, Knopf, 1943.

SMITH, ARTHUR H., *China and America Today*, New York, Revell, 1907.

SNELL, JOHN L., *Illusion and Necessity: The Diplomacy of Global War, 1939-45*, Boston, Houghton Mifflin, 1963.

SNOW, EDGAR, *Far Eastern Front*, New York, Smith & Haas, 1933.

——, *Red Star Over China*, New York, Modern Library, 1944 (first published 1938).

——, *The Battle for Asia*, New York, Random, 1941.

——, *Journey to the Beginning*, New York, Random, 1958.

——, *Random Notes on Red China, 1936-45*, Cambridge, Harvard Univ. Press, 1957.

STEELE, A. T., *The American People and China*, New York, Council on Foreign Relations (McGraw-Hill), 1966.

STILWELL, JOHN E., *Stilwell Genealogy*, vol. III, *The History of Captain Nicholas Stilwell, Son of Lieutenant Nicholas Stilwell, and His Descendants*, privately printed, New York, 1930.

STILWELL, JOSEPH W., *The Campaign in Burma, March 10 to June 1, 1942*, Headquarters, American Army Forces, China, Burma and India, unpublished. (This is the suppressed report of the First Burma Campaign.)

——, *History of the CBI Theater, 21 May 1942 to 25 October 1945*, unpublished. This is "The Stilwell Report" of which a revision and additions were made by Colonel Mason Wright in November 1945. A copy of the original is at the Hoover Library (with a number of sections removed by the Department of Defense) and another copy is at NA, Modern Military Records Division. The revised version is on file at OCMH. For a full description of the contents, see Notes to Chapter 20.

STILWELL, JOSEPH W. (ed. Theodore White), *The Stilwell Papers*, New York, Sloane, 1948.

STILWELL, WINIFRED A., "Family Story," unpublished manuscript.

STIMSON, HENRY L., *The Far Eastern Crisis*, New York, Harper, 1936.

STIMSON, HENRY L., and BUNDY, McGEORGE, *On Active Service in Peace and War*, New York, Harper, 1947.

STONE, JAMES H., ed., *Crisis Fleeting* (reports by medical officers in CBI), Washington, Office of the Surgeon General, 1969.

STORRY, RICHARD, *The Double Patriots: A Study of Japanese Nationalism*, Boston, Houghton Mifflin, 1957.

STUART, JOHN LEIGHTON, *Fifty Years in China*, New York, Random, 1946.

SYKES, CHRISTOPHER, *Orde Wingate*, New York, World, 1959.

TANG LEANG-LI, *The Inner History of the Chinese Revolution*, New York, Dutton, 1930.

THOMAS, LOWELL, *Old Gimlet Eye: The Adventures of Smedley D. Butler*, New York, Farrar & Rinehart, 1933.

TONG, HOLLINGTON K., *Dateline China*, New York, Rockport, 1950.

——, ed., *China, After Seven Years of War*, New York, Macmillan, 1945.

TOYNBEE, ARNOLD, *A Journey to China*, London, Constable, 1931

TROTSKY, LEON, *Problems of the Chinese Revolution*, New York, Pioneer, 1932.

TSOU, TANG, *America's Failure in China, 1941-50*, Univ. of Chicago Press, 1963.

TULLY, GRACE, *FDR, My Boss*, New York, Scribner's, 1949.

U.S. DEPARTMENT OF THE ARMY, HISTORICAL DIVISION, *U.S. Army in the World War, 1917-19*, vols. 1, 8, 9, 12-15, Washington, 1948.

U.S. DEPARTMENT OF THE ARMY, HISTORICAL DIVISION (OCMH), *U.S. Army in World War II*, multiple volumes, Washington, various dates. See under CLINE, MATLOFF, MORTON, ROMANUS and SUNDERLAND, WATSON.

U.S. CONGRESS, 81ST, 2ND SESSION, SUBCOMMITTEE OF THE COMMITTEE ON FOREIGN RELATIONS, *Hearings on Loyalty of Employees of the State Department*, Washington, GPO, 1950.

U.S. CONGRESS, 82ND, 1ST SESSION, *Military Situation in the Far East*, Hearings of the Committee on Armed Services and the Committee on Foreign Relations of the Senate, Part 3. (Testimony of General Hurley, 21 June 51, pp. 2859-81.) Washington, GPO, 1951.

U.S. CONGRESS, 82ND, 1ST SESSION, SENATE JUDICIARY COMMITTEE (INTERNAL SECURITY SUBCOMMITTEE), *Hearings on Institute of Pacific Relations*, Washington, GPO, 1951.

U.S. CONGRESS, 89TH, 1ST SESSION. See MORGENTHAU.

U.S. MILITARY ACADEMY, *The Centennial at West Point, 1802-1902*, Washington, GPO, 1904.

———, "The Howitzer," Class of 1904 Yearbook.

U.S. DEPARTMENT OF STATE (FAR EASTERN SERIES 30), *United States Relations with China, 1944-49* (White Paper), Washington, GPO, 1949.

U.S. DEPARTMENT OF STATE, *Foreign Relations of the United States*, annual series, Washington, GPO, various dates. Cited as USFR.

———, *Foreign Relations of the United States, Cairo-Tehran 1943*, Washington, GPO, 1961.

———, *Foreign Relations of the United States, 1942, China; 1943, China; 1944, China*, 3 vols., Washington, GPO, 1956-68. Cited as USFRC with year.

VARG, PAUL A., *Missionaries, Chinese and Diplomats, 1890-52*, Princeton Univ. Press, 1958.

———, *The Making of a Myth: The United States and China, 1897-1912*. East Lansing, Michigan State Univ. Press, 1968.

WATSON, MARK S., *Chief of Staff: Prewar Plans and Preparations*, Washington, Dept. of the Army, Historical Division, 1950.

WEDEMEYER, GENERAL ALBERT C., *Wedemeyer Reports!*, New York, Holt, 1958.

WELLES, SUMNER, *Seven Decisions That Shaped History*, New York, Harper, 1950.

WERTENBAKER, CHARLES, "The China Lobby," *The Reporter*, 15 April 1952.

WHITE PAPER. See U.S. DEPARTMENT OF STATE, *United States Relations with China*.

WHITE, THEODORE H., and JACOBY, ANNALEE, *Thunder Out of China*, New York, Sloane, 1961 (first published 1946).

WILLIAMS, GENERAL ROBERT P., MC, "Diary, 1941-45" and "One Man's CBI: A Different Kind of War," unpublished manuscripts, Hoover Library, Stanford, California.

WILLIAMS, S. WELLS, *The Middle Kingdom*, 2 vols., New York, Scribner's, 1883.

WILLKIE, WENDELL, *One World*, New York, Simon & Schuster, 1943.

WINFIELD, GERALD F., *China: The Land and the People*, New York, Sloane and American Institute of Pacific Relations, 1948.

WOODHEAD, H. G. W. (editor of *The Peking & Tientsin Times*), *The China Yearbook, 1928,* Tientsin, Tientsin Press; Univ. of Chicago Press, 1928.

WOODWARD, SIR LLEWELLYN, *British Foreign Policy in the Second World War*, London, HMSO, 1962. (Official history based on access to official documents.)

YOUNG, ARTHUR N., *China and the Helping Hand 1937-45*, Cambridge, Harvard Univ. Press, 1963.

Notes

In the interest of space I have not (except in special cases) given references for the quotations from Stilwell's diaries, letters and other writings. This was a reluctant decision since the date and source of each quotation exist in my files but to have included them would have nearly doubled the length of these Notes. Nor are references given for the standard facts of history such as the origins of the Chinese Revolution or the events of the Washington Conference. I have tried to confine the Notes to quotations (other than those from Stilwell) and to statements of fact or description whose source is not standard or self-evident.

The works of all authors cited in the Notes may be found under those authors' names in the Bibliography. I hope the reader will find this a simpler and more usable method than the deplorable "op. cit." system which requires interminable leafing back through pages of footnotes in search of the original "cit.," usually ending in a paroxysm of irritation before the source can be located. When an author has published two or more successive books on the same subject not formally labeled Vols. I, II and III, as in the case of Borg, Bryant, Langer and Gleason, Matloff, Seagrave and others, these are cited as (for example) Seagrave* and Seagrave** according to the order listed in the Bibliography; or by an identifying word from the title, as in the case of Collis, Snow and others.

When a source is obvious, as in the case of a participant mentioned by name in connection with a particular event who is also the author of a work listed in the Bibliography, I have not always thought it necessary to cite the reference.

The basic personal records of Stilwell's military career, like those of every officer, are in his 201 File, made available to me by the Adjutant General's Office with the consent of Mrs. Stilwell.

ABBREVIATIONS USED IN THE NOTES

BB	Stilwell's Black Book
B&W	Stilwell's Black and White Books
FDRL	Franklin D. Roosevelt Library
HP	Hornbeck Papers
M-Diary	*Morgenthau Diary, China*
NA	National Archives
NYT	*The New York Times*
R&S	Romanus and Sunderland
S-Diary	Stilwell's daily diary (unpublished)
SP	*The Stilwell Papers* (published version)
USFR	*Foreign Relations of the United States*, annual series
USFRC	*Foreign Relations of the United States*, China series
WD	War Department

Prologue: THE CRISIS

PAGE

1   *Roosevelt's message to Chiang*: full text, R&S**, 383-84.

3   *"If I can prove the Chinese soldier"*: Darrell Berrigan, "Uncle Joe Pays Off," *Sat. Eve. Post*, 17 Jun 44.

5   *Hurley's report of interview*: S-Diary, 12 Sep 44.

I

1 Foundations of an Officer

Family records, letters and other papers dealing with Stilwell's parentage and youth are in Carmel files B-1–5.

10   *"Business sagacity"*: J. Stilwell, *Genealogy*, III, 131.

10   *"Father was impressive"*: Mrs. Wilder to author.

11   *Words of a classmate*: William R. Wigley, letter to "Nan," 25 May 42, in West Point Archives.

11   *Yonkers High paid the football team*: *ibid.* Joe's athletic activities are recorded in one of a series of articles on school sports by Gus T. Stahl in the *Yonkers Herald*, 9 Apr 28.

11   *Dr. Baker's report*: copy in Carmel B-1.

12   *Stayed in bed for a week*: Hubbard, 77.

13   *Hazing at West Point*: 56th Congress, 2nd Session, HR, Report No. 2768, 9 Feb 01.

15   *Stilwell's demerits*: USMA, Corps of Cadets, *Register of Delinquencies*, Nos. 38, 38½.

16   *Root's principles*: Jessup, *Elihu Root*, I, 253.

17   *Life at Army posts*: *Army-Navy Journal*, Dupuy, Janowitz, Pogue, I, *passim*.

17   *Ranking officer's wife poured coffee*: K. Marshall, 8.

18   *"Scarcely conscious" of the right to vote*: Maj. G. S. Carpenter, "Major Thoughts on the Relation of the Soldier to Politics," *Journal of the Military Service Institute of the U.S.*, vol. 21 (1897), 277.

20   *Efficiency Reports*: NA, RG 94, AGO 530007.

20   *"Everyday intercourse with Frenchmen"*: letter to Military Secretary, US Army, 25 Feb 06, and reply, 21 Apr 06, NA, MSO.

21   *Requests to go "beyond the seas"*: NA, RG 94, 17 and 19 Feb 07, MSO; 23 and 25 May 07, 28 and 30 Apr 08, 30 Apr and 4 May 09, all AGO; also Carmel B-1.

21   *"Confidential Mission"*: NA, RG 165, File 4493-A; also RG 94, AGO 530007.

23   Further requests to go "beyond the seas" and other correspondence dealing with his career during this period are also in NA, RG 94 and 165.

2 Visitor to Revolution: CHINA, 1911

31   *Open Door, origin of the phrase*: Tyler Dennett, *Life of Hay*, 295.

31   *"America Assists the East"*: F. T. Gates, described as Mr. Rockefeller's secretary, *Outlook*, 9 Sep 05, qtd. Smith, 239.

33   *Millard*: articles in *Scribner's*, January, February, March 1901, qtd. Beale, 187.

33   *"Stolen, sacked, pillaged"*: Minister Rockhill to Mrs. Henry Cabot Lodge, 2 Dec 00, qtd. Beale, 187-88.

34   *John Hay on China*: Morse and McNair, 780.

34   *Theodore Roosevelt quoted*: to B. I. Wheeler, 17 Jun 05, qtd. Beale, 174.

35   *An up-river Treaty Port*: Rasmussen, 39.

35   *"Her weakness will endanger"*: Pelissier, 247.

36   *"He did not have a Chinese mind"*: qtd. Snow, *Journey*, 95.

36   *Li Yuan-hung under the bed*: Tang Leang-li, 81.

37   *American correspondent quoted*: NYT, 10 Nov 11.

40   *John Foord quoted*: NYT, 20 Oct 11.

41   *Rebel leader in Hankow quoted*: NYT, 15 Oct 11.

41   *Joint Resolution of Congress*: USFR 1912, 71.

3 The Great War: ST. MIHIEL AND SHANTUNG

42　　*Restless as ever*: Stilwell's persistent requests for overseas leave or detached service of various kinds are to be found in NA, RG 94, AGO file; also Carmel A-1.

43　　*"A very capable officer"*: Lt. Col. Lucian Holt, Efficiency Report for 1914, 201 File.

44　　*Hunter Liggett on training*: Liggett, 211.

44　　*"No swivel chair job"*: letter from Office of C/S, WD, 25 Aug 17, Carmel A-2.

46　　*Count Okuma quoted*: statement published by *Shin Nippon*, November 1914, qtd. Hornbeck, mem, 25 Nov 41, HP, File "Japan Official Statements."

47　　*"Disease and chagrin"*: Powell, 32.

50　　*"Never took thirty years"*: O'Connor, 170.

50　　*Stimson at Langres*: Stimson Diary and War Letters for February 1918 (Yale). His stay at Langres overlapped Stilwell's for four days, 23-27 Feb.

52　　*Major Belhomme's letter*: to Joseph Stilwell, Jr., 16 Jan 62, Carmel B-5.

55　　*Not "at his best or second best"*: Liggett, 159.

56　　*Schmeercase in the newspapers*: Reuters in *London Evening Journal*, 16 Sep 18; also in Paris *Herald* and French papers. A rather imaginative version of the affair is given by Hubbard, 80-83.

57　　*"Nothing but praise of your section"*: to AG, GHQ, AEF, 28 Apr 19, Carmel A-2; also special Efficiency Report by Wells in 201 File.

58　　*Shantung episode*: for the Chinese reaction see Millard, Chiang Monlin, Reinsch; for the American side see Fleming, Hosack, *Current Opinion* (September, November 1919).

59　　*"A conspiracy to rob" and other comments*: *Literary Digest*, 2 Aug 19.

59　　*Hearst press quoted*: ibid.

60　　*Senators Johnson and Borah quoted*: *NYT*, 21 Sep and 3 Oct 19; also Fleming, 328.

60　　Current Opinion: September 1919, 138.

4 Assignment to Peking: YEARS OF THE WARLORDS, 1920-23

The articles published by the magazine *Asia* are a valuable source for China in the 1920s.

61　　*Conversation with Chauncey Fenton*: as told by Stilwell to Brooks Atkinson, *NYT*, 17 Jan 43.

62   *MID requirements*: Collier, 34, 37-40; also Lt. Warren J. Clear, "Oriental Language Detail," *Infantry Journal*, August 1923.

62   *"Rape of Shantung," etc.*: *New York Mail*, New York *Sun*, Washington *Post*, Chicago *Tribune*, qtd. *Current Opinion*, September 1919.

62   *Harding's speech*: *NYT*, 22 Oct 20.

63   *Chinese language*: I am indebted for this explanation to Col. David D. Barrett.

66   *"The years that were fat"*: see Kates in Bibliography.

66   *The Language School curriculum*: report by Stilwell, 1 Jan 21, to MID, forwarded to MacMurray, then Chief of Far Eastern Division, State Department, by Sherman Miles, chief of MID, with covering letter describing Stilwell as "our best man out there." Johnson Papers, vol. 2. Other reports on the program by Stilwell in NA, RG 165, MID file.

67   *"A soft unearthly music"*: Finney, 108.

67   *Executions*: Rasmussen, 75.

68   *A picture of George Washington*: Booker, 63; see also Rodney Gilbert, "Arms and the Men in China," *Asia*, September 1922; Peffer, "Currents and Characters in China," *Asia*, January 1922.

69   *Feng and Wu at banquet*: Powell, 85.

69   *Wu's army*: Booker, 76.

70   *Military performance*: Selle, 81, 90.

71   *Part St. Paul, part Bryan*: Peffer, "Currents and Characters," *Asia*, January 1922, 72.

72   *"Bands of staggering skeletons"*: Rasmussen, 74.

72   *"Leave the work for foreign committees"*: *NYT*, 26 Dec 20, VI, 2.

72   *Wilson quoted*: 9 Dec 20, Ray Stannard Baker and William E. Dodd, *The Public Papers of Woodrow Wilson* (New York, Harper, 1925-27), VI, 227.

72   *Building the Yellow River Road*: Stilwell, "Opening China for Gas-Wagons," *Asia*, July 1924; also article by S. Hancock, civil engineer, assistant to Maj. Stilwell, in *The Oriental Motor*, Shanghai, September 1921, Carmel A-3.

74   *Profile of Yen Hsi-shan*: "Who's Who in the China Situation," *Infantry Journal*, April 1928.

74   *"Has China Found a Moses?"*: *Asia*, April 1924, article under that title.

74   *Yen entertains foreign visitors*: Booker, 109.

75   *Mrs. Stilwell's account*: "Family Story," 100.

75   Stilwell's sketches quoted in this section include "General Dope," "The Shih Li Pu Beggars," "The Amateur Doctor," "An Unorthodox Chinese Diary" (Shensi).

76   *Stilwells "different"*: Mrs. John Magruder, interview with author.

77   North China Daily News: clipping enclosed in letter from John Goette, 18 Dec 32, Carmel A-3.

78   *Feng's rule in Shensi*: Holcombe, 74ff.; Pelissier, 294; Sheridan, *passim*.

83   *"The best vote-getter"*: Powell, 71.

84   *The Washington Conference*: Bland, Griswold, Leopold, Morse and McNair, Nevins, Powell, Pusey; also HP, File "Japan, Press Clippings, 1922-24."

87   *Trip to Vladivostok*: According to the records of the NA, Stilwell's report was "destroyed by a War Department action dated 9 Jun 28."

88   *Toynbee's quatrain*: Toynbee, 253.

5 THE "CAN DO" REGIMENT AND
The Rise of Chiang Kai-shek, 1926-29

91   *Suicides at Leavenworth*: Marshall to Stimson, 27 Oct 41, Stimson Diary, 35.

91   *"Common sense and a sense of humor"*: Col. George Byroade, Efficiency Report, 8 Jul 26, 201 File.

91   *Correspondence with Whipple*: Carmel A-4.

93   *Chiang called "Billiken"*: John Emmerson to author.

93   *Whampoa*: Liu, 8-15.

94   *Slogans*: unsigned account of visit, 23 Mar 27, Bingham Papers.

95   *"Physique of an elephant"*: Chiang Monlin, 145.

95   *"With my heart thumping"*: *ibid.*, 147.

95   *"Thirty percent by fighting"*: account from Bingham Papers, cited above.

95   *Eugene Chen*: Sheean, *Personal History*, 207; *Peking and Tientsin Times*, 24 Jan 27.

96   *"The same question for which we fought"*: mem by Mr. Wm. R. Johnson, a missionary from Nanchang, 16 Sep 27, Johnson Papers.

96   *Johns Hopkins assembly*: Borg*, 74-79.

96   *"Powerful influence," etc.*: Bland, 93; Borg*, 81ff.

96   *"Elected assemblies"*: Bland, 256.

97   *Christmas Memorandum*: Borg*, 229.

98   *Press comment*: Baltimore Sun, 10 Jan, 22 Mar 27; New York *World*, 30 Jan 27; qtd. Borg*, 259, 261.

98   *Fifteenth Infantry customs*: Finney, *passim*; files of *Sentinel*; items listed under Fifteenth Infantry in Bibliography.

99   *"Cohabiting with low caste women"*: report to WD, 17 Jan 27, NA, RG 94, Box 483.

100   *Tea-drinking s.o.b.'s*: a paraphrase by Gen. Timberman, who served in the 15th Infantry, 1925-28, in interview with author.

100   *"Reduce the fat men of the regiment"*: to Stilwell, 6 Oct 28, Carmel A-5.

100   *"Vital necessity"*: report of 12 Dec 27.
100   *Request to leave campsite unpoliced*: Col. Barrett, who served in the 15th Infantry, 1931-34, to author.
101   *General Connor's report*: 15 Jun 26, NA, RG 94, Box 483.
102   *"The most military looking man"*: Finney, 122.
102   *Marshall's dinner party*: Mrs. Stilwell to author.
102   *Marshall to Pershing*: 26 Dec 26, qtd. Pogue, I, 243.
103   *Butler's reply to press*: qtd. Powell, 146.
103   *"The whirlwinds were gathering"*: Buck, 208.
104   *MacMurray quoted*: USFR 1927, 164-68.
104   *"Red Wave on the Yangtze"*: title of a series by Putnam Weale in the *North China Daily News*, qtd. Powell, 144.
104   *"Peasants will rise like a tornado"*: qtd. Clubb, 135.
105   *Raid on the Soviet Embassy*: Clubb, 136.
105   *Kellogg quoted*: 18 and 25 Apr 27, USFR 1927, 205, 210-11.
105   *Coolidge speech*: qtd. Borg*, 423.
106   *Joseph Grew quoted*: USFR 1927, 201.
106   *Borah quoted*: Borg*, 190.
106   *Castner asks for reinforcements*: 10 Apr 27, NA, RG 94, China File Box 483.
106   *"If a Marine so much"*: Thomas, 291.
107   *Credentials*: In requesting credentials for Stilwell from General Chu Yu-pu, Commander-in-Chief for the Preservation of Peace and Order in Chihli Province, General Castner gave as the ostensible purpose of his mission that he was to meet Senator Hiram Bingham of Connecticut, then visiting China, and escort him to Tientsin (Carmel A-4). This has survived in the archives as the reason for Stilwell's journey to Hsuchow, although Senator Bingham, who was then in the Yangtze area, could not at this time have traveled north by rail. Stilwell met him subsequently in Tientsin when Bingham reached north China, traveling probably by ship from Shanghai.
107   *Chang Tsung-chang's attributes*: Abend, 65; Holcombe, 101; Barrett, "Soldiers of Fortune."
108   *White Russians*: Finney, 123-24; Barrett, "Soldiers of Fortune."
114   *Stilwell's report on mission*: to CG USAFC, 16 Jun 27, NA, RG 94, 40 China; also in Carmel A-4.
114   *MacMurray's and Castner's commendation*: MacMurray's was added to Castner's official commendation, 2 Jul 27, 201 File.
116   *Chiang Kai-shek's proposals of marriage*: Snow, *Journey*, 85.
116   *Chiang–Soong wedding*: Hahn, 140-42.
116   *Chang Tso-lin prepares to be Emperor*: Abend, 57; Stuart, 110-11.
117   *Castner's forced marches*: report by Castner to WD, 12 Dec 27, NA, RG 94, China File Box 483; also Gens. Boatner and Timberman to author.
117   *"One of the most popular officers"*: Sentinel, 25 May 28.

117   *"Brilliant and incisive"*: Finney, 133.

118   *"Strategic retreat"*: *Sentinel*, 20 Apr 28.

119   *"Unbearable sting"*: qtd. in one (11 May 28) of a series of reports to Stilwell on political developments from an informant signing himself "Interpreter"; Carmel A-6.

119   *Chang Tso-lin retreats with rolling stock*: ibid., 2 Jun 28; also Finney, 134.

120   *"Thunderous silence"*: Col. Barrett to author.

120   *"The new disorder of things"*: George Atcheson, Jr., to Hornbeck, 4 Jul 28, HP, File "Atcheson, G."

122   *Handball championship*: *Sentinel*, 13 Apr 29.

6 "Vinegar Joe," 1929-35

123   *"Intense desire to get my hands"*: Pogue, I, 251.

124   *"Move, shoot and communicate"*: Gen. Timberman, interview with author.

124   *"Wicked memory"*: K. Marshall, 9.

125   *Infantry Journal*: Stilwell's articles: "Caterpillar or Scorpion," November–December 1932; "Annual Maneuvers at Benning," July–August 1933; "Counsel for the Defense," *Cavalry Journal*, March–April 1933.

125   *"A genius for instruction" and Marshall's other judgments*: Efficiency Report for July 1929–June 1930, 201 File.

125   *Wells' letter*: 6 Mar 46, written with reference to a newspaper photograph of Stilwell at the surrender on the *Missouri*, Carmel B-19.

126   *Missionary story*: obituary in *Baltimore Sun*, 13 Oct 46.

127   *"Close to a misanthrope"*: Gen. Roberts, interview with author.

129   *"Mumbles in its beard"*: Gen. Betts, interview with author.

130   *Marshall asked three times by Commandant to relieve Stilwell*: Marshall interview with R&S, 6 Jul 49.

130   *Marshall's Efficiency Reports*: 30 Jun 31 and 15 Jun 32, in 201 File.

133   *"Forced into bitter rebellion"*: from a report based on three years' study of the Chinese press, 1930-32; Clubb, *Communism in China as Reported from Hankow in 1932* (New York, Columbia Univ. Press, 1968).

134   *Emperor wanted Inukai to curb Army*: Storry, 109.

134   *Something "wonderful" for world peace*: Morison, 375.

134   *Tardieu, "a long way off"*: ibid., 370.

135   *"Dumped" or "deposited," etc.*: ibid., 376, n. 14.

136   *"Sticking pins in tigers"*: Morison, 382.

136   *Stimson quoted*: *Far Eastern Crisis*, 88-90.

136   *"Did nothing to show the shame"*: Morison, 390, n. 35.

137   *"Soft and pudgy," etc.*: Diary, 11, 12 and 15 Feb 32, qtd. Ferrell, 248.

138   *Prince Kung*: Fairbank, Reischauer and Craig, 174.

139   *"Brad, why do you want to go"*: Gen. Bradley, interview with author.

140   *"He took us seriously"*: Paul Jones to author.

140   *"We have never received better instruction"*: letter of Imperial Valley Chapter of Reserve Officers Assn., 6 Oct 34, Carmel A-10.

140   *Marshall "tired of seeing mediocrity"*: letter of 31 Oct 34, qtd. Pogue, I, 285.

141   *"How intensely interesting"*: letter of Col. L. D. Gassner, C/S, IVth Corps Area, 11 Jan 35, Carmel A-10.

141   *Hull, "a respectful and friendly spirit"*: qtd. Borg*, 523.

7 MILITARY ATTACHÉ: China's Last Chance, 1935-37

144   *General Han Fu-chu in Shantung*: Abend, 221.

144   *General Sung Che-yuan and the Japanese*: Snow, *Battle*, 10-14; Bisson, 3.

147   *T. V. Soong to Abend*: Abend, 215.

147   *"Dead but not buried"*: ibid., 225.

147   *Half the people died before thirty*: White, *Thunder*, xix; Winfield, 112.

147   *Hupeh, five changes of governor, etc.*: Li Tsung-jen, #41, 12-14.

148   *Mme. Kung's commission, and profits with Mme. Chiang*: Peck to "Colleagues," 19 Mar 36, HP, File "Peck"; also Peck to Hornbeck, 24 Feb 36, Johnson Papers, vol. 38.

148   *Johnson on Soong*: MemCon with J. Lossing Buck, 13 May 38, *ibid.*

148   *Johnson's motto*: Snow, *Journey*, 150.

148, 149 *"Every bit of leadership" and "cold-blooded act"*: to Hornbeck, 31 Jul 35 and 13 Jul 36, HP, File "Johnson"; also in Johnson Papers, vol. 24.

148   *Japan's smuggling campaign*: Powell, 288-89.

149   *"Too late, too late"*: to Hornbeck, 24 Feb 36, Johnson Papers, vol. 28.

149   *"Forces them to use force"*: to Hornbeck, 3 Dec 35, Johnson Papers, vol. 24.

150   *Myth of the China market*: Griswold, 469.

150   *Cadogan quoted*: MemCon, 4 Mar 35, Johnson Papers, vol. 38.

150   *"Two elements in Japan"*: Hull, I, 276.

150-51 *Hull's year-end statement*: *NYT*, 5 Dec 35.

151   *The December demonstration and rise of nationalist resistance*: Bisson, 71; Snow, *Journey*, 144-45; Borg**, 159-62.

152   *Preparations in Szechwan*: Hornbeck mem, 5 Mar 36, HP, File, "Armed Forces."

152   *Chiang sent word to Johnson*: Johnson to Hornbeck, 19 Oct 36, HP, File "Johnson."

152   *"You are probably the only one"*: letter of Tam Sai-fan of Standard Oil Vacuum Co., 24 May 36, Carmel A-11.

153   *"No evidence of planned defense"*: USFR 1936, 223.

155   *Chang Hsueh-liang's private plane*: Leonard, 51, 164.

155   *Stilwell's report on Manchuria*: 18 Sep 36, USFR 1936, 301-302.

156   *Hull's reply, "interested in peace"*: mem by Hull, 2 Oct 36, *ibid.*, 330-31.

156   *Stilwell's report on Chinese officer's proposal*: 13 Jul 36, Carmel A-11.

157   *Communists' campaign in Shansi*: Griffith, 48.

157   *Stilwell's report on Shansi*: G-2 No. 9322, 13 Mar 36, Carmel A-12.

158   Shanghai Evening Post and Mercury: qtd. Borg**, 213.

158   *Colonel Lynch's report*: NA, RG 94, China File 1926-29, Box 481.

158-59   *Ringwalt's report*: qtd. Borg**, 205.

159   *Mao's talk with Snow*: Red Star, 455.

160   *Russia's role in saving Chiang*: Snow, *Random Notes*, 1-2; Powell, 276. For other accounts of the kidnapping see Bertram, *passim*, and Snow, *Red Star*.

161   *Washington's reaction*: Borg**, 530.

161   *Johnson's reports on Sian*: 11 May 37 and 25 Jun 37, USFR 1937, 87, 122. Stilwell's report is G-2 No. 9510, 25 Jan 37.

161   *General Sugiyama quoted*: from *Japan Advertiser*, 20 May 37, qtd. Bisson, 2.

163   *"Knows China better than any other officer"*: letter to Col. Fay W. Brabson, 9 Jul 37, Carmel A-12.

8 MILITARY ATTACHÉ: Sino-Japanese War, 1937-39

All correspondence relating to Stilwell's dispute with MID is in Carmel files A-12–17 and B-10.

164   *Boatride on Pei Hai Lake*: Goette, 3-4.

166   *"So that the world would get a true picture"*: Col. Barrett to author.

166   *Chiang's proclamation*: qtd. Bisson, 21.

166   *Bugles sounded in Peiping*: Snow, *Battle*, 16-18.

166   *Japanese bombing of Nankai University*: *Peking and Tientsin Times*, qtd. Bisson, 33-34.

168   *Japanese savagery at Paoting*: ibid., 279-80, 294.

168   *Chiang's motives at Shanghai*: Li Tsung-jen, #33, 9-10, 15, and #34, 13; Liu, 147; Abend, 245-46.

169   *"The tragedy of the retreat"*: Li Tsung-jen, #33, 9-10.

169   *One of the most memorable war pictures*: Life, 4 Oct 37.

170   *Hirota's speech and other Japanese statements*: HP, File "Japan Official Statements 1930s-40s" and File "China's Relations with Japan, 1930s."

170-71   *Taylor on Stilwell*: Gen. Taylor, interview with author.

173   *Chinese soldiers pushing train*: ibid.

173 *"Amoral drift"*: speech of 25 Apr 35, qtd. Stimson-Bundy, 311-12.

173 *A navy "so strong"*: Hull, I, 456.

174 *Delano history*: Crow, *Foreign Devils*, 21-27; Dennett, 579, 588; Kleeman, 21-22; Gunther, *Roosevelt*, 87.

174 *Chinese furnishings at Hyde Park*: Elizabeth B. Drewry to author.

174 *Roosevelt told Moley*: Moley, 95.

174 *Conferred with Stimson*: Welles, 67; Stimson-Bundy, 302.

174 *"Even more incensed"*: Welles, 8, 69.

175 *Carlson, "mutual confidence" and "mature graciousness"*: Twin Stars, 276, 130.

175 *Carlson's letters to FDR*: FDRL, PPF-4951 "Carlson."

176 *"From the heart," "love of liberty," etc.*: Carlson, *Twin Stars*, 158.

176 *Isolationist letters*: HP, mem, 30 Sep 37, File "China, Relations with Japan, 1930s."

176-77 *"It's a terrible thing"*: Rosenman, 167.

177-78 *Sack of Nanking*: Varg, *Missionaries*, 257-60; Powell, 297-98; Pelissier, 380; Snow, *Battle*, 56-59.

178 *Chiang on "ultimate victory"*: qtd. Bisson, 289.

179 *Peace overtures*: Johnson to Hornbeck, 2 Mar 38, HP, File "Johnson 1938"; also Bisson, 336.

179 *Johnson, "The present Chinese Government"*: to Hornbeck, 2 Mar 38, HP, File "Johnson 1938."

180 *Roosevelt considered seizing Japanese assets*: Blum, I, 486.

180 *Showdown should be postponed*: Welles, 74.

180 *Ludlow Resolution*: Hull, I, 563-64.

180 *"Doing the right thing"*: NYT, 8 Feb 38.

182 *Belden "sad, ragged, torn"*: John Davies to author.

182 *Agnes Smedley on Stilwell*: Smedley, 207.

184 *Carlson "disgusted"*: to FDR, 23 Sep 38, FDRL, *loc. cit.*

184 *Johnson on Carlson's toast and Chinese attitude*: to Hornbeck, 22 Mar 38, HP, File "Johnson 1938."

185 *Mme. Chiang on "real power"*: Gen. Dorn, who was a guest at the tea party, to author.

185 *Lanchow mission*: preliminary correspondence and Stilwell's report, 16 Apr 38, "Observations at Lanchow," in Carmel A-13; Welles, MemCon with FDR, 25 Feb and 4 Mar 38, FDRL, PSF "China 1938-40"; also in this file, WD mem, 20 Apr 38, on Stilwell's report; also Hull to Johnson, 15 Jun 38.

186 *Taierchuang, "mad with joy" and "battle cries"*: Li Tsung-jen, #35, 24.

186 *Casualties*: G-2 report by Dorn, 10 Apr 38, Carmel A-13.

186 *Falkenhausen "tearing his hair"*: Carlson, 152.

187 *Stilwell's interview with Li Tsung-jen*: Li Tsung-jen, #36, 13.

187 *Yellow River dikes blown at Chengchow*: Forman, 246-48; Belden, *Time to Die*, 179.

188 *European observer on missionary impact*: qtd. Steele, 54.

188   *Missionary Review of the World*: September 1938, qtd. Varg, 255.

188   *"There are no Communists left"*: qtd. Snow, *Journey*, 229.

189   *Carlson, "whether Eastern Asia"*: *Twin Stars*, 301.

189   *Opinion polls*: Bailey, *Man in the Street*, 9.

189   *Hull refused T. V. Soong*: Blum, I, 219.

190   *Buck to Morgenthau*: "Interview with Colonel Stilwell," Hankow, 30 Aug 38, Morgenthau Diary, vol. 138, unpub., FDRL.

190   *Morgenthau, "a bare chance"*: Blum, I, 510, 527.

190-91   *Tilly Hoffman's report*: to Barrett, n.d., Carmel A-13.

191   *A "people's defense" of Hankow*: Chalmers Johnson, 36-38; for other sources on the siege, see Snow, *Battle*, 105; Smedley, 227-35.

193-94   *Stilwell's report summarizing the war*: G-2 No. 6900, 25 Sep 38 and No. 9702, 17 Nov 38, Carmel A-14.

194   *"Completely let down"*: Johnson to Hornbeck, 9 Jan 39, HP, File "Johnson."

194   *Chiang's message to Roosevelt*: Hornbeck to Hull, conveying message from Chinese Ambassador, 18 Oct 38, HP, File "Chiang Kai-shek."

195   *"Reforming its personnel"*: *New York Herald Tribune*, 3 Nov 38.

195   *Wang Ching-wei's mission*: Li Tsung-jen, #37, 13.

196   *"Failed to awaken"*: *New York Herald Tribune*, 7 Nov 38.

196   *Japanese "have begun to feel"*: ibid.

196   *Removal to west China*: White, *Thunder*, 57-59.

197   *G-2 report on Chiang Kai-shek*: No. 9716, 24 Jan 39, Carmel A-17.

198   *Meeting with Chennault*: Chennault, 85-86 (who mistakenly dates the meeting in the following winter when Stilwell was no longer in China).

198   *Stilwell's visit to General Okamura*: Gen. Munson to author.

199   *Craigie "utterly weary"*: Abend, 33.

199   *Drowned body in the river*: Mrs. Clubb to author.

200   *Promotion*: officially dated 5 Aug 39. In a postwar interview with R&S (13 Jul 49), Marshall said he had promoted Stilwell over the protests of McCabe, who had wanted to remove him as Military Attaché. Marshall was "not impressed by the very elegant set of stuffed shirts" in McCabe's circle and put little credence in the validity of McCabe's derogatory Efficiency Reports on Stilwell.

200   *Congratulatory letters*: major of Infantry—Thomas Austin; colonel of Artillery—Leroy Collins; officer of ONI, signature illegible, letter dated Quantico 9 Aug 39; all, with many others, in Carmel B-11.

II

Stilwell's Diary and its Supplements are the basic source for the events, meetings, discussions, decisions and disputes in which he participated, as well as for his quoted comments thereon. Since this may be taken for granted, they are cited only when the source might not be obvious or when the circumstance is of special significance. For the period covered by Part Two much of this material has been published, or quoted in published form, either in the volumes by Romanus and Sunderland or in *The Stilwell Papers* edited by Mr. White. Where a reference seemed indicated, I have cited the published version where it exists, for the convenience of the reader.

9 The Rush to Prepare 1939-41

203   *Army ranked 19th*: World Almanac for 1938, 706.

203   *"Status of a third rate power"*: Marshall's Biennial Report, 1939-41, 16-18.

204   *Thayer, "to make good soldiers"*: qtd. Dupuy, 124.

204   *"Good eating"*: Col. Trevor Dupuy, who was present, to author.

204   *Footnote*: Peck to Hornbeck, 28 Mar 26; Ringwalt to Peck, 5 Apr 36; HP, File "Peck."

206   *Grew, "pressure for an embargo"*: Grew, 299.

206   *Judd's speeches*: Varg, *Missionaries*, 271.

207   *"Resolutely backed up by naval force"*: Committee on East Asia, Bulletin 28, November 1940, qtd. Varg, *ibid.*, 262.

207   *Grew's public speech in Tokyo*: Grew, 300.

207   *Knox, "unthinkable"*: Langer and Gleason*, 471.

208   *Third Army maneuvers in Louisiana*: NYT, 7 and 26 May 40; News-week, 13 May 40; also Lt. Francis G. Smith, *History of the Third Army*, Study No. 17, Historical Section, AGF, 1946.

208   *"One of the most amazing encirclements"*: T. A. Price, staff correspondent of *The News* (not otherwise identified), 10 May 40, Carmel Scrapbook.

209   *Chief umpire's critique*: Army and Navy Journal, 1 Jun 40, 962.

209   *Divisional commander's bet*: Eisenhower, 8.

209   *General Strong predicted*: qtd. Snell, 74.

210   *General Tojo*: qtd. Langer and Gleason**, 28.

211   *"Uniting of all these regions"*: Langer and Gleason*, 603.

212   *"He would be ruined in any case"*: Linebarger, 267.

213   *"Cold-blooded"*: Gen. Arms to author. In contrast, Dean Rusk, who served in Delhi HQ of CBI, thought that one of Stilwell's faults as a commander was that he was too kindly to incompetents if they were loyal: "He didn't have ice in his veins like Marshall" (interview with author).

213 *"You had to; he had it"*: Col. Harris Wiltamuth (7th Division) to author.

213 *"Black cat" talk*: Eldridge (PR officer for 7th Division), 21.

214 *Falkenhausen on Japanese*: qtd. Carlson, *Twin Stars*, 151.

214 *Carlson's comments*: ibid., 31-32, 275, 301-302.

214 *Colonel Mott*: Mott, 103.

214 *"Predatory powers"*: qtd. Iriye, 207.

214 *United States "would be drawn in"*: Stimson-Bundy, 366.

215 *"All four agreed"*: ibid., Sherwood, 397.

215 *Admiral Yamamoto*: A. Russell Buchanan, *The United States and World War II* (New York, Harper, 1964) I, 37.

215 *Japanese begin planning Pearl Harbor*: ibid.

215 *Chiang asks for air force*: telegrams of 18, 20, 23 Oct 40, qtd. Langer and Gleason**, 296-97.

216 *Communists "taking advantage"*: Johnson to State, 20 Oct 40, qtd. R&S*, 9.

216 *"Three all" principle*: Chalmers Johnson, 57-59. (This book contains much valuable material on the Japanese occupation and the hatred it engendered in the Chinese populace.)

217 *Chennault's meeting with Mme. Chiang*: Chennault, 4.

218 *Soong's requirements for air force*: R&S*, 13-15.

218 *"Counter-offensive I am preparing"*: Langer and Gleason**, 303.

218 *"500 stars"*: Blum, II, 365.

218 *Hornbeck on sympathizers*: mem to SecNav, 16 Apr 42, HP, File "McHugh."

218 *Stimson, "I wanted so much"*: Stimson Diary, 6 Nov 41.

219 *Roosevelt, "Is he still willing"*: Blum, II, 367.

219 *"To demand an end to aggression"*: ibid., 365.

219 *Hull, Morgenthau, Soong, Lothian on B-17 proposal*: ibid., 366-67.

219 *Stimson and Marshall on B-17s*: ibid., Langer and Gleason**, 304.

220 *China Defense Supplies*: Wertenbaker.

221 *"Chinese military self-sufficiency"*: Magruder to Marshall, 11 Aug 41, R&S*, 29.

221 *Thirty Division program*: CBI History, Master Narrative; also R&S*, 25-42.

222 *General Sliney's report*: 10 Dec 41, R&S*, 36-44 (together with other AMMISCA reports to the same effect).

222 *"Fatally defective"*: Schuirmann to State, 4 Apr, USFRC 42, 31.

222 *Free-lance correspondent on Burma Road*: Vanya Oakes, in "The Wrong News about Asia," *Asia*, April 1944, 151.

222 *Arnstein's report*: in *Life*, 6 Oct 41; others on Burma Road: Sherwood, 289, 405; R&S*, 47; Eldridge, 25-30.

223 *Marshall and Stimson predict Russian defeat*: Stimson to FDR, 23 Jun 41, in Stimson Diary 34. Stimson wrote that he had spent the day in conference with the War Plans Division and the Chief of Staff. "Here is their estimate of controlling facts: 1) Ger-

many will be thoroughly occupied in beating Russia for a minimum of one month and a maximum of three months."

225   *California maneuvers*: *NYT*, 1 and 26 Jun 41; Eldridge, biographical essay on Stilwell in *Time* files.

225   *Stilwell rated No. 1*: Gen. Wilson's Efficiency Report, December 40–June 41, 201 File.

226   *Joint Board's opinion*: Sherwood, 412.

226   *Yarnell on Lattimore*: letter of 29 Apr 41, HP, File "Yarnell"; other letters on this appointment in FDRL, PSF "China 41-42."

226   *Lattimore's report*: *ibid.*, PSF "Currie."

227   *Chiang appeals for help*: 2 Nov 41, *ibid.*, PSF "China 41-42"; Langer and Gleason**, 840; Chiang to Soong for conveying to Knox and Stimson, 25 Nov 41, M-Diary, I, 530.

228   *Gauss on China's resistance*: Gauss to State, 11 Sep 41, HP, File "China: Relations with U.S."

10 "I'll Go Where I'm Sent"
DECEMBER–FEBRUARY 1941-1942

It may be assumed that all official communications for which references are not specifically cited in this and the following sections are to be found in R&S.

230   *"Fight 'em off with oranges?"*: Dorn, "Walkout."

232   *Marshall's judgment of Stilwell*: interview with R&S, 6 Jul 49.

232   *First of nine corps commanders*: Stilwell, B&W I, 27. The list was shown him by Mark Clark, who had been designated by Marshall to rate commanding officers.

232   *In the Kremlin "no one knew what to do"*: Svetlana Alliluyeva, *Letters to a Friend* (New York, Harper, 1967).

233-34   *News of Pearl Harbor in China*: Han Suyin, 235; Peck, 353; "Armistice Day," White, *Thunder*, 152; Gen. McNally, then language officer in Kweiyang, to author.

234   *Chiang's proposal for Allied strategy*: R&S*, 56-57.

234   *Roosevelt's list of United Nations*: Sherwood, 452.

235   *Niemeyer Mission*: Woodward, 419; text in M-Diary, I, 619-22.

235   *British suspect a trick*: Sherwood, 457.

235   *"Be fatal to have"*: Bryant*, 235.

236   *Wavell in Chungking*: Magruder to President, SecWar and C/S, 25 Dec 41; Lattimore to Currie, 11 Dec 41, FDRL, " 'Safe' China." On this meeting see also Feis, 25; R&S*, 55; Stimson Diary, 29 Dec 41; Wavell to Churchill, 25 Jan 42, in Churchill, IV, 134.

237   *Anglo-Chinese dispute over Lend-Lease*: R&S*, 57-60; Feis, 11.

237   *Marshall to Wavell*: FDRL, " 'Safe' China."

238   *Gauss on "shock" and "indignation"*: to State, 17 Jan 42; also Vincent to Gauss, 24 Jan, USFRC 42, 4, 10.

238   *Roosevelt feared Asia gravitating to Japan*: Sherwood, 455.

238   *"If China goes under"*: Elliott Roosevelt, 53.

239   *FDR and Churchill "differed strongly"*: Churchill, IV, 153; Sherwood, 716.

239   *FDR conversation with Snow*: Snow, *Journey*, 253-57.

239   *"Compel the Chinese people"*: to Morgenthau, 6 Dec 34, Nixon, II, 306.

239   *FDR's China policy*: Judge Rosenman, interview with author; also Marshall on same, R&S*, 62, n. 40.

239   *Colonial empires past*: Sherwood, 573.

239   *China as an equal*: Welles, 155.

240   *British Empire was finished*: Burns, 208.

240   *"I reacted so strongly"*: Churchill, IV, 209.

240   *Primary responsibility for China*: Hopkins Papers, qtd. R&S*, 86, n. 13.

240   *"Wild and half-baked"*: Bryan*, 236.

240   *One-word lesson, "China"*: Churchill, IV, 134.

241   *Drum episode*: Drum Papers, qtd. R&S*, 63-68; Stimson Diary, 6 Jan 42; Pogue and Dorn to author.

242   *Marshall's view of China's potential*: interview with R&S, 13 Jul 49.

243   *"Joe, you have 24 hours"*: Dorn, "Walkout."

243   *Meeting of Stimson and Stilwell*: Stimson Diary, 14 Jan 42; also Stimson-Bundy, 530.

244   *More important than Singapore*: Churchill, IV, 53, 56.

245   *Chiang and Soong on Stilwell's appointment*: Stimson Diary, 19, 22, 24 Jan 42; R&S*, 66, 72-73 (nn. 74, 75, 77, 78); White Paper, 469.

245   *Admiral Miles' instructions*: Miles, 18.

245   *A British historian*: Collis, *Burma*, 76.

246   *Stilwell's strategy for Far East*: mem for C/S, 6 Jan 42, *CBI History*, Sec. 3, App. III; mem for C/S, 31 Jan 42, R&S*, 75.

246   *Stilwell's instructions*: *CBI History*, Master Narrative; Marshall to Stilwell, 9 Feb 42, R&S*, 74; designation as CG USAF-CBI dated 1 and 4 Feb 42, 201 File.

246   *Origins of Hump air route*: Stimson Diary, 30 Jan 42; Soong to FDR, 31 Jan 42, R&S*, 77; Sherwood, 513; USFRC 42, 13; Harriman to President, 31 Jan 42, in Mr. Harriman's papers.

247   *Chinese initiate the "back-country road"*: R&S*, 76-78.

248   *Dispute over Chennault's command*: B&W II, 9 Feb 42 (*SP*, 37); also R&S*, 73, n. 79.

249   *Meeting with President*: SP, 36; also Stimson to FDR, 2 Feb 42, FDRL, OF "150 China 42."

249   *Roosevelt characteristics*: Gunther, 26; Sherwood, 249; Mrs. Halsted, interview with author.

249   *FDR letter to a friend*: to Fred I. Kent, Governor of Federal Reserve Bank of New York, Nixon, II, 585.

250   *FDR in 1944, "I do not want the United States"*: qtd. Matloff**, 491.

250   *China drew loudest applause*: Sherwood, 458.

250   *Chinese communiqués on Hong Kong*: *NYT*, 16 Dec 41: "A savage Chinese attack is in full swing in the Tamshui area 25 miles north of Hong Kong" and has forced the Japanese "to retire from some of their positions outside Canton." AP from Chungking, quoting official Chinese Central News agency.

250   *Chiang on Indochina*: "Proposed Campaign in Indo-China," documents, 8 Jan–6 Feb, USFRC 42, 749-60.

250-51 Magruder on "make-believe": to WD, 10 Feb, USFRC 42, 13-16.

251   *"Fascist dictatorship"*: Griswold, 382.

251   *No journalist "wishing well to China"*: Sheean, *Thunder*, 345.

251   *$500-million loan*: Feis, 22-23; Blum, III, 87-100; Stimson-Bundy, 531; Stimson Diary, 3 and 5 Feb 42; State Dept. comment, 28 Feb, USFRC 42, 474.

252   *Magruder, China no military asset*: to AGWar, 3 Feb 42, *CBI History*, Sec. 3.

254   *Wavell reported "inferiority complex"*: Churchill, IV, 101.

254   *Air raid from Outer Mongolia*: Arnold to President, 28 Jan 42, FDRL, PSF " 'Safe' China."

255   *Singapore "worst disaster"*: Churchill, IV, 92.

11 "A Hell of a Beating"

MARCH–MAY 1942

257   *Indian units trained for desert war*: Slim, 8.

257   *Burma as "impenetrable barrier"*: Mountbatten, 12.

258   *Burning of Lend-Lease stores*: R&S*, 84.

258   *Dorman-Smith's last dinner*: Collis, *Burma*, 105.

258   *"We Asiatics"*: ibid., 26.

259   *Gandhi to Chiang Kai-shek*: USFRC 42, 33-34; Chiang to Ambassador in London (Wellington Koo), 24 Feb 42, FDRL, Tully file "Chiang Kai-shek."

261   *"No one ever saw a fat Chinese"*: Steele, 25.

261   *China's deterioration*: Tsou, 49-53.

262   *"Intense distaste"*: Steele, 27

262   *Gauss "hard to fool" and "because he is cold"*: mem by Hornbeck, 8 May 42, HP, File "Gauss."

262   *"Only a minor asset"*: to State, 14 Jul 42, *ibid.*, File "Leahy."

262   *Ho Ying-chin nicknamed Grandma*: Li Tsung-jen, #24, 10.

264   *Condition of the Chinese armies*: report by Mme. Sun Yat-sen, HP,

File "Armed Forces China"; Gauss to State, 14 Jan, USFRC 44, 5; Miles, 153; Stilwell, *passim*.

267   *"Extreme delicacy"*: USFRC 42, 29.

269   *Sliney, "one of the best"*: Slim, 118.

269   *Number of generals at British Headquarters*: Stilwell, *Burma Campaign*.

270   *Tu Li-ming to Dorman-Smith*: Collis, *Burma*, 122.

270   *Alexander at Dunkirk*: *Current History*, October 1942; Churchill, IV, 166-67, 169.

273   *Press conference in Chungking*: Harrison Forman in *NYT*, 21 Mar 42.

274   *RAF withdrew to India*: Stilwell, *Burma Campaign*.

275   *Chiang's favorite advice*: letter of Mme. Chiang, 16 Mar 42, Hoover, File 13.

275   *"The bastards have caught me"*: Eldridge, 55.

275   *Slim's talk with Merrill*: Belden, 33.

276   *"Obstinate as a team of mules"*: Slim, 36.

276   *Aide to Wavell sees sinister atmosphere*: Collis, *Burma*, 142.

278   *The Chinese "parasites"*: Alexander, "Report," 94.

278   Lien tso fa: Liu, 13.

278-79   *Hsueh Yueh and G—mo's interference*: Li Tsung-jen, #41, 30.

280   *Newspaper headlines*: Carmel Scrapbook, AP from Delhi, 20 Mar 42 (unidentified newspapers).

280   *Stilwell's seal*: B&W II, 49, undated; see *SP*, 117, n. 6 by White.

280   *Officers of the 38th*: Col. —— and colleagues in interview with author.

281   *Madame's letter*: 8 Apr 42, Carmel A-21.

281   *Mrs. Luce's article*: *Life*, 6 and 15 Jun 42.

282   *Mandalay after the bombing*: Dorn, "Walkout."

282   *Chiang to Churchill*: to Wellington Koo for transmission to PM, 17 Apr 42, FDRL, PSF "China 41-42."

284   *Watermelons*: S-Diary; Dorn, "Walkout"; see also Mme. Chiang's comment, p. 352 of this book.

284   *Japanese treatment of prisoners*: Davies mem, "Burma Campaign," August 1942, HP, File "Davies."

285   *"Sir Childe Harold Alexander"*: 10 Apr 42, Carmel A-21.

285   *Louis Johnson's report*: 26 May, USFRC 42, 57.

285   *"Completely antiforeign overnight"*: HP, File "McHugh."

285-86   *Marshall et al. on Tenth Air Force*: Matloff*, 202.

286   *Plan for training Chinese troops in India*: Marshall to FDR, 29 Apr 42, forwarding radio from Stilwell, FDRL, PSF " 'Safe' China."

287   *Doolittle raid, Chiang's objection*: reports by Bissell, 11 and 16 Apr 42 and other correspondence, *ibid.*; Marshall to CKS, 17 Apr, USFRC 42, 32.

288   *Alexander to General Tu*: Alexander, "Report," 94.

289   *"Unhappy" and "sulky"*: Dorn, "Walkout."

289 *Ava bridge prepared for demolition since February*: Kirby, II, 179, n. 1.

289-90 *Alexander and Stilwell during air raid*: Dorn, "Walkout."

290 *State of funk*: Eldridge, 81.

290 *"The Boss should tell the Chinese"*: ibid., 90.

291 *Telling Darrell Berrigan*: Sat. Eve. Post, 17 Jun 44.

291 *"If I run out now"*: Jones to author.

292 *Alexander's farewell statement*: Current History, October 1944.

292 *"Resignedly playing solitaire"*: Eldridge, 88.

292 *Scott and Haynes*: Scott, 208.

292 *C-47s (DC-3s)*: The Douglas C-47 was one of the many military conversions of the commercial DC-3. Designed to carry heavy cargo, its top speed was about 220 m.p.h. When fitted with folding benches, it could carry 28 fully equipped troops.

292-98 *The walkout*: S-Diary throughout; for other primary accounts, Dorn, Belden, Eldridge, Seagrave, information from Jones to author; letter of General Williams to Mrs. Williams, 30 May 42, lent to author. Originals of Stilwell's last radio messages in Hoover, File 123.

298 *"Looking like the wrath of God"*: Providence Journal, editorial 20 May 42.

298 *Marshall's message*: 13 May 42, Carmel A-21.

299 *Instructions to AMMISCA of May 9*: AC/S, OPD, mem to WD Message Center, HP, File "Marshall."

300 *Newspaper headlines*: based on UP from Chungking, Carmel Scrapbook, unidentified newspapers.

300 San Francisco Chronicle *and* NYT *editorials*: 15 Oct 46 and 26 May 42, respectively.

12 The Client

JUNE–OCTOBER 1942

301 *"Keeping China in the War"*: R&S*, 152.

301 *Stilwell's plan for reconquest*: to Stimson, 25 May 42, Stimson Papers; CBI History, Master Narrative.

302 *"Exalted concept of true soldiering"*: Sevareid, 322.

302 *"Ill-fated strategy of attack"*: Liu, 179.

303 *China justified in remaining passive*: Peck, 381, 386.

303 *Chiang's message of May 25*: Matloff*, 227.

303 *Madame to Currie*: USFRC 42, 55.

304 *Chiang asks for Hopkins*: ibid., 57.

304 *Roosevelt to Arnold*: 5 May 42, FDRL, " 'Safe' China."

304 *Gauss, "undeclared peace"*: to SecState, 7 Mar, USFRC 42, 27; mem by Hornbeck, 7 May 42, ibid., 41.

305   *Statement of military failings*: text in R&S*, 153.

305   *"Quite a few should be shot"*: to Stimson, 25 May 42, Stimson Papers.

305-306   *Stilwell's plan of reform*: text in R&S*, 154.

306n.   *Von Seeckt's recommendations*: Liu, 93, 99.

307   *"Some regenerative idea"*: SP, 19 Jun 42, 116.

308   *Soong to Stilwell*: R&S*, 168.

308   *"I need everything"*: Arnold, 329.

309   *Pilots caught in tree tops*: Peers, 123.

309   *"Scuttling pompously"*: Chennault, 153.

309   *Feud with Bissell*: Gauss to State, 29 Aug, USFRC 42, 146.

309   *"Kick in the teeth"*: McHugh to ONI, 11 Oct 42, McHugh Papers.

310   *Chennault to Madame*: 27 Nov 41, Chennault Papers.

310   *Report on Chinese air cadets*: 5 May 42, *ibid.*

310   *"Examine the optimums"*: qtd. in a souvenir history of AVG published in 1967 by the Flying Tigers Organization, Chennault Papers, AVG, Misc.

310   *Letter to Stilwell*: Chennault, 211.

310   *"Full authority"*: *ibid.*

310   *"15 Nippon planes every day"*: 13 May 42, Chennault Papers, AVG.

312   *Three Demands crisis*: CBI History, Master Narrative; SP, 119-22; R&S*, 168-72; Vincent (28 Jun), Hull (1 Jul), Gauss (2 Jul), FDR (4 Jul), USFRC 42, 91-92, 95-96, 109.

313   *Rumors set afloat*: Gauss, 11 Jul, *ibid.*, 110.

313   *Gauss, "bluff"*: *ibid.*; SP, 126.

313   *Chou En-lai quoted*: M-Diary, 22 Apr 42, II, 872-73.

313   *Attempt to divest Stilwell of Lend-Lease*: SP, 126-27, 130; R&S*, 175-79.

316   *Lung Yun and Madame as hostage*: Col. Thomas Arms, Jr. (instructor with Y-force) to author.

317   *Chiang did not want a well-trained army*: Stilwell to Marshall, 23 Jul 43, qtd. R&S*, 353; Davies, "Conversation with Chinese Attaché," USFRC 43, 62.

318   *Letter to Stimson, "unvarnished truth"*: 27 Jun 42.

318   *Four-point military plan*: 30 Jul 42, Hoover, File 15; text in R&S*, 182.

319   *"It is not anticipated"*: 6 Aug 41, R&S*, 41.

319   *British "have no intention"*: 31 Jul, "CBI: A Reappraisal," USFRC 42, 129-31; see also Gauss to State, 3 Aug, *ibid.*, 121.

319   *Dorn to War Department, August 4*: R&S*, 182-83.

320   *Chou En-lai to Davies*: USFRC 42, 102.

321   *Cyril Rogers*: Snow, *Journey*, 216.

321   *"90 percent untrue"*: White, *Thunder*, 112.

322   *Maxwell Hamilton*: 16 Feb, USFRC 42 ,19.

322   *Gauss, "dismiss this as rot"*: 11 Jul, *ibid.*, 112.

322   *Dr. Van Slyke*: 9 Jun 42, FDRL, PSF "Currie."

323   *"If anything happens"*: 3 Aug, USFRC 42, 119-23.

323   *Currie's recommendations*: R&S*, 186.

323   *FDR, "the problem of personalities"*: FDR to Currie, 12 Sep 42, FDRL, OF "150 China 42."

324   *British "reappraisal"*: Gauss, conversation with British Ambassador, 4 Sep, USFRC 42, 148.

324   *Marshall on Currie's visit*: interview with R&S, 6 Jul 49.

324   *FDR to Marshall on Stilwell*: Roosevelt, *Letters*, II, 1350.

324   *"Harmony in Chungking"*: to FDR, 6 Oct, USFRC 42, 154.

13 "Peanut and I on a Raft"

AUGUST 1942–JANUARY 1943

326   *22nd Division physical condition*: Eldridge, 143; *SP,* note by White, 137.

327   *"Put 50 in a plane naked"*: S-Diary, 14 Sep 42.

327   *Conditions of flight*: *CBI History,* "Fillers"; Gen. Wheeler, interview with author.

328   *"Thank God we don't speak Chinese"*: Eldridge, 142.

328-29   *Resentments at Ramgarh*: Seagrave**, 50; Ho Yungchi, 40; Liu, 185.

329   *Americans shocked at punishments*: Gen. Boatner to author.

329   *Stilwell addresses troops*: Col. —— and Lt. Col. —— of 38th Division, interview with author.

331   *Willkie considered "highest rank"*: Hornbeck mem, 31 Oct 42, on speech by Gardner Cowles (who accompanied Willkie), HP, File "China, Relations with U.S."

332   *General Hsiung quoted*: Han Suyin, 287.

332-35   *Incidents of Willke's visit (unless otherwise noted)*: Willkie, 117-49; see also Peck, 433.

333   One World *sales*: Burns, 328. I am indebted to Professor Burns for two other sources on the phenomenal sales of Willkie's book, viz.: Donald Bruce Johnson, *The Republican Party and Wendell Willkie* (1960), 236, and Ellsworth Barnard, *Wendell Willkie* (1966), 412.

333   *Military review for Willkie*: NA, film, 208 UN 21.

333   *War Ministry cocktail party*: the late Joseph Barnes (who accompanied Willkie) to author.

334   *"Cold battlefields"*: Thoburn Wiant, AP, *NYT,* 1 Nov 44.

335   *Willkie urges Madame to accompany him*: J. C. Vincent, interview with author.

336   *Stilwell to Byroade*: Byroade, interview with author.

336   *"Sian is to the north of Kunming"*: Scott, 260.

337   *Chennault's letter of October 8*: Chennault, 212-15.

338   *Marshall, "just nonsense"*: interview with R&S, 6 Jul 49.

338-39   *McHugh's intervention*: report to ONI, 11 Oct 42, McHugh Papers.

In a letter to Knox of 1 Aug 42 McHugh had written that he felt "pushed out" by Stilwell, which may have partly accounted for this action.

339   *Marshall infuriated*: R&S*, 148.

339   *President read the document*: McHugh to Chennault, 11 Mar 43, McHugh Papers. As a result of Marshall's angry protest, Admiral King issued an order prohibiting McHugh from serving again in CBI (mem for Mr. Chester, 26 Jan 45, *ibid.*). This was later rescinded after Stilwell's return, when McHugh secured his consent.

339   *ATC "will never be able"*: to Stimson, 6 Oct 42, Stimson Papers. This letter, which forcefully argued the necessity of reopening the land route through Burma, was passed on by Stimson to the President (covering letter of 17 Oct 42).

339-40   *Stimson interview with Soong*: 10 Oct 42, R&S*, 229.

340   *"Develop more of patience"*: 6 Oct 42, Carmel A-21.

340   *"Boom from Burma"*: CBI History, OSS Narrative, Annex B, Sec. 2.

340   *"He never told me what to do"*: Gen. Wheeler to author.

341   *"Sleeve-jerking"*: Eldridge, 149.

342   *Chinese map includes north Burma*: Woodward, 425, n. 2.

342   *A million Indian laborers*: Kirby, II, 301.

344   *Plan of campaign for Hankow*: R&S*, 241.

344   *Memoranda for Soong*: 27 Dec 42, Hoover, File 133; 2 Jan 43, Carmel A-22.

345   *"I read your profane message"* (*and Stilwell's letter of 28 Nov 42, to which this was a reply*): R&S*, 245, 247.

346   *Roberts on British*: Matloff*, 347.

346-47   *Canceling the campaign*: R&S*, 259.

347   *DSC ceremony*: NYT, 17 Jan 43, editorial 19 Jan 43; Time, 25 Jan 43.

347   *Citation*: WD General Orders No. 3, 15 Jan 43.

14 The President's Policy

JANUARY-MAY 1943

349   *Letter from Mrs. Quinn*: FDRL, OF "150 China 43."

349   *"Goddam it," said a Congressman*: Time, 1 Mar 43; other accounts, State Dept. press summary, 24 Feb 43.

350   *Lord Halifax*: Woodward, 425, n. i.

350   *Madame's tour*: Tong, Dateline, 188-91; Sandburg in Washington Post, 14 Mar 43.

350   *Madame's talk with Hopkins*: Sherwood, 644, 660-61, 706; Hopkins mems, 24 and 30 Nov 43, Hopkins Papers.

351   *Madame at White House and Waldorf*: Tully, 33-35.

351   *"You never saw a facial expression"*: Dorn to author.

351   *FDR did not want Madame "too close"*: Mrs. Halsted to author.

351   *"Hard as steel"*: Eleanor Roosevelt, 249.

351-52 *Dinner table*: ibid.

352   *Madame on watermelon incident*: Marshall interview with R&S, 6 Jul 49.

352   *Leahy and Stimson quoted*: Leahy, 154; Stimson Diary, 4 May 43.

352   *Press conference*: verbatim report, State Dept. Radio Bulletin, No. 43, 19 Feb 43; Sevareid (who was present) to author.

352   *English cigarets*: Blum, III, 106.

352-53 *"Just crazy to get her out"*: ibid.

353   *FDR's four principles*: Welles, 151-52.

353   *"New epoch"*: Feis, 62.

353   *Atcheson, "seriously deteriorating"*: to State, 28 May 43, HP, File "Leahy." (A copy of this report was sent by Hornbeck to Leahy in the White House.)

354   *Pearl Buck's letter*: Blum, III, 105.

354   *White's Honan report*: FDRL, PSF "China."

355   *Atcheson urges a "determined offensive"*: 28 May 43, cited above.

356   *"Could not stand another Bataan" and "a situation might arise"*: R&S*, 270.

356   *Statements of the British and Admiral King*: ibid., qtd. Feis, 55-56.

356   *Arnold-Somerville-Dill mission*: SP, 196; Arnold, 407, 409, 413, 417-27; Sherwood, 681; Feis, 56-57, Blum, III, 194.

357   *Chinese Air Force*: Gauss mem, 13 Mar 43, HP, File "Gauss."

357   *Russians complained*: Davies to Stilwell, 11 Jul, USFRC 42, 115.

357   *Chiang to Roosevelt, February 7*: R&S*, 276.

357-58 *Wavell summary*: ibid., 277.

358   *Arnold to Stilwell*: 1 Mar 43, Carmel A-22.

358   *Roosevelt to Alsop*: Roosevelt, *Letters*, II, 1361.

358   *Alsop's letters*: 10 Dec 42 ("before I have reached China"), 1 Mar 43, Hopkins Papers, Chinese Affairs.

358   *Begged to be recalled*: to Stettinius, 12 Jan 43, HP, File "Alsop."

359   *"Munching a porcupine"*: Bryant*, 494.

359-60 *Roosevelt orders priority for Chennault*: R&S*, 279-82. Roosevelt's "Sultan of Morocco" letter, Stilwell's letter to Marshall of 15 Mar 43 and Marshall's reply to President are all here.

362   *Legion of Merit for Stilwell*: mem of A/G, 28 Oct 43, 201 File; R&S* 282, n. 51.

362   *Davies predicted*: Report on Stilwell Mission, 9 Mar 43, Carmel A-22.

362   *Condition of the 30 divisions*: S-Diary, 21 Jun 43 (*SP*, 208-209) and *passim*.

363   *Loss by death or desertion*: Liu, 137.

363   *Kunming Training Center*: CBI History, Master Narrative; Stilwell to Stimson, 21 Mar 43, Stimson Papers.

363   *American instructor quoted*: Col. Thomas Arms, Jr., to author.

363   *Interpreters' strike*: ibid.

364   *Lung Yun and rubber tires*: Ravdin, 202.

364   *Building the Road*: Seagrave**, 15-27; *CBI History,* Master Narrative; R&S*, 341-45; Gen. Wheeler to author.

365   *Stilwell at the Polo Ground Mess*: Jones to author; *New York Herald Tribune,* 16 Jun 43, UP from Chungking. This correspondent wrote that Stilwell's "determination to assure the best possible treatment for men at the front is one of the reasons for his tremendous popularity."

365   *"Am I through in China?" and other notes*: Carmel A-22 and A-25.

366   *Ho Ying-chin diverts armies*: *CBI History,* Master Narrative; *SP,* 208.

366   *Chennault and Stilwell summoned to Washington*: SP, 203; R&S*, 317; *NYT* editorial, 30 Apr 43.

367   *Chiang-Chennault program*: R&S*, 319.

367   *Chiang's "personal assurance"*: ibid., 320.

367   *Stilwell's memorandum for President*: 1 May 43, Hoover, File 61; text in R&S*, 323-24.

367-68 *Stilwell's poor performance*: Marshall interview with R&S, 6 Jul 49; Gen. Deane (then secretary to Combined Chiefs) to author.

368   *Stimson's conversation with Stilwell*: Stimson Diary, 30 Apr 43.

368   *Stimson's telephone call and letter to President*: Stimson Diary, 3 May 43.

369   *"Possibility of collapse"*: Leahy, 157.

369   *"We are his suckers"*: undated mem summarizing the Conference, Hoover, File 61.

369   *"By-pass" Burma, Singapore the "only prize"*: Churchill, IV, 793; VI, 143.

369   *Anthony Eden*: Sherwood, 716.

370   *King could "raise holy hell"*: Gunther, 45.

370   *King believed in Stilwell*: King, 436, n. 12.

370   *Marshall on relations with President*: interview with R&S, 13 Jul 49.

370   *Stilwell only one to call him George*: Gen. Wedemeyer to author.

370   *Marshall's quarrel with Hopkins, Chennault a "paid employee"*: Sherwood, 739, 405.

370   *Marshall's opinions of Chennault and Alsop*: interview with R&S, 13 Jul 49.

371   *TRIDENT*: BB, 13 (*SP*, 204-205); Stimson Diary, 21 and 22 May 43; R&S*, 320-35; Leahy, 161, 172; Churchill, IV, chap. 20; Hoover, File 61. The USFR volume on the TRIDENT Conference was not yet published at the time this book was in preparation.

371   *FDR asks opinions of Chiang Kai-shek*: Chennault, 220.

372   *Eugene Meyer's dinner*: Davies, 81st Congress, Loyalty Hearings, 2095.

373 *Meeting with Churchill*: S-Diary, 22 May 43, and mem for Stimson, Carmel A-22.

373 *Churchill on Stilwell*: Sherwood, 958n.

373 *Reportedly threw teapots*: 8 Jul 43, Stimson Papers.

373 *"Check on their tactics"*: *NYT*, 1 Jun 43.

374 *"The other me"*: S-Diary, 29 May 43.

15 Stilwell Must Go

JUNE–OCTOBER 1943

375 *ATC fliers' attitude*: Peers, 107-109; Eldridge, 174-76.

376 *Pipeline*: A record of the extraordinary labor and ingenuity involved in laying the line over the river gorges of north Burma exists in Signal Corps Film HRE-7.

377 *Average American in China*: White, *Thunder*, 161; Isaacs, *No Peace*, chap. 1, "American Soldiers in Asia."

377 *Chinese attitude*: Stevens to State (1 Apr), Penfield to State (6 May), Rice to State (2 Oct), USFRC 44, 48, 68, 163.

377 *"Caching gas"*: Report of Col. Vincent, HQ, Forward Echelon Command, 29 Jul 43, Chennault Papers, 14th AF.

377 *Smuggling and Bordello affair*: BB, "Chennault's Whore House," 18-19; *CBI Roundup*, 21 Dec 44; Chennault Papers, CID File; Report by Theater Inspector General, Col. S. F. Griswold, Kunming, 1 Jul 43, to CG USAF, CBI.

378 *Talk with Chiang Monlin*: in full in *SP*, 214-15.

380 *"Field Chief of Staff"*: undated draft mem for Marshall, "Situation as of June 43," Carmel A-22; R&S*, 341.

381 *Chiang's Legion of Merit*: Film 208 UN 64.

381 *Citation*: WD General Orders No. 38, 12 Jul 43.

381 *Letter to Marshall of July 23*: R&S*, 353.

382 *Yeh Ming-ch'en*: Fairbank, Reischauer and Craig, 170, n. 1.

382 *"Generally worthless"*: After a joint staff conference in London, Davies reported to Stilwell that British planners thought the Chinese "generally worthless in the prosecution of the war against Japan." Davies mem, "Policy Conflicts Among the United Nations," September 1943, Carmel A-22.

382 *Winant to Davies*: ibid.

382-83 *Roosevelt dissatisfied and conference of July 15*: Sherwood, 739.

383 *SEAC lines of command*: Mountbatten, 5; Stilwell in BB, 44, refers to a radio from Marshall calling the arrangement "cock-eyed."

383 *Davies' analysis of Britain*: "Anglo-American Cooperation in East Asia," 15 Nov 43, Carmel A-22.

385 *Wingate's publicity and losses*: Sykes, 367, 450.

385   *"We must all eat some crow" and Handy addendum*: 26 Aug 43, Carmel A-22; R&S*, 366.

385   *Soong at Quebec*: Marshall interview with R&S, 6 Jul 49.

386   *Stilwell's long-range plan*: "Role of China in the Defeat of Japan," Hoover, File 211.

387   *Refused to pressure Marshall*: Eldridge, 200.

387   *Senator Lodge's talk*: mem, 7 Oct 43, HP, File "China Relations with U.S."

387   *Americans were discovering*: Peffer, "Our Distorted View of China," *NYT Magazine*, 7 Nov 43.

387   OPD's "Re-analysis": Matloff**, 326, n. 56.

388   *Stilwell's plan for joint Kuomintang-Communist action*: R&S*, 368.

388   *Chou En-lai's reiterated invitation*: Davies mem, "Conversation with Chou En-lai," 16 Mar 43, Hoover, File 67.

388   *Rumors of civil war*: Feis, 88-89.

388   *Stilwell asks for directive*: 7 and 13 Jul, 5 and 12 Aug 43, qtd. Matloff**, 199.

389   *"Mismanagement and corruption"*: to State, 22 Sep, USFRC 44, 161.

389-90   *Soong's plan for removal of Stilwell*: Feis, 77-78; R&S*, 375.

390   *White House priority No. 1*: Currie to Tully, 1 Jul 43, FDRL, PSF "China 43-45."

390   *"Dear George" letter*: R&S*, 375, n. 54.

391   *Marshall rejects Soong plan*: R&S*, 375.

391   *Soong had President's promise*: 82nd Congress, IPR Hearings, Alsop testimony, 18 Oct 51, 1414.

391   *Marshall and Stimson consider recall*: Stimson to Stilwell, 25 Oct 43, Carmel A-22; R&S*, 376.

391   *"Everything seems to go wrong"*: 15 Oct 43, R&S*, 382.

391   *Eight-point plan for reform*: "Program for China," 29 Sep 43, full text in R&S*, 372-73.

392   *Mountbatten told by Irwin*: Evans, 105.

392   *"You watch him, Wedemeyer"*: Eldridge, 173.

392   *"Unnecessarily primitive"*: Slim, 221.

393   *Sun demands removal of Boatner*: Ho Yungchi, 64; R&S*, 374; R&S**, 31.

393   *"Heavenly surcease"*: 12 Oct 43, Stimson Papers.

394   *Stilwell's memos to G–mo*: 26 Sep and 6 Oct 43, Hoover, File 13.

394   *Recall crisis*: BB, 74; SP, 231-35; Somervell to OCMH, qtd. R&S*, 376; Mountbatten, 5; Mountbatten to author.

395   *Cartier vanity case*: Mountbatten to FDR, 23 Oct 43, FDRL, PSF "Britain 43-45."

395   *Roosevelt's reply*: Roosevelt, *Letters*, II, 1468.

16 China's Hour at Cairo
NOVEMBER–DECEMBER 1943

397   *Chiang to be met before Stalin*: Feis, 104.

397   *Hurley as a "tame Republican"*: Ambassador Harriman to author.

398   *Records as Military Attaché rated Wei*: "Some Notes on Chinese Commanders," an informal typewritten collection assembled from various sources on nine leading figures including, besides Wei, Yen Hsi-shan, Ku Chu-tung, Chang Fa-kwei, Li Tsung-jen, Hsueh Yueh and Ch'en Ch'eng, Carmel A-13.

399   *Dorn, "the obvious remedy"*: mem, "Future Training of Chinese Troops," 11 Nov 43, Hoover, File 206; reports of 7 Aug and 27 Oct, Hoover, File 215; R&S*, 352.

399   *Stilwell's program for Cairo*; R&S**, 56-57.

400   *Awed participant*: Harold Macmillan, *The Blast of War* (New York, Harper, 1967), 357.

400   *War Department views on China*: "Role of China in the Defeat of Japan," CCS mem, 22 Nov 43, qtd. Matloff**, 350.

400   *Roosevelt wanted success for China*: McIntire, 167; Sherwood, 773.

401   *"Great triumph"*: to Mountbatten, 8 Nov 43, FDRL, PSF.

401   *"Our one great objective"*: Sherwood, 779; also Welles, 151; Elliott Roosevelt, 154.

401   *"First real Oriental"*: M-Diary, II, 1414.

401   *As he appeared to Brooke and Churchill*: Bryant**, 51-52; Churchill, V, 328-29.

402   *Chiang wanted Bonins*: Matloff**, 343.

403   *Madame not satisfied with interpreters*: Bryant**, 53.

403   *Marshall's angry outburst*: session of 24 Nov 43, *SP*, 255; Matloff**, 350; White Paper, 255.

403   *Madame's appearance*: Bryant**, 53.

404   *"Ghastly waste of time"*: ibid., 55.

404   *Mountbatten's interview with Chiang*: Mountbatten to author.

404-405 *Stilwell's notes for meeting with FDR*: Data Book, Carmel, qtd. R&S**, 63.

405   *FDR on Marines*: Stilwell ms., "Story of J. Peene, Sr.," qtd. R&S**, 64.

405   *FDR agrees to equip 90 divisions*: ibid.; Matloff**, 350; Feis, 122, n. 14.

405   *"FDR is not interested"*: Data Book, qtd. R&S**, 65.

406   *"Driven absolutely mad"*: qtd. R&S**, 65.

406   *Churchill recorded in his own minutes*: Churchill, V, 328.

406   *Marshall's conversation with Stilwell*: S-Diary, 21 Nov 43.

407   *FDR to Bullitt*: Beatrice Farnsworth, *William C. Bullitt and the Soviet Union* (Bloomington, Indiana Univ. Press, 1967), 3.

407   *FDR motives at Tehran*: Sherwood, 776-80.

407   *Stalin "getable"*: ibid., 799.

407   *Stalin on the Chinese*: Feis, 107.

408   *Boatner's radiogram*: BB, 90; Eldridge, 189; Gen. McNally to author.

408   *Circumstances in the field*: Col. —— of the 38th Division to author.

409   *"BUCCANEER is off"*: Churchill, V, 412; King, 525.

409   *"To weigh the evidence on his desk"*: Ambassador Harriman to author.

409   *Marshall offers to transfer Stilwell*: Marshall interview with R&S, 6 Jul 49; R&S**, 73.

409   *FDR talking*: full text in *SP*, 251-54; original is headed, "Story of J. Peene, Sr." (the name of Stilwell's grandfather), Carmel, A-22.

410   *Chiang demands $1-billion loan*: to FDR, 9 Dec 43, R&S**, 74-75.

411   *Gauss on loan*: 22 Dec 43, M-Diary, 983; Feis, 122.

411   *Fiasco of previous loan and Treasury reaction*: Blum, III, 103, 107, 109-112; M-Diary, 980, 1022-24.

411   *Gauss quoted*: 15 Dec 43, FDRL, PSF "China 43-45."

411   *Morgenthau's memorandum*: Blum, III, 113; M-Diary, 960, 1006; full text in White Paper, 488-89.

412   *Chiang refuses Y-force*: R&S**, 80.

412-13 *Dispute over payment for airfields*: Blum, III, 110-19. The suggestions of Somervell and Clay at the meeting of January 20 are given verbatim in M-Diary, 1031; see also 1028, 1034, 1038, 1272. In USFRC 44 the dispute occupies 125 pages, 824-950. Documents in White Paper, 492-509.

413   *"Some very good offers"*: Blum, III, 117.

413   *Building the airfields*: Winfield, 195-98; Signal Corps Film, 111 SM 40.

413   *Stilwell proposed as negotiator*: Blum, III, 119.

17 The Road Back

DECEMBER 1943–JULY 1944

415   *Pershing incident*: O'Connor, 103.

418   *"Had to have the air to eat"*: Jones to author.

419   *In Slim's opinion*: Slim, 180, 217, 222.

420   *"Because we had only six regiments"*: Boatner to Stilwell, 2 Dec 43, qtd. R&S**, 122.

420   *"Wherever Stilwell went"*: Seagrave**, 94.

420   *Parade with Japanese heads on poles*: Boatner to author.

421   *Ate "like the birds"*: UP by Jack Guinn from NCAC HQ, 24 Aug 44 (unidentified newspaper, Carmel Scrapbook).

421   *"Special attention to people at the bottom"*: Col. —— of 38th Division, interview with author.

421   *"Dig up 150 ceiling fans"*: Stilwell to Sultan, 8 Jun 44, Hoover, File 120.

421   *Chinese patients not to be searched*: Ravdin, 174.

422   *Wingate on Chinese cheerfulness*: Sykes, 369.

423   *Chinese requisitions usually double*: The 38th Division's list in December was 280 percent in excess of numerical strength (R&S**, 107).

423   *"After the airboys learned"*: Jones to author.

423   *Roosevelt "the poorest administrator"*: qtd. Burns, 321.

424   *Giffard reputed among Americans*: Dean Rusk, interview with author.

424   *"A lesson" and "surly obstinacy"*: Slim, 178-79.

424   *Stilwell's willingness to fight under Slim*: ibid.

424   *"Two people" and "He had courage"*: ibid., 36, 98.

425   *"His own worst enemy"*: Marshall interview with R&S, 6 Jul 49.

425   *"You will find below the surface"*: Marshall to Mountbatten, 26 Jan 44, OCS, GCM, WDCSA 091.713.

425   *Wingate's angry comment*: Ogburn, 60.

425-26 *Fergusson's account*: qtd. Sykes, 499-500.

427   *Roosevelt to Chiang, January 14*: qtd. Feis, 127.

428   *Churchill on Burma*: Churchill, V, 560-61, 573.

428   *Alsop to Hopkins*: 1 Sep 43 and 14 Jan 44, Hopkins Papers.

429   *"Monocled aplomb"*: New York Sun, qtd. Current Biography, 1945.

429   *AXIOM conference of January 31*: Wedemeyer, 258; Mountbatten, 31; R&S**, 164.

430-31 *Boatner's interview with Roosevelt*: Boatner to author; see also Stettinius to Hull, 23 Feb, USFRC 44, 25.

431   *Roosevelt to Churchill*: Churchill, V, 562, 574.

432   *"If I had a pack"*: Eldridge, 213; see also Darrell Berrigan, "Uncle Joe Pays Off," *Sat. Eve. Post*, 17 Jun 44.

432   *"A street address in Los Angeles"*: Ogburn, 61.

433   *Merrill a "born leader"*: Ravdin, 179.

433   *Make-up of the GALAHAD force*: Stone, ed., Reports of Capts. Hopkins and Stelling, Battalion Medical Officers, 295, 303, 311.

433   *Shooting through the train windows*: Ogburn, 72.

433   *"Simply and quietly"*: ibid., 88.

433   *"Aw, to hell with this"*: Tillman Durdin, *NYT*, 30 Apr 44.

434   *"Very simple. Keep going"*: Col. —— of 38th Division, interview with author.

434   *"When he told you what to do"*: Gen. Arms, interview with author.

434   *"Every drop hurt me"*: Eldridge, 215.

434   *He said to Paul Jones*: Jones to author.

435   *"Not with you, you dirty bastard"*: Yank, 6 Oct 44.

435   *Wingate's Order of the Day*: Sykes 522-23; Evans, 151n.

435   *Chiang's order of March 6*: R&S**, 176.

435   *Mountbatten's concern for publicity*: Ralph Arnold, 153.

436   *"To keep my campaign going for a week"*: Eldridge, 229. Mount-
        batten's visit was recorded by Signal Corps Film 18 CS 1083.

437   *"A god-damn duck-hunter"* and *"poor old man"*: Eldridge, 216;
        Time, 21 Oct 46.

437   *"Fire in his belly"* and *disruptive to Allied causes*: Mountbatten, in-
        terview with author.

437   *"A grand old warrior"*: qtd. R&S**, 170.

437   *Upset by the smell of corpses*: Stilwell to Win, 10 Mar 44, Carmel
        B-14.

437   *"Busted the Limey in the eye"*: Eldridge, 202.

439   *General Sultan's question*: R&S**, 174.

439   *Mountbatten, "great urgency"*: ibid., 177; Mountbatten, 51.

439   *Chiang's reply to Roosevelt*: 27 Mar 44, full text in R&S**, 308.

440   *Stilwell's birthday*: Signal Corps Film 1762; text of telegrams in Car-
        mel A-23.

441   *"If the Japs are behind us"*: *CBI History*, Master Narrative.

441   *The meeting at Jorhat*: Slim, 236; S-Diary, 3 Apr 44.

442   *Wingate to Slim*: Evans 164-65, n.; Slim, 234.

442   *Opinion of Colonel Demetriadi*: interview with author.

443   *"Put us all on the same beam"*: April 1944, Hoover, File 124, Sec. 1.

443   *Unfavorable comment in Chungking*: Gauss to State, 17 and 24 Apr,
        USFRC 44.

443   *Roosevelt to Chiang, April 3*: R&S**, 310.

443   *Threat to cut off Lend-Lease*: ibid., 312-14; *CBI History*, Master
        Narrative; Stilwell to Marshall, 11 Apr 44, Hoover, File 124,
        Sec. 1.

444   *Dorn's letters*: 28 and 29 Apr 44, Hoover, File 35.

444   *Stilwell's radio*: 27 Apr 44, Hoover, File 124, Sec. 1.

445   *"Danger—above everything"*: Ogburn, 5.

445   *"Our own battalion commander"*: Stone, ed., Report of Captain
        Henry Stelling, MC, 370.

445   *"If necessary at the expense"*: Ogburn, 226.

446   *Mountbatten replied "impossible"* and *"unsound"*: R&S**, 200.

446   *Admiral King quoted*: King, 541.

448   *Mountbatten's Order of the Day*: NYT, 20 May 44; *Churchill's
        query*: V, 569.

449   *March to Myitkyina*: Peers, 166.

449   *"Pitiful but still splendid"*: qtd. R&S**, 230.

450   *"Smell their way to the field"*: Seagrave**, 137.

450   *"I had him in my rifle sights"*: Ogburn, 279.

451   *"Terrified of the Japs"*: 15 Jun 44, from NCAC correspondence in
        Gen. Boatner's possession.

451   *Order to return GALAHAD convalescents to duty*: Stone, ed., Re-
        port of Colonel Tracy S. Voorhees, JAGD, 383-86.

451   *"Red flag to a bull"*: Ogburn, 279.

451   *"GI's favorite"*: *Yank*, 6 Oct 44.

451   *Cancels rule against pets*: Tillman Durdin, *NYT*, 30 Apr 44.

451   *Chiang summons Stilwell "immediately"*: Ferris to Stilwell, 3 Jun 44, Hoover, File 131.

452   *Noel Coward episode*: Hoover, Files 130-31; Wheeler's letter in Carmel A-23.

452-53   *Dorn's reports on Y-force*: 11 May and 8 Jun 44, Carmel A-23.

18 "The Future of All Asia Is at Stake"

JUNE–SEPTEMBER 1944

455   *Young Generals' plot*: Gauss to State (24 Jan and 3 Feb), Service (3 and 10 Feb), USFRC 44, 312, 319-26, 334-36.

456   *American foreign service reports*: Gauss (28 Jan and 1 Feb), Sprouse (28 Jan), A. S. Chase (30 May), Langdon (14 Jul), Service (20 Mar), USFRC 44, 11, 38-39, 318ff., 331-34, 439-41, 476-77; also White, *Thunder*, 71; Peck, 417, 476, 553-54.

456   *Laborers at airfields*: Peck, 450.

456   *"I'd like to get a year's leave"*: Peck, 514.

456   *Foreign correspondents' protest*: Tong, 242, 247-50.

457   *Crisis surfacing in Chungking*: Gauss, 8 Jan, 16 Feb, 22 Sep, USFRC 44, 160-62, 341-42, 451.

457   *Fourteenth Air Force report on Honan*: R&S**, 327.

457   *Embassy observer in Sian*: Rice, 11 Nov, USFRC 44, 193-94.

458   *Service's summarizing report*: mem to Asst. C/S G-2, 2 Jun 44, Hoover, File 125.

458   *"Hopelessly inadequate"*: qtd. R&S**, 366.

459   *Chiang demands, Marshall refuses diversion of tonnage from B-29s*: all quotations from R&S**, 364-70, except "bleeding us white" from a later entry in Stimson Diary, 3 Oct 44.

459   *Lack of air transport in Europe*: Marshall interview with R&S, 6 Jul 49.

459   *Collect a force of 250,000*: Merrill interview with R&S, 20 Apr 48; R&S***, 57.

460   *"Prolonged kiss of death"*: Peck, 498.

460   *Gauss, "I confess"*: 15 Jun, USFRC 44, 100.

460   *Gauss instructed on June 15*: USFRC 44, 102-105; Feis, 143.

461   *"Not committed to support"*: mem by Edmund Clubb, Division of Chinese Affairs, 19 May, USFRC 44, 792; Feis, 142.

462   *Stalin assured Harriman*: Feis, 140-41.

462   *Communists might win*: White Paper, 64-65.

462   *Chiang reported preparing to attack*: *CBI History*, Master Narrative.

462-63   *Mission to Yenan*: Davies, 24 Jun 43 and 15 Jan 44, R&S**, 302-303; Timberman to author; Gauss (27 Jan and 11 Feb), FDR to CKS (9 Feb), CKS "facilitates" (22 Feb), USFRC 44, 313-14, 329-30, 348-49.

463   *Hsiao I-shu on Communists*: Dorn to author.

463   *Dixie Mission*: Barrett, "Dixie Mission," 19; FDR to CKS, 5 Apr, USFRC 44, 394.

464   *Wallace mission*: Roosevelt's motives, Rosenman, 438-39; purpose, Stettinius, 21 and 24 May, USFRC 44, 224, 230; CBI HQ requests pressure, Ferris to Stilwell, 17 Jun 44, Hoover, File 119; conversations with CKS, full texts in White Paper, 549-59.

465   *Wallace not in sympathy*: John Carter Vincent, who accompanied Wallace, to author: Wallace "didn't mix at all with CKS. He had no use for him or for the regime which he believed was rotten."

465   *"Deeply moved"*: Wallace report, 28 Jun, USFRC 44, 225.

465   *Chennault and Alsop on hand*: Chennault, 231.

465   *Stilwell invites Wallace*: Stilwell to Davies (16 Jun 44), to Jones (22 Jun 44), Hoover, File 119.

465   *Wallace recommended*: report of 28 Jun 44 cited above.

465   *Composed by Alsop*: Alsop, *Atlantic Monthly*, April 1952.

466   *"Usual poison"*: qtd. Stimson Diary, 2 Aug 44.

466   *Wallace's second report*: 10 Jul, USFRC 44, 244.

466   *Langdon's report*: 1 Aug, USFRC 44, 493-97.

466   *"Stuck with a regime"*: 81st Congress, Loyalty Hearings, John K. Fairbank testimony, 2412.

466   *Service's brief for Wallace*: "The Situation in China and Suggestions Regarding American Policy," 20 Jun, USFRC 44.

467   *Fear of Japanese continuing to fight in China*: Marshall, Third Biennial Report, 209. For the same view held by Nimitz see Samuel Lubell, "Vinegar Joe and the Reluctant Dragon," *Sat. Eve. Post*, 24 Feb 45.

467   *Brooke wants Stilwell relieved*: Marshall interview with R&S, 6 Jul 49; Bryant**, 162.

467   *Proposal to enlarge Stilwell's command*: All official messages in the command crisis are in R&S**, 378-86, 413-22. Stilwell's undated notes and drafts of his messages to Marshall are in Carmel A-23–24.

467   *Footnote, Alexander's remark*: Gen. Boatner to author.

469   *"What I am trying to find out"*: Morgenthau, "Presidential Diary," 28 Jun 44, Morgenthau Estate (unpub.).

470   *Delivery by senior officer in Chungking*: Marshall to Stilwell, 7 May 44, Hoover, File 131.

471   *"Today a fateful decision"*: typewritten copy of a telegram, no date or letterhead, Hopkins Papers, Chinese Affairs; also qtd. by Sherwood, 804.

471   *Soong to Gauss*: Gauss, 12 Jul, USFRC 44, 125.

471-72 *What Stilwell hoped for from enlarged command*: Hearn interview with R&S, 26 Nov 48; Timberman interview with author.

472 *Pai Ch'ung-hsi, "real command"*: *CBI History*, Master Narrative.

472 *Dispute with Chennault over arms for ground forces*: All communications in this episode are quoted from R&S**, 371-72, 402-403, 412.

473 *"Let them stew"*: to Hearn, 21 Aug 44, R&S**, 412. Hearn's paraphrase of this message in relaying it to Chennault became the basis of a *cause célèbre*. In the course of transmission or of coding and decoding, the key word in the sentence "He [Stilwell] is working on a proposition which might give this spot a real face-lifting" came through as "face-lossing" (*sic*). On the head of this pin Chennault and Alsop strenuously erected a monument to the villainy of Stilwell. OCMH has since verified the original wording of the radio message.

473 *Emotions in Kandy*: Eldridge, 289.

473 *"Get me a jeep"*: S. Dillon Ripley to author.

474 *Brooke, "It is clear"*: Bryant**, 185.

474 *"Sleek, smart and prosperous"*: Ralph Arnold, 130.

473 *Stimson wrote*: 22 Aug 44, Carmel A-23.

475 *Comparison with Iliad*: SP, 312.

475 *Li Chi-shen's proposed secession*: R&S**, 408-409, 411-12; USFRC 44, 150-51, 467, 505-506, 510, 512-15.

476 *Journalists' reports from Yenan*: qtd. by State to Gauss, 19 and 23 Jul, USFRC 44, 479-80; *NYT*, 1 Jul, 6, 14, 23 Aug, 25 Sep, 6 Oct 44.

477 *DIXIE Mission reports*: Service, 28 Jul, 23 and 31 Aug, forwarded by Gauss to State, 1 Sep, USFRC 44, 517-23, 527-32, 536-43, 610-12.

477 *Mao on American landings*: 23 Aug, USFRC 44, 612.

478 *"Better men physically"*: 81st Congress, Loyalty Hearings, Dorn testimony, 2166.

478 *Marshall proposes Hurley*: Marshall interview with R&S, 6 Jul 49.

479 *Hurley asks to be made Ambassador*: Stettinius to Hull, 3 Aug and mem of 9 Aug, USFRC 44, 247-48.

479 *Stimson comments*: Stimson Diary, 3 Aug 44.

479 *Roosevelt, "I know my men"*: Morgenthau, "Presidential Diary," 3 Oct 39, Morgenthau Estate (unpub.).

479 *FDR asks for Nelson*: Marshall interview with R&S, 6 Jul 49.

479 *"You get three years in Washington"*: M-Diary, 1265.

480 *Hopkins talk with Davies*: mem by Davies, 4 Sep 44, Carmel A-24.

480 *"Trusting no one but himself"*: Gauss, 31 Jul, USFRC 44, 493.

480 *Reported arrangements with Japanese*: R&S***, 8.

481 *Chiang not anxious for American landings*: Service for Wallace, 20 Jun, USFRC 44.

481-82 *Hurley and Nelson explain intentions*: Stilwell, undated notes, Carmel A-23.

19 The Limits of "Can Do"

SEPTEMBER–NOVEMBER 1944

483   *Hurley opened negotiations*: All official communications in the com-
       mand crisis—except as supplemented below—are quoted from
       R&S**, 422-72, which contains the most complete published
       documentation of the developments, and gives the full text of
       most of the documents. Originals of Roosevelt's messages to
       Chiang Kai-shek of 6 Jul, 23 Aug, 16 Sep, 5 and 18 Oct 44 are
       in FDRL, Map Room Papers. Stilwell's record from day to day
       is in *SP*, 325-49, except for his unpublished notes, for which
       references are given below.

483   *Sir Horace Seymour*: Woodward, 426.

484   *Chiang and conscripts*: Linebarger mem for Col. Dickey, 8 Sep 44,
       Hoover, File 158.

484   *138 dead in Kunming*: Langdon, 13 Oct, USFRC 44, 173.

484   *"More real power in China"*: SP, 328.

485   *Gauss, problem of Communists*: 28 Sep, USFRC 44, 601.

485   *Stilwell on use of Communists*: R&S**, 429.

485   *"If CKS and Co"*: draft of eyes-alone radio, n.d., Hoover, File 115.

485   *Chou En-lai to Service*: report of 28 Jul, USFRC 44.

486   *Chennault, "true unification"*: 21 Sep 44, FDRL, PSF "War Dept.
       Chennault."

486   *Roosevelt-Carlson letters*: FDRL, PSF "China 43-45."

488   *Defeat in east China*: White, "Disaster in the East," in *Thunder*, 179-
       98.

489   *OSS unit finds warehouses*: ibid., 196.

489   *"Crazy little bastard"*: SP, 330, and notes of 10 Sep 44, Carmel A-24.

490   *"Plain talk" with Soong*: notes of 16 Sep 44, Carmel A-23, and SP,
       331.

490   *Chiangs' marital rift*: NYT, 30 Nov and 11 Dec 44.

491   *No U.S. units for CBI*: Matloff**, 478. OPD Strategy Section rec-
       ommended on 31 Aug 44 that U.S.-Chinese forces should be
       withdrawn from Burma after reaching Lashio so that the British
       could reconquer their own colonial territory without American
       involvement.

493   *Stilwell took the message to Huang Shan*: According to Hurley's ex
       post facto account (82nd Congress, Hearings on Military Situa-
       tion in Far East, 2865-80), the Generalissimo was just about to
       place his seal on Stilwell's commission as commander of the Chi-
       nese armies when he was interrupted by Stilwell's delivery of the
       message. Since all Chiang's effort was directed toward not giving
       Stilwell the command, this version suffers from inherent improb-
       ability. Hurley's several postwar testimonies, given to various
       Congressional investigations in the highly charged atmosphere

following the Communist victory in China, grew and changed over the years, becoming progressively richer the further removed they were in time from the event. His later testimony is infirm ground for the historian.

496   *Nelson promised Chiang*: Stilwell to Marshall, 2 Oct 44, Carmel A-24. Referring to the meeting of the Standing Committee on 2 Oct (see below), Stilwell radioed, "Gauss has learned that at a private meeting CKS told his Council that he would not appoint an American commander and that Nelson had promised him control of Lend-Lease." Although Gauss did not include this promise in his official report, he did forward a transcript of the conversations between Nelson and Chiang.

497   *Hurley listened receptively*: White, *Thunder*, 223. Hurley repeated Chiang's charges against Stilwell to White "as if he believed them."

497   *"Anyone who crowds him"*: to Marshall, 26 Sep 44, Carmel A-24.

499   *Chiang's speech to the Standing Committee*: Gauss, 3 Oct, USFRC 44, 265-66.

499   *Merrill's report of Quebec*: S-Diary, 4 Oct 44; Merrill interview with R&S, 20 Apr 48.

499   *"Sharp rejoinder"*: Stimson Diary, 3 Oct 44.

499   *Joint Chiefs considered abandoning China*: ibid.

500   *Stimson indignant*: ibid.

500   *Stimson "pretty sure" Chiang would not accept*: ibid., 4 Oct 44.

501   *"If you sustain Stilwell"*: Hurley to FDR, 13 Oct 44; full text in 82nd Congress, Hearings on Military Situation in Far East, 2879-81.

501   *"Losing China's potential effort"*: 10 Oct 44, Carmel A-24.

501   *"Direct and positive" orders*: Leahy, 272

501   *"Must not indefinitely underwrite"*: mem by Davies, 15 Nov, USFRC 44, 690.

502   *Marshall's orders for secret departure*: Gen. Frank McCarthy (Marshall's aide) to Pogue, 7 Aug 67.

503   *"Will I be allowed to make a statement?"*: Data Book.

503   *"They want to fight the Japanese"*: 16 Oct 44, Carmel A-24.

503   *Gauss, "Some of our Army officers"*: 24 Oct, USFRC 44, 657.

503   *Stilwell's letters to Chennault, Chu Teh, Auchinleck*: Hoover, File 135.

503   *Gauss' motives for resignation*: Service, interview with author.

503   *Proposed decoration*: 201 File.

504   *"Bitched it up"*: Data Book.

504   *Stilwell's departure*: White, *Thunder*, 225.

505   *Dorn to Bergin*: 23 Oct 44, Carmel B-14.

505   *"I foresee trouble"*: Stimson Diary, 23 Oct 44.

505   *"Dirtiest in history"*: qtd. Rosenman, 504; also on campaign, Gunther, 351; Sherwood, 828-30

505   *Atkinson's return*: 81st Congress, Loyalty Hearings, Atkinson testimony, 2420, and interview with author.

506   *Gauss' resignation*: Grew to Gauss, 31 Oct, USFRC 44, 856.

506   *Press comment*: Harsch, 31 Oct 44; Wiant, *NYT*, 1 Nov 44; Judd, *Time*, 13 Nov 44.

506   *Roosevelt's press conference*: full text, FDRL, Press Conferences, vol. 24; *NYT* editorial, 14 Nov 44.

506   *Stilwell's return*: McCarthy to Pogue, 7 Aug 67; Stimson Diary, 3 Nov 44.

506   *"The most difficult task"*: Stimson-Bundy, 530.

507   *"The less you say"*: Surles to Stilwell, 10 Nov 44, Carmel A-24.

507-508   *Pan Yu-kan, Pick, Cooper, Tseng*: all in Carmel B-14.

508   *"Doing a job for Uncle Joe"*: Maj. E. T. Hancock, 3 Nov 44, *ibid.*

509   *"Too weak to rule"*: a Chinese friend to Judd, mem by Vincent, 17 Oct, USFRC 44, 174.

509   *Hsiung quoted*: Hsiung, xv.

20 "We Ought to Get Out—*NOW*"

1945-46

510   *Judge Vinson*: S-Diary, 21 Mar 45.

511   *Opening of the Road*: Signal Corps Film 111 CR3 (Combat Report No. 3), "The Stilwell Road" (from the building of the Burma Road in 1937 to the opening at Kunming in 1945); *NYT*, 21 Jan 45.

511   *G—mo's proclamation*: qtd. Feis, 275.

511   *U.S. Headquarters India-Burma, official order*: 3 Mar 45, Circular 22.

511   *Letter from Sultan*: 30 Jan 45, Carmel A-27.

511   *"Curtain was down"*: Mrs. Simon B. Buckner to author.

511   *"Nothing can be done in China"*: Stimson Diary, 13 Dec 44.

512   *"Unless we stand clear"*: notes of January 1945, Carmel A-27.

512   *"A letter for General Handy"*: biographical résumé by Jim Shepley, 12 Oct 46, *Time* files.

512   History of the CBI Theater: The copies at Hoover and OCMH do not entirely conform in organization and arrangement, but the basic scheme is the same. Section One consists of the Master Narrative (still classified as of 1967) of 215 pages divided into seventeen chapters in more or less chronological form. Section Two (Two and Three in OCMH copy) consists of 31 topical chapters dealing with the Road, Pipelines, Y-Force, Z-Force, Ramgarh, the several Air Forces, Lend-Lease, GALAHAD, the two Burma campaigns, political reports, China Exchange, Ad-

ministrative and Staff reports, Historical and Political Setting (the last four mentioned remain classified) and other subjects.

512   *"There was no American"*: Steele, 30

512   *Atcheson telegram*: full text in White Paper, 87-92; Feis, 268-71; 82nd Congress, Hearings on Military Situation in Far East, Hurley testimony, 2905-2906.

513   *"Organize, lead and command"*: Gen. McClure, Wedemeyer's C/S, to Gen. Ch'en Ch'eng, new Minister of War, MemCon, 14 Dec, USFRC 44, 741-43.

514   *Hurley on Communist party*: qtd. Feis, 265.

514   *Stettinius advised President*: mem, 4 Jan 45, Feis 219-20.

514   *Ho Ying-chin's "ridiculous" estimates*: mem by Augustus Chase, 22 Sep, USFRC 44, 583.

515   *Invasion of Japan necessary*: Leahy, 158; Matloff**, 501, 512.

515   *"Set up a new Japanese state"*: Deane, 225.

515   *As Stalin frankly said*: Feis, 243.

516   *Legion of Merit*: WD General Orders No. 12, 24 Feb 45; *NYT*, 11 Feb 45.

516   *To his aide, a grudging approval*: Richard Young to author.

516   *Wedemeyer "making a case"*: S-Diary, 23 Jan 45.

517   *Recall of Ramgarh division*: R&S***, 62.

517   *Wedemeyer's reports*: ibid., 52, 165.

517   *"It will boil down to me"*: S-Diary, 4 Apr 45. The speaker was Gen. Gruber, a veteran of the first Burma campaign.

518   *Defeat of Japan considered 15 months distant*: Rear Adm. Ellis Zacharias, *Behind Closed Doors* (New York, Putnam, 1950), 56-57.

519   *Okinawa casualties*: Louis Snyder, *The War, 1939-45* (New York, Messner, 1960), 484.

519   *"Pooh pooh" said MacArthur*: S-Diary Supplement, 19 Jun 45, Carmel B-19.

520   *Ideas on tactical aviation*: notes, June–July 1945, Carmel A-29.

520   *Chennault's letter of resignation*: addressed to Wedemeyer, labeled "Top Secret—Eyes Alone"; copy in Carmel A-27.

520   *A "pressing necessity"*: Feis, 325.

521   *Chiang queried Washington about Stilwell*: S-Diary, 13 Aug 45, on information from MacArthur.

521   *Visiting correspondents*: Theodore White and A. T. Steele.

522   *Visit to Japan and on board* Missouri: letters to Win, 3 and 7 Sep 45, Carmel B-19.

523   *Request to go to Peking*: Marshall to Stilwell, 2 Oct 45, Carmel A-30.

523   *Hurley's resignation*: text of his letter of resignation, White Paper, 581-84.

523   *Nominated by* Army Times: clipping, n.d., Carmel Scrapbook.

523-24   *Hurley's accusations*: *NYT*, 26 Nov 45.

524   *Chefoo incident:* Feis, 365-66.

524   *Colonel Yeaton's judgment:* ibid., 358.

525   *SWNCC directive:* ibid., 375.

525   *"Fighting is becoming more bitter":* ibid., 377.

525   *Hurley senses conspiracy:* ibid., 409.

525   *"Deserving Democrat":* Hurley's testimony, 82nd Congress, Hearings on Military Situation in Far East, 21 Jun 51, 2937.

526   *Amerasia case:* Wertenbaker.

526   *Marshall's instructions:* Feis, 418-20.

527   *Stilwell's talk with Byroade:* Byroade to author.

528   *Stilwell's death:* Time, 21 Oct 46; *Atlanta Constitution,* 15 Oct 46; Merrill, Carlson (Carmel Scrapbook).

529   *Memorial service in China:* Charles J. Simpson, a member of the Military Advisory Group who was present, to author.

529   *Aid to China in year after V-J Day:* White Paper, 225-29.

529   *Number of Nationalist troops moved:* Tsou, 308.

529   *"Simply does not know what is going on":* talk to Business Advisory Council, 12 Jun 47, qtd. David Lillienthal, *Journals* (New York, Harper, 1964), II, 200-201.

529   *"Dominant group of reactionaries":* White Paper, 687.

530   *Marshall opposed to American military intervention:* Tsou, 475-76.

530   *Americans denounced for prolonging civil war:* ibid., 477-78.

530   *"World's worst leadership":* ibid., 483.

530   *"Dedicate their lives to this task":* ibid., 490.

530   *Madame asks for $3 billion:* ibid., 492.

530-31   *General Peers quoted:* Peers, 152-53.

INDEX

For well-known Chinese names, the aspirates (') used in romanized spelling to indicate the pronunciation of consonants have not been used consistently in the text. On the assumption that they might have the same irritating effect on the reader as they have on the author, I have preferred in most cases the conventionalized·newspaper style without the aspirate, leaving the correct form to appear in the Index.

For persons whose dates cannot be ascertained, the following system has been used: for those born before and including the year 1885, the dates are expressed as (b. 1883), etc.; for those born 1886 and after, the dates are expressed as (1886-   ), etc.

This American Past edition of
Stilwell and the American Experience in China, 1911–1945
The text was set on the Linotype in various sizes of Times Roman.
The display face used throughout the book is Horizon,
in varying weights. The book was printed and bound by
Kingsport Press, Kingsport, Tennessee
on acid-free paper furnished by P. H. Glatfelter Company.
Brick & Ballerstein, Inc., Long Island City, New York,
manufactured the slipcase.

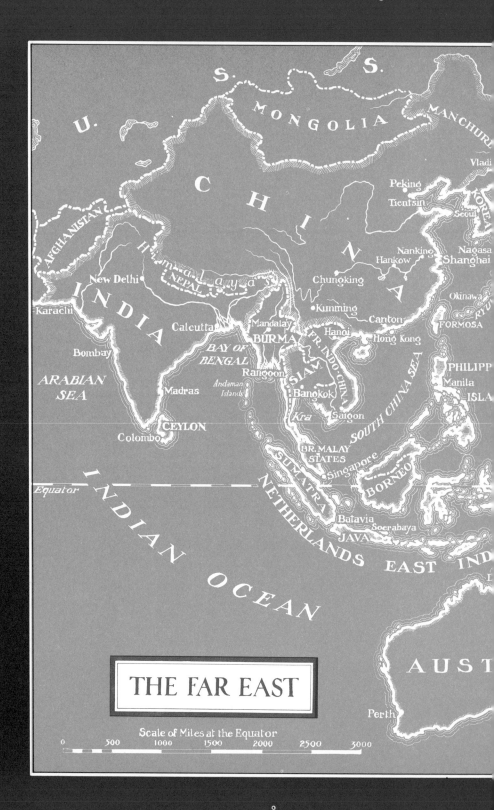

THE FAR EAST

Scale of Miles at the Equator

0   500   1000   1500   2000   2500   3000